What Is Addiction?

D1073704

What Is Addiction?

edited by Don Ross, Harold Kincaid, David Spurrett, and Peter Collins

A Bradford Book
The MIT Press
Cambridge, Massachusetts
London, England

© 2010 Massachusetts Institute of Technology

All rights reserved. No part of this book may be reproduced in any form by any electronic or mechanical means (including photocopying, recording, or information storage and retrieval) without permission in writing from the publisher.

MIT Press books may be purchased at special quantity discounts for business or sales promotional use. For information, please email special_sales@mitpress.mit.edu or write to Special Sales Department, The MIT Press, 55 Hayward Street, Cambridge, MA 02142.

This book was set in Stone Serif and Stone Sans on 3B2 by Asco Typesetters, Hong Kong.
Printed and bound in the United States of America.

Library of Congress Cataloging-in-Publication Data

What is addiction? / edited by Don Ross ... [et al.].
    p.   cm.
"A Bradford book."
Includes bibliographical references and index.
ISBN 978-0-262-51311-1 (pbk. : alk. paper)
1. Substance abuse. 2. Compulsive behavior. 3. Cognitive neuroscience. 4. Neurosciences—
Social aspects. I. Ross, Don, 1962–.
RC564.W497   2010
616.86—dc22   2009014712

10   9   8   7   6   5   4   3   2   1

Contents

Introduction: What Is Addiction?

Don Ross and Harold Kincaid

In Western culture, the addict has been a stock cultural figure for many years. Consider, for example, the book (1949) and film (1955) versions of *The Man with the Golden Arm*. The central character, played in the film by Frank Sinatra, is introduced as a former heroin user who has shaken off his dependence while in prison. He expects his release from jail to mark a new beginning for him as a musician. However, encounters with and pressures from his exploitative old cronies, and his morally confused and deceptive wife, lead him to relapse. In short order his virtues, ambitions, and judgment evaporate in the face of his desperation to obtain and use his drug. He steals; he blows his carefully cultivated musical opportunity; he has brushes with the law and is ultimately (falsely) accused of murder. In the end he finds a third chance at a well-ordered life, thanks to the intervention of an angelic woman; but first, at her insistence, he must undergo a harrowing ordeal of withdrawal.

The Man with the Golden Arm is comparatively optimistic. In many subsequent, less sentimental, popular depictions of addiction, there is no suggestion of redemption. The superb film of 2000, *Requiem for a Dream*, pursues its heroin-entrapped characters from heights of romantic joy and tenderness to disfigurement, degradation, self-hatred, and psychic collapse. They are last seen in fetal positions, one following the amputation of his infected arm in a prison hospital.

Addiction on this well-rehearsed conception is a pit into which any heedless person might fall. It represents a moral failing to the extent that lack of caution is moralized. But we are typically asked to sympathize with addicted characters for two reasons. First, the punishment is out of proportion to the sin; mere fecklessness is not usually taken to justify humiliation and personal destruction. Second, the addicts' stupidity is corrected by new knowledge as their condition overwhelms them, but their enlightenment comes too late—addiction is nemesis. Thus the more recent of the addiction narratives described above has the arc of classical tragedy.

Scientific knowledge tends to undermine dramatic purity. Nothing more exotic than statistically careful prevalence studies were needed to determine that the overwhelming majority of people diagnosed as addicts eventually break their dependence without ever seeking clinical assistance, let alone angelic salvation. The supposedly relentless grip of addiction has typically been explained in later twentieth-century artistic treatments by invoking the dogma of 12-step programs,[1] according to which addiction is a "disease" that can be kept at bay but never cured. This, however, has contributed to undermining the nemesis image, as a side effect of sweeping medicalization of less terrifying patterns of experience. Popular usage in some countries—certainly in the United States—now has it that anything any person does more often than is thought reasonable from the reference point of the describer is "addicted" to the behavior in question. It is of course possible to imagine someone's life devoured by an "addiction" to (for example) building model trains, but it would require rare skill to do so without mixing elements of farce into the tragedy.

Thus in the less credulous corners of contemporary culture there has been deflation in the import, and even the plausibility, of the idea of addiction. The psychiatric profession has generally reverted to the alternative construct of "dependence," which distances clinical response from both the tragic image and the skeptical backlash.

Doubts that addiction might be anything other than a cultural organizing principle for storytelling can be philosophically motivated (Fingarette 1988). Skepticism is often expressed about whether addiction *in general* has any common objective structure. Perhaps, for example, all cases of nicotine dependence are neurochemically similar, but "addictions" to tobacco, cocaine, and gambling have nothing in common except judgments by observers that the "victims" of these conditions smoke, snort, and bet more often than the observer deems prudent. The fact that many putative addictions follow similar behavioral courses doesn't necessarily impress the skeptic, who might in response cite Ian Hacking's (1999) work on interactive or "looping" kinds. Hacking surveys a range of cases in which social construction of a certain kind of person induces some people to conform to the expectations built into the construction, which further stabilizes the construction, and so on, in a self-reinforcing spiral. As Hacking would emphasize, if this goes on in the case of addiction, it is not grounds for concluding that addicts don't really exist—quite the contrary.[2] However, it would imply that addiction is in the first place a social kind rather than a biomedical one. In many people's view, this is directly relevant to the question of whether people who conform to the type should be regarded mainly as victims or mainly as authors of their own conditions.

With the exception of the final three chapters, this is not a book of philosophical essays. It is instead devoted mainly to presenting the range of available scientific evidence on which opinions about the philosophical issues should be based. The evidence in question comes from a range of disciplinary perspectives: neuroscience, genetics, behavioral psychology, behavioral economics, and psychiatry. All of these perspectives are represented here. Only following these surveys do we turn to discussions of their philosophical import.

Some readers may be surprised by the degree of attention devoted in the book to pathological gambling. This reflects the growing status of that condition as a test case for claims about addiction as a unitary phenomenon (Ross et al. 2008). No scientific evidence links intense interest in sex or shopping to the "classic" drug addictions. Thus these phenomena are consistent with the view that the popular addiction concept simply metaphorically extends the real dependence of individuals on exogenous sources of certain biochemicals. However, this is not true of pathological gambling (or, more recently, overeating). Here there is no dependence on exogenous substances; yet there is strong behavioral and neurobiological evidence that pathological gambling and substance dependence share a common set of features.

The chapters by Bickel and Yi, Bellegarde and Potenza, Redish, Ross, and Petry all adhere to the perspective that there is a shared set of characteristics common to substance dependences and pathological gambling. On the other hand, none of them defends the view that addiction as generally conceived has a *simple* unifying structure. In particular, Redish surveys evidence for multiple neurodynamical and neurochemical vulnerabilities that partly cut across the different addictions, but also partly divide them. Ross argues that although the popular idea of addiction is indeed overly liberal in its extension—with potentially problematic implications for public health—there is a core neurochemical signature that characterizes drug dependencies and pathological gambling (and probably overeating).

Addiction could have a unifying basis even if that basis is not a localizable neural dysfunction. This is the view defended directly in the chapter by Heyman, according to which addiction follows a standard behavioral course because it is a natural human vulnerability generated by the structure of evolved human decision-making dispositions. These same structural properties, according to Heyman, explain why and how most addicts recover on their own as they get older, unless they are afflicted with comorbid psychiatric disorders. Goldman et al. survey a broad literature on anticipatory processing—the psychological states that precede action—and argue that this focus integrates cognitive and information processing perspectives with motivational/emotional approaches. They then discuss a range of addiction studies and show how their approach sheds light on these findings. Chapters by Rachlin, Ainslie, and Spurrett and Murrell extend and enrich this perspective. Monterosso and coauthors, however, close the distance (as does Ross's chapter) between behaviorally grounded and neuroscientifically grounded accounts. The chapter by Kincaid and Sullivan reemphasizes the importance of social context in framing addiction, while in no way denying the relevance of neuroscientific or genetic findings.

We can sketch in somewhat more detail the contents of the chapters by focusing on the levels or kinds of factors to which their authors turn in explaining addiction. They differ in the extent to which they emphasize the following causal influences:

1. genetic, either in terms of specific genes that confer greater vulnerability to addiction, or less direct evidence for heritability;
2. molecular neurobiological, that is, biochemical changes at the level of the neuron;
3. systems neurobiological, that is, brain regions and/or circuits and their functions;
4. picoeconomic dynamics, that is, subpersonal goal-seeking systems competing in ways that interact to explain the behavior of the whole person;
5. psychological or cognitive processes at the level of whole person, such as "executive functioning"; and
6. social and cultural factors.

Most and perhaps all of the contributors agree that addiction is multifactoral, but they differ on how far any particular influence can succeed in explaining given key aspects of addiction by itself.

Finally, as noted earlier, an underlying thread running through discussions of both questions canvassed in the book—Is addiction one thing or many?; and, To what extent can addiction be identified with localizable brain dysfunctions?—is the degree to which addiction should be regarded as voluntary. As a broad generalization, authors in this book tend to think of addiction as under personal-level control to the extent that they emphasize its distinctive properties as behavioral rather than neural—thus, to the extent that they are skeptical about reductionism. Heyman and Manson are most explicit on this point. Ainslie denies that sudden cravings are like a reflex and argues instead that they too result from the processes he sees underlying all choice. On the other hand, to the extent that addiction is partly explained by genetic vulnerability, as argued by MacKillop and coauthors, most commentators would suggest that there must be some corresponding diminution of personal responsibility. Schroeder argues explicitly that addicts are, in effect, "mugged" by their midbrain reward systems, conceived as forces acting outside the scope of their rationality. The reader may infer support for this view in the scientific evidence surveyed by Bickel and Yi, Bellegarde and Potenza, and Ross. However, the prospect that addicts need to be divided into two groups—a relatively homogeneous group of hard-core addicts and another heterogeneous group of individuals with some addictive behaviors—suggests that loss of control may vary between the two groups. Orthogonally, emphasis on addiction as a social problem, as suggested by Kincaid and Sullivan and by Manson, may to some extent imply transfer of control of addiction away from the individual—but in the "upward" rather than "downward" direction.

We cannot suppose that the chapters in the book, taken collectively, offer a definitive answer to the question "What is addiction?" That would be an ambition that is clearly beyond the reach of our present imperfect knowledge. But we submit that the surveys and essays we have assembled demonstrate a sweeping recent advance, across several fronts, over the simplistic conception embedded in popular dramatic treatments.

Collins, in his concluding chapter on the philosophical foundations of public policy on addiction, reminds us that the cultural stereotype of the addict remains a potent force in the formation of public policy. The problem on which he puts his finger is not that addicts are necessarily treated inhumanely (though of course many drug addicts, especially in the United States, are shamefully persecuted by the criminal justice system). In general, the rise of the medicalized concept of addiction in the popular mind has been helpful in that respect. Rather, the problem is that many people appeal to an amorphous concept of addiction that leads to systematic confusion of genuine public health problems with perennial moral issues around the limits of liberal tolerance and the demand for public order. Collins suggests that although philosophical clarification can help contain this confusion up to a point, ultimately we depend on advances in scientific understanding to guide better policy. The chapters in this book make clear that the demand will not go unsatisfied.

Notes

1. E.g., the regimen prescribed by Alcoholics Anonymous.

2. If it were such grounds, then we'd have an equally good basis for saying that there are "really" no lawyers or conservatives or Jews, either.

References

Fingarette, H. (1988). *Heavy Drinking: The Myth of Alcoholism as a Disease.* Berkeley: University of California Press.

Hacking, I. (1999). *The Social Construction of What?* Cambridge, MA: Harvard University Press.

Ross, D., Sharp, C., Vuchinich, R., and Spurrett, D. (2008). *Midbrain Mutiny: The Picoeconomics and Neuroeconomics of Disordered Gambling.* Cambridge, MA: MIT Press.

1 Neuroeconomics of Addiction: The Contribution of Executive Dysfunction

Warren K. Bickel and Richard Yi

Your lights are on, but you're not home
Your will is not your own
Your heart sweats and teeth grind
Another kiss and you'll be mine
Whoa, you like to think that you're immune to the stuff, oh yeah
It's closer to the truth to say you can't get enough
You know you're gonna have to face it, you're addicted to love
—Robert Palmer, "Addicted to Love"

The word "addict" comes from Roman law where an individual is bound to his or her creditor in lieu of payment of debt. Indeed, this was one way that an individual became a slave in ancient times. The more contemporary concept of a "slave to drugs" provides an important vantage point for considering the problems of drug addiction. However, in suggesting that the addict is not able to exert control of his or her circumstances, this vantage point may not capture an important feature of addiction. Addicts can clearly exert some control over circumstances and make both healthy and unhealthy choices. We will argue that the range of choices of addicts, which overlaps with those choices made by nonaddicted individuals, is constrained. This restricted range of choices is not foreign to us, though we may often think those choices are ill advised under a variety of circumstances. Let us consider some of the choices that addicts often make: sharing needles, engaging in risky sexual activities, participating in theft and criminal activities, placing important relationships in jeopardy, and ignoring the health consequences of what they do (Simon and Burns 1997). These choices may result in negative consequences and contribute to the estimated 245-billion-dollar cost of addiction to the U.S. economy (Harwood, Fountain, and Livermore 1998).

The goal of our chapter is to suggest that the unhealthy choices of addicts result from two separate and competing processes—one that is hyperactive and one that is hypoactive. The hyperactive process results from excessive activity in the limbic reinforcement system. The hypoactive process results from decreased activity in the prefrontal cortex associated with executive functions. Considerable scientific effort has been exerted in the study of the hyperactive process and considerably less in the study of the hypoactive system. In this chapter, we will try to emphasize the less-examined hypoactive executive function processes, or as expressed in addicts, executive dysfunction. We will use the four questions of Tinbergen (1951) as an organizing concept and structure for this chapter. Tinbergen, the Nobel Prize–winning ethnologist, said that to explain a behavior requires that it be understood in four dimensions. The first question refers to mechanism—what brain regions underlie a behavior? The second question addresses development—how is the behavior related to age? The third question addresses evolution—what is the evolutionary basis for the behavior? The last question refers to adaptation—how does the environment alter the behavior?

Mechanism: Addiction as Competition of Two Brain Systems

The mechanism of addiction is the first of Tinbergen's categories of questions and explanations we will address. "Mechanism" here refers to the association between specific brain structures and addiction. A number of recent theories conceptualize addiction as an emergent phenomenon resulting from the interaction of two brain systems. Jentsch and Taylor (1999) proposed that drug seeking behavior is a consequence of the combination of amplified incentive value bestowed upon drug and drug-related cues (via reward processing by the amygdala) and impaired ability to inhibit behavior (due to frontal cortical dysfunction). Similarly, Bechara (2005) has proposed that willpower to resist drugs, and lack thereof, is a function of the interaction of impulsive and reflective systems, represented by the amygdala and the ventromedial prefrontal cortex, respectively. In this conceptualization, the amygdala is the critical structure for somatic signaling of immediate outcomes, while the ventromedial prefrontal cortex is critical for somatic signaling of delayed outcomes.

Here, we outline and provide supporting evidence of a similar two-brain-system theory of drug addiction that is largely influenced by the work of Bechara (2005) and Jentsch and Taylor (1999): the competing neural systems hypothesis (Bickel et al. 2007). Similar to Bechara (2005), we propose an "impulsive" system that is responsible for behaviors concerning immediate outcomes; the neuroanatomical representation of this system is the limbic system, particularly the extended amygdala and ventral striatum. The contrasting system, responsible for deliberative processes, is called the "executive" system (to emphasize the importance of executive function); the neuroanatomical representation of this system is the prefrontal cortex, particularly the ventromedial prefrontal cortex, orbitofrontal cortex, and dorsolateral prefrontal cortex.[1]

Executive function has been employed and defined in a variety of ways, ranging from frontal lobe functions (Struss and Benson 1986) to defining it by its components, such as effortful and flexible organization and strategic planning (Denckla 1994; see Barkley 1997 for a review of the history of executive functions). A central theme of many of these views is that the executive system permits consideration of factors not directly cued by present contingencies (Denckla 1994; Dennett 1995). Recognizing that the processes that comprise executive functioning may differ in the absence of a singular definition, we will define executive function as the class of self-directed behaviors for the cross-temporal organization of behavior (self-regulation). Therefore, an executive action is a self-directed action that functions to alter behavior and change future outcomes (Barkley 1997, 2004). We propose that drug addiction is a result of the larger relative influence of the impulsive system (with correspondingly diminished influence of the executive system), where immediate, largely positive outcomes of drug consumption are emphasized relative to the delayed, largely negative outcomes of drug dependence.

Increased Activity of the Impulsive System

Evidence for the domination of addicts' behavior and cognition by an impulsive system includes an overwhelming volume of data from multiple sources and analytical levels that has identified drug reinforcement and the processes associated with it as a fundamental component of addiction (Everitt and Robbins 2005; Wise 1980). These processes have been closely identified with dopamine signaling, and associated with activity in evolutionarily old reinforcement structures including the amygdala, dorsolateral striatum, nucleus accumbens, ventral pallidum, and related structures.

The role of the amygdala and related structures involves the trigger or attachment of somatic states to environmental events or cues (Bechara 2005; Bechara, Damasio, Damasio, and Lee 1999). Even secondary reinforcers that have no biological basis for triggering a somatic signal (e.g., money) can develop the trigger/attachment mechanism via the amygdala (Bechara 2004). Conditioned approach behavior to drug cues has been shown to be related to abnormal activity in the amygdala and ventral striatum, suggesting "exaggerated processing of the incentive value of substance-related cues" (Bechara 2005, 1459; Everitt 1999). Moreover, other addiction research using brain-imaging technology has demonstrated that the amygdala is overresponsive to reward (London et al. 2000). Observations of this sort have led to the hypothesis that limbic structures associated with the midbrain dopamine pathway form an important set of nuclei that signal the valence (positive or negative) of immediate outcomes (Bechara 2005; Bechara and Damasio 2005; McClure et al. 2004).

A "neuronal substrate for the rewarding or reinforcing properties of drugs of abuse" (Jentsch and Taylor 1999, 373), the ventral striatum has been implicated as another important structure in the development of addiction. A substantial body of evidence indicates that the reinforcing properties of drugs of dependence are due to the transmission of dopamine within this system (Dalley et al. 2007; Leshner and Koob 1999; Leyton et al. 2002), and that chronic drug consumption affects the dopaminergic function in the ventral striatum (e.g., Kalivas and Stewart 1991; Nestler 2004; Wolf 1998), which in turn may affect later behavioral output to obtain the drug (Garavan et al. 2000; Robinson and Berridge 1993; Schultz, Dayan, and Montague 1997). The role of dopamine in the ventral striatum also appears to be central in drug relapse (Dettling et al. 1995; Heinz et al. 2004; Ito et al. 2002).

Decreased Activity of the Executive System

In addiction, the executive system is marked by its limited role in and contribution to choice and decisions. This recent conceptualization in the study of addiction and its recognition by the application of brain-imaging technologies (Volkow, Fowler, and Wang 2004) suggest that "hyposensitivity to reward in the PFC mediates the reduced self-control reported by the cocaine abusers" (Goldstein et al. 2007, 49) as well as other addicted individuals. Neuroimaging studies generally observe decreased activity among addicts relative to controls in those regions that compose the prefrontal cortex, which is an evolutionarily younger brain region found in humans and higher mammals. For example, studies have demonstrated decreased activity or volumetric reduction of the prefrontal cortex among the addicted (Bickel, Kowal, and Gatchalian 2006; Fein, Di Sclafani, and Meyerhoff 2002; Franklin et al. 2002; Goldstein and Volkow 2002; Volkow and Fowler 2000).

The ventromedial prefrontal cortex is part of an extended neural circuit linking systems for memory and emotion/affect, and influencing decision making (Bechara, Tranel, Damasio, and Damasio 1996; Damasio 1996). The ventromedial prefrontal cortex triggers somatic states gathering information from memories, cognition, and knowledge (Bechara 2005; Bechara, Damasio, and Damasio 2003), incorporating this information in the decision-making process. Patients with ventromedial prefrontal cortex lesions discount or neglect future consequences of decisions (Bechara et al. 1999; Bechara, Tranel, and Damasio 2000) and exhibit decision-making deficiencies (Ackerly 2000; Fellows 2006; Harlow 1999).

The dorsolateral prefrontal cortex is responsible for cognitive control (MacDonald et al. 2000), functioning with memory to suppress or shape emotional reaction (Bechara 2004). The dorsolateral prefrontal cortex interacts with working memory, and this memory system in addition to a number of other functions may relate to appropriate selection of upcoming actions based on success in the past (Rowe et al. 2000). In fact, drug abusers with deficits in working memory also exhibit compromised decision making (Bechara and Martin 2004; Martin et al. 2003); damage to the dorsolateral prefrontal cortex results in compromised decision making (Clark, Cools, and Robbins 2004; Manes et al. 2002).

Evidence of Executive Dysfunction among Addicts

According to the proposed competing neural systems hypothesis, addiction results in part from a hyperactive impulsive system with exaggerated autonomic responses to drug-related cues (Bechara 2001, 2003) and a hypoactive executive system (e.g., prefrontal cortex), such that the impulsive system overwhelms the executive system, with corresponding emphasis on immediate outcomes and consequences. Likewise, Bechara (2005) suggests that if signals triggered by the impulsive system were relatively strong, they would have the capacity to hijack the top-down, goal-driven cognitive resources needed for normal operation and exercising the willpower to resist drugs. The processes that might result in decreased executive function may be several non-mutually exclusive phenomena including premorbid dysfunction perhaps as a result of genetics, drug- and dose-related morphological changes in the brain (e.g., toxicity), altered development of the executive system, and consequences of disuse (e.g., atrophy) consistent with the use-dependent plasticity observed in the cortex (Weiller and Rijntjes 1999). The empirical evidence of executive dysfunction in substance-abusing individuals provides substantial support for this perspective, encompassing a wide array of specific impairments in addicted individuals. These include high rate of temporal discounting (see Bickel and Yi, in press, for an argument that temporal discounting be added as an executive function), risky decision making (assessed with the Iowa Gambling Task[2]), diminished response inhibition (Stroop Task[3]), diminished working memory (recall tasks), and inflexible thinking (Wisconsin Card Sorting Task).

Temporal discounting refers to the intuitive idea that an outcome that is temporally delayed loses its value as the delay to receipt of the outcome gets longer. A high rate of temporal discounting provides an explanation for why a drug abuser chooses the immediate satisfaction of drug consumption in lieu of the larger but delayed satisfaction of sobriety (e.g., better health). Future discounting is greater in drug-dependent populations including cocaine dependents (Coffey et al. 2003), opioid dependents (Kirby, Petry, and Bickel 1999; Madden et al. 1997), problem drinkers (Petry 2001a; Vuchinich and Simpson 1998), and cigarette smokers (Baker, Johnson, and Bickel 2003; Bickel, Odum, and Madden 1999; Mitchell 1999). Pathological and problem gamblers also future discount rewards more than normals (Dixon, Marley, and Jacobs 2003; Petry 2001b). The Iowa Gambling Task (an analogue for risky decision making[4]) requires participants to pick a card from one of four stacks of cards, where each deck has a specific probability of winning or losing some hypothetical money amount, with a resulting expected probability of net gains or losses. Over a series of trials, choice by a self-controlled individual should trend toward the two "good" decks that result in a net gain and away from the two "bad" decks that result in a net loss; impulsive individuals show no such shift in behavior. An extensive body of research has found that individuals with an impulse control disorder more frequently choose from the disadvantageous decks (e.g., Best, Williams, and Coccaro 2002). This observation has also been observed with cocaine-dependent individuals (Mintzer and Stitzer 2002), with diminished medial prefrontal cortex and dorsolateral prefrontal cortex activation (Bolla et al. 2003), as well as cocaine and heroin polysubstance abusers (Verdejo-Garcia, Perales, and Perez-Garcia 2007).

Goldstein and Volkow (2002) suggest that addiction results in an inability to inhibit behavior related to the drug of dependence, indicating the response inhibition may be an executive function that is impaired as a result of drug dependence. Using various analogues of response inhibition such as the Stroop task, the Stop task,[5] and the Go/No-Go task,[6] various drug-dependent populations have been found to exhibit response inhibition deficiencies. Drugs of abuse associated with these groups include: methamphetamine (Monterosso et al. 2005; Salo et al. 2002; Simon et al. 2000), cocaine (Fillmore and Rush 2002; Kaufman et al. 2003), alcohol and pathological gambling (Goudriaan et al. 2006), cigarettes (Spinella 2002), and opioids (Mintzer and Stitzer 2002). As noted previously, working memory and its use for future behaviors is associated with DLPC function. Deficits of normal function have been observed with methamphetamine (Chang et al. 2002; Kalechstein, Newton, and Green 2003; Simon et al. 2000), MDMA (Wareing, Fisk, and Murphy 2000), cocaine (Hester and Garavan 2004), opioids (Mintzer and Stitzer 2002), and substance addictions in general (Bechara and Martin 2004). The Wisconsin Card Sorting Task (WCST) is a neuropsychological assessment of "flexible thinking" (Berg 1948), requiring various intact executive functions of the frontal lobe. The WCST requires individuals to correctly sort cards, one at a time, according to a rule. Each card displays a number of colored geometric figures, and individuals must sort according to color (e.g.) based on "correct/incorrect" feedback in the absence of explicit direction that color is the rule for sorting. Deficiency in this task has been observed in users of marijuana (Bolla et al. 2002), alcohol and stimulants (Bechara and Damasio 2002), and heroin (Lyvers and Yakimoff 2003).

Implications of Diminished Executive Function for Treatment Response
Evidence supports the importance of executive dysfunction among the addicted. Between 50 and 80 percent of individuals with alcohol disorders experience mild to severe neurocognitive impairments (Bates et al. 2006); similar impairments are observed in studies of cocaine and methamphetamine dependence as well (Aharonovich et al. 2006; Gonzalez et al. 2004). The prevalence of these impairments of executive function may provide an explanation for treatment failure among patients (Lundqvist 1995). Indeed, diminished executive function may interfere with the ability to assimilate and participate in treatment (Verdejo-Garcia et al. 2004). Inability to inhibit responding or having a short temporal view may lead addicted individuals to exhibit impatience and frustration with the treatment process and sessions. Similarly, diffi-

culty in planning may render patients unresponsive to several aspects of cognitive-behavioral therapy (CBT) that require planning and other executive skills. Also, lapses of memory may prevent patients from implementing CBT strategies for avoiding relapse, while a lack of cognitive flexibility may make it difficult to implement new modes of behaving (Lundqvist 1995; Verdejo-Garcia et al. 2005).

A variety of studies support the relationship of neuropsychological impairments to poor treatment outcomes. For example, a large study (N = 1,726) from Project MATCH found that neuropsychological impairment led to less treatment compliance and lower self-efficacy, which more proximally predicted drinking. The analyses suggested that patients with and without cognitive impairments had different pathways of recovery (Bates et al. 2006). These results are similar to other previously reported outcomes where neuropsychological impairment was related to greater attrition, violations of clinic rules, and poor treatment outcomes (Aharonovich et al. 2006; Aharonovich, Nunes, and Hasin 2003; Fals-Stewart and Schafer 1992; Fals-Stewart et al. 1994; Teichner et al. 2002). Such findings are evident even with mild cognitive dysfunctions (>1.0 standard deviation) (Aharonovich et al. 2006). These and other findings have led Bates and colleagues to conclude that addiction treatments need to be modified or developed to facilitate this important aspect of recovery (Bates et al. 2004). However, the need for neurocognitive rehabilitation may not be readily apparent to treatment staff because counselors are unable to detect such deficits (Fals-Stewart 1997).

Ontogeny: Development-related Pattern in Discounting and Correlated Brain Region

The ontogeny of addiction is the second of Tinbergen's categories of questions and explanations we address. For this dimension, issues of ontogeny refer to the developmental changes in executive function as well as addiction that may explain behavior. Given the development of executive function and related brain structures that occurs in childhood (Anderson 2002; Casey, Galvan, and Hare 2005; Casey, Tottenham, Liston and Durston 2005), behavior consistent with suboptimal executive function may result from an underdeveloped neural circuitry responsible for cross-temporal planning of behavior (Chambers, Taylor, and Potenza 2003). Conceptualized as a high rate of temporal discounting, poor cross-temporal planning of behavior has been found to vary as a function of age. In the first study examining the developmental trend of temporal discounting, Green et al. (1994) collected discounting measures from 6th graders, college students, and senior citizens. The highest rate of temporal discounting was observed in adolescents, with decreasing discounting with increasing age. Said another way, the young prefer immediate rewards relative to older individuals. This general developmental pattern in discounting has been replicated (Green, Myerson, and Ostaszewski 1999; Scheres et al. 2006), and other studies have further specified the age/discounting relationship, finding that temporal discounting rapidly decreases between childhood and adulthood (into the 30s; Green and Myerson 1996), and may increase again in later years (Read and Read 2004).

As discussed previously, specific brain regions may be involved in differential rates of temporal discounting. Some recent research has examined the developmental pattern of brain regions proposed in our competing neural systems hypothesis, and this research indicates that the higher temporal discounting, and thus greater impulsiveness, observed in childhood and adolescence has neural correlates. Most of these observations support the competing neural systems hypothesis. Ernst et al. (2005) examined brain activation involved in reward-related processes using fMRI, finding stronger activation in response to rewards in nucleus accumbens (NAc) of adolescents compared to adults. In a similar study, Galvan et al. (2006) observed exaggerated NAc activity to reward-value manipulations with diminished and diffuse activation of orbital frontal cortex for adolescents (compared to adults). The authors suggest that "different developmental trajectories for these regions may relate to the increased impulsive and risky behaviors observed during [adolescence]" (6889), with relatively disproportionate activation in subcortical systems rather than control systems, resulting in actions based on immediate rewards. Better response inhibition has been associated with greater activation in regions of the prefrontal cortex that are also correlated with age (Marsh et al. 2006), suggesting that changes in frontostriatal structure and activity that accompany age may underlie normal development and accompanying improvement in self-control. Casey et al. (2006) provide a review of developmental brain function.

Age-related Changes in Drug Use and Other Risky Behaviors Consistent with Developmental Pattern

Under the conceptualization that risky or impulsive behaviors indicate a preference for immediate over delayed rewards, the age-related changes in incidence of risky or impulsive behaviors is consistent with the neurological development observed between adolescence and adulthood. Adolescents exhibit a host of impulsive behaviors (Arnett 1992, 1999) that diminish in frequency as a function of age. Among others, these include risky driving (Jessor, Turbin, and Costa 1997; Williams 1998), committing crime (Daly and Wilson 2001; Hirschi and Gottfredson 1983), and drug use (Hill and Chow 2002; Kowal et al., in prep.; Warner et al. 1995).

Laboratory assessments have confirmed the developmental pattern of impulsive behaviors. As noted previously, the Iowa Gambling Task (IGT) is thought to be a good measure of risk-taking behavior, and has shown an improvement in performance as a function of age. Overman et al. (2004) found a steady improvement in IGT performance from 6th grade to adulthood, with preference for the "good" deck increasing as age increased. Similar observations have been obtained by Crone and van der Molen (2004), Crone et al. (2005), and Hooper et al. (2004). Although 3- to 6-year-old children have been extensively studied with modified versions of the IGT (see Bunch, Andrews, and Halford 2007; see also Kerr and Zelazo 2004; Zelazo and Frye 1997), we leave out this discussion because of evidence that brain regions directly relevant for executive function are not developing during this time period (Gogtay et al. 2004). Crone and van der Molen (2004) have ruled out other possible explanations besides changes in impulsiveness for the developmental shift. They point to "developmental increase in the sensitivity to future consequences, positive or negative, that could not be explained by developmental changes in working memory capacity or inductive reasoning" (251), concluding that children fail to consider future rewards in a manner similar to individuals with ventromedial prefrontal cortex lesions.

Evolution: Discounting and Executive Function

The evolution of executive function relevant to addiction is the third of Tinbergen's categories of questions and explanations we address. For this dimension, we examine the evolutionary fitness of executive function, and how addiction might co-opt these functions (specifically temporal discounting) to adversely affect behavior. We begin by considering one theory on the evolution of the human brain and how the development of the cerebral cortex and related executive function might confer an evolutionary advantage. We conclude with a brief discussion of how addiction might diminish this evolutionary advantage by abating the influence of executive control on temporal discounting.

Paleoneurology and comparative neuroanatomy indicate that brain evolution included not only increases in overall size, but development of newer structures to handle changing and expanding evolutionary pressures. Robert Jastrow (1981) outlines the evolution of the human brain thus: The reptilian brain of 300 million years ago was responsible for the processes that affect survival. These processes included searching for food and sex, fight-or-flight responses, etc. The mammalian brain of 200 million years ago maintained the survival processes of the reptilian brain, but added new processes for mammalian life such as taking care of progeny. The brain of man's immediate ancestors (120 million years ago) includes a more developed cerebral cortex surrounding the old reptilian brain, responsible for flexible behavioral outputs controlled by what we might call executive functioning. Of particular relevance is the newest part of the cerebral cortex, the neocortex. The neocortex plays a role in higher-order processes such as memory, attention, perceptual awareness, language, and consciousness.

If the evolution of the brain was a function of natural selection, one might ask why this evolution occurred. Stated differently, what is the evolutionary advantage of the development of cortical regions of the brain and related executive function? There is little question that significant costs are associated with expanding overall brain size and specific brain structures as well as maintaining them thereafter. Brain tissue, with a much higher metabolic rate than the cells in the rest of the human body (Aiello and Wheeler 1995), places significant pressure on the ability of the organism to meet the dietary threshold for survival. Given the importance of food for survival, it would seem that anything that increases rather than decreases this demand would negatively affect survival chances, and be naturally selected against. For brain development to continue in the face of this challenge suggests that the evolved brain confers advantages for survival and procreation beyond the associated costs.

Numerous theories speculate on the evolutionary processes or pressures that may have led to the natural selection of the evolved human brain. We will focus our review on a relatively recent theory on the evolution of the brain called the *social brain hypothesis* (Dunbar 1998). Group living bestows a degree of advantage over solitary living (e.g., minimization of predatory risk). However, successful group living requires that individuals are able not only to meet individual survival requirements, but also to engage in behavioral synchronization and cooperation with others. Therefore, the social brain hypothesis posits that sociality confers reproductive fitness; ability to engage in coordinated group behavior improves not only the evolutionary fitness of the group, but the fitness of the individuals engaging in social behaviors. The additional computational demands of complex social interactions were naturally selected for, that is, executive functioning regions of the brain.

Dunbar (1998, 2003) and Dunbar and Shultz (2007) review research in support of the social brain hypothesis. For instance, a study of baboons in Kenya (Silk, Alberts, and Altmann 2003) found that sociality in female baboons was positively associated with the number of progeny that survived until 12 months of age (indicating a good chance of surviving into adulthood). Among primates, the relative size of the neocortex is correlated with a host of indices of social group complexity including overall size, prevalence of social play, and frequencies of coalitions, tactical deception, and social learning (see review in Dunbar and Shultz 2007). It appears that as group and clique size and complexity increase, the cross-temporal organization of behavior (resulting in successful engagement in sociality) that is covered by the cortical regions of the brain becomes more important for survival and prosperity.

Research in the field of functional neuroanatomy indicates a substantial body of evidence that disruptions of the neocortex result in exhibitions of socially inappropriate behavior or inability to correctly perceive others' behavior (Damasio et al. 1991; Grafman, Litvan, and Stark 1995). Anderson et al. (1999) observed that damage to the prefrontal cortex during infancy resulted in adolescent and adult behavior marked by physical and verbal abuse (to others), theft, deceit, risky sexual behavior, accrual of financial debt, and a lack of meaningful relationships. Mah et al. (2004) found that patients with lesions to orbitofrontal cortex or dorsolateral prefrontal cortex demonstrated impaired social perception when making judgments based on nonverbal cues. Stone et al. (1998) found deficits in social reasoning in patients with bilateral lesions of the orbitofrontal cortex. When fully developed and functioning correctly, the prefrontal cortex appears to allow for socially appropriate behavior (Wood 2003), which, stated differently, is the ability to consider the immediate and delayed outcomes for alternative courses of action; individuals with malfunctioning prefrontal cortex (via lesion) reveal insensitivity to the delayed consequences of their choice (Bechara, Damasio, Damasio, and Anderson 1994; Bechara, Tranel, and Damasio 2000). In other words, engaging in appropriate social behavior is a form of delaying gratification. Individuals with normally developed and functioning prefrontal cortex are able to consider future consequences of behavior and thus behave in a socially appropriate manner; individuals with prefrontal cortex dysfunction are not able to do so.

Psychologists have also proposed that social and intertemporal behaviors are related. Rachlin, who has extensively studied self-control (nominally, the ability to defer smaller-immediate for larger-delayed rewards and/or the ability to cross-temporally organize behavior in order to maximize benefit), has speculated that social and cross-temporal behaviors are related: specifically, that altruism (or what might be called positive social behavior) is similar to self-control. Rachlin (2000, 2002) argues that what might be considered altruism is really self-controlled behavior within a social context with reciprocity. Buckner and Carroll (2007) suggest that the ability to project oneself into the future (prospection, relevant to temporal discounting) is related to the ability to conceive another's point of view (relevant to social interaction). Both processes appear to be under the governance of the prefrontal cortex, and require the projection of oneself to an alternative point of view (Mesulam 2002). Research on the relationship between the ability to delay gratification (via temporal discounting) and behavior in social dilemmas supports this perspective (Harris and Madden 2002; Yi, Johnson, and Bickel 2005).

Environmental and Cultural Factors: Modulators of Executive Function

The last of Tinbergen's questions addresses environmental adaptation and how it supports reproductive success. This is the most speculative section of this chapter since there is little data that directly address this matter. For the purposes of this chapter, we want to consider how different current environmental circumstances may influence executive function and thus reproductive success. First, we note that environmental adaptations that did not promote reproductive success would ultimately lead to extinction. However, to be relevant to humans and to the questions that we are addressing in this chapter, we must consider the relationship between culture and executive function. But before addressing that directly, we will address how cultures and reproductive success may operate.

Clearly, cultures that survive must meet a minimum threshold of reproductive success such that the population of subsequent generations does not decrease in number.

Indeed, any cultural adaptation that increases reproduction will be favored. Perhaps not surprisingly, this threshold allows a broad range of conditions. Recognizing that genetically the members of two different cultures are essentially the same, let us consider a contemporary family farmer in the United States and a contemporary member of the Yanomamö, a hunter/gatherer tribe that lives on the border between Brazil and Venezuela (see Beinhocker 2006 for more details regarding Yanomamö and comparisons to Western culture).

Our contemporary farmer has written language, works industriously using larger pieces of equipment during the growing season, must plant the crops, maintain them during the season, and plan to sell the food as well as likely save some portion of it for personal or family use. The farmer has a vast array of economic choices in terms of different items she or he could purchase. In contrast, the Yanomamö member has no written language, works industriously using stone tools to hunt and gather whenever food is needed, and counts in units of one, two, or many (Beinhocker 2006). The economic choices of the Yanomamö member are limited, likely by orders of magnitude, relative to the contemporary farmer (ibid.). Importantly, both contemporary American farmers and the Yanomamö continue to reproduce and survive. Thus, they both meet the minimal threshold of evolutionary adaptation, indicating, first, that successful cultures can be quite diverse.

The second point is that although these two cultures both require skills and effort, they likely produce different demands on the development of executive function. The role of executive function is to organize behavior cross-temporally, and the temporal view of the farmer is likely longer relative to the hunter/gatherers since the economic returns of farmers are more delayed. Indeed, Tucker examined the discount rate of farmers and hunter/gatherers among native groups of Madagascar (Tucker 2006), finding that hunter/gatherers discounted the future significantly more than farmers. This observation is important and suggests that culture, and in particular economic activity within that culture, can influence consideration of the future and with it likely executive functions. To the extent that foraging can be considered a more marginal economic activity, it may be related to prior observations that lower-income individuals have shortened consideration of the future.

With the assumption that culture influences consideration of the future, we can begin to speculate about how our contemporary culture influences our perspective on the future. Clearly, since the 1950s, an ever increasing array of technological and social changes has occurred that may diminish aspects of executive function in at least some segments of advanced societies. We have made the case previously (Bickel and Marsch 2000) that our consumer culture (namely, the desire to get things right away and the use of electronic media) is changing our environmental demands, and that this tendency may reduce concentration, attention, and consideration of the future. To our knowledge, there have not been any studies examining discounting or other executive functions in those who use extensive media technology versus those who do not. However, individuals who do not exercise those executive functions may be at risk for addiction or other disorders. If the numbers of such individuals are substantial, then we should see evidence in the population. We consider three types of behaviors that could be influenced by the cultural trends: drug dependence, obesity, and declining personal savings. To the extent that these changes in consumer culture have been progressive, there should be evidence of greater problems in the recent past than in the more distant past.

Drug Dependence

Using data from the National Comorbidity Study, Warner and colleagues (1995) assessed the prevalence of drug use and dependence of over 8,000 individuals. Specifically, a structured psychiatric diagnostic interview was administered to a nationally representative, noninstitutionalized sample that ultimately composed four U.S. birth cohorts including Cohort I (born 1966–1975), Cohort II (born 1956–1965), Cohort III (born 1946–1955), and Cohort IV (born 1936–1945). Cohort IV (born pre-World War II) was found to have the lowest prevalence of drug use and lifetime dependence drug use with dependence increasing in each later cohort. The greatest prevalence of lifetime drug dependence was with Cohort I (the cohort born most recently).

Obesity

Using the National Health and Nutrition Examination Survey, studies have examined the epidemiology of obesity in children and adults (Centers for Disease Control and Prevention 2004; Flegal, Wei, and Ogden 2002; Hedley et al. 2004; Ogden et al. 2002). Those indicated that the prevalence of overweight children (6–11 years of age) quadrupled between 1963–1970 and 1999–2002. For that same time period the prevalence of overweight adolescents (12–19 years) tripled. Obesity among adults doubled in prevalence from 1976–1980 to 1999–2002.

Declining Household Saving

According to the Bureau of Economic Analysis, Department of Commerce, the household saving rate was 7 percent in 1960–1979. Each subsequent time frame showed progressive decline in savings until it was less than zero (−0.3 percent) in 2005.

Collectively, these data are consistent with the notion that our culture can influence our use of executive functions. The growing prevalence of several important public health and financial challenges is also consistent with our environment placing demands that put more people at risk of failing to cope adequately with those challenges. One perhaps more insidious point to consider is that these changes in the environment (niche construction) are being driven by the demands of consumers. Thus we may be indirectly producing enduring changes in the environment that do not support the development of executive function.

Conclusion

In this chapter, we sought to synthesize several diverse areas together with the goal of providing a view of executive function that illustrates the diverse set of factors and forces that influence executive function and may lead to executive dysfunction. In the conceptualization provided here, executive dysfunction is an important component of addiction and perhaps other disorders. We illustrated the mechanism that is associated with decreases in executive function (decreased activity in prefrontal cortex). We provided evidence that these executive functions come online later in the process of development which may be in part the reason adolescents engage in risky behaviors such as drug use. We reviewed the evidence that executive function evolved to support community and socialization, which in turn suggests that executive dysfunction may be related to challenges in the social sphere. Finally, in what we see as a more speculative discussion, we propose that culture can influence consideration of the future (a central element of executive function). In this view culture can either extend or constrict consideration of the future and as such may make more or fewer people susceptible to other diseases or disorders.

This chapter, in part because of the nascent aspects of the study of executive dysfunction in addiction, raises many more questions than it answers. Among the most interesting questions from our perspective are ones that are essentially therapeutic in nature: (1) Can executive dysfunction be improved by training, medication, or direct stimulation of the brain (e.g., transcranial magnetic stimulation and/or biofeedback)? (2) If such training or medications improve executive function, which area of the brain will show increased activity? (3) Could successful therapy for improving executive function be a useful component of a comprehensive prevention program for addiction? (4) Could these treatments or programs be successfully applied to executive dysfunction associated with other disorders (e.g., attention-deficit/hyperactivity disorder [ADHD])? Collectively, the answers to these questions will provide an understanding of the importance of executive dysfunction for the development of addiction and its role in its treatment.

Acknowledgments

This research was supported by NIDA grants R37 DA 006526-18, R01 DA 11692-09, R01 DA022386-02, R03 DA021707-01, Wilbur Mills Chair Endowment, and in part by the Arkansas Biosciences Institute, a partnership of scientists from Arkansas Children's Hospital, Arkansas State University, the University of Arkansas-Division of Agriculture, the University of Arkansas, Fayetteville, and the University of Arkansas for Medical Sciences. The Arkansas Biosciences Institute is the major research component of the Tobacco Settlement Proceeds Act of 2000.

Notes

1. In the present volume, A. David Redish provides evidence of both orbitofrontal cortex and ventral striatum as important brain regions in the neural subsystem responsible for flexible, goal-directed behavior and expectation of outcomes.

2. Along with the Wisconsin Card Sorting Task, the Iowa Gambling Task is described in detail later in this chapter.

3. Stroop tasks require that the individual inhibit a prepotent verbal response (e.g., reading a visually presented color word) and replace it with a different verbal response (e.g., identify the ink color of the visually presented word).

4. There is some debate regarding what the Iowa Gambling Task measures (see, e.g., Colombetti 2008; Dunn et al. 2006).

5. Participants are presented with a "Go" stimulus indicating that they should respond. On some trials, a "Stop" stimulus is presented immediately after the Go stimulus, indicating that the participant should inhibit the response signaled by the initial Go stimulus.

6. Participants are presented with S+ and S− stimuli. The appropriate action to S+ is a response; the appropriate action to S− is no response.

References

Ackerly, B. A. (2000). *Political Theory and Feminist Social Criticism*. New York: Cambridge University Press.

Aharonovich, E., Hasin, D. S., Brooks, A. C., Liu, X., Bisaga, A., and Nunes, E. V. (2006). Cognitive deficits predict low treatment retention in cocaine dependent patients. *Drug and Alcohol Dependence* 81 (3): 313–322.

Aharonovich, E., Nunes, E., and Hasin, D. (2003). Cognitive impairment, retention, and abstinence among cocaine abusers in cognitive-behavioral treatment. *Drug and Alcohol Dependence* 71 (2): 207–211.

Aiello, L. C., and Wheeler, P. (1995). The expensive-tissue hypothesis. *Current Anthropology* 36 (2): 199–221.

Anderson, P. (2002). Assessment and development of executive function. *Child Neuropsychology* 8 (2): 71–82.

Anderson, S. W., Bechara, A., Damasio, H., Tranel, D., and Damasio, A. R. (1999). Impairment of social and moral behavior related to early damage in human prefrontal cortex. *Nature Neuroscience* 2 (11): 1032–1037.

Arnett, J. (1992). Reckless behavior in adolescence: A developmental perspective. *Developmental Review* 12 (4): 339–373.

Arnett, J. (1999). Adolescent storm and stress, reconsidered. *American Psychologist* 54 (5): 317–326.

Baker, F., Johnson, M. W., and Bickel, W. K. (2003). Delay discounting in current and never-before cigarette smokers: Similarities and differences across commodity, sign, and magnitude. *Journal of Abnormal Psychology* 112 (3): 382–392.

Barkley, R. A. (1997). Behavioral inhibition, sustained attention, and executive functions: Constructing a unifying theory of ADHD. *Psychological Bulletin* 121 (1): 65–94.

Barkley, R. A. (2004). Adolescents with attention-deficit/hyperactivity disorder: An overview of empirically based treatments. *Journal of Psychiatric Practice* 10 (1): 39–56.

Bates, M. E., Barry, D., Labouvie, E. W., Fals-Stewart, W., Voelbel, G., and Buckman, J. F. (2004). Risk factors and neuropsychological recovery in clients with alcohol use disorders who were exposed to different treatments. *Journal of Consulting and Clinical Psychology* 72 (6): 1073–1080.

Bates, M. E., Pawlak, A. P., Tonigan, J. S., and Buckman, J. F. (2006). Cognitive impairment influences drinking outcome by altering therapeutic mechanisms of change. *Psychology of Addictive Behaviors* 20 (3): 241–253.

Bechara, A. (2001). Neurobiology of decision-making: Risk and reward. *Seminars in Clinical Neuropsychiatry* 6: 205–216.

Bechara, A. (2003). Risky business: Emotion, decision-making, and addiction. *Journal of Gambling Studies* 19: 23–51.

Bechara, A. (2004). The role of emotion in decision-making: Evidence from neurological patients with orbitofrontal damage. *Brain and Cognition* 55 (1): 30–40.

Bechara, A. (2005). Decision making, impulse control, and loss of willpower to resist drugs: A neurocognitive perspective. *Nature Neuroscience* 8 (11): 1458–1463.

Bechara, A., and Damasio, A. R. (2005). The somatic marker hypothesis: A neural theory of economic decision. *Games and Economic Behavior* 52: 336–372.

Bechara, A., and Damasio, H. (2002). Decision-making and addiction (part I): Impaired activation of somatic states in substance dependent individuals when pondering decisions with negative future consequences. *Neuropsychologia* 40 (10): 1675–1689.

Bechara, A., Damasio, H., and Damasio, A. R. (2003). Role of the amygdala in decision-making. *Annals of the New York Academy of Sciences* 985: 356–369.

Bechara, A., Damasio, A. R., Damasio, H., and Anderson, S. W. (1994). Insensitivity to future consequences following damage to human prefrontal cortex. *Cognition* 50 (1–3): 7–15.

Bechara, A., Damasio, H., Damasio, A. R., and Lee, G. P. (1999). Different contributions of the human amygdala and ventromedial prefrontal cortex to decision-making. *Journal of Neuroscience* 19 (13): 5473–5481.

Bechara, A., and Martin, E. M. (2004). Impaired decision making related to working memory deficits in individuals with substance addictions. *Neuropsychology* 18 (1): 152–162.

Bechara, A., Tranel, D., and Damasio, H. (2000). Characterization of the decision-making deficit of patients with ventromedial prefrontal cortex lesions. *Brain* 123 (11): 2189–2202.

Bechara, A., Tranel, D., Damasio, H., and Damasio, A. R. (1996). Failure to respond autonomically to anticipated future outcomes following damage to prefrontal cortex. *Cerebral Cortex* 6: 215–225.

Beinhocker, E. (2006). *The Origin of Wealth*. London: Random House.

Berg, E. A. (1948). A simple objective technique for measuring flexibility of thinking. *Journal of General Psychology* 39: 15–22.

Best, M., Williams, J. M., and Coccaro, E. F. (2002). Evidence for a dysfunctional prefrontal circuit in patients with an impulsive aggressive disorder. *Proceedings of the National Academy of Sciences* 99 (12): 8448–8453.

Bickel, W. K., Kowal, B. P., and Gatchalian, K. M. (2006). Understanding addiction as a pathology of temporal horizon. *Behavior Analyst Today* 7 (1): 32–47.

Bickel, W. K., and Marsch, L. A. (2000). The tyranny of small decisions: Origins, outcomes and proposed solutions. In W. K. Bickel and R. E. Vuchinich, eds., *Reframing Health Behavior Change with Behavioral Economics*, 341–391. New Jersey: Lawrence Erlbaum.

Bickel, W. K., Miller, M. L., Yi, R., Kowal, B. P., Lindquist, D. M., and Pitcock, J. A. (2007). Behavioral and neuroeconomics of drug addiction: Competing neural systems and temporal discounting processes. *Drug and Alcohol Dependence* 90S: S85–S91.

Bickel, W. K., Odum, A. L., and Madden, G. J. (1999). Impulsivity and cigarette smoking: Delay discounting in current, never, and ex-smokers. *Psychopharmacology* 146: 447–454.

Bickel, W. K., and Yi, R. (in press). Temporal discounting as a measure of executive function: Insights from the competing neuro-behavioral decision system hypothesis of addiction. In D. Houser and K. McCabe, eds., *Neuroeconomics: Advances in Health Economics and Health Services Research*. Bingley: Emerald Publishing.

Bolla, K. I., Brown, K., Eldreth, D., Tate, K., and Cadet, J. L. (2002). Dose-related neurocognitive effects of marijuana use. *Neurology* 59: 1337–1343.

Bolla, K. I., Eldreth, D. A., London, E. D., Kiehl, K. A., Mouratidis, M., Contoreggi, C., Matochik, J. A., Kurrian, V., Cadet, J. L., Kimes, A. S., Funderburk, F. R., and Ernst, M. (2003). Orbitofrontal cortex dysfunction in abstinent cocaine abusers performing a decision-making task. *NeuroImage* 19 (3): 1085–1094.

Buckner, R. L., and Carroll, D. C. (2007). Self-projection and the brain. *Trends in Cognitive Sciences* 11 (2): 49–57.

Bunch, K. M., Andrews, G., and Halford, G. S. (2007). Complexity effects on the children's gambling task. *Cognitive Development* 22 (3): 376–383.

Casey, B. J., and Durston, S. (2006). From behavior to cognition to the brain and back: What have we learned from functional imaging studies of attention deficit hyperactivity disorder? *American Journal of Psychiatry* 163: 957–960.

Casey, B. J., Galvan, A., and Hare, T. A. (2005). Changes in cerebral functional organization during cognitive development. *Current Opinion in Neurobiology* 15 (2): 239–244.

Casey, B. J., Tottenham, N., Liston, C., and Durston, S. (2005). Imaging the developing brain: What have we learned about cognitive development? *Trends in Cognitive Sciences* 9 (3): 104–110.

Centers for Disease Control and Prevention (2004). Prevalence of overweight and obesity among adults with diagnosed diabetes—United States, 1988–1994 and 1999–2002. *Morbidity and Mortality Weekly Report* 53 (45): 1066–1068.

Chambers, R. A., Taylor, J. R., and Potenza, M. N. (2003). Developmental neurocircuitry of motivation in adolescence: A critical period of addiction vulnerability. *American Journal of Psychiatry* 160 (6): 1041–1052.

Chang, L., Ernst, T., Speck, O., Patel, H., DeSilva, M., Leonido-Yee, M., and Miller, E. N. (2002). Perfusion MRI and computerized cognitive test abnormalities in abstinent methamphetamine users. *Psychiatry Research: Neuroimaging* 114 (2): 65–79.

Clark, L., Cools, R., and Robbins, T. W. (2004). The neuropsychology of ventral prefrontal cortex: Decision-making and reversal learning. *Brain and Cognition* 55 (1): 41–53.

Coffey, S. F., Gudleski, G. D., Saladin, M. E., and Brady, K. T. (2003). Impulsivity and rapid discounting of delayed hypothetical rewards in cocaine-dependent individuals. *Experimental and Clinical Psychopharmacology* 11 (1): 18–25.

Crone, E. A., Bunge, S. A., Latenstein, H., and van der Molen, M. W. (2005). Characterization of children's decision making: Sensitivity to punishment frequency, not task complexity. *Child Neuropsychology* 11 (3): 245–263.

Crone, E. A., and van der Molen, M. W. (2004). Developmental changes in real life decision making: Performance on a gambling task previously shown to depend on the ventromedial prefrontal cortex. *Developmental Neuropsychology* 25 (3): 251–279.

Dalley, J. W., Fryer, T. D., Brichard, L., Robinson, E. S. J., Theobald, D. E. H., Laane, K., Pena, Y., Murphy, E. R., Shah, Y., Probst, K., Abakumova, I., Aigbirhio, F. I., Richards, H. K., Hong, Y., Baron, J. C., Everitt, B. J., and Robbins, T. W. (2007). Nucleus accumbens D2/3 receptors predict trait impulsivity and cocaine reinforcement. *Science* 315 (5816): 1267–1270.

Daly, M., and Wilson, M. (2001). Risk-taking, intrasexual competition, and homicide. *Nebraska Symposium on Motivation* 47: 1–36.

Damasio, A. R. (1996). The somatic marker hypothesis and the possible functions of the prefrontal cortex. *Philosophical Transactions of the Royal Society B: Biological Sciences* 351: 1413–1420.

Damasio, H., Kuljis, R. O., Yuh, W., Van Hoesen, G. W., and Ehrhardt, J. (1991). Magnetic resonance imaging of human intracortical structure in vivo. *Cerebral Cortex* 1 (5): 374–379.

Denckla, M. B. (1994). Measurement of executive function. In G. R. Lyon, ed., *Frames of Reference for the Assessment of Learning Disabilities: New Views on Measurement Issues*, 117–142. Baltimore: Paul H. Brookes.

Dennett, D. (1995). *Darwin's Dangerous Idea: Evolution and the Meanings of Life.* New York: Simon and Schuster.

Dettling, M., Heinz, A., Dufeu, P., Rommelspacher, H., Graf, K. J., and Schmidt, L. G. (1995). Dopaminergic responsivity in alcoholism: Trait, state, or residual marker? *American Journal of Psychiatry* 152 (9): 1317–1321.

Dixon, M. R., Marley, J., and Jacobs, E. A. (2003). Delay discounting by pathological gamblers. *Journal of Applied Behavior Analysis* 36 (4): 449–458.

Dunbar, R. (1998). The social brain hypothesis. *Evolutionary Anthropology* (6): 178–190.

Dunbar, R. (2003). *Why Are Apes So Smart? Primate Life Histories and Socioecology.* Chicago: University of Chicago Press.

Dunbar, R., and Shultz, S. (2007). Understanding primate brain evolution. *Philosophical Transactions of the Royal Society B: Biological Sciences* 362 (1480): 649–658.

Ernst, M., Nelson, E. E., Jazbec, S., McClure, E. B., Monk, C. S., Leibenluft, E., Blair, J., and Pine, D. S. (2005). Amygdala and nucleus accumbens in response to receipt and omission of gains in adults and adolescents. *Neuroimage* 25: 1279–1291.

Everitt, B. J. (1999). Associative processes in addiction and reward: The role of amygdala and ventral striatum subsystems. *Annals of the New York Academy of Sciences* 877: 412–438.

Everitt, B. J., and Robbins, T. W. (2005). Neural systems of reinforcement for drug addiction: From actions to habits to compulsion. *Nature Neuroscience* 8 (11): 1481–1489.

Fals-Stewart, W. (1997). Ability of counselors to detect cognitive impairment among substance-abusing patients: An examination of diagnostic efficiency. *Experimental and Clinical Psychopharmacology* 5 (1): 39–50.

Fals-Stewart, W., and Schafer, J. (1992). The relationship between length of stay in drug-free therapeutic communities and neurocognitive functioning. *Journal of Clinical Psychology* 48 (4): 539–543.

Fals-Stewart, W., Schafer, J., Lucente, S., Rustine, T., and Brown, L. (1994). Neurobehavioral consequences of prolonged alcohol and substance abuse: A review of findings and treatment implications. *Clinical Psychology Review* 14: 755–778.

Fein, G., Di Sclafani, V., and Meyerhoff, D. J. (2002). Prefrontal cortical volume reduction associated with frontal cortex function deficit in 6-week abstinent crack-cocaine dependent men. *Drug and Alcohol Dependence* 68 (1): 87–93.

Fellows, L. K. (2006). Deciding how to decide: Ventromedial frontal lobe damage affects information acquisition in multi-attribute decision making. *Brain* 129 (4): 944–952.

Fillmore, M. T., and Rush, C. R. (2002). Impaired inhibitory control of behavior in chronic cocaine users. *Drug and Alcohol Dependence* 66 (3): 265–273.

Flegal, K. M., Wei, R., and Ogden, C. (2002). Weight-for-stature compared with body mass index-for-age growth charts for the United States from the Centers for Disease Control and Prevention. *American Journal of Clinical Nutrition* 75 (4): 761–766.

Franklin, T. R., Acton, P. D., Maldjian, J. A., Gray, J. D., Croft, J. R., Dackis, C. A., O'Brien, C. P., and Childress, A. R. (2002). Decreased gray matter concentration in the insular, orbitofrontal, cingulate, and temporal cortices of cocaine patients. *Biological Psychiatry* 51 (2): 134–142.

Galvan, A., Hare, T. A., Parra, C. E., Penn, J., Voss, H., Glover, G., and Casey, B. J. (2006). Earlier development of the accumbens relative to orbitofrontal cortex might underlie risk-taking behavior in adolescents. *Journal of Neuroscience* 26 (25): 6885–6892.

Garavan, H., Pankiewicz, J., Bloom, A., Cho, J. K., Sperry, L., Ross, T. J., Salmeron, B. J., Risinger, R., Kelley, D., and Stein, E. A. (2000). Cue-induced cocaine craving: Neuroanatomical specificity for drug users and drug stimuli. *American Journal of Psychiatry* 157 (11): 1789–1798.

Gogtay, N., Giedd, J. N., Lusk, L., Hayashi, K. M., Greenstein, D., Vaituzis, A. C., NugentIII, T. F., Herman, D. H., Clasen, L. S., Toga, A. W., Rapoport, J. L., and Thompson, P. M. (2004). Dynamic mapping of human cortical development during childhood through early adulthood. *Proceedings of the National Academy of Sciences of the United States of America* 101 (21): 8174–8179.

Goldstein, R. Z., and Volkow, N. D. (2002). Drug addiction and its underlying neurobiological basis: Neuroimaging evidence for the involvement of the frontal cortex. *American Journal of Psychiatry* 159 (10): 1642–1652.

Goldstein, R. Z., Alia-Klein, N., Tomasi, D., Zhang, L., Cottone, L. A., Maloney, T., et al. (2007). Is decreased prefrontal cortical sensitivity to monetary reward associated with impaired motivation and self-control in cocaine addiction? *American Journal of Psychiatry* 164 (1): 43–51.

Gonzalez, R., Rippeth, J. D., Carey, C. L., Heaton, R. K., Moore, D. J., Schweinsburg, B. C., Cherna, M., and Grant, I. (2004). Neurocognitive performance of methamphetamine users discordant for history of marijuana exposure. *Drug and Alcohol Dependence* 76 (2): 181–190.

Goudriaan, A. E., Oosterlaan, J., de Beurs, E., and van den Brink, W. (2006). Neurocognitive functions in pathological gambling: A comparison with alcohol dependence, Tourette syndrome and normal controls. *Addiction* 101 (4): 534–547.

Grafman, J., Litvan, I., and Stark, M. (1995). Neuropsychological features of progressive supranuclear palsy. *Brain and Cognition* 28 (3): 311–320.

Green, L., Fry, A. F., and Myerson, J. (1994). Discounting of delayed rewards: A life-span comparison. *Psychological Science* 5: 33–36.

Green, L., and Myerson, J. (1996). Exponential versus hyperbolic discounting of delayed outcomes: Risk and waiting time. *American Zoologist* 36 (4): 496–505.

Green, L., Myerson, J., and Ostaszewski, P. (1999). Amount of reward has opposite effects on the discounting of delayed and probabilistic outcomes. *Experimental Psychology: Learning, Memory, and Cognition* 25 (2): 418–427.

Harlow, J. M. (1999). Passage of an iron rod through the head. *Journal of Neuropsychiatry and Clinical Neurosciences* 11 (2): 281–283.

Harris, A. C., and Madden, G. J. (2002). Delay discounting and performance on the prisoner's dilemma game. *The Psychological Record* 52: 429–440.

Harwood, H. J., Fountain, D., and Livermore, G. (1998). Economic costs of alcohol abuse and alcoholism. *Recent Developments in Alcoholism* 14: 307–330.

Hedley, A. A., Ogden, C. L., Johnson, C. L., Carroll, M. D., Curtin, L. R., and Flegal, K. M. (2004). Prevalence of overweight and obesity among US children, adolescents, and adults, 1999–2002. *Journal of the American Medical Association* 291 (23): 2847–2850.

Heinz, A., Siessmeier, T., Wrase, J., Hermann, D., Klein, S., Grusser-Sinopoli, S. M., Flor, H., Braus, D. F., Buchholz, H. G., Grunder, G., Schreckenberger, M., Smolka, M. N., Rosch, F., Mann, K., and Bartenstein, P. (2004). Correlation between dopamine D2 receptors in the ventral striatum and central processing of alcohol cues and craving. *American Journal of Psychiatry* 161 (10): 1783–1789.

Hester, R. K., and Garavan, H. (2004). Executive dysfunction in cocaine addiction: Evidence for discordant frontal, cingulated, and cerebellar activity. *Journal of Neuroscience* 24 (49): 11017–11022.

Hill, E. M., and Chow, K. (2002). Life-history theory and risky drinking. *Addiction* 97 (4): 401–413.

Hirschi, T., and Gottfredson, M. (1983). Age and explanation of crime. *American Journal of Sociology* 89 (3): 552–584.

Hooper, C. J., Luciana, M., Conklin, H. M., and Yarger, R. S. (2004). Adolescents' performance on the Iowa Gambling Task: Implications for the development of decision making and ventromedial prefrontal cortex. *Developmental Psychology* 40 (6): 1148–1158.

Ito, R., Dalley, J. W., Robbins, T. W., and Everitt, B. J. (2002). Dopamine release in the dorsal striatum during cocaine-seeking behavior under the control of a drug-associated cue. *Journal of Neuroscience* 22 (14): 6247–6253.

Jastrow, R. (1981). *The Enchanted Loom: Mind in the Universe.* New York: Simon and Schuster.

Jentsch, J. D., and Taylor, J. R. (1999). Impulsivity resulting from frontostriatal dysfunction in drug abuse: Implications for the control of behavior by reward-related stimuli. *Psychopharmacology* 146: 373–390.

Jessor, R., Turbin, M. S., and Costa, F. M. (1997). Predicting developmental change in risky driving: The transition to young adulthood. *Applied Developmental Science* 1 (1): 4–16.

Kalechstein, A. D., Newton, T. F., and Green, M. (2003). Methamphetamine dependence is associated with neurocognitive impairment in the initial phases of abstinence. *Journal of Neuropsychiatry and Clinical Neuroscience* 15 (2): 215–220.

Kalivas, P. W., and Stewart, J. (1991). Dopamine transmission in the initiation and expression of drug- and stress-induced sensitization of motor activity. *Brain Research Reviews 16* (3): 223–244.

Kaufman, J. N., Ross, T. J., Stein, E. A., and Garavan, H. (2003). Cingulate hypoactivity in cocaine users during a go-nogo task as revealed by event-related functional magnetic resonance imaging. *Journal of Neuroscience* 23 (21): 7839–7843.

Kerr, A., and Zelazo, P. D. (2004). Development of "hot" executive function: The children's gambling task. *Brain and Cognition* 55 (1): 148–157.

Kirby, K. N., Petry, N. M., and Bickel, W. K. (1999). Heroin addicts have higher discount rates for delayed rewards than non-drug using controls. *Journal of Experimental Psychology: General* 128: 78–87.

Kowal, B. P., Gatchalian, K. M., Badger, G. J., Mongeon, J., and Bickel, W. K. (in preparation). Is drug use a developmental disorder? An evolutionary approach.

Leshner, A. I., and Koob, G. F. (1999). Drugs of abuse and the brain. *Proceedings of the Association of American Physicians* 111 (2): 99–108.

Leyton, M., Boileau, I., Benkelfat, C., Diksic, M., Baker, G., and Dagher, A. (2002). Amphetamine-induced increases in extracellular dopamine, drug wanting, and novelty seeking: A PET/[11C]raclopride study in healthy men. *Neuropsychopharmacology* 27: 1027–1035.

London, E. D., Ernst, M., Grant, S., Bonson, K., and Weinstein, A. (2000). Orbitofrontal cortex and human drug abuse: Functional imaging. *Cerebral Cortex* 10 (3): 334–342.

Lundqvist, T. (1995). Specific thought patterns in chronic cannabis smokers observed during treatment. *Life Sciences* 56 (23–24): 2141.

Lyvers, M., and Yakimoff, M. (2003). Neuropsychological correlates of opioid dependence and withdrawal. *Addictive Behaviors* 28 (3): 605–611.

MacDonald, A. W., Cohen, J. D., Stenger, V. A., and Carter, C. S. (2000). Dissociating the role of the dorsolateral prefrontal and anterior cingulate cortex in cognitive control. *Science* 288 (5472): 1835–1838.

Madden, G. J., Petry, N. M., Badger, G. J., and Bickel, W. K. (1997). Impulsive and self-control choices in opioid-dependent patients and non-drug-using control participants: Drug and monetary rewards. *Experimental and Clinical Psychopharmacology* 5 (3): 256–262.

Mah, L., Arnold, M. C., and Grafman, J. (2004). Impairment of social perception associated with lesions of the prefrontal cortex. *American Journal of Psychiatry* 161 (7): 1247–1255.

Manes, F., Sahakian, B., Clark, L., Rogers, R., Antoun, N., Aitken, M., and Robbins, T. (2002). Decision-making processes following damage to the prefrontal cortex. *Brain* 125 (3): 624–639.

Marsh, R., Zhu, H., Schultz, R. T., Quackenbush, G., Royal, J., Skudlarski, P., and Peterson, M. D. (2006). A developmental fMRI study of self-regulatory control. *Human Brain Mapping* 27: 848–863.

Martin, E. M., Pitrak, D. L., Rains, N., Grbesic, S., Pursell, K., Nunnally, G., and Bechara, A. (2003). Delayed nonmatch-to-sample performance in HIV-seropositive and HIV-seronegative polydrug abusers. *Neuropsychology* 17 (2): 283–288.

McClure, S. M., Laibson, D. L., Loewenstein, G., and Cohen, J. D. (2004). Separate neural systems value immediate and delayed monetary rewards. *Science* 306 (5695): 503–507.

Mesulam, M. (2002). The human frontal lobes: Transcending the default mode through contingent encoding. In D. T. Stuss and R. T. Knight, eds., *Principles of Frontal Lobe Function*, 8–30. Oxford: Oxford University Press.

Mintzer, M. Z., and Stitzer, M. L. (2002). Cognitive impairment in methadone maintenance patients. *Drug and Alcohol Dependence* 67 (1): 41–51.

Mitchell, S. H. (1999). Measures of impulsivity in cigarette smokers and nonsmokers. *Psychopharmacology* 146: 455–464.

Monterosso, J. R., Aron, A. R., Cordova, X., Xu, J., and London, E. D. (2005). Deficits in response inhibition associated with chronic methamphetamine abuse. *Drug and Alcohol Dependence* 79 (2): 273–277.

Nestler, E. J. (2004). Molecular mechanisms of drug addiction. *Neuropharmacology* 47 (Supplement 1): 24–32.

Ogden, C. L., Flegal, K. M., Carroll, M. D., and Johnson, C. L. (2002). Prevalence and trends in overweight among US children and adolescents, 1999–2000. *Journal of the American Medical Association* 288 (14): 1728–1732.

Overman, W. H. (2004). Sex differences in early childhood, adolescence, and adulthood on cognitive tasks that rely on orbital prefrontal cortex. *Brain and Cognition* 55 (1): 134–147.

Petry, N. M. (2001a). Delay discounting of money and alcohol in actively using alcoholics, currently abstinent alcoholics, and controls. *Psychopharmacology* 154 (3): 243–250.

Petry, N. M. (2001b). Pathological gamblers, with and without substance use disorders, discount delayed rewards at high rates. *Journal of Abnormal Psychology* 110 (3): 482–487.

Rachlin, H. (2000). *The Science of Self-Control*. Cambridge, MA: Harvard University Press.

Rachlin, H. (2002). Altruism and selfishness. *Behavioral and Brain Sciences* 25 (2): 239–250.

Read, D., and Read, N. L. (2004). Time discounting over the lifespan. *Organized Behavior and Human Decision Processes* 94: 22–32.

Robinson, T. E., and Berridge, K. C. (1993). The neural basis of drug craving: An incentive-sensitization theory of addiction. *Brain Research Reviews* 18: 247–291.

Rowe, J. B., Toni, I., Josephs, O., Frackowiak, R. S. J., and Passingham, R. E. (2000). The prefrontal cortex: Response selection or maintenance within working memory? *Science* 288 (5471): 1656–1660.

Salo, R., Nordahl, T. E., Possin, K., Leamon, M., Gibson, D. R., Galloway, G. P., Flynn, N. M., Henik, A., Pfefferbaum, A., and Sullivan, E. V. (2002). Preliminary evidence of reduced cognitive inhibition in methamphetamine-dependent individuals. *Psychiatry Research* 111 (1): 65–74.

Scheres, A., Dijkstra, M., Ainslie, E., Balkan, J., Reynolds, B., Sonuga-Barke, E., and Castellanos, F. X. (2006). Temporal and probabilistic discounting of rewards in children and adolescents: Effects of age and ADHD symptoms. *Neuropsychologia* 44 (11): 2092–2103.

Schultz, W., Dayan, P., and Montague, P. R. (1997). A neural substrate of prediction and reward. *Science* 275 (5306): 1593–1599.

Silk, J. B., Alberts, S. C., and Altmann, J. (2003). Social bonds of female baboons enhance infant survival. *Science* 302 (5648): 1231–1234.

Simon, C. D., Carnell, J., Brethen, P., Rawson, R. A., and Ling, W. (2000). Cognitive impairment in individuals currently using methamphetamine. *American Journal on Addictions* 9: 222–231.

Simon, D., and Burns, E. (1997). *The Corner: A Year in the Life of an Inner-City Neighborhood*. New York: Broadway Books.

Spinella, M. (2002). Correlations between orbitofrontal dysfunction and tobacco smoking. *Addiction Biology* 7 (4): 381–384.

Stone, V. E., Baron-Cohen, S., and Knight, R. T. (1998). Frontal lobe contributions to theory of mind. *Journal of Cognitive Neuroscience* 10 (5): 640–656.

Struss, D. T., and Benson, D. F. (1986). *The Frontal Lobes*. New York: Raven Press.

Teichner, G., Horner, M. D., Roitzsch, J. C., Herron, J., and Thevos, A. (2002). Substance abuse treatment outcomes for cognitively impaired and intact outpatients. *Addictive Behaviors* 27 (5): 751–763.

Tinbergen, N. (1951). *The Study of Instinct*. Oxford: Clarendon Press.

Tucker, B. (2006). A future discounting explanation for the persistence of a mixed foraging-horticulture strategy among the Mikea of Madagascar. In D. J. Kennett and B. Winterhalder, eds., *Behavioral Ecology and the Transition to Agriculture*, 22–40. Berkeley: University of California Press.

Verdejo-Garcia, A. J., Lopez-Torrecillas, F., Aguilar de Arcos, F., and Perez-Garcia, M. (2005). Differential effects of MDMA, cocaine, and cannabis use severity on distinctive components of the executive functions in polysubstance users: A multiple regression analysis. *Addictive Behaviors* 30 (1): 89–101.

Verdejo-Garcia, A. J., Lopez-Torrecillas, F., Gimenez, C. O., and Perez-Garcia, M. (2004). Clinical implications and methodological challenges in the study of the neuropsychological correlates of cannabis, stimulant, and opioid abuse. *Neuropsychology Review* 14 (1): 1–41.

Verdejo-Garcia, A. J., Perales, J. C., and Perez-Garcia, M. (2007). Cognitive impulsivity in cocaine and heroin polysubstance abusers. *Addictive Behaviors* 32 (5): 950–966.

Volkow, N. D., and Fowler, J. S. (2000). Addiction, a disease of compulsion and drive: Involvement of the orbitofrontal cortex. *Cerebral Cortex* 10 (3): 318–325.

Volkow, N. D., Fowler, J. S., and Wang, G. J. (2004). The addicted human brain viewed in the light of imaging studies: Brain circuits and treatment strategies. *Neuropharmacology* 47 (Supplement 1): 3–13.

Vuchinich, R. E., and Simpson, C. A. (1998). Hyperbolic temporal discounting in social drinkers and problem drinkers. *Experimental and Clinical Psychopharmacology* 6 (3): 292–305.

Wareing, M., Fisk, J. E., and Murphy, P. N. (2000). Working memory deficits in current and previous users of MDMA ("ecstasy"). *British Journal of Psychology* 91 (2): 181–188.

Warner, L. A., Kessler, R. C., Hughes, M., Anthony, J. C., and Nelson, C. B. (1995). Prevalence and correlates of drug use and dependence in the United States: Results from the national comorbidity survey. *Archives of General Psychiatry* 52 (3): 219–229.

Weiller, C., and Rijntjes, M. (1999). Learning, plasticity, and recovery in the central nervous system. *Experimental Brain Research V1* 28 (1): 134–138.

Williams, A. F. (1998). Risky driving behavior among adolescents. In R. Jessor, ed., *New Perspectives on Adolescent Risk Behavior*, 221–237. Cambridge: Cambridge University Press.

Wise, R. A. (1980). Action of drugs of abuse on brain reward systems. *Pharmacology, Biochemistry, and Behavior* 13: 213–223.

Wolf, M. E. (1998). The role of excitatory amino acids in behavioral sensitization to psychomotor stimulants. *Progress in Neurobiology* 54 (6): 679–720.

Wood, J. N. (2003). Social cognition and the prefrontal cortex. *Behavioral and Cognitive Neuroscience Reviews* 2 (2): 97–114.

Yi, R., Johnson, M. W., and Bickel, W. K. (2005). Relationship between cooperation in an iterated prisoner's dilemma game and the discounting of hypothetical outcomes. *Learning and Behavior* 33 (3): 324–336.

Zelazo, P. D., and Frye, D. (1997). Cognitive complexity and control: A theory of the development of deliberate reasoning and intentional action. In M. Stamenov, ed., *Language Structure, Discourse, and the Access to Consciousness*, 113–153. Amsterdam and Philadelphia: John Benjamins.

2 Neurobiology of Pathological Gambling

Jennifer D. Bellegarde and Marc N. Potenza

For as long as people have been gambling, some have persisted in gambling despite experiencing serious adverse consequences related to their gambling. For example, approximately 3,600 years ago, some Mayans continued to gamble despite losing their property and wagering their wives and children (Hill and Clark 2001). This level of risk-taking and associated devastation raises the question of why such gamblers do not stop gambling prior to experiencing such significant losses. Today, with a growing awareness of potential risks associated with gambling, questions arise as to why individuals begin gambling in the first place.

The DSM-IV-TR (American Psychiatric Association Committee on Nomenclature and Statistics 2000) classifies pathological gambling (PG) as an "Impulse Control Disorder Not Elsewhere Classified." This category also includes kleptomania, pyromania, intermittent explosive disorder, and trichotillomania. Although one prevailing model considers these disorders as obsessive-compulsive spectrum disorders (Hollander and Wong 1995), it has been suggested that PG and other impulse control disorders (ICDs) might be conceptualized as behavioral or non-drug addictions (Grant et al. 2006; Potenza 2006).

Substance use disorders and ICDs such as PG share important features including persisting behavior despite adverse consequences, diminished or loss of control over the behavior, compulsive engagement in the behavior, and craving or appetitive urge states. Of particular interest to this chapter are data showing that ICDs and substance use disorders may share certain neurobiological features and processes (Brewer and Potenza 2008; Williams and Potenza 2008).

Pathological Gambling as a "Behavioral Addiction"

By definition, gambling is the process of placing something of value—most commonly money—at risk in the hopes of gaining something of greater value (Potenza, Kosten, and Rounsaville 2001). Excessive forms of gambling are sometimes described as compulsive, problematic, or pathological. PG is the diagnostic term adopted by the

American Psychiatric Association (American Psychiatric Association Committee on Nomenclature and Statistics 2000). Historically, this term was selected in favor of "compulsive gambling" (a term more widely used at the time of the introduction in the DSM in 1980) in part to distinguish the disorder from obsessive-compulsive disorder (OCD—American Psychiatric Association Committee on Nomenclature and Statistics 1980). Currently, a diagnosis of PG requires the presence of five or more inclusionary criteria reflecting persistent and recurrent maladaptive gambling behaviors that cannot be better accounted for by a manic episode (the exclusionary criterion). The inclusionary criteria include a preoccupation with gambling; repeated unsuccessful attempts to either control, cut back, or stop gambling; needing to gamble larger amounts over time to achieve the desired effect (tolerance); and restlessness or irritability when attempting to cut back or stop gambling (withdrawal). Other criteria consist of gambling as a way of escape or to relieve a dysphoric mood and the phenomenon of "chasing," which entails trying to win back recent gambling losses through more gambling. Lying to conceal the extent of gambling, committing illegal acts to finance gambling, jeopardizing or losing significant relationships or opportunities, and relying on others to relieve a desperate financial situation caused by gambling are also embodied in the inclusionary criteria for PG (American Psychiatric Association Committee on Nomenclature and Statistics 2000).

Like the inclusionary criteria for substance dependence, those for PG target aspects of tolerance, withdrawal, interference in major areas of life functioning, and repeated unsuccessful attempts to cut back or quit. Similar to individuals with substance use problems, those with PG often experience problems in legal, financial, and marital domains. Although some diagnostic criteria may appear more unique to PG, some similarities may be seen. This is the case with chasing, a concept that might be akin to drug-chasing behaviors during drug "runs," although further research is needed to examine this hypothesis. Unlike substance use disorders (SUDs) that carry a separate diagnostic category for less severe forms of substance use (i.e., substance abuse), the DSM-IV-TR does not include diagnostic criteria for excessive gambling not meeting criteria for PG, although the term "problem gambling" has been used in this context. However, the term has in some circumstances been used inclusive of PG and at others exclusive of PG, thus complicating comparisons across studies (Potenza, Kosten, and Rounsaville 2001).

Beyond shared diagnostic criteria, both individuals with PG and those with SUDs score high on measures of impulsivity (Steel and Blaszczynski 1998; Petry 2001), demonstrate "telescoping" characterized by a faster rate of progression from initial to problematic behavior in women compared with men (Potenza, Steinberg, et al. 2001; Tavares et al. 2001), and show lower prevalence estimates in older adults and higher estimates in adolescents and young adults (Potenza 2006). PG and SUDs frequently co-occur (Petry, Stinson, and Grant 2005; Desai and Potenza 2008; Petry 2007). Other co-occurring psychiatric disorders include antisocial personality, mood, anxiety, and psychotic disorders (Petry, Stinson, and Grant 2005; Desai and Potenza 2008; Scherrer et al. 2007). PG and SUDs frequently share personality features including impulsiveness and sensation-seeking (Petry 2001; Nordin and Nylander 2007). Some studies have found that PG subjects score highly on measures associated with compulsivity (e.g., harm avoidance—Potenza 2007; Tavares and Gentil 2007; Blanco et al. in press). However, compulsive features in PG appear more closely related to impaired control over mental activities and urges/worries about losing control over motor behaviors rather than compulsions like hand-washing and checking, which are typically seen in OCD (Blanco et al. in press). Whereas population-based studies have found increased odds between PG and SUDs, population-based studies have typically not found an increased association between OCD and PG (Cunningham-Williams et al. 1998; Potenza, Koran, and Pallanti in press; Kim and Grant 2001).

Neurodevelopmental Vulnerabilities

Youth Gambling and Risk Behaviors

Prevalence studies indicate that most youths have gambled, although the majority have not experienced adverse consequences due to problematic gambling (Wilber and Potenza 2006). It is a cause for concern, however, that adolescent rates of pathological gambling may be more than three times higher than those in adults. Past-year estimates of serious gambling problems among youths range between 3% and 9% compared to prevalence estimates for adult pathological gambling between less than 1% and 3% (Gupta and Deverensky 1998; Shaffer and Hall 2001). Because PG, substance use, and other risk behaviors frequently co-occur in adolescents (Proimos et al. 1998; Cunningham-Williams and Cottler 2001), it has been suggested that certain neurodevelopmental features may predispose youth to developing problematic addictive behaviors such as PG (Chambers and Potenza 2003).

Impulsivity, Decision Making, and Gambling

The mechanisms underlying adolescent vulnerability to PG may be expressed as a general clinical motif or behavioral trait that extends to adolescent SUD or other psychiatric disorders (Chambers, Taylor, and Potenza 2003; Chambers, Krystal, and Self 2001). Impaired impulse control is an example of one such motif. Impulsivity has been defined as "a predisposition toward rapid, unplanned reactions to internal or external stimuli, [with diminished] regard to the negative consequences of these reactions to the impulsive individual or to others" (Moeller et al. 2001, 1784). Impulsivity has relevance to multiple psychiatric disorders including ICDs, SUDs, bipolar disorder, attention deficit hyperactivity disorder, borderline personality disorder, among others (Jentsch and Taylor 1999; Sonuga-Barke 2005). It is also a behavioral trait commonly associated with adolescence given that impulsivity has been shown to increase in adolescence and then decrease with age (Clayton 1992).

Aspects of impulsivity and related constructs can be measured in multiple ways using self-reports and behavioral tasks. Factor analyses have identified two (Reynolds et al. 2006) or three (Reynolds, Penfold, and Patak in press) domains including "impulsive decision making," "impulsive inattention," and "impulsive disinhibition." Self-report and behavioral measures within and across these domains of impulsivity often do not correlate with one another or do so relatively weakly (Krishnan-Sarin et al. 2007). Tasks assessing aspects of impulsivity have been used in PG subjects. For example, performance on the Stroop Color-Word Interference Task, a test of cognitive control involving attention, conflict monitoring, and impulse control, has been found to distinguish PG and control subjects (Forbush et al. 2008). During Stroop performance, PG and control subjects are most distinguished by activation of the ventromedial prefrontal cortex, with PG subjects showing less activation than controls (Potenza, Leung, et al. 2003). This region of the prefrontal cortex has been implicated in other studies of PG, impulsive aggression, and disadvantageous decision making (Brewer and Potenza 2008), and is a region showing important maturational changes during adolescence (Chambers and Potenza 2003).

Gambling can be conceptualized as a form of action-oriented decision making in which impulsivity can play a significant role. This decision-making process may be divided into three components or stages. First, input received is put into a contextual framework. Second, within this framework, the processing and evaluating of various options with regard to representations and responses takes place. And third, output, which consists of the action-oriented decision made during the processing stage, is planned and implemented. The output thus may consist of a motor or behavioral response. The second stage is host to a complex motivational circuitry that is important in understanding impulsivity in PG. In PG, impulsivity may result in disadvantageous action-oriented decision making that translates into faulty risk-benefit assessment and the accompanied behavioral action (Chambers and Potenza 2003).

Neurodevelopmental Changes during Adolescence

Adolescence is a developmental stage where motivation for experimentation and where the curiosity about and desire to pursue novelty is an important motivational force for the learning processes involved in the journey toward adulthood. It may also contribute to a vulnerability for addiction (Clayton 1992).

One possibility is that the brain regions involving the representation of novelty and promoting motivational drives are more effective at driving behavior during adolescence than during adulthood (Chambers and Potenza 2003). Dopamine (DA) released into the nucleus accumbens (NAc) may flag novelty and provide the "go" signal to pursue it (Panksepp 1998). Studies suggest that the mesolimbic DA system is strongest during adolescence, which may in part explain the high incidence of novelty-associated behaviors (Cote and Crutcher 1991). A more robust DA system in adolescents may also heighten pharmacological sensitization during drug experimentation, making youths more vulnerable to substance addiction (Johnson and Muffler 1997). Neurobiological data also suggest a skewed maturation process of the DA system compared to the serotonin (5-HT) system during adolescence (Takeuchi et al. 2000). DA functioning may promote motivational drives while 5-HT may limit behavioral engagement. A stronger DA system at this stage in neurodevelopment may therefore contribute to enhanced motivational drive and impulsivity (Chambers and Potenza 2003).

Sex hormones likely play an important role in impulsive behaviors in adolescents. The high concentration of sex hormone receptors in the hippocampus, the ventral striatum, and the hypothalamic region in conjunction with rising levels of sex hormones during puberty may contribute to an increased sensitivity to novelty and impulsivity (Giedd et al. 1996; Panksepp 1998; Chambers, Taylor, and Potenza 2003) . These factors in conjunction with the relative immaturity of frontal cortical regions may contribute to adolescent PG, SUDs, and other impulsive or risky behaviors. Additional anatomical brain changes also likely contribute. Neuroimaging studies have found that both the ratio of lateral ventricle to brain volume and the density of white matter increase during adolescence, most likely due to myelination in frontal cortical regions (Giedd et al. 1996; Paus et al. 1999). These changes increase the speed and efficiency of action potential propagation during this developmental stage, which most likely also help to promote learning and adaptation (Paus et al. 1999). It is possible that the same neurodevelopmental processes that promote the necessary experimentation, learning, and adaptation of adolescence needed to enable children to move toward adulthood are the same processes that render adolescents vulnerable to addiction and ICDs such as PG.

Neurochemistry

Neurotransmitters

Serotonin (5-HT)   Historically, serotonin (5-HT) has been considered to play a central role in impulse control and impulse control disorders (DeCaria, Begaz, and Hollander 1998; Potenza 2008). Serotonergic dysfunction is hypothesized to contribute to impairments in the control or cessation of certain behaviors. Serotonergic neurons project from the raphe nucleus to various brain regions including the hippocampus, amygdala, and frontal cortex. In animals, forebrain 5-HT depletion facilitates impulsive choice, and the indirect 5-HT agonist fenfluramine decreases impulsive behavior (Poulos, Parker, and Le 1996; Mobini et al. 2000). In humans, individuals with impulsive features and early-onset alcoholism have on average low levels of the 5-HT metabolite 5-hydroxyindolacetic acid (5-HIAA) (Linnoila et al. 1983; Coccaro et al. 1990). Data suggest that altered 5-HT function contributes to PG.

Lower levels of 5-HIAA have been found in CSF samples of PG subjects when compared to healthy controls. However, this difference was only observed after controlling for tapping time, which was increased in the PG group (Nordin and Eklundh 1999). The administration of metachlorophenylpiperazine (m-CPP), which acts as a partial agonist with high affinity for 5-HT$_1$ and 5-HT$_2$ receptors, is followed by reports of a behavioral "high" and increased prolactin levels in individuals with PG as compared to healthy control subjects (Pallanti et al. 2006). Genetic studies involving the serotonin transporter gene (5-HTTLPR) also suggest an involvement of 5-HT in PG (Perez de Castro et al. 1997), although findings from early molecular genetic studies of PG have not been consistently replicated; see, for example, studies of dopamine-related genes (Comings 1998; da Silva Lobo et al. 2007).

Clinical trials of PG have shown mixed results regarding the efficacy of serotonin reuptake inhibitors (SRIs) such as paroxetine, escitalopram, sertraline, and fluvoxamine. Among placebo-controlled trials, several have found SRIs to be more efficacious than placebo in reducing PG symptoms, while other studies reported no clear benefit of active drug over placebo (Hollander et al. 2000; Blanco et al. 2002; Kim et al. 2002; Grant et al. 2003; Grant and Potenza 2006; Brewer, Grant, and Potenza 2008). Although small sample size and limited temporal durations of studies may limit the interpretation of SRI findings, it is also conceivable that divergent results may be due in part to differences in subpopulations of people with PG. It has been suggested that certain groups of individuals with PG may respond preferentially to SRIs. Preliminary data consistent with this notion come from a study of escitalopram in individuals with PG and co-occuring anxiety disorders (Grant and Potenza 2006).

Dopamine (DA) Dopamine (DA) has been implicated in rewarding and reinforcing behaviors and drug addiction. Dopaminergic neurons projecting from the ventral tegmental area (VTA) to the nucleus accumbens (NAc), via the medial forebrain bundle, appear important in the processing and reinforcement of rewards, given that disruptions of DA transmission, either along the axonal routes or at receptor sites, decrease the reward value of DA (Nestler and Aghajanian 1997). From these and other data, a role for DA in PG has been hypothesized.

Decreased levels of DA, in conjunction with elevated levels of DA metabolites 3,4-dihydroxyphenylacetic acid (DOPAC) and homovanillic acid (HVA) have been observed in the CSF of pathological gamblers. These differences, however, were largely negligible once adjusting for CSF flow rate (Bergh et al. 1997; Nordin and Eklundh 1999).

Amphetamine, a drug that influences DA and norepinephrine neurotransmission, has been reported to cross-prime for gambling behavior in pathological gamblers, suggesting that promotion of DA transmission may be important in increasing PG behaviors (Zack and Poulous 2004). The same group reported that the DA receptor antagonist haloperidol enhances the rewarding and priming effects in PG, raising questions about the nature of a role for DA in PG (Zack and Poulos 2007). DA agonists such as pramipexole and ropinirole have been associated with PG and other ICDs (e.g., binge-eating, compulsive shopping, compulsive sex) in Parkinson's disease (Voon et al. 2006; Potenza, Voon, and Weintraub 2007). However, as other factors (age at onset of Parkinson's disease, ICDs prior to onset of Parkinson's disease, personal or familial history of alcoholism, impulsivity measures) have been associated with ICDs in Parkinson's disease, more research is needed to understand the extent to which dopaminergic therapies, the pathophysiology of Parkinson's disease, or other factors contribute to ICDs in Parkinson's disease.

Gamma-aminobutyric acid (GABA) and Glutamate   Gamma-aminobutyric acid (GABA), the major inhibitory neurotransmitter in the brain, is synthesized from glutamate by the action of glutamic acid decarboxylase (GAD). Roy et al. found that cerebrospinal fluid (CSF) GABA levels did not differ in male PGs and healthy controls (Roy et al. 1989). In apparent contrast, Nordin and Sjödin found increased GABA levels in PGs (Nordin and Sjödin 2007). Together, these findings indicate that although GABA has been implicated in PG, additional research is needed to determine a precise role and the clinical implications.

Data suggest an anatomical and functional link between GABA and the dopaminergic systems implicated in substance use disorders (Sofuoglu and Kosten 2006). Glutamate (glutamic acid), the GABA precursor and the major excitatory neurotransmitter in the brain and spinal cord, may be involved in both ICDs and SUDs. Glutamate within the NAc may mediate reward-seeking behavior by modulating the release of DA (Baker et al. 2002; McFarland, Lapish, and Kalivas 2003). Pharmacological treatment studies using N-acetylcysteine, a compound with glutamatergic properties, has shown preliminary efficacy in the treatments of PG and cocaine addiction (LaRowe et al. 2006; Grant, Kim, and Odlaug 2007). One suggested mode of action is that N-acetylcysteine increases extracellular levels of glutamate by stimulating the inhibitory metabotropic glutamate receptors, which then reduces the synaptic release of glutamate. Additional research is needed to investigate the efficacy and tolerability of glutamatergic drugs in the treatment of PG and other ICDs, as well as to investigate directly their mechanisms of action.

Norepinephrine and Stress
Noradrenergic mechanisms have been postulated to contribute to PG (DeCaria, Begaz, and Hollander 1998). Early studies of men with PG found high levels of norepinephrine and its metabolites in individuals with PG and a correlation between these

biochemical measures and personality measures of extraversion (Roy et al. 1988, 1989). More recent studies of stress response pathways in PG suggest noradrenergic dysfunction, with higher peripheral norepinephrine levels and higher blood levels of epinephrine in PG subjects compared to controls during gambling and on gambling-concentrated days (Meyer et al. 2004; Krueger, Schedlowski, and Meyer 2005). Cardiovascular and hypothalamic-pituitary-adrenal axis activity was measured in male gamblers during an actual gambling session and a control condition where subjects played for points rather than money. Compared to the control condition, during gambling heart rate and cortisol levels significantly increased at gambling onset and remained elevated throughout the gambling session. The authors also reported that subjects with higher impulsivity scores showed significantly higher heart rate levels compared to a low-impulsivity subgroup. In addition, a positive correlational relationship was found between gambling severity and impulsivity. In a similar experiment using the same gambling session and control condition, endocrine measures were taken during gambling at baseline, at 30, 60, 90 minutes, and after the session. Norepinepherine levels increased at the onset of gambling for all subjects, but the increase was most significant for the problem gamblers throughout sampling.

As is the case with drug addiction, PG is often associated with elevated life stressors. Consistent with that finding, the rise of morning cortisol from awakening to 30 min following awakening was greater in problem and pathological gamblers than in recreational gamblers (Wohl et al. 2008). Taken together, these findings are consistent with a role for the stress response and noradrenergic systems involvement in PG, possibly relating to arousal and excitement.

Opioid Systems

Opioidergic pathways, implicated in the mediation of hedonic, rewarding and reinforcing behaviors, may contribute to PG. Problem gamblers have shown elevated levels of the endogenous opioid β-endorphin during gambling (Shinohara et al. 1999). Opioid antagonists such as naltrexone and nalmefene have shown efficacy with respect to ameliorating PG symptoms in placebo-controlled trials (Kim et al. 2001; Grant et al. 2006). As in the case of alcohol dependence, individuals with strong gambling urges at treatment onset seem to respond preferentially to opiate antagonists (Kim et al. 2001).

Neuropeptides

Few studies have examined whether there is a role for central neuropeptides in PG. Nordin and Sjödin evaluated CSF levels of sulphated cholecystokinin (CCK) octapeptide (CCK-8S), CCK tetrapeptide (CCK-4), and neuropeptide Y (NPY). Compared with healthy controls, PG subjects did not show increased levels of NPY, but did show higher concentrations of CCK-8S and CCK-4 (Nordin and Sjödin 2007). As CCK and

NPY may contribute to the regulation of reward behavior, further studies of these peptides as they relate to specific aspects of impulsivity, PG, and other ICDs are needed (ibid.).

Taurine, an amino acid with inhibitory effects in the nervous system, has been investigated in PG. One initial study reported that taurine levels were lower in PG subjects than in healthy controls (Nordin and Eklundh 1996). More recently, Nordin and Sjödin reported that PG subjects have higher levels of CSF taurine (Nordin and Sjödin 2006). As some of the research methods differed in both studies, further investigation is needed to clarify the nature of taurine function in PG.

Monoamine Oxidase (MAO)

The monoamine oxidases (MAOs, types A and B) are involved in the metabolism of norepinephrine, 5-HT, and DA. Reports have suggested that PG subjects have lower levels of platelet MAO compared to healthy controls (Carrasco et al. 1994; Blanco et al. 1996). Low platelet MAO activity, predominantly consisting of MAO type B and thought to reflect 5-HT function, may be a biological predisposition for impulsivity in pathological gamblers (Blanco et al. 1996). Molecular genetic studies have suggested a role for allele variants of the MAO-A-encoding gene in PG, especially for severe forms of the disorder (Ibanez et al. 2000; Pérez de Castro et al. 2002).

Neuroimaging Studies

Relatively few neuroimaging studies of PG have been published. One functional magnetic resonance imaging (fMRI) study showed decreased activity in the ventral striatum and ventromedial prefrontal cortex in PG subjects compared to healthy control subjects during a simulated gambling task (Reuter et al. 2005). These findings are consistent with earlier investigations that found relatively diminished activation of the ventromedial prefrontal cortex in PG during Stroop performance (Potenza, Leung et al. 2003) and when shown videotapes of gambling stimuli (Potenza, Steinberg et al. 2003). Similarly, cocaine-dependent subjects either with co-occuring PG or without show relatively diminished activation of the ventromedial prefrontal cortex during performance of the Iowa Gambling Task (IGT) (Tanabe et al. 2007).

Seven pathological gamblers were imaged using positron emission tomography (PET) while participating in a computerized blackjack task during both monetary and non-monetary (points only) conditions (Hollander et al. 2005). Results suggested that gambling for money was generally associated with significantly greater prefrontal activation than gambling for points alone. However, similar findings have been reported in opioid addicts compared to healthy controls (Martin-Soelch et al. 2001), suggesting that these findings are not exclusive to PG and may extend to other populations including those with drug addictions.

Using a block design and fMRI, Crockford et al. acquired images of 13 PG subjects and 10 healthy controls while participants viewed alternating short gambling and nature scenes (Crockford et al. 2005). Pathological gamblers showed increased activity in the right dorsolateral prefrontal cortex (DLPFC) (including inferior frontal gyrus, medial frontal gyrus, the right parahippocampal gyrus, and left occipital cortex, including fusiform gyrus). In a separate study of gambling urges using a videotape paradigm that simulates interpersonal interactions, individuals with PG differed from those without with respect to behavioral and neural measures (Potenza, Steinberg et al. 2003). Behaviorally, PG subjects differed most in their subjective responses to the gambling as opposed to the sad and happy tapes, with PG subjects reporting stronger urges to gamble following viewing of the gambling tapes. Neural differences were most substantial during the initial period of tape viewing, prior to the subjective onset of motivational or emotional response. During viewing of the gambling tape, PG as compared to control subjects showed relatively diminished activation of frontal cortex, basal ganglia, and thalamus. These findings are different from those of cue provocation studies of subjects with obsessive-compulsive disorder in which relatively greater activations of these regions are observed. When the neural correlates of gambling urges in PG were directly compared with those of cocaine cravings in cocaine dependence, similar brain regions were identified (Potenza 2008). For example, relatively diminished activation of the ventral striatum was observed in PG and cocaine-dependent subjects compared to their control groups, reminiscent of findings during reward-processing tasks (Reuter et al. 2005; Potenza 2008).

Neuropsychology and Neurocognition

Executive Functioning (EF)

Specific EF tasks have been linked to impairments of the prefrontal cortex or the subcortical and cortical networks that project into the prefrontal networks. Such associations have been found using various methodologies such as lesion studies and neuroimaging. Multiple studies suggest that pathological gamblers exhibit EF impairments in areas of inhibition, cognitive flexibility, and planning.

Response inhibition appears to be impaired in PG as evidenced by performance with the stop signal task, circle tracing task, and the Stroop color-word test. For example, pathological gamblers have been found to perform worse than control subjects on the Stroop Color-Word Interference Task (Forbush et al. 2008). A similar result was found during the Reverse Stroop test, further demonstrating decreased response inhibition (Kertzman et al. 2006).

Cognitive flexibility also appears to be impaired in PG. This is evidenced by performance on the Wisconsin Card Sorting Task (WCST) (Goudriaan et al. 2006; Marazziti et al. 2008; Forbush et al. 2008). Pathological gamblers are slower than healthy control subjects in realizing that the pattern rule has changed and take longer to adapt to the new rule. In the time it takes them to adapt, they commit a larger number of perseveration errors (Goudriaan et al. 2006). Pathological gamblers also perform disadvantageously on measures of verbal fluency, as measured by the Controlled Oral Word Association Test, which is another measure of cognitive flexibility (Goudriaan et al. 2006).

In the Tower of London task, pathological gamblers show deficits in planning compared to healthy control subjects, a finding similar to that in subjects with alcohol dependence (Goudriaan et al. 2006). In this task, subjects must arrange a structure to conform to a prearranged configuration in as few steps as possible. Pathological gamblers' scores decrease significantly more than healthy controls with increasing levels of difficulty.

Decision Making

The Iowa Gambling Task (IGT) assesses risk/reward decision making, and PG subjects perform disadvantageously on the IGT compared to healthy control subjects (Goudriaan et al. 2006). PG subjects also demonstrate risky decision making in the Game of Dice task (Brand et al. 2005). This assessment is similar to the IGT, but differs from the traditional IGT in the fact that instructions explicitly explain to participants the rules of reward and reinforcement and provide them with probabilities to guide their choices. Despite this transparency, PG subjects demonstrate significantly more long-term disadvantageous decisions than healthy controls (Brand et al. 2005). Goudriaan et al. specifically examined feedback processing using reaction time analyses on the IGT and the Card Playing Task, a task measuring perseveration for reward. PG subjects demonstrated diminished performance on those tasks and showed a deficit in feedback processing (Goudriaan et al. 2005). The perseveration errors on the IGT and the Game of Dice task, even in the presence of conscious knowledge of the rules, is consistent with clinical impressions that individuals with PG continue to gamble despite knowing that they will typically lose.

Delay discounting evaluates the temporal decay of the value of rewards within individuals. In delay-discounting tasks, subjects must choose between a small reward now or a larger reward to be awarded at a later time. Outcomes that are delayed may be less effective in directing or influencing behavior, and the extent to which this is the case varies across individuals (Reynolds and Schiffbauer 2004). Delay discounting has been observed in a wide range of substance-dependent populations including alcohol, smoking, and cocaine (Reynolds 2006). In general, substance-dependent individuals discount significantly more than non-substance-dependent individuals, and when monetary rewards are substituted for a drug of choice, substance-dependent individuals discount even more rapidly (Madden et al. 1997).

Studies suggest similarities between PG and SUD subjects on measures of delay discounting. Pathological gamblers were found to discount rewards more rapidly than healthy controls (Petry 2001). SUD and PG may have additive effects on delay discounting. In one study, SUD subjects who also had PG discounted more than subjects who only had a SUD (Petry and Casarella 1999). In a second study, the sample consisted of subjects with a primary diagnosis of PG with and without a secondary diagnosis of SUD. Results of that study showed that PG subjects with SUD discounted more than those with PG only (Petry 2001). Thus, results have shown that pathological gamblers discount at a higher rate than healthy controls and that the discounting can be exacerbated by a secondary diagnosis of SUD. In addition, as with studies of delay discounting in SUD populations, severity of PG symptoms correlates positively with rates of delay discounting (Alessi and Petry 2003). Therefore, those with more severe PG discount monetary rewards more rapidly than those with less severe illness.

Self-report measures also suggest that PG subjects are more impulsive than control subjects. For example, PG subjects score higher than healthy controls on the Barratt Impulsivity Scale (BIS) (Fuentes et al. 2006; Forbush et al. 2008) and the impulsiveness and/or sensation-seeking measures on personality questionnaires (Potenza, Steinberg et al. 2003; Forbush et al. 2008).

Hemispheric Dysregulation

It has been suggested that hemispheric dysregulation is related to impaired impulse control (IC). Because PG is classified as an IC disorder, some have attempted to investigate whether pathological gamblers show differential hemispheric activation induced by various task requirements. Using electroencephalography (EEG), Goldstein et al. showed that compared to controls, PGs demonstrated deficits in degree of EEG activation in response to simple verbal versus spatial tasks (Goldstein et al. 1985). In addition to displaying less hemispheric activation, PGs also showed reversal of normal hemispheric differentiation. These findings mirrored what has been found in children with attention-deficit/hyperactivity disorder (ADHD), who, like PGs, exhibit impulsivity (Carlton and Goldstein 1987).

Genetics

As with most psychiatric disorders, pathological gambling seems to be the result of a complex interaction between genetic and environmental factors. Genetic studies of PG are in their early stages and, in many cases, limited by small sample size.

Family Studies

Family studies are used to investigate the inheritance of traits or disorders by examining the blood relatives of the affected individual. Two assessment methods may be used. With the family-history method, information is obtained by asking the proband (the affected individual) questions about his or her family members. With the family-study method, information is obtained by direct questioning of the proband's relatives through interviews. Family studies can be used to deduce information on the familial segregation of the trait being studied. They cannot, however, enable us to differentiate between genetic and environmental factors. An additional type of family study involves comparing the frequency of the trait studied in the relatives (usually first-degree) of the proband and comparing that to similarly obtained data from the relatives of control subjects (Risch 1994).

PG has been associated with parental gambling (Lesieur and Heineman 1988; Jacobs et al. 1989; Lesieur and Blume 1990; Lesieur et al. 1991). Gambino et al. examined the frequency of perceived addictive problems of relatives in a population of 93 substance users in the Veteran's Affairs system (Gambino et al. 1993). Gambling behavior was assessed using the South Oaks Gambling Screen. This scale allowed the identification of probable problem (subclinical) gamblers (score $= 3 \le x \le 4$) and probable pathological gamblers (score $= >5$). Using this scoring scheme, 17.3% of participants ($n = 16$) were deemed probable pathological gamblers and 14% ($n = 13$) were deemed probable problem gamblers. Subjects who reported parental gambling problems were 3 times more likely to be probable pathological gamblers, and subjects who reported having grandparents with gambling problems were 12 times more likely.

Other studies have sought to evaluate the effect of childhood exposure to gambling in families. In one such study, Gupta and Derevensky evaluated 477 children between the ages of 9 and 14 who reported gambling on a regular basis (Gupta and Derevensky 1997). Of the sample, 86% reported gambling with their family members. No data were reported regarding PG diagnosis. However, the large proportion of subjects having reported gambling with relatives raises questions regarding the influence of family environment in the development of a gambling disorder. The same authors found a 4.7% prevalence of PG in a sample of 817 secondary school students (Gupta and Derevensky 1998). They found that those with a PG diagnosis were also more likely to have reported a parental gambling problem. An independent study found that among adolescents screening positive for a gambling problem, those self-reporting a gambling problem were more likely to report having a family member with a gambling problem (Cronce et al. 2007). Studies using adult samples have also reported an association between PG and parental gambling problems (Volberg and Steadman 1988; Ohtsuka et al. 1997). In addition, several studies have linked adult problem gambling with exposure to gambling during childhood (Hraba and Lee 1995).

Several studies have also reported high rates of gambling disorders in first-degree relatives of pathological gamblers. For example, a family-history method analysis of 14 PGs revealed that more than 9% of their first-degree relatives had some form of gambling disorder (Shaffer and Hall 2001; Black, Moyer, and Schlosser 2003). In a larger sample of 31 gender-matched PGs and 193 first-degree relatives, using a combination of both family-history and family-interview methods, Black et al. found that among first-degree relatives of PGs, 8.3% met the criteria for PG and 12.4% for any gambling disorder. A gender-matched control group exhibited rates of 2.1% for PG and 3.5% for any gambling disorder (Black et al. 2006). To our knowledge, all published family studies of PG have shown a higher frequency of gambling-related problems in relatives than what would be expected in the general population.

Twin Studies

Twin studies can help investigators distinguish between genetic and environmental factors by enabling them to determine the extent to which genetic factors are responsible for the development of a certain trait or disorder (phenotype). Monozygotic (identical) twins share 100% of their genotype whereas dizygotic (fraternal) twins share, on average, 50% of their genome. In cases where genetic factors predominantly account for phenotypical variance, monozygotic twins should show significantly greater similarity than should dizygotic twins.

A large twin study of PG was conducted using the Vietnam Era Twin (VET) registry (Eisen et al. 1998). The registry consisted of 3,359 male twin pairs. This study found that genetic factors most likely accounted for between 35% and 54% of the liability for developing any of the symptoms of PG. They also specifically examined each PG symptom. For example, the authors found that "gambling larger amounts than intended" could be explained by genetic factors (55%) and environmental factors (45%). This study is thus another way of determining that PG most likely results from a complex contribution of both genetics and environment. In the VET registry sample, the heritability factor estimate for PG was determined to be 46%.

A smaller sample of 92 male and 63 female twins found possible gender differences in genetic predisposition for PG (Winters and Rich 1998). Subjects were queried about their past-year gambling. For males, genetic factors were determined to be significantly responsible for so-called high action gambling (e.g., slots, roulette), but genetic influence was not significant for low action games such as sports betting. For females, no significant genetic influence was found for either high or low action games. Because the sample size was small and the gambling behavior was not extensively examined, these results should be considered with caution.

The VET sample was further examined to evaluate the continuity of PG diagnosis (Slutske et al. 2000). Analyses showed that the risk for PG was significantly higher for a twin whose co-twin demonstrated symptoms of subclinical PG as opposed to those whose co-twin displayed no PG symptoms. This provided support for the hypothesis that subclinical (problem gambling) and PG constitute a continuum and may share risk factors.

VET data also indicate that a significant portion of the liability for PG is accounted for by that for alcohol dependence. Men with some PG symptoms were more likely to

have alcohol dependence than those with no PG symptoms. The risk for alcohol dependence was similarly more elevated in co-twins having exhibited PG symptoms
than those who did not. This may suggest that a genetic locus involved in susceptibility to PG may also make persons more susceptible to alcoholism. Similar investigations have found common genetic contributions to PG and antisocial behaviors and
PG and major depressive disorder, suggesting overlapping genetic factors may be involved in the predisposition for PG and both externalizing and internalizing disorders,
respectively.

Molecular Genetics

A small number of molecular genetics studies of PG have investigated the roles of specific candidate genes related to neurotransmitter systems. The D2A1 D_2 receptor gene
allele and the dopamine DdeI allele of the D_1 receptor gene have been found more frequently in PG subjects as opposed to control ones (Comings et al. 1996). The *Taq*I A
polymorphism of the A1 allele of the D_2 receptor gene has been linked to PG and various substance addictions, such as alcohol, cocaine, and nicotine dependence (Blum et
al. 1995). A variable number tandem repeat (VNTR) polymorphism located in exon III
of the D_4 receptor gene has been found to be associated with PG (Perez de Castro et al.
1997; Comings et al. 1999). Studies have linked this polymorphism to impulsivity,
novelty-seeking, vulnerability to substance addiction in adolescence, and cue-elicited
craving both for food and drugs, although not consistently (Williams and Potenza
2008). As more recent studies using more well-defined methodologies have not replicated some of these initial findings, more research is needed to understand the precise
role in PG of genetic factors related to DA function (da Silva Lobo et al. 2007).

A gender-related difference has been reported with respect to the promoter region of
the serotonin transporter gene (5-HTTLPR); a less functional short variant was found
more frequently in PG males, but not in females (Pérez de Castro et al. 2002). Further
gender-related differences were found with respect to the gene encoding MAO-A. Males
with a severe form of PG showed a 3 repeat allele in the promoter region of the MAO-A
gene 30 base pairs VNTR and exhibited a polymorphism in the first intron (Ibanez et
al. 2000; Pérez de Castro et al. 2002). These molecular genetic studies should be interpreted cautiously given methodological limitations, which may include small sample
sizes, the potential for false-positive results due to type I error, incomplete characterization of participants, and inconsistent consideration of allelic differences attributable to
racial differences.

Conclusion

An improved understanding is emerging of the neurobiology of pathological gambling
and its relationship to that of other psychiatric disorders. Future studies using various
methodologies such as neuroimaging and genetics will enable us to better understand

the etiology of PG and help us to devise optimal treatment strategies for individuals with PG. The identification of subpopulations of PG is an important goal that, in conjunction with a better understanding of co-occurring psychiatric disorders, may help to develop more targeted treatment strategies. Identification of genetic factors may help not only in targeting effective treatments, but also in the development of more effective prevention efforts.

References

Alessi, S., and Petry N. M. (2003). Pathological gambling severity is associated with impulsivity in a delay discounting procedure. *Behavioral Process* 64: 345–354.

American Psychiatric Association Committee on Nomenclature and Statistics (1980). *Diagnostic and Statistical Manual of Mental Disorders*, 3rd ed. Washington, D.C.: American Psychiatric Association.

American Psychiatric Association Committee on Nomenclature and Statistics. (2000). *Diagnostic and Statistical Manual of Mental Disorders*, 4th ed.—text revision. Washington, D.C.: American Psychiatric Association.

Baker, D. A., Xi, Z.-X., Shen, H., Swanson, C. J., and Kalivas, P. W. (2002). The origin and neuronal function of in vivo nonsynaptic glutamate. *Journal of Neuroscience* 22 (20): 9134–9141.

Bergh, C., Eklund, T., Sodersten, P., and Nordin, C. (1997). Altered dopamine function in pathological gambling. *Psychological Medicine* 27 (2): 473–475.

Black, D. W., Monahan, P. O., Temkit, M. H., and Shaw, M. (2006). A family study of pathological gambling. *Psychiatry Research* 141 (3): 295.

Black, D. W., Moyer, T., and Schlosser, S. (2003). Quality of life and family history in pathological gambling. *Journal of Nervous Mental Disorders* 191 (2): 124–126.

Blanco, C., Orensanz-Munoz, L., Blanco-Jerez, C., and Saiz-Ruiz, J. (1996). Pathological gambling and platelet MAO activity: A psychobiological study. *American Journal of Psychiatry* 153 (1): 119–121.

Blanco, C., Petkova, E., Ibanez, A., and Saiz-Ruiz, J. (2002). A pilot placebo-controlled study of fluvoxamine for pathological gambling. *Annals of Clinical Psychiatry* 14: 9–15.

Blanco, C., Potenza, M. N., Kim, S. W., Ibanez, A., Zaninelli, R., Saiz-Ruiz, J., and Grant, J. E. (in press). A pilot study of impulsivity and compulsivity in pathological gambling. *Psychiatry Research*.

Blum, K., Sheridan, P. J., Wood, R. C., Braverman, E. R., Chen, T., and Comings, D. E. (1995). Dopamine D_2 receptor gene variants: Association and linkage studies studies in impulsive-addictive-compulsive behavior. *Pharmacogenetics* 5: 121–141.

Brand, M., Kalbe, E., Labudda, K., Fujiwara, E., Kessler, J., and Markowitsch, H. J. (2005). Decision-making impairments in patients with pathological gambling. *Psychiatry Research* 133 (1): 91.

Brewer, J. A., Grant, E., and Potenza, M. N. (2008). The treatment of pathological gambling. *Addictive Disorders and Their Treatment* 7: 1–14.

Brewer, J. A., and Potenza, M. N. (2008). The neurobiology and genetics of impulse control disorders: Relationships to drug addictions. *Biochemical Pharmacology* 75: 63–75.

Carlton, P. L., and Goldstein, L. (1987). Physiological determinants of pathological gambling. In T. Galski, ed., *A Handbook of Pathological Gambling*. Springfield, IL: Charles C. Thomas.

Carrasco, J. L., Saiz-Ruiz, J., Hollander, E., Cesar, J., and Lopez-Ibor, J. J. J. (1994). Low platelet monoamine oxidase activity in pathological gambling. *Acta Psychiatrica Scandinavica* 90 (6): 427–431.

Chambers, R., and Potenza, M. (2003). Neurodevelopment, impulsivity, and adolescent gambling. *Journal of Gambling Studies* 19 (1): 53–84.

Chambers, R. A., Krystal, J. H., and Self, D. W. (2001). A neurobiological basis for substance abuse comorbidity in schizophrenia. *Biological Psychiatry* 50 (2): 71.

Chambers, R. A., Taylor, J. R., and Potenza, M. N. (2003). Developmental neurocircuitry of motivation in adolescence: A critical period of addiction vulnerability. *American Journal of Psychiatry* 160 (6): 1041–1052.

Clayton, R. (1992). Transitions and drug use: Risk and protective factors. In M. Glantz and R. Pikens, eds., *Vulnerability to Drug Abuse*, 15–52. Washington, D.C.: American Psychological Association.

Coccaro, E., Siever, L. J., Klar, H. M., Maurer, G., Cochrane, K., Cooper, T. B., Mohs, R. C., and Davis, K. L. (1990). Serotonergic studies in patients with affective and personality disorders: Correlates with suicidal and impulsive aggressive behavior. *Archives of General Psychiatry* 46: 587–599.

Comings, D. E. (1998). The molecular genetics of pathological gambling. *CNS Spectrums* 3 (6): 20–37.

Comings, D. E., Gonzalez, N., Wu, S., Gade, R., Muhleman, D., Saucier, G., Johnson, P., Verde, R., Rosenthal, R. J., Lesieur, H. R., Rugle, L. J., Miller, W. B., and MacMurray, J. (1999). Studies of the 48 Bp repeat polymorphism of the DRD4 gene in impulsive, compulsive, addictive behaviors: Tourette Syndrome, ADHD, pathological gambling, and substance abuse. *American Journal of Human Genetics* 88: 358–368.

Comings, D. E., Rosenthal, R. J., Lesieur, H. R., Rugle, L. J., Muhleman, D., Chiu, C., Dietz, G., and Gade, R. (1996). A study of the dopamine D_2 receptor gene in pathological gambling. *Pharmacogenetics* 6 (3): 223–234.

Cote, L., and Crutcher, M. D. (1991). The basal ganglia. In E. R. Kandel, J. H. Schwartz, and T. M. Jessell, eds., *Principles of Neural Science*, 647–659. Norwalk, CT: Appleton and Lange.

Crockford, D. N., Goodyear, B., Edwards, J., Quickfall, J., and el-Guebaly, N. (2005). Cue-induced brain activity in pathological gamblers. *Biological Psychiatry* 58 (10): 787.

Cronce, J. M., Corbin, W. R., Steinberg, M. A., and Potenza, M. N. (2007). Self-perception of gambling problems among adolescents identified as at-risk or problem gamblers. *Journal of Gambling Studies* 23 (4): 363–375.

Cunningham-Williams, R. M. and Cottler, L. B. (2001). The epidemiology of pathological gambling. *Seminars in Clinical Neuropsychiatry* 6: 155–166.

Cunningham-Williams, R. M., Cottler, L. B., Compton, W. M., and Spitznagel, E. L. (1998). Taking chances: Problem gamblers and mental health disorders—results from the St. Louis Epidemiologic Catchment Area Study. *American Journal of Public Health* 88 (7): 1093–1096.

da Silva Lobo, D., Vallada, H. P., Knight, J., Martins, S. S., Tavares, H., Gentil, V., and Kennedy, J. L. (2007). Dopamine genes and pathological gambling in discordant sib-pairs. *Journal of Gambling Studies* 23: http://lib.bioinfo.pl/pmid:17394052.

DeCaria, C. M., Begaz, T., and Hollander, E. (1998). Serotonergic and noradrenergic function in pathological gambling. *CNS Spectrums* 3 (6): 38–47.

Desai, R., and Potenza, M. N. (2008). Gender differences in the associations between past-year gambling problems and psychiatric disorders. *Social Psychiatry and Psychiatric Epidemiology* 43 (3): 173–183.

Eisen, S. A., Lin, N., Lyons, M. J., Scherrer, J., Griffith, K., True, W. R., Goldberg, J., and Tsuang, M. T. (1998). Familial influences on gambling behavior: An analysis of 3359 twin pairs. *Addiction* 93: 1375–1384.

Forbush, K. T., Shaw, M., Graeber, M. A., Hovick, L., Meyer, V. J., Moser, D. J., Bayless, J., Watson, D., and Black, D. W. (2008). Neuropsychological characteristics and personality traits in pathological gambling. *CNS Spectrums* 13 (4): 306–315.

Fuentes, D., Tavares, H., Artes, R., and Gorenstein, C. (2006). Self-reported and neuropsychological measures of impulsivity in pathological gambling. *Journal of the International Neuropsychological Society* 12: 907–912.

Gambino, B., Fitzgerald, R., Shaffer, H. J., Renner, J., and Courtnage, P. (1993). Perceived family history of problem gambling and scores on SOGS. *Journal of Gambling Studies* 9 (2): 169–184.

Giedd, J. N., Snell, J. W., Lange, N., Rajapakse, J. C., Casey, B. J., Kozuch, P. L., Vaituzis, A. C., Vauss, Y. C., Hamburger, S. D., Kaysen, D., and Rapoport, J. L. (1996). Quantitative magnetic resonance imaging of human brain development: Ages 4–18. *Cerebral Cortex* 6: 551–560.

Goldstein, L., Manowitz, P., Nora, R., Swartzburg, M., and Carlton, P. L. (1985). Differential EEG activation and pathological gambling. *Biological Psychiatry* 20 (11): 1232–1234.

Goudriaan, A. E., Oosterlaan, J., de Beurs, E., and van den Brink, W. (2005). Decision making in pathological gambling: A comparison between pathological gamblers, alcohol dependents, persons with Tourette Syndrome, and normal controls. *Cognitive Brain Research* 23 (1): 137.

Goudriaan, A. E., Oosterlaan, J., de Beurs, E., and van den Brink, W. (2006). Neurocognitive functions in pathological gambling: A comparison with alcohol dependence, Tourette Syndrome and normal controls. *Addiction* 101 (4): 534–547.

Grant, J., Kim, S. W., Potenza, M. N., Blanco, C., Ibanez, A., Stevens, L. C., and Zaninelli, R. (2003). Paroxetine treatment of pathological gambling: A multi-center randomized controlled trial. *International Clinical Psychopharmacology* 18: 243–249.

Grant, J., and Potenza, M. N. (2006). Escitalopram treatment of pathological gambling with co-occurring anxiety: An open-label pilot study with double-blind discontinuation. *International Clinical Psychopharmacology* 21: 203–209.

Grant, J., Potenza, M. N., Hollander, E., Cunningham-Williams, R., Numinen, T., Smits, G., and Kallio, A. (2006). Multicenter investigation of the opioid antagonist nalmefene in the treatment of pathological gambling. *American Journal of Psychiatry* 163: 303–312.

Grant, J. E., Brewer, J. A., and Potenza, M. N. (2006). The neurobiology of substance and behavioral addictions. *CNS Spectrums* 11 (12): 924–930.

Grant, J. E., Kim, S. W., and Odlaug, B. L. (2007). N-acetyl cysteine, a glutamate-modulating agent, in the treatment of pathological gambling: A pilot study. *Biological Psychiatry* 62 (6): 652.

Gupta, R., and Derevensky, J. L. (1997). Familial and social influences on juvenile gambling behavior. *Journal of Gambling Studies* 13 (3): 179–192.

Gupta, R., and Derevensky, J. L. (1998). Adolescent gambling behavior: A prevalence study and an examination of the correlates associated with problem gambling. *Journal of Gambling Studies* 14: 319–345.

Hill, W. D.,and Clark, J. E. (2001). Sports, gambling, and government: America's first social compact? *American Anthropologist* 103 (2): 331–345.

Hollander, E., and Wong C. M. (1995). Obsessive-compulsive spectrum disorders. *Journal of Clinical Psychiatry* 56 (Suppl. 4): 3–6.

Hollander, E., DeCaria, C. M., Finkell, J. N., Begaz, T., Wong, C. M., and Cartwright, C. (2000). A randomized double-blind fluvoxamine/placebo crossover trial in pathological gambling. *Biological Psychiatry* 47: 813–817.

Hollander, E., Pallanti, S., Rossi, N. B., Sood, E., Baker, B. R., and Buchsbaum, M. S. (2005). Imaging monetary reward in pathological gamblers. *World Journal of Biological Psychiatry* 6 (2): 113–120.

Hraba, J., and Lee, G. (1995). Problem gambling and policy advice: The mutability and relative effects of structural, associational, and attitudinal variables. *Journal of Gambling Studies* 11 (2): 105–121.

Ibanez, A., de Castro, I. P., Fernandez-Piqueras, J., Vlanco, C., and Saiz-Ruiz, J. (2000). Pathological gambling and DNA polymorphic markers at MAO-A and MAO-B genes. *Molecular Psychiatry* 5: 105–109.

Jacobs, D. F., Marston, A. R., Singer, R. D., Widaman, K., Little, T., and Veizades, J. (1989). Children of problem gamblers. *Journal of Gambling Behavior* (Special issue: Gambling and the family) 5 (4): 261–268.

Jentsch, J., and Taylor, J. R. (1999). Impulsivity resulting from frontostriatal dysfunction in drug abuse: Implications for the control of behavior by reward-related stimuli. *Psychopharmacology* 146: 373–390.

Johnson, B. D., and Muffler, J. (1997). Sociocultural. In J. H. Lowinson, P. Ruiz, R. B. Millman, and J. G. Langrod, eds., *Substance Abuse: A Comprehensive Textbook*, 107–117. Baltimore: Williams and Wilkins.

Kertzman, S., Lowengrub, K., Aizer, A., Nahum, Z. B., Kotler, M., and Dannon, P. N. (2006). Stroop performance in pathological gamblers. *Psychiatry Research* 142 (1): 1.

Kim, S. W., Grant, J. E. (2001). Personality dimensions in pathological gambling disorder and obsessive-compulsive disorder. *Psychiatry Research* 104(3): 205.

Kim, S. W., Grant, J. E., Adson, D. E., and Shin, Y. C. (2001). Double-blind naltrexone and placebo comparison study in the treatment of pathological gambling. *Biological Psychiatry* 49 (2001): 914–21.

Kim, S., Grant, J. E., Adson, D. E., Shin, Y. C., and Zaninelli, R. (2002). A double-blind, placebo-controlled study of the efficacy and safety of paroxetine in the treatment of pathological gambling disorder. *Journal of Clinical Psychiatry* 63 (6): 501–507.

Krishnan-Sarin, S., Reynolds, B., Duhig, A. M., Smith, A., Liss, T., McFetridge, A., Cavallo, D. A., Carroll, K. M., and Potenza, M. N. (2007). Behavioral impulsivity predicts treatment outcome in a smoking cessation program for adolescent smokers. *Drug and Alcohol Dependence* 88 (1): 79.

Krueger, T. H. C., Schedlowski, M., and Meyer, G. (2005). Cortisol and heart rate measures during casino gambling in relation to impulsivity. *Neuropsychobiology* 52 (4): 206.

LaRowe, S. D., Mardikian, P., Malcolm, R., Myrick, H., Kalivas, P., McFarland, K., Saladin, M., McRae, A., and Brady, K. (2006). Safety and tolerability of N-acetylcysteine in cocaine-dependent individuals. *American Journal on Addictions* 15 (1): 105–110.

Lesieur, H. R., and Blume, S. B. (1990). Characteristics of pathological gamblers identified among patients on a psychiatric admissions service. *Hospital and Community Psychiatry* 41 (9): 1009–1012.

Lesieur, H. R., Cross, J., Frank, M., Welch, M., White, C. M., Rubenstein, G., Moseley, K., and Mark, M. (1991). Gambling and pathological gambling among university students. *Addictive Behaviors* 16 (6): 517–527.

Lesieur, H. R., and Heineman, M. (1988). Pathological gambling among youthful multiple substance abusers in a therapeutic community. *British Journal of Addiction* 83 (7): 765–771.

Linnoila, M., Virkunnen, M., Scheinen, M., Nuutila, A., Rimon, R., and Goodwin, F. (1983). Low cerebrospinal fluid 5 hydroxy indolacetic acid concentrations differentiates impulsive from non impulsive violent behavior. *Life Science* 33: 2609–2614.

Madden, G. J., Petry, N. M., Badger, G. J., and Bickel, W. K. (1997). Impulsive and self-control choices in opioid-dependent patients and non-drug-using control patients: Drug and monetary rewards. *Experimental and Clinical Psychopharmacology* 5 (3): 256–262.

Marazziti, D., Dell'Osso, M. C., Conversano, C., Consoli, G., Vivarelli, L., Mungai, F., Di Nasso, E., and Golia, F. (2008). Executive function abnormalities in pathological gamblers. *Clinical Practice and Epidemiology in Mental Health* 4 (7).

Martin-Soelch, C., Chevalley, A. F., Kunig, G., Missimer, J., Magyar, S., Mino, A., Schultz, W., and Leenders, K. L. (2001). Changes in reward-induced brain activation in opiate addicts. *European Journal of Neuroscience* 14 (8): 1360–1368.

McFarland, K., Lapish, C. C., and Kalivas, P. W. (2003). Prefrontal glutamate release into the core of the nucleus accumbens mediates cocaine-induced reinstatement of drug-seeking behavior. *Journal of Neuroscience* 23 (8): 3531–3537.

Meyer, G., Schwertfeger, J., Exton, M. S., Janssen, O. E., Knapp, W., Stadler, M. A., Schedlowski, M., and Kruger, T. H. (2004). Neuroendocrine response to casino gambling in problem gamblers. *Psychoneuroendocrinology* 29: 1272–1280.

Mobini, S., Chiang, T. J., Al-Ruwaitea, A. S., Ho, M. Y., Bradshaw, C. M., and Szabadi, E. (2000). Effect of central 5-hydroxytryptamine depletion on inter-temporal choice: A quantitative analysis. *Psychopharmacology* 149 (3): 313–318.

Moeller, F., Barratt, E. S., Dougherty, D. M., Schmitz, J. M., and Swann, A. C. (2001). Psychiatric aspects of impulsivity. *American Journal of Psychiatry* 158: 1783–1793.

Nestler, E., and Aghajanian, G. (1997). Molecular and cellular basis of addiction. *Science* 278: 58–63.

Nordin, C., and Eklundh, T. (1996). Lower CSF taurine levels in male pathological gamblers than in healthy controls. *Human Psychopharmacology* 11 (5): 401–403.

Nordin, C., and Eklundh, T. (1999). Altered CSF 5-HIAA disposition in pathologic male gamblers. *CNS Spectrums* 4 (12): 25–33.

Nordin, C., and Nylander, P.-O. (2007). Temperament and character in pathological gambling. *Journal of Gambling Studies* 23 (2): 113–120.

Nordin, C., and Sjodin, I. (2006). Altered csf taurine function in pathological gambling. *Journal of Psychiatric Research* 40 (5): 473.

Nordin, C., and Sjödin, I. (2007). CSF cholecystokinin, γ-aminobutyric acid, and neuropeptide y in pathological gamblers and healthy controls. *Journal of Neural Transmission* 114 (4): 499–503.

Ohtsuka, K., Bruton, E., DeLuca, L., and Borg, V. (1997). Sex differences in pathological gambling using gaming machines. *Psychological Reports* 80 (3 Pt 1): 1051–1057.

Pallanti, S., Bernardi, S., Quercioli, L., DeCaria, C., and Hollander, E. (2006). Serotonin dysfunction in pathological gamblers: Increased prolactin response to oral m-CPP versus placebo. *CNS Spectrums* 11 (12): 956–964.

Panksepp, J. (1998). Seeking: Systems and anticipatory states of the nervous system. In *Affective Neuroscience*, 144–163. New York: Oxford University Press.

Paus, T., Zijdenbos, A., Worsley, K., Collins, D. L., Blumenthal, J., Giedd, J. N., Rapoport, J. L., and Evans, A. C. (1999). Structural maturation of neural pathways in children and adolescents: In vivo study. *Science* 283: 1908–1911.

Pérez de Castro, I., Ibáñez, A., Saiz-Ruiz, J., and Fernández-Piqueras, J. (2002). Concurrent positive association between pathological gambling and functional DNA polymorphisms at the mao-a and the 5-ht transporter genes. *Molecular Psychiatry* 7: 927–928.

Perez de Castro, I., Ibáñez, A., Torres, P., Saiz-Ruiz, J., and Fernandez-Piqueras, J. (1997). Genetic association study between pathological gambling and a functional DNA polymorphism at the D_4 receptor gene. *Pharmacogenetics* 7 (5): 345–348.

Petry, N. M. (2001). Pathological gamblers, with and without substance use disorders, discount delayed rewards at high rates. *Journal of Abnormal Psychology* 110 (3): 482–487.

Petry, N. M. (2007). Gambling and substance use disorders: Current status and future directions. *American Journal on Addictions* 16 (1): 1–9.

Petry, N. M., and Casarella, T. (1999). Excessive discounting of delayed rewards in substance abusers with gambling problems. *Drug and Alcohol Dependence* 56: 25–32.

Petry, N. M., Stinson, F. S., and Grant, B. F. (2005). Co-morbidity of DSM-IV pathological gambling and other psychiatric disorders: Results from the national epidemiologic survey on alcohol and related conditions. *Journal of Clinical Psychiatry* 66 (5): 564–574.

Potenza, M. N. (2006). Should addictive disorders include non-substance-related conditions? *Addiction* 101 (Suppl. 1): 142–151.

Potenza, M. N. (2007). Impulsivity and compulsivity in pathological gambling and obsessive-compulsive disorder. *Revista Brasileira de Psiquiatria* 29: 105–106.

Potenza, M. N. (2008). The neurobiology of pathological gambling and drug addiction: An overview and new findings. *Philosophical Transactions of the Royal Sociaty of London B* 363: 3181–3189.

Potenza, M. N., Koran, L. M., and Pallanti, S. (under review). The relationship between obsessive-compulsive and impulse control disorders: A current understanding and future research directions. *Psychiatry Research*.

Potenza, M. N., Kosten, T. R., and Rounsaville, B. J. (2001). Pathological gambling. *Journal of the American Medical Association* 286 (2): 141–144.

Potenza, M. N., Leung, H.-C., Blumberg, H. P., Peterson, B. S., Fulbright, R. K., Lacadie, C. M., Skudlarski, P., and Gore, J. C. (2003). An fMRI Stroop task study of ventromedial prefrontal cortical function in pathological gamblers. *American Journal of Psychiatry* 160 (11): 1990–1994.

Potenza, M. N., Steinberg, M. A., McLaughlin, S. D., Wu, R., Rounsaville, B. J., and O'Malley, S. S. (2001). Gender-related differences in the characteristics of problem gamblers using a gambling helpline. *American Journal of Psychiatry* 158 (9): 1500–1505.

Potenza, M. N., Steinberg, M. A., Skudlarski, P., Fulbright, R. K., Lacadie, C. M., Wilber, M. K., Rounsaville, B. J., Gore, J. C., and Wexler, B. E. (2003). Gambling urges in pathological gambling: A functional magnetic resonance imaging study. *Archives of General Psychiatry* 60 (8): 828–836.

Potenza, M. N., Voon, V., and Weintraub, D. (2007). Drug insight: Impulse control disorders and dopamine therapies in Parkinson's disease. *Nature Clinical Practice Neurology* 3: 664–672.

Poulos, C. X., Parker, J. L., and Le, A. D. (1996). Dexfenfluramine and 8-oh-dpat modulate impulsivity in a delay-of-reward paradigm: Implications for a correspondence with alcohol consumption. *Behavioral Pharmacology* 7 (4): 395–399.

Proimos, J., DuRant, R. H., Pierce, J. D., and Goodman, E. (1998). Gambling and other risk behaviors among 8th- to 12th-grade students. *Pediatrics* 102 (2): e23.

Reuter, J., Raedler, T., Rose, M., Hand, I., Glascher, J., and Buchel, C. (2005). Pathological gambling is linked to reduced activation of the mesolimbic reward system. *Natural Neuroscience* 8 (2): 147.

Reynolds, B. (2006). A review of delay-discounting research with humans: Relations to drug use and gambling. *Behavioural Pharmacology* 17 (8): 651–667.

Reynolds, B., Ortengren, A., Richards, J. B., and de Wit, H. (2006). Dimensions of impulsive behavior: Personality and behavioral measures. *Personality and Individual Differences* 40 (2): 305.

Reynolds, B., Penfold, R. B., and Patak, M. (in press). Dimensions of impulsive behavior in adolescents: Laboratory behavioral assessments. *Experimental Clinical Psychopharmacology*.

Reynolds, B., and Schiffbauer, R. (2004). Measuring state changes in human delay discounting: An experiential discounting task. *Behavioral Processes* 67: 343–356.

Risch, N. J. (1994). Mapping genes for psychiatric disorders. In C. R. Cloniger and E. S. Gershon, eds., *Genetic Approaches to Mental Disorders*. Washington, D.C.: American Psychiatric Press.

Roy, A., Adinoff, B., Roehrich, L., Lamparski, D., Custer, R., Lorenz, V., Barbaccia, M., Guidotti, A., Costa, E., and Linnoila, M. (1988). Pathological gambling. A psychobiological study. *Archives of General Psychiatry* 45 (4): 369–373.

Roy, A., de Jong, J., and Linnoila, M. (1989). Extraversion in pathological gamblers: Correlates with indexes of noradrenergic function. *Archives of General Psychiatry* 46 (8): 679–681.

Roy, A., de Jong, J., Ferraro, T., Adinoff, B., Gold, P., Rubinow, D., and Linnoila, M. (1989). CSF GABA and neuropeptides in pathological gamblers and normal controls. *Psychiatry Research* 30 (2): 137–144.

Scherrer, J. F., Slutske, W. S., Xian, H., Waterman, B., Shah, K. R., Volberg, R., and Eisen, S. A. (2007). Factors associated with pathological gambling at 10-year follow-up in a national sample of middle-aged men. *Addiction* 102 (6): 970–978.

Shaffer, H., and Hall M. N. (2001). Updating and refining prevalence estimates of disordered gambling behavior in the United States and Canada. *Canadian Journal of Public Health* 92: 168–172.

Shinohara, K., Yanagisawa, A., Kagota, Y., Gomi, A., Nemoto, K., Moriya, E., Furusawa, E., Furuya, K., and Tersawa, K. (1999). Physiological changes in pachinko players; Beta-endorphin, catecholamines, immune system substances, and heart rate. *Applied Human Science* 18 (2): 37–42.

Slutske, W. S., Eisen, S., True, W. R., Lyons, M. J., Goldberg, J., and Tsuang, M. (2000). Common genetic vulnerability for pathological gambling and alcohol dependence in men. *Archives of General Psychiatry* 57: 666–674.

Sofuoglu, M., and Kosten, T. R. (2006). Emerging pharmacological strategies in the fight against cocaine addiction. *Expert Opinion on Emerging Drugs* 11: 91–98.

Sonuga-Barke, E. J. S. (2005). Causal models of attention-deficit/hyperactivity disorder: From common simple deficits to multiple developmental pathways. *Biological Psychiatry* 57 (11): 1231.

Steel, Z., and Blaszczynski, A. (1998). Impulsivity, personality disorders, and pathological gambling severity. *Addiction* 93 (6): 895–905.

Takeuchi, Y., Matsushita, H., Sakai, H., Kawano, H., Yoshimoto, K., and Sawada, T. (2000). Developmental changes in cerebrospinal fluid concentrations of monoamine-related substances revealed with a coulochem electrode array system. *Journal of Child Neurology* 15 (4): 267–270.

Tanabe, J., Thompson, L., Claus, E., Dalwani, M., Hutchison, K., and Banich, M. T. (2007). Prefrontal cortex activity is reduced in gambling and nongambling substance users during decision-making. *Human Brain Mapping* 28 (12): 1276–1286.

Tavares, H., and Gentil, V. (2007). Pathological gambling and obsessive-compulsive disorder: Towards a spectrum of disorders of volition. *Revista Brasileira de Psiquiatria* 29: 107–117.

Tavares, H., Zilberman, M. L., Beites, F. J., and Gentil, V. (2001). Gender differences in gambling progression. *Journal of Gambling Studies* 17 (2): 151–159.

Volberg, R. A., and Steadman, H. J. (1988). Refining prevalence estimates of pathological gambling. *American Journal of Psychiatry* 145 (4): 502–505.

Voon, V., Hassan, K., Zurowski, M., Duff-Canning, S., de Souza, M., Fox, S., and Lang, A. E. (2006). Prospective prevalence of pathological gambling and medication association in Parkinson's disease. *Neurology* 66: 1750–1752.

Wilber, M. K., and Potenza, M. N. (2006). Adolescent gambling: Research and clinical implications. *Psychiatry* 3 (10): 40–48.

Williams, W. A., and Potenza, M. N. (2008). The neurobiology of impulse control disorders. *Revista Brasileira de Psiquiatria* 30: 24–30.

Winters, K. C., and Rich, T. (1998). A twin study of adult gambling behavior. *Journal of Gambling Studies* 14 (3): 213–225.

Wohl, M. J., Matheson, K., Young, M. M., and Anisman, H. (2008). Cortisol rise following awakening among problem gamblers: Dissociation from comorbid symptoms of depression and impulsivity. *Journal of Gambling Studies* 24 (1): 79–90.

Won Kim, S., and Grant, J. E. (2001). Personality dimensions in pathological gambling disorder and obsessive-compulsive disorder. *Psychiatry Research* 104 (3): 205.

Zack, M., and Poulos, C. X. (2004). Amphetamine primes motivation to gamble and gambling-related semantic networks in problem gamblers. *Neuropsyhcopharmacology* 29: 195–207.

Zack, M., and Poulos, C. X. (2007). A D_2 antagonist enhances the rewarding and priming effects of a gambling episode in pathological gamblers. *Neuropsychopharmacology* 32 (8): 1678.

3 Genetic Influences on Addiction: Alcoholism as an Exemplar

James MacKillop, John E. McGeary, and Lara A. Ray

Introduction

The identification of DNA as the substrate of inheritance (Watson and Crick 1953) and subsequent decoding of the human genome (Venter et al. 2001) were scientific watersheds that have already led to major breakthroughs in understanding human behavior. This applies to both normal and disordered behavior, including addictive behavior. Empirical research has unequivocally demonstrated a substantial influence of genetic factors on addictive behavior (Haile, Kosten, and Kosten 2007; Kreek, Nielsen, and LaForge 2004; Lobo and Kennedy 2006; Saxon, Oreskovich, and Brkanac 2005). The goal of the current chapter is to conceptually review this evidence, integrating various lines of behavioral genetic research and critically discussing the strengths and weaknesses of the current knowledge in the field. To the extent possible, our objective is to provide both breadth and depth, focusing on the conceptual approaches applied, the methodologies used, and the empirical findings to date. However, given the sheer volume of research in this area, surveying the evidence for genetic influences on all forms of addictive behavior is beyond the scope of a single chapter. Instead, the focus will be on alcoholism, or alcohol dependence according to the Diagnostic and Statistical Manual (American Psychiatric Association 2000), as an exemplar of an addictive disorder. Alcoholism was selected because the literature in this area is extensive and persuasive, and it is also representative of findings on the genetics of addiction in other domains.

The chapter is divided into three general sections. The first section will focus on several sources of evidence indicating substantial genetic influences on alcoholism from various methodological approaches. This includes findings from genetic epidemiology studies, nonhuman animal research, genetic linkage analysis, and case-control association studies. This literature has produced clear evidence of genetic risk for alcoholism, but has also revealed a pattern of genetic influences that is polygenic and multifactorial. The second section will focus on recent research that is seeking to uncover specific genetic factors that contribute to risk for alcoholism. In particular, we will review recent efforts to identify intermediate phenotypes, or "endophenotypes," which may elucidate the mechanistic processes that connect variation in gene function to variation in alcohol use and misuse. This is a less extensive area of research, but it is also at the vanguard of the field because of its potential to trace specific influences from the genome to the disorder itself. Based on the findings reviewed in the first two sections, the final section will discuss the implications of genetic influences for theories of alcoholism and clinical approaches.

Converging Evidence of Polygenic Genetic Influences on Alcoholism

There are a number of sources of evidence that indicate a substantial role of genetic factors in the etiology of alcoholism, albeit often obliquely. These include genetic epidemiological studies, such as twin and adoption studies; studies using nonhuman animal models of alcoholism, which use selective breeding and other experimental techniques to study dimensions of alcohol-related behavior; linkage studies, which examine commonly inherited portions of the genome in affected individuals compared to controls; and case-control association studies, which directly examine the frequency of candidate polymorphisms in affected individuals and controls. Each of these areas will be discussed in turn.

Evidence that alcoholism runs in families has been reported for several decades (e.g., Cotton 1979), but is inherently limited by the confounding of genetic and environmental factors: children of alcoholics both potentially inherit genes predisposing them to alcoholism and are exposed to alcoholic households that may also confer increased risk for alcoholism via an array of environmental processes. Epidemiological genetic research has been able to address this confound using adoption studies, which examine the rates of alcoholism in individuals with and without a family history of alcoholism who are adopted into nonalcoholic families. The difference in diagnostic status of the biological parent creates a natural experiment in which the effect of biological family's environmental influences can be effectively reduced to nil and the effect of family history of alcoholism, or "genetic loading," can be isolated. These studies have repeatedly revealed substantially greater rates of alcoholism in adoptees with a positive family history relative to controls (Cadoret et al. 1985; Cadoret, Troughton, and O'Gorman 1987; Cloninger, Bohman, and Sigvardsson 1981; Goodwin et al. 1973; Sigvardsson, Bohman, and Cloninger 1996), although this effect has been somewhat less consistent for female adoptees (e.g., Bohman, Sigvardsson, and Cloninger 1981; Sigvardsson, Bohman, and Cloninger 1996). In terms of magnitude, the difference in odds-ratio of developing alcoholism has been as much as 6–8 times higher in individuals with a positive family history who are adopted into nonalcoholic families (Cadoret et al. 1985; Cadoret, Troughton, and O'Gorman 1987).

Genetic epidemiological studies have also made significant contributions to understanding the influence of genetic influences via twin studies, where the prevalence of alcoholism is examined in monozygotic (i.e., identical) twins, who have almost identical genomes,[1] to dizygotic (i.e., fraternal) twins, who share, on average, 50% of their genetic variation. Like adoption studies, twin studies take advantage of these genotypic differences as a natural experiment. This approach has consistently shown significantly greater concordance rates for alcoholism in monozygotic twins of alcoholics compared to dizygotic twins (Heath et al. 1997; Hrubec and Omenn 1981; Kendler et al. 1997; Pickens et al. 1991). For example, Kendler et al. (1997) found approximately double the risk of alcoholism between monozygotic twins compared to dizygotic twins in a sample of almost 9,000 twin pairs. Twin studies also have the advantage of permitting estimates of heritability (i.e., predicted variance attributable to genetics in a sample), and the existing literature suggests that about 50–60% of the risk for alcoholism is attributed to genetics (for a review, see McGue 1999).

A second, and highly persuasive, line of research implicating genetic factors in alcoholism comes from animal models. This approach traces its roots to research using a selective breeding methodology to clarify the genetic bases of an array of different aspects of behavior and cognition. An early example of this approach is Tryon's (1940) studies on "maze bright" and "maze dull" rats, which demonstrated that successively mating rodents who performed well on mazes (bright rats) with other high-performing rats and doing the same with low-performing (dull) rats led to increasingly distinct strains of rats that exemplified the selective trait (high or low maze performance). Applied to alcoholism, a large literature has developed demonstrating that preference for alcohol varies considerably among rodents and that selective breeding can lead to highly distinct strains in terms of alcohol-related characteristics (for a review, see Crabbe 2003). For example, at one end of the spectrum, the C57BL/6J strain of mice has consistently exhibited a high preference for alcohol, whereas at the other, the DBA/2J strain consistently exhibits very low alcohol preference (Belknap, Crabbe, and Young 1993). In the literature, the C57BL/6J mice are often referred to as "alcohol-preferring" mice. In addition, the selective breeding approach has been successful in developing strains that provide animal models of various dimensions of alcohol-related behavior, such as proneness to withdrawal seizures or initial sensitivity to alcohol (Crabbe 2003).

Thus, like twin and adoption studies, the evidence that alcohol preference and other aspects of alcohol-related behavior are highly sensitive to selective breeding in non-human animals demonstrates that genetic factors play a substantial role in the expression of these phenotypes. Importantly, beyond the classic selective breeding technique, animal models of alcoholism can also be experimentally informative by using an array of innovative contemporary genetic strategies to clarify the underlying genetic influences. This includes quantitative trait loci (QTL) mapping, gene expression profiling, and targeted and random mutagenesis. These approaches have generated promising findings in terms of identifying specific genes underlying variation in alcohol-related behavior in rodents (e.g., Fehr et al. 2002, 2004; Shirley et al. 2004).

There are, however, limitations to animal models of alcoholism. Perhaps the most notable limitation is the lack of clarity in the connection between the alcohol-related behaviors observed in animal models and in humans. Specifically, it is unclear if the genetically mediated manifestations of alcohol-related behavior observed in rodents are fundamentally the same in humans. It is possible that selective breeding successfully results in rodent strains that bear only phenomenological similarities to humans, but are actually guided by genetic factors that are not in play for humans. As such, animal models provide a very powerful proof-of-concept that many aspects of alcohol consumption are substantially under genetic control, but whether there is close genetic homology between animal models and human variability in drinking cannot be unambiguously ascertained at this point. This is not to diminish the advances using this strategy. Beyond demonstrations in principle, animal models permit an entire experimental enterprise for investigating alcohol-related phenomena in ways that are impossible in humans. Furthermore, translational efforts to understand the etiology and improve the treatment of alcoholism rely on, and often start with, animal models of addictions. For now, however, the disconnect between the animal models and human alcoholism remains a limitation of this area.

Thus, a joint limitation of both genetic epidemiological research and animal models of addiction is that they represent strong but essentially oblique evidence of genetic influences on alcoholism. In the case of epidemiological research, genetic influences represent aggregates that typically cannot be deconstructed into specific genes. In the case of animal models, the parallels between the animal models and human alcoholism have not been definitively established. In order to identify the specific genes that are implicated in alcoholism, two complementary strategies have commonly been used, namely genetic linkage analysis and case-control genetic association studies.

At one end of the experimental spectrum, linkage studies can be used to examine the entire genome for linkage between a phenotype of interest (e.g., alcoholism) and genetic variation. Linkage analysis consists of examining evenly spaced polymorphic markers across the genomes of individuals who are positive (i.e., probands) and negative for the phenotype within a family to find chromosomal regions that tend to be shared among affected relatives but not shared among unaffected relatives. In other words, linkage analysis seeks to find chromosomal locations that are relevant to the transmission of the disease liability by identifying which genetic markers of known locations tend to be transmitted along with the disease phenotype within families. Importantly, the transmission of the marker among affected relatives needs to be significantly greater than the transmission of the marker than is expected by chance.

"Log of odds" (LOD) scores are used as a quantitative index of linkage, with higher scores indicating greater evidence of linkage; the conventional LOD score criterion is three or higher. In turn, these relatively large chromosomal regions can then be mined to identify the specific genes that underlie the different frequencies between groups.

To date, the most significant linkage study on alcoholism is the Collaborative Study on the Genetics of Alcoholism (COGA), which included an initial sample of 105 families with multiple alcoholic members and a replication sample of 157 additional families, with a total enrollment of over 2,000 individuals (Foroud et al. 2000; Reich et al. 1998). Using a diagnosis of alcoholism as the phenotype of interest, COGA identified a number of areas of linkage, particularly on chromosomes 1 and 7 (Foroud et al. 2000; Reich et al. 1998), but also demonstrated that there was little evidence for small numbers of genetic loci that exerted high-magnitude effects and clearly accounted for differences between alcoholics and controls. More recently, the COGA project has been an invaluable resource for moving beyond the diagnostic phenotype of alcoholism and mapping genetic variability underlying alternative phenotypes that are relevant to the pathophysiology of alcoholism itself (e.g., Dick et al. 2002; Saccone et al. 2000), as will be discussed further below.

At the other end of the experimental spectrum are case-control association studies, which target specific genes of interest and compare the allele frequencies in individuals who have a disorder ("cases") to individuals who do not have the disorder ("controls"). This is based on the premise that alleles that contribute to alcoholism will be disproportionately present in affected individuals, and, conversely, alleles that protect against alcoholism will be disproportionately prevalent in unaffected individuals. Given its relative simplicity, this research strategy has been extensively applied to alcoholism and has revealed a wide array of genes that appear to underlie genetic influences (e.g., George et al. 1993; Town et al. 1999). However, although individual studies have been promising, the case-control literature as a whole has been bedeviled by conflicting findings.

A highly illustrative example is that of the DRD2 *Taq*I A polymorphism and its association with alcoholism risk. In this case, an initial case control study by Blum et al. (1990) reported that one variant in the dopamine D_2 receptor gene (DRD2) *Taq*I A polymorphism was dramatically more prevalent in alcoholics compared to controls. Specifically, the minor A1 version of the gene was present in 77% of the alcoholic sample, but in only 28% of controls, which generated enormous scientific and popular interest. Postmortem studies have subsequently revealed that A1+ individuals exhibit significantly decreased D_2 receptor availability (Noble et al. 1991; Thompson et al. 1997), and neuroimaging studies have indicated lower D_2 receptor density (Noble et al. 1997) and reduced mean glucose metabolism in brain regions associated with high dopaminergic activity (Jonsson et al. 1999), all suggesting a plausible functional basis for possession of the A1 allele conferring greater risk. A large number of studies have also subsequently investigated its relationship to alcoholism, both with replications (Amadeo et al. 1993; Blum et al. 1991; Comings et al. 1991; Ishiguro et al. 1998; Kono et al. 1997; Neiswanger, Hill, and Kaplan 1995; Noble et al. 1994; Parsian et al. 1991; Higuchi et al. 1994b) and with many failures to replicate (Arinami et al. 1993; Bolos et al. 1990; Chen et al. 1996; Chen, Chien, and Hwu 2001; Cook et al. 1992; Cruz et al. 1995; Edenberg et al. 1998; Gelernter and Kranzler 1999; Gelernter et al. 1991; Goldman et al. 1992; Goldman et al. 1997; Lee et al. 1999; Lobos and Todd 1998; Lu et al. 1996; Parsian, Cloninger, and Zhang 2000; Sander et al. 1995, 1999; Schwab et al. 1991; Suarez et al. 1994; Turner et al. 1992; Waldman, Robinson, and Rhee 1999).

It has been speculated that these equivocal findings may be because the A1 allele is disproportionately common in severe alcoholics (Noble 2000), but this hypothesis is difficult to test based on varying definitions of severity; and findings that have included dimensions of severity have been inconsistent (Dick and Foroud 2003). In addition, a complicating factor has been that A1 frequency varies considerably by racial and ethnic ancestry. This raises the possibility of population stratification in the positive findings (Goldman et al. 1993), an experimental confound in which differences in the frequency of an allele among affected individuals spuriously emerge because of different racial/ethnic compositions of case and control groups and corresponding differences in allele frequencies (Hutchison et al. 2004). For example, if an allele is disproportionately more prevalent in African-American individuals and the group of alcoholic cases has a disproportionately higher percentage of African-American participants, a genetic association could emerge spuriously on the basis of race, not disease liability itself. Most recently, an additional complicating factor has been the finding that the DRD2 *Taq*I A polymorphism is actually not located in the DRD2 gene, but is in an adjacent protein kinase gene, ANKK1 (Neville, Johnstone, and Walton 2004).

Clearly the relationship between the DRD2 *Taq*I A polymorphism and alcoholism is neither as robust nor as straightforward as it was initially thought, and recent efforts have been made to square these conflicting findings. Two recent meta-analyses have surveyed the literature on this candidate gene, finding significant but modest positive associations. Young et al. (2004) examined 55 studies including almost 10,000 subjects, finding a significant association with substance abuse in general. Munafò, Matheson, and Flint (2007) examined 40 studies, finding a significant association with alcoholism, even after excluding the first positive finding, although this was somewhat qualified by some evidence for publication bias. Based on these reviews, on balance, the A1 allele of the *Taq*I A polymorphism does appear to be generally associated with alcoholism, albeit accounting for approximately .2% of phenotypic variance in risk for alcoholism (Munafò, Matheson, and Flint 2007). This is substantially lower than the earlier, much more optimistic, estimates of over 20% (Noble 2000).

With regard to the recent evidence of the polymorphism actually being located in the ANKK1 gene, one plausible hypothesis that has been initially borne out by two recent studies (Dick et al. 2007; Gelernter et al. 2006) is that the *TaqI* A variant may be nonrandomly correlated with nearby polymorphisms in the DRD2 gene or part of a DRD2–linked haplotype of genes commonly inherited together, both of which would explain its relationship to D_2 receptor characteristics. Such nonrandom associations are referred to as linkage disequilibrium (LD). High, but not collinear (i.e., one to one), LD with a functional variant in the DRD2 gene could substantially clarify the mixed empirical findings since each sample would have a variable level of association with the active polymorphism. Alternatively, it is possible that the *TaqI* A polymorphism itself influences dopaminergic neurotransmission (Munafò, Matheson, and Flint 2007; Neville, Johnstone, and Walton 2004), although the mechanism by which this might take place is unclear. Unfortunately, the general pattern of findings with regard to the *TaqI* A polymorphism, where initially promising findings are followed by repeated failures to replicate, is highly representative of case-control association studies for multiple candidate genes (e.g., Arias, Feinn, and Kranzler 2006; van der Zwaluw et al. 2007). Similar to linkage studies, the genetic association literature for alcoholism suggests that any single gene is unlikely to have a large effect on alcoholism liability.

Taken together, the picture that emerges from the empirical research using the aforementioned research strategies is paradoxical. Alcoholism is clearly substantially influenced by genetic factors, with reliable estimates of heritability of about 50–60% (Kendler et al. 2003; Knopik et al. 2004; McGue 1999), and animal studies demonstrating potent genetic influences on an array of alcohol-related phenotypes. Conversely, however, linkage and association studies have not identified a single major locus, or small number of major loci, suggesting that the genetic influence on alcoholism liability is conferred by many genes, not just a few, each contributing small- to medium-sized influences. At this point, there is no evidence of an "alcoholism gene" and little promise that one will emerge. Thus, the major task at hand is characterizing the apparently multifarious genetic influences on alcoholism (Dick and Foroud 2003; Hines et al. 2005).

Understanding Genetic Influences on Alcoholism via an Intermediate Phenotype Approach

Based on the preceding findings, a high priority in research on the genetics of alcoholism is decomposing the substantial statistical risk in terms of heritability into the specific genetic causes of increased genetic liability. As Crabbe (2003, 291) has commented, "one does not inherit risk: one inherits specific risk-promoting or risk-protective genes," and it is these genes, and the functional consequences of variation in these genes, that are of greatest interest. In this section, we will review the recent findings characterizing the nature of genetic risk and protective factors. We will first discuss a conceptual approach recently applied in this area—an intermediate phenotype approach—and provide a framework for identifying general and specific genetic influences on alcoholism. Then, we will review the empirical findings on intermediate phenotypes relating to alcoholism. Finally, we will discuss potential interactions that may add further complexity to fully characterizing genetic influences on alcoholism, such as epistatic (gene-by-gene) and gene-by-environment (G × E) interactions.

An Intermediate Phenotype Approach to the Genetics of Alcoholism

One approach to elucidating genetic influences on psychiatric disorders that is increasingly being used is the intermediate phenotype, or "endophenotype," approach (Gottesman and Gould 2003; Flint and Munafò 2007; Hines et al. 2005). This approach seeks to characterize genetic influences by identifying specific functional processes (i.e., intermediate phenotypes, endophenotypes) that are responsible for a genetic variant's proximal influence on a disorder. This approach is based on the assumption that psychiatric diagnoses may be useful for describing a clinical syndrome and communication among clinicians, but they may not be useful phenotypes for genetic studies as the current DSM-IV symptoms tell us little about the underlying neurobiology and pathophysiology of the disorder (Dick and Foroud 2003; Hines et al. 2005). For most psychiatric syndromes, there are many permutations of symptoms that may result in a diagnosis, resulting in considerable heterogeneity among individuals diagnosed with a condition. Indeed, the existing heterogeneity in terms of alcoholism has been the basis for ongoing efforts to characterize dominant subtypes (e.g., Babor and Caetano 2006). Furthermore, the psychiatric diagnosis of alcoholism, alcohol dependence, has been criticized as overemphasizing the pharmacological properties of all psychoactive drugs over repeated administrations (i.e., tolerance, withdrawal), rather than core behavioral features of addiction (O'Brien, Volkow, and Li 2006). As such, there is a multitude of pathways to the diagnosis of alcoholism, referred to as equifinality from a developmental perspective (Windle and Davies 1999), in which genetic factors may plausibly play diverse roles leading to a common pattern of maladaptive alcohol use. Taken together, the diagnosis of alcoholism is a relatively diffuse phenotype that is considerably distal from individual genes. To use the common metaphor, the imprecise nature of diagnosis as a phenotype has made it difficult to parse genetic "signal" from "noise." Therefore, by focusing on identifying more narrowly defined phenotypes that reflect both genetic and behavioral variation, an intermediate phenotype approach attempts to identify the functional influences of risk-conferring and risk-preventing genes. Moreover, a focus on intermediate phenotypes has the potential to simultaneously identify the pathophysiological mechanisms underlying the disorder, unlike the relatively opaque phenotype of diagnosis.

Although the terms intermediate phenotype and endophenotype have been used more or less interchangeably so far, they are not synonyms. Etymologically, Gottesman and Shields (1973) introduced the concept of an endophenotype in reference to understanding the genetic risk for schizophrenia. The term was intended to refer to an internal, genetically mediated process that was not readily observable but that could be objectively and reliably assessed, and was robustly connected to the disorder under consideration. In addition, the conventional criteria for an endophenotype include that it should be heritable, stable (i.e., present even when the disease is not), and evident in nonaffected family members at a higher prevalence than in the population in general, reflecting transmission patterns of familial association and cosegregation (Gottesman and Gould 2003). In contrast, intermediate phenotypes refer to the general category of phenomena that are empirically related to genetic variation and diagnostic variation (presence or absence of the diagnosis or symptoms), which includes both endophenotypes and candidate variables that have not as yet been determined to meet the preceding criteria. Thus, endophenotypes reflect a subclass of intermediate phenotypes, which in turn reflect a subclass of phenotypes (Goldman and Ducci 2007). We will discuss both variables that can be considered endophenotypes and other promising intermediate phenotypes. Although there are many potential intermediate phenotypes, we will focus only on those studies that have both identified a variable of clear relevance to alcoholism and have demonstrated empirical evidence of specific genes that contribute to variation in that more narrow phenotype.

Prior to doing so, however, we will provide a framework for understanding the ways in which genetic variables may exert influences in three broad domains. As depicted in table 3.1, genetic influences on alcohol use may come in a number of forms that vary in their specific relevance to alcohol and the point at which alcohol is processed. The first domain pertains to variables that are not specifically related to alcohol. Rather, they are predisposing factors to a number of forms of addiction and other related psychopathology. This is in part based on the high rates of comorbidity among types of addictive behavior and other types of psychopathology (e.g., Grant et al. 2004), suggesting potentially pleiotropic genetic influences (i.e., individual genetic variants resulting in multiple phenotypic expressions). However, there is also direct empirical support for such nonspecific influences. Twin studies have also shown that common genetic factors may underlie vulnerability to alcohol and drug dependence. The genetic correlation between alcohol and drug dependence was partially explained by the genetic risk both disorders share with adolescent conduct disorder (Button et al. 2007). An alternative conceptualization of this covariation is that conduct disorder represents an early, adolescent manifestation of the same genetic loading that influences adult alcohol dependence later in life (Dick et al. 2006b). Genetic factors underlying alcohol and nicotine dependence were also found to overlap substantially (True et al. 1999). A large twin study investigating genetic and environmental risk factors underlying the comorbidity among ten lifetime psychiatric disorders, including alcohol and drug dependence, concluded that the pattern of comorbidity between substance use disorders

Table 3.1

A conceptual framework for investigating the genetics of alcoholism via an intermediate phenotype approach. Converging findings suggest that an array of genetic factors contribute to alcoholism, including general (nonspecific) risk factors for externalizing psychopathology and specific alcohol-related risk factors. Candidate intermediate phenotypes represent the apparent mechanisms functionally relating the candidate genes to alcohol-related outcomes. The lists of candidate intermediate phenotypes and genes respectively pertain to one another, but are intended to be illustrative, not exhaustive.

	Intermediate Phenotypes for Alcoholism		
Specificity	Nonspecific	Alcohol-specific	
Domain:	General Dispositional Factors	Alcohol Pharmacokinetics	Alcohol Pharmacodynamics
Candidate Intermediate Phenotypes:	Attenuated Resting Beta-frequency	Metabolism of Alcohol	Low Response to Alcohol
	Attenuated P300 Event-related Potentials	Metabolism of Acetaldehyde	Amplified Subjective Effects of Alcohol
	Substance Cue Reactivity		
Candidate Genes:	GABRA2	ADH1B	5HTTLPR and GABRA6
	CHRM2	ALDH2	OPRM1
	DRD4 VNTR		

and other highly prevalent externalizing psychiatric disorders are largely due to common genetic risk factors (Kendler et al. 2003). Common genetic factors underlying vulnerability to frequently comorbid disorders suggests that disorders that are correlated at the phenotypic level may also be correlated at the genotypic level, reflecting pleiotropic influences. Likewise, intermediate phenotypes may reflect this by conferring risk to various forms of psychopathology.

In contrast to nonspecific genetic influences, the two additional domains of genetic influences reflect genetic effects are specific to alcoholism, first in the area of the pharmacokinetics of alcohol (i.e., the movement of alcohol through the body and its metabolism) and the second in terms of the pharmacodynamics of alcohol (i.e., the neuropharmacological actions of alcohol). The basis for distinguishing between these categories is because they can be loosely thought of as successively dependent on each other in the chronology of drinking. Nonspecific genetic factors putatively contribute to the probability of engaging in an array of behaviors, including drinking alcohol. Then, once alcohol is consumed, genetically influenced pharmacokinetic factors affect its subsequent processing and metabolic responses to its ingestion. Finally, after alcohol enters the central nervous system, genetically influenced pharmacodynamic factors affect its psychoactive effects. Importantly, however, these are not strictly chronological relationships and the variables in these different domains interact with each other. Within this framework, we consider that aggregate genetic risk for an individual reflects an emergent property of the specific risk-promoting and risk-preventing genes in each of these domains, and that these genes can have additive, multiplicative, or and even opposing effects, as will be evident in the following sections.

Genetic Variation Affecting General Dispositional Factors Conferring Risk for Alcoholism

As noted above, the first source of genetic influences comes in the form of variables that are not specifically related to alcohol per se, but pertain to broader dispositional variables that may influence the probability that an individual may use alcohol or develop alcoholism. An ostensibly good example might be dimensions of personality, such as novelty-seeking, that are associated with an array of different forms of substance use (e.g., Conway et al. 2003; Galen, Henderson, and Whitman 1997; Gurpegui et al. 2007) and plausibly could contribute to other forms of psychopathology, such as attention-deficit hyperactivity disorder, disruptive behavior disorders, or antisocial personality disorder, for example. However, generally speaking, personality variables as intermediate phenotypes have not been supported in the literature. A large number of promising associations have been reported, but many have subsequently failed to replicate. In a recent review and meta-analysis of 46 studies of genetic polymorphisms and dimensions of personality, Munafò et al. (2003) found limited evidence for consistent relationships. This may be due to similar problems as those with psychiatric diagnosis, with personality traits potentially being too diffuse to be closely connected with one gene or a small number of genes. In other words, personality traits may be akin to other complex behavioral phenotypes, like diagnostic phenotypes, and therefore subject to the same problems with regard to genetic association findings. In addition, because personality is typically assessed using self-report inventories, subjective interpretations of the items may contribute to ambiguous relationships between personality and individual genes. More progress has been made in identifying intermediate phenotypes that are more narrowly and objectively defined, particularly in the areas of brain electrophysiology and anticipatory reactions to substance cues. These phenotypes are arguably more homogeneous as a function of their closer proximity to neurobiological processes underlying disease liability.

In the first case, there is strong empirical support for variations in both resting-state and event-related electrophysiological brain oscillations, as alcoholism endophenotypes and recent studies have successfully identified specific genes underlying this variation (e.g., Edenberg et al. 2004; Jones et al. 2004, 2006; Porjesz et al. 2002). Brain oscillations are assessed using electroencephalography (EEG) and reflect dynamic changes in large numbers of neurons firing in concert, either in general during a resting state or in response to a stimulus. Several different types of brain oscillations can be reliably detected and have been demonstrated to be both highly heritable (van Beijsterveldt et al. 1996), ranging from 76–89%, and to be associated with alcoholism status (Bauer 2001; Costa and Bauer 1997; Propping, Kruger, and Mark 1981; Winterer et al. 1998; Rangaswamy et al. 2002) and other forms of psychopathology (e.g., Bauer and Hesselbrock 1993). This has been evident in terms of two types of brain oscillations, the resting-state beta frequency and the P300 event-related potential (ERP).

With regard to the resting-state beta frequency, the beta waveform is believed to reflect the balance of activation between excitatory neurons projecting from the cortex to subcortical regions of the brain and inhibitory interneurons (Porjesz and Begleiter 2003), which communicate only to other local neurons. Neurochemically, the topography of the beta wave is thought to be determined as a result of variation in GABAergic activation (Whittington et al. 2000). Resting-state beta frequency has been demonstrated to be significantly higher in alcoholics (Bauer 2001; Costa and Bauer 1997; Propping, Kruger, and Mark 1981; Rangaswamy et al. 2002; Winterer et al. 1998) and offspring of alcoholics (Finn and Justus 1999; Gabrielli et al. 1982; Rangaswamy et al. 2004). In addition, resting-state beta frequency has been found to be unrelated to duration of abstinence (Rangaswamy et al. 2002), suggesting that it is a trait variable. In the context of the COGA project, participants underwent EEG assessments, and linkage analysis indicated significant linkage on a portion of chromosome 4 where the $GABA_A$ receptor gene GABRA2 is located (Porjesz et al. 2002). Subsequently, single nucleotide polymorphism (SNP) analysis revealed that this same gene was significantly associated with alcoholism (Edenberg et al. 2004), drug addiction (Agrawal et al. 2006), and conduct disorder (CD) (Dick et al. 2006b). These findings suggest that variation in the GABRA2 gene affects the probability of developing these behavioral disorders by affecting an individual's level of neural excitability (Porjesz and Rangaswamy 2007). From a functional standpoint, this variation is thought to predispose individuals to greater CNS disinhibition, or alternatively, CNS hyperexcitability, that in turn contributes to a general predisposition to externalizing disorders (Porjesz and Rangaswamy 2007).

In addition to resting-state beta waveforms, the P300 event-related potential (ERP) waveform that occurs between 300 and 700 milliseconds as a response to a significant stimulus has also been implicated as an intermediate phenotype for alcoholism. The P300 putatively reflects several important aspects of information processing, with the amplitude of the P300 believed to reflect inhibition of responses to irrelevant stimuli (Porjesz and Begleiter 2003). In terms of the parameters of the P300, the earlier and larger the waveform, the greater the inhibitory processing, and alcoholics reliably demonstrate truncated P300 ERPs (Begleiter and Porjesz 1999), as is also the case for children who are at risk for alcoholism (Begleiter et al. 1984; Polich, Pollock, and Bloom

1994; Rangaswamy et al. 2007). Importantly, the P300 waveform consists of two specific types of oscillations (Porjesz and Begleiter 2003), delta and theta, both of which have been demonstrated to be lower among alcoholics and those with externalizing disorders (Porjesz et al. 2005).

In terms of its localization, the P300 is believed to originate in the frontal cortex, hippocampus, and amygdala (Porjesz and Begleiter, 2003), and appears to be subserved by acetylcholinergic neurotransmission (Fellous and Sejnowski 2000). Similar to the resting beta frequency, the functional outcome of diminished P300 waveform is believed to be due to greater central nervous system disinhibition resulting in disturbed impulse regulation (Porjesz and Begleiter 2003). This is supported by a recent report of a significant inverse correlation between self-reported impulsivity and P300 ERP (Chen et al. 2007). As with resting beta frequency, the COGA project allowed for linkage analysis of the P300 ERP, and found strong evidence of linkage on chromosome 7, specifically implicating the acetylcholinergic gene CHRM2 (Jones et al. 2004, 2006), which has also been demonstrated to be associated with alcoholism and other forms of externalizing disorders (Dick et al. 2008; Wang et al. 2004). In addition, CHRM2 has since been independently found to be associated with alcoholism, drug dependence, and affective disorders in a separate sample (Luo et al. 2005). Thus, these findings implicate specific genetic influences on *trait* disinhibition (during a resting state [beta frequency]), and greater *state* disinhibition (in response to a stimulus [P300 ERP]), thereby increasing risk for alcoholism and other related disorders.

The second relevant nonspecific intermediate phenotype pertains to anticipatory reactions to substance-related cues. In this case, a large empirical literature has demonstrated that individuals with substance use histories exhibit potent biobehavioral reactions to substance cues (for a review, see Carter and Tiffany 1999; see also the chapter by Goldman et al. in this volume), including large magnitude increases in craving and smaller magnitude changes in psychophysiological arousal and affect. Reactivity to substance cues putatively reflects anticipatory reactions to environmental stimuli that signal reward and is believed to be a significant motivational factor in ongoing substance use and posttreatment relapse (for a review, see MacKillop and Monti 2007). Cue reactivity has been demonstrated to be positively associated with severity of addictive behavior (Glautier and Drummond 1994; Monti et al. 1987; Rankin, Stockwell, and Hodgson 1982) and, in a recent study of the causes of posttreatment relapse, giving in to temptation in the presence of cues was the most frequent individual cause for adults and among the most frequent causes for adolescents (Ramo and Brown 2008). Moreover, cue reactivity has been demonstrated to be highly variable among individuals at similar levels of severity, with some individuals exhibiting negligible reactions and others exhibiting dramatic increases in motivation (Avants et al. 1995; Shiffman et al. 2003; Monti et al. 1999; Rohsenow et al. 1992).

Although many of the criteria of endophenotype status have not been empirically demonstrated for substance cue reactivity, it has considerable promise as an intermediate phenotype and a number of studies have suggested that the variable number of tandem repeats (VNTR) polymorphism in the dopamine D_4 receptor gene (DRD4) is related to substance cue reactivity. The DRD4 VNTR polymorphism refers to a hypervariable portion of exon III, varying from 2 to 11 repeats with trimodal distribution of 2, 4, and 7 repeat alleles. Basic research on the DRD4 VNTR polymorphism has suggested that the 7 repeat allele is associated with less sensitive D_4 receptors in terms of inhibiting intracellular cyclic AMP (Asghari et al. 1995) and generally lower receptor functionality (Van Craenenbroeck et al. 2005).

In an initial report, Hutchison et al. (2002) found that possession of at least one "long" version allele (i.e., 7 repeats or longer; DRD4-L) was associated with greater reactivity to smoking cues, including greater craving, arousal, and attention paid to the smoking stimuli. Subsequently, additional studies demonstrated that DRD4-L individuals show exaggerated reactivity to alcohol (Hutchison et al. 2006; McGeary et al. 2006) and heroin (Shao et al. 2006) cues. In addition, there is evidence that DRD4-L status influences reactivity to food cues among binge eaters (Sobik, Hutchison, and Craighead 2005). Consistent with a positive moderating role of DRD4-L genotype, in a recent study, DRD4 VNTR status was found to interact with the individual's level of alcohol craving, such that as craving increased, DRD4-L individuals exhibited disproportionately high preference for alcohol in a behavioral economic alcohol self-administration task (MacKillop et al. 2007). From a neuroanatomical standpoint, a recent study using functional magnetic resonance imaging (fMRI) reported that DRD4-L status was associated with greater activation of right superior frontal gyrus and right insula in reaction to smoking cues (McClernon et al. 2007). Similarly, an fMRI paradigm also revealed that DRD4-L individuals exhibited greater reactivity to alcohol cues (Filbey et al. 2008), although the differential increases were in the in the orbitofrontal cortex, anterior cingulate gyrus, and striatum.

Taken together, these studies provide converging evidence that DRD4-L status is generally associated with greater anticipatory reactions to environmental cues signaling reward. This relationship provides insight into the role of DRD4 VNTR status in the development and maintenance of alcoholism and other forms of addictive behavior: DRD4-L individuals appear to be predisposed to greater cue reactivity, which may dynamically increase the probability that an individual chooses to drink, smoke, or engage in an array of appetitive behaviors. Of note, addressing one of the premises of the intermediate phenotype approach, there is little evidence that links the DRD4 VNTR polymorphism and alcoholism in the strict diagnostic sense (Dick and Foroud 2003), but this is not surprising if its role is related to a subtle component of appetitive behavior, namely reactions to reward-related cues, which would not be anticipated to be solely responsible for alcoholism.

Importantly, although these findings are promising, caution should be exercised in definitively identifying augmented cue reactivity as an intermediate phenotype subserved by DRD4 VNTR genotype. One recent study has not supported the relationship (van den Wildenberg et al. 2007), and the overall literature is relatively small and confined to a few research groups. Confirming this relationship will rely on the convergence of findings in a larger number of independent studies.

Genetic Variation Affecting the Pharmacokinetics of Alcohol

A second source of genetic influences on alcohol use and abuse comes in the form of genetically mediated differences in the pharmacokinetics of alcohol, or the metabolism of alcohol as it travels through the body. The metabolic breakdown of alcohol is primarily a three-step hepatic process in which the ingested alcohol is first broken down via oxidation into acetaldehyde by the enzyme alcohol dehydrogenase (ADH), and is then further metabolized into acetate and excretable by-products by the enzyme aldehyde dehydrogenase (ALDH). The genes responsible for these enzymes exert important influences on the neurobehavioral effects of alcohol because they determine the speed with which alcohol and its metabolites pass through the body and into the central nervous system. As such, functional variation in the genes coding for ADH and ALDH are relevant to alcohol's psychoactive effects. Indeed, the most robust findings on the genetic basis of risk for alcoholism have been found in relation to the genes responsible for the pharmacokinetics of alcohol. The increased consistency of the findings that implicate more biologically driven phenotypes, such as alcohol metabolism, further supports the need for continued refinement of phenotypes for behavioral disorders in order to more successfully and reliably identify specific genes.

Of the ADH and ALDH enzymes, the genetic influences that are best characterized are for the ALDH enzyme. Two ALDH enzymes are responsible for metabolizing acetaldehyde, and are encoded by two genes, ALDH2 and ALDH1A1, located on chromosomes 12 and 9, respectively. ALDH2 has two variants, ALDH2-1 and ALDH2-2, of which the latter reflects a lysine-to-glutamate substitution resulting in an inactive form of the enzyme that cannot metabolize acetaldehyde into acetate. Importantly, this variant is dominant, such that even individuals with only one copy of the ALDH2-2 (heterozygotes) demonstrate almost no ALDH2 activity in the liver (Crabb et al. 1989). As a result, ALDH2-2 carriers experience a buildup of acetaldehyde following alcohol consumption, which causes an array of unpleasant effects, including flushing, headache, tachycardia, and nausea, among others. Importantly, this aversive reaction to alcohol has been robustly demonstrated to have a protective effect against alcoholism in a number of studies, such that ALDH2-2 carriers are less likely to develop alcoholism (e.g., Chen et al. 1999; Luczak, Glatt, and Wall 2006; Thomasson et al. 1991). In terms of the specific magnitude, a recent meta-analysis of over 4,000 individuals found that ALDH2-2 genotype reduced the risk of alcoholism to between one-fourth and one-ninth of the risk among noncarriers (Luczak, Glatt, and Wall 2006). Indeed, for ALDH2-2 homozygotes, only a very small number cases of alcoholism have been identified (Luczak, Glatt, and Wall 2006). This protective effect generally pertains to individuals of East Asian ancestry for whom possession of the ALDH2-2 allele is common; it is relatively rare among individuals of European or African ancestry (Oota et al. 2004). Interestingly, despite its strong protective effect, there is evidence that ALDH2 status interacts with environmental influences. Higuchi et al. (1994a) found that from 1979 to 1992 the percentage of Japanese alcohol-dependent individuals who possessed an ALDH2-2 allele increased from 2.5% to 13%, suggesting that greater social acceptability of alcohol use in Japanese culture may have reduced the protective effect of this genetic variant. Similarly, in a recent study of Asian-American college students, ALDH2 genotype status was not associated with differences in alcohol use (Hendershot et al. 2005), suggesting that acculturation may also moderate the polymorphism's influence.

Based on these potent effects via variation in the ALDH2 gene, there is also considerable interest in the ALDH1A1 gene. Unlike the ALDH2 gene, which is responsible for enzymatic activity in the mitochondria, ALDH1A1 is responsible for enzymatic activity in the cytosol (Edenberg 2007). However, variants of the ALDH1A1 gene occur at relatively low frequencies and findings to date have been mixed. Ehlers et al. (2004) found that Southwest California Indians possessing the less functional enzymatic variant (i.e., resulting in greater acetaldehyde buildup) experienced a protective effect against alcoholism. In contrast, Hansell et al. (2005) did not find a protective effect in an Australian community sample. At this point, although variation in ALDH1A1 may be related to risk for alcoholism, the data are far from definitive.

Beyond variation in the genes responsible for the enzymatic metabolism of acetaldehyde, there is also considerable evidence that genetic variation at the first step in the metabolism of alcohol plays a significant role in risk for alcoholism. As noted above, alcohol is initially broken down via oxidation by alcohol dehydrogenase (ADH). Of the multiple forms of the ADH, the class I isozymes (ADH1A, ADH1B, and ADH1C) are believed to play the major role in metabolizing alcohol (Edenberg 2007; Lee et al. 2006). The genes responsible for these enzymes are closely located on chromosome 4, and both the ADH1B and ADH1C genes (coding for the respective isoenzymes) appear to have functional polymorphisms. In the case of ADH1B, three polymorphisms of the gene have been identified. Of these, two (ADH1B-2, ADH1B-3) have been associated with faster enzymatic activity compared to the ADH1B-1 allele, with both resulting in an approximately 75- to 90-fold greater turnover rate. In the case of ADH1C, two variants have been studied, ADH1C-1 and ADH1C-2, and there is evidence that ADH1C-2 is associated with approximately half the alcohol turnover compared to ADH1C-1 (Edenberg 2007). Of note, a third variant of the ADH1C gene has been identified in Native Americans (Osier et al. 2002), but it has not been studied in great detail. In addition to independently increasing the rate of alcohol metabolism, variation in the ADH1B and ADH1C genes epistatically affects the speed at which an individual metabolizes alcohol into acetaldehyde. For example, a man who is homozygous for the ADH1B-2 and ADH1C-1 alleles is estimated to have a speed of oxidation that is eight times faster than a man who is homozygous for the ADH1B-1 and ADH1C-2 alleles (Lee et al. 2006).

The consequences of possession of genetic variants that affect ADH enzymatic activity are similar to those for variants that affect ALDH activity. Possession of the ADH1B-2 allele has been demonstrated to reduce the risk of alcoholism in East Asians (Luczak, Glatt, and Wall 2006; Thomasson et al. 1991; Whitfield 2002), for whom the frequency of this allele is high. Again, the basis for these protective effects is believed to be acetaldehyde accumulation: more rapid oxidation of alcohol results in greater blood levels of acetaldehyde, and, in turn, flushing, headache, tachycardia, and nausea in response to alcohol ingestion. In addition, although the minor allele frequency is lower in other ethnic groups, this protective effect has also been demonstrated for individuals of European and African ancestry (Whitfield 2002) and individuals of Jewish descent (Hasin et al. 2002; Luczak et al. 2002). Similarly, Edenberg et al. (2006) found that possession of the ADH1B-3 allele reduces the risk of alcoholism in African Americans, although not among Europeans, and Wall, Carr, and Ehlers (2003) found the ADH1B-3 allele had a protective effect among Southwest American Indians. With regard to ADH1C, there is evidence that the faster metabolism of alcohol via possession of the ADH1C-1 allele has protective effects in Asians, but this allele is in high linkage disequilibrium with ADH1B-2, which is believed to be responsible for this protective effect (Chen et al. 1999; Choi et al. 2005; Osier et al. 1999).

Taken together, the preceding genetic variants related to the pharmacokinetics of alcohol have been determined to substantially affect an individual's risk for alcoholism by influencing alcohol metabolism and its neurobehavioral correlates. A central step in the metabolism of alcohol includes its oxidation into acetaldehyde, and allelic variation that either results in slower breakdown of acetaldehyde (ALDH-related genes) or faster initial accumulation of acetaldehyde (ADH-related genes) largely determines whether an individual will experience the aversive symptoms accompanying excessive acetaldehyde buildup upon alcohol consumption. This relationship is prototypical of an intermediate phenotype approach. Specific genetic polymorphisms can be identified and traced to intervening processes that specifically affect risk for alcoholism, albeit in this case via a protection-conferring rather than risk-conferring direction. Although substantially more remains to be understood about the genes responsible for alcohol's metabolism, the robust findings in this area demonstrate the importance of these specific alleles and, more broadly, the importance of considering genes responsible for a drug's pharmacokinetics as part of an individual's genetic liability for addiction.

Genetic Variation Affecting the Pharmacodynamics of Alcohol

Beyond the processes of metabolism, once alcohol enters the brain its psychoactive effects are a result of its neuropharmacological actions (i.e., pharmacodynamics). Until relatively recently, alcohol's effects were believed to take place via altering neural membrane permeability; now, however, there is extensive evidence that that alcohol has specific effects on neurotransmitter release and receptor function (Boehm, Valenzuela, and Harris 2005; Gianoulakis 2001). Neuroanatomically, these effects are most relevant in the ascending mesocorticolimbic reward axis, which originates in the ventral tegmental area (VTA) and projects into the nucleus accumbens (NAcc) and forebrain structures such as the anterior cingulate and prefrontal cortex (Gardner 2005; Hyman et al. 2006). Activity in this brain region is believed to subserve reward-related learning and the positively reinforcing stimulant effects common to drugs of addictive potential, including alcohol, cocaine, opiates, and marijuana (Gardner 2005; Hyman, Malenka, and Nestler 2006). In the context of this reward pathway, multiple neurotransmitter systems play diverse roles in alcohol's effects. For example, alcohol directly increases the release of dopamine (DA) in the VTA and NAcc (Kohl et al. 1998; Weiss et al. 1993; Weiss and Porrino 2002), but DA release is also under tonic GABAergic inhibitory control and glutamatergic control (Krystal et al. 2003). In addition, GABA neurons in the VTA are themselves under inhibitory control of opioidergic neurons from the arcuate nucleus, which also directly release endorphins in the NAcc and increase NAcc dopamine release (Jamensky and Gianoulakis 1997). Further, serotonin appears to serve as a modulator of dopamine release in this pathway, and increased levels of serotonin amplify the subjective effects of alcohol (e.g., LeMarquand, Pihl, and Benkelfat 1994). These diverse neuropharmacological actions account for alcohol's multifarious psychoactive effects over the course of the blood alcohol curve, ranging from reinforcing effects, such as stimulation and anxiolysis, to aversive effects, such as sedation and cognitive/motoric impairment (e.g., Holdstock and de Wit 1998; Martin et al. 1993). Moreover, these diverse effects provide a large number of neurobiological processes that may be influenced by genetic factors (Boehm, Valenzuela, and Harris 2005; Gianoulakis 2001).

It is here that the third domain of genetic influences on alcoholism has been evident. Genetic variation that affects the functionality of these neurotransmitter systems may alter alcohol's psychoactive effects and, in turn, alcoholism liability. In this case, the intermediate phenotypes of greatest interest are individual differences in the subjective experiences of alcohol's psychoactive effects, as measured using human laboratory paradigms. Research in this area to date has focused on both attenuated and amplified subjective responses to alcohol as endophenotypes.

In the first case, there is a strong empirical basis for low response to alcohol early in an individual's drinking career as a genetically mediated behavioral risk factor for alcoholism. Low response is typically defined as attenuated response to alcohol's subjective and behavioral effects of alcohol intoxication (Schuckit and Gold 1988) and has been demonstrated in individuals who are at risk for alcoholism, including children of alcoholics, Native Americans, and Koreans (Chiu et al. 2004; Ehlers et al. 1999; Erblich and Earleywine 1999; Schuckit and Smith 2000; Wall et al. 1999). Low response has been demonstrated to be reliable when measured over time and to have a heritability of approximately 60% (Heath et al. 1999; Viken et al. 2003). Moreover, four longitudinal investigations have found that low response to alcohol measured in the laboratory predicted alcohol-related problems over a decade later (Volavka et al. 1996; Heath et al. 1999; Rodriguez, Wilson, and Nagoshi 1993; Schuckit and Smith 2000). The putative basis for the increased risk via low response to alcohol is a predisposition for greater amounts of alcohol to be necessary for intoxication and lower sensitivity to the unpleasant effects of alcohol, even at higher levels of blood-alcohol concentration. Response to alcohol in this area has typically been assessed using the Subjective High Assessment Scale (SHAS), and recent studies have suggested that performance on the SHAS is most highly correlated with the unpleasant sedative effects of alcohol (Conrod, Peterson, and Pihl 2001), supporting the notion that low responders to alcohol may be less sensitive to the sedative effects of alcohol. From a mechanistic standpoint, the greater alcohol consumption resulting from low response is believed to result in greater tolerance for alcohol and greater probability of spending time with heavy-drinking peers, in both cases further reinforcing heavier drinking and, in turn, increasing risk for alcoholism (Schuckit, Smith, and Kalmijn 2004).

Unfortunately, despite strong evidence of low response as an endophenotype and considerable efforts in this area, the specific genes that contribute to low response to alcohol have not been definitively identified. A number of candidates have been identified in terms of variations in neurotransmitter systems and second-messenger systems (Schuckit, Smith, and Kalmijn 2004), but two studies have suggested that the most promising genes are the serotonin transporter gene (5HTTLPR) on chromosome 17 and the $GABA_{A\alpha6}$ subunit gene (GABRA6) on chromosome 5. Schuckit et al. (1999) conducted a 15-year follow-up on individuals who had been definitively identified as having high or low response to alcohol at age 20 and found that polymorphisms in the two aforementioned genes were significantly associated with both low response to alcohol and alcohol use disorder status at age 35. Subsequently, this study was expanded with 45 additional subjects, which supported the initial results (Hu et al. 2005). Persuasively, of the total sample of 86, all individuals with the relevant 5HTTPR and GABRAA alleles exhibited both low response to alcohol in the laboratory and met criteria for an alcohol use disorder at the 15-year follow-up (Hu et al. 2005). Despite these promising findings, however, these are only small studies. At this point, although level of response to alcohol represents one of the earliest behavioral endophenotypes for alcoholism and one of its most reliable risk factors documented to date, the specific genes that underlie low response require considerable further elucidation.

In contrast to findings that implicate diminished response to alcohol in risk liability models, very interesting findings have recently emerged in the area of enhanced sensitivity to the rewarding effects of alcohol as an intermediate phenotype of variation in the opioid mu receptor gene, OPRM1. Of particular interest has been the OPRM1 A118G[2] (Asn40Asp) polymorphism in exon 1, which is believed to be functional although with some ambiguity. Possession of a G allele has been associated with decreased functionality in the form of lowered mRNA and protein yield (Zhang et al. 2005), but an earlier study suggested that the A-to-G substitution affects receptor binding affinity for endogenous ligand β-endorphin leading to a gain in function. Based on the substantial role of the endogenous opioid system in alcohol's pharmacodynamics, Ray and Hutchison (2004) investigated differences in subjective responses to intravenous alcohol based on OPRM1 genotype in hazardous drinkers and found significantly greater alcohol sensitivity among carriers of the G allele (AG/GG). Specifically, AG/GG individuals were found to report greater subjective intoxication, stimulation, sedation, and positive mood effects of alcohol across the rising limb of the blood-alcohol curve. Ray and Hutchison (2007) have subsequently replicated these findings in an independent sample, again finding that AG/GG individuals exhibit greater subjective intoxication and alcohol-induced "high." These findings are also corroborated by a recent study demonstrating greater alcohol-induced stimulation in rhesus macaques with the primate homologue of OPRM1-AG/GG genotype (Barr et al. 2007). Taken together, these studies suggest that in the same way that there is evidence that some individuals are predisposed to exhibit a diminished response to alcohol's sedative effects, others are predisposed to experience alcohol's rewarding effects more potently, although it is unclear the extent to which these findings are reciprocally related.

Importantly, there is much that remains to be known about how OPRM1 genotype relates to genetic risk for alcoholism per se. Recent meta-analyses have not demonstrated a clear relationship between OPRM1 genotype status and alcoholism (Arias, Feinn, and Kranzler 2006; van der Zwaluw et al. 2007), but as we noted earlier, alcoholism endophentoypes and the associated genes that may subserve them represent subtle components of alcohol-related behavior that may have complex relationships to diagnosis itself. In the case of sensitivity to the rewarding effects of alcohol, it may serve as an important predictor of heavier use, thereby increasing the risk of abuse. Moreover, these reward-mediated behavioral mechanisms may be especially important during the earlier stages of alcohol use and abuse. Alternatively, in light of the findings relating to low response to alcohol as a risk factor, it is possible that greater sensitivity to alcohol's rewarding effects as a result of OPRM1-G genotype may potentially serve as a protective factor or only selectively confer risk among certain individuals. Interestingly, taken together, research on sensitivity to alcohol's effects as an intermediate phenotype suggests that sensitivity may be best understood on a continuum based on various genetic factors. A final consideration is that although the consistency of Ray and Hutchison's

(2004, 2007) findings suggests that they are robust, caution must still be exercised given the small number of studies in this area.

Interactions Adding Further Complexity to Understanding Genetic Influences

The preceding findings reflect some of the most promising intermediate phenotypes for alcoholism and may facilitate deconstructing the large statistical genetic risk of alcoholism into the particulate influences of individual genes underlying that risk. Although only a comparatively small number of studies have been conducted in this area, an intermediate phenotype-driven approach appears to be the most promising strategy for elucidating specific genetic influences on alcoholism. However, in addition to the challenge of identifying valid intermediate phenotypes, there are several other scientific challenges to this approach that are worth bearing in mind. In particular, we will focus on two challenges that are specific to research in this area: interactions between multiple genes that multiplicatively increase risk (i.e., gene-by-gene, or epistatic, interactions) and gene-by-environment interactions.

In the first case, epistatic interactions can be defined as a multiplicative relationship between possession of two or more specific genetic polymorphism and an outcome variable of interest, such as an alcoholism diagnosis or an intermediate phenotype. For example, possession of one genetic variant may confer risk only in the presence or absence of another variant, or, less categorically, a variant's influence may by amplified or attenuated by the presence of one or more other variants. This is a problem because most studies examine one, or only a small number of polymorphisms, and cannot concurrently examine the thousands of other variants that essentially represent non-randomly assigned independent variables. For example, although variation in the dopamine D_4 receptor gene has generally not been found to be associated with alcoholism (Dick and Foroud 2003), Muramatsu et al. (1996) found an interaction between possession of the protective ALDH2-2 genotype and DRD4 VNTR status resulting in greater risk for alcoholism. This may explain differences in the level of protective effects from ALDH2-2 across individuals and varying findings in terms of DRD4 VNTR genotype. A second relevant example of an epistatic interaction can be seen in a recent study on the neurogenetic basis of impulsivity. Eisenberg et al. (2007) found an epistatic interaction of the DRD2 *Taq*I A polymorphism and the DRD4 VNTR polymorphism, such that possession of both minor versions, putatively conferring greater risk, was associated with substantially greater impulsivity as measured by a behavioral economic measure of impulsivity. This is relevant because alcohol misusers have been found to display significantly more impulsive responding using this measure (Field et al. 2007; Petry 2001; Vuchinich and Simpson 1998), as have individuals with an array of addictive disorders (for a review, see Bickel and Marsch 2001). Notably, it has been unclear whether these differences reflect an antecedent or consequence of addictive behavior (Bickel and Marsch 2001), and these data suggest that innate differences in discounting may exist prior to addictive behavior. In both cases, these studies revealing gene-by-gene interactions demonstrate the importance of considering multiple genetic variables because in both cases, the exclusion of either gene would have substantially altered the findings. Further, these findings exemplify the critical role that alternative unmeasured genes may play, potentially explaining the mixed results in genetic association studies.

The second challenge to research on the genetics of addiction in general is that of gene-by-environment (G × E) interactions, or multiplicative relationships that are contingent on possession of a specific genotype and specific environmental experience, either historical or current. A number of high-magnitude G × E interactions have been demonstrated in psychiatric genetics (e.g., Caspi et al. 2002; Foley et al. 2004), and such interactions pose a challenge because they may substantially amplify or suppress the observed role of a gene in the etiology of a disorder. For example, in the case of alcoholism, it is plausible that possession of a certain genotype may only be relevant based on certain developmental experiences, such as regular alcohol consumption before a certain age or a traumatic experience. If this is the case, the role of the gene could be minimal under most circumstances and substantial for the individuals with the environmental exposure. Thus, in samples where relatively few subjects have the pertinent environmental or developmental history, the observed role of the gene will be negligible; and, equally, in samples where many subjects have the pertinent environmental history, the observed role of the candidate will be very prominent. In both cases, the observed associations will reflect spurious relationships insofar as they do not accurately reflect the actual interaction.

Although specific G × E interactions have not been unambiguously identified in terms of alcoholism, provocative findings have emerged from both nonhuman and human studies. The 5HTTLPR polymorphism in the gene coding for the serotonin transporter comes in short and long forms, with the former resulting in approximately a 50% decrease in serotonin transporters and, in turn, greater levels of synaptic serotonin (Lesch et al. 1996). Possession of the short form of this polymorphism has been associated with G × E interactions relating to affective disorders in humans (Kendler et al. 2005; Caspi et al. 2003). More importantly, in nonhuman primates (macaques), possession of a short version of 5HTTLPR and exposure to early life stress in the form of emotional deprivation results in greater alcohol consumption (Barr et al. 2004). In terms of human studies, marital status and religiosity have been found to attenuate the effects of additive genetics on alcohol use (Heath, Eaves, and Martin 1998; Koopmans et al. 1999). Likewise, recent results from the COGA project revealed that marital status moderates the effects of the GABRA2 genotype on alcohol dependence, such that the effects of genotype were magnified among individuals who were married (Dick et al. 2006a). The authors hypothesize that genetic risk for alcoholism may become more salient among individuals in a lower risk environment (e.g., those stably married). In addition, behavioral genetics research has shown that the effect of genetic factors on behavior can vary significantly across development. For example, a study of Finnish twins found that genetics accounted for only one fifth of the variance in drinking initiation at age 14, but that genetic factors accounted for one third of the variability in drinking patterns at age 16, and accounted for half of the variability in drinking behavior at age 18 (Rose et al. 2001). These findings highlight the importance of considering developmental factors when studying genetic and environmental factors underlying substance use and abuse. Given the virtually unlimited number of potential $G \times E$ interactions from a practical standpoint, such influences represent a major challenge to psychiatric genetics in general and alcoholism research in particular. Further, the potential for $G \times E$ interactions underscores the importance of both gathering detailed data on each individual's environment and actively exploring potential $G \times E$ relationships.

In both cases, these challenges represent what are essentially "third-variable" confounds, or the inadvertent confounding of an observed relationship between two variables by a third, unobserved, variable. In the case of epistatic interactions, the third variable represents an additional gene and could plausibly include third-order (three-way) interactions and beyond. In the case of $G \times E$ interactions, the third variable represents a developmental event or environmental condition that is unaccounted for and plays a prominent role. In both cases, these interactive relationships reflect the other side of the coin in terms of the enormous potential that access to the genome brings, namely, the substantial scientific challenges that accompany incorporating genetic influences.

Implications of Evidence of Genetic Influences on Alcoholism

The implications of the preceding findings on the genetic influences in alcoholism and the apparent mechanisms by which this takes place are manifold, but they can be broadly grouped into two distinct categories, theoretical and clinical. In the first case, from a Kuhnian (1962) standpoint, the study of alcoholism is preparadigmatic insofar as a large number of theories of alcoholism currently exist (e.g., Leonard and Blane 1999), with no single accepted account. The most dominant theories are neurobiological (e.g., Hyman, Malenka, and Nestler 2006; Robinson and Berridge 2001), affective (e.g., Baker et al. 2004), developmental (e.g., Vanyukov et al. 2003), cognitive (e.g., Goldman 2002), and reinforcement-based (e.g., Higgins, Heil, and Lussier 2004). These approaches commonly agree that the etiology of alcoholism is of multifactorial provenance, including biological, psychological, and social processes (biopsychosocial risk). However, this agreement does not constitute a single integrated theoretical approach and studies directly testing competing theories with differential predictions are rare, in part because theories of alcoholism often exist on different levels of analysis.

Across the etiological theories of alcoholism, the existing findings on the disorder's genetic underpinnings suggest that any plausible theory of alcoholism must incorporate and integrate genetic influences. This is not a challenge in the case of neurobiological theories of alcoholism, where genetic factors are typically incorporated, and the same is true of developmental theories, where the assembly of the individual's genome represents the first point in development. However, a number of major theoretical approaches do not incorporate the role of genetic influences, and we would argue that to the extent that any theory of alcoholism neglects to address the role of genetics, it must be considered incomplete. This is not to say that genetic factors cannot be incorporated into most theories that do not specify a genetic role; rather, it is simply the case that attempts to do so have not been made.

Beyond the theoretical implications, the accumulated evidence of substantial genetic influences has major implications for clinical approaches to alcoholism, both in terms of prevention and treatment. In the case of prevention, the substantial level of genetic influence suggests that genetic research may play an increasing role in identifying individuals who are predisposed to higher or lower risk for alcoholism. In identifying genes that are clearly and robustly associated with alcoholism, progress may also be made in improving secondary prevention efforts (i.e., targeted prevention for at-risk individuals). Moreover, identifying risk-conferring genes and the mechanisms underlying risk will provide clear targets for preventive interventions. For example, given the substantial shared genetic influences on externalizing disorders and advances in identifying genes associated with neural disinhibition (Edenberg et al. 2004; Porjesz et al. 2002), prevention programs focusing directly on that diathesis would appear to have great promise.

Importantly, advances in understanding the genetics of alcoholism also have the potential of improving the cost effectiveness of prevention programs. Primary (i.e., universal) prevention efforts have the advantage of addressing an entire population but are, by definition, not targeted at specific individuals. However, the evidence reviewed earlier in the chapter indicates that risk for alcoholism is far from equal across individuals. Identifying individuals who are at greater risk and specifically providing prevention efforts would allow greater allocation of resources to individuals who are at the greatest risk for alcoholism. This applies also to secondary prevention efforts for clear environmental predictors of risk, such as early onset of drinking (e.g., Hingson, Heeren, and Winter 2006). Thus, in general, an emphasis on specific risk factors, genetic or environmental, or combinations thereof, has the implication that the most promising and cost-effective prevention strategy is secondary prevention: identifying individuals at risk and providing preventive interventions that address the specific processes that confer risk.

For treatment, there are similar implications. As progress is made at identifying the specific genetic contributions, so too will it be important to incorporate what is known about the underlying genetic processes into forms of treatment. One area of considerable promise is that of pharmacogenetics, or the study of interactions between specific medications and genetic variation (Aitchison and Gill 2003). For example, disulfiram (commercial name, Antabuse) is a compound that exerts its effects via the same pharmacokinetic pathway described with regard to possession of an ALDH2-2 allele. In the context of alcohol's metabolism, disulfiram is an aldehyde dehydrogenase blocker that results in an increase in acetaldehyde after ingested alcohol is initially oxidized into acetylaldehyde via alcohol dehydrogenase. This results in the aversive syndrome of symptoms from acetaldehyde buildup (e.g., nausea, flushing, tachycardia), creating an acutely aversive consequence of alcohol consumption and putatively serving as a deterrent. It essentially induces the same effect as possession of the low-activity variants of ALDH2 gene. Unfortunately, a major limitation of disulfiram's use in practice is compliance, which is often low (Suh et al. 2006) although this varies depending on the patient sample (e.g., Fuller et al. 1986).

Although disulfiram pharmacotherapy represents an example of using a medication to mimic a known genetically influenced protective factor, a more clear example of applying a pharmacogenetic approach comes from recent research on individual differences in reactions to naltrexone pharmacotherapy for alcoholism. Individual responses to naltrexone have been heterogeneous (for a review, see Rohsenow 2004), and several recent studies have suggested that functional variation in OPRM1, the mu opioid receptor gene, may be responsible for some of these differences. OPRM1 is a particularly good candidate because naltrexone is a pure mu opioid receptor agonist (Goldman et al. 2005), among other receptor targets. Focusing on the OPRM1 +118A/G polymorphism, Oslin et al. (2003) found that alcoholics possessing at least one G allele exhibited significantly lower rates of relapse on naltrexone and a longer time to resume heavy drinking. More recently, Ray and Hutchison (2007) found that naltrexone selectively diminished the subjective effects of alcohol in AG/GG individuals. Replicating the finding that OPRM1 AG/GG individuals exhibit more pronounced positive subjective effects of alcohol (Ray and Hutchison 2004), naltrexone was found to attenuate those differences to the point that A allele homozygotes and G allele carriers (heterozygotes and homozygotes) were functionally equivalent (Ray and Hutchison 2007). Importantly, the initial clinical findings reported by Oslin et al. (2003) have been recently replicated in the COMBINE study of concurrent naltrexone and acamprosate pharmacotherapy for alcoholism, suggesting that carriers of the G allele of the OPRM1 gene were more responsive to naltrexone for the treatment of alcoholism (Anton et al. 2008). This finding has been further affirmed via a follow-up haplotype-based analysis (Oroszi et al. 2009). In each case, these studies reveal a differential clinical benefit for individuals possessing at least one G allele. Although these studies are recent and require systematic replication, they nonetheless demonstrate that one promising strategy for ameliorating genetically mediated risk for alcoholism may be directly targeting these genetic influences and their biobehavioral expression (i.e., via endophenotypes) through pharmacological interventions (Goldman et al. 2005; Kenna, McGeary, and Swift 2004a,b).

Less obvious but equally important is the parallel implication for tailored psychosocial treatments that are informed by a better understanding of genetic diatheses. As with a pharmacogenetic approach, if the biobehavioral mechanisms underlying genetic risk can be clearly characterized, implementing specific behavioral approaches to address these processes could prove to be most effective. For example, as noted previously, possession of the long version of the DRD4 VNTR genotype appears to be associated with more pronounced reactions to appetitive targets (e.g., Hutchison et al. 2002, 2006; McGeary et al. 2006). From a clinical standpoint, such reactions have previously been approached using extinction-based cue exposure treatment (e.g., Drummond and Glautier 1994; Monti et al. 1993), but with only limited success (for a review and meta-analysis, see Tiffany and Conklin 2000). This may be because of the substantial heterogeneity in individuals' reactions to substance cues (Avants et al. 1995; Monti et al. 1999; Rohsenow et al. 1992; Shiffman et al. 2003), which has typically not been accounted for in clinical trials. Thus, it may be possible that cue exposure treatment is not a useful approach for all alcoholics, but may be selectively useful for those individuals who possess a long DRD4 VNTR variant and experience more potent cue-elicited urges. Although this is necessarily speculative at this point, the larger point is that the substantial evidence of genetic influences on alcoholism implies a greater focus on gene-by-treatment interactions, both for pharmacological and psychosocial treatments.

In spite of the great promise that genetic research has for advancing the prevention and treatment of alcoholism, it is important also to sound a note of caution. Each of the preceding prospects would depend on much more common genetic testing and perhaps even widespread genetic screening. This raises an array of social and ethical issues that would need to be fully considered and addressed before proceeding, and the evidentiary basis for genetically informed prevention or treatment would need to be definitive. As we have repeatedly emphasized throughout this review, the complexity of genetic influences on alcoholism cannot be understated and the literature is replete with highly promising findings that have not been consistent over time. At this point, it would be premature to make any general recommendations for specific gene-by-treatment combinations, no matter how promising the initial findings may be. Fully translating advances in the genetics of alcoholism into clinical advances remains a prospect that will require considerable further research to realize.

Conclusions

The objective of this chapter was to review the genetics of addiction by assembling the converging lines of evidence on the genetics of alcoholism as an exemplar of the literature in general. Moreover, we sought to do so with a particular emphasis on research on the mechanisms of genetic effects via an intermediate phenotype approach. What emerges from the literature can at first glance appear to be a study in contradictions: unambiguous evidence of substantial genetic influences from twin studies, adoption studies, and nonhuman animal models, but elusive and unreliable findings in studies of specific individual genes. However, rather than being paradoxical, the state of the literature can be understood as attesting to the complexity of genetic influences on addiction. The behavioral and physiological disturbances observed in individuals with alcoholism, and addicts more generally, may be syndromal, but they vary tremendously and appear to be multifariously influenced by a large number of genes exerting typically small effects. Moreover, these effects are not uniform and may be a function of pleiotropic effects resulting in susceptibility to various forms of psychopathology or may specifically affect risk for addiction to a particular substance. To address this complexity, the intermediate phenotype approach represents a highly promising strategy for deconstructing genetic risk into constituent genes and mechanisms, albeit with the attendant challenges and the potential limitations noted throughout this review. Fully understanding genetic influences on addiction and applying that knowledge will only come through sustained pursuit and characterization of the genes and processes that underlie the risk for and protection against addiction.

Acknowledgments

The authors gratefully acknowledge the assistance of Lauren Wier, MPH, in the preparation of this chapter. The preparation of this chapter was supported by a grant from the Alcoholic Beverage Medical Research Foundation (JM), a career award from the National Institute on Alcohol Abuse and Alcoholism (JM), a Research Career Scientist Award from the Department of Veterans Affairs (JEM), and a training grant from the National Institute on Alcohol Abuse and Alcoholism (LAR).

Notes

1. Interestingly, although monozygotic twins are often presumed to be identical, there is evidence that is not entirely the case. For example, differences in copy number variations between monozygotic twins have been identified, which may explain observed differences between the two twins (Bruder et al. 2008). Thus, monozygotic twins are probably better thought of as simply having extremely similar, not identical, genomes.

2. Although this SNP is commonly referred to as A118G (Asn40Asp), it has recently been determined that the OPRM1 protein may contain an additional 62 amino acids. This has resulted in the new designation of this SNP according to the NCBI Human Genome Assembly 36 as A355G (Asn102Asp).

References

Agrawal, A., Edenberg, H. J., Foroud, T., Bierut, L. J., Dunne, G., Hinrichs, A. L., Nurnberger, J. I., Crowe, R., Kuperman, S., Schuckit, M. A., et al. (2006). Association of GABRA2 with drug dependence in the collaborative study of the genetics of alcoholism sample. *Behavioral Genetics* 36 (5): 640–650.

Aitchison, K., and Gill, M. (2003). Pharmacogenetics in the postgenomic era. In R. Plomin, J. C. DeFries, I. W. Craig, and P. McGuffin, eds., *Behavioral Genetics in the Postgenomic Era*. Washington, D.C.: American Psychological Association.

Amadeo, S., Abbar, M., Fourcade, M. L., Waksman, G., Leroux, M. G., Madec, A., Selin, M., Champiat, J. C., Brethome, A., Leclaire, Y., et al. (1993). D_2 dopamine receptor gene and alcoholism. *Journal of Psychiatric Research* 27 (2): 173–179.

American Psychiatric Association (2000). *Diagnostic and Statistical Manual of Mental Disorders*, 4th edition. Washington, D.C.

Anton, R. F., Oroszi, G., O'Malley, S., Couper, D., Swift, R., Pettinati, H., and Goldman, D. (2008). An evaluation of mu-opioid receptor (OPRM1) as a predictor of naltrexone response in the treatment of alcohol dependence: Results from the Combined Pharmacotherapies and Behavioral Interventions for Alcohol Dependence (COMBINE) study. *Archives of General Psychiatry* 65 (2): 135–144.

Arias, A., Feinn, R., and Kranzler, H. R. (2006). Association of an Asn40Asp (A118G) polymorphism in the mu-opioid receptor gene with substance dependence: A meta-analysis. *Drug and Alcohol Dependence* 83 (3): 262–268.

Arinami, T., Itokawa, M., Komiyama, T., Mitsushio, H., Mori, H., Mifune, H., Hamaguchi, H., and Toru, M. (1993). Association between severity of alcoholism and the A1 allele of the dopamine D_2 receptor gene *Taq*I A RFLP in Japanese. *Biological Psychiatry* 33 (2): 108–114.

Asghari, V., Sanyal, S., Buchwaldt, S., Paterson, A., Jovanovic, V., and Van Tol, H. H. (1995). Modulation of intracellular cyclic AMP levels by different human dopamine D_4 receptor variants. *Journal of Neurochemistry* 65 (3): 1157–1165.

Avants, S. K., Margolin, A., Kosten, T. R., and Cooney, N. L. (1995). Differences between responders and nonresponders to cocaine cues in the laboratory. *Addictive Behaviors* 20 (2): 215–224.

Babor, T. F., and Caetano, R. (2006). Subtypes of substance dependence and abuse: Implications for diagnostic classification and empirical research. *Addiction* 101 (Suppl. 1): 104–110.

Baker, T. B., Piper, M. E., McCarthy, D. E., Majeskie, M. R., and Fiore, M. C. (2004). Addiction motivation reformulated: An affective processing model of negative reinforcement. *Psychological Review* 111 (1): 33–51.

Barr, C. S., Newman, T. K., Lindell, S., Shannon, C., Champoux, M., Lesch, K. P., Suomi, S. J., Goldman, D., and Higley, J. D. (2004). Interaction between serotonin transporter gene variation and rearing condition in alcohol preference and consumption in female primates. *Archives of General Psychiatry* 61 (110): 1146–1152.

Barr, C. S., Schwandt, M., Lindell, S. G., Chen, S. A., Goldman, D., Suomi, S. J., Higley, J. D., and Heilig, M. (2007). Association of a functional polymorphism in the mu-opioid receptor gene with alcohol response and consumption in male rhesus macaques. *Archives of General Psychiatry* 64 (3): 369–376.

Bauer, L. O. (2001). Predicting relapse to alcohol and drug abuse via quantitative electroencephalography. *Neuropsychopharmacology* 25 (3): 332–340.

Bauer, L. O., and Hesselbrock, V. M. (1993). EEG, autonomic and subjective correlates of the risk for alcoholism. *Journal of Studies on Alcohol* 54 (5): 577–589.

Begleiter, H., and Porjesz, B. (1999). What is inherited in the predisposition toward alcoholism? A proposed model. *Alcoholism: Clinical and Experimental Research* 23 (7): 1125–1135.

Begleiter, H., Porjesz, B., Bihari, B., and Kissin, B. (1984). Event-related brain potentials in boys at risk for alcoholism. *Science* 225 (4669): 1493–1496.

Belknap, J. K., Crabbe, J. C., and Young, E. R. (1993). Voluntary consumption of ethanol in 15 inbred mouse strains. *Psychopharmacology (Berlin)* 112 (4): 503–510.

Bickel, W. K., and Marsch, L. A. (2001). Toward a behavioral economic understanding of drug dependence: Delay discounting processes. *Addiction* 96(1): 73–86.

Blum, K., Noble, E. P., Sheridan, P. J., Finley, O., Montgomery, A., Ritchie, T., Ozkaragoz, T., Fitch, R. J., Sadlack, F., Sheffield, D., et al. (1991). Association of the A1 allele of the D_2 dopamine receptor gene with severe alcoholism. *Alcohol* 8 (5): 409–416.

Blum, K., Noble, E. P., Sheridan, P. J., Montgomery, A., Ritchie, T., Jagadeeswaran, P., Nogami, H., Briggs, A. H., and Cohn, J. B. (1990). Allelic association of human dopamine D_2 receptor gene in alcoholism. *Journal of the American Medical Association* 263 (15): 2055–2060.

Boehm II, S. L., Valenzuela, C. F., Harris, and R. A. (2005). Alcohol: Neurobiology. In J. H. Lowinson, P. Ruiz, R. B. Millman, and J. G. Langrod, eds., *Substance Abuse: A Comprehensive Textbook*, 4th edition. Baltimore, MD: Williams and Wilkins.

Bohman, M., Sigvardsson, S., and Cloninger, C. R. (1981). Maternal inheritance of alcohol abuse: Cross-fostering analysis of adopted women. *Archives of General Psychiatry* 38 (9): 965–969.

Bolos, A. M., Dean, M., Lucas-Derse, S., Ramsburg, M., Brown, G. L., and Goldman, D. (1990). Population and pedigree studies reveal a lack of association between the dopamine D_2 receptor gene and alcoholism. *Journal of the American Medical Association* 264 (24): 3156–3160.

Bond, C., LaForge, K. S., Tian, M., Melia, D., Zhang, S., Borg, L., Gong, J., Schluger, J., Strong, J. A., Leal, S. M., et al. (1998). Single-nucleotide polymorphism in the human mu opioid receptor gene alters beta-endorphin binding and activity: Possible implications for opiate addiction. *Proceedings of the National Academy of Sciences USA* 95 (16): 9608–9613.

Bruder, C. E., Piotrowski, A., Gijsbers, A. A., Andersson, R., Erickson, S., de Ståhl, T. D., Menzel, U., Sandgren, J., von Tell, D., Poplawski, A., et al. (2008). Phenotypically concordant and discordant monozygotic twins display different DNA copy-number-variation profiles. *American Journal of Human Genetics* 82: 763–771.

Button, T. M., Rhee, S. H., Hewitt, J. K., Young, S. E., Corley, R. P., and Stallings, M. C. (2007). The role of conduct disorder in explaining the comorbidity between alcohol and illicit drug dependence in adolescence. *Drug and Alcohol Dependency* 87 (1): 46–53.

Cadoret, R. J., O'Gorman, T. W., Troughton, E., and Heywood, E. (1985). Alcoholism and antisocial personality: Interrelationships, genetic and environmental factors. *Archives of General Psychiatry* 42 (2): 161–167.

Cadoret, R. J., Troughton, E., and O'Gorman, T. W. (1987). Genetic and environmental factors in alcohol abuse and antisocial personality. *Journal of Studies on Alcohol* 48 (1): 1–8.

Carter, B. L., and Tiffany, S. T. (1999). Cue-reactivity and the future of addiction research. *Addiction* 94 (3): 349–351.

Caspi, A., McClay, J., Moffitt, T. E., Mill, J., Martin, J., Craig, I. W., Taylor, A., and Poulton, R. (2002). Role of genotype in the cycle of violence in maltreated children. *Science* 297 (5582): 851–854.

Caspi, A., Sugden, K., Moffitt, T. E., Taylor, A., Craig, I. W., Harrington, H., McClay, J., Mill, J., Martin, J., Braithwaite, A., et al. (2003). Influence of life stress on depression: moderation by a polymorphism in the 5-HTT gene. *Science* 301 (5631): 386–369.

Chen, A. C., Porjesz, B., Rangaswamy, M., Kamarajan, C., Tang, Y., Jones, K. A., Chorlian, D. B., Stimus, A. T., and Begleiter, H. (2007). Reduced frontal lobe activity in subjects with high impulsivity and alcoholism. *Alcoholism: Clinical and Experimental Research* 31 (1): 156–165.

Chen, C. C., Lu, R. B., Chen, Y. C., Wang, M. F., Chang, Y. C., Li, T. K., and Yin, S. J. (1999). Interaction between the functional polymorphisms of the alcohol-metabolism genes in protection against alcoholism. *American Journal of Human Genetics* 65 (3): 795–807.

Chen, C. H., Chien, S. H., and Hwu, H. G. (1996). Lack of association between *Taq*I A1 allele of dopamine D_2 receptor gene and alcohol-use disorders in atayal natives of Taiwan. *Alcoholism: Clinical and Experimental Research* 67 (5): 488–490.

Chen, W. J., Chen, C. H., Huang, J., Hsu, Y. P., Seow, S. V., Chen, C. C., and Cheng, A. T. (2001). Genetic polymorphisms of the promoter region of dopamine D_2 receptor and dopamine transporter genes and alcoholism among four aboriginal groups and Han Chinese in Taiwan. *Psychiatric Genetics* 11 (4): 187–195.

Chiu, T. M., Mendelson, J. H., Sholar, M. B., Mutschler, N. H., Wines, J. D., Hesselbrock, V. M., and Mello, N. K. (2004). Brain alcohol detectability in human subjects with and without a paternal history of alcoholism. *Journal of Studies on Alcohol* 65 (1): 16–21.

Choi, I. G., Son, H. G., Yang, B. H., Kim, S. H., Lee, J. S., Chai, Y. G., Son, B. K., Kee, B. S., Park, B. L., Kim, L. H., et al. (2005). Scanning of genetic effects of alcohol metabolism gene (ADH1B and ADH1C) polymorphisms on the risk of alcoholism. *Human Mutations* 26 (3): 224–234.

Cloninger, C. R., Bohman, M., and Sigvardsson, S. (1981). Inheritance of alcohol abuse. Cross-fostering analysis of adopted men. *Archives of General Psychiatry* 38 (8): 861–868.

Comings, D. E., Comings, B. G., Muhleman, D., Dietz, G., Shahbahrami, B., Tast, D., Knell, E., Kocsis, P., Baumgarten, R., Kovacs, B. W., et al. (1991). The dopamine D_2 receptor locus as a modifying gene in neuropsychiatric disorders. *Journal of the American Medical Association* 266 (13): 1793–1800.

Conrod, P. J., Peterson, J. B., and Pihl, R. O. (2001). Reliability and validity of alcohol-induced heart rate increase as a measure of sensitivity to the stimulant properties of alcohol. *Psychopharmacology (Berlin)* 157 (1): 20–30.

Conway, K. P., Kane, R. J., Ball, S. A., Poling, J. C., and Rounsaville, B. J. (2003). Personality, substance of choice, and polysubstance involvement among substance dependent patients. *Drug and Alcohol Dependence* 71 (1): 65–75.

Cook, B. L., Wang, Z. W., Crowe, R. R., Hauser, R., and Freimer, M. (1992). Alcoholism and the D_2 receptor gene. *Alcoholism: Clinical and Experimental Research* 16 (4): 806–809.

Costa, L., and Bauer, L. (1997). Quantitative electroencephalographic differences associated with alcohol, cocaine, heroin, and dual-substance dependence. *Drug and Alcohol Dependence* 46 (1–2): 87–93.

Cotton, N. S. (1979). The familial incidence of alcoholism: A review. *Journal of Studies on Alcohol* 40 (1): 89–116.

Crabb, D. W., Edenberg, H. J., Bosron, W. F., and Li, T. K. (1989). Genotypes for aldehyde dehydrogenase deficiency and alcohol sensitivity: The inactive ALDH2(2) allele is dominant. *Journal of Clinical Investigation* 83 (1): 314–316.

Crabbe, J. C. (2003). Finding genes for complex behaviors: Progress in mouse models of the addictions. In R. Plomin, J. DeFries, I. Craig, and P. McGuffin, eds., *Behavioral Genetics in the Postgenomic Era*. Washington, D.C.: American Psychological Association.

Cruz, C., Camarena, B., Mejia, J. M., Paez, F., Eroza, V., Ramon De La Fuente, J., Kershenobich, D., and Nicolini, H. (1995). The dopamine D2 receptor gene *Taq*I A1 polymorphism and alcoholism in a Mexican population. *Archives of Medical Research* 26 (4): 421–426.

Dick, D. M., Agrawal, A., Schuckit, M. A., Bierut, L., Hinrichs, A., Fox, L., Mullaney, J., Cloninger, C. R., Hesselbrock, V., Nurnberger, J. I., Jr., et al. (2006a). Marital status, alcohol dependence, and GABRA2: Evidence for gene-environment correlation and interaction. *Journal of Studies on Alcohol* 67 (2): 185–194.

Dick, D. M., Aliev, F., Wang, J. C., Grucza, R. A., Schuckit, M., Kuperman, S., Kramer, J., Hinrichs, A., Bertelsen, S., Budde, J. P., et al. (2008). Using dimensional models of externalizing psychopathology to aid in gene identification. *Archives of General Psychiatry* 65 (3): 310–318.

Dick, D. M., Bierut, L., Hinrichs, A., Fox, L., Bucholz, K. K., Kramer, J., Kuperman, S., Hesselbrock, V., Schuckit, M., Almasy, L., et al. (2006b). The role of GABRA2 in risk for conduct disorder and alcohol and drug dependence across developmental stages. *Behavioral Genetics* 36 (4): 577–590.

Dick, D. M., and Foroud, T. (2003). Candidate genes for alcohol dependence: A review of genetic evidence from human studies. *Alcoholism: Clinical and Experimental Research* 27 (5): 868–879.

Dick, D. M., Nurnberger, J., Jr., Edenberg, H. J., Goate, A., Crowe, R., Rice, J., Bucholz, K. K., Kramer, J., Schuckit, M. A., Smith, T. L., et al. (2002). Suggestive linkage on chromosome 1 for a quantitative alcohol-related phenotype. *Alcoholism: Clinical and Experimental Research* 26 (10): 1453–1460.

Dick, D. M., Wang, J. C., Plunkett, J., Aliev, F., Hinrichs, A., Bertelsen, S., Budde, J. P., Goldstein, E. L., Kaplan, D., Edenberg, H. J., et al. (2007). Family-based association analyses of alcohol dependence phenotypes across DRD2 and neighboring gene ANKK1. *Alcoholism: Clinical and Experimental Research* 31 (10): 1645–1653.

Doyle, A. E., Faraone, S. V., Seidman, L. J., Willcutt, E. G., Nigg, J. T., Waldman, I. D., Pennington, B. F., Peart, J., and Biederman, J. (2005). Are endophenotypes based on measures of executive functions useful for molecular genetic studies of ADHD? *Journal of Child Psychology and Psychiatry* 46 (7): 774–803.

Drummond, D. C., and Glautier, S. (1994). A controlled trial of cue exposure treatment in alcohol dependence. *Journal of Consulting and Clinical Psychology* 62 (4): 809–817.

Edenberg, H. J. (2007). The genetics of alcohol metabolism: Role of alcohol dehydrogenase and aldehyde dehydrogenase variants. *Alcohol Research and Health* 30 (1): 5–13.

Edenberg, H. J., Dick, D. M., Xuei, X., Tian, H., Almasy, L., Bauer, L. O., Crowe, R. R., Goate, A., Hesselbrock, V., Jones, K., et al. (2004). Variations in GABRA2, encoding the alpha 2 subunit of the GABA(A) receptor, are associated with alcohol dependence and with brain oscillations. *American Journal of Human Genetics* 74 (4): 705–714.

Edenberg, H. J., Foroud, T., Koller, D. L., Goate, A., Rice, J., Van Eerdewegh, P., Reich, T., Cloninger, C. R., Nurnberger, J. I., Jr., Kowalczuk, M., et al. (1998). A family-based analysis of the association of the dopamine D_2 receptor (DRD2) with alcoholism. *Alcohol: Clinical and Experimental Research* 22 (2): 505–512.

Edenberg, H. J., Xuei, X., Chen, H. J., Tian, H., Wetherill, L. F., Dick, D. M., Almasy, L., Bierut, L., Bucholz, K. K., Goate, A., et al. (2006). Association of alcohol dehydrogenase genes with alcohol dependence: A comprehensive analysis. *Human Molecular Genetics* 15 (9): 1539–1549.

Ehlers, C. L., Garcia-Andrade, C., Wall, T. L., Cloutier, D., and Phillips, E. (1999). Electroencephalographic responses to alcohol challenge in Native American Mission Indians. *Biological Psychiatry* 45 (6): 776–787.

Ehlers, C. L., Spence, J. P., Wall, T. L., Gilder, D. A., and Carr, L. G. (2004). Association of ALDH1 promoter polymorphisms with alcohol-related phenotypes in southwest California Indians. *Alcohol: Clinical and Experimental Research* 28 (10): 1481–1486.

Eisenberg, D. T., Mackillop, J., Modi, M., Beauchemin, J., Dang, D., Lisman, S. A., Lum, J. K., and Wilson, D. S. (2007). Examining impulsivity as an endophenotype using a behavioral approach: A DRD2 *Taq*I A and DRD4 48-bp VNTR association study. *Behavioral and Brain Functions* 3 (2).

Erblich, J., and Earleywine, M. (1999). Children of alcoholics exhibit attenuated cognitive impairment during an ethanol challenge. *Alcohol: Clinical and Experimental Research* 23 (3): 476–482.

Fehr, C., Shirley, R. L., Belknap, J. K., Crabbe, J. C., and Buck, K. J. (2002). Congenic mapping of alcohol and pentobarbital withdrawal liability loci to a <1 centimorgan interval of murine chromosome 4: Identification of Mpdz as a candidate gene. *Journal of Neuroscience* 22 (9): 3730–3738.

Fehr, C., Shirley, R. L., Metten, P., Kosobud, A. E., Belknap, J. K., Crabbe, J. C., and Buck, K. J. (2004). Potential pleiotropic effects of Mpdz on vulnerability to seizures. *Genes, Brain, and Behavior* 3 (1): 8–19.

Fellous, J. M., and Sejnowski, T. J. (2000). Cholinergic induction of oscillations in the hippocampal slice in the slow (0.5–2 Hz), theta (5–12 Hz), and gamma (35–70 Hz) bands. *Hippocampus* 10 (2): 187–197.

Field, M., Christiansen, P., Cole, J., and Goudie, A. (2007). Delay discounting and the alcohol Stroop in heavy drinking adolescents. *Addiction* 102 (4): 579–586.

Filbey, F. M., Ray, L., Smolen, A., Claus, E. D., Audette, A., and Hutchison, K. E. (2008). Differential neural response to alcohol priming and alcohol taste cues is associated with DRD4 VNTR and OPRM1 genotypes. *Alcoholism: Clinical and Experimental Research* 32 (7): 1113–1123.

Finn, P. R., and Justus, A. (1999). Reduced EEG alpha power in the male and female offspring of alcoholics. *Alcohol: Clinical and Experimental Research* 23 (2): 256–262.

Flint, J., and Munafò, M. R. (2007). The endophenotype concept in psychiatric genetics. *Psychological Medicine* 37 (2): 163–180.

Foley, D. L., Eaves, L. J., Wormley, B., Silberg, J. L., Maes, H. H., Kuhn, J., and Riley, B. (2004). Childhood adversity, monoamine oxidase a genotype, and risk for conduct disorder. *Archives of General Psychiatry* 61 (7): 738–744.

Foroud, T., Edenberg, H. J., Goate, A., Rice, J., Flury, L., Koller, D. L., Bierut, L. J., Conneally, P. M., Nurnberger, J. I., Bucholz, K. K., et al. (2000). Alcoholism susceptibility loci: confirmation studies in a replicate sample and further mapping. *Alcohol: Clinical and Experimental Research* 24 (7): 933–945.

Fuller, R. K., Branchey, L., Brightwell, D. R., Derman, R. M., Emrick, C. D., Iber, F. L., James, K. E., Lacoursiere, R. B., Lee, K. K., Lowenstam, I., et al. (1986). Disulfiram treatment of alcoholism: A Veterans Administration cooperative study. *Journal of the American Medical Association* 256 (11): 1449–1455.

Gabrielli, W. F., Jr., Mednick, S. A., Volavka, J., Pollock, V. E., Schulsinger, F., and Itil, T. M. (1982). Electroencephalograms in children of alcoholic fathers. *Psychophysiology* 19 (4): 404–407.

Galen, L. W., Henderson, M. J., and Whitman, R. D. (1997). The utility of novelty seeking, harm avoidance, and expectancy in the prediction of drinking. *Addictive Behaviors* 22 (1): 93–106.

Gardner, E. L. (2005). Brain-reward mechanisms. In J. H. Lowinson, P. Ruiz, R. B. Millman, and J. G. Langrod, eds., *Substance Abuse: A Comprehensive Textbook*, 4th ed. Baltimore, MD: Williams and Wilkins.

Gelernter, J., and Kranzler, H. (1999). D$_2$ dopamine receptor gene (DRD2) allele and haplotype frequencies in alcohol dependent and control subjects: No association with phenotype or severity of phenotype. *Neuropsychopharmacology* 20 (6): 640–649.

Gelernter, J., O'Malley, S., Risch, N., Kranzler, H. R., Krystal, J., Merikangas, K., Kennedy, J. L., and Kidd, K. K. (1991). No association between an allele at the D$_2$ dopamine receptor gene (DRD2) and alcoholism. *Journal of the American Medical Association* 266 (13): 1801–1807.

Gelernter, J., Yu, Y., Weiss, R., Brady, K., Panhuysen, C., Yang, B. Z., Kranzler, H. R., and Farrer, L. (2006). Haplotype spanning TTC12 and ANKK1, flanked by the DRD2 and NCAM1 loci, is strongly associated to nicotine dependence in two distinct American populations. *Human Molecular Genetics* 15 (24): 3498–3507.

George, S. R., Cheng, R., Nguyen, T., Israel, Y., and O'Dowd, B. F. (1993). Polymorphisms of the D$_4$ dopamine receptor alleles in chronic alcoholism. *Biochemical and Biophysical Research Communications* 196 (1): 107–114.

Gianoulakis, C. (2001). Influence of the endogenous opioid system on high alcohol consumption and genetic predisposition to alcoholism. *Journal of Psychiatry and Neuroscience* 26 (4): 304–318.

Glautier, S., and Drummond, D. C. (1994). Alcohol dependence and cue reactivity. *Journal of Studies on Alcohol* 55 (2): 224–229.

Goldman, D., Brown, G. L., Albaugh, B., Robin, R., Goodson, S., Trunzo, M., Akhtar, L., Lucas-Derse, S., Long, J., Linnoila, M., et al. (1993). DRD2 dopamine receptor genotype, linkage disequilibrium, and alcoholism in American Indians and other populations. *Alcoholism: Clinical and Experimental Research* 17 (2): 199–204.

Goldman, D., Dean, M., Brown, G. L., Bolos, A. M., Tokola, R., Virkkunen, M., and Linnoila, M. (1992). D$_2$ dopamine receptor genotype and cerebrospinal fluid homovanillic acid, 5-hydroxyindoleacetic acid and 3-methoxy-4-hydroxyphenylglycol in alcoholics in Finland and the United States. *Acta Psychiatrica Scandinavica* 86 (5): 351–357.

Goldman, D., and Ducci, F. (2007). Deconstruction of vulnerability to complex diseases: Enhanced effect sizes and power of intermediate phenotypes. *Scientific World Journal* 7: 124–130.

Goldman, D., Oroszi, G., O'Malley, S., and Anton, R. (2005). COMBINE genetics study: The pharmacogenetics of alcoholism treatment response: Genes and mechanisms. *Journal of Studies on Alcohol (Supplement)* 15: 56–64; discussion 33.

Goldman, D., Urbanek, M., Guenther, D., Robin, R., and Long, J. C. (1997). Linkage and association of a functional DRD2 variant [Ser311Cys] and DRD2 markers to alcoholism, substance abuse, and schizophrenia in Southwestern American Indians. *American Journal of Medical Genetics* 74 (4): 386–394.

Goldman, M. S. (2002). Expectancy and risk for alcoholism: The unfortunate exploitation of a fundamental characteristic of neurobehavioral adaptation. *Alcoholism: Clinical and Experimental Research* 26 (5): 737–746.

Goodwin, D. W., Schulsinger, F., Hermansen, L., Guze, S. B., and Winokur, G. (1973). Alcohol problems in adoptees raised apart from alcoholic biological parents. *Archives of General Psychiatry* 28 (2): 238–243.

Gottesman, I. I., and Gould, T. D. (2003). The endophenotype concept in psychiatry: Etymology and strategic intentions. *American Journal of Psychiatry* 160 (4): 636–645.

Gottesman, I. I., and Shields, J. (1973). Genetic theorizing and schizophrenia. *British Journal of Psychiatry* 122 (566): 15–30.

Grant, B. F., Stinson, F. S., Dawson, D. A., Chou, S. P., Ruan, W. J., and Pickering, R. P. (2004). Co-occurrence of 12-month alcohol and drug use disorders and personality disorders in the United States: Results from the National Epidemiologic Survey on Alcohol and Related Conditions. *Archives of General Psychiatry* 61 (4): 361–368.

Gurpegui, M., Jurado, D., Luna, J. D., Fernandez-Molina, C., Moreno-Abril, O., and Galvez, R. (2007). Personality traits associated with caffeine intake and smoking. *Progress in Neuropsychopharmacology and Biological Psychiatry* 31 (5): 997–1005.

Haile, C. N., Kosten, T. R., and Kosten, T. A. (2007). Genetics of dopamine and its contribution to cocaine addiction. *Behavioral Genetics* 37 (1): 119–145.

Hansell, N. K., Pang, D., Heath, A. C., Martin, N. G., and Whitfield, J. B. (2005). Erythrocyte aldehyde dehydrogenase activity: Lack of association with alcohol use and dependence or alcohol reactions in Australian twins. *Alcohol and Alcoholism* 40 (5): 343–348.

Hasin, D., Aharonovich, E., Liu, X., Mamman, Z., Matseoane, K., Carr, L., and Li, T. K. (2002). Alcohol and ADH2 in Israel: Ashkenazis, Sephardics, and recent Russian immigrants. *American Journal of Psychiatry* 159 (8): 1432–1434.

Heath, A. C., Bucholz, K. K., Madden, P. A., Dinwiddie, S. H., Slutske, W. S., Bierut, L. J., Statham, D. J., Dunne, M. P., Whitfield, J. B., and Martin, N. G. (1997). Genetic and environmental contributions to alcohol dependence risk in a national twin sample: Consistency of findings in women and men. *Psychological Medicine* 27 (6): 1381–1396.

Heath, A. C., Eaves, L. J., and Martin, N. G. (1998). Interaction of marital status and genetic risk for symptoms of depression. *Twin Research* 1 (3): 119–122.

Heath, A. C., Madden, P. A., Bucholz, K. K., Dinwiddie, S. H., Slutske, W. S., Bierut, L. J., Rohrbaugh, J. W., Statham, D. J., Dunne, M. P., Whitfield, J. B., et al. (1999). Genetic differences in alcohol sensitivity and the inheritance of alcoholism risk. *Psychological Medicine* 29 (5): 1069–1081.

Hendershot, C. S., MacPherson, L., Myers, M. G., Carr, L. G., and Wall, T. L. (2005). Psychosocial, cultural, and genetic influences on alcohol use in Asian American youth. *Journal of Studies on Alcohol* 66 (2): 185–195.

Higgins, S. T., Heil, S. H., and Lussier, J. P. (2004). Clinical implications of reinforcement as a determinant of substance use disorders. *Annual Review of Psychology* 55: 431–461.

Higuchi, S., Matsushita, S., Imazeki, H., Kinoshita, T., Takagi, S., and Kono, H. (1994a). Aldehyde dehydrogenase genotypes in Japanese alcoholics. *Lancet* 343 (8899): 741–742.

Higuchi, S., Muramatsu, T., Murayama, M., and Hayashida, M. (1994b). Association of structural polymorphism of the dopamine D_2 receptor gene and alcoholism. *Biochemical and Biophysical Research Communications* 204 (3): 1199–1205.

Hines, L. M., Ray, L., Hutchison, K., and Tabakoff, B. (2005). Alcoholism: The dissection for endophenotypes. *Dialogues in Clinical Neuroscience* 7 (2): 153–163.

Hingson, R. W., Heeren, T., and Winter, M. R. (2006). Age at drinking onset and alcohol dependence: Age at onset, duration, and severity. *Archives of Pediatric and Adolescent Medicine* 160 (7): 739–746.

Holdstock, L., and de Wit, H. (1998). Individual differences in the biphasic effects of ethanol. *Alcoholism: Clinical and Experimental Research* 22 (9): 1903–1911.

Hrubec, Z., and Omenn, G. S. (1981). Evidence of genetic predisposition to alcoholic cirrhosis and psychosis: Twin concordances for alcoholism and its biological end points by zygosity among male veterans. *Alcoholism: Clinical and Experimental Research* 5 (2): 207–215.

Hu, X., Oroszi, G., Chun, J., Smith, T. L., Goldman, D., and Schuckit, M. A. (2005). An expanded evaluation of the relationship of four alleles to the level of response to alcohol and the alcoholism risk. *Alcoholism: Clinical and Experimental Research* 29 (1): 8–16.

Hutchison, K. E., LaChance, H., Niaura, R., Bryan, A., and Smolen, A. (2002). The DRD4 VNTR polymorphism influences reactivity to smoking cues. *Journal of Abnormal Psychology* 111 (1): 134–143.

Hutchison, K. E., Ray, L., Sandman, E., Rutter, M. C., Peters, A., Davidson, D., and Swift, R. (2006). The effect of olanzapine on craving and alcohol consumption. *Neuropsychopharmacology* 31 (6): 1310–1317.

Hutchison, K. E., Stallings, M., McGeary, J., and Bryan, A. (2004). Population stratification in the candidate gene study: Fatal threat or red herring? *Psychological Bulletin* 130 (1): 66–79.

Hyman, S. E., Malenka, R. C., and Nestler, E. J. (2006). Neural mechanisms of addiction: The role of reward-related learning and memory. *Annual Review of Neuroscience* 29: 565–598.

Ishiguro, H., Arinami, T., Saito, T., Akazawa, S., Enomoto, M., Mitushio, H., Fujishiro, H., Tada, K., Akimoto, Y., Mifune, H., et al. (1998). Association study between the −141C Ins/Del and *Taq*I A polymorphisms of the dopamine D_2 receptor gene and alcoholism. *Alcoholism: Clinical and Experimental Research* 22 (4): 845–848.

Jamensky, N. T., and Gianoulakis, C. (1997). Content of dynorphins and kappa-opioid receptors in distinct brain regions of C57BL/6 and DBA/2 mice. *Alcoholism: Clinical and Experimental Research* 21 (8): 1455–1464.

Jones, K. A., Porjesz, B., Almasy, L., Bierut, L., Dick, D., Goate, A., Hinrichs, A., Rice, J. P., Wang, J. C., Bauer, L. O., et al. (2006). A cholinergic receptor gene (CHRM2) affects event-related oscillations. *Behavioral Genetics* 36 (5): 627–639.

Jones, K. A., Porjesz, B., Almasy, L., Bierut, L., Goate, A., Wang, J. C., Dick, D. M., Hinrichs, A., Kwon, J., Rice, J. P., et al. (2004). Linkage and linkage disequilibrium of evoked EEG oscillations with CHRM2 receptor gene polymorphisms: Implications for human brain dynamics and cognition. *International Journal of Psychophysiology* 53 (2): 75–90.

Jonsson, E. G., Nothen, M. M., Grunhage, F., Farde, L., Nakashima, Y., Propping, P., and Sedvall, G. C. (1999). Polymorphisms in the dopamine D_2 receptor gene and their relationships to striatal dopamine receptor density of healthy volunteers. *Molecular Psychiatry* 4 (3): 290–296.

Kendler, K. S., Kuhn, J. W., Vittum, J., Prescott, C. A., and Riley, B. (2005). The interaction of stressful life events and a serotonin transporter polymorphism in the prediction of episodes of major depression: A replication. *Archives of General Psychiatry* 62 (5): 529–535.

Kendler, K. S., Prescott, C. A., Myers, J., and Neale, M. C. (2003). The structure of genetic and environmental risk factors for common psychiatric and substance use disorders in men and women. *Archives of General Psychiatry* 60 (9): 929–937.

Kendler, K. S., Prescott, C. A., Neale, M. C., and Pedersen, N. L. (1997). Temperance board registration for alcohol abuse in a national sample of Swedish male twins, born 1902 to 1949. *Archives of General Psychiatry* 54 (2): 178–184.

Kenna, G. A., McGeary, J. E., and Swift, R. M. (2004a). Pharmacotherapy, pharmacogenomics, and the future of alcohol dependence treatment, Part 1. *American Journal of Health-System Pharmacy* 61 (21): 2272–2279.

Kenna, G. A., McGeary, J. E., and Swift, R. M. (2004b). Pharmacotherapy, pharmacogenomics, and the future of alcohol dependence treatment, Part 2. *American Journal of Health-System Pharmacy* 61 (22): 2380–2388.

Knopik, V. S., Heath, A. C., Madden, P. A., Bucholz, K. K., Slutske, W. S., Nelson, E. C., Statham, D., Whitfield, J. B., and Martin, N. G. (2004). Genetic effects on alcohol dependence risk: Reevaluating the importance of psychiatric and other heritable risk factors. *Psychological Medicine* 34 (8): 1519–1530.

Kohl, R. R., Katner, J. S., Chernet, E., and McBride, W. J. (1998). Ethanol and negative feedback regulation of mesolimbic dopamine release in rats. *Psychopharmacology (Berlin)* 139 (1–2): 79–85.

Kono, Y., Yoneda, H., Sakai, T., Nonomura, Y., Inayama, Y., Koh, J., Sakai, J., Inada, Y., Imamichi, H., and Asaba, H. (1997). Association between early-onset alcoholism and the dopamine D_2 receptor gene. *American Journal of Medical Genetics* 74 (2): 179–182.

Koopmans, J. R., Slutske, W. S., van Baal, G. C., and Boomsma, D. I. (1999). The influence of religion on alcohol use initiation: Evidence for genotype × environment interaction. *Behavioral Genetics* 29 (6): 445–453.

Kreek, M. J., Nielsen, D. A., and LaForge, K. S. (2004). Genes associated with addiction: Alcoholism, opiate, and cocaine addiction. *Neuromolecular Medicine* 5 (1): 85–108.

Krystal, J. H., Petrakis, I. L., Krupitsky, E., Schutz, C., Trevisan, L., and D'Souza, D. C. (2003). NMDA receptor antagonism and the ethanol intoxication signal: From alcoholism risk to pharmacotherapy. *Annals of the New York Academy of Sciences* 1003: 176–184.

Kuhn, T. S. (1962). *The Structure of Scientific Revolutions*. Chicago: University of Chicago Press.

Lee, J. F., Lu, R. B., Ko, H. C., Chang, F. M., Yin, S. J., Pakstis, A. J., and Kidd, K. K. (1999). No association between DRD2 locus and alcoholism after controlling the ADH and ALDH genotypes in Chinese Han population. *Alcoholism: Clinical and Experimental Research* 23 (4): 592–599.

Lee, S. L., Chau, G. Y., Yao, C. T., Wu, C. W., and Yin, S. J. (2006). Functional assessment of human alcohol dehydrogenase family in ethanol metabolism: Significance of first-pass metabolism. *Alcoholism: Clinical and Experimental Research* 30 (7): 1132–1142.

LeMarquand, D., Pihl, R. O., and Benkelfat, C. (1994). Serotonin and alcohol intake, abuse, and dependence: Findings of animal studies. *Biological Psychiatry* 36 (6): 395–421.

Leonard, K. E., and Blane, H. T. (eds.) (1999). *Psychological Theories of Drinking and Alcoholism*. New York: Guilford Press.

Lesch, K. P., Bengel, D., Heils, A., Sabol, S. Z., Greenberg, B. D., Petri, S., Benjamin, J., Müller, C. R., Hamer, D. H., and Murphy, D. L. (1996). Association of anxiety-related traits with a polymorphism in the serotonin transporter gene regulatory region. *Science* 274 (5292): 1527–1531.

Lobo, D. S., and Kennedy, J. L. (2006). The genetics of gambling and behavioral addictions. *CNS Spectrums* 11 (12): 931–939.

Lobos, E. A., and Todd, R. D. (1998). Association analysis in an evolutionary context: Cladistic analysis of the DRD2 locus to test for association with alcoholism. *American Journal of Medical Genetics* 81 (5): 411–419.

Lu, R. B., Ko, H. C., Chang, F. M., Castiglione, C. M., Schoolfield, G., Pakstis, A. J., Kidd, J. R., and Kidd, K. K. (1996). No association between alcoholism and multiple polymorphisms at the dopamine D2 receptor gene (DRD2) in three distinct Taiwanese populations. *Biological Psychiatry* 39 (6): 419–429.

Luczak, S. E., Glatt, S. J., and Wall, T. L. (2006). Meta-analyses of ALDH2 and ADH1B with alcohol dependence in Asians. *Psychological Bulletin* 132 (4): 607–621.

Luczak, S. E., Shea, S. H., Carr, L. G., Li, T. K., and Wall, T. L. (2002). Binge drinking in Jewish and non-Jewish white college students. *Alcoholism: Clinical and Experimental Research* 26 (12): 1773–1778.

Luo, X., Kranzler, H. R., Zuo, L., Wang, S., Blumberg, H. P., and Gelernter, J. (2005). CHRM2 gene predisposes to alcohol dependence, drug dependence and affective disorders: Results from an extended case-control structured association study. *Human Molecular Genetics* 14 (16): 2421–2434.

MacKillop, J., Menges, D. P., McGeary, J. E., and Lisman, S. A. (2007). Effects of craving and DRD4 VNTR genotype on the relative value of alcohol: An initial human laboratory study. *Behavioral Brain Functions* 3: 11.

MacKillop, J., and Monti, P. M. (2007). Advances in the scientific study of craving for alcohol and tobacco: From scientific study to clinical practice. In P. M. Kavanagh, ed., *Translation of Addictions Sciences into Practice*. Amsterdam: Elsevier Press.

Martin, C. S., Earleywine, M., Musty, R. E., Perrine, M. W., and Swift, R. M. (1993). Development and validation of the Biphasic Alcohol Effects Scale. *Alcoholism: Clinical and Experimental Research* 17 (1): 140–146.

McClernon, F. J., Hutchison, K. E., Rose, J. E., and Kozink, R. V. (2007). DRD4 VNTR polymorphism is associated with transient fMRI-BOLD responses to smoking cues. *Psychopharmacology (Berlin)* 194 (4): 433–441.

McGeary, J. E., Monti, P. M., Rohsenow, D. J., Tidey, J., Swift, R., and Miranda, R., Jr. (2006). Genetic moderators of naltrexone's effects on alcohol cue reactivity. *Alcoholism: Clinical and Experimental Research* 30 (8): 1288–1296.

McGue, M. (1999). Behavioral genetics models of alcoholism and drinking. In K. E. Leonard and H. T. Blane, eds., *Psychological Theories of Drinking and Alcoholism*, 2nd ed. New York: Guilford Press.

Monti, P. M., Binkoff, J. A., Abrams, D. B., Zwick, W. R., Nirenberg, T. D., and Liepman, M. R. (1987). Reactivity of alcoholics and nonalcoholics to drinking cues. *Journal of Abnormal Psychology* 96 (2): 122–126.

Monti, P. M., Rohsenow, D. J., Hutchison, K. E., Swift, R. M., Mueller, T. I., Colby, S. M., Brown, R. A., Gulliver, S. B., Gordon, A., and Abrams, D. B. (1999). Naltrexone's effect on cue-elicited craving among alcoholics in treatment. *Alcoholism: Clinical and Experimental Research* 23 (8): 1386–1394.

Monti, P. M., Rohsenow, D. J., Rubonis, A. V., Niaura, R. S., Sirota, A. D., Colby, S. M., Goddard, P., and Abrams, D. B. (1993). Cue exposure with coping skills treatment for male alcoholics: A preliminary investigation. *Journal of Consulting and Clinical Psychology* 61 (6): 1011–1019.

Munafò, M. R., Clark, T. G., Moore, L. R., Payne, E., Walton, R., and Flint, J. (2003). Genetic polymorphisms and personality in healthy adults: A systematic review and meta-analysis. *Molecular Psychiatry* 8 (5): 471–484.

Munafò, M. R., Matheson, I. J., and Flint, J. (2007). Association of the DRD2 gene *Taq*1A polymorphism and alcoholism: A meta-analysis of case-control studies and evidence of publication bias. *Molecular Psychiatry* 12 (5): 454–461.

Muramatsu, T., Higuchi, S., Murayama, M., Matsushita, S., and Hayashida, M. (1996). Association between alcoholism and the dopamine D_4 receptor gene. *Journal of Medical Genetics* 33 (2): 113–115.

Neiswanger, K., Hill, S. Y., and Kaplan, B. B. (1995). Association and linkage studies of the *Taq*I A1 allele at the dopamine D_2 receptor gene in samples of female and male alcoholics. *American Journal of Medical Genetics* 60 (4): 267–271.

Neville, M. J., Johnstone, E. C., and Walton, R. T. (2004). Identification and characterization of ANKK1: A novel kinase gene closely linked to DRD2 on chromosome band 11q23.1. *Human Mutations* 23 (6): 540–545.

Noble, E. P. (2000). Addiction and its reward process through polymorphisms of the D_2 dopamine receptor gene: A review. *European Psychiatry* 15 (2): 79–89.

Noble, E. P., Blum, K., Ritchie, T., Montgomery, A., and Sheridan, P. J. (1991). Allelic association of the D_2 dopamine receptor gene with receptor-binding characteristics in alcoholism. *Archives of General Psychiatry* 48 (7): 648–654.

Noble, E. P., Gottschalk, L. A., Fallon, J. H., Ritchie, T. L., and Wu, J. C. (1997). D_2 dopamine receptor polymorphism and brain regional glucose metabolism. *American Journal of Medical Genetics* 74 (2): 162–166.

Noble, E. P., Syndulko, K., Fitch, R. J., Ritchie, T., Bohlman, M. C., Guth, P., Sheridan, P. J., Montgomery, A., Heinzmann, C., Sparkes, R. S., et al. (1994). D_2 dopamine receptor *Taq*I A alleles in medically ill alcoholic and nonalcoholic patients. *Alcohol and Alcoholism* 29 (6): 729–744.

O'Brien, C. P., Volkow, N., and Li, T. K. (2006). What's in a word? Addiction versus dependence in DSM-V. *American Journal of Psychiatry* 163 (5): 764–765.

Oota, H., Pakstis, A. J., Bonne-Tamir, B., Goldman, D., Grigorenko, E., Kajuna, S. L., Karoma, N. J., Kungulilo, S., Lu, R. B., Odunsi, K., et al. (2004). The evolution and population genetics of the ALDH2 locus: Random genetic drift, selection, and low levels of recombination. *Annals of Human Genetics* 68 (Pt 2): 93–109.

Oroszi, G., Anton, R. F., O'Malley, S., Swift, R., Pettinati, H., Couper, D., Yuan, Q., and Goldman, D. (2009). OPRM1 Asn40Asp predicts response to naltrexone treatment: A haplotype-based approach. *Alcoholism: Clinical and Experimental Research* 33 (3): 383–393.

Osier, M., Pakstis, A. J., Kidd, J. R., Lee, J. F., Yin, S. J., Ko, H. C., Edenberg, H. J., Lu, R. B., and Kidd, K. K. (1999). Linkage disequilibrium at the ADH2 and ADH3 loci and risk of alcoholism. *American Journal of Human Genetics* 64 (4): 1147–1157.

Osier, M. V., Pakstis, A. J., Goldman, D., Edenberg, H. J., Kidd, J. R., and Kidd, K. K. (2002). A proline-threonine substitution in codon 351 of ADH1C is common in Native Americans. *Alcoholism: Clinical and Experimental Research* 26 (12): 1759–1763.

Oslin, D. W., Berrettini, W., Kranzler, H. R., Pettinati, H., Gelernter, J., Volpicelli, J. R., and O'Brien, C. P. (2003). A functional polymorphism of the mu-opioid receptor gene is associated with naltrexone response in alcohol-dependent patients. *Neuropsychopharmacology* 28 (8): 1546–1552.

Parsian, A., Cloninger, C. R., and Zhang, Z. H. (2000). Functional variant in the DRD2 receptor promoter region and subtypes of alcoholism. *American Journal of Medical Genetics* 96 (3): 407–411.

Parsian, A., Todd, R. D., Devor, E. J., O'Malley, K. L., Suarez, B. K., Reich, T., and Cloninger, C. R. (1991). Alcoholism and alleles of the human D_2 dopamine receptor locus: Studies of association and linkage. *Archives of General Psychiatry* 48 (7): 655–663.

Petry, N. M. (2001). Delay discounting of money and alcohol in actively using alcoholics, currently abstinent alcoholics, and controls. *Psychopharmacology (Berlin)* 154 (3): 243–250.

Pickens, R. W., Svikis, D. S., McGue, M., Lykken, D. T., Heston, L. L., and Clayton, P. J. (1991). Heterogeneity in the inheritance of alcoholism: A study of male and female twins. *Archives of General Psychiatry* 48 (1): 19–28.

Polich, J., Pollock, V. E., and Bloom, F. E. (1994). Meta-analysis of P300 amplitude from males at risk for alcoholism. *Psychological Bulletin* 115 (1): 55–73.

Porjesz, B., Almasy, L., Edenberg, H. J., Wang, K., Chorlian, D. B., Foroud, T., Goate, A., Rice, J. P., O'Connor, S. J., Rohrbaugh, J., et al. (2002). Linkage disequilibrium between the beta frequency of the human EEG and a GABAA receptor gene locus. *Proceedings of the National Academy of Sciences of the USA* 99 (6): 3729–3733.

Porjesz, B., and Begleiter, H. (2003). Alcoholism and human electrophysiology. *Alcohol Resolution Health* 27 (2): 153–160.

Porjesz, B., and Rangaswamy, M. (2007). Neurophysiological endophenotypes, CNS disinhibition, and risk for alcohol dependence and related disorders. *Scientific World Journal* 7: 131–141.

Porjesz, B., Rangaswamy, M., Kamarajan, C., Jones, K. A., Padmanabhapillai, A., and Begleiter, H. (2005). The utility of neurophysiological markers in the study of alcoholism. *Clinical Neurophysiology* 116 (5): 993–1018.

Propping, P., Kruger, J., and Mark, N. (1981). Genetic disposition to alcoholism. An EEG study in alcoholics and their relatives. *Human Genetics* 59 (1): 51–59.

Ramo, D. E., and Brown, S. A. (2008). Classes of substance abuse relapse situations: A comparison of adolescents and adults. *Psychology of Addictive Behaviors* 22 (3): 372–379.

Rangaswamy, M., Jones, K. A., Porjesz, B., Chorlian, D. B., Padmanabhapillai, A., Kamarajan, C., Kuperman, S., Rohrbaugh, J., O'Connor, S. J., Bauer, L. O., et al. (2007). Delta and theta oscillations as risk markers in adolescent offspring of alcoholics. *International Journal of Psychophysiology* 63 (1): 3–15.

Rangaswamy, M., Porjesz, B., Chorlian, D. B., Wang, K., Jones, K. A., Bauer, L. O., Rohrbaugh, J., O'Connor, S. J., Kuperman, S., Reich, T., et al. (2002). Beta power in the EEG of alcoholics. *Biological Psychiatry* 52 (8): 831–842.

Rangaswamy, M., Porjesz, B., Chorlian, D. B., Wang, K., Jones, K. A., Kuperman, S., Rohrbaugh, J., O'Connor, S. J., Bauer, L. O., Reich, T., et al. (2004). Resting EEG in offspring of male alcoholics: Beta frequencies. *International Journal of Psychophysiology* 51 (3): 239–251.

Rankin, H., Stockwell, T., and Hodgson, R. (1982). Cues for drinking and degrees of alcohol dependence. *British Journal of Addiction* 77 (3): 287–296.

Ray, L. A., and Hutchison, K. E. (2004). A polymorphism of the mu-opioid receptor gene (OPRM1) and sensitivity to the effects of alcohol in humans. *Alcoholism: Clinical and Experimental Research* 28 (12): 1789–1795.

Ray, L. A., and Hutchison, K. E. (2007). Effects of naltrexone on alcohol sensitivity and genetic moderators of medication response: A double-blind placebo-controlled study. *Archives of General Psychiatry* 64 (9): 1069–1077.

Reich, T., Edenberg, H. J., Goate, A., Williams, J. T., Rice, J. P., Van Eerdewegh, P., Foroud, T., Hesselbrock, V., Schuckit, M. A., Bucholz, K., et al. (1998). Genome-wide search for genes affecting the risk for alcohol dependence. *American Journal of Medical Genetics* 81 (3): 207–215.

Robinson, T. E., and Berridge, K. C. (2001). Incentive-sensitization and addiction. *Addiction* 96 (1): 103–114.

Rodriguez, L. A., Wilson, J. R., and Nagoshi, C. T. (1993). Does psychomotor sensitivity to alcohol predict subsequent alcohol use? *Alcoholism: Clinical and Experimental Research* 17 (1): 155–161.

Rohsenow, D. J. (2004). What place does naltrexone have in the treatment of alcoholism? *CNS Drugs* 18 (9): 547–560.

Rohsenow, D. J., Monti, P. M., Abrams, D. B., Rubonis, A. V., Niaura, R. S., Sirota, A. D., and Colby, S. M. (1992). Cue elicited urge to drink and salivation in alcoholics: Relationship to individual differences. *Advances in Behavior Research and Therapy* 14: 195–210.

Rose, R. J., Dick, D. M., Viken, R. J., Pulkkinen, L., and Kaprio, J. (2001). Drinking or abstaining at age 14? A genetic epidemiological study. *Alcoholism: Clinical and Experimental Research* 25 (11): 1594–1604.

Saccone, N. L., Kwon, J. M., Corbett, J., Goate, A., Rochberg, N., Edenberg, H. J., Foroud, T., Li, T. K., Begleiter, H., Reich, T., et al. (2000). A genome screen of maximum number of drinks as an alcoholism phenotype. *American Journal of Medical Genetics* 96 (5): 632–637.

Sander, T., Harms, H., Podschus, J., Finckh, U., Nickel, B., Rolfs, A., Rommelspacher, H., and Schmidt, L. G. (1995). Dopamine D_1, D_2, and D_3 receptor genes in alcohol dependence. *Psychiatric Genetics* 5 (4): 171–176.

Sander, T., Ladehoff, M., Samochowiec, J., Finckh, U., Rommelspacher, H., and Schmidt, L. G. (1999). Lack of an allelic association between polymorphisms of the dopamine D_2 receptor gene and alcohol dependence in the German population. *Alcoholism: Clinical and Experimental Research* 23 (4): 578–581.

Saxon, A. J., Oreskovich, M. R., and Brkanac, Z. (2005). Genetic determinants of addiction to opioids and cocaine. *Harvard Review of Psychiatry* 13 (4): 218–232.

Schuckit, M. A., and Gold, E. O. (1988). A simultaneous evaluation of multiple markers of ethanol/placebo challenges in sons of alcoholics and controls. *Archives of General Psychiatry* 45 (3): 211–216.

Schuckit, M. A., Mazzanti, C., Smith, T. L., Ahmed, U., Radel, M., Iwata, N., and Goldman, D. (1999). Selective genotyping for the role of 5-HT2A, 5-HT2C, and GABA alpha 6 receptors and the serotonin transporter in the level of response to alcohol: A pilot study. *Biological Psychiatry* 45 (5): 647–651.

Schuckit, M. A., and Smith, T. L. (2000). The relationships of a family history of alcohol dependence, a low level of response to alcohol and six domains of life functioning to the development of alcohol use disorders. *Journal of Studies on Alcohol* 61 (6): 827–835.

Schuckit, M. A., Smith, T. L., and Kalmijn, J. (2004). The search for genes contributing to the low level of response to alcohol: Patterns of findings across studies. *Alcoholism: Clinical and Experimental Research* 28 (10): 1449–1458.

Schwab, S., Soyka, M., Niederecker, M., Ackenheil, M., Scherer, J., and Wildenauer, D. B. (1991). Allelic association of human dopamine D$_2$-receptor DNA polymorphism ruled out in 45 alcoholics. *American Journal of Human Genetics* 49 (203): 2055–2060.

Shao, C., Li, Y., Jiang, K., Zhang, D., Xu, Y., Lin, L., Wang, Q., Zhao, M., and Jin, L. (2006). Dopamine D$_4$ receptor polymorphism modulates cue-elicited heroin craving in Chinese. *Psychopharmacology (Berlin)* 20 (3): 286–312.

Shiffman, S., Shadel, W. G., Niaura, R., Khayrallah, M. A., Jorenby, D. E., Ryan, C. F., and Ferguson, C. L. (2003). Efficacy of acute administration of nicotine gum in relief of cue-provoked cigarette craving. *Psychopharmacology (Berlin)* 166 (4): 343–350.

Shirley, R. L., Walter, N. A., Reilly, M. T., Fehr, C., and Buck, K. J. (2004). Mpdz is a quantitative trait gene for drug withdrawal seizures. *Nature Neuroscience* 7 (7): 699–700.

Sigvardsson, S., Bohman, M., and Cloninger, C. R. (1996). Replication of the Stockholm Adoption Study of alcoholism: Confirmatory cross-fostering analysis. *Archives of General Psychiatry* 53 (8): 681–687.

Sobik, L., Hutchison, K., and Craighead, L. (2005). Cue-elicited craving for food: A fresh approach to the study of binge eating. *Appetite* 44 (3): 253–261.

Suarez, B. K., Parsian, A., Hampe, C. L., Todd, R. D., Reich, T., and Cloninger, C. R. (1994). Linkage disequilibria at the D$_2$ dopamine receptor locus (DRD2) in alcoholics and controls. *Genomics* 19 (1): 12–20.

Suh, J. J., Pettinati, H. M., Kampman, K. M., and O'Brien, C. P. (2006). The status of disulfiram: A half of a century later. *Journal of Clinical Psychopharmacology* 26 (3): 290–302.

Thomasson, H. R., Edenberg, H. J., Crabb, D. W., Mai, X. L., Jerome, R. E., Li, T. K., Wang, S. P., Lin, Y. T., Lu, R. B., and Yin, S. J. (1991). Alcohol and aldehyde dehydrogenase genotypes and alcoholism in Chinese men. *American Journal of Human Genetics* 48 (4): 677–681.

Thompson, J., Thomas, N., Singleton, A., Piggott, M., Lloyd, S., Perry, E. K., Morris, C. M., Perry, R. H., Ferrier, I. N., and Court, J. A. (1997). D$_2$ dopamine receptor gene (DRD2) *TaqI* A polymorphism: Reduced dopamine D$_2$ receptor binding in the human striatum associated with the A1 allele. *Pharmacogenetics* 7 (6): 479–484.

Tiesinga, P. H., Fellous, J. M., Jose, J. V., and Sejnowski, T. J. (2001). Computational model of carbachol-induced delta, theta, and gamma oscillations in the hippocampus. *Hippocampus* 11 (3): 251–274.

Tiffany, S. T., and Conklin, C. A. (2000). A cognitive processing model of alcohol craving and compulsive alcohol use. *Addiction* 95 (Suppl. 2): S145–153.

Town, T., Abdullah, L., Crawford, F., Schinka, J., Ordorica, P. I., Francis, E., Hughes, P., Duara, R., and Mullan, M. (1999). Association of a functional mu-opioid receptor allele (+118A) with alcohol dependency. *American Journal of Medical Genetics* 88 (5): 458–461.

True, W. R., Xian, H., Scherrer, J. F., Madden, P. A., Bucholz, K. K., Heath, A. C., Eisen, S. A., Lyons, M. J., Goldberg, J., and Tsuang, M. (1999). Common genetic vulnerability for nicotine and alcohol dependence in men. *Archives of General Psychiatry* 56 (7): 655–661.

Tryon, R. (1940). Genetic differences in maze-learning rats. *Yearbook, National Society for the Study of Education* 39: 111–119.

Turner, E., Ewing, J., Shilling, P., Smith, T. L., Irwin, M., Schuckit, M., and Kelsoe, J. R. (1992). Lack of association between an RFLP near the D_2 dopamine receptor gene and severe alcoholism. *Biological Psychiatry* 31 (3): 285–290.

van Beijsterveldt, C. E., Molenaar, P. C., de Geus, E. J., and Boomsma, D. I. (1996). Heritability of human brain functioning as assessed by electroencephalography. *American Journal of Human Genetics* 58 (3): 562–573.

van Beijsterveldt, C. E., and van Baal, G. C. (2002). Twin and family studies of the human electro-encephalogram: A review and a meta-analysis. *Biological Psychology* 61 (1–2): 111–138.

Van Craenenbroeck, K., Clark, S. D., Cox, M. J., Oak, J. N., Liu, F., and Van Tol, H. H. (2005). Folding efficiency is rate-limiting in dopamine D_4 receptor biogenesis. *Journal of Biological Chemistry* 280 (19): 19350–19357.

van den Wildenberg, E., Janssen, R. G., Hutchison, K. E., van Breukelen, G. J., and Wiers, R. W. (2007). Polymorphisms of the dopamine D_4 receptor gene (DRD4 VNTR) and cannabinoid CB1 receptor gene (CNR1) are not strongly related to cue-reactivity after alcohol exposure. *Addiction Biology* 12 (2): 210–220.

van der Zwaluw, C. S., van den Wildenberg, E., Wiers, R. W., Franke, B., Buitelaar, J., Scholte, R. H., and Engels, R. C. (2007). Polymorphisms in the micro-opioid receptor gene (OPRM1) and the implications for alcohol dependence in humans. *Pharmacogenomics* 8 (10): 1427–1436.

Vanyukov, M. M., Tarter, R. E., Kirisci, L., Kirillova, G. P., Maher, B. S., and Clark, D. B. (2003). Liability to substance use disorders: 1. Common mechanisms and manifestations. *Neuroscience and Biobehavioral Review* 27 (6): 507–515.

Venter, J. C., Adams, M. D., Myers, E. W., Li, P. W., Mural, R. J., Sutton, G. G., Smith, H. O., Yandell, M., Evans, C. A., Holt, R. A., et al. (2001). The sequence of the human genome. *Science* 291 (5507): 1304–1351.

Viken, R. J., Rose, R. J., Morzorati, S. L., Christian, J. C., and Li, T. K. (2003). Subjective intoxication in response to alcohol challenge: Heritability and covariation with personality, breath alcohol level, and drinking history. *Alcoholism: Clinical and Experimental Research* 27 (5): 795–803.

Volavka, J., Czobor, P., Goodwin, D. W., Gabrielli, W. F., Jr., Penick, E. C., Mednick, S. A., Jensen, P., and Knop, J. (1996). The electroencephalogram after alcohol administration in high-risk men and the development of alcohol use disorders 10 years later. *Archives of General Psychiatry* 53 (3): 258–263.

von Stein, A., and Sarnthein, J. (2000). Different frequencies for different scales of cortical integration: From local gamma to long range alpha/theta synchronization. *International Journal of Psychophysiology* 38 (3): 301–313.

Vuchinich, R. E., and Simpson, C. A. (1998). Hyperbolic temporal discounting in social drinkers and problem drinkers. *Experimental and Clinical Psychopharmacology* 6 (3): 292–305.

Waldman, I. D., Robinson, B. F., and Rhee, S. H. (1999). A logistic regression extension of the transmission disequilibrium test for continuous traits: Application to linkage disequilibrium between alcoholism and the candidate genes DRD2 and ADH3. *Genetic Epidemiology* 17 (Suppl. 1): S379–384.

Wall, T. L., Carr, L. G., and Ehlers, C. L. (2003). Protective association of genetic variation in alcohol dehydrogenase with alcohol dependence in Native American Mission Indians. *American Journal of Psychiatry* 160 (1): 41–46.

Wall, T. L., Johnson, M. L., Horn, S. M., Carr, L. G., Smith, T. L., and Schuckit, M. A. (1999). Evaluation of the self-rating of the effects of alcohol form in Asian Americans with aldehyde dehydrogenase polymorphisms. *Journal of Studies on Alcohol* 60 (6): 784–789.

Wang, J. C., Hinrichs, A. L., Stock, H., Budde, J., Allen, R., Bertelsen, S., Kwon, J. M., Wu, W., Dick, D. M., Rice, J., et al. (2004). Evidence of common and specific genetic effects: Association of the muscarinic acetylcholine receptor M2 (CHRM2) gene with alcohol dependence and major depressive syndrome. *Human Molecular Genetics* 13 (17): 1903–1911.

Watson, J. D., and Crick, F. H. (1953). Molecular structure of nucleic acids: A structure for deoxyribose nucleic acid. *Nature* 171 (4356): 737–738.

Weiss, F., Lorang, M. T., Bloom, F. E., and Koob, G. F. (1993). Oral alcohol self-administration stimulates dopamine release in the rat nucleus accumbens: Genetic and motivational determinants. *Journal of Pharmacology and Experimental Therapeutics* 267 (1): 250–258.

Weiss, F., and Porrino, L. J. (2002). Behavioral neurobiology of alcohol addiction: Recent advances and challenges. *Journal of Neuroscience* 22 (9): 3332–3327.

Whitfield, J. B. (2002). Alcohol dehydrogenase and alcohol dependence: Variation in genotype-associated risk between populations. *American Journal of Human Genetics* 71 (5): 1247–1250; author reply 1250–1251.

Whittington, M. A., Traub, R. D., Kopell, N., Ermentrout, B., and Buhl, E. H. (2000). Inhibition-based rhythms: Experimental and mathematical observations on network dynamics. *International Journal of Psychophysiology* 38 (3): 315–336.

Windle, M., and Davies, P. (1999). Developmental theory and research. In K. E. Leonard and T. H. Blane, eds., *Psychological Theories of Drinking and Alcoholism.* New York: Guilford Press.

Winterer, G., Kloppel, B., Heinz, A., Ziller, M., Dufeu, P., Schmidt, L. G., and Herrmann, W. M. (1998). Quantitative EEG (QEEG) predicts relapse in patients with chronic alcoholism and points to a frontally pronounced cerebral disturbance. *Psychiatry Research* 78 (1–2): 101–113.

Young, R. M., Lawford, B. R., Nutting, A., and Noble, E. P. (2004). Advances in molecular genetics and the prevention and treatment of substance misuse: Implications of association studies of the A1 allele of the D_2 dopamine receptor gene. *Addictive Behaviors* 29 (7): 1275–1294.

Zhang, Y., Wang, D., Johnson, A. D., Papp, A. C., and Sadee, W. (2005). Allelic expression imbalance of human mu opioid receptor (OPRM1) caused by variant A118G. *Journal of Biological Chemistry* 280 (38): 32618–32624.

4 Addiction as a Breakdown in the Machinery of Decision Making

A. David Redish

The Broken Decision Making Hypothesis

I start from the assumption that one of the major reasons for the evolution of the nervous system and the brain was to guide actions based on the immediately available information (sensory stimuli) in the light of previous experience (memory) and internal signals (needs, goals) that would further survival, procreation, and success of the genome—in other words, to make decisions. However, nervous systems are, by necessity, physical systems, particularly pharmacological systems, and thus pharmacological interventions can manipulate and bypass decision-making calculations to drive maladaptive decisions. I will argue, below, that it is the set of pharmacological chemicals that access failure points in the decision-making machinery that have been defined as the drugs of abuse. In addition, these decision-making processes were evolved in limited contexts; there is no reason to assume that they are optimal. I will argue, below, that there are experiential sequences that can drive an agent[1] to make incorrect choices, which can lead to problem gambling.

This chapter will first review the neurophysiology of decision making in mammals, and then will proceed to review a set of identifiable failure points within the system. Although we will acknowledge specific drugs of abuse and problem behaviors as we pass through the failure points, the relationship between failure points, drugs, and problem behaviors is complex. Our understanding of the full interaction between drugs, problem behaviors, and the decision-making system is still incomplete and will require more research (see Redish, Jensen, and Johnson 2008, for a larger review). The primary argument made here is that addiction should be considered in the light of *vulnerabilities in the machinery of the decision-making system*. The broken decision making hypothesis implies that if we want to understand addiction, then we need to understand the natural decision-making system, so that we can identify the vulnerabilities therein.

What Is a Decision?

Fundamentally, a decision is the selection of what action one should take at a given time. Of course, choosing not to act is still an act, and thus we will always include the null action as an available choice. This definition is general enough to encompass many experimental paradigms, including classical animal learning tasks, spatial (maze) tasks, multiple-choice paradigms, serial-choice tasks, forced-choice tasks, and go/no-go tasks. It is useful for interpreting data from rats on mazes and monkeys in visually cued paradigms, as well as larger, more human-cognitive decisions, such as a young couple buying a house, high school students deciding which college to go to, or a retiree deciding whether to bet that last bit of life savings on the pull of the one-armed bandit.

Many theories of decision making have been proposed, both from the normative perspective, in which the calculations of future possibilities are used to select the best choice (Bellman 1958; Becker and Murphy 1988; Sutton 1992; Sutton and Barto 1998), and from the descriptive perspective, in which heuristics are used to explain the actual decisions made by humans (Kahneman, Slovic, and Tversky 1982; Kahneman and Tversky 2000; Bernheim and Rangel 2004). Normative theories arise from the hypothesis that a suboptimal agent would be outcompeted by an optimal agent. However, what defines optimality is a complex issue requiring an understanding of the evolutionary milieu (including the dynamics and history of the species, Maynard-Smith 1982; Stephens and Krebs 1987; Weiner 1995), as well as other interacting species (including predators, prey, and conspecifics, Darwin 1871; Giraldeau and Caraco 2000). Additionally, the computation to identify the optimal choice may itself contain a cost, which may make heuristics more successful evolutionarily (Simon 1955; Gigerenzer and Goldstein 1996; Gigerenzer 2001). As pointed out by Gould (1980, 1983), evolution is not optimal—to succeed, an agent need merely be better (and luckier) than other agents. Extensive research has suggested that memory, estimation of the future, and even reward-recognition show serious deviations from straightforward normative systems in humans (for reviews, see Ainslie 1992, 2001; Kahneman, Slovic, and Tversky 1982; Kahneman and Tversky 2000; Schacter 2001; and Gilovich, Griffin, and Kahneman 2002).

The hypothesis that addiction arises from vulnerabilities in decision-making processes goes beyond the suggestion that humans make errors in decision making—not all drugs are abused, not all behaviors are continued despite terrible consequences, and there is a remarkable variability in the symptoms of addiction (Lowinson et al. 1997; Tarter, Ammerman, and Ott 1998; Volkow and Li 2005; Koob and Le Moal 2006). The present hypothesis suggests, instead, that the key to addiction is an interaction between the pharmacological effects of certain drugs and the physical machinery underlying the decision-making system. We thus start from the assumption that there is an interaction between the neurophysiology of the decision-making machine and addiction (Berke 2003; Kelley 2004; Hyman 2005; Kalivas and Volkow 2005; Koob and Le Moal 2006; Redish, Jensen, and Johnson 2008). This assumption means that we first need a neurophysiological understanding of the actual decision-making process. We will therefore start from a descriptive rather than a normative perspective. Our description of the decision-machine will be based primarily on the animal learning literature because there is more available neurophysiological data therein.

Theoretically, a decision must balance expected reward, expected costs, and the risks of each. Primarily, a decision is based on the value of the various choices, value being defined as expected reward minus expected cost.[2] The calculation of both expected reward and expected cost will need to take into account both the probability of receiving the reward or paying the cost as well as any delays before the reward is received or the costs are paid. These delays relate to the issue of the risk of receiving the reward (what is the probability of actually getting it?) and the risk of paying the cost (what is the probability that one won't need to pay it or that other rewards will have come in to make the cost less burdensome?).

Importantly, however, one cannot know the future, and therefore one cannot know the actual probability of receiving a reward or the actual cost that will be paid; thus one cannot know the actual value of a decision. Instead, one must *predict* the value of a decision. This prediction must be based on past experience. Thus, the first step of any decision must entail a recognition of the similarities and differences between the agent's current situation and its experience.

Categorizing Situations

Fundamentally, the definition of a situation is a classification process, a recognition that the current situation is similar to these previously experienced situations and different from those other previously experienced situations. Computationally, models of classification in cognitive systems have been based on a prototype-centered process (Ashby and Maddox 2005; Hertz, Krogh, and Palmer 1991; Kéri 2003; Lakoff 1990; Redish et al. 2007). An abstract prototype-centered model can be implemented neurally through content-addressable memories (Kohonen 1980; Hopfield 1982; Hertz, Krogh, and Palmer 1991). These models are based on positive coupling between neurons representing similar instances and global (or broad) inhibitory processes (Grossberg 1976; Wilson and Cowan 1973; Hertz, Krogh, and Palmer 1991). They can be described through attractor dynamics in high-dimension spaces—incomplete or unstable states will evolve through time into stable *attractor states*. Stable states are associated with remembered information (here identified situations). The set of similar input patterns (here cues) that settle to the same final state (thus classified as the same situation) define a *basin of attraction*. The resistance of this final state to noise defines the depth of the basin and can be said to form a sort of inertia in the system.

Making Decisions

Once the agent has successfully classified the situation, it has to identify the potential actions available to it and select an action to take. This process requires some combination of prediction, expectation, and evaluation, leading to action-selection. Each of these stages can be extended or truncated. For example, an agent could fully trace the future possibilities out into the extended future, until it reaches an expectation of reward that it could evaluate in the context of its current needs[3] (Tolman 1932; Koene et al. 2003; Daw, Niv, and Dayan 2005). It could then select the action that would take the first steps to this reward. This search process would obviously require an extensive computation that could take a long time to calculate. Alternatively, an agent could truncate the prediction component and cache in its memory an association of the value of taking a given action in a given situation for a given need (Sutton and Barto 1998; Daw, Niv, and Dayan 2005). In fact, the agent could truncate all the stages except action-selection, simply remembering the most successful action it had taken in previous experience with the current situation (Hull 1943). Although this would be computationally inexpensive (it is just a simple table-lookup operation), it is also inflexible and dangerous unless the agent is sure of its choices.

A number of researchers have suggested that these two extremes are realized separately by neural subsystems: (1) [*planning*] a flexible (goal-directed) system that learns quickly but acts slowly and allows complex decision planning, flexible responses, and a consideration of expected outcomes; and (2) [*habit*] a less flexible (stimulus-response) system that learns slowly but can act quickly (O Keefe and Nadel 1978; Squire 1987; Redish 1999; Poldrack and Packard 2003; Daw, Niv, and Dayan 2005; Redish, Jensen, and Johnson 2008).

Planning strategies   If the agent has the time available, or if it requires the flexibility that this extended search operation requires, it can take the time to predict expectations, calculate the value from those expectations given its current needs, and then select actions based on those calculated values. The flexible system has been most extensively described in the rodent in two literatures: devaluation, in which the value of a goal is changed (Colwill and Rescorla 1990; Balleine and Dickinson 1998; Schoenbaum, Setlow, and Ramus 2003), and cognitive mapping, in which navigation to a goal remains flexible in response to the presence of obstacles and to changes in starting point (O'Keefe and Nadel 1978; Redish 1999). Recent models of the devaluation phenomenon and of cognitive map-based navigation have suggested that they both arise from a planning-capable system that directly allows the consideration of possibilities (Jensen and Lisman 1998, 2005; Koene et al. 2003; Daw, Niv, and Dayan 2005; Redish and Johnson 2007; Buckner and Carroll 2007; Zilli and Hasselmo 2008). These models suggest that some structure is providing the animal with a prediction of the consequences of its actions, from which an evaluation of the goal can be reached, and a decision made. This prediction is likely occurring in frontal cortex (Daw, Niv, and Dayan 2005), hippocampus (Jensen and Lisman 1998, 2005; Koene et al. 2003), or through an interaction between them (Buckner and Carroll 2007).

Early descriptions of the behavior of rats making spatial decisions described transient pause-and-look behaviors at decision points early in learning (vicarious trial and error [VTE], Meunzinger 1938; Tolman 1938). Learning increased nonlinearly at approximately the same set of trials during which VTE behaviors were seen (Tolman 1938; Gallistel, Fairhurst, and Balsam 2004). Tolman (1932, 1938, 1939, 1948) suggested that these behaviors were indicative of the evaluation of expectancies of the consequences of the animal's actions. We have recently observed that hippocampal neurons transiently encoded positions forward of the animal while rats paused at choice points and showed VTE behaviors, which may reflect the search processes considering the available choices (Johnson and Redish 2007).

However, hippocampal lesions do not seem to affect changing values of future expectancies (Corbit and Balleine 2000). Nor did we observe any relationship between the future choices reflected in hippocampal neural activity and the actual decisions made by the animal (Johnson and Redish 2007). Therefore, we concluded that evaluation is most likely occurring in other structures. Plausible candidates include orbitofrontal cortex (Schoenbaum, Roesch, and Stalnaker 2006; Padoa-Schioppa and Assad 2006), ventral striatum (Mogenson, Jones, and Yim 1980; O'Doherty et al. 2004), and an interaction between them (Kalivas and Volkow 2005). Manipulations of both orbitofrontal cortex and ventral striatum affect evaluation processes (Corbit, Muir, and Balleine 2001; Kalivas and Volkow 2005; Calu et al. 2007), and neural activity in both structures reflect future values (Nicola et al. 2004a,b; Plassmann, O'Doherty, and Rangel 2007; Padoa-Schioppa and Assad 2006), and future goals (Lavoie and Mizumori 1994; Feierstein et al. 2006; Ramus et al. 2007; German and Fields 2007, van der Meer and Redish 2009). However, the exact mechanism underlying evaluation in the planning system is still unknown. Similarly, the mechanism by which actions are selected from a flexible expectancy-based evaluation system are also unknown. But flexible action-selection is known to require both ventral striatum (Mogenson, Jones, and Yim 1980) and dorsomedial striatum (Devan and White 1999; Hikosaka et al. 1999; Ragozzino, Jih, and Tzavos 2002; Yin and Knowlton 2006).

Habit strategies   If an agent is going to be in the same situation and make the same decision over and over again, it is inefficient to spend the time to search through future possibilities, evaluate those possibilities, and select among them each time the agent encounters that situation. Instead, the agent can simply cache the values of actions in a given situation (Sutton and Barto 1998; Daw, Niv, and Dayan 2005) or even simply associate a given action with a given situation (Hull 1943). This is obviously much less flexible than the planning system detailed above, but it is also much simpler and faster.

Computationally, action-selection within the habit system can be a table-lookup operation. More dynamically, the appropriate action to associate with a given situation can be learned through temporal-difference algorithms, in which the expected values of situation-action associations are learned through value-prediction-error signals, calculated as the difference between the expected value of taking an action in a given situation and the value observed after actually taking the action (Sutton and Barto 1998; Montague, Dayan, and Sejnowski 1996; Schultz, Dayan, and Montague 1997; Suri and Schultz 1999; Doya 2000; Daw 2003; Daw, Niv, and Dayan 2005).[4] These models change the expected values of situation-action pairs in order to drive value-prediction-error signals to zero (Sutton and Barto 1998).

The less-flexible habit system has been extensively studied in both the primate and the rodent and has been identified as involving cortico-striatal loops, particularly involving the lateral aspects of striatum (Packard and McGaugh 1992; Graybiel 2000; White and McDonald 2002). Dopamine signals parallel these value-prediction error signals remarkably well (Montague et al. 1995; Montague, Dayan, and Sejnowski 1996; Barto 1995; Schultz, Dayan, and Montague 1997; Schultz 1998). Neurons in these structures develop correlates to situation-action relationships slowly, particularly in response to highly regular stimulus-action associations (Schultz and Romo 1992; Jog et al. 1999; Hikosaka et al. 1999; Schultz, Tremblay, and Hollerman 2003; Schmitzer-Torbert and Redish 2004; Samejima et al. 2005; Barnes et al. 2005; Hikosaka, Nakamura, and Nakahara 2006; Schmitzer-Torbert and Redish 2008).

Early theories, however, suggested that the planning and habit systems are two extremes of a continuum (Tolman 1932, 1938; Simon 1955). Supporting this continuum hypothesis, fMRI correlational data has found a continuum of future-consideration time-courses ranging from ventroanterior to dorsoposterior striatum in the human (Tanaka et al. 2004). Whether the planning (flexible) and habit (stimulus-response) systems are two extremes of a continuum or form an explicit competitive dichotomy, we can identify multiple failure modes within this prediction, expectation, evaluation, action-selection decision-making system.

Failure Modes of the Decision-making System

The decision-making machine described above is, first and foremost, a physical machine. It is implemented in a neurophysiological substrate, with specific neuronal firing patterns and specific pharmacological properties encoding specific information (variables) used to select the appropriate actions.

The description of the decision-making machine, above, has divided it into three separable systems, *situation-recognition*, *planning*, and *habit*. Correct decision making depends on the integrity of each of these systems. All three systems (situation-recognition, planning, habit) have failure points through which drugs, cues, and reward-sequences can drive incorrect (addictive) choices. So far, we have identified eight key vulnerabilities in the system:[5]

1. changing needs (moving away from homeostasis and/or changing allostatic set points);
2. mimicking the euphoric reward signals;
3. overvaluation of actions or expectancies within a situation;
4. incorrect separation of situations;
5. lack of recognition of changing situations;
6. overfast discounting processes;
7. changing learning rates; and
8. a mismatch in the balance of planning and habit decision systems.

These vulnerabilities provide a taxonomy of potential problems with decision-making systems. Although each vulnerability can drive an agent to return to the addictive choice, each vulnerability will also produce characteristic symptoms. Different drugs, different behaviors, and different individuals are likely to access different vulnerabilities. This has implications for an individual's susceptibility to addiction and the transition to addiction, for the potential for relapse, and for the potential for treatment.

(1)   Known failure modes: Changing needs   Evaluation of outcomes requires satisfaction of needs. Because drug-use can change the represented needs of the agent, drugs can change the predicted value when value is calculated from expectancies (thus taking into account those needs).

Because organisms are evolved to maintain critical parameters at a set level under large challenges, changes that drive an agent away from the stored target level will drive the agent to restore itself to that target level. If the changes are immediate but the set-point remains unchanged, the failure mode is one of "homeostasis." The well-known crash that occurs after acute delivery of opiates (even the first delivery) is an example of homeostatic changes (Azolosa, Stitzer, and Greenwald 1994; Harris and Gewirtz 2005; Koob and Le Moal 2006). Homeostatic changes produce a need to return the system back to the original target level, analogous to hunger or thirst. However, whereas the perceived effect is clearly very real, the actual need may be illusory (as the emotional crash that follows opiate delivery, which feels like it needs to be treated with another dose of opiates).

Extended use can also drive the system to a new expected target level. Here, the system has changed to expect a new level, which, once removed, produces a need to return it to the new, incorrect, levels. This is then an "allostatic" failure mode (Ahmed and Koob 2005; Koob and Le Moal 2006). For example, the changes in cholinergic receptor levels that occur with chronic nicotine use (Benowitz 1996) will drive the system to depend on higher than normal nicotine levels for normal functioning. Many smokers titrate their nicotine intake to ensure specific nicotine levels within their bodies (Schmitz, Schneider, and Jarvik 1997).

Changing needs will primarily drive effects within the flexible, planning system because reacting to quickly changing needs requires the ability to reevaluate value in the context of specific needs, which requires expectancies. It is possible, however, that continued drug-taking due to the changed-needs vulnerability could slowly train up the habit system, leading to a shift in drug-use from the compulsive, needs-based vulnerability to a more robotic, habit-based vulnerability, independent of corrective changes in homeostatic or allostatic set-points.

(2)   Known failure modes: Mimicking reward   Any reinforcement learning system needs a means of recognizing receipt of reward. A drug that directly mimicked this reward-signal would be a powerful reinforcer of behaviors leading to that drug.

This hypothesized reward signal is likely to be related to the qualia of euphoric pleasure and dysphoric displeasure (Berridge and Robinson 1998, 2003). We can thus identify this signal with subjective, hedonic signals. That identification suggests that this signal is likely to be carried in part by the endogenous opioid system (Berridge and Robinson 1998, 2003; Kelley et al. 2002). μ-receptor agonists are rewarding and euphorigenic, whereas κ-receptor agonists are aversive and dysphoric (Chavkin, James, and Goldstein 1982; Mucha and Herz 1985; Bals-Kubik, Herz, and Shippenberg 1989; Herz 1997, 1998; Kieffer 1999; De Vries and Shippenberg 2002). Opioid antagonists reduce facial expressions made in response to sweet and bitter stimuli (Berridge and Robinson 2003), and also reduce the reported qualia of hedonic pleasure associated with eating sweet substances, without interfering in taste discrimination (Arbisi, Billington, and Levine 1999; Levine and Billington 2004). Obviously, a pharmacological agent that mimicked the positive side of this evaluation signal would be misinterpreted as a delivered reward, and actions that led to receipt of that pseudo-reward would gain value as if it were a real reward. It is likely that this is one of the vulnerabilities accessed by morphine, heroin, and the other abused opiates, all of which are μ-opioid receptor agonists (Negus et al. 1993; Jaffe, Knapp, and Ciraulo 1997; van Ree, Gerrits, and Vanderschuren 1999). Thus, although organisms never evolved to take μ-opioid receptor agonists, such agonists are misinterpreted as providing a strong reward signal, leading to the incorrect seeking of those agonists.

A drug that mimics reward will show properties similar to normal rewards in that the reward signal can be correctly predicted given the appropriate cues. Thus, for example, the reward-mimicking component will drive value-prediction error only when unexpected. A drug accessing the reward-mimicking vulnerability will enable a strong memory of and expectancy for the reward, which could lead to craving (Redish and Johnson 2007). The expectation of drug-receipt can also lead to allostatic preparation for the drug (which occurs for heroin, Meyer and Mirin 1979; Siegel 1988; and for alcohol, Hunt 1998). This cue-driven expectancy can explain the cue-dependence of heroin craving (O'Brien et al. 1977; Childress et al. 1988, 1992; Grant et al. 1996) and the increased likelihood for heroin overdoses in nonfamiliar drug-taking situations (Siegel et al. 1982).

(3) Known failure modes: Overvaluation The calculation of future value of an action depends on a complex process relating to stored memories of rewards (expectancies, see above), to motivational signals, and to cached expected values of situation-action pairs (Sutton and Barto 1998; Daw, Niv, and Dayan 2005; Berridge 2006; Redish and Johnson 2007). Any mechanism by which the value of an action within a given situation increases extraordinarily will drive overselection of that action.

Overvaluation can affect both the planning (search and expectancy-based) and habit (cached value) systems (Bernheim and Rangel 2004; Redish 2004; Berridge 2006; Redish, Jensen, and Johnson 2008). At this point, computational models of the planning system are still very limited (Koene et al. 2003; Johnson and Redish 2005; Daw, Niv, and Dayan 2005; Zilli and Hasselmo 2008), but experimental evidence suggests that dopamine (Berridge 2006), ventral striatum (Lavoie and Mizumori 1994; O'Doherty et al. 2004; van der Meer and Redish 2009), and the orbitofrontal cortex (Schoenbaum and Roesch 2005; Padoa-Schioppa and Assad 2006; Plassmann, O'Doherty, and Rangel 2007; Sakagami and Pan 2007) are all involved in evaluation of future rewards in the planning system. Incorrect signals arriving from orbitofrontal cortex have been hypothesized to drive overvaluation of expected drug-related outcomes (Volkow, Fowler, and Wang 2003; Kalivas and Volkow 2005; Schoenbaum, Roesch, and Stalnaker 2006). Both orbitofrontal cortex (Volkow and Fowler 2000; Stalnaker et al. 2006) and ventral striatum (Peoples et al. 1999; Carelli 2002; German and Fields 2007) show profound changes in activity with continued drug use. A number of abused drugs directly produce dopamine signals in ventral striatum (Pidoplichko et al. 1997; Stuber, Wightman, and Carelli 2005; Cheer et al. 2007a; Keath et al. 2007).

As reviewed above, computational models of habit-based learning systems are quite sophisticated, based in large part on the temporal difference reinforcement learning algorithm (Sutton and Barto 1998; Daw 2003), in which a value-prediction error signal is reduced to zero. If dopamine does signal value-prediction-error within these systems (Montague, Dayan, and Sejnowski 1996; Schultz, Dayan, and Montague 1997; Schultz 1998), then drugs that produce dopamine neuropharmacologically (which would theoretically bypass the calculation of value-prediction-error) will drive overvaluation of actions leading to taking those drugs (Redish 2004). Cocaine, amphetamine, nicotine, and many other drugs lead to fast dopamine release pharmacologically (Ritz et al. 1987; Kuhar, Ritz, and Sharkey 1988; Mansvelder, Keath, and McGehee 2002; Mansvelder and McGehee 2002), even when those drug-events are already predicted (Stuber, Wightman, and Carelli 2005; Cheer et al. 2007a,b), in contrast to food-rewards, which do not produce dopamine signals to well-predicted rewards (Schultz 1998, 2002).

Because action-selection in the planning system is more flexible than in the habit system, overvaluation in each system may lead to different observable clinical consequences. Nevertheless, developing overvaluation will lead to overselection of drug-related choices, to a willingness to pay high costs for drug-receipt, and to a developing inelasticity of drug-taking relative to costs (Redish 2004).

(4)   Known failure mode: The illusion of control   If an agent misidentifies a changing cue as the cause of observed wins and losses, the agent may incorrectly believe it can control those wins and losses by controlling that cue.

This failure mode arises when the agent incorrectly identifies differences between situations. For example, imagine an agent playing a slot machine with a button that has no relation to reward delivery. The agent may randomly experience a different proportion of winning plays with the button pressed than with the button unpressed (or vice versa). This difference may lead the agent to incorrectly identify the button as an important control for winning and losing on the slot machine. The button may be particularly difficult to ignore if it provides signals to the user (such as flashing lights), even if those signals are stated as being unrelated to reward delivery (Griffiths 1994; Parke and Griffiths 2004; Dickerson and O'Connor 2006). This leads to superstitions and the *illusion of control* (Langer and Roth 1975; Custer 1984; Wagenaar 1988; Sylvain, Ladouceur, and Biosvert 1997; Redish et al. 2007). The more potential cues there are available to identify situations, the more likely an agent is to misidentify differing reward contingencies as arising from different situations.

Newer gambling machines are designed to provide more cues rather than fewer (Parke and Griffiths 2004; Rivlin 2004; Dickerson and O'Connor 2006). Early theories of gambling based on simple Pavlovian and instrumental associations would have suggested that faster, simpler lever-reward sequences would lead to more gambling (Pavlov 1927; Ferster and Skinner 1957; Dickerson and O'Connor 2006). In contrast, the hypothesis that gambling arises from an "illusion of control" vulnerability suggests that more complex machines with extra (even unrelated) cues will be harder to predict and more susceptible to the illusion of control. Slot-machine gamblers and gamblers playing skill games are more likely to show irrational cognitive beliefs about control than nongamblers and those playing explicitly non-skill games (e.g., lotteries) (Walker 1992; Toneatto et al. 1997; Raylu and Oei 2002). The illusion of control vulnerability predicts that the most pernicious gambling machines will be those with cues that provide limited but incomplete predictability. Newer gambling machines have become more and more complex over time, with some approaching the complexity of some video games (Rivlin 2004; Dickerson and O'Connor 2006). With experience, these cues can become secondary rewards in their own right, and can hook unsuspecting users into trying to figure out just how to predict the (unpredictable) win.

Theoretical analyses of learning suggest that unexpected delivery of positive rewards (reinforcement) leads to associations, but lack of delivery of expected reward (disappointment) leads to reassessment of the situation (Redish et al. 2007). This observation in problem gamblers has been termed *hindsight bias* in which gamblers explain away losses through the back-identification of differential cues (Custer 1984; Wagenaar 1988). Hindsight bias may explain the importance of *near misses* as a driving force in continuation of gambling phenomena (Parke and Griffiths 2004). Many problem gamblers have experienced a statistically unlikely sequence of wins followed by devastating losses (Custer 1984; Wagenaar 1988). Such a reward sequence will lead to development of an association and subsequent attempted analysis of the differences between the winning and losing conditions. Computational models based on content-addressable situation-categorization mechanisms faced with statistically unlikely winning sequences can show relapsing and remitting gambling activity, including very high losses after the big strike (Redish et al. 2007). These agents are attempting to find again that magical situation in which all the cues lined up perfectly and they won big.

(5)   Known failure modes: Inability to recognize changing situations   If, on the other hand, a situation has changed, but the agent does not recognize the changed situation, the agent may continue responding even at high cost.

Many gamblers and drug addicts refuse to acknowledge changes in their underlying situations and fail to reverse their choices, even under adverse conditions (Wagenaar 1988; Potenza, Kosten, and Rounsaville 2001; Dickerson and O'Connor 2006). This persistence in the face of change can be related to misexpectations of reward delivery probabilities or to a misunderstanding of the independence of probabilistic trials. This is related to the well-known sequential probability error in which subjects expect a sequence of probable events to even out (Langer and Roth 1975), as so beautifully shown in the opening scene of Tom Stoppard's *Rosencrantz and Guildenstern Are Dead* in which Rosencrantz and Guildenstern argue about whether dozens of coin tosses coming up heads in a row are a consequence of random processes or a sign of their impending doom.

A similar and related process may be occurring in the *partial reinforcement extinction effect*, in which an agent trained to respond to receive reward but now no longer receiving reward for the response (extinction) continues responding longer if the reward was only delivered with a low probability during training (Mackintosh 1974; Domjan

1998). Behavioral extinction has long been identified as recognition of changes between acquisition and extinction conditions (Capaldi 1957, 1958; Bouton 2002, 2004; Redish et al. 2007). Computationally, these effects can be shown to derive from the information available to the animal justifying the differentiation from a single situation to two situations (Fuhs and Touretzky 2007). Computational models based on content-addressable situation-categorization mechanisms faced with a change in the statistics of winning do not always recognize the change and can continue responding including paying very high losses after winning (Redish et al. 2007).

Clinically, these failure modes may relate to the observation of *chasing* (Lesieur 1977; Custer 1984; Wagenaar 1988), in which gambling continues in the face of devastating losses. The agent continues to believe that its original hypothesis is correct and the losses will be replaced if only it continues playing. This error can be particularly pernicious if the agent has an incorrect hypothesis about the predictability of the win.

(6)   Known failure modes: Deficits in discounting processes   To make a correct decision, a decision system must to take into account the probability and the delay before an expected reward will be received (Stephens and Krebs 1987; Ainslie 1992, 2001; Sozou 1998). Both the planning and habit systems require correct discounting processes to correctly evaluate future rewards. Faster discounting rates would increase the calculated value of short-term pleasures and decrease the calculated value of long-term costs. Addicts generally discount faster than nonaddicts (Kirby, Petry, and Bickel 1999; Alessi and Petry 2003; Madden, Bickel, and Critchfield in press). Discounting processes can account for changes in plans as the drug becomes more proximal and more available (Ainslie 1992, 2001).

(7)   Known failure modes: Changes in learning rate   Any learning process has a critical computational factor that controls the speed at which information is changed. This is termed the *learning rate*. Slower learning rates allow for increased stability in the face of noise, whereas faster learning rates allow for increased responsivity to changing signals (O'Reilly and McClelland 1994; Hertz, Krogh, and Palmer 1991; Duda, Hart, Stork 2001).

Both planning and habit learning systems include fundamental learning rates within their algorithms. Planning systems must learn to associate situation-action-situation relationships (so as to correctly predict effects of actions taken within a given situation). Drugs that temporarily increase the learning rate within the planning system could increase the likelihood that agents would search drug-related choices, which could lead to drug-seeking and obsession (Redish and Johnson 2007).

Habit systems must learn to associate actions with situations and cues within those situations. A drug that temporarily increased learning rates during the presence of the drug could lead to increased stimulus-action associations (Gutkin, Dehaene, and

Changeux 2006). Similarly, if continued drug-use decreased learning rates, it could become particularly difficult to unlearn those problematic associations (or to learn alternate associations) (Gutkin, Dehaene, and Changeux 2006).

(8) Known failure modes: Balances between systems Accurate behavior requires a correct balance between flexible but computationally expensive (planning) and rigid but fast-reacting (habit) systems. Some tasks require planning strategies (e.g., the Morris water maze, Morris 1981; Redish 1999), whereas other tasks require habit strategies (e.g., mirror writing, the serial-reaction time task, Cohen and Squire 1980; Knopman and Nissen 1991; Knowlton, Mangels, and Squire 1996). Changes in strategy have long been studied in the transition from planning to habit strategies in many maze-related and sequence-learning tasks (Packard and McGaugh 1996; Hikosaka et al. 1999; Schmitzer-Torbert and Redish 2002), and in devaluation experiments (Balleine and Dickinson 1998; Killcross and Coutureau 2003), and from habit back to planning strategies in behavioral inhibition (Gray and McNaughton 2000) and go/no-go tasks (Iversen and Mishkin 1970; Goldman, Rosvold, and Mishkin 1970; Isoda and Hikosaka 2007). A mismatch in the balance between future-searching [planning] and cached-value [habit] systems can produce profound deficits in the ability to interrupt cached-behaviors (Brass and Haggard 2007; Isoda and Hikosaka 2007) or to react appropriately to changes in cue and reward distributions (Hirsh 1974; Corbit and Balleine 2000; Corbit, Muir, and Balleine 2001; Ragozzino et al. 2002; Yin et al. 2005).

Drugs that selectively impair systems needed for the future-searching process (such as hippocampus and prefrontal cortex, both of which are targeted by alcohol [Hunt 1998; Oscar-Berman and Marinkovic 2003; White 2003]) or which selectively strengthen cached value systems (a suggested consequence of amphetamine, Nelson and Killcross 2006) will lead to decision making that is less flexible, less able to take variable consequences into account, and less able to inhibit and return from habitlike responding.

Implications for Individual Diagnosis and Treatment

The primary implication of the theory proposed here is that addiction is a multi-spectrum disorder with many underlying endophenotypes, all of which show the same basic final phenomenology: the continued use of drugs or the continued pursuit of problematic behaviors. All three systems (situation-recognition, flexible planning systems, slowly learned habit systems) have failure-points through which drugs, cues, and reward-sequences can drive incorrect (addictive) choices. Even though each vulnerability can drive the agent toward the drug or problematic behavior, the underlying mechanism (and reason) is different. These differences should be manifest in differentiable clinical observables.

For example, this theory predicts that craving will be clinically separable from relapse. If we assume that craving is a clinical sign of the expectance of a specific reward of very high value, then craving occurs when the search process in the planning system identifies a potential high-value reward (Redish and Johnson 2007). Because the planning system is flexible, recognition of a path to an outcome does not necessarily lead to taking that path. Thus, craving can occur without relapse. Because relapse can also be driven by the habit system, which does not include expectancies, relapse can occur without craving. Thus the dependence of craving within planning systems, the inherent flexibility of the planning system, and the multiple pathways to relapse through both planning and habit systems imply that craving and relapse should be clinically dissociable processes.

Relapse can also occur through the situation-recognition system. The potential suddenness of relapse (Lowinson et al. 1997; Goldstein 2000) suggests that even in recovered addicts, much like the fast reinstatement of behavior after extinction, the drug-seeking association is not forgotten (Gawin 1991; Redish et al. 2007). The cessation of drug seeking may also utilize a changing of the situation classification much like behavioral extinction does. Redish et al. (2007) have suggested that, as with extinction, the key to recovery from addiction is a changing of the situation representation, which allows different consequences (i.e., natural rewards predominating over drug rewards) and actions (i.e., not drug seeking) to be associated with a given situation. Relapse, then, would occur when the subject reclassifies a given situation as similar (equivalent) to the earlier drug-associated situation, and the subject is reminded of its previous experience. This cued renewal of responding is a key part of many clinical models of relapse (Childress et al. 1988, 1992, 1993; O'Brien et al. 1992). Both drug craving and relapse are known to be strongly influenced by drug-associated cues (Childress et al. 1988, 1992, 1993) and by context (O'Brien et al. 1992). Avoiding casinos is a key to avoiding gambling relapses (Dickerson and O'Connor 2006). Dickerson and O'Connor (2006) describe a gambler that successfully maintained control of gambling urges by driving a new route home that avoided driving by a local casino. Thus, a key implication of the situation classification module is the potential for cued relapse of recovered (successfully "extinguished") behaviors.

Not all subjects who try drugs become addicted (Koob and Le Moal 2006). Estimates range from <5% for users of psychedelic drugs to >30% for users of tobacco (Anthony, Warner, and Kessler 1994). Even within the animal-based self-administration paradigm, in a cocaine-delivery experiment, less than 20% of rats were willing to pay a high cost for drugs (Deroche-Gamonet, Belin, and Piazza 2004), even though the rats received the same physical experiences and were presumably relatively genetically similar.

One of the major open questions in addiction entails understanding these differences, and understanding why some people are more susceptible to addiction (whether to a specific addiction such as alcohol or cocaine or to addictions in general; Volkow and Li 2005). Addiction shows strong heritability (Koob and Le Moal 2006), tied to known (and unknown) genetics (Crabbe 2002; Goldman, Oroszi, and Ducci 2005). Of course, a susceptible agent who never tries drugs will never fall victim to the recurring vulnerability in the decision-making system and thus will not become an addict. Thus, addiction arises from an interaction between the genetics of the individual and the experience (social, physical) of the individual.

The vulnerabilities theory proposed here suggests that the continued pursuit of drugs or problematic behaviors may be due to many potential decision-making failures. Which vulnerabilities the subject has fallen victim to will depend on the individual's predisposition (genetics, social background) and the drug or behavioral effects on the system itself. For example, three different dopamine polymorphisms can make subjects more or less able to learn from positive examples (DARPP-32, involved in striatal D_1 receptor functionality), from negative examples (DRD2, involved in striatal D_2 receptor functionality), or more or less able to switch under changing reward probabilities (COMT, involved in prefrontal dopamine function) (Frank et al. 2007). Each of these genetic polymorphisms will affect the susceptibility to different drug- and reward-paradigms.

Addiction treatment will require a regimen specifically designed to address the vulnerabilities active within the individual. Homeostatic and allostatic vulnerabilities will likely require pharmacological treatment to rebalance the system. Overvaluation will require treatment to change the recall and reevaluation processes, as well as mechanisms with which to strengthen alternative choices available. Miscategorization of situations will likely require treatments aimed at executive function and its role in recategorizing situations.

I propose that the clinical treatment of addiction should not be addressed to the general "addicted population," nor to specific drugs of abuse, but rather to the specific constellation of vulnerabilities active within the individual. Although the set of failure-modes identified in this chapter is certainly incomplete, the hypothesis presented here (that addiction arises from vulnerabilities in the neurophysiological machinery underlying decision making) suggests a research paradigm that can address both the definition of addiction itself as well as addiction treatment.

Conclusion: Defining Addiction as Vulnerabilities in the Decision-making Process

Definitions of addiction were originally based on continued use despite the stated desire to change (Ainslie 1992; Goldstein 2000; Koob and Le Moal 2006). But, of course, many addicts deny that they have a problem, even though they clearly need help. In fact, the first step of many treatment programs is the admission of a problem (e.g., Alcoholics Anonymous; Narcotics Anonymous). Nor are all actions that are continued despite the stated desire to stop are traditionally termed "addiction"—most people would rather stay home to play with their kids but continue to go to work. (Presumably this is due to the knowledge of future consequences.) This suggests that although the stated desire to change may be related to addiction, it cannot be the defining characteristic.

In addition, defining addiction as a mismatch between stated desires and actions precludes the ability of nonhuman animals (without language) to be addicted. Many researchers have thus suggested a definition of addiction based on continued use despite devastatingly negative consequences (Leshner 1997; Robinson 2004; Koob and Le Moal 2006; ICD-10; DSM-IV-TR). Animals readily self-administer[6] the same substances that humans do (Weeks 1962; Koob and Le Moal 2006), such as cocaine (Woolverton 1992); nicotine (Goldberg, Spealman, and Goldberg 1981; Caggiula et al. 2001); heroin (Wise 1989); even caffeine (Griffiths and Woodson 1988), and are even willing to pay abnormally high prices for it (Deroche-Gamonet, Belin, and Piazza 2004; Vanderschuren and Everitt 2004). However, many behaviors done despite devastating consequences are celebrated. Examples include the actions of saints, freedom marchers, dissidents, and jailed poets. This suggests that although continued drug use despite terrible consequences may be related to addiction, it cannot be the defining characteristic.

Instead, I suggest that addiction be defined as failures of the decision-making system due to identifiable vulnerabilities. For example, according to the theory reviewed above, heroin (among other consequences) mimics the μ-opioid-driven reward signal. Animals (including humans) did not evolve to be rewarded for heroin. Instead, animals evolved to use internal μ-opioid agonists as the signal for reward. Heroin just happens to trip that internal signal, making heroin appear (incorrectly) as a very strong positive reward.

In recent years, many researchers have argued for the concept of addiction as a disease (Leshner 1997; Hyman 2005). The vulnerabilities theory proposed here fits well within that concept in that it suggests that addiction entails failure modes within the decision-making machinery. This means that it is, if not a disease per se, at least a damaged part of the machine that potentially could be fixed with appropriately guided treatment.

Acknowledgments

I thank John Ferguson, Adam Johnson, Zeb Kurth-Nelson, Steve Jensen, and Matthijs van der Meer for comments on a draft of this chapter. This work was supported by a Sloan Fellowship, a Career Development Award from the University of Minnesota TTURC (NCI/NIDA P50 DA01333), and NIH R01 DA024080.

Notes

1. Following the cognition literature, I use the term "agent" to refer to any decision maker, whether it be a person, an animal, a computer simulation, or robot. Agency is used without any prejudice or presumption regarding free will.

2. Humans have been shown to treat expected rewards and expected costs differently, even when the final total future value is the same (Kahneman and Tversky 1979). These effects will have important consequences for specific time courses and treatment of addiction, but are not critical for the first-order descriptions given here.

3. This search process, of course, depends on memory-recall processes. Limitations in the search for available actions can lead to the potential for returning to the same potential action, which can be termed a form of *obsession* (Redish and Johnson 2007).

4. Recent models have also looked at hypothetical actions and fictive learning signals, in which agents update not just the actual action, but also similar (Sutton and Barto 1998; Johnson and Redish 2005), or different (Lohrenz et al. 2007) actions. For example, if an agent considers putting money in stocks, but decides to put it in bonds instead, and the stock market rises while the bond market falls, then the agent can update both the action taken (putting money in bonds) and the action considered (putting money in stocks) after the observation (see, for example, Lohrenz et al. 2007; Chiu, Lohrenz, Montague 2008).

5. This list is almost certainly incomplete. More details and an expanded list of potential vulnerabilities can be found in the discussion and response sections of Redish, Jensen, Johnson 2008.

6. The self-administration paradigm has been called into question from its very inception due to the absence of other non-drug options. However, it remains the primary animal test used throughout the literature. In the last year, experiments have shown that animals given the choice between drugs (cocaine, heroin) and strong sweet tastes (saccharin) will switch to saccharin choice, even after extended cocaine (Lenoir et al. 2007) or heroin (Lenoir and Ahmed 2007) experience. Whether this is due to problems with the self-administration paradigm (Gardner 1997) or to the addictive nature of sweet tastes (Mintz 1986; Pelchat 2002; Grigson 2002) is unknown at this time.

References

Ahmed, S. H., and Koob, G. F. (2005). Transition to drug addiction: A negative reinforcement model based on an allostatic decrease in reward function. *Psychopharmacology* 180: 473–490.

Ainslie, G. (1992). *Picoeconomics*. Cambridge: Cambridge University Press.

Ainslie, G. (2001). *Breakdown of Will*. Cambridge: Cambridge University Press.

Alcoholics Anonymous. http://www.alcoholics-anonymous.org. (Accessed December 6, 2008.)

Alessi, S. M., and Petry, N. M. (2003). Pathological gambling severity is associated with impulsivity in a delay discounting procedure. *Behavioural Processes* 64 (3): 345–354.

Anthony, J. C., Warner, L. A., and Kessler, R. C. (1994). Comparative epidemiology of dependence on tobacco, alcohol, controlled substances, and inhalants: Basic findings from the National Comorbidity Survey. *Experimental and Clinical Psychopharmacology* 2 (3): 244–268.

Arbisi, P. A., Billington, C. J., and Levine, A. S. (1999). The effect of naltrexone on taste detection and recognition threshold. *Appetite* 32 (2): 241–249.

Ashby, F. G., and Maddox, W. T. (2005). Human category learning. *Annual Reviews: Psychology* 56: 149–178.

Azolosa, J. L., Stitzer, M. L., and Greenwald, M. K. (1994). Opioid physical dependence development: Effects of single versus repeated morphine pretreatments and of subjects' opioid exposure history. *Psychopharmacology* 114 (1): 71–80.

Balleine, B. W., and Dickinson, A. (1998). Goal-directed instrumental action: Contingency and incentive learning and their cortical substrates. *Neuropharmacology* 37 (4–5): 407–419.

Bals-Kubik, R., Herz, A., and Shippenberg, T. (1989). Evidence that the aversive effects of opioid antagonists and κ-agonists are centrally mediated. *Psychopharmacology* 98: 203–206.

Barnes, T. D., Kubota, Y., Hu, D., Jin, D. Z., and Graybiel, A. M. (2005). Activity of striatal neurons reflects dynamic encoding and recoding of procedural memories. *Nature* 437: 1158–1161.

Barto, A. G. (1995). Adaptive critics and the basal ganglia. In J. C. Houk, J. L. Davis, and D. G. Beiser, eds., *Models of Information Processing in the Basal Ganglia*, 215–232. Cambridge, MA: MIT Press.

Becker, G. S., and Murphy, K. M. (1988). A theory of rational addiction. *Journal of Political Economy* 96 (4): 675–700.

Bellman, R. (1958). On a routing problem. *Quarterly Journal of Applied Mathematics* 16 (1): 87–90.

Benowitz, N. L. (1996). Pharmacology of nicotine: Addiction and therapeutics. *Annual Review of Pharmacology and Toxicology* 36: 597–613.

Berke, J. D. (2003). Learning and memory mechanisms involved in compulsive drug use and relapse. In J. Wang, ed., *Drugs of Abuse: Analysis of Neurological Effects*. Totowa: Humana.

Bernheim, B. D., and Rangel, A. (2004). Addiction and cue-triggered decision processes. *American Economic Review* 94 (5): 1558–1590.

Berridge, K. C. (2006). The debate over dopamine's role in reward: The case for incentive salience. *Psychopharmacology* 191 (3): 391–431.

Berridge, K. C., and Robinson, T. E. (1998). What is the role of dopamine in reward: Hedonic impact, reward learning, or incentive salience? *Brain Research Reviews* 28: 309–369.

Berridge, K. C.,and Robinson, T. E. (2003). Parsing reward. *Trends in Neurosciences* 26 (9): 507–513.

Bouton, M. E. (2002). Context, ambiguity, and unlearning: Sources of relapse after behavioral extinction. *Biological Psychiatry* 52: 976–986.

Bouton, M. E. (2004). Context and behavioral processes in extinction. *Learning and Memory* 11 (5): 485–494.

Brass, M., and Haggard, P. (2007). To do or not to do: The neural signature of self-control. *Journal of Neuroscience* 27 (34): 9141–9145.

Buckner, R. L., and Carroll, D. C. (2007). Self-projection and the brain. *Trends in Cognitive Sciences* 11 (2): 49–57.

Caggiula, A. R., Donny, E. C., White, A. R., Chaudhri, N., Booth, S., Gharib, M. A., Hoffman, A., Perkins, K. A., and Sved, A. F. (2001). Cue dependency of nicotine self-administration and smoking. *Pharmacology, Biochemistry, and Behavior* 70 (4): 515–530.

Calu, D. J., Stalnaker, T. A., Franz, T. M., Singh, T., Shaham, Y., and Schoenbaum, G. (2007). Withdrawal from cocaine self-administration produces long-lasting deficits in orbitofrontal-dependent reversal learning in rats. *Learning and Memory* 14 (5): 325–328.

Capaldi, E. J. (1957). The effect of different amounts of alternating partial reinforcement on resistance to extinction. *American Journal of Psychology* 70 (3): 451–452.

Capaldi, E. J. (1958). The effect of different amounts of training on the resistance to extinction of different patterns of partially reinforced responses. *Journal of Comparative and Physiological Psychology* 51 (3): 367–371.

Carelli, R. M. (2002). Nucleus accumbens cell firing during goal-directed behaviors for cocaine vs. natural reinforcement. *Physiology and Behavior* 76 (3): 379–387.

Chavkin, C., James, I. F., and Goldstein, A. (1982). Dynorphin is a specific endogenous ligand of the kappa opioid receptor. *Science* 215 (4531): 413–415.

Cheer, J. F., Aragona, B. J., Heien, M. L. A. V., Seipel, A. T., Carelli, R. M., and Wightman, R. M. (2007a). Coordinated accumbal dopamine release and neural activity drive goal-directed behavior. *Neuron* 54 (2): 237–244.

Cheer, J. F., Wassum, K. M., Sombers, L. A., Heien, M. L. A. V., Ariansen, J. L., Aragona, B. J., Phillips, P. E. M., and Wightman, R. M. (2007b). Phasic dopamine release evoked by abused substances requires cannabinoid receptor activation. *Journal of Neuroscience* 27 (4): 791–795.

Childress, A. R., Ehrman, R., Rohsenow, D. J., Robbins, S. J., and O'Brien, C. P. (1992). Classically conditioned factors in drug dependence. In J. H. Lowinson, P. Ruiz, and R. B. Millma, eds., *Substance Abuse: A Comprehensive Textbook*, 56–69. Baltimore: Williams and Wilkins.

Childress, A. R., Hole, A. V., Ehrman, R. N., Robbins, S. J., McLellan, A. T., and O'Brien, C. P. (1993). Cue reactivity and cue reactivity interventions in drug dependence. *NIDA Research Monographs* 137: 73–94.

Childress, A. R., McLellan, A. T., Ehrman, R., and O'Brien, C. P. (1988). Classically conditioned responses in opioid and cocaine dependence: A role in relapse? *NIDA Research Monographs* 84: 25–43.

Chiu, P. H., Lohrenz, T. M., and Montague, P. R. (2008). Smokers' brains compute but ignore, a fictive error signal in a sequential investment task. *Nature Neuroscience* 11 (4): 514–520.

Cohen, N. J., and Squire, L. R. (1980). Preserved learning and retention of pattern-analyzing skill in amnesia: Dissociation of knowing how and knowing that. *Science* 210: 207–210.

Colwill, R. M., and Rescorla, R. A. (1990). Effect of reinforcer devaluation on discriminative control of instrumental behavior. *Journal of Experimental Psychology: Animal Behavior Processes* 16 (1): 40–47.

Corbit, L. H., and Balleine, B. W. (2000). The role of the hippocampus in instrumental conditioning. *Journal of Neuroscience* 20 (11): 4233–4239.

Corbit, L. H., Muir, J. L., and Balleine, B. W. (2001). The role of the nucleus accumbens in instrumental conditioning: Evidence of a functional dissociation between accumbens core and shell. *Journal of Neuroscience* 21 (9): 3251–3260.

Crabbe, J. C. (2002). Genetic contributions to addiction. *Annual Review of Psychology* 53 (1): 435–462.

Custer, R. L. (1984). Profile of the pathological gambler. *Journal of Clinical Psychiatry* 45 (12, sec. 2): 35–38.

Darwin, C. (1871). *The Descent of Man.* London: J. Murray.

Daw, N. D. (2003). Reinforcement learning models of the dopamine system and their behavioral implications. Ph.D. thesis, Carnegie Mellon University.

Daw, N. D., Niv, Y., and Dayan, P. (2005). Uncertainty-based competition between prefrontal and dorsolateral striatal systems for behavioral control. *Nature Neuroscience* 8: 1704–1711.

Deroche-Gamonet, V., Belin, D., and Piazza, P. V. (2004). Evidence for addiction-like behavior in the rat. *Science* 305 (5686): 1014–1017.

Devan, B. D., and White, N. M. (1999). Parallel information processing in the dorsal striatum: Relation to hippocampal function. *Journal of Neuroscience* 19 (7): 2789–2798.

De Vries, T. J., and Shippenberg, T. S. (2002). Neural systems underlying opiate addiction. *Journal of Neuroscience* 22 (9): 3321–3325.

Dickerson, M., and O'Connor, J. (2006). *Gambling as an Addictive Behavior.* Cambridge: Cambridge University Press.

Domjan, M. (1998). *The Principles of Learning and Behavior*, 4th edition. Pacific Grove: Brooks/Cole.

Doya, K. (2000). Reinforcement learning in continuous time and space. *Neural Computation* 12: 219–245.

DSM-IV-TR (2000). *Diagnostic and Statistical Manual of Mental Disorders.* Washington, D.C.: American Psychiatric Association.

Duda, R. O., Hart, P. E., and Stork, D. G. (2001). *Pattern Classification*. New York: Wiley.

Feierstein, C. E., Quirk, M. C., Uchida, N., Sosulski, D. L., and Mainen, Z. F. (2006). Representation of spatial goals in rat orbitofrontal cortex. *Neuron* 60 (4): 495–507.

Ferster, C. B, and Skinner, B. F. (1957). *Schedules of Reinforcement*. Appleton-Century-Crofts.

Frank, M. J., Moustafa, A. A., Haughey, H. M., Curran, T., and Hutchison, K. E. (2007). Genetic triple dissociation reveals multiple roles for dopamine in reinforcement learning. *Proceedings of the National Academy of Sciences* 104 (41): 16311–16316.

Fuhs, M. C., and Touretzky, D. S. (2007). Context learning in the rodent hippocampus. *Neural Computation* 19 (12): 3172–3215.

Gallistel, C. R., Fairhurst, S., and Balsam, P. (2004). Inaugural Article: The learning curve: Implications of a quantitative analysis. *Proceedings of the National Academy of Sciences, USA* 101 (36): 13124–13131.

Gardner, E. L. (1997). Brain-reward mechanisms. In J. H. Lowinson, P. Ruiz, R. B. Millman, and J. G. Langrod, eds., *Substance Abuse: A Comprehensive Textbook*, 48–96. Baltimore: Williams and Wilkins.

Gawin, F. H. (1991). Cocaine addiction: Psychology and neuropsychology. *Science* 251 (5001): 1580–1586.

German, P. W., and Fields, H. L. (2007). Rat nucleus accumbens neurons persistently encode locations associated with morphine reward. *Journal of Neurophysiology* 97 (3): 2094–2106.

Gigerenzer, G. (2001). The adaptive toolbox: Toward a darwinian rationality. *Nebraska Symposium on Motivation* 47: 113–146.

Gigerenzer, G., and Goldstein, D. G. (1996). Reasoning the fast and frugal way: Models of bounded rationality. *Psychological Review* 103: 650–669.

Gilovich, T., Griffin, D., and Kahneman, D., eds. (2002). *Heuristics and Biases: The Psychology of Intuitive Judgement*. Cambridge: Cambridge University Press.

Giraldeau, L. A., and Caraco, T. (2000). *Social Foraging Theory*. Princeton: Princeton University Press.

Goldberg, S. R., Spealman, R. D., and Goldberg, D. M. (1981). Persistent behavior at high rates maintained by intravenous self-administration of nicotine. *Science* 214: 573–575.

Goldman, D., Oroszi, G., and Ducci, F. (2005). The genetics of addictions: Uncovering the genes. *Nature Reviews Genetics* 6 (7): 521–532.

Goldman, P. S., Rosvold, H. E., and Mishkin, M. (1970). Evidence for behavioral impairment following prefrontal lobectomy in the infant monkey. *Journal of Comparative and Physiological Psychology* 70 (3): 454–463.

Goldstein, A. (2000). *Addiction: From Biology to Drug Policy*. New York: Oxford University Press.

Gould, S. J. (1980). *The Panda's Thumb*. New York: Norton.

Gould, S. J. (1983). *Hen's Teeth and Horse's Toes*. New York: Norton.

Grant, S., London, E. D., Newlin, D. B., Villemagne, V. L., Liu, X., Contoreggi, C., Phillips, R. L., Kimes, A. S., and Margolin, A. (1996). Activation of memory circuits during cue-elicited cocaine craving. *Proceedings of the National Academy of Sciences, USA* 93 (21): 12040–12045.

Gray, J., and McNaughton, N. (2000). *The Neuropsychology of Anxiety*. Oxford: Oxford University Press.

Graybiel, A. (2000). The basal ganglia. *Current Biology* 10 (14): R509–R511.

Griffiths, M. D. (1994). The role of cognitive bias and skill in fruit machine gambling. *British Journal of Psychology* 85 (3): 351–370.

Griffiths, R. R., and Woodson, P. P. (1988). Reinforcing properties of caffeine: Studies in humans and laboratory animals. *Pharmacology Biochemistry and Behavior* 29 (2): 419–427.

Grigson, P. S. (2002). Like drugs for chocolate: Separate rewards modulated by common mechanisms? *Physiology and Behavior* 76 (3): 389–395.

Grossberg, S. (1976). Adaptive pattern classification and universal recoding: I. Parallel development and coding of neural feature detectors. *Biological Cybernetics* 23: 121–134.

Gutkin, B. S., Dehaene, S., and Changeux, J. P. (2006). A neurocomputational hypothesis for nicotine addiction. *Proceedings of the National Academy of Sciences, USA* 103 (4): 1106–1111.

Harris, A. C., and Gewirtz, J. C. (2005). Acute opioid dependence: Characterizing the early adaptations underlying drug withdrawal. *Psychopharmacology* 178 (4): 353–366.

Hertz, J., Krogh, A., and Palmer, R. G. (1991). *Introduction to the Theory of Neural Computation*. Reading, MA: Addison-Wesley.

Herz, A. (1997). Endogenous opioid systems and alcohol addiction. *Psychopharmacology* 129: 99–111.

Herz, A. (1998). Opioid reward mechanisms: A key role in drug abuse? *Canadian Journal of Physiology and Pharmacology* 76 (3): 252–258.

Hikosaka, O., Nakahara, H., Rand, M. K., Sakai, K., Lu, X., Nakamura, K., Miyachi, S., and Doya, K. (1999). Parallel neural networks for learning sequential procedures. *Trends in Neurosciences* 22 (10): 464–471.

Hikosaka, O., Nakamura, K., and Nakahara, H. (2006). Basal ganglia orient eyes to reward. *Journal of Neurophysiology* 95: 567–584.

Hirsh, R. (1974). The hippocampus and contextual retrieval of information from memory: A theory. *Behavioral Biology* 12: 421–444.

Hopfield, J. J. (1982). Neural networks and physical systems with emergent collective computational abilities. *Proceedings of the National Academy of Sciences, USA* 79: 2554–2558.

Hull, C. L. (1943). *Principles of Behavior.* New York: Appleton-Century-Crofts.

Hunt, W. A. (1998). Pharmacology of alcohol. In R. E. Tarter, R. T. Ammerman, and P. J. Ott, eds., *Handbook of Substance Abuse: Neurobehavioral Pharmacology,* 7–22. New York: Plenum.

Hyman, S. E. (2005). Addiction: A disease of learning and memory. *American Journal of Psychiatry* 162: 1414–1422.

ICD-10 (1992). *International Classification of Diseases.* World Health Organization.

Isoda, M., and Hikosaka, O. (2007). Switching from automatic to controlled action by monkey medial frontal cortex. *Nature Neuroscience* 10: 240–248.

Iversen, S. D., and Mishkin, M. (1970). Perseverative interference in monkeys following selective lesions of the inferior prefrontal convexity. *Experimental Brain Research* 11 (4): 376–386.

Jaffe, J. H., Knapp, C. M., and Ciraulo, D. A. (1997). Opiates: Clinical aspects. In J. H. Lowinson, P. Ruiz, R. B. Millman, and J. G. Langrood, eds., *Substance Abuse: A Comprehensive Textbook,* 158–166. Baltimore: Williams and Wilkins.

Jensen, O., and Lisman, J. E. (1998). An oscillatory short-term memory buffer model can account for data on the Sternberg task. *Journal of Neuroscience* 18 (24): 10688–10699.

Jensen, O., and Lisman, J. E. (2005). Hippocampal sequence-encoding driven by a cortical multi-item working memory buffer. *Trends in Neurosciences* 28 (2): 67–72.

Jog, M. S., Kubota, Y., Connolly, C. I., Hillegaart, V., and Graybiel, A. M. (1999). Building neural representations of habits. *Science* 286: 1746–1749.

Johnson, A., and Redish, A. D. (2005). Hippocampal replay contributes to within session learning in a temporal difference reinforcement learning model. *Neural Networks* 18 (9): 1163–1171.

Johnson, A., and Redish, A. D. (2007). Neural ensembles in CA3 transiently encode paths forward of the animal at a decision point. *Journal of Neuroscience* 27 (45): 12176–12189.

Kahneman, D., Slovic, P., and Tversky, A., eds. (1982). *Judgement under Uncertainty: Heuristics and Biases.* Cambridge: Cambridge University Press.

Kahneman, D., and Tversky, A. (1979). Prospect theory: an analysis of decision under risk. *Econometrica* 47 (2): 263–292.

Kahneman, D., and Tversky, A., eds. (2000). *Choices, Values, and Frames.* Cambridge: Cambridge University Press.

Kalivas, P. W., and Volkow, N. D. (2005). The neural basis of addiction: A pathology of motivation and choice. *American Journal of Psychiatry* 162: 1403–1413.

Keath, J. R., Iacoviello, M. P., Barrett, L. E., Mansvelder, H. D., and McGehee, D. S. (2007). Differential modulation by nicotine of substantia nigra versus ventral tegmental area dopamine neurons. *Journal of Neurophysiology* 98 (6): 3388–3396.

Kelley, A. E. (2004). Memory and addiction: Shared neural circuitry and molecular mechanisms. *Neuron* 44: 161–179.

Kelley, A. E., Bakshi, V. P., Haber, S. N., Steininger, T. L., Will, M. J., and Zhang, M. (2002). Opioid modulation of taste hedonics within the ventral striatum. *Physiology and Behavior* 76 (3): 365–377.

Kéri, S. (2003). The cognitive neuroscience of category learning. *Brain Research Reviews* 43 (1): 85–109.

Kieffer, B. L. (1999). Opioids: First lessons from knockout mice. *Trends in Pharmacological Sciences* 20 (1): 19–26.

Killcross, S., and Coutureau, E. (2003). Coordination of actions and habits in the medial prefrontal cortex of rats. *Cerebral Cortex* 13 (8): 400–408.

Kirby, K. N., Petry, N. M., and Bickel, W. K. (1999). Heroin addicts have higher discount rates for delayed rewards than non-drug-using controls. *Journal of Experimental Psychology: General* 128 (1): 78–87.

Knopman, D. L., and Nissen, M. J. (1991). Procedural learning is impaired in Huntington's disease: Evidence from the serial reaction time task. *Neuropsychologia* 29 (3): 245–254.

Knowlton, B. J., Mangels, J. A., and Squire, L. R. (1996). A neostriatal habit learning system in humans. *Science* 273: 1399–1402.

Koene, R. A., Gorchetchnikov, A., Cannon, R. C., and Hasselmo, M. E. (2003). Modeling goal-directed spatial navigation in the rat based on physiological data from the hippocampal formation. *Neural Networks* 16 (5–6): 577–584.

Kohonen, T. (1980). *Content-Addressable Memories*. New York: Springer.

Koob, G. F., and Le Moal, M. (2006). *Neurobiology of Addiction*. London: Elsevier Academic Press.

Kuhar, M. J., Ritz, M. C., and Sharkey, J. (1988). Cocaine receptors on dopamine transporters mediate cocaine-reinforced behavior. In D. Clouet, K. Asghar, and R. Brown, eds., *Mechanisms of Cocaine Abuse and Toxicity*, 14–22. Rockville, MD: National Institute on Drug Abuse.

Lakoff, G. (1990). *Women, Fire, and Dangerous Things*. Chicago: University of Chicago Press.

Langer, E. J., and Roth, J. (1975). Heads I win, tails it's chance: The illusion of control as a function of the sequence of outcomes in a purely chance task. *Journal of Personality and Social Psychology* 32 (6): 951–955.

Lavoie, A. M., and Mizumori, S. J. Y. (1994). Spatial-, movement-, and reward-sensitive discharge by medial ventral striatum neurons in rats. *Brain Research* 638: 157–168.

Lenoir, M., and Ahmed, S. H. (2007). Supply of a nondrug substitute reduces escalated heroin consumption. *Neuropsychopharmacology* (published online October 2007).

Lenoir, M., Serre, F., Cantin, L., and Ahmed, S. H. (2007). Intense sweetness surpasses cocaine reward. PLoS ONE 2(8): e698.

Leshner, A. I. (1997). Addiction is a brain disease, and it matters. *Science* 278 (5335): 45–47.

Lesieur, H. (1977). *The Chase: Career of the Compulsive Gambler*. Norwell, MA: Anchor Press.

Levine, A. S., and Billington, C. J. (2004). Opioids as agents of reward-related feeding: A consideration of the evidence. *Physiology and Behavior* 82: 57–61.

Lohrenz, T., McCabe, K., Camerer, C. F., and Montague, P. R. (2007). Neural signature of fictive learning signals in a sequential investment task. *Proceedings of the National Academy of Sciences, USA* 104 (22): 9493–9498.

Lowinson, J. H., Ruiz, P., Millman, R. B., and Langrod, J. G., eds. (1997). *Substance Abuse: A Comprehensive Textbook*, 3rd edition. Baltimore: Williams and Wilkins.

Mackintosh, N. J. (1974). *The Psychology of Animal Learning*. Academic Press.

Madden, G., Bickel, W., and Critchfield, T., eds. (in press). *Impulsivity: Theory, Science, and Neuroscience of Discounting*. Washington, D.C.: APA books.

Mansvelder, H. D., Keath, J. R., and McGehee, D. S. (2002). Synaptic mechanisms underlie nicotine-induced excitability of brain reward areas. *Neuron* 33: 905–919.

Mansvelder, H. D., and McGehee, D. S. (2002). Cellular and synaptic mechanisms of nicotine addiction. *Journal of Neurobiology* 53 (4): 606–617.

Maynard-Smith, J. (1982). *Evolution and the Theory of Games*. Cambridge: Cambridge University Press.

Meunzinger, K. F. (1938). Vicarious trial and error at a point of choice. I. A general survey of its relation to learning efficiency. *Journal of Genetic Psychology* 53: 75–86.

Meyer, R., and Mirin, S. (1979). *The Heroin Stimulus*. New York: Plenum.

Mintz, S. W. (1986). *Sweetness and Power*. New York: Viking.

Mogenson, G. J., Jones, D. L., and Yim, C. Y. (1980). From motivation to action: Functional interface between the limbic system and the motor system. *Progress in Neurobiology* 14: 69–97.

Montague, P. R., Dayan, P., Person, C., and Sejnowski, T. J. (1995). Bee foraging in uncertain environments using predictive Hebbian learning. *Nature* 377 (6551): 725–728.

Montague, P. R., Dayan, P., and Sejnowski, T. J. (1996). A framework for mesencephalic dopamine systems based on predictive Hebbian learning. *Journal of Neuroscience* 16 (5): 1936–1947.

Morris, R. G. M. (1981). Spatial localization does not require the presence of local cues. *Learning and Motivation* 12: 239–260.

Mucha, R. F., and Herz, A. (1985). Motivational properties of kappa and mu opioid receptor agonists studied with place and taste preference conditioning. *Psychopharmacology* 86: 274–280.

Narcotics Anonymous. http://www.na.org. (Accessed on December 6, 2008.)

Negus, S., Henriksen, S., Mattox, A., Pasternak, G., Portoghese, P., Takemori, A., Weinger, M., and Koob, G. (1993). Effect of antagonists selective for mu, delta, and kappa opioid receptors on the reinforcing effects of heroin in rats. *Journal of Pharmacology and Experimental Therapeutics* 265 (3): 1245–1252.

Nelson, A., and Killcross, S. (2006). Amphetamine exposure enhances habit formation. *Journal of Neuroscience* 26 (14): 3805–3812.

Nicola, S. M., Yun, I. A., Wakabayashi, K. T., and Fields, H. L. (2004a). Cue-evoked firing of nucleus accumbens neurons encodes motivational significance during a discriminative stimulus task. *Journal of Neurophysiology* 91 (4): 1840–1865.

Nicola, S. M., Yun, I. A., Wakabayashi, K. T., and Fields, H. L. (2004b). Fiiring of nucleus accumbens neurons during the consummatory phase of a discriminative stimulus task depends on previous reward predictive cues. *Journal of Neurophysiology* 91 (4): 1866–1882.

O'Brien, C. P., Childress, A. R., McLellan, A. T., and Ehrman, R. (1992). A learning model of addiction. In C. P. O'Brien and J. H. Jaffe, eds., *Research Publications: Association for Research in Nervous and Mental Disease*, vol. 70, 157–177. New York: Raven Press.

O'Brien, C. P., Testa, T., O'Brien, T. J., Brady, J. P., and Wells, B. (1977). Conditioned narcotic withdrawal in humans. *Science* 195: 1000–1002.

O'Doherty, J., Dayan, P., Schultz, J., Deichmann, R., Friston, K., and Dolan, R. J. (2004). Dissociable roles of ventral and dorsal striatum in instrumental conditioning. *Science* 304 (5669): 452–454.

O'Keefe, J., and Nadel, L. (1978). *The Hippocampus as a Cognitive Map*. Oxford: Clarendon Press.

O'Reilly, R. C., and McClelland, J. L. (1994). Hippocampal conjunctive encoding, storage, and recall: Avoiding a trade-off. *Hippocampus* 4 (6): 661–682.

Oscar-Berman, M., and Marinkovic, K. (2003). Alcoholism and the brain: An overview. *Alcohol Research and Health* 27 (2): 125–134.

Packard, M. G., and McGaugh, J. L. (1992). Double dissociation of fornix and caudate nucleus lesions on acquisition of two water maze tasks: Further evidence for multiple memory systems. *Behavioral Neuroscience* 106 (3): 439–446.

Packard, M. G., and McGaugh, J. L. (1996). Inactivation of hippocampus or caudate nucleus with lidocaine differentially affects expression of place and response learning. *Neurobiology of Learning and Memory* 65: 65–72.

Padoa-Schioppa, C., and Assad, J. A. (2006). Neurons in the orbitofrontal cortex encode economic value. *Nature* 441: 223–226.

Parke, J., and Griffiths, M. (2004). Gambling addiction and the evolution of the "near miss." *Addiction Research and Theory* 12 (5): 407–411.

Pavlov, I. (1927). *Conditioned Reflexes*. Oxford: Oxford University Press.

Pelchat, M. L. (2002). Of human bondage: Food craving, obsession, compulsion, and addiction. *Physiology and Behavior* 76 (3): 347–352.

Peoples, L. L., Uzwiak, A. J., Gee, F., and West, M. O. (1999). Tonic firing of rat nucleus accumbens neurons: Changes during the first two weeks of daily cocaine self-administration sessions. *Brain Research* 822: 231–236.

Pidoplichko, V. I., DeBiasi, M., Williams, J. T., and Dani, J. A. (1997). Nicotine activates and desensitizes midbrain dopamine neurons. *Nature* 390: 401–404.

Plassmann, H., O'Doherty, J., and Rangel, A. (2007). Orbitofrontal cortex encodes willingness to pay in everyday economic transactions. *Journal of Neuroscience* 27 (37): 9984–9988.

Poldrack, R. A., and Packard, M. G. (2003). Competition among multiple memory systems: Converging evidence from animal and human studies. *Neuropsychologia* 41: 245–251.

Potenza, M. N., Kosten, T. R., and Rounsaville, B. J. (2001). Pathological gambling. *Journal of the American Medical Association* 286 (2): 141–144.

Ragozzino, M. E., Jih, J., and Tzavos, A. (2002). Involvement of the dorsomedial striatum in behavioral flexibility: Role of muscarinic cholinergic receptors. *Brain Research* 953 (1–2): 205–214.

Ragozzino, M. E., Ragozzino, K. E., Mizumori, S. J. Y., and Kesner, R. P. (2002). The role of the dorsomedial striatum in behavioral flexibility for response and visual cue discrimination learning. *Behavioral Neuroscience* 116: 105–115.

Ramus, S. J., Davis, J. B., Donahue, R. J., Discenza, C. B., and Waite, A. A. (2007). Interactions between the orbitofrontal cortex and hippocampal memory system during the storage of long-term memory. *Annals of the New York Academy of Sciences* 1121: 216–231.

Raylu, N., and Oei, T. P. S. (2002). Pathological gambling a comprehensive review. *Clinical Psychology Review* 22 (7): 1009–1061.

Redish, A. D. (1999). *Beyond the Cognitive Map: From Place Cells to Episodic Memory*. Cambridge, MA: MIT Press.

Redish, A. D. (2004). Addiction as a computational process gone awry. *Science* 306 (5703): 1944–1947.

Redish, A. D., Jensen, S., and Johnson, A. (2008). A unified framework for addiction: Vulnerabilities in the decision process. *Behavioral and Brain Sciences* 31: 415–437, with discussion and response 437–487.

Redish, A. D., Jensen, S., Johnson, A., and Kurth-Nelson, Z. (2007). Reconciling reinforcement learning models with behavioral extinction and renewal: Implications for addiction, relapse, and problem gambling. *Psychological Review* 114 (3): 784–805.

Redish, A. D., and Johnson, A. (2007). A computational model of craving and obsession. *Annals of the New York Academy of Sciences* 1104 (1): 324–339.

Ritz, M. C., Lamb, R. J., Goldberg, S. R., and Kuhar, M. J. (1987). Cocaine receptors on dopamine transporters are related to self-administration of cocaine. *Science* 237: 1219–1223.

Rivlin, G. (2004). The chrome-shiny, lights-flashing, wheel-spinning, touch-screened, drewcarey-wisecracking, video-playing, sound events -packed, pulse-quickening bandit. *New York Times*, May 9.

Robinson, T. E. (2004). Neuroscience: Addicted rats. *Science* 305 (5686): 951–953.

Sakagami, M., and Pan, X. (2007). Functional role of the ventrolateral prefrontal cortex in decision making. *Current Opinion in Neurobiology* 17 (2): 228–233.

Samejima, K., Ueda, Y., Doya, K., and Kimura, M. (2005). Representation of action-specific reward values in the striatum. *Science* 310 (5752): 1337–1340.

Schacter, D. L. (2001). *The Seven Sins of Memory*. Boston: Houghton Mifflin.

Schmitz, J. M., Schneider, N. G., and Jarvik, M. E. (1997). Nicotine. In J. H. Lowinson, P. Ruiz, R. B. Millman, and J. G. Langrod, eds., *Substance Abuse: A Comprehensive Textbook*, 276–294. Baltimore: Williams and Wilkins.

Schmitzer-Torbert, N. C., and Redish, A. D. (2002). Development of path stereotypy in a single day in rats on a multiple-T maze. *Archives Italiennes de Biologie* 140: 295–301.

Schmitzer-Torbert, N. C., and Redish, A. D. (2004). Neuronal activity in the rodent dorsal striatum in sequential navigation: Separation of spatial and reward responses on the multiple-T task. *Journal of Neurophysiology* 91 (5): 2259–2272.

Schmitzer-Torbert, N. C., and Redish, A. D. (2008). Task-dependent encoding of space and events by striatal neurons is dependent on neural subtype. *Neuroscience* 153 (2): 349–360.

Schoenbaum, G., and Roesch, M. (2005). Orbitofrontal cortex, associative learning, and expectancies. *Neuron* 47 (5): 633–636.

Schoenbaum, G., Roesch, M., and Stalnaker, T. A. (2006). Orbitofrontal cortex, decision making, and drug addiction. *Trends in Neurosciences* 29: 116–124.

Schoenbaum, G., Setlow, B., and Ramus, S. J. (2003). A systems approach to orbitofrontal cortex function: Recordings in rat orbitofrontal cortex reveal interactions with different learning systems. *Behavioural Brain Research* 146 (1–2): 19–29.

Schultz, W. (1998). Predictive reward signal of dopamine neurons. *Journal of Neurophysiology* 80: 1–27.

Schultz, W. (2002). Getting formal with dopamine and reward. *Neuron* 36: 241–263.

Schultz, W., Dayan, P., and Montague, R. (1997). A neural substrate of prediction and reward. *Science* 275: 1593–1599.

Schultz, W., and Romo, R. (1992). Role of primate basal ganglia and frontal cortex in the internal generation of movements: I. Preparatory activity in the anterior striatum. *Experimental Brain Research* 91: 363–384.

Schultz, W., Tremblay, L., and Hollerman, J. R. (2003). Changes in behavior-related neuronal activity in the striatum during learning. *Trends in Neurosciences* 26 (6): 321–328.

Siegel, S. (1988). Drug anticipation and the treatment of dependence. *NIDA Research Monographs* 84: 1–24.

Siegel, S., Hinson, R. E., Krank, M. D., and McCully, J. (1982). Heroin "overdose" death: Contribution of drug-associated environmental cues. *Science* 216 (4544): 436–437.

Simon, H. (1955). A behavioral model of rational choice. *Quarterly Journal of Economics* 69: 99–118.

Sozou, P. D. (1998). On hyperbolic discounting and uncertain hazard rates. *Royal Society London* B 265: 2015–2020.

Squire, L. R. (1987). *Memory and Brain*. New York: Oxford University Press.

Stalnaker, T. A., Roesch, M. R., Franz, T. M., Burke, K. A., and Schoenbaum, G. (2006). Abnormal associative encoding in orbitofrontal neurons in cocaine-experienced rats during decision-making. *European Journal of Neuroscience* 24 (9): 2643–2653.

Stephens, D. W., and Krebs, J. R. (1987). *Foraging Theory*. Princeton: Princeton University Press.

Stoppard, T. (1991). *Rosencrantz and Guildenstern Are Dead*. New York: Grove Press. First performed 1967.

Stuber, G. D., Wightman, R. M., and Carelli, R. M. (2005). Extinction of cocaine self-administration reveals functionally and temporally distinct dopaminergic signals in the nucleus accumbens. *Neuron* 46: 661–669.

Suri, R. E., and Schultz, W. (1999). A neural network model with dopamine-like reinforcement signal that learns a spatial delayed response task. *Neuroscience* 91 (3): 871–890.

Sutton, R. S., ed. (1992). Special issue on reinforcement learning, vol. 8(3/4) of *Machine Learning*. Boston: Kluwer Academic Publishers.

Sutton, R. S., and Barto, A. G. (1998). *Reinforcement Learning: An Introduction*. Cambridge, MA: MIT Press.

Sylvain, C., Ladouceur, R., and Biosvert, J. M. (1997). Cognitive and behavioral treatment of pathological gambling: A controlled study. *Journal of Consulting and Clinical Psychology* 65 (5): 727–732.

Tanaka, S. C., Doya, K., Okada, G., Ueda, K., Okamoto, Y., and Yamawaki, S. (2004). Prediction of immediate and future rewards differentially recruits cortico-basal ganglia loops. *Nature Neuroscience* 7: 887–893.

Tarter, R. E., Ammerman. R. T., and Ott, P. J., eds. (1998). *Handbook of Substance Abuse: Neurobehavioral Pharmacology*. New York: Plenum.

Tolman, E. C. (1932). *Purposive Behavior in Animals and Men*. New York: Appleton-Century-Crofts.

Tolman, E. C. (1938). The determiners of behavior at a choice point. *Psychological Review* 45 (1): 1–41.

Tolman, E. C. (1939). Prediction of vicarious trial and error by means of the schematic sowbug. *Psychological Review* 46: 318–336.

Tolman, E. C. (1948). Cognitive maps in rats and men. *Psychological Review* 55: 189–208.

Toneatto, T., Blitz-Miller, T., Calderwood, K., Dragonetti, R., and Tsanos, A. (1997). Cognitive distortions in heavy gambling. *Journal of Gambling Studies* 13 (3): 253–266.

van der Meer, M. A. A., and Redish, A. D. (2009). Covert expectation-of-reward in rat ventral striatum at decision points *Frontiers in Integrative Neuroscience* 3 (1): 1–15.

Vanderschuren, L. J. M. J., and Everitt, B. J. (2004). Drug seeking becomes compulsive after prolonged cocaine self-administration. *Science* 305 (5686): 1017–1019.

van Ree, J. M., Gerrits, M. A. F. M., and Vanderschuren, L. J. M. J. (1999). Opioids, reward and addiction: An encounter of biology, psychology, and medicine. *Pharmacological Reviews* 51 (2): 341–396.

Volkow, N., and Li, T. K. (2005). The neuroscience of addiction. *Nature Neuroscience* 8 (11): 1429–1430.

Volkow, N. D., and Fowler, J. S. (2000). Addiction, a disease of compulsion and drive: Involvement of the orbitofrontal cortex. *Cerebral Cortex* 10 (3): 318–325.

Volkow, N. D., Fowler, J. S., and Wang, G. J. (2003). The addicted human brain: Insights from imaging studies. *Journal of Clinical Investigation* 111 (10): 1444–1451.

Wagenaar, W. A. (1988). *Paradoxes of Gambling Behavior*. London: Erlbaum.

Walker, M. B. (1992). Irrational thinking among slot machine players. *Journal of Gambling Studies* 8 (3): 245–261.

Weeks, J. R. (1962). Experimental morphine addiction: Method for automatic intravenous injections in unrestrained rats. *Science* 138 (3537): 143–144.

Weiner, J. (1995). *The Beak of the Finch: A Story of Evolution in Our Time*. New York: Vintage.

White, A. M. (2003). What happened? Alcohol, memory blackouts, and the brain. *Alcohol Research and Health* 27 (2): 186–196.

White, N. M., and McDonald, R. J. (2002). Multiple parallel memory systems in the brain of the rat. *Neurobiology of Learning and Memory* 77: 125–184.

Wilson, H. R., and Cowan, J. D. (1973). A mathematical theory of the functional dynamics of cortical and thalamic tissue. *Kybernetik* 13: 55–80.

Wise, R. A. (1989). Opiate reward: Sites and substrates. *Neuroscience and Biobehavioral Reviews* 13 (2–3): 129–133.

Woolverton, W. L. (1992). Cocaine self-administration: Pharmacology and behavior. *NIDA Research Monographs* 124: 189–202.

Yin, H. H., and Knowlton, B. J. (2006). The role of the basal ganglia in habit formation. *Nature Reviews Neuroscience* 7: 464–476.

Yin, H. H., Ostlund, S. B., Knowlton, B. J., and Balleine, B. W. (2005). The role of the dorsomedial striatum in instrumental conditioning. *European Journal of Neuroscience* 22 (2): 513–523.

Zilli, E. A., and Hasselmo, M. E. (2008). Modeling the role of working memory and episodic memory in behavioral tasks. *Hippocampus* 18 (2): 193–209.

5 Economic Models of Pathological Gambling

Don Ross

1 Introduction

Pathological gambling (PG) is a kind of "ideal puzzle" for the economic model of the consumer. The pathological gambler takes pains to engage in activity that transparently has negative expected returns if utility varies positively with money. She also, typically, spends further resources on commitment devices designed to interfere with her gambling. These properties together describe an agent that is a kind of perfect foil for the rationally maximizing consumer. Recently, aspects of the neuropathology underlying the strange economic agency of the pathological gambler are becoming better understood. Thus PG is an ideal test-bed phenomenon for working out relationships between economic modeling based on constrained optimization of utility and the new neuroscience of behavior.

This chapter will proceed as follows. In section 2 I will explain why PG raises a puzzle for the standard microeconomic modeling framework, and why this puzzle potentially sheds light on deep issues at the intersection of economics and neuroscience. Section 3 outlines the prevailing neuroeconomic model of reward learning in the brain's dopaminergic system. In section 4 I indicate grounds, based on this model, for suggesting that PG may be the basic, instead of a derivative or merely honorary, form of addiction. Section 5 returns to economics, surveying currently popular economic models of addiction and indicating why we are at an impasse with respect to choosing amongst them. Section 6 proposes a path for further economic model development, based in neuroscience and inspired by the proposal to regard PG as the core manifestation of addiction.

2 PG and Economic Behavior

PG is widely spoken of as a form of addiction. Popularly, this is often regarded as a mere analogy. On the basis of evidence from neuroscience (to be discussed later), such an understanding of the association between PG and classic (substance) addictions is too weak. People suffering from "full-blown" PG—that is, people who are preoccupied with gambling on a daily basis and find it dominating (and typically ruining) the rest of their lives—show signature brain properties identical to those that mark cocaine addicts. Ross et al. (2008) argue that PG is in fact the core, "baseline" form of addiction, with each distinctive substance addiction best modeled as a complicating case of gambling addiction.

Based on the arguments by Ross et al. (2008), I will make the following two assumptions. First, there is a *qualitative* difference between addicted gamblers and people who merely occasionally lose more money at gambling than they or their families consider ratifiable *ex post*. That is, gambling addiction does not simply lie on one end of a continuum that shades gradually into mere intermittent reckless wagering. I will reserve the term "PG" as designating the condition of people who suffer from an observable brain disorder to be described below. It may be thought that this decision with respect to classification automatically takes PG out of the domain of economics and deposits it into the domain of neuroscience alone. Part of the point of this chapter is to show why this is not so. Second, an implication of this classification policy is that PG may be a relatively minor public health problem, probably affecting less than 1% of any population that has been rigorously surveyed for prevalence. (Because I am interpreting "rigorously" very stringently, I allude here to only a small sample of surveys of rather few global populations: Australia, New Zealand, the United Kingdom, and a few Canadian provinces and American states.) Nevertheless, one available motivation for studying PG is its relevance for modeling a range of much more prevalent behavioral patterns—including addiction in general, which is surely a major public health issue on nearly anyone's evaluative scale.

The utility-maximizing agent of standard microeconomic theory is held to be "rational" in the sense of having intertemporally consistent preferences. This agent will, up to the limits of the accuracy of her information about the consumption opportunities her environment will provide, allocate her resources over time in such a way that she'll get the highest possible welfare over the course of her life as an agent. In this framework, the economic analyst interprets chronic impulsivity and addiction as expressions of preferences that, given the distribution of opportunity costs in the world, happen to make the agent's life hard. If we see a person waste away from alcoholism, application of the model directs us to infer that this person considers drunkenness to be worth very high opportunity costs. Like any other utility maximizer, she gets as much welfare overall as is possible for her, given this preference. That she becomes less and less well off over time (against her own subjective reference point) is because alcohol consumption causes tolerance to increase, so the opportunity cost of the same high, for which her preference must persist lest she exhibit inconsistency, rises steadily during the history of drinking. In this frame, so far as the alcoholic's harm to herself is concerned, the only policy response by others that isn't cruel and oppressive is to try to avoid unnecessary increases in the price of drinks, and to help her minimize her opportunity costs by assisting her to avoid situations that are potentially dangerous or embarrassing. It would make no moral sense in this framework for others to help the agent avoid alcohol, since (once potential harm to second and third parties is minimized) this would just amount to lowering her welfare. This way of applying the traditional economic model of utility maximization to addiction was developed in formal detail by Becker (1976) and Becker and Murphy (1988).

This model unfortunately mispredicts the typical course of addiction. Most addicts don't just consume their substance of abuse until they've run out of all resources due to their high preference for the substance persisting as their budget runs down. Instead, most of them spend resources trying to stop consuming their substance of abuse. It isn't impossible for models like Becker's to accommodate this. One might conjecture, for example, that some or most addicts periodically stop consumption so they can recalibrate their tolerance levels and then temporarily enjoy their highs less expensively.[1] This move requires the expected-utility-maximizing account of addiction to furnish a special explanation of why most addicts eventually successfully quit. Rational-addict theories *must* infer from this that addicts did not initially know that addiction was going to be bad, and only learned this through experiencing lower welfare levels than they expected. Again, this is possible; but then this is difficult to reconcile with the strong tendency of addicts to *relapse*. We must suppose on the one hand that each time an alcoholic stops drinking but then relapses, she's aiming to get drunk more cheaply for a while. But then, on the other hand, we must hypothesize that when she at last stops once and for all, this was because she *finally* realized that she was doing herself more harm than good. If she never stops once and for all, we have to suppose that she was *not* doing herself more harm than good, in her own terms. Thus, to capture addiction in a traditional economic model, it seems we must characterize the most common course of addiction as involving a radical psychological discontinuity between unsuccessful and successful attempts at quitting: the former are for the sake of enhanced enjoyment of the addiction, and the latter result from a decision to abandon this enjoyment. Unfortunately for the ease of modeling, this psychological hypothesis is entirely ad hoc and has no empirical evidence in its favor. The distressed addict must be considered either ignorant or inconsistent.[2]

There is a straightforward general strategy for economically modeling inconsistent people. This is to drop the assumption that the relevant economic agent is identical with a whole person's whole biography; the person can be broken up into interacting subagents on either or both synchronic or diachronic dimensions (Strotz 1956; Schelling 1978, 1980, 1984; Ainslie 1992, 2001; Ross 2005, forthcoming). An analogy can be drawn here between people and countries. We all know that countries often behave irrationally—erecting self-harming barriers to imports, for example, or alternately debauching the fiscus and enforcing unpopular belt-tightening shocks—due to the interactions of rational citizens acting in pursuit of their parochial interests. Nevertheless, for many purposes, especially macroeconomic policy analysis, economists model countries as agents.

If the person is divided into agents synchronically, she becomes a *community* of agents. If the person is divided diachronically, she becomes a *sequence* of agents. In either case, we model the whole person using game theory: her so-called *molar* behavior is treated as a dynamic equilibrium of bargaining games among synchronic or diachronic agents (or, in principle, both). Given any set of assumptions weaker than perfect information and rational expectations, one can build a game to rationalize any observed outcome as a Nash equilibrium. Thus the problem with breaking the person into subagents is the opposite of the problem we face when we leave the person's agency unified. In the latter case, we can't find any model that handles all of the data about addiction at once. With the former approach, we get a plethora of models among which behavioral data don't decide.

In earlier work (Ross 2005, 2006; Ross et al. 2008) I have discussed the relationship between *picoeconomics* and *neuroeconomics*. The term "picoeconomics" was coined by Ainslie (1992) to denote applications of game theory to multiagent models of intertemporal inconsistency as described above. The identities of picoeconomic subpersonal agents are directly inferred from goals attributed at the personal scale. Thus, for example, a person trying to quit smoking may have her behavior explained as the result of interaction between an agent interested in having a cigarette and another agent that prefers to quit. The first agent might strengthen its prospects by forming a coalition with an agent interested in going to the bar, where a smoking lapse is more likely, while the more prudent agent might advance its cause by teaming up with an interest in going jogging. Whereas picoeconomics thus begins from the level of manifest behavior, neuroeconomics (Glimcher 2003; Montague and Berns 2002; Montague, King-Cassas, and Cohen 2006) appeals to the ontology of anatomical and functional brain areas developed by neuroscience and identifies subpersonal agents with functionally delineated groups of neurons (especially neurotransmitter systems). These agents also cooperate against a general background of conflict over a scarce resource, namely blood hemoglobin flow. The utility functions of these units are implicit under a linear or dynamic programming interpretation of the algorithms they compute when physically healthy. Determination of these algorithms, mainly by comparing mathematical models with neuroimaging data, is the basic activity of the neuroeconomist.

The existence of two strategies for dividing the person into subagents is methodologically helpful, because it potentially allows us to use one family of models as a source of constraints on the other. Picoeconomic agents are identified "top down," from what psychologists call the "molar" level. Neuroeconomic agents are identified "bottom up," from what psychologists call the "molecular" level. We cannot simply assume straightforward *reduction* of picoeconomic agents to neuroeconomic ones because their utility functions don't range over the same domains: picoeconomic agents have utility functions over returns to molar-level behavioral alternatives, whereas neuroeconomic agents simply compete to maximize their own activity levels. Nevertheless, choice among neuroeconomic models based on brain data offers a potential basis for selection among picoeconomic models, as we will see.

Suppose we conceptualize addiction generally, and PG specifically, as disorders of consumption scheduling. This may ultimately be a simplification, but it is the natural simplification from which *economic* modeling begins. In neuroeconomics, this directs our attention to the so-called *reward system* in the brain, which may be roughly identified with the dopaminergic neurotransmitter system that projects from midbrain areas to orbitofrontal and prefrontal cortex. The evolved task of this system is to comparatively value alternative allocations of attention, motor response and consumption, which at this level of analysis are seamlessly integrated rather than separated. Models here are algorithms by which the system is taken to estimate the expected opportunity costs of attending to one stimulus rather than another and of preparing one motor response rather than another. In the next section I will outline the basic neuroeconomic model of the reward system. Subsequently I will describe an account of PG as a hysteresis response of the system thus modeled.

3   The Neuroeconomics of Reward

Neuroscientists individuate "systems" in the brain by identifying generic functional responses with relatively encapsulated neurotransmitter pathways. The reward system is distinguished as a pathway that transmits signals using the neurotransmitter dopamine. Activity in midbrain areas that people share with other vertebrates, the ventral tegmental area (VTA) and pars compacta of substantia nigra (SNpc), releases dopamine in response to *surprising* magnitudes of *learned* contingencies. These signals project most directly to the ventral striatum (VS) and especially to the nucleus accumbens (NAcc). For reasons to be explained later, persistently high concentrations of dopamine in NAcc are a basic neural signature of addiction. The reward system's dopamine signal also projects to prefrontal cortex (PFC), where it appears to produce, at least in nonaddicts, a serotonin signal that acts as an opponent process. I will say more about this opposition later.

fMRI evidence (McClure, Daw, and Montague 2003) strongly suggests that the reward system implements *temporal difference learning* (henceforth "TD") (Sutton and Bartow 1998). This denotes a family of functions that relate a situation at a particular time s_t to a time-discounted sum of expected rewards (idealized as numeric measures r of received utility) that can be earned into the future. Suppose, following McClure, Daw, and Montague (2003), that t, $t+1$, $t+2$, etc. represent times on some arbitrary measurement scale. Then the TD equation is

$$V^*(s_t) = E[r_t + \gamma r_{t+1} + \gamma^2 r_{t+2} + \gamma^3 r_{t+3} + \cdots]$$

which we close by writing

$$V^*(s_t) = E[r_t + \gamma V^*(s_{t+1})].$$

This describes the procedure by which the reward-system learning algorithm continuously inputs new information to keep refining its estimate of V^* to get a particular stream of actual temporal valuations V. From this we can define a measure δ of the extent to which the value estimates of two successive states and a reward experienced by the system are consistent with one another:

$$\delta(t) = r_t + \gamma V(s_{t+1}) - V(s_t),$$

where δ is an error signal that pushes $V(s)$ toward better estimates as it gets more data. If $V(s_{t+1})$ turns out to be better than expected, then $\delta(t)$ will be positive, thus indicating that $V(s_t)$ needs to be adjusted upward. If $V(s_{t+1})$ turns out to be worse than expected, $\delta(t)$ will be negative and $V(s_t)$ will be adjusted downward. If $\delta(t) = 0$ then of course no learning occurs.

The reward system appears to integrate all of the following functions: (i) learning environmental cues that predict reward, (ii) learning comparative values of rewards, (iii) focusing attention on cues that predict rewards, and (iv) motivating the system to act on the basis of these cues (thanks to projection from the dopamine system to motor neurons). It is currently unclear whether it does so by bolting together a TD (or similar) learning algorithm with a separate algorithm for estimating reward rate (as in Daw 2003), or by implementing a single more complex rule, as in the Predictor-Valuation (PV) model of Montague and Berns (2002). Given the possibilities left open by present empirical knowledge, we can treat the latter either as a direct molecular account of one learning process, or as an account one level up in the molar direction of a vector function that decomposes into more molecular processes of rate estimation and temporal point estimation.

The PV model is characterized as follows. Suppose $R(x, n)$ estimates the value of a reward distributed at various possible times $x, y, z, \ldots, n$ in the future, scaled according to the uncertainty attending to the intervals between the estimation point and each time, as in:

$$R(x, n; D) = \int_{-\infty}^{+\infty} dy\, G(x - y, (x - n)D) r(y)$$

where $G(z, b) = (2\pi b)^{-1/2} \exp\{-z^2/2b\}$ and D is a constant. Then the value $F(n)$ the brain attaches to getting a particular predictor signal at perceptual time n is given by:

$$F(n) = \int_{n}^{+\infty} dx\, e^{-q(x-n)} \int_{-\infty}^{+\infty} dy\, G(x - y_1(x - n)D)\rho(y) = \int_{n}^{+\infty} dx\{e^{-q(x-n)}\}\{R(x, n; D)$$

$$= \int_{n}^{+\infty} dx\ \{\text{discount future time } x \text{ relative to perceptual time } n\}$$

$$\times \{\text{diffused version of reward estimate } \rho(x) \text{ for some } x \text{ and } n\}$$

Interestingly, as Montague and Berns point out, this functional form corresponds to the Black-Scholes model of portfolio option pricing. This helps to make vivid the *economic* character of the processes as modeled by neuroeconomics. PV is essentially a model of the reward system's estimate of the expected opportunity costs of attending to one stimulus rather than another and of preparing one motor response rather than another. (It seems that, in light of the brain's architecture, these opportunity costs can't be factored out separately.)

4   Neuroeconomics of Addiction and PG

PV describes the reward system as essentially a consumer of *micro-scale novelty*—that is, of favorable contrasts in stimulus timing and magnitude relative to baselines established by regularities in experience. A useful image here is of a kitten drawn along by a person dangling and jerking a string in front of its eyes (useful also for the point that the kitten would lose interest if the string jerked too metronomically—perhaps, in evolutionary terms, because this is indicative of the stimulus not being alive). Given the reward system's integration of so many basic inputs to behavior—attention, salience persistence, valuation, and motor priming—one is naturally led to raise the following question: why aren't most whole people (i.e., the collections of the subagents) driven by their dopamine responses to be myopic novelty seekers?

The answer, hinted at earlier, is that opponent systems with different utility functions usually prevent the reward system from seizing exclusive control of behavior. Circuits in orbitofrontal cortex (OFC) and possibly ventromedial prefrontal cortex (VMPFC) (though see Horn et al. 2003) appear to inhibit impulsivity through integration of cognition[3] (which suppresses hypothalamic input to VTA and SNpc) and emotion (especially fear of risk; Shiv et al. 2005). As noted previously, serotonin seems to be the neurotransmitter that carries the relevant signal, probably abetted by GABA neurons (Gulledge and Jaffe 2001; Yang, Seamans, and Gorelova 1999).

The basic trigger mechanism for addiction seems to be that continuous floods of dopamine into NAcc depress serotonin levels in OFC and VMPFC and thereby reduce inhibition of impulse: the reward system is given greater influence over behavior. In the case of stimulant drugs (cocaine, amphetamines) extra dopamine is directly introduced in NAcc. Alcohol, nicotine, and opiates work on more indirect pathways that disturb neurotransmitter ratios and increase NAcc dopamine concentration by that mechanism. All these widespread addictive agents thereby crowd out salience of stimuli that don't predict drugs, and focus action on, enhance the perceived value of, and direct orientation toward stimuli that do (Koob, Paolo Sanna, and Bloom 1998). The basic mechanism works as follows. In ventral striatum and VMPFC neurons are normally held quiet by negative resting membrane potentials (called "K+" currents) unless pushed into depolarized states by inflow from cerebral cortex and thalamus. When these neurons are depolarized dopamine excites them; when they're polarized dopamine dampens them further. Thus motivation is sensitive to cognitive judgments. But the reward system then amplifies these initial judgments if they're reinforced.

This describes the process by which the reward system simultaneously learns to pursue a target obsessively and increases the relative valuation of stimuli that predict it. However, it does not yet explain the steady state of addiction in which the addict finds difficulty pursuing alternative rewards, in particular the social ones associated with recovery, even when these are made intermittently salient enough to induce attempts at reform. Kalivas, Volkow, and Siemans (2005) report work that refines our understanding of behavioral attentional gating in addicts by separating its two underlying neurochemical substrates. Activation patterns in recovered rat cocaine addicts presented with cocaine-associated cues suggest that dopamine release in the projection from PFC to NAcc is responsible for strongly cueing the learned expectation of reward in response to the cues, while adaptations in glutamate synapses in NAcc reduce plasticity and impair the animals' abilities to learn to respond to alternative rewards. According to Siemans and Yang (2004) dopamine action gives rise to two possible states in VMPFC depending on which of two groups of receptors, D1 or D2, predominates. If D2 reception predominates, then multiple excitatory inputs promote VMPFC output to NAcc. If D1 reception predominates, then all signals below a high threshold are inhibited. In cocaine withdrawal, protein signaling to D2 receptors is reduced, thus inducing the animal to seek stimuli that can clear the high D1 threshold—namely, stimuli associated with cocaine. Here, then, is a neurochemical model of the mechanism by which withdrawal gives rise to cravings. A craving is nothing more nor less than the phenomenology associated with the reward system's pulling attention back toward the addictive target, and away from the alternative motivators on which cortical systems are trying to focus. Thus the reward system not only, as stated above, amplifies initial judgments that are reinforced; it also makes them difficult to behaviorally revise. This begins to explain the recovered addicts' characteristic struggle with relapse.

Further details have come to light on the way in which dopamine and glutamate neurons complement one another in subserving reward learning and in generating addiction (Kelley 2004). Cells in NAcc and VMPFC on which dopamine and glutamate neurons jointly synapse act as coincidence detectors in associative learning; essentially, an animal or person is motivated to act when dopamine and glutamate signals agree with one another in sending positive signals. Dopamine neurons respond to *global* saliences, that is, overall states of the world that suggest reward prospects. Glutamate, by contrast, responds to specific sensory information, and "teaches" the system to respond to new information with a similar profile. (As with any other neurotransmitter system, this teaching occurs by modification of synaptic potentials.) Glutamate thereby lays down episodic memories that are guides to subsequent actions, and so "stamps in" the dopaminergic response by modifying synapses to be alert to distinctive sensory predictors. Thus the smoker cannot bear to finish a meal without lighting up, the drinker cannot pass the bar without going in, and the gambler experiences a compulsive rush when she hears jangling coins or sees flashing neon.

Powerful though the reward system is in regulating behavior, however, it is not normally in charge. Though dopamine concentration in NAcc is necessary for addiction, it is not sufficient for it; after all, stimulant drugs produce high concentrations of dopamine in NAcc of nonaddicts, and most people who are exposed to addictive substances or gambling do not become addicts. Goldstein and Volkow (2002) review a now substantial body of evidence that heavy consumption of drugs or gambling tips into addiction when *repeated* NAcc dopamine concentrations cause long-term changes in PFC circuits so as to impair inhibition of subcortical responses. One of the ways that some drugs do this is as directly as possible: stimulants, alcohol, and opiates physically destroy some prefrontal circuitry. More subtly, consumption of addictive substances appears to cause reformation of dendritic links as a result of which normal cortical inhibition of the amygdala is reduced (Robinson et al. 2001; Rosenkranz and Grace 2001; Miller and Cohen 2001). In effect, addiction not only hijacks the reward system, but sabotages the systems that might check its influence. The explanation of addiction's relentless grip even on people who have been clean long enough to have shaken off all physiological dependence is thus completed.

Adding this evidence to that which we have reviewed on the dopamine-glutamate mechanism in NAcc, Goldstein and Volkow (2002) construct an integrated model of addiction which they call "impaired response inhibition and salience attribution" (I-RISA). This model links the neural processes underlying four distinct aspects of addiction to substances: intoxication, craving, compulsive drug administration, and withdrawal. The main distinctive general feature of intoxication is dopamine concentration in NAcc. Craving is then the learned association between the drug reward and various stimulus contingencies, based on modified synaptic potentials in amygdala, hippocampus, thalamus, anterior cingulate, and OFC. Compulsive drug administration is then the consequence of the reward system having learned to treat the addictive target as an overwhelmingly salient reward acting semiautonomously in controlling behavior. Strong glutamate responses then support withdrawal symptoms which include dysphoria, anhedonia, impaired cognition, and irritability. As noted earlier, fear of withdrawal is almost certainly not the main factor in maintaining addiction.

Instead, as a result of the resculpting of prefrontal circuits that reduces cortical inhibition of the midbrain, the cravings induced by the addiction-trained reward system, against which alternative rewards have difficulty competing, are often sufficient to provoke relapse after periods of abstinence. Because of the way in which the reward system learns, cravings are induced by any of the cues with which the target of addiction was associated during learning (Chiamulera 2004).

The focus of the past few paragraphs has been broadly hydraulic, a story told in terms of interacting functional systems. Though this allowed us to abstract away from biochemical details (which were merely referred to rather than described), the relevance of the neuroeconomic model may have faded from view. However, its importance becomes evident when we now ask why *some* but not *most* behavioral patterns that (unlike drugs) involve no introduction of exogenous chemical interferences can trigger addictive response.

Notice that nothing has in fact been said as yet about why some *drugs* are addictive. We have implicitly dismissed appeals to physiological dependence by pointing out that physiologically recovered addicts typically must pay significant costs to try to avoid relapse and are thus still economic puzzles. As Wise (2002) argues, a similar point can be made about identifying the addicted condition with neuroadaptations that attenuate frontal control, as described above. Rewarding properties of direct stimulants are learned extremely quickly; after as few as two or three electrical stimulations to hypothalamus, rats will begin frantically pressing levers for further such stimulation and ignoring food and water. In these cases neuroadaptations cannot yet have occurred at the point where pursuit of the reward appears to be compulsive. Thus the neurochemistry of addiction as just reviewed has *described* addiction but not *explained* it. This is where the neuroeconomic perspective rises to the occasion. Instead of explaining PG by reference to drug addiction, we will explain drug addiction in terms of a neuroeconomic account of PG.

Let us sharpen the question before us by means of a contrast. Gambling is genuinely addictive for a minority of people; interpersonal sex is probably not potentially addictive for anyone.[4] Why?

The crucial conceptual step is to distinguish reward for the molar economic agent—the person—from reward for a molecular agent—such as the dopamine system. Folk psychology often reduces reward to imagined shots of hedonic delight. (Early neoclassical economists made this same identification, but quickly came to think of utility in a more abstract sense.) However, as Wise (2002) stresses, rewards at the level of neural agents are "unsensed incentives." The point of this phrase, in the context of reflections on targets of addiction, is that although people sense the *hedonic* consequences of drugs or of an exciting bet, they are not directly conscious of what is rewarding about them *to their brains*. In the case of addictive gambling, folk psychology leads us to wonder what it is that the gambler gets that keeps attracting her to gamble more. Is it thrills, or money, or relief from boredom, or what? This is the wrong question to ask if we want to understand gambling *addiction*.

In light of the PV model of the reward system, in neuroeconomics the distinction between a reward and a predictor of a reward is subtle to the point of vanishing. Rewards are units of information that "by association establish otherwise neutral stimuli as things to be approached" (Wise 2002, 233). The reward system is a device for leading animals to approach certain things rather than others, and it encodes no distinction between what is of ultimate benefit and what predicts an experience the animal is conditioned to repeat. In the case of animals that must adapt to changing environments, the system has a bias for—takes as rewarding—any predictor of *novel* experiences that are not aversive. People, furthermore, are the ultimate novelty-seekers, their freakishly large brains signifying their status as the only animals in whom exaggerated drive for cognitive exploration is the basic species-specific adaptation. This emerges directly in the dopaminergic system's design: dopamine is not released by familiar stimuli but by positive surprises. Furthermore, as Wise reminds us, since the *sensed* properties of the "reward" in the folk sense (i.e., the food in the mouth, the orgasm, the drug high, the receipt of the winnings at the window) are not typically surprising, the system becomes unresponsive to them. So saying as we do that the dopaminergic system responds to predictors of reward is actually a bit misleading. What we call "predictors of reward" at the *molar* level are (when positively surprising) the rewards themselves at the *molecular* level.

What gambling fundamentally consists in is paying for a surprise that is simple enough for the primitive dopamine system to understand with minimal or no help from frontal processing. This requires that odds in the gambler's favor not be *too* high, and it may be important to the reward that they're negative. This doesn't imply that the gambler doesn't prefer winning to losing. All people who like gambling, and not just gambling addicts, want two things at once that they can't have both of: to win every bet, and to participate in processes where there's a high risk of losing. On reflection, is this apparently perverse preference structure so unprecedented? How many people want, in general, exciting lives but in which nothing seriously threatens them? However, that is an analogy at the personal level, whereas the roots of addiction lie elsewhere. In the gambling addict, the reward system has triumphed over other parts of the brain and wrestled away control of behavior. Now it directly pursues maximization of its own utility function by taking a simple action—pulling the slot-machine lever—that *guarantees* a surprise.

We should now be able to see why, when people discover that there are institutions where they can buy such direct manipulation of the dopaminergic system, hysteresis is induced in some of them. By contrast, interpersonal sex reverses the relevant contingencies: because fine-grained scheduling involves negotiation and interpersonal signaling, there is no *simple* action the reward system can initiate that then reliably delivers a surprise. Of course, *romance*, as opposed to just *sex*, offers rich veins for surprise and is endlessly intriguing to most people. But romantic responses are highly complex and involve most of the brain; they are not, like slot-machine play or roulette, off-line indulgences for the dopamine system.

For the precise sense in which puzzles arise for neuroeconomists *before* the insight that what's rewarding to the reward system and what's rewarding to the person are two different kinds of thing, consider a discussion by Ahmed (2004). Reviewing Redish's (2004) neuroeconomic model of cocaine addiction, which directly applies associative TD learning following Montague, Dayan, and Sejnowski (1996), Ahmed points out that the model depends on the fact that cocaine directly causes dopamine release in NAcc, and so predicts strong reward regardless of any other contingencies. But then, Ahmed wonders, what about "addictions to ordinary rewards, such as fatty foods, which, unlike cocaine, produce a dopamine signal that can be accommodated" (2004, 1902)? It is not obvious that fatty foods are a good example of stimulants that directly produce dopamine signals the brain can accommodate; fatty foods may stimulate the addictive response without cognitive mediation just like cocaine. However, the answer to Ahmed's question if we replace fatty foods by gambling is straightforward. Given what reward *means* in the midbrain, and given what gambling *is* from this point of view, it too is guaranteed to predict strong reward come what may. By contrast, the *person* gets what she regards as her reward from gambling—a cash win—only a minority of the time.

What about addictive drugs, then? The course of behavioral effects exerted by them is highly regular and stereotypical. Again, however, we should not look for the surprises they induce at the level of the person, but at the level of the reward system. Addictive drugs disrupt the internal clock by which the brain measures intervals against which reward rates are estimated. (Note that time scales relevant to patterns of midbrain dopamine release are very short.) Since it is still unclear how reward rate estimation and reward delivery point estimation are integrated in the dopamine system, here the high-level neuroeconomic account outruns neurochemical substantiation and detail, so caution is required. But it should be evident that there are two basic ways in which an economically simple agent (which does not imply a *chemically* simple *machine*) such as the reward system can be surprised. On the one hand, the environment may deliver salient stimuli in forms it doesn't expect at all or—as in the case with gambling—in familiar forms on time schedules it can't predict. On the other hand, the environment may deliver familiar rewards on schedules that *seem* unpredictable to the system because it logs them against a jittering clock.

The crucial requirement on an addictive target is that it trips the reward circuit into hysteresis: a self-amplifying causal process driven by positive feedback. In the case of drugs, their chemical influence on NAcc dopamine levels *happens to be* the mechanism by which hysteresis is induced. If this were the *only* mechanism for such hysteresis, then there would be no harm in our identifying addictive properties with intrinsic chemical properties. But the phenomenon of gambling addiction refutes this conceptual move. The intrinsic chemical properties of drugs are, in this sense, *distractions* from the elementary structure of addiction. They are of course important, and we should expect that they will greatly complicate development of neuropharmacological responses to addictive drugs. But principles of theory development direct us to deal with basic cases of phenomena first and turn to complications later. These considerations suggest that gambling addiction should move to a position of central focus in addiction research.[5]

This completes the outline of the neuroeconomic account of what addiction and PG *are*. Notice, however, that nothing has yet been said about how it is that the overwhelming majority of people control their reward systems and avoid addiction. There is a straightforward reason for this: where environmental circumstances favoring dopaminergic mutiny are in place, it is the *person*—the molar-scale agent—whose strategies are relevant. Thus we must partly shift our attention from the neuroeconomic scale. I say "partly" because, as we will see, neuroeconomics provides useful input to selection among molar-scale models.

5   Behavioral Economics of Addiction

As noted in section 2, the most common molar-scale account of addiction in current behavioral economics is picoeconomics. What distinguishes a picoeconomic account from alternatives is that it models the challenge for the person trying to control her reward system around properties of her discount function. Based on experimental work, Herrnstein and Prelec (1992) and Ainslie (1992) argued that the default intertemporal discount function for an individual animal is not the standard exponential curve of financial economics but a hyperbola as captured by Mazur's (1987) formula:

$$v_i = \frac{A_i}{1 + kD_i}$$

where v_i, A_i, and D_i respectively represent the present value of a delayed reward, the amount of a delayed reward, and the delay to the reward from a reference point. k is a constant specific to an individual agent. With respect to the shape of the hyperbolae generated by the function, k is a parameter controlling the steepness of discounting. Hyperbolic intertemporal discounting allows for (though it does not entail) intertemporal preference reversals when agents choose between smaller, sooner rewards (SSRs) and larger, later ones (LLRs). A pair of temporally spaced rewards a [t_1], b [t_2], for which the person's utility function gives $b \succ a$ at a point well out into the future from the current reference point, where the slope of the discount function is relatively gentle, may stand in the relation $a \succ b$ as the time of a's possible consumption comes closer to the reference point, where discounting is steeper. Here b is an LLR—say, paying off the home mortgage—and a is an SSR—for example, going to the casino with a substantial stake. Ainslie's "pure" picoeconomic modeling approach represents this situation as a bargaining game between two synchronous subpersonal interests, one of which (the "short-range interest") has a utility function such that SSR $\succ$ LLR while the other (the "long-range interest") has the opposite preference ordering over these alternatives. In this model the personal utility function drops out of the picture altogether. The short-range and long-range interests are forced to bargain because the former depends on resources harvested by the latter. However, their bargaining game has the structure of a Prisoner's Dilemma (PD): if the long-range interest will allow the short-range interest to obtain a payoff at *some* point, then the short-range interest prefers to obtain its pay-off now, but that amounts to defection in the PD; if the long-range interest will never indulge the short-range interest in future then the short-range interest is also best off defecting at the first opportunity. Thus defection on any bargain with the long-range interest is a dominant strategy for the short-range interest. This in turn implies that the long-range interest never maximizes by indulging the short-range one.

If this is taken as the standard model of all people, then it predicts that addiction and other pathologies of impulsivity (e.g., chronic procrastination) are inescapable for everyone. Of course this describes a counterfactual. Ainslie thus hypothesizes that coalitions of long-range interests and (new) short-range interests form around *personal rules*. A personal rule is essentially a limited side-payment to a short-range interest. For example, a person may establish a personal rule to visit the casino only every second Saturday, and to gamble only with a fixed budget on those days. Personal rules can be made consistent with the assumption of hyperbolic personal discounting if present behavior *predicts* future behavior. In that case, the person can derive *present* satisfaction from evidence that the personal rule is in place, making it a currently valuable asset. If the rule is broken, then this asset is damaged or destroyed at the reference point for discounting, where its value *might* thus dominate the value of the competing SSR.

From the *economic* perspective this account requires that we identify a place in the model for the person—the agent that holds the personal rule as an asset—despite the fact that the personal utility function is unrepresented in the bargaining game among interests. The most direct way of doing this is to combine the picoeconomic model with the "team reasoning" model of Bacharach (2006). Suppose that the interest in gambling, though it always prefers gambling now to gambling later (and is thus a short-range interest in that sense), has some *standing* interest in *gambling*. Then it faces the problem that it cannot expect any later gambling unless it allows long-range interests some scope to harvest resources. Given these assumptions, the person can emerge from the bargaining dynamics as a corporate institution with which the short- and long-range interests partly identify. Formally, as Bacharach shows, this must amount (if it is to be coherent as noncooperative game theory) to the claim that where personal rules are effective the bargaining game among the implicated interests has the structure of an Assurance Game instead of a PD. This approach may seem difficult to reconcile with Ainslie's view of short-range interests as persisting for only as long as their immediate objects are live options. One of his favorite examples is an annoying interest in scratching an itch, which will fade entirely if even briefly ignored; unless the itch is caused by a foreign irritant, as most itches are not, the interest in scratching *is* the itch. Thus it exists only for a few seconds. However, commitment to coherent modeling does not require denial that interests can be fleeting; we need only insist that interests controllable by team reasoning persist for long enough to achieve behavioral expression (as reflected in the Assurance Game payoffs). Though some people are good at ignoring itches, this does not seem to involve any bargaining with them.

Picoeconomics as promoted by Ainslie and others (e.g., Rachlin 2000, Ross 2005) does not have explicit foundations in neuroscience. Because picoeconomic subpersonal agents have access to all of the computational resources of the person, they cannot be identified with specific brain regions. Furthermore, picoeconomic interests are individuated by reference to their environmentally embedded objects. This means that their identity criteria include aspects of their ecological contexts. Parts of the brain cannot be individuated in this way.[6]

What, then, are we to make of a situation in which we have two economic accounts of addiction, each on a different scale of analysis, that do not seem to speak to one another? We find several kinds of bridges proposed in the literature to date, which variously require more or less drastic amendments to picoeconomics.

The first family of accounts have their technical foundations in work by Laibson (1997). His original motivation was unrelated to addiction, but was instead motivated by interest in capturing the qualitative property of hyperbolic discounting—specifically, switches in preference rankings from LLRs to SSRs merely in consequence of the passage of time—without resort to a hyperbolic function. The basis for this interest was in turn pragmatic: in any given problem setting, Mazur's formula has many possible solutions because the k parameter collapses average steepness and "bowedness" of the discount curve, so consumption functions that incorporate hyperbolic discounting are not guaranteed to converge. Laibson showed that the qualitative account of picoeconomics is captured by an alternative discount function of the so-called β–δ or *quasi-hyperbolic* form, borrowed from Phelps and Pollack (1968). This class of functions is expressed by

$$v_i = A_i \beta \delta^D$$

where v_i represents the present value of a delayed reward, A_i the amount of that reward, β a constant discount factor for all delayed rewards, δ a per-period exponential discount factor, and D the delay of the reward. Where $\beta = 1$ the equation reduces to standard exponential discounting. Where $\beta < 1$ discounting is initially steeper up to some inflection point. β–δ discounting predicts that value drops precipitously from no delay to a one-period delay, but then declines more gradually (and exponentially) over all periods thereafter.

One possible way of applying β–δ to discounting preserves its original purely pragmatic spirit. Hyperbolic discounting is taken to be the correct molar-scale account of discounting, with β–δ discounting then treated simply as an approximation for the sake of making conventional economic analysis tractable. This interpretation does not address the relationship between picoeconomics and neuroeconomics. A similar remark applies to models in which the synchronic division of the person proposed by Ainslie is replaced by a purely diachronic division closer to the earlier accounts of Strotz (1956) and Schelling (1978, 1980, 1984). Phelps and Pollock developed the β–δ model in the first place to study intergenerational wealth transfers; and addiction and PG can readily be modeled as such a problem for a person decomposed diachronically into subagents. The present agent, like the present generation, discounts its own utility at the β rate, while setting policy for later agents (generations) whose utility it discounts at the δ rate. Models of this kind, applied to the more general class of addiction-like phenomena, can be found in the work of Laibson (1998), Laibson, Repetto, and Tobacman (1998), and O'Donoghue and Rabin (1999).

More recently, however, Laibson and colleagues have exploited β–δ discounting to try to unite molar-scale and molecular-scale economic models. McClure et al. (2004) interpret some fMRI data they obtained as suggesting that "limbic" brain areas discount more steeply than "cortical" areas.[7] They then propose that hyperbolic discounting at the molar scale be understood as an aggregation of the tug of war between neurally realized β-discounting ("limbic") and δ-discounting ("cortical") subagents. This idea can in turn be given either of two generic kinds of interpretation in economic modeling.

On the first interpretation, we *reduce* the picoeconomic interests involved in addiction to the brain's rival discounting systems. This amounts to *eliminating* picoeconomic models of addiction and PG in favor of neuroeconomic ones. Philosophically, this would amount to a commitment to find a neural site for the kind of personal agency involved in the formation of personal rules, since people quite evidently *do* formulate, express, and use such rules. (Consider, for example, the facilities for self-banning from casinos that are required by law in most jurisdictions in the English-speaking world.) One might hypothesize that a neurally realized site of "consciousness" is in play here. However, there is no scientific support for the idea that consciousness is *locally* implemented in the brain, and there are grounds for suspecting that the concept of consciousness involved here is rooted in suspect philosophical interpretations of folk psychology (Dennett 1991).

A more interesting interpretation of the McClure et al. proposal associates it with a family of models that are currently very popular among behavioral economists. These in effect put the prefrontal/midbrain agent outside the boundary of the personal agent: β-discounting is understood as an *exogenous* challenge to personal utility maximization.[8] Loewenstein (1996, 1999) (along with Read [2001]) points out that only certain sorts of goods are hyperbolically discounted at the molar scale: for example, desserts (Hoch and Loewenstein 1991) and hamburgers (Read 2001), but not petrol (Hoch and Loewenstein) or computer paper (Read).[9] The former sorts of reward are referred to as "visceral": they are perceptible *as* rewards with minimal cognitive processing. If personal utility is identified with valuation resulting from relatively cognitive or "cold" processing, then the siren call of visceral satisfactions can be treated as a form of *disutility* to the person, a threat to successful maximization lying in ambush in the "external" environment within the brain.

There are several worked-out economic models that unpack this general idea in different specific ways. Gul and Pesendorfer (2001, 2005) provide the most direct such approach. Their model defines a "temptation" as a choice option with the property that its presence in the choice set makes an agent worse off, either because this results in her making a worse choice than she would have made in the option's absence, or because to cope with the option the agent must incur a cost of "self-control." Thus the (molar) agent is incentivized to take steps to avoid encountering temptations. These may include personal-rule formation, along with other generic devices itemized by Ainslie (1992): precommitment, control of attention, and preparation of emotion. Despite predicting some of the same the same behavioral phenomena, as Gul and Pesendorfer (2001) point out, the picoeconomic model admits no role for self-control *in their sense*, that is, as resistance "at the point of choice" (so to speak) to a storm of visceral temptation. In the picoeconomic model, overcoming "weakness of will" is identified with reconfiguration of commodity spaces, with personal rules being added to consumption bundles. On Gul and Pesendorfer's model, by contrast, choice is distinct from the action or failure of willpower, which thus has nothing directly to do with discounting. Of all existing accounts, this is the only model of addiction that requires no revisions to standard consumer theory: the agent discounts exponentially, and can be as far-sighted as the modeler likes and the data warrant relative to her modeling convention.

A second approach that implicitly makes prefrontal processing exogenous to the economic agent is promoted by Loewenstein (1999), and explains the addict's self-control problem as an informational deficit. According to Loewenstein, cognitive memory for visceral intensity is systematically unreliable. In consequence, people routinely underestimate the effect that past and future visceral states will have on future behavior, thus neglecting to incorporate their influence in making present choices. For example, an abstinent substance abuser may reinitiate consumption in part because he fails to remember the effect of past craving on drug use, and thus underestimates how much future craving will make it difficult to quit. This psychological hypothesis admits readily of an economic interpretation based around *self-signaling* (Prelec and Bodner 2003). This can in turn be modeled either in a unified or multiple agency setting. In the multiple (diachronic) agent context, present agents with some degree of special concern for their descendent agents choose prudently because prudent choice now *predicts* prudent choice later, and the *present* agent gets lightly discounted *present* utility from this reassurance. As in picoeconomics, this explains personal rules as presently valuable assets. However, the potential value of self-signaling depends neither on hyperbolic discounting nor on dividing the person into intertemporally multiple agents. As Bénabou and Tirole (2004) demonstrate rigorously, self-signaling can be justified by any imperfection in an agent's knowledge about her own capacity to cope with temptations.

Bernheim and Rangel (2004) point out a generic deficit in all of the models reviewed so far in this section: none indicate what is *special* about *addictive* targets. (This objection applies, as it were, twice over to picoeconomic accounts that do not draw the distinction between visceral and nonvisceral rewards.) One possible response is to claim that all visceral rewards are potentially addictive (which would require finding at least a few actual people addicted to most of them, under at least some non-ad-hoc system of classification). Bernheim and Rangel interpret the psychological evidence differently. They argue that addictive drugs are special in chemically causing the dopamine system to systematically overpredict the expected reward given a cue for drug intake (e.g., clinking ice cubes, the sight of a needle, or the smell of someone else's tobacco). Here we at last find economic modeling at the molar level making direct contact with the two themes from earlier sections of the present chapter: the details of the neuroeconomic model of the dopamine system, and the contention that, in light of these details, PG is the basic form of addiction. Bernheim and Rangel's account perpetuates, and indeed emphasizes, the tradition of treating substance addiction as basic.

Before considering the implications of PG as basic addiction for this family of current economic models of self-control, a further problem for the integration of neuroeconomic and picoeconomic models of addiction must be mentioned. Recall that the original McClure et al. hypothesis continues to interpret addiction and related pathologies of impulsivity in terms of *discounting*. However, Glimcher, Kable, and Louie (2007) have recently reported fMRI data that they interpret as indicating that neurons in both midbrain and prefrontal areas in fact implement similar discount functions as the molar subject. They find, as have others (Hariri et al. 2006), variability in activation levels in striatum between subjects, which correlates with variability in molar steepness of discounting. (A similar degree of behavioral variability had earlier been demonstrated by Simpson and Vuchinich [2000].) However, they find no areas in which activation levels are correlated with steeper or shallower discount functions than those inferred from molar behavior. Glimcher et al. interpret these findings as directly challenging the McClure et al. hypothesis, and indeed generalize this doubt: not only does it undermine the idea of distinct δ and β discounting areas in the brain, but also, they say, the very existence of "separable neural agents that could account for multiple selves that are used to explain hyperbolic-like discounting behavior" (Glimcher, Kable, and Louie 2007, 143).

The implications of this evidence and its interpretation for picoeconomics are somewhat subtle. Recall that the multiple selves of picoeconomics are molar-scale objects, individuated by reference to ecologically embedded effects. In light of this, it is important that Glimcher et al. generalize their negative suggestion above quite carefully as follows: "This finding argues strongly against the hypothesis that the sub-personal interests, with different discount functions, are instantiated as discrete neural systems *at the proximal algorithmic level*" (ibid.; their emphases). The real challenge from neuroeconomics is to the conception of addiction as a pathology of *discounting*. This is consistent with Glimcher et al.'s cautiously suggesting that their data might support a model of the Gul and Pesendorfer variety.

6   PG as Basic Addiction: Implications for Integrated Economic Modeling

It is too early for anyone to be able to confidently forecast the way in which behavioral economics and neuroeconomics will be integrated in a general model of addictive consumption. In this concluding section, I aim simply to put a new proposal on the table, based on the specific suggestion of section 4 that PG be interpreted as the basic form of addiction.

As described in section 5, the currently most popular economic models of addiction rely on a strong distinction between visceral and more "cognitive" rewards. They either implicitly or explicitly identify the person as the agent with a utility function ranging over the latter, thus preserving the tradition that conceptualizes economics as the science of *rational*—here interpreted as both far-sighted and *deliberate*—choice. On these models, the problem posed for the *person* by visceral rewards is that they tend to be processed *automatically* by older brain systems. This automatic processing has virtues of speed (Benhabib and Bisin 2004), but in the presence of visceral rewards that produce addiction, requires control if personal utility is to be maximized. Such control is costly. People, presumably due to a mix of genetic and environmentally contingent factors, have different budget constraints when facing these costs. Some—in tendency, those whose budget constraints are tightest—become addicts.

This general account makes no specific reference to discounting. It does, however, explain why, at least where visceral rewards are concerned, consumption schedules are frequently consistent with models of hyperbolic discounting. All one need hypothesize to make this weak connection is that temptations exert their force only at short intertemporal distances by comparison with cognitively ratified rewards.

As noted, the only existing model in this family that explains why a specific *subset* of the visceral rewards are distinctively addictive is that of Bernheim and Rangel (2004).

This explanation relies on hypothesized specific properties of some drugs. Suppose instead, however, that PG is the basic addiction, in the sense suggested in section 4. That is, suppose that the roots of addiction lie in the organism's discovery of a simple action it can take that *reliably* delivers a *salient* (i.e., "attention-grabbing") signal whose properties of interest (a big win? a small win? a loss?), and micro-scale timing (i.e., moment of delivery within an interval frame) it cannot predict. Suppose that addictive drugs mimic PG by disrupting the stability of the clock used by the brain to learn reward expectancy. How, if at all, does this idea relate to picoeconomics? And does it lend itself to neuroeconomic modeling and testing?

TD learning does not predict a discovery, due to Gallistel (1990), that conditioning outcomes in animal learning are timescale invariant. This means that responses from a given animal will be the same in two otherwise identical learning conditions if the interval durations between cues and rewards in one condition are a constant multiple of the durations of the other. In general, TD learning has been framed as a model of classical associative conditioning, after Rescorla and Wagner (1972). By contrast with associative models, Scalar Expectancy Theory (SET) (Gibbon 1977) and Rate Estimation Theory (RET) (Gallistel 1990), as unified in Gallistel and Gibbon (2000), are *timing* models of conditioning phenomena. According to such models, animals represent the durations of intervals and the rates of relevant events, and conditioned responding occurs as a function of the comparison of rates of reinforcement. Animals are drawn to environments with higher such rates by gradient climbing, rather than forming explicit associations between stimuli and conditioned responses. For ease of reference, I will call the unification of SET and RET "G-learning."

G-learning is naturally compatible with melioration, the basic mechanism underlying hyperbolic discounting, since melioration is just choice of whichever behavioral patterns among those perceived as alternatives optimize current reward rate. Now, picoeconomics is in the first place a theory of consumption, not a learning theory. This is a fundamental source of the difficulty we have encountered in finding neuroeconomic foundations for it. The neuroeconomic model of reward predicts that the tendency to impulsive consumption should be in some way a function of the dopamine system's learning of relationships between cues and rewards, which is implemented by locking in attention on cues. Picoeconomic theory has no account of the *learning* of hyperbolic discounting; one supposes it is an innate disposition.

Thus it is potentially significant that G-learning offers a timing theory of reward learning. Sanabria and Killeen (2005), commenting critically on Ainslie's model of molar appetite, note that "a key property of signals of reinforcement is that they become both conditioned reinforcers, or CRs, and conditioned stimuli, eliciting approach" (661). This leads them to ask "Is this the behavioral substrate of desire, of appetite? If so, then Ainslie's hyperbolic interests, Skinner's CRs, and Pavlov's CSs are the same entity. A theory of one is a theory of all" (661). Ainslie (2005) responds favorably to the suggestion and enlarges on it, commending Sanabria and Killeen for

mentioning the opportunity [raised by picoeconomics] to revise "the hoary study of CRs [conditioned responses]." I judge such a revision to be among [my theory's] most important implications.... [F]or the selection of responses, the potential of brief temporary preferences to lure organisms into responses that are aversive overall, could let us do without the *deux ex machina* of a second, "conditioned" selective principle that is so often invoked to explain aversive, involuntary or maladaptive processes.... The model of aversion as a rapidly cycling addiction comprising reward and inhibition of reward lets us add conditioned processes to the marketplace of rewarded processes. (667)

G-learning, to the extent that it applies directly to the reward system, suggests a natural way of unifying the molar and the molecular accounts of entrapment by processes that generate continuous reward rate uncertainty. A recent computational model of the reward system by Daw (2003), which has among its aims to make G-learning and TD learning complementary, offers a clue as to how this might work. In Daw's model G-learning is taken to precede, and indeed to enable, TD learning. Suppose an animal has learned a function that predicts a reward at t, where the function in question decomposes into models of two stages: one applying to the interval between the conditioned and the unconditioned stimulus, and one applying to the interval between the unconditioned stimulus and the next conditioned stimulus. Then imagine that a case occurs in which at t nothing happens. Should the animal infer that its model of the world needs revision, perhaps to a one-stage model, or should it retain the model and regard the omission as noise or error? In Daw's account the animal uses G-learning to select a world model: whichever such model matches behavior that yields the higher reward rate will be preferred to alternatives. Given this model as a constraint, TD learning can then predict the temporal placement of rewards ("when"-learning). This hybrid approach allows Daw to drop two unbiological features of the original Montague, Dayan, and Sejnowski (1996) model of TD learning by the dopamine system: tapped-line delay timing and exogenously fixed trial boundaries, which are plausible only in the sparse and controlled setup of the laboratory. This is surely progress, as it is doubtful that anyone ever took these two properties for anything other than modeling conveniences.

Now let us speculate. If the reward system can only settle into stable "when"-learning after selecting a world model, how might it respond to the environment of the casino? Each pull of the lever constitutes an experiment in reward rate estimation. If wins were never forthcoming, this would not be interesting. If wins were always forthcoming, the reward rate would be estimated, TD learning would run, and dopamine firing would stabilize to the cue. Of course, a casino in which one always wins is simply nirvana; a rational agent would stay there and no issue of addiction would arise. However, in a real casino, the system can fall into the following trap. Suppose it models each gambling station as a new environment for reward-rate estimation. This gives it a natural mission: search all such environments for the highest reward rate. For these to be learned, every pull of the lever must be treated as a trial, as a predictor of surprise. Attention will be directed to these cues. TD learning will run on each conjectured reward-rate environment, but never stabilize. The system has effectively stumbled into a filling station for dopamine.

If people turn out to be vulnerable to this sort of process, how might we best model it economically? First, note that it would be natural to represent the resulting consumption scheduling using a hyperbolic discounting function. After all, the underlying process literally *is* melioration. However, characterizing the process in terms of *discounting* is an accurate high-level *description* but does not get to grips with the *economic* properties of the underlying mechanism. If people use their frontal cognitive resources —along with, I would add, external control devices furnished by social norms and institutions (see Ross 2009)—to suppress tendencies to be entrapped by jiggling intervals, then the basic insight behind the family of economic models reviewed earlier (in section 5) would be upheld. This family is formally generalized by Benhabib and Bisin (2004). At the same time, the different intuitive stories that are presented with the more specific models we considered might come to be regarded as *overly* specific. We would not necessarily be driven to say with Bernheim and Rangel that addiction rests on a *mistake*, for no particular misprediction is indicated when the person is induced to sample reward rates. Nor does addiction necessarily require inaccurate memory of the power of meliorative entrapment, as in Loewenstein's account; the addict who dries out and then relapses may have full knowledge of what she is getting back into, but simply fail to muster the mental stamina required to maintain maximization, in the same logical sense in which a baseball player fails to maximize on a given occasion because he doesn't hit the ball hard enough. The fully axiomatized dynamic model of Gul and Pesendorfer may well apply to the economic problem of an agent tempted to experimentally meliorate, though it relies on stronger assumptions than the general model of Benhabib and Bisin.

There is a first, obvious course of neuroscientific studies suggested by the above hypothesis. We should design fMRI experiments to investigate the question of whether reward learning in the midbrain and prefrontal dopamine circuit is timescale invariant. Does the dopamine spike transfer from a reward to its cue after the same number of trials if trial–intertrial ratios are held constant while intervals themselves are varied? If the answer is yes, how then does dopamine signaling respond when reward magnitudes vary stochastically within different intervals conditioned to the same cues?

A model of PG as basic addiction, grounded on a timing model of reward learning, can only become a properly *economic* theory, amenable to being interrogated for consistency with the Gul and Pesendorfer and Benhabib and Bisin theories, if it is rendered in terms of choices between alternatives rather than conditioning (as in Gallistel 1990). Fortunately, the early accounts of timing models of learning were presented using the language of conditioning merely for pedagogical reasons, in order to be comparable with standard psychological results. But the intended interpretation of the new learning rules is algorithmic; the learning subject in both Gallistel and Gibbon (2002) and Daw (2003) is a Bayesian estimator. Meanwhile, Caplin and Dean (2007) have taken the first steps in an ambitious program to construct an axiomatic theory of choice-driven neural learning. As they point out, this will permit central tenets of theories to be tested instead of merely particular parametrizations. Thus convergence is occurring from both sides of the interdisciplinary partnership toward what might once have looked like a square circle: an *economic* model of an agent's *deciding* to have her money pumped by a process she knows to be rigged and which she expects to regret.

Acknowledgments

Thanks to Rudy Vuchinich, Carla Sharp, David Spurrett, Peter Collins, and Nelleke Bak.

Notes

1. Massing (2000) describes heroin addicts who explain recurrent entrance into rehabilitation programs, followed by renewed use, in this way. These junkies self-characterize as fully rational: they expect to pursue this cycle for as long as they have resources to do so.

2. The *non*distressed addict, who never tries to stop, is handled without difficulty by the Becker and Murphy model.

3. Especially, perhaps, cognition concerning the future; see Fellows and Farah 2004. Of particular interest in the present context is the fact that their results suggest that VMPFC activity has no effect on discounting, but instead promotes awareness of expected future contingencies. This is an instance of a case for attributing different economic properties to different parts of the brain.

4. In the United States there is widespread popular, therapeutic, and nonneuroscientific social science discussion of, and practice oriented around, so-called sex addiction. But there is no neuroscientific evidence for it. Obviously, there are people who devote great time and energy to pursuit of sex. This is not evidence of addiction. Sex has a number of crucial disanalogies with targets of addiction. One of these is that fine manipulation of the reward contingency is not under an individual's own control. Admittedly, this objection does not apply to masturbation or consumption of pornography. It is possible that there are masturbation and/or pornography addicts; but, again, I am aware of no neuroscientific evidence for this at present. Widespread belief in sex addiction is confined to the United States and the United Kingdom and seems to have its entire basis in cultural ideology. See Ross et al. 2008, chapter 8.

5. Goldstein and Volkow (2002, 1645) make this same point.

6. There is a large literature on the more general version of this issue among philosophers, which they call the problem of "wide versus narrow content." See McClamrock 1995.

7. I have put "limbic" and "cortical" in scare quotes because, as Paul Glimcher emphasizes in correspondence, the idea that the brain can be neatly partitioned in this way is obsolete. One could express the spirit (though not quite the literal content) of McClure et al.'s proposal in more accurate neuroscientific terminology by substituting "prefrontal or basal" for "limbic" and "frontal" for "cortical."

8. Models of this type may or may not interpret the prefrontal/midbrain systems as economic agents; at the molar scale where these models are focused, nothing empirical hangs on this. But I agree with Glimcher (2003) that commitment to "real" neuroeconomics requires genuine *economic* modeling of every brain unit that is treated as functionally modular.

9. People convinced that the whole human species is blithely ignoring a coming catastrophe following "peak oil" might presumably disagree with this assertion about petrol.

References

Ahmed, S. (2004). Addiction as compulsive reward prediction. *Science* 306: 1901–1902.

Ainslie, G. (1992). *Picoeconomics*. Cambridge: Cambridge University Press.

Ainslie, G. (2001). *Breakdown of Will*. Cambridge: Cambridge University Press.

Ainslie, G. (2005). Précis of *Breakdown of Will*. *Behavioral and Brain Sciences* 28: 635–673.

Bacharach, M. (2006). *Beyond Individual Choice*. Princeton: Princeton University Press.

Becker, G. (1976). *The Economic Approach to Human Behavior*. Chicago: University of Chicago Press.

Becker, G., and Murphy, K. (1988). A theory of rational addiction. *Journal of Political Economy* 96: 675–700.

Bénabou, R., and Tirole, J. (2004). Willpower and personal rules. *Journal of Political Economy* 112: 848–886.

Benhabib, J., and Bisin, A. (2004). Modeling internal commitment mechanisms and self-control: A neuroeconomics approach to consumption-saving decisions. *Games and Economic Behavior* 52: 460–492.

Bernheim, B. D., and Rangel, A. (2004). Addiction and cue-triggered decision processes. *American Economic Review* 94: 1558–1590.

Caplin, A., and Dean, M. (2007). The neuroeconomic theory of learning. *American Economic Review* 97: 148–152.

Chiamulera, C. (2004). Cue reactivity in nicotine and tobacco dependence: A "multiple-action" model of nicotine as a primary reinforcement and as an enhancer of the effects of smoking-associated stimuli. *Brain Research Reviews* 48: 74–97.

Daw, N. (2003). Reinforcement learning models of the dopamine system and their behavioral implications. Doctoral dissertation, Carnegie Mellon University, Pittsburgh.

Dennett, D. (1991). *Consciousness Explained.* Boston: Little, Brown.

Fellows, L., and Farah, M. (2004). Dissociable elements of human foresight: A role for the ventro-medial frontal lobes in framing the future, but not in discounting future rewards. *Neurophyscholo-gia* 43: 1214–1221.

Gallistel, C. (1990). *The Organization of Learning.* Cambridge, MA: MIT Press.

Gallistel, C., and Gibbon, J. (2000). Time, rate, and conditioning. *Psychological Review* 107: 289–344.

Gallistel, C., and Gibbon, J. (2002). *The Symbolic Foundations of Conditioned Behavior.* Mahwah, NJ: Lawrence Erlbaum.

Gibbon, J. (1977). Scalar expectancy theory and Weber's Law in animal timing. *Psychological Review* 84: 279–335.

Glimcher, P. (2003). *Decisions, Uncertainty, and the Brain.* Cambridge, MA: MIT Press.

Glimcher, P., Kable, J., and Louie, K. (2007). Neuroeconomic studies of impulsivity: Now or just as soon as possible? *American Economic Review* 97: 142–147.

Goldstein, R., and Volkow, N. (2002). Drug addiction and its underlying neurobiological basis: Neuroimaging evidence for the involvement of the prefrontal cortex. *American Journal of Psychiatry* 159: 1642–1652.

Gul, F., and Pesendorfer, W. (2001). Temptation and self control. *Econometrica* 69: 1403–1436.

Gul, F., and Pesendorfer, W. (2005). The simple theory of temptation and self-control. http://www.princeton.edu/~pesendor/finite.pdf

Gulledge, A., and Jaffe, D. (2001). Multiple effects of dopamine on layer V pyramidal cell excitabil-ity in rat prefrontal cortex. *Journal of Neurophysiology* 86: 586–595.

Hariri, A., Brown, S., Williamson, D., Flory, J., de Wit, H., and Manuck, S. (2006). Preference for immediate over delayed rewards is associated with magnitude of ventral striatal activity. *Journal of Neuroscience* 26: 13213–13217.

Herrnstein, R., and Prelec, D. (1992). A theory of addiction. In G. Loewenstein and J. Elster, eds., *Choice Over Time,* 331–361. New York: Russell Sage Foundation.

Hoch, S., and Loewenstein, G. (1991). Time-inconsistent preferences and consumer self-control. *Journal of Consumer Research* 17: 492–507.

Horn, N., Dolan, M., Elliott, R., Deakin, J., and Woodruff, P. (2003). Response inhibition and impulsivity: An fMRI study. *Neuropsychologia* 4: 1959–1966.

Kalivas, P., Volkow, N., and Siemans, J. (2005). Unmanageable motivation in addiction: A pathol-ogy in prefrontal-accumbens glutamate transmission. *Neuron* 45: 647–650.

Kelley, A. (2004). Memory and addiction: Shared neural circuitry and molecular mechanisms. *Neuron* 44: 161–179.

Koob, G., Paolo Sanna, P., and Bloom, F. (1998). Neuroscience of addiction. *Neuron* 21: 467–476.

Laibson, D. (1997). Golden eggs and hyperbolic discounting. *Quarterly Journal of Economics* 112: 443–477.

Laibson, D. (1998). Life-cycle consumption and hyperbolic discount functions. *European Economic Review* 42: 861–871.

Laibson, D., Repetto, A., and Tobacman, J. (1998). Self-control and saving for retirement. *Brookings Papers on Economic Activity* 1: 91–196.

Loewenstein, G. (1996). Out of control: Visceral influences on behavior. *Organizational Behavior and Human Decision Processes* 65: 272–292.

Loewenstein, G. (1999). A visceral account of addiction. In J. Elster and O.-J. Skog, eds., *Getting Hooked: Rationality and Addiction*, 235–264. Cambridge: Cambridge University Press.

Massing, M. (2000). *The Fix*. Los Angeles: University of California Press.

Mazur, J. (1987). An adjusting procedure for studying delayed reinforcement. In M. Commons, J. Mazur, J. Nevin, and H. Rachlin, eds., *Quantitative Analysis of Behavior Vol. 5: The Effect of Delay and of Intervening Events on Reinforcement Value*, 55–73. Hillsdale, NJ: Lawrence Erlbaum Associates.

McClamrock, E. (1995). *Existential Cognition*. Chicago: University of Chicago Press.

McClure, S., Daw, N., and Montague, P. R. (2003). A computational substrate for incentive salience. *Trends in Neuroscience* 26: 423–428.

McClure, S., Laibson, D., Loewenstein, G., and Cohen, J. (2004). Separate neural systems value immediate monetary rewards. *Science* 306: 503–507.

Miller, E., and Cohen, J. (2001). An integrative theory of prefrontal cortex function. *Annual Review of Neuroscience* 24: 167–202.

Montague, P. R., and Berns, G. (2002). Neural economics and the biological substrates of valuation. *Neuron* 36: 265–284.

Montague, P. R., Dayan, P., and Sejnowski, T. (1996). A framework for mesencephalic dopamine systems based on predictive Hebbian learning. *Journal of Neuroscience* 16: 1936–1947.

Montague, P. R., King-Casas, B., and Cohen, J. (2006). Imaging valuation models in human choice. *Annual Review of Neuroscience* 29: 417–448.

O'Donoghue, T., and Rabin, M. (1999). Incentives for procrastinators. *Quarterly Journal of Economics* 114: 769–816.

Phelps, E., and Pollack, R. (1968). On second-best national saving and game equilibrium growth. *Review of Economic Studies* 35: 201–208.

Prelec, D., and Bodner, R. (2003). Self-signaling and self-control. In G. Loewenstein, D. Read, and R. Baumeister, eds., *Time and Decision*, 277–298. New York: Russell Sage Foundation.

Rachlin, H. (2000). *The Science of Self-Control*. Cambridge, MA: Harvard University Press.

Redish, A. (2004). Addiction as a computational process gone awry. *Science* 306: 1944–1947.

Read, D. (2001). Is time-discounting hyperbolic or subadditive? *Journal of Risk and Uncertainty* 23: 5–32.

Rescorla, R., and Wagner, A. (1972). A theory of Pavlovian conditioning: Variations in the effectiveness of reinforcement and nonreinforcement. In A. Black and W. Prokasy, eds., *Classical Conditioning II: Current Research and Theory*, 64–99. New York: Appleton Century Crofts.

Robinson, I., Gorny, G., Milton, E., and Kolb, B. (2001). Cocaine self-administration alters the morphology of dendrites and dendritic spines in the nucleus accumbens and neurocortex. *Synapse* 39: 257–266.

Rosenkranz, J., and Grace, A. (2001). Dopamine attenuates prefrontal cortical suppression of sensory inputs to the basolateral amygdala of rats. *Journal of Neuroscience* 21: 4090–4103.

Ross, D. (2005). *Economic Theory and Cognitive Science: Microexplanation*. Cambridge, MA: MIT Press.

Ross, D. (2006). The economics of the sub-personal: Two research programs. In B. Montero and M. White, eds., *Economics and the Mind*, 41–57. London: Routledge.

Ross, D. (2009). Integrating the dynamics of multi-scale economic agency. In H. Kincaid and D. Ross, eds., *The Oxford Handbook of Philosophy of Economic Science*, 245–279. Oxford: Oxford University Press.

Ross, D., Sharp, C., Vuchinich, R., and Spurrett, D. (2008). *Midbrain Mutiny: The Picoeconomics and Neuroeconomics of Disordered Gambling*. Cambridge, MA: MIT Press.

Sanabria, F., and Killeen, P. (2005). Freud meets Skinner: Hyperbolic curves, elliptical theories, and Ainslie interests. *Behavioral and Brain Sciences* 28: 660–661.

Schelling, T. (1978). Economics, or the art of self-management. *American Economic Review* 68: 290–294.

Schelling, T. (1980). The intimate contest for self-command. *Public Interest* 60: 94–118.

Schelling, T. (1984). Self-command in practice, in policy, and in a theory of rational choice. *American Economic Review* 74: 1–11.

Shiv, B., Loewenstein, G., Bechara, A., Damasio, H., and Damasio, A. (2005). Investment behavior and the negative side of emotion. *Psychological Science* 16: 435–439.

Siemans, J., and Yang, C. (2004). The principal features and mechanisms of dopamine modulation in the prefrontal cortex. *Progress in Neurobiology* 74: 1–57.

Simpson, C., and Vuchinich, R. (2000). Reliability of a measure of temporal discounting. *The Psychological Record* 50: 3–16.

Strotz, R. (1956). Myopia and inconsistency in dynamic utility maximization. *Review of Economic Studies* 23: 165–180.

Sutton, R., and Bartow, A. (1998). *Reinforcement Learning: An Introduction.* Cambridge, MA: MIT Press.

Wise, R. (2002). Brain reward circuitry: Insights from unsensed incentives. *Neuron* 36: 229–240.

Yang, C., Siemans, J., and Gorelova, N. (1999). Developing a neuronal model for the pathophysiology of schizophrenia based on the nature of electrophysiological actions of dopamine in the prefrontal cortex. *Neuropsychopharmacology* 21: 161–194.

6 Addiction: A Latent Property of the Dynamics of Choice

Gene M. Heyman

Introduction

The Great Lisbon Earthquake of 1755 prompted some of the first attempts to explain a natural disaster scientifically. Eighteenth-century, Enlightenment intellectuals suggested natural causes, such as expanding underground gases and explosive mixtures of chemical deposits and water. However, the quake was also interpreted as yet more evidence for the widely held view that natural disasters were the work of wrathful gods, showing their might and punishing evildoers. Today this debate is largely settled. It is generally accepted that momentous changes in the physical environment can be understood by the same principles that apply to their more moderate counterparts. The theory of plate tectonics explains earthquakes as well as the slow drift of the continents across the globe; the principles of heat exchange help explain hurricanes as well as the moderating diurnal shifts from warm sunny days to cool breezy nights.

In this chapter I take the same natural science approach to addiction that has proven so useful in the physical sciences. The governing idea is that the principles that describe everyday choice also describe addiction. That is, we need not assume disease or even psychological deficits to explain self-destructive drug use. Rather, addiction is a latent property of the rules of choice. These rules usually produce reasonable outcomes, and under some circumstances, they even yield optimal outcomes. However, under certain conditions these same principles lead to excessive, self-destructive outcomes. When one of the options is heroin or cocaine and there is a breakdown of protective social forces, the rules that describe everyday choice predict periods of drug binging alternating with periods of abstinence. The principles also predict why drugs like heroin and cocaine are more likely than other substances to support self-destructive behavior and even details of drug use such as the excuses that often accompany relapse. However, before describing how the logic of choice leads to addiction, a few preliminary matters need to be attended to.

My account of choice and addiction depends on the following preliminaries: a list of criteria for distinguishing between voluntary and involuntary activities, a list of criteria for distinguishing between addicted and nonaddicted drug users, and an understanding of what researchers have learned about the time course of addiction and the factors that predict whether addiction persists or comes to an end. The definitional issues will be discussed first.

Part I: How to Tell Whether an Activity Is Voluntary and Whether a Drug User Is Addicted

The Voluntary/Involuntary Continuum: A Sampler

The two columns of table 6.1 identify behaviors that differ in the degree to which they are voluntary. The right column identifies activities that are universally recognized as voluntary. The left column identifies activities that to varying degrees are recognized as involuntary. For instance, Patty Hearst claimed that she did not voluntarily rob a bank but was brainwashed by her kidnapers, the Symbionese Liberation Army, and coerced upon threat of death. The jury didn't believe her, but others did. (Willie Sutton said he robbed banks because "that's where the money is.") On the other hand, probably everyone agrees that reflexive, defensive eye blinks—also in the left column—are involuntary. Although the table entries are heterogeneous, they share a common property. To varying degrees they vary in frequency as a function of their consequences. The items in the right column rise and fall with mathematical precision as a function of reward and punishment (e.g., Herrnstein 1970). In contrast, the frequencies of the items in the left column vary little or not at all as a function of their consequences. For instance, imagine that you are offered $10 to not blink in response to a jet of air

Table 6.1

Involuntary activities	Voluntary activities
blink	wink
patellar reflex	kick
blush	put on rouge
food elicited key peck	instrumental key peck
cause an accidental death	murder someone
Patty Hearst's bank robbery	Willie Sutton's bank robbery
thrifty metabolism obesity	overeating obesity
insulin receptor number/affinity plasticity	exercise that leads to changes in insulin receptors
whooping crane mating dance	Times Square dancing chicken dance
vomit up food	search for food
frigid lake induced decrease in the temperature of the liver	jumping into a frigid lake
infant's reflexive smile	adult's social smile
compulsive hand washing	conventional hand washing

aimed at your eye. You can't do it. Double, triple, or quadruple the offer, and you still can't do it. Blinks are reflexive, elicited responses that depend on the stimulus conditions, not their costs and benefits. If there ever were creatures that ruminated over whether they should blink or not as a projectile hurtled toward their eyes, they have long been replaced by hardwired blinkers.

For some of the entries in the left (involuntary) column, it is possible to imagine a scenario in which they actually belong in the right, voluntary column. Taking Patty Hearst at her word ("I was coerced"), it is not out of the question to argue that had she really believed in the rule of law, she would have refused to comply with her kidnappers' commands. She could have stood on principle, even if it meant her own demise. The Southwest Pima—also in the left column—are "thrifty" metabolizers. They efficiently turn food into immediately usable calories, storing the leftover nutrients as fat. This is a useful adaptation for environments frequented by droughts and privation. However, it leads to obesity and diabetes under current conditions of ever present fast-food retail outlets. Nevertheless, the Pima could maintain a reasonable body weight if only they engaged in vigorous exercise several hours a day and went on starvation diets on a regular basis (thereby simulating their old way of life). After all, scores of prisoners have successfully completed hunger strikes to protest inhumane prison conditions.

The question of whether the symptoms of obsessive-compulsive disorder (OCD, also in the left column) are under voluntary control raises different issues. With the help of a therapist, the majority of OCD sufferers can put their compulsions to rest (e.g., Seligman, Walker, and Rosenhan 2001). There are successful pharmacological and behavioral treatments. The behavioral treatments seem to offer more lasting effects in that the methods can continue to work after treatment is over. However, the approach requires much from the patients. They have to confront the conditions that induce the obsessive, anxiety-provoking ideas and feelings. This suggests that those who do not take advantage of treatment are, perhaps, doing so in order to avoid anxiety. Or, put another way, it could be said that they are choosing to remain obsessive. Thus, a number of the entries in the left, involuntary column, are hard to classify.

The underpinnings of volition: Neural and practical   The table and commentary suggest three different ways for an activity to be considered involuntary, where involuntary means not susceptible to the influence of behavioral consequences. The first is the degree to which the neural circuits permit reward and punishment to influence the behavior. For example, there are two types of facial expressions: social/elicited and social/instrumental (Rinn 1984). Blind babies smile reflexively in response to social interactions. Later in life, blind children learn to monitor their facial expressions according to social norms, even to the point of disguising their actual emotions (e.g., Cole, Jenkins, and Shott 1989). These different smiles have their proximal underpinnings in different neural control networks. The emotion-induced expressions rely largely on subcortical pathways, whereas the neural pathway for volitional facial movements includes the motor strip of the cortex, an area of the brain that has many connections with structures that are involved in learning and memory (Rinn 1984). But the table also makes it clear that neural pathways fail to provide a full account of the voluntary/involuntary distinction. There is also a matter of feasibility. It seems legitimate to say that there is no real choice when all but one alternative entails great and immediate harm. For instance, assuming that Patty Hearst's real choices were participating in the robbery or death, it is reasonable to say that she was not a voluntary participant in the robbery. Similarly, it seems unreasonable to say the Pima are choosing to be fat when the only way to be slim is weekly fasts. The OCD case is borderline. I think it is reasonable to say that if recovery from OCD typically depends on treatment, then OCD symptoms should be considered involuntary. That is, if most OCD sufferers require professional clinical help to reduce their compulsions then the compulsions are, by the feasibility standard, involuntary.

Is Addiction Voluntary Drug Use?

Table 6.1 and commentary provide some rules for determining whether drug use in addicts is voluntary. First, are the behaviors that comprise drug seeking and drug consumption susceptible to reward and punishment? Second, are the measures needed to curb drug use in addicts within the boundaries of acceptable behavior? For instance, do everyday rewards and punishments bring drug use to a halt in addicts, or must the consequences entail cruel and inhumane measures? Obviously this issue entails historical and cultural matters so that the answer may vary according to time and place. Third, is treatment usually a necessary component of recovery?

Simple observation tells us that the activities that comprise drug seeking and drug consumption are "wired up" so as to be highly susceptible to the influence of punishment and reward. Hustling for resources, tracking down a dealer, drinking, injecting, and smoking are learned, motivated activities that vary as a function of reward and punishment. There is nothing innate about going into a store to buy liquor or sticking a needle in one's arm. But now consider these activities as means to an intoxicated state. What does it take to deter a heavy drinker from going to the store to buy gin in order to get drunk, or a heavy drug user from sticking a needle in his arm to get high on heroin? Will familiar everyday rewards and punishments do the job, or does it take draconian methods to keep a heroin addict off of heroin? Third, do addicts need professional assistance in order to quit using drugs? If draconian methods and/or professional assistance are prerequisite for quitting then it is reasonable, according to table 6.1 and the supporting discussion, to call addiction involuntary drug use. To answer these questions, we need to look at studies of how addicts behave. But to do this, we need to know how to identify addicts.

The Criteria for Identifying Addicts: The American Psychiatric Association's *Diagnostic and Statistical Manual of Mental Disorders*

The American Psychiatric Association's nosological handbook (1994), titled the *Diagnostic and Statistical Manual of Mental Disorders*, has become the gold standard for identifying psychiatric disorders for clinicians, researchers, and the courts. The manual substitutes the term "substance dependence" for "addiction." It begins its description of substance dependence in the following words:

The essential feature of Substance Dependence is a cluster of cognitive, behavioral, and physiological symptoms indicating that the individual continues use of the substance despite significant substance-related problems. There is a pattern of repeated self-administration that usually results in tolerance, withdrawal, and compulsive drug-taking behavior. (176)

Following this passage is a list of seven observable, measurable signs related to drug use, such as tolerance, withdrawal, using more drug than initially intended, or failing to stop using after vowing to do so. If three or more of these symptoms are present in the previous twelve months then the drug user is considered drug dependent. These classification rules have proven reliable and useful. Direct tests of interclinician reliability reveal high correlations (e.g., Spitzer, Forman, and Nee 1979; Spitzer, Williams, and Skodol 1980), and research based on these criteria has led to systematic findings. Those who meet the criteria for addiction reliably differ from those who do not meet the criteria (e.g., Anthony and Helzer 1991). Thus, it is reasonable to use the APA criteria for distinguishing addicts from nonaddicts. Indeed there is no better set of guidelines to go by.

Part II: On the Nature of Addiction

Is Addiction a Chronic, Relapsing Disease?

Scientific research papers, clinical texts, and National Institute on Drug Abuse (NIDA) public service announcements typically describe addiction as a "chronic, relapsing disease." These claims are not without empirical support. In clinic outcome studies, individuals in treatment for addiction often resume drug use within a year or so of the end of treatment or simply never stop using drugs despite treatment (e.g., Hunt, Barnett, and Branch 1971; Robins 1993; Wasserman et al. 1998). However, most individuals who meet the APA criteria for addiction do not enter treatment (Anthony and Helzer 1991). For instance, the most recent large-scale survey of psychiatric health in the United States estimated that only 16% of those who met the lifetime criteria for addiction had been in treatment for one or more days (Stinson, Grant, and Dawson 2005; Stinson et al. 2006). This raises the possibility that the clinic studies are based on an unrepresentative sample of drug users, and as most of what is known about drug use is based on clinic samples, the broader suggestion is that current views of addiction are based on atypical addicts. In particular, perhaps clinic addicts are less likely to quit using drugs than nonclinic addicts. If so then the current perception that addiction is a chronic disorder is based on an unrepresentative population. This hypothesis can be checked by evaluating the course of addiction in drug users who were identified at random, independent of whether they entered treatment. Four national psychiatric surveys recruited subjects in just this way.

Toward an Unbiased Estimate of Whether Addiction Is a Chronic, Relapsing Disorder
The studies were sponsored and supported by the various federal health institutes devoted to the study and treatment of drug problems (e.g., Kessler et al. 2005a,b; Robins and Regier 1991; Stinson, Grant, and Dawson 2005; Stinson et al. 2006; Warner et al. 1995). The researchers' overarching scientific goal was to obtain valid information about the prevalence of psychiatric disorders and their correlates. Subjects were recruited according to criteria that would produce a sample that approximated the demographic characteristics of the nation. In the first of these surveys groups that were considered more vulnerable to psychiatric problems were oversampled, such as prison populations (e.g., Anthony and Helzer 1991). The interviews followed semistructured, research-based guidelines that were designed to produce DSM diagnoses (e.g., Robins and Regier 1991). Sample sizes varied from about 8,000 (Kessler et al. 2005a,b) to more than 40,000 individuals (Stinson, Grant, and Dawson 2005; Stinson et al. 2006). In a foreword to the summary report of the initial (and precedent-setting) ECA survey, Daniel X. Freedman, longtime editor of the *Archives of American Psychiatry* and a leading spokesman for science-based clinical practice, wrote:

Here then is the soundest fundamental information about the range, extent and variety of psychiatric disorders ever assembled. In psychiatry, no single volume of the twentieth century has such importance and utility not just for the present but for the decades ahead. (Robins and Regier 1991, xxiv)

Freedman's words are important. If the data are, as he says, the "soundest fundamental information" available on the "extent of psychiatric disorders" then they promise to answer the question of whether addiction is a chronic relapsing disorder.

I calculated "remission" rates on the basis of estimated lifetime dependence rates and current dependence rates. For instance, the percentage of addicts in remission at the time of the interview is, by definition, the quotient: (*lifetime addicted – currently addicted*)/*lifetime addicted*. For the ECA study, which was conducted in the early 1980s, the criterion for current dependence was minimal, just one or more symptoms. For the other three surveys, the criterion for current dependence was the same as for lifetime dependence: three or more symptoms. Figure 6.1 shows the results.

The percentages vary from about 59% to 80%, which is to say the majority of those who ever met the criteria for dependence did not do so at the time of the surveys. The

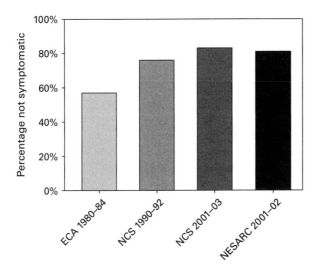

Figure 6.1
Percentage of individuals who met lifetime but not current criteria for drug abuse and dependence in national epidemiological studies.

details are worth some attention, as they are relevant to the question of whether the remission results are reliable.

The ECA had the highest rate of those still addicted (41%). Their criterion was one symptom whereas the other studies used the more standard rule of three or more symptoms. Thus, the results are sensible. When researchers used a more liberal standard for dependence, rates of dependence were higher. Moreover, it is possible to check if the markedly lower ECA remission rate is more a matter of method than fact. The NCS investigators recalculated current dependence rates using the ECA one-symptom rule. If the data are orderly, remission rates should decrease and approximate those of the ECA study. This is exactly what happened. Put another way, if the ECA researchers had used the more standard three-symptom rule, their remission rates would have been more like the other three studies.

However, the main point is that most of those who met lifetime criteria for addiction did not do so at the time of the interview. As the average age in these surveys was about 42 years old, most should still be addicted if addiction were in fact a chronic disease. This is puzzling. How can the most extensive systematic studies fail to support an idea that is so widely accepted? Perhaps the surveys are misleading. On the other hand, the surveys, despite their potential value to the understanding of addiction, go unmentioned in those reports that describe addiction as a chronic relapsing disease. The first step then at sorting this out is to see if in fact the results shown in figure 6.1 could be misleading. I first tested the idea that somehow (see below) the remission rates reflect a

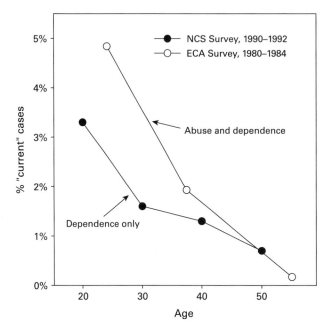

Figure 6.2
Current cases as a function of age.

temporary rather than permanent halt in drug use, and second I evaluated whether drug-specific remission rates would show the expected pattern for all but marijuana. Figures 6.2 and 6.3 test these hypotheses.

Was remission temporary? Figure 6.2 shows current cases of dependence as a function of age (Anthony and Helzer 1991; Warner et al. 1995). This tests the possibility that the high remission rates really reflect a pattern in which relatively short periods of heavy drug use are followed by relatively long periods of abstinence. Given sufficiently biased "time-on/time-off" ratios, a one-shot interview could, in principle, produce misleading high remission rates. However, if one year of remission typically stretched into a lifetime of remission then the prevalence of current cases of addiction among lifetime addicts should plummet as a function of age. The graph shows two different cohorts. This provides a check for historical trends. For both cohorts, the overall percentage of current cases plummets. By age 30 more than half of those who were addicted at age 20 no longer are using illicit drugs in a clinically significant manner.

Are the high remission rates due to marijuana smokers? Figure 6.3 tests whether remission rates vary markedly as a function of the type of drug that is abused. Perhaps

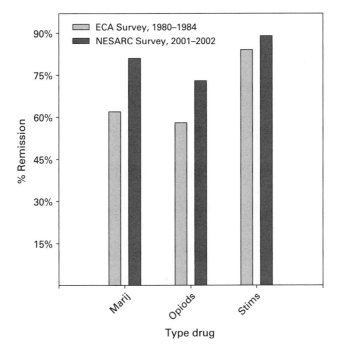

Figure 6.3
Type of drug.

those who met the criteria for marijuana dependence remit, whereas heavy stimulant and opiate users do not, thereby preserving the conventional view of addiction for the "harder" drugs. The figure shows the results for the two surveys that provided data for specific drug groups. These are also the two largest studies (Anthony and Helzer 1991; Stinson, Grant, and Dawson 2005; Stinson et al. 2006). Remission is about the same for marijuana, opiates, and stimulants. However, these and similar surveys show that remission rates are lower and less age-dependent for the two legal addictive drugs, alcohol and cigarettes (e.g., Helzer, Burnam, and McEvoy 1991). This suggests that access to drugs and the correlates of illegality play an important role in the persistence of drug use, even in those who are addicted.

Summary of remission (resolution) results These results do not say that all heavy illicit drug users automatically stop using drugs as they approach the end of their twenties. Clearly a significant number of individuals remain heavy illicit drug users into their forties and beyond. Those who do not quit include the clinic populations that have figured so heavily in the addiction literature, and they may also include the homeless and recidivist criminal offenders. But the vast majority of individuals who meet the criteria for addiction are neither in jail nor homeless. Thus, the data say that most individuals who meet the criteria for addiction stop using at about age 30 or younger. Importantly, this same result was found in every major scientific population survey conducted over the last thirty years. These studies are models of current best practices. They randomly selected subjects; they used the APA criteria for classifying psychiatric disorders; and they employed interview techniques that have a strong track record for reliability and validity (e.g., Robins and Regier 1991; Spitzer, Forman, and Nee 1979; Spitzer, Williams, and Skodol 1980).

The Typical Correlates of Quitting Illicit Drugs: Draconian Punishments or the Mounting Pressures of Adult Life?

According to the four most recent national surveys of mental health in the United States, most addicts stop using illicit drugs at clinically significant levels by the time they reach their early thirties. As most of those who quit illicit drug use did not seek treatment, a reasonable inference is that the correlates of quitting were related to the various obligations and liabilities of age and maturity. Children, spouses, the need for employment and the various other liabilities and responsibilities that accompany getting older interfere with getting high on a regular basis, particularly if the drug is illegal. This inference suggests the more general point that addiction rates will vary markedly as a function of situational factors. Several lines of evidence support this inference. Biographies, ethnographic studies of drug-using populations, and large-scale surveys all point to everyday events as the correlates of quitting drugs among addicts. Some of the highlights of this large literature include the following.

William Burroughs (1959) vividly likened his state of mind as an addict to that of a rabid dog's state of mind. Just as a rabid dog cannot be tamed into not biting, the drug addict cannot be restrained from taking more drugs:

A dope fiend is a man in total need of dope. Beyond a certain frequency need knows absolutely no limit or control. In the words of total need: *"Wouldn't you?"* Yes you would. You would lie, cheat, inform on your friends, steal, do *anything* to satisfy total need. Because you would be in a state of total sickness, total possession, and not in a position to act in any other way. Dope fiends are sick people who cannot act other than they do. A rabid dog cannot choose but bite. (xxxix)

However, when Burroughs's stipend from home came to an end, he could no longer afford dope. Rather than take a job or turn to crime, he quit opiates. Toneatto and his colleagues (1999) studied the correlates of quitting cocaine in untreated former cocaine addicts. The control group was untreated current cocaine addicts. The two groups did not differ in terms of demographics, pharmacological history, or psychiatric characteristics. Rather, recovery was correlated with cognitive processes. Those who quit were more likely to report that they had spent some time "weighing the pros and cons" of continued cocaine use and had decided in favor of the cons. There were no particular triggering events for quitting. Rather, it was a matter of everyday life events. Those who quit decided that everyday life would be better without cocaine. (But note this presumes that there are alternatives to cocaine.) Biernacki (1986) reports somewhat similar findings for a population of former heroin users, and Waldorf, Reinarman, and Murphy (1991) obtained comparable results for a population of former San Francisco Bay Area cocaine users.

For most individuals conventional responsibilities and heavy drug use are at odds. Over time the pressures of earning an income and maintaining ties with family and friends overwhelm the benefits that the drugs provide. Of course, this isn't true for everyone. For one thing not everyone has familial or occupational obligations, and as emphasized in the section on choice, drug use itself may have irreparably severed the addict's ties with family and occupation. However, these cases appear to be in the minority so that the survey results support the inference that the weight of the everyday ends up overwhelming drug use for most addicts.

Additional Psychiatric Disorders Distinguish Addicts Who Quit from Those Who Do Not

The issue of what distinguishes addicts who quit from those who do not is little studied, although it has to be one of the most (if not the most) relevant topics for the understanding of addiction and for research-based treatment design. Interestingly, the few available studies that used DSM criteria for identifying addicts (e.g., Carroll and Rounsaville 1992; Rounsaville and Kleber 1985) did not find differences in pharmacological history. Rather the research supports the conclusion that addicts who quit are much less likely to suffer from additional psychiatric disorders than those who do not quit (e.g., Heyman 2001; Regier et al. 1990). This fits in with the data presented so far. If quitting is a matter of choice then quitting depends on the availability of better choices. Psychiatric disorders undermine the ability to find better alternatives to drugs. Thus, it makes sense for the presence of additional psychiatric disorders to show up as the strongest predictor of the persistence of drug use in addicts.

The correlation between clinic addicts and psychiatric disorders is relevant to two points made at the beginning of this chapter regarding widely shared understandings of addiction and research studies that recruit their subjects from clinics. The two observations go hand in hand. Clinic addicts are much less likely to stop using drugs than nonclinic addicts. The comorbidity data help explain why this is the case. When addiction is coupled with additional disorders, it is much harder to quit drugs. The more general message is that whether addiction persists depends on individual differences. For most addicts drug use comes to a halt; for those with additional medical problems it is much less likely to come to a halt. This is sensible, but it is a sensibility that is missing from most of the writing on addiction.

Effective Clinic Treatments Mimic the Natural Recovery Results

The point of this review is not to say that drug addicts do not need help or that drug treatment is of little use. Rather the review shows that the correlates of quitting are often everyday circumstances. This suggests an approach to treatment. Assuming that the right interpretation of the literature is that drug use in addicts persists as a function of its costs and benefits, then treatments that alter the consequences of drug use should prove effective. The inference has no shortage of empirical support.

There are several effective pharmacotherapies for addiction (e.g., Dole and Nyswander 1967; Fiore et al. 1994; Pettinati et al. 2006). These all work by the same principle. They alter receptor dynamics so as to reduce the reward value of the drug, thereby shifting preference to nondrug activities. For example, methadone binds to opiate receptors. This mollifies withdrawal symptoms and attenuates the intensity of heroin's positive hedonic effects, particularly the rush. As a result heroin is less rewarding.

There are several proven behavioral therapies for addiction. These include Alcoholics Anonymous and its various relatives, voucher programs, and treatments that combine random drug testing with financial penalties. Alcoholics Anonymous and voucher programs are best known. They differ in numerous respects but both establish viable alternatives to drug use. In AA it is an alcohol-free social life. The voucher programs establish individually tailored activities, such as hobbies (e.g., Alcoholics Anonymous 1976; Higgins et al. 2000). The penalty programs are less well known but highly effective for addicts who have much to lose if they test positive for drug use. Figure 6.4 summarizes the results of treatment programs for physicians and airplane pilots. The

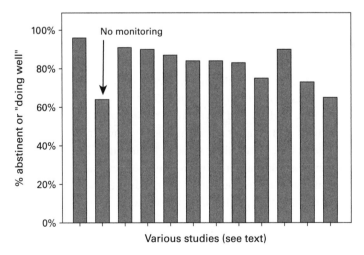

Figure 6.4
Abstinence when evidence of drug use can result in job loss.

common component in these treatment plans was testing for drug use (which in all but one case was random) and the contingency that a positive test could result in the suspension of professional activities. The studies were cited in a book on drug abuse in "professionals" (Coombs 1997). The graph shows that success rates averaged about 90% for those programs that included random testing. These results are not in accord with the claim that "addiction is a chronic relapsing disease," but they do fit with the view that addicts voluntarily persist in self-destructive drug use.

Summary of Part II: On the Nature of Addiction

The sources in this review have included biographies, ethnographic studies, and large-scale surveys. Each approach tells, in its own way, the same story. Drug use in addicts typically resolves before the user is much past thirty years old, and most often does so without the help of professional intervention. This suggests that the correlates of quitting are largely everyday events—the sort of occurrences that influence most decisions. Studies of recovery from addiction support this inference. As the costs of drug use increase and the benefits decrease, the addict is increasingly likely to quit. However, this finding leads to an apparently nonsensical conclusion. If drug use in addicts remains voluntary then they must have been engaged in voluntary self-destructive behavior. From the point of view that voluntary actions are guided by their consequences, this doesn't make sense. That is, given the definition that voluntary acts are those acts that are subject to their consequences then voluntary acts should extinguish once their costs outweigh their benefits. If addiction is a disorder then its costs must outweigh its benefits. Hence, addiction should never emerge or if it does emerge it should extinguish quickly. It does, as we just saw, extinguish, but not that quickly. Drug use that meets the criteria for addiction is robust and often persists for several years or more. This is puzzling. How can behavior that is maintained by its costs and benefits persist when the costs outweigh the benefits? As the empirical findings seem quite solid, the conceptual problem must hold the key to this riddle. Perhaps a more nuanced account of voluntary action is in order. The next section of this chapter focuses on the nature of voluntary action. The analysis leads to the result that addiction and other forms of excessive consumption are inherent in the principles that guide choice.

Part III: Choice and Addiction

Three Basic Features of Voluntary Behavior

This section presents an analysis of choice and addiction. It is based on three elementary features of voluntary behavior and proceeds in three steps. First the features are combined and displayed in graphs that plot the relationship between preference and the values of the competing options. Second, I trace out the logical implications of the graphs for choice in general and addiction in particular. Third, I consider a few empirical tests of the analysis as it applies to addiction. These tests focus on behavioral phenomena that are unique to addiction. The results help explain why addicts continue to use drugs when they could improve their lot by cutting back or stopping altogether. More generally, the analysis helps solve a particular version of the general problem of voluntary self-destructive behavior. The model shows that excessive consumption levels are inherent to choice, and that depending on the properties of the commodities at hand, the degree of excess can be great. The three observations are as follows:

Many of the variables that influence choice change in value as a function of having been chosen, or consumed, or simply of time itself   Voluntary activities are goal oriented. The goals have value in the sense that they attract preferences. The values change as a function of the preferences. For instance, behaviors motivated by biological goals, such as satisfying hunger, reduce hunger, those motivated by cognitive concerns, say curiosity, reduce curiosity (at least locally), and similar dynamics apply to other wants, desires, and interests. The relationships need not follow a simple function, and the functions linking consumption and value need not slope downward. Potato chips augment the desire for more potato chips, at least at first, and activities that involve skills and/or knowledge, such as piano playing or birdwatching, often provide greater and greater enjoyment as skill and/or knowledge increase. However, whatever the shape of the function linking choice and goal values, it is usually if not always the case that the values that guide our choices change as a function of the choices we make.

For a series of choices there is more than one way of framing the possible options
Given a series of choices between two or more items, it is possible to frame the choice locally or globally. The local frame of reference pits one item against the other. The global frame of reference combines the items so that the choice is between aggregates composed of different proportions of each item. For example, given apples and oranges, we can choose either one or the other, or we can organize the apples and oranges into bundles, and ask "should I commit to a basket of four oranges and six apples or a basket composed of two oranges and eight apples?" In economics textbooks, consumers are described as taking the market basket approach (e.g., Baumol and Blinder 1994; Samuelson 1967), whereas in experiments and in many everyday situations, individuals more often frame their options as items rather than market baskets even though they are in situations that involve a series of choices (e.g., Herrnstein et al. 1993; Heyman and Dunn 2002; Heyman and Tanz 1995; Vaughan 1981; Vaughan and Herrnstein 1987). Although the issue of framing options as items or aggregates has not been much discussed, it can make a great difference in terms of overall preference

and overall benefits. For example, it is possible to arrange choice experiments in which the item-by-item frame of reference yields exclusive preference for one item, whereas the aggregate frame of reference yields exclusive preference for the other item (e.g., Herrnstein et al. 1993; Heyman and Dunn 2002). Material presented in this chapter and elsewhere (Heyman 2003) shows that differences in the nature of the available commodities determine the degree to which frame of reference matters. For instance, when the available options include addictive drugs, frame of reference matters a great deal.

Individuals choose the best option As "best" is not independently defined, this may seem a tautological statement. However, it is a useful and commonplace observation. It helps establish a quantitative account of choice and furthers, I believe, our understanding of human behavior.

These three observations were combined to provide an account of everyday choice and of addiction. In keeping with the idea that addiction is a function of general principles of choice and does not require special rules, the everyday situation will be described first. The goal is to introduce the principles and then show that under certain circumstances these principles lead to addiction. The everyday example, eating out at restaurants, is based on an example initially introduced by Herrnstein (1990). More generally, the analysis presented here borrows and builds on Herrnstein and Prelec's (1992) account of addiction and distributed choice.

The Three Observations Predict That Choice Is Governed by Competing Equilibrium States

Figures 6.5 and 6.6 embody the three characteristics of voluntary behavior that were just reviewed. The first shows the relationship between choice and the value of eating out. Assume two restaurants and that the value of each cuisine changes as a function of how frequently it is sampled. For simplicity, the relationship between choice and value is linear. And as a way of depicting satiation and other consumption-dependent declines in value, the lines slope downward. Of course, there is any number of possible shapes to the value functions, but these complexities do not alter the conclusions discussed in this chapter.

On the x-axis of each graph is the number of times each restaurant was selected in the most recent ten meals. (The x-axis is a moving window that is updated with every choice.) The y-axis for the left panel shows the value of each meal when the options are framed as a series of independent choices. The right panel shows the same restaurants for the same consumer (that is, his or her tastes are the same), but now the restaurants are aggregated into competing combinations or market baskets, composed of ten restaurants each (a meal plan). For example, the leftmost point is a 10-Italian/ 0-Chinese meal plan, whereas the midpoint on the x-axis marks off a 5-Italian/

5-Chinese meal plan. Consequently, the y-axis for this graph shows the value of each of eleven possible combinations of Chinese and Italian meals. As noted below these values are obtained by weighting the value of a meal by the number or times it is consumed. The equations are given next. The symbol x stands for the number of times that the diner went to the Chinese restaurant in the last 10 meals, Vc is the value of a Chinese meal given that it had been selected x times in the last 10 meals, Vi is the value of an Italian meal given that it has been selected $10 - x$ times in the last 10 meals, and $Vmealplan$ is the value of a meal plan composed of x Chinese meals and $10 - x$ Italian meals:

$$Vc = (10 - 0.9x) \tag{1a}$$

$$Vi = 4.5 - 0.15(10 - x) = 3 + 0.15x \tag{1b}$$

$$Vmealplan = xVc + (10 - x)Vi \tag{2}$$

Summary   In each graph the choice rule is the same: choose the option that has the higher value. However, in the left panel options are framed as individual meals, whereas in the right panel, options are framed as aggregates composed of different proportions of Chinese and Italian meals.

There are two possible equilibria—the world of choice is ambiguous   Figure 6.5 shows that each approach leads to an equilibrium. In the one-meal-at-a-time frame of reference, the diner switches restaurants when the one most recently visited has a

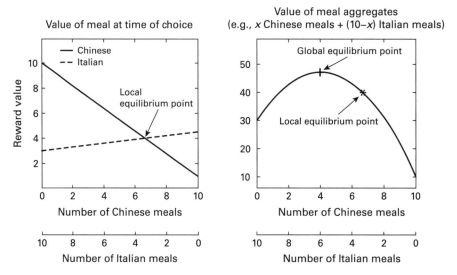

Figure 6.5

lower expected value. This drives overall preference to the point that each restaurant provides an equally good meal. This is where the lines cross. The crossing point is also the distribution of choices predicted by the matching law (Herrnstein 1970), a highly general choice rule (discussed later in this chapter). The dynamic process that yields matching (and the crossing point equilibrium) is referred to as "melioration," a term that captures the idea that individuals choose whatever is best at the moment (e.g., Vaughan 1981, Vaughan and Herrnstein 1987). The meal plan approach also leads to an equilibrium. Its equilibrium is the combination of meals that produces the highest overall value. However, the equilibria for the two approaches are not the same. The meal-at-a-time approach yields an overall preference for Chinese food; the meal-plan approach yields an overall preference for Italian food. Importantly, the differences are not economically neutral. The meal-plan approach earns about 20% more eating pleasure. The increment in value is not due to any change in the restaurants or the consumers' tastes. For example, the equations for the value of a meal are the same in the left and right panel (e.g., $Vc = 10 - 0.9x$ in both panels). Rather, the difference is entirely due to how the consumer frames his or her options. Thus, a shift in the frame of reference can, by itself, lead to changes in overall preference and overall benefits.

The Psychology of Local and Global Bookkeeping

Before applying this analysis to drugs, it would be useful to add some "psychology" to the graph and also address a concern that is likely to have occurred to some readers. Following the dictum that there are "no free lunches," the market basket approach must have a catch. It does not seem plausible to increase earnings by 20% by simply reimagining the structure of the options.

There are costs. First, the market basket approach is considerably more complex than the meal-at-a time approach. For instance, in the restaurant problem the item-by-item equilibrium is a function of simply choosing the best of two options on each trial, whereas the global equilibrium entails eleven possible outcomes, each ten meals long. It would take a great deal of time to sample each ten meal combination and a good deal of record keeping to keep tabs on their respective values. There are, though, various strategies for simplifying the meal-plan comparisons. For example, a quantity used in economics, referred to as marginal utility, leads to the same preference equilibrium as does the best aggregate, but with much less computation. However, this measure remains considerably more complex than the meal-at-a-time approach, and, more important and more interesting, there is evidence that consumers do not track marginal utilities whereas there is evidence that under certain conditions, they do track market baskets or some feature of market baskets (other than marginal utility). For example, in several experiments with college students, Rachlin and his colleagues found that when they arranged the temporal pattern of choice trials to highlight the aggregate structure of a series of choices, the subjects began making choices as predicted by a market basket frame of references (e.g., Kudadjie-Gyamfi and Rachlin 1996; Rachlin and Siegel 1994). Heyman and Tanz (1995) obtained similar results in a study with pigeons in which the aggregate structure of a series of choices was highlighted by the color of the stimulus lights.

Second, there is a temporal factor that favors the meal-at-a-time frame of reference. The advantages provided by the meal with the higher value arrive right away. In contrast, the advantages that accompany choosing the best series of meals build up slowly, and on occasion, this frame of reference requires taking the meal that is currently not favored. For example, if five of the last ten meals were Chinese, the graph says that on the next night out, the Chinese meal would provide more pleasure. However, the meal plan approach says that there should be six Italian meals for every four Chinese meals. Hence, to get the best eating experience, as measured over a series of meals, diners must occasionally eat at the restaurant that they currently like second best. It is not obvious how this is managed, but however it is, effort must be involved. For example, the opportunity for the better meal is either ignored or the forgone pleasure is reinterpreted as a sign that tomorrow holds the promise of an even better Chinese meal.

An Analysis of Choice Based on Fundamental Features of Voluntary Behavior Does Not Look Like Rational Choice

In economics and behavioral biology and some areas of psychology it is often assumed that individuals are global optimizers—which, in the terms of figure 6.5, is a way of saying that individuals take the meal-plan approach to choice. This is at least partially at odds with the vision of individual choice presented in these pages. The restaurant graph says that it is possible for choice to stabilize at a distribution that is suboptimal; that shifts in the frame of reference can lead to a shift in the distribution of choices (overall preference); and that the contingencies that guide voluntary action are inherently ambiguous. Given choice-dependent changes in value, it is always possible to draw up two "best" choice policies. These observations predict that consumers will often experience ambivalence and labile preferences, and end up at a suboptimal local equilibrium, although at each opportunity they made what seemed the best choice. These two visions of individual behavior reflect different origins. The idea that individuals are global optimizers has its roots in the idea that rationality serves as a reasonable foundational assumption for understanding human behavior (e.g., Ferguson and Gould 1975; Samuelson 1967). The analysis presented here combines rationality ("choose what is best") with elementary features of voluntary action—namely that the values that guide choice are not stable and that in a series of choices, items can be framed as items or as aggregates.

Drug Use as Depicted by the "Meal-at-a-Time" and "Meal-Plan" Analysis

Figure 6.6 demonstrates that the three principles that generated the restaurant graph can generate a graph that approximates the American Psychiatric Association's (1994)

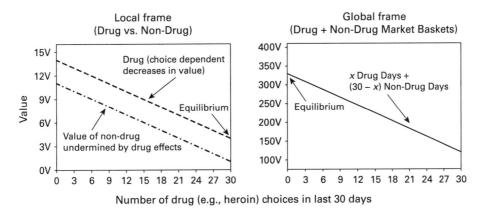

Figure 6.6
Number of drug (e.g., heroin) choices in the last thirty days.

account of addiction. The origins of the graph are experiments on choice. Herrnstein and his colleagues (1993) arranged a two-button choice procedure in which monetary rewards changed in value as a function of the subject's choices. Responses at one button reduced the monetary payoffs at both buttons, whereas responses at the other button increased the monetary payoffs at both buttons. Although they did not relate their study to addiction or other forms of excessive behavior, their contingency, displayed in figure 6.6, provides a close analogy to the verbal account of substance dependence found in the *Diagnostic and Statistical Manual of Mental Disorders*.

Graphing addiction   In figure 6.6, the x-axes measure the number of days an individual took drugs in the last thirty days. Note that as before, each x-axis is a moving window so that it reflects the most recent thirty choices, not necessarily the first thirty opportunities to use the drug. The y-axis in the left panel lists the current values of drug days and nondrug days. These values change as a function of the number of times the drug was used. In the right panel, the y-axis is the value of different combinations of drug days and nondrug days. For example at $x = 10$, the y-axis reveals the value of 10 drug days and 20 nondrug days, and at $x = 11$, the y-axis now shows the value of 11 drug days plus 19 nondrug days, etc. Thus, the idea of the left panel is that the individual chooses what to do one day at a time, whereas the perspective of the right panel is that the individual makes choices according to a 30-day lifestyle: "do I want to be high all the time, some of the time, or none of the time?" From here on out it will be simpler and more appropriate to refer to the "meal-at-a-time" frame of reference as "local bookkeeping" or "day-at-a-time" frame of reference, and the "meal-plan" frame of reference as "global bookkeeping" or "lifestyle" frame of reference. The equations that generated the lines for the two panels are in the endnote.[1]

The left panel shows what the APA account of addiction "looks" like   In the left panel, the top downward-sloping line represents the value of the drug and the bottom downward-sloping line represents the value of various competing nondrug activities. That the line representing the value of the drug is higher says that the drug is preferred (which is essential for a choice-based account of addiction), and that it slopes downward says that tolerance has decreased the value of the drug.

The line that depicts the value of nondrug activities also slopes downward. This is a literal translation of the cardinal feature of the APA account of addiction. Recall that according to the APA, the central feature of addiction is: *that drug use continues despite mounting negative consequences*. The graph assigns these negative consequences to the competing activities, because this is in fact what happens. The direct consequences of drug use, such as intoxication and withdrawal symptoms, interfere with the ability to function, particularly in conventional social situations. It is difficult to converse with customers or tend to family duties while drunk or hungover. The downward slope also captures the indirect, socially mediated liabilities of drug use. These include legal consequences, such as an arrest record, and the stigma that often accompanies heavy drug use. Individuals with a criminal record for drug offenses and a reputation for shooting up or drinking heavily tend to have fewer opportunities. For example, because of federal regulations, students with drug offenses on their records have a more difficult time obtaining loans for college study. Put more generally, addictive drug use undermines the value of legitimate activities that normally would compete with drug use. Thus, the value of the drug, although declining, remains higher than the value of the (shrinking) nondrug alternatives. In the end, the drug is chosen exclusively—a full-out binge.

Note that these dynamics differ from those in the restaurant problem. Eating Chinese food did not lead to binging on Chinese food because after a while Italian food was better. However, drugs do not let the competition get better. Rather, they make the competition worse. Thus, as shown in figure 6.6, drug use can lead to a situation in which the drug is the only commodity "left standing." The pattern looks exactly like an "out of control, drug binge." But reward value and choice, not compulsion, are the driving forces.

A lifestyle frame of reference predicts abstinence   The right panel shows the same two commodities from the perspective of organizing them into aggregates composed of series of 30 consecutive days. This represents decisions framed as competing lifestyles. In this framework, the best option is just the opposite of the best option in the local bookkeeping approach: never use drugs. The equilibrium is 0 days of drug plus 30 days of nondrug activities. Again, it should be emphasized that nothing has changed other than the frame of reference. The person in the right panel who never uses heroin likes heroin just as much as the person in the left panel who uses heroin every day.

(The equation for the value of heroin in both panels is $Vh = 14 - 0.33x$, where x is the number of days heroin was used in the last 30 days.) However, the person represented by the right panel considers heroin from the perspective of its influence on subsequent nondrug days as well as its influence on subsequent heroin days, which is to say, the decision is a lifestyle decision. (The corresponding equation is $xVh + (30 - x)Vnh$, where Vnh is the value of a nondrug day.)

Summary: Ambiguity, Relapse, and Abstinence

The choice rule for each graph is take what is best. However, the outcomes could not be more different: always use heroin/never use heroin. From the perspective of the right panel, the individual in the left panel could not be doing worse, and, from the perspective of the right panel, the reason is that he or she is doing so poorly is excessive drug use. From the perspective of the left panel, heroin is the best choice. Again, it should be emphasized that heroin has the same value on a day-to-day basis in both panels. Thus, frame of reference accounts for what seems like a compulsive, out-of-control pattern of drug use.

Two possible equilibrium states and the temporal pattern of heavy drug use   One of the implications of this analysis is that the contingencies that guide voluntary action are inherently ambiguous. This is because under most conditions, the local and global equilibria diverge, although often not by much (the analysis supporting this point is not presented in this chapter).

As it is always possible for conditions to change so that the frame of reference changes, the fact that the local and global equilibria are usually different means that there is always the potential for preference to shift from one equilibrium to the other. Consequently, it is more accurate to say that the equilibria that attend choice are "semistable" or inherently labile. For instance, the ever-present local equilibrium ensures that there is an ever-present threat of relapse (for the abstinent drug user), and conversely, the ever-present global equilibrium ensures that the heavy drug user could quit all at once. Together these observations suggest that drug use will often vacillate between periods of heavy use and periods of abstinence. This is what is observed.

If the Local Frame of Reference Supports Self-Destructive Patterns of Behavior, Why Does It Persist?

Addiction is a disposition. It reflects the accumulating consequences of a series of choices. One drink does not imply alcoholism, just as one day without a drink does not imply temperance. According to the analysis presented here, those who use drugs self-destructively fail to frame their choices in a way that is commensurate with the dispositional character of addiction. They make their choices one at a time, as if they were always taking the drug just once. In contrast, those who do not fall victim to the seductive powers of drugs treat drugs, and commodities like them, dispositionally. They choose a safe rate of consumption, which is to say, they choose a rate (and it may be zero) that does not undermine other important concerns. But given that the local frame of reference yields such poor results when one of the choices is an addictive drug, it is puzzling that this approach to decisions persists. Shouldn't all drug users learn that they have to take into consideration a drug's lifestyle value as well as its current value? These points suggest that the factors that prop up local bookkeeping must be powerful. Next I list three reasons why the local frame of reference persists despite its liabilities.

The perceptual structure of experience favors item-by-item choices   Perceptual experience seems largely to follow the outlines of items and individual activities, not aggregates made up of items and activities. Restaurants exist as independent units; the opportunities to use heroin arrive one at a time. Conversely, the aggregate "eight Chinese meals plus two Italian meals" is not a naturally occurring unit. Similarly, the bundle "three days of heroin plus twenty-seven nondrug days" is not a naturally occurring unit. To be sure, one can create multiday meal plans and multiday drug-use plans, but these are abstractions. They require thinking ahead, imagined consequences, and new categories that compound unlike activities and objects: "first I will mow the lawn, then reward myself with an hour on the courts." By definition, abstractions are less vivid, and less compelling than tangible goods and activities. Local bookkeeping is in accord with the natural fracture lines of nature. In contrast, global bookkeeping requires a reworking of the world as it is perceived and experienced. These comments point out that local bookkeeping options—items and activities—are more salient, and this in turn suggests that saliency directly or indirectly reinforces local bookkeeping.

Hyperbolic discounting and the difficulty of detecting delayed costs   As demonstrated in numerous studies, the motivational pull of behavioral consequences declines steeply as a function of delay (see Ainslie 1975, 1992; Green and Myerson 2004; Rachlin 2000). A characteristic of all addictive drugs is that their positive effects come quickly if not immediately, whereas their costs are greatly delayed. For example, cigarettes provide virtually instantaneous benefits (taste, nicotine, and the sensory pleasures of inhaling smoke), whereas their costs are probabilistic and take years if not decades to show up (cancer and other diseases). As a result, smoking can persist for some time before its true costs are realized.

The failure to take advantage of socially mediated guidelines that promote the global equilibrium   The global reward options are complex. Recall, for example, that in the restaurant problem there were eleven candidates for the best global meal plan. However, there is a way around these difficulties. Recall that in the restaurant and addiction graphs (figures 6.5 and 6.6), the local equilibrium was to the right of the global equilibrium. This suggests (and it can be proven) that any practice that reduces consumption of the most favored item or activity will push the local equilibrium toward the global equilibrium. Socially mediated rules on appetites are usually restrictive. They stress moderation, temperance, and in some cases outright abstinence. Social mores and even laws restrict when and where sex can occur, and to varying degrees social customs do the same for all other appetites. (This is not to deny Dionysian cultural traditions, but these do not seem as pervasive or powerful as those stressing temperance.) Thus, an individual can ensure that he or she will not end up at the local equilibrium by simply following, perhaps blindly, culturally mediated teachings on appetites. Indeed this analysis provides a convenient story for why humans are willing to support social institutions that limit their own freedoms, and why humans are so socially docile, either by learning or inheritance or both.

But what about individuals who reject mainstream societal prohibitions on appetites? According to this analysis of social mores, they will have a much more difficult time avoiding the local equilibrium. They will have to find the global equilibrium on their own, and the graphs reveal that this is not easy. Thus, local bookkeeping may also be sustained by antisocial attitudes. However, it should be added that these issues are very complex. For example, nonconventional value systems, such as those found in spiritual movements, often reject intoxicating drugs. This suggests that any value system, including nonconventional ones, that promotes behaviors that are more in line with global bookkeeping will end up rejecting addictive drugs. In any case, society offers values and practices that help people avoid the penalties inherent to local bookkeeping. These methods simply require adherence to the norms. This is a much simpler approach than sorting out the best policy regarding one's needs and appetites from scratch.

Summary

There are good reasons for the local frame of reference to persist if not dominate most decision making. The decision process is simpler, the true costs are often hard to detect at first, and the options are framed so as to fit well if not precisely with perceptual experience. However, logic and experience also reveal that pitfalls will eventually emerge. Fortunately, the level of overall benefits associated with the local and global equilibria are not that different for most commodities. However, for a few commodities, the local equilibrium is seriously deficient. We say that these commodities are dangerous, and accordingly, they are often the target of informal and legal prohibitions. One way around the danger's posed by seriously suboptimal local equilibria is to "nibble at the edges" until a safe level of consumption is arrived at. Or one can simply adhere to the prohibitions, relying on tradition for how to pursue one's own appetites.

Part IV: Evidence and Predictions That Support the Local/Global Analysis of Appetites and Addiction

Behavioral Studies

If the analysis presented in these pages is correct then voluntary actions should gravitate to the local or global equilibrium. The local equilibrium is equivalent to the matching law predictions (see, e.g., Herrnstein 1990). The matching law predictions have been summarized in various books and review articles (Davison and McCarthy 1988; Herrnstein 1970, 1990; Williams 1988). They hold for different species, different reinforcers, in laboratory settings, in nonlaboratory settings, and are now the subject of research in economics, psychopharmacology, and neuroscience. There is no shortage of support for the prediction that choice gravitates to the local equilibrium.

The global equilibrium describes the ideal distribution of choices. However, it was pointed out that the perceptual structure of experience is more in accord with locally framed options. This predicts that experimenters can push subjects from the local to the global equilibrium by arranging stimulus conditions that highlight the aggregate structure of a series of choices. There are several experiments in which subjects distributed their choices as predicted by the global equilibrium. As predicted by the discussion of the "natural fracture lines of experience," the experimenters arranged stimuli that corresponded to the abstract, aggregate structure of a series of choices (e.g., Heyman and Tanz 1995; Rachlin and Siegel 1994).

One line of experiments and naturalistic studies reveals that choice distributions settle in at the local equilibrium (e.g., the matching law literature). Another line shows that under certain conditions, choice distributions settle in at the global equilibrium or at some point in between the local and global predictions. The two literatures fit together nicely. The natural or default choice allocation is the one predicted by the simple rule: "choose the best item or activity." Economic analyses reveal the liabilities of local bookkeeping and the advantages of paying attention to choice-dependent changes in value. Thus, when the default approach to choice is supplemented by analysis and/or prudential (socially mediated) rules, the global equilibrium or an approximation of it emerges (see Prelec and Herrnstein 1991 for a fascinating discussion of this issue).

The Local/Global Analysis Predicts Spontaneous Recovery and the Rationalizations That Accompany Relapse

The local/global analysis predicts specific features of addiction as well as the overall pattern of drug binges and periods of abstinence. Next, I review two predictions. They are good test cases because they distinguish addiction from other disorders. One is spontaneous recovery. The other is the utterance that often accompanies relapse: "this is the last time."

Spontaneous remission   It was pointed out that shifts in the frame of reference could lead to abrupt changes in the pattern of drug use. For a currently abstinent but previously heavy drug user, a shift to the local frame of reference implies relapse. Conversely, for a currently heavy drug user, a shift to a global frame of reference implies abstinence, which is likely to be labeled "spontaneous recovery," particularly if the antecedents of the shift in the frame of reference are obscure. Assuming that choice plays much more of a role in addiction than other psychiatric disorders, these observations imply that addiction will be the disorder most closely linked with spontaneous recovery. A number of findings support this prediction.

To test whether addiction was the psychiatric disorder most closely linked to spontaneous recovery, I did a search in the digital reference source, *psychINFO*. The search terms "addiction or dependence or alcoholism" and "spontaneous recovery" triggered 29 hits. In contrast, the same search with "obsessive-compulsive disorder" and "Tourettes" as substitutes for the addictions triggered just three hits. More interesting, addiction seems to be the only psychiatric disorder listed in the DSM that has been a source of new terms for spontaneous recovery. The phrases "going cold turkey" and "kicking the habit" refer to the process of going off heroin and have remained within the domain of addiction. No one talks about going "cold turkey" in relationship to OCD or schizophrenia, but they do talk about "going cold turkey" in regard to smoking. The implication is that people do quit heroin and smoking all at once, but not OCD.

The vocabulary of relapse   Just as there are specific terms for quitting drugs, there are also verbal formulas linked to relapse. Those who plan to quit drugs but don't, typically preface their next drink or shot of heroin with the words, "this is the last time," or "I will start my detox tomorrow." An interesting feature of this excuse is that it is so robust. Although hackneyed and usually misleading, it seems not to lose its power. This is curious. How can an utterance that is so transparently misleading continue to survive? The local/global analysis provides some hints. The key idea is in a kind of logical trick that resolves the conflicting demands of local and global bookkeeping.

Global bookkeeping provides the best strategy when outcomes depend on a series of choices. However, we also saw that this can mean taking the second-best choice on some trials. This creates a conflict between what is best now and what is best overall. The ideal solution would be to somehow enjoy both what is best now and what is best overall. On many trials this is the case (see, for example, figure 6.5). However, there are always some trials when the two approaches call for different choices, and for some commodities and some people these occasions may be rather frequent. For instance, according to Alcoholics Anonymous there is a population of drinkers who are either teetotalers or helpless drunks; they cannot drink socially. However, even for this population there is one occasion in which the conflict between local and global dissolves. The last choice in a series has no future consequences. Logically, it is a singlet. If it really is the last opportunity to have a drink then the "alcoholic" can safely have a drink. Thus, it is possible to justify any local decision that is at odds with a global decision if it is framed as the "last time." On any true last time this is legitimate. However, in advance it is hard to tell whether this time is really the last time. Accordingly, the preface to relapse and not quitting drugs are the words: "this is the last time."

Why Drugs?

Nothing has been said about why drugs are the most likely focus for excessive, self-destructive consumption patterns. This may seem a fault of the analysis. It does not specify any particular substance or activity. However, there is a connection. If we ask what sort of commodities fit the addiction graph, the answer is commodities that undermine the value of competing commodities. This point then leads to the observation that drugs are particularly good at spoiling competing reinforcers.

First, according to the analysis presented in the previous section of this chapter, excessiveness and addiction depend on the relationship between the local and global equilibria. The distance between the two equilibria along the x-axis defines the degree of excessiveness, and the distance along the y-axis defines the degree of inefficiency or self-destructiveness. Second, the restaurant and addiction graphs reveal that these differences reflect the properties of the available commodities and activities. For instance, recall that individuals who adopted a local bookkeeping approach to the restaurant problem ate too much Chinese food. However, their gluttony pales in comparison to the degree of excessiveness that emerged in the heroin addiction graph, figure 6.6. The implication is that something about heroin (as displayed in the graph) promoted excessiveness. Inspection reveals that this "something" is that heroin undermined the value of the competing nondrug rewards. Preference for heroin increased even though its value declined because it spoiled the value of the competing activities.

Thus, the question of "why are drugs the most likely focus of addictive behavior?" can be rephrased as "why are drugs the commodities that are most likely to undermine the value of competing rewards?" The answers are various versions of the fact that addictive drugs interact directly with neurons, the biological substrates of behavior. Cocaine and heroin bind directly to receptor sites. This means that their effects are virtually immediate (once they reach the receptor) and given that common dose levels are several orders of magnitude greater than the circulating levels of the neurotransmitters that normally bind to the receptor sites, the drug effects are immense, producing psychological states that are not obtainable by other means. The immediate consequences of these intense drug effects are intoxication and acute withdrawal states. Both interfere with competing activities, particularly conventional ones. The long-term consequences of the drug effects are chronic withdrawal conditions and toxic reactions, such as illness and psychological disturbance. These consequences also undermine non-drug competing activities. Finally, because the drugs act directly on the neural underpinnings of behavior they do not (with the exception of alcohol[2]) trigger satiating mechanisms. This leaves judgment as the only counterweight to consumption. However, intoxicating drugs undermine judgment. Thus, drugs that act on the central nervous system are particularly good at setting in motion forces that push the local equilibrium to the right of and below the global equilibrium.

Summary

The goals of this chapter were threefold: (1) to introduce readers to important but not well-known findings regarding the time course of addiction and the correlates of quitting drugs, (2) to develop a model of choice, and (3) to apply the model to addiction. The key results were that the contingencies that guide choice are ambiguous; that when one of the options is an addictive drug, everyday choice processes can lead to drug binging and a pattern of consumption that closely matches the American Psychiatric Association's description of addiction; and that differences in how choices are framed (either as items or aggregates) can have a profound effect on the overall distribution of choices and the overall returns on those choices, all else the same. According to these observations, addiction is not the result of a disease process or even of faulty decision making. It is the result of a kind of perverse interaction between the rules of choice and rewarding commodities and activities that have the capacity to undermine competing activities.[3]

Given that everyday decision processes are a sufficient condition for addiction and that most people have used alcohol and/or an addictive illegal drug, logic says that most people should become addicts. However, most people do not become addicts. The reason is not lack of access. Virtually everyone has had an alcoholic drink or an illegal addictive drug at least once, and a good portion of the population partakes of these substances on a regular basis. This implies that there are powerful antiaddiction processes at work. This chapter pointed out two. First, if individuals frame their choices in terms of lifestyle consequences, referred to here as global bookkeeping, then making the best choice implies a non-self-destructive consumption pattern—thereby ruling out addiction. Second, social proscriptions on appetites tend to push consumption toward the global equilibrium. Hence, it is possible to avoid the dangers of local bookkeeping by simply following social conventions regarding drug use. Values such as prudence and respect for the law support this approach. These observations suggest that social factors and values play an important role in drug use.

The applied implications of the analysis presented in this chapter are that prevention programs should enhance nondrug interests and that treatment programs should focus on decreasing the relative reward value of the drug. There are many programs that focus on the relative reward value of the drug. These include pharmacotherapies that reduce the reward value of the drug, and behavioral programs that increase the reward value of abstinence (e.g., Alcoholics Anonymous 1976; Higgins et al. 2000; Silverman et al. 2002). As with OCD, logic says that the behavioral programs are essential since they offer methods that can work after treatment is formally over. Possibly these programs would be more available in an environment in which addiction was not presented as a disease. In any case, to call a disorder a disease when it is possible to bring about a "cure" by rearranging factors that influence the reward value of the symptoms is likely to prove counterproductive in the long run. That we don't cure Tourettes syndrome by rewarding "not-ticing," but do bring addiction to a halt by rewarding abstinence, will eventually become apparent to all. It also might be useful to point out that there is no perfect solution to drug problems. Economics and psychology tell us that if addictive drugs provide psychological benefits that are not readily available elsewhere, there will be a demand for them. Political realities tell us that in liberal democracies, this demand will find a way to express itself. Thus, what is possible are measures that decrease the likelihood that the demand for intoxication turns into addiction. According to this chapter, these measures should be based on global bookkeeping consumption rates but packaged so that they appear as local bookkeeping options.

Notes

1. The equation for the value of the drug is $(14 - 0.33x)$, where x is the number of drug days. The equation for the value of nondrug competing activities is $(11 - 0.33x)$. Note that choosing the drug, x, leads to a decrease in the value of all commodities, as implied by the APA account of addiction.

2. Alcohol differs from the other addictive drugs in that it does not directly bind to receptor sites.

3. Smoking may not seem to fit this account. Cigarettes differ from other addictive drugs in that they are not intoxicating, and in fact are highly compatible with virtually any other activity, from horseback riding to sitting at a desk. What this shows is that they have created a niche in which they are the only occupant. Hence, having no competition, they are always chosen. Thus, they do not need to undermine the competition; it didn't exist in the first place.

References

Ainslie, G. W. (1975). Specious reward: A behavioral theory of impulsiveness and impulse control. *Psychological Bulletin* 82 (4): 463–496.

Ainslie, G. W. (1992). *Picoeconomics: The Strategic Interaction of Successive Motivational States within the Person.* Cambridge: Cambridge University Press.

Alcoholics Anonymous (1976). *Alcoholics Anonymous: The Story of How Many Thousands of Men and Women Have Recovered from Alcoholism.* New York: A.A. World Services.

American Psychiatric Association. (1994). *Diagnostic and Statistical Manual of Mental Disorders: DSM-IV*, 4th ed. Washington, D.C.: American Psychiatric Association.

Anthony, J. C., and Helzer, J. E. (1991). Syndromes of drug abuse and dependence. In L. N. Robins and D. A. Regier, eds., *Psychiatric Disorders in America: The Epidemiologic Catchment Area Study*, 116–154. New York: Free Press.

Baumol, W. J., and Blinder, A. S. (1994). *Economics: Principles and Policy*, 6th ed. Fort Worth: Dryden Press.

Biernacki, P. (1986). *Pathways from Heroin Addiction: Recovery without Treatment*. Philadelphia: Temple University Press.

Burroughs, W. S. (1959). *Naked Lunch*. New York: Grove Weidenfeld.

Carroll, K. M., and Rounsaville, B. (1992). Contrast of treatment-seeking and untreated cocaine abusers. *Archives of General Psychiatry* 49: 464–471.

Cole, P. M., Jenkins, P. A., and Shott, C. (1989). Spontaneous expressive control in blind and sighted children. *Child Development* 60: 683–688.

Coombs, R. H. (1997). *Drug-impaired Professionals*. Cambridge, MA: Harvard University Press.

Davison, M., and McCarthy, D. (1988). *The Matching Law: A Research Review*. Hillsdale, NJ: Lawrence Erlbaum.

Dole, V. P., and Nyswander, M. E. (1967). Heroin addiction—a metabolic disease. *Archives of Internal Medicine* 120: 19–24.

Ferguson, C. E., and Gould, J. P. (1975). *Microeconomic Theory*. Homewood, IL: Richard D. Irwin.

Fiore, M. C., Smith, S. S., Jorenby, D. E., and Baker, T. B. (1994). The effectiveness of the nicotine patch for smoking cessation: A meta-analysis. *Journal of the American Medical Association* 271: 1940–1947.

Green, L., and Myerson, J. (2004). A discounting framework for choice with delayed and probabilistic rewards. *Psychological Bulletin* 130: 769–792.

Helzer, J. E., Burnam, A., and McEvoy, L. T. (1991). Alcohol abuse and dependency. In L. N. Robins and D. A. Regier, eds., *Psychiatric Disorders in America: The Epidemiologic Catchment Area Study*, 81–115. New York: Free Press.

Herrnstein, R. J. (1970). On the law of effect. *Journal of the Experimental Analysis of Behavior* 13: 243–266.

Herrnstein, R. J. (1990). Rational choice theory: Necessary but not sufficient. *Journal of the American Psychologist* 45: 356–367.

Herrnstein, R. J., Loewenstein, G. F., Prelec, D., and Vaughan, W. (1993). Utility maximization and melioration: Internalities in individual choice. *Journal of Behavioral Decision Making* 6: 149–185.

Herrnstein, R. J., and Prelec, D. (1992). A theory of addiction. In G. Loewenstein and J. Elster, eds., *Choice Over Time*, 331–360. New York: Russell Sage Foundation.

Heyman, G. M. (2001). Is addiction a chronic, relapsing disease? Relapse rates, estimates of duration, and a theory of addiction. In P. Heymann and W. Brownsberger, eds., *Drug Addiction and Drug Policy*, 81–117. Cambridge, MA: Harvard University Press.

Heyman, G. M. (2003). Consumption dependent changes in reward value: A framework for understanding addiction. In R. E. Vuchinich and N. Heather, eds., *Choice, Behavioral Economics, and Addiction*, 95–127. Amsterdam, Netherlands: Pergamon/Elsevier Science.

Heyman, G. M., and Dunn, B. (2002). Decision biases and persistent illicit drug use: An experimental study of distributed choice and addiction. *Drug and Alcohol Dependence* 67: 193–203.

Heyman, G. M., and Tanz, L. (1995). How to teach a pigeon to maximize overall reinforcement rate. *Journal of the Experimental Analysis of Behavior* 64: 277–297.

Higgins, S. T., Wong, C. J., Badger, G. J., Ogden, D. E., and Dantona, R. L. (2000). Contingent reinforcement increases cocaine abstinence during outpatient treatment and 1 year of follow-up. *Journal of Consulting and Clinical Psychology* 68 (1): 64–72.

Hunt, W. A., Barnett, L. W., and Branch, L. G. (1971). Relapse rates in addiction programs. *Journal of Clinical Psychology* 27 (4): 455–456.

Kessler, R. C., Berglund, P., Demler, O., Jin, R., Merikangas, K. R., and Walters, E. E. (2005a). Lifetime prevalence and age-of-onset distributions of DSM-IV disorders in the national comorbidity survey replication. *Archives of General Psychiatry* 62: 593–602.

Kessler, R. C., Chiu, W. T., Demler, O., Merikangas, K. R., and Walters, E. E. (2005b). Prevalence, severity, and comorbidity of 12-month DSM-IV disorders in the national comorbidity survey replication. *Archives of General Psychiatry* 62: 617–627.

Kudadjie-Gyamfi, E., and Rachlin, H. (1996). Temporal patterning in choice among delayed outcomes. *Organizational Behavior and Human Decision Processes* 65: 61–67.

Pettinati, H., O'Brien, C. P., Rabinowitz, A. R., Wortman, S. P., Oslin, D. W., Kampman, K. M., and Dackis, C. A. (2006). The status of naltrexone in the treatment of alcohol dependence: Specific effects on heavy drinking. *Journal of Clinical Psychopharmacology* 26: 610–625.

Prelec, D., and Herrnstein, R. J. (1991). Preferences and principles, alternative guidelines for choice. In R. Zeckhauser, ed., *Strategic Reflections on Human Behavior*, 319–340. Cambridge, MA: MIT Press.

Rachlin, H. C. (2000). *The Science of Self-control*. Cambridge, MA: Harvard University Press.

Rachlin, H., and Siegel, E. (1994). Temporal patterning in probabilistic choice. *Organizational Behavior and Human Decision Processes* 59: 161–176.

Regier, D. A., Farmer, M. E., Rae, D. S., Locke, B. Z., Keith, S. J., and Judd, L. L. (1990). Comorbidity of mental disorders with alcohol and other drug abuse. Results from the epidemiologic catchment area (ECA) study. *Journal of the American Medical Association* 264 (19): 2511–2518.

Rinn, W. E. (1984). The neuropsychology of facial expression: A review of the neurological and psychological mechanisms for producing facial expressions. *Psychological Bulletin* 95 (1): 52–77.

Robins, L. N. (1993). Vietnam veterans' rapid recovery from heroin addiction: A fluke or normal expectation? *Addiction* 88: 1041–1954.

Robins, L. N., and Regier, D. A. (1991). *Psychiatric Disorders in America: The Epidemiologic Catchment Area Study*. New York: Free Press.

Rounsaville, B. J., and Kleber, H. D. (1985). Untreated opiate addicts: How do they differ from those seeking treatment? *Archives of General Psychiatry* 42: 1072–1077.

Samuelson, P. A. (1967). *Economics*, 7th ed. New York: McGraw-Hill.

Seligman, M. E. P., Walker, E. F., and Rosenhan, D. L. (2001). *Abnormal Psychology*, 4th ed. New York: W.W. Norton.

Silverman, K., Svikis, D., Wong, C. J., Hampton, J., Stitzer, M. L., and Bigelow, G. E. (2002). A reinforcement-based therapeutic workplace for the treatment of drug abuse: Three-year abstinence outcomes. *Experimental and Clinical Psychopharmacology* 10: 228–240.

Spitzer, R. L., Forman, J. B., and Nee, J. (1979). DSM-III field trials: I. Initial interrater diagnostic reliability. *American Journal of Psychiatry* 136: 815–817.

Spitzer, R. L., Williams, J. B., and Skodol, A. E. (1980). DSM-III: The major achievements and an overview. *American Journal of Psychiatry* 137: 151–164.

Stinson, F. S., Grant, B. F., and Dawson, D. A. (2005). Comorbidity between DSM-IV alcohol and specific drug use disorders in the United States: Results from the National Epidemiologic Survey on Alcohol and Related Conditions. *Drug and Alcohol Dependence* 80: 105–116.

Stinson, F. S., Grant, B. F., Dawson, D. A., Ruan, W. J., Huang, B., and Saha, T. (2006). Comorbidity between DSM-IV alcohol and specific drug use disorders in the United States: Results from the National Epidemiologic Survey on Alcohol and Related Conditions. *Alcohol Research and Health* 29 (2): 94–106.

Toneatto, T., Sobell, L. C., Sobell, M. B., and Rubel, E. (1999). Natural recovery from cocaine dependence. *Psychology of Addictive Behaviors: Journal of the Society of Psychologists in Addictive Behaviors* 13: 259–268.

Vaughan, W. (1981). Melioration, matching, and maximization. *Journal of the Experimental Analysis of Behavior* 36 (2): 141–149.

Vaughan, W., Jr., and Herrnstein, R. J. (1987). Stability, melioration, and natural selection. In L. Green and J. H. Kagel, eds., *Advances in Behavioral Economics*, 185–215. Norwood, NJ: Ablex Publishing.

Waldorf, D., Reinarman, C., and Murphy, S. (1991). *Cocaine Changes: The Experience of Using and Quitting*. Philadelphia: Temple University Press.

Warner, L. A., Kessler, R. C., Hughes, M., Anthony, J. C., and Nelson, C. B. (1995). Prevalence and correlates of drug use and dependence in the United States: Results from the National Comorbidity Survey. *Archives of General Psychiatry* 52: 219–229.

Wasserman, D. A., Weinstein, M. G., Havassy, B. E., and Hall, S. M. (1998). Factors associated with lapses to heroin use during methadone maintenance. *Drug and Alcohol Dependence* 52: 183–192.

Williams, B. A. (1988). Reinforcement, choice, and response strength. In S. S. Stevens and R. C. Atkinson, eds., *Stevens' Handbook of Experimental Psychology: Learning and Cognition*, 2nd ed., 167–244. New York: Wiley.

7 Addiction and Altruism

Howard Rachlin

My Lecture Game

The relationship between addiction and altruism is perhaps best illustrated by the ten-person Prisoner's Dilemma game I play with audiences whenever I give a lecture or talk at a colloquium. First I say that the purpose of the exercise is to get everyone into the same mood—and that mood is ambivalence. Then I hand out blank index cards to ten random members of the audience and I ask everybody else (as I ask the reader) to imagine that they had gotten a card. I then say that their job is to write either an X or a Y on the card, as they choose, subject to the following rules:

1. If you choose Y you will receive $100 times N.
2. If you choose X you will receive $100 times N plus a bonus of $300.
3. N equals the number (of the 10 players) who choose Y.

I say regretfully that the money is purely hypothetical and then I point out several properties of this game. First, I strongly emphasize that for any particular player it is always better to choose X. By choosing X a player will subtract 1 from N and thereby lose $100 but more than make up for that loss by the $300 bonus. The net gain for choosing X is therefore $200. *"And this holds regardless of what anyone else chooses."* I say this slowly, loudly, and twice. I pause after saying it and, as far as possible, stare each member of the audience in the eye, effectively daring them to dispute the point; but no one ever does challenge it. It is perfectly true. I then emphasize the point further by saying that any lawyer would advise them to choose X.

Then I say: "However, if everyone obeyed their lawyers and chose X, N would equal zero and each person would earn just $300, whereas if everyone disobeyed their lawyers and chose Y, N would equal 10 and each person would earn $1,000. Hence the dilemma."

I point out, truly, that there is no right or wrong answer. Then I tell them to mark their cards, letting no one see what they have written. I say that if anyone asks what they have chosen they should flip a mental coin and reply X or Y randomly. Their

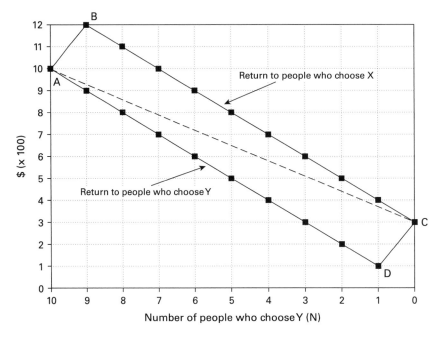

Figure 7.1
Contingencies of the ten-person Prisoner's Dilemma game I play with lecture audiences.

choice will be completely anonymous. No one will ever know what they have chosen or how much they have (hypothetically) earned. Then I collect the cards.

I have played this game dozens and dozens of times: with college students; with professors of psychology; with philosophers; with Italian socialist economists; with Japanese psychologists. The median response is 6 *Y*s to 4 *X*s plus or minus 2 either way. I then put up the chart shown in figure 7.1 and use it to look up the earnings of the *X* and *Y* choosers. For example, with 6 *Y*-choosers, $N = 6$ and each *Y*-chooser gets $600 while each of the 4 *X*-choosers gets $900. For obvious reasons, an *X*-choice is called a "defection" and a *Y*-choice is called a "cooperation." Although the money earned is hypothetical, laboratory experiments with real money (albeit in lesser amounts) have found significant numbers of cooperations in one-shot prisoner's dilemma games such as this one (Camerer 2003).

Sometimes, depending on the circumstances, I try to lead a discussion (without revealing what anyone actually chose) of why a person should choose *Y* in this game. They cannot claim that a *Y*-chooser's reputation would be enhanced since the choices are completely anonymous. They cannot claim to be influencing other players' choices in future games since they know that the game will be played only once during my lecture and then the audience will disperse. Many in the audience do say, despite all my efforts to forestall it, that they would choose Y if they believed that everyone else would choose Y. This rationale, on the face of it, is a non sequitur. Since the difference between the outcomes of an X and a Y choice is absolutely constant, what anyone else chooses in this game should, in theory, not influence their choice. (As my mother used to ask, "If all the other kids jump off the roof, should you jump off the roof?") What others do in this game will have a strong effect on a player's earnings. But what others do is irrelevant to what *you* should (in theory) do—you should defect. It is certainly incontrovertible that if a person chooses Y he will be happy if everyone else chooses Y and he earns \$1,000. But would he be happier in such a case than he would be if he alone had chosen X and earned \$1,200? If so, why? It seems as if the enhanced earnings of *others* (the extra \$900 paid to the other players due to each player's Y-choice) at a sacrifice of \$200 for themselves has an effect on people's behavior.

Fehr and Fischbacher (2003) define altruism as "costly acts that confer economic benefits on other individuals." Choosing Y—cooperating—in this game is truly an altruistic act by this definition. And many people in the audience do cite a reason that might fall into this category. An audience member might raise her hand and say that any truly altruistic person would choose Y; certainly choosing Y benefits other individuals. In terms of money paid out, if it were real, each choice of Y would cost me (or NIH) \$700. The dashed line in the figure shows this average as a function of the number of Y-choosers. I would save the \$300 bonus for the Y-chooser but, by the increase in N, would have to pay \$100 more to each player, a total of \$1,000. The group as a whole nets an extra \$700 for each Y-chooser, an average of \$70 per player. If the money were being used for a group activity (say to fund a party) it would make sense in every way to choose Y (the dashed line is at a maximum at $N = 10$). But, as it stands, providing that gain of \$100 to each *other* member of the group (\$900 in all) costs any individual player \$200. And, since the choice is anonymous, the Y-chooser gets no credit for the sacrifice (the "costly act"). So why choose Y?

The answer is that although my lecture game is a one-shot game, players may not treat it as a one-shot game. They may ask themselves not what should I choose in this game, but what should I choose in these sorts of games in general. If we made each decision in life solely on the basis of its own reinforcement, we would never act altruistically. We would never give to public radio or television. We would never vote. We would never carry our litter to the garbage can. We would never leave a tip at a restaurant to which we did not expect to return.

The proper question to ask is, is it better to choose Y-like choices as a general rule than to choose X-like choices as a general rule? My lecture game was set up as a one-shot choice. But there is really no such thing as a one-shot choice. When the game began I said nothing about its context. But all choices must be embedded in a context. Each player was free to place the game in any context he or she wished.

In real life, reinforcement acts not on individual responses but on patterns of responses. In the animal lab, where a rat's food is contingent on pressing a lever, the rat chooses not between this press and this nonpress, but between a high rate of lever-pressing along with a high rate of eating and a low rate of lever-pressing along with a low rate of eating (Rachlin 1978). Similarly, in my lecture game, Y-choosers choose not between this X and this Y but between Xs generally and Ys generally. *This* choice was just part of a general pattern of choices. And, as a general pattern, it may well pay to act altruistically. In Hillary Mantel's (2005) excellent novel, *Beyond Black*, the main character has been kind to a pathetic, homeless man who was later found hanged. The hanging was caused somehow by the actions of a group of fiends (servants of the devil). The fiends are later discussing the matter. One of them says to the other (p. 410), "You failed to see that little bugger [the hanged man] was her good deed. And what's the result? She's looking to commit a few others. They get in the habit... see? It's sad. But they get the taste for it."

You may argue that, given a human tendency toward altruism, this molar conception of learned altruism is unnecessary. You may say that the lecture game reveals only that for the 6 of 10 people on the average who chose Y, a gain of $900 for the other players may be worth a sacrifice of $200 for themselves—irrespective of the behavior of others. Indeed, as I will show further on, trade-offs between one's own smaller benefit and the larger benefit of others are common and easily measurable. But such a simple trade-off cannot be the reason why some people choose Y. Had the game been repeated four or five times, we would find more and more defection (Camerer 2003). That is, more and more Y-choosers would become X-choosers even though the basic trade-off ($900 for others at a cost of $200 for oneself) does not change as the game is repeated. This is because, when the game is repeated, the context of each game becomes the other games played. (For a single flower in a room, the context is the room. For a flower in a bouquet, the context is the other flowers.) Where others are repeatedly defecting, it pays to defect. However, where others are repeatedly cooperating, it pays to cooperate because otherwise you will either cause them to defect in the future or they will boot you from further repetitions of the game.

You may well object at this point to say that this explanation makes the Y-choosers in my one-shot lecture game into pretty ignorant people. Is it not patently clear that this is a one-shot game? It seems as if, after all, the X-choosers are correct in their choice and the Y-choosers are incorrect. Y-choosers seem to have put my lecture game into the wrong context—as shown by the fact that they tend to become X-choosers as the game is repeated. To answer this objection I will argue that choosing Y in my lecture game is really an act of self-control.

It is possible to distinguish between *altruism* and *social cooperation* in terms of repeated games like my lecture game. If a game were never to be repeated, cooperation would be altruistic; a player's cooperation could have no influence on the other

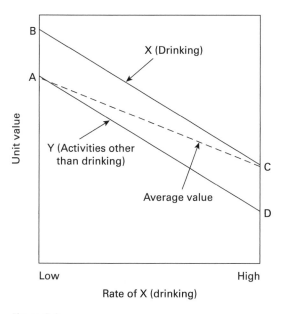

Figure 7.2
The alcoholic's dilemma. As drinking rate increases, the value of having a drink (shown on line BC) and the value of not having (or refusing) a drink (shown on line AD) both decrease. But the value of having a drink is always higher than that of not having a drink, and the value of the average state (as shown by the dashed line) is maximum at a low drinking rate.

players' subsequent choices and would never be reinforced. However, where games are repeated, cooperation may be reinforced by another player's subsequent cooperation. In that case, cooperation would not be truly altruistic, and is called here *social cooperation*. Nevertheless, since I insist that there is no such thing as a true one-shot game, all instances of altruism are actually instances of social cooperation. I explain altruism as really social cooperation over a wide temporal extent—wider than the duration of any laboratory experiment.

Self-Control and Altruism

Figure 7.2 is a highly simplified version of Herrnstein and Prelec's (1992) primrose path model of self-control as applied to alcoholism. The model is clearly analogous to my lecture game illustrated in figure 7.1. The difference lies in the abscissa. In the case of Figure 7.2, instead of the percentage of players defecting (choosing X) we have the percentage of defections (choosing to drink) by a single "player" (the alcoholic) over a relatively long period of time—the rate of drinking. The leftmost point starts not at zero rate but at the rate when drinking becomes harmful. As in figure 7.1, the ordinate shows value. As rate of drinking increases, the value of each particular drink (line BC) goes down due to the buildup of tolerance. At the same time, the value of everything other than drinking (line AD), such as health, physical well being, social relations, and job performance, also goes down. Under the conditions illustrated in figure 7.2 (see Rachlin 2000 for other scenarios), regardless of the rate of drinking, having a drink is always more valuable than not having a drink. At point A, when the alcoholic is relatively sober, having a drink is immediately pleasurable (is positively reinforcing). At point C, when the addict is completely drunk, having a drink merely prevents the addict from feeling worse (is negatively reinforcing). The triangle ABC defines an area of positive reinforcement. An alcoholic starting at point A, who repeatedly chooses the most valuable of available activities (always to drink), will proceed along "the primrose path" (ABC) to point C where drinking and not drinking as well are low valued. The triangle ACD defines an area of negative reinforcement.

The dashed line shows the addict's average state as drinking increases. Clearly it is better to be at point A than at point C. An alcoholic at point C would like to return to point A where both everyday life and the pleasure of drinking are much better, but he can only do so along path CDA (which might be called "the straight and narrow path") where immediately less-valued alternatives must continuously be chosen. There are thus two motives for moving along path CDA. One is to return to point A and become relatively sober (a social drinker, say); the other is to attain point B where drinking is pleasurable again. But of course point B is an unstable point. As soon as a person moves from A to B there seems to be no reason not to move still further down the primrose path and then all the way to point C. And then the cycle begins all over again: the painful straight and narrow path until the addictive act once again becomes sufficiently positively reinforcing; the slide down the primrose path as positive reinforcement gradually becomes negative reinforcement (perhaps not all the way to point C); the climb again—perhaps not all the way to point A—in an endless series.

Although the labels on figure 7.2 are in terms of alcoholism, they may apply to any kind of addiction. You could substitute cigarette smoking, heroin, cocaine, gambling, and so on, within the basic primrose path model.

What then prevents all of us from becoming addicts? How is it possible to choose among abstract entities such as *rates* of drinking, smoking, gambling, using heroin or cocaine rather than between this particular act and that particular act? Although it is certainly better to choose among abstract patterns of acts, it is particular acts that have to be done. And we have to do them one by one. How do we manage to choose among abstract patterns rather than particular acts? The answer is that the temporal extent of the decision to drink, to smoke, to gamble, and so on, or to abstain from these activities differs from person to person. When people choose not between having this drink and refusing it (not between points along the solid lines BC and AD in figure 7.2, which are always resolved in favor of the higher-valued drink) but among various drinking rates (that is, points along the dotted line of figure 7.2, which is clearly resolved in favor of the peak at point A), their behavior is labeled "self-controlled."

Although we know very well by now how reinforcement increases our tendency to do particular acts, it is far from clear how reinforcement can increase patterns of acts—especially when the value of those whole patterns goes contrary to that of each and every one of their components—as in figure 7.2. As the gestalt psychologists said (Koffka 1955), the value of the whole may exceed the sum of the values of its parts. Suppose that a person prefers listening to any of 20 three-minute popular songs to any particular three-minute section of some one-hour symphony. Suppose also that the person prefers listening to the whole symphony to listening to the same 20 three-minute songs one after the other. Then listening to the symphony would be an act of self-control. Certainly some people listen to symphonies under these conditions. How do they manage to start listening to the symphony and to avoid switching, while it is going on, to a three-minute song that, by our assumption, they prefer during the next three minutes? If it is particular acts that need to be done, how do those particular acts of symphony listening, of less value in themselves than popular-song listening, get shaped into a more valuable pattern? I will return to this question in the final section of the chapter. First, it is necessary to delineate more clearly between self-control and altruism.

Choices to engage in addictive behavior are *defections*, not from the interests of a group of people over social space, but from the same person's interests over a period of time. Choices not to engage in addictive behavior are *cooperations*, not with other people's interests, but with the same person's interests over a period of time (Ainslie 2001). Cooperation with others over social space (i.e., altruistic choices), shown in figure 7.1, is analogous to cooperation with yourself over time (i.e., self-control), shown in figure 7.2. Figure 7.3 makes this analogy explicit. In the case of altruism the dots in

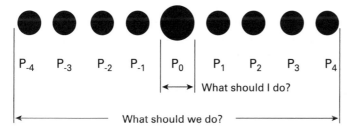

Figure 7.3
The large dot (P_0) stands for the individual at the present time. The wider or narrower range of dots (P_{-N} to P_N) stand for wider or narrower bases of choice over which value is maximized—either in time or in social distance. Maximization of value over the wider range is labeled self-control (in time) or altruism (in social space). Maximization of value over the narrower range is labeled addiction (in time) or selfishness (in social space).

the diagram designate *individuals distributed in social space*. The large dot stands for the person. Let us call that person P_0. The small dots $(P_1, P_2, P_3, \ldots, P_N \ldots)$ stand for other people; the closer a small dot is to the large dot, the closer is the social bond between that person and P_0.

In the case of self-control, the dots in the diagram designate *a single individual at different times*. The large dot stands for P_0 now. The small dots stand for a single person P_0 at different times in the future; the closer a small dot is to the large dot, the sooner is that future time. People differ from each other both in the extent of their cooperation with others over social space (altruism) and in the extent of their cooperation with themselves over time (self-control). These spatial and temporal extents may be measured by discount functions.

Social and Delay Discount Functions

By definition, (a) the wider your responsiveness to temporal contingencies, the more self-control you have, and (b) the wider your responsiveness to social space, the more altruistic you are. In neither case are there any hard and fast boundaries but a falling-off of common interest as the group gets larger and larger. A person's responsiveness in time or social space can be quantified by discount functions that measure this falling-off.

Figure 7.4 shows (a) social and (b) delay discount functions (from Rachlin and Jones 2008). The social discount function was obtained by first asking participants to imagine that they had made a list of 100 people closest to them with number 1 their closest friend or relative and number 100 perhaps only someone they passed regularly on the street (but not actually make the list). Then they were asked to make a series of choices between varying amounts of (hypothetical) money for themselves and $75 for a specific person on their list (for example, person 10). Initially, for half of the participants, the amount for themselves was $85 (versus $75 for person N); for the other half of the participants, the amount for themselves was $5 (versus $75 for person N). Participants generally preferred high amounts for themselves to $75 for person N but preferred $75 for person N to very low amounts for themselves. We then systematically lowered (raised) the amount for the participant. As an initially high amount for themselves was lowered, participants crossed over and preferred the $75 for person N. (As an initially low amount for themselves was raised, participants crossed over and preferred the higher amount for themselves.) Then we repeated the process for other Ns. The points in figure 7.4a are median crossover points for all participants as a function of social distance (N). As N increased, the crossover point decreased. That is, the greater the social distance between the participant and the receiver of the $75, the less altruistic participants indicated they would be. The decrease followed a hyperbolic function (the solid line in figure 7.4a). The equation of that function is: $v = V/(1 + k_{social}N)$

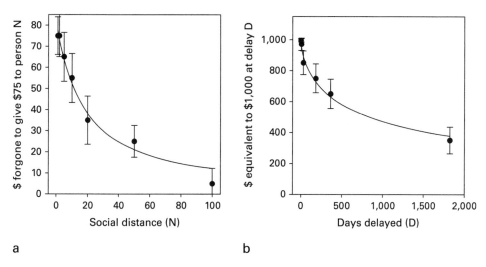

Figure 7.4

a. Median indifference points between $75 for a person at social distance N (given on the abscissa) and an amount of money (shown on the ordinate) for the participant. The line is the best-fitting hyperbolic discount function. b. Median indifference points between $1,000 delayed by D days (given on the abscissa) and an amount of money (shown on the ordinate) now. The line is the best-fitting hyperbolic discount function.

where V is the intercept of the function on the ordinate, v is the crossover point, and k_{social} is a constant measuring "selfishness" (inversely proportional to altruism).

According to Hamilton's Rule (1964), given that organisms behave so as to maximize the survival of their genes, altruism in nature should depend on probability of genetic overlap (r) between giver and receiver. The crossover point, where an animal is indifferent between a smaller reward (v) for itself and a larger reward (V) for another animal, should be where $v = rV$. Hamilton's Rule may be rewritten as the hyperbolic equation: $v = V/(1 + R)$ where R is the odds against genetic overlap. But in complex human social systems, which vary widely both between and within cultures, genetic overlap is less important for altruism than common interest within the social system. That is, in human societies, you would give up some fraction of a reward for another person (perhaps not even a relative, maybe a member of the same athletic team) whose own interests overlap with yours. The amount you would give up depends on the degree of overlap. Thus, probability of genetic overlap should be replaced, in human social systems, by a coefficient of common interest (n) within the social system: $v = nV$. Like r, n is a probability (i.e., a fraction ranging from 0 to 1.0). And, mathematically equivalent, $v = V/(1 + N')$ where N' is the odds against overlap of common interest. When we ask participants to imagine they had made a list of their closest friends and relatives, they may be thought of as estimating such overlap: $N' = k_{social}N$, where k_{social} is a person's tendency to see a common interest between himself and another person. Some support for these speculations is the fact that the resulting hyperbolic equation $[v = V/(1 + k_{social}N)]$ so precisely describes both group and individual social discount functions (Rachlin and Jones 2008).[1]

A delay discount function is shown in figure 7.4b. Participants (Stony Brook undergraduates) balanced a higher amount for themselves (V) to be obtained at a later time (D) with a smaller amount for themselves at the present time. A crossover point (v), obtained by a corresponding method to the social discount function of figure 7.4a, indicated equivalence between a large, delayed reward ($1,000 in this case) and a smaller but immediate reward. The hyperbolic equation that describes delay crossover points $[v = V/(1 + k_{delay}D^s)]$ is like the one that describes social crossover points (except for the nonunity exponent, s, which equaled 0.8 for the data of figure 7.4b). As other chapters in this volume show, steepness of delay discounting predicts degree of addictive behavior—that is, lack of self-control. And, just as delay discounting measures addiction, so social discounting measures altruism.

In a public goods game (Jones 2007), 96 participants (Stony Brook undergraduates) were asked to imagine that they were given $100 any part of which they could place in a box to be passed around the room. After the box was passed to all participants the experimenter would double the money in it and distribute it among all of the participants regardless of how much money they had contributed. Any individual participant would receive whatever he or she had retained plus the distribution. If all participants contributed all of their money, each would receive $200. If none contributed at all each would receive $100. Each player in this game would maximize her own reward by contributing nothing and maximize the reward to the group as a whole by contributing all $100. In addition to playing this public goods game, each participant was given a social discounting questionnaire. Individual functions, fitted to the data of each participant revealed a wide range of k_{social} values. Jones (2007) found a significant negative correlation between a participant's k_{social} and the amount of money that person was willing to donate in the public goods game. The steeper a participant's social discount function (the higher his or her k_{social}), the less money that participant contributed in the PGG.

Given the analogy between altruism and self-control illustrated in figure 7.3, a question arises: Are people more generous to their future selves or to other people? Is social discounting essentially steeper than delay discounting? Looking at discount functions alone, this question is impossible to answer. The abscissas of figure 7.4a and 7.4b are incommensurable. Days of delay and social distance are not only different scales; they are different types of scale. Although it is possible to experimentally convert the ordinal scale of figure 7.4a to absolute distance (a ratio scale like that of figure 7.4b: Jones 2007), there is no answer to the question: How much distance is equal to how much time? (You would have to ask, with respect to what speed?)

Nevertheless, social discounting and delay discounting may be compared experimentally using a procedure in which the same game is played in two ways: one way, against the player's future self; another way, against another player. We turn to such a comparison now.

Self-Control and Social Cooperation Compared Experimentally

The object of this series of experiments (Brown and Rachlin 1999) was to compare self-control with social cooperation by humans playing a game. The game was played either by a single player ("alone") to study self-control, or by a pair of players ("together") to study social cooperation. The participants were all female Stony Brook undergraduates.

The game board is diagrammed in figure 7.5. It consisted of a rectangular plastic tray divided into four compartments ("boxes"). Each box contained three items: a red or green index card with a picture of a door ("red doors" or "green doors"); a red or green key; 1, 2, 3, or 4 nickels. (In subsequent experiments, 1, 2, 5, or 6 nickels were in the boxes.) The upper boxes both contained red doors; the lower boxes both contained green doors. The left boxes both contained red keys; the right boxes both contained green keys. Note that each right box held one more nickel than the box to its left, and each upper box held two more nickels than the one below it. All the items in the boxes were visible to the players.

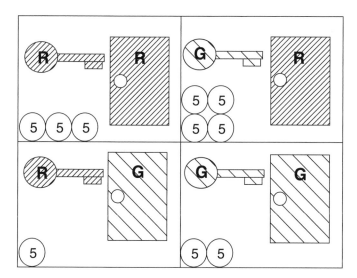

Figure 7.5
Diagram of game board used by Brown and Rachlin (1999).

The Self-Control Game ("Alone")

Each trial began with the apparatus as pictured in figure 7.5. To start, a player was given a red key. The player could use that key to "open" one or the other red door (to choose either the upper left or upper right box). The used key was then surrendered to the experimenter. If the upper left box was chosen, the player surrendered his original key and was permitted to take the 3 nickels and the (new) red key from that box. If the upper right box was chosen the player was permitted to take the 4 nickels and the green key from that box. Then the nickels and key taken were replaced in the box by the experimenter and the next trial began. If a red key had been received on the previous trial, the player could again choose between the two red doors as before; if a green key had been received on the previous trial, the player could use the key to "open" one or the other green doors (to choose a key and nickels from either the lower left or lower right box).

The alone game is a self-control procedure; the behavior leading to the higher current reward (choosing the right box with 2 or 4 nickels plus a green key) conflicted with the behavior that maximized overall reward (choosing the left box with 1 or 3 nickels plus a red key). Choosing the right box always earned the player one more nickel than choosing the left box did, but at the cost of obtaining a green key. With the green key the player paid for the 1-nickel gain (for choosing the right box) on the previous trial with an average 2-nickel loss (having to choose between the lower boxes) on the present trial.

The best overall strategy in the alone game is always to choose the left box, always receive a red key, and always earn 3 nickels. Always choosing the right box yields a fixed return of 2 nickels per trial. Alternating between the left and right boxes yields an average return of 2.5 nickels $[(4 + 1)/2]$ per trial. Only on the very last trial does it pay to choose the right box, but the participants did not know when the experiment would end.

The alone version of the game duplicates the contingencies of a Prisoner's Dilemma game against an opponent playing "tit-for-tat." Tit-for-tat says, cooperate on the first trial, and from then on cooperate if your opponent cooperated on the previous trial and defect if your opponent defected on the previous trial. Consider what it would be like to play a repeated Prisoner's Dilemma game against an opponent who plays tit-for-tat. If you were to cooperate on the present trial you would be able to choose next time between the higher rewards (because the other player will have cooperated). If you were to defect on the present trial you would be forced to choose next time between the lower two rewards (because the other player will have defected). These are the very contingencies set up by the keys and doors of the alone condition.

Because current choice of the lower available reward always leads to a higher next-trial reward, current choice in the alone game depends on the degree to which the (higher) next-trial reward is discounted. Because it cannot be obtained until the next trial, the higher future reward may be discounted by delay. But another possible source of discounting is probabilistic discounting. A player may currently discount higher future reward by the probability that she herself will fail to choose the lower reward on subsequent trials. Suppose a player has repeatedly chosen the higher current-trial reward in the past, earning 2 nickels per trial. If she chooses the lower current-trial reward on this trial only, and the higher current-trial reward on all subsequent trials, she will earn 1 nickel on this trial, 4 nickels on the next trial (for an average of 2.5 nickels), then return to 2 nickels per trial. This might not be enough incentive to choose the 1 nickel on the current trial. But if she chooses the lower current reward on this trial and continues to do so, she will eventually earn 3 nickels per trial, a 50% increase. This may well be a sufficient incentive to choose the 1 nickel now. However, if by past experience a player believes it unlikely that she will choose the lower current-trial reward in the future, there is little incentive to do so in the present.

Probabilistic discounting may apply as well in everyday self-control situations. If by past experience a dieter believes it highly improbable that high calorie foods will be resisted tomorrow and on subsequent days, there is little reason to resist them today. See Ainslie 2001 for a generalization of this reasoning to all forms of self-control.

The Social Cooperation Task ("Together")

The game as played by two players together was the same as when played alone, except that the two players, playing on a single game board, made choices on alternate trials. After using her key to open a box, each player took the nickels in the box for herself and then handed the key to the other player. Thus, after the first trial, whether a player was permitted to choose between the upper boxes (3 or 4 nickels) or between the lower boxes (1 or 2 nickels) depended on the other player's choice on the previous trial. The players were not allowed to discuss the game. Their only means of communication was through the choices they made.

Playing the game together, income would be maximized (at 3 nickels per trial) for each player if both players repeatedly chose the left box (cooperated). However, the individual player would always gain more on the present trial by choosing the right box (defecting). The penalty for defecting, of having to choose between the lower boxes, is suffered not by the player who defected but by the other player, who inherits the green key.

There is an ambivalence in the together game as there is in the alone game. A player wants to choose the right box with the higher number of nickels (2 rather than 1 or 4 rather than 3). That is, she wants to defect. But she also wants to have a red key (to be able to choose between 4 and 3 nickels rather than between 2 and 1). She will only have a red key if her partner had chosen the left box (if her partner had cooperated) on the previous trial. Since her partner has the very same motives, one way for a player to get her partner to cooperate on the next trial might be to cooperate herself on the present trial. Thus, each player has a reason to defect and a reason to cooperate.

But cooperating is the very worst strategy in this game, unless the other player also cooperates. Therefore the only reason to cooperate (within the demands of the game) is to influence the other player to cooperate subsequently. The reward for cooperating in the social cooperation version of the game must be discounted not only by the delay to the player's next turn but also by the probability that the other player will reciprocate.

People's estimation of the probability of other people's future cooperation, however, might be expected to be lower than their estimation of the probability of their own future cooperation. For this reason, a player who cooperates with her own future self in the alone game (who consistently chooses the lower current-trial reward) may defect from the interests of her partner in the together game. This was what we found.

Four groups of participants were tested in a standard "transfer" design. One group played the game alone for 40 trials. Another group played the game together for 40 trials. The third group played alone for 20 trials (first phase) and then together for 20 trials (second phase). The fourth group played together for 20 trials (first phase) and then alone for 20 trials (second phase). Figure 7.6 shows the results averaged over four-trial blocks. Participants playing alone came to cooperate on about 60% of the trials, whereas participants playing together cooperated on about 20% of the trials. When participants were switched from playing alone to playing together, cooperation decreased. When participants were switched from playing together to playing alone, cooperation increased. Experience in the first phase with one condition seemed to have no effect on behavior on the second phase with the other condition.

Then, with new participants, we redid the entire experiment as before except we increased the number of nickels in the two upper boxes (with the red doors) to 5 and 6 (rather than the 3 and 4 shown, in figure 7.5). This manipulation maintained the self-control (and Prisoner's Dilemma) contingencies but increased the larger delayed reward (the reward for cooperation). The reason for increasing the larger reward was to make sure that the alone condition presented a true conflict of motives rather than just a cognitive problem—a problem in practical arithmetic. If the alone condition were a true self-control problem, increasing the amount of the larger-later reward should increase self-control as it has done in many self-control experiments. If the alone condition is just a problem in practical arithmetic, increasing the amount of the larger-later reward should have no effect. In a practical arithmetic problem, correct answers are not increased by increasing the amounts. (If Johnny goes to the store with $10 to buy groceries, just as many children will get the right answer as if he goes to the store with $20.) The results of Brown's second experiment, with 5 and 6 nickels

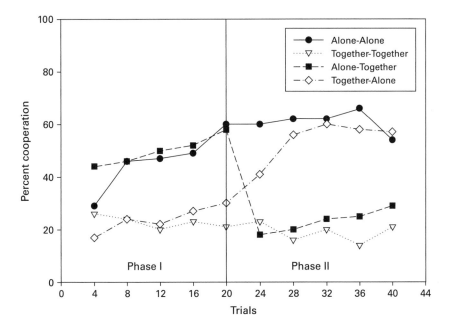

Figure 7.6
Results obtained by Brown and Rachlin (1999) with rewards of 1, 2, 3, and 4 nickels as shown in figure 7.5.

in the upper boxes, are shown in figure 7.7. Now participants in the alone condition cooperated on about 80% of the trials, rather than the 60% cooperation found with the smaller next-trial rewards—evidence that the alone condition does indeed test self-control.

What about the together condition? Increasing the amount of the next-trial rewards had no effect on cooperation of participants playing together; they still cooperated on about 20% of the trials. Recall that the benefit of cooperation in the together condition is realized only if the other player reciprocates. A crucial variable in the together game is a player's subjective estimation of the probability that, if she cooperates, the *other* player will cooperate too. It is not surprising that increasing the amount of the next-trial reward (the reward to the *other* player) did not increase this subjective probability.

In summary, the results of these experiments imply that a crucial variable distinguishing self-control from social cooperation is the probability of reciprocation of cooperation and defection. In self-control situations, where reciprocation is under the control of a single person, this probability may be high. Most people perceive a common interest between themselves today and themselves tomorrow. But in Prisoner's

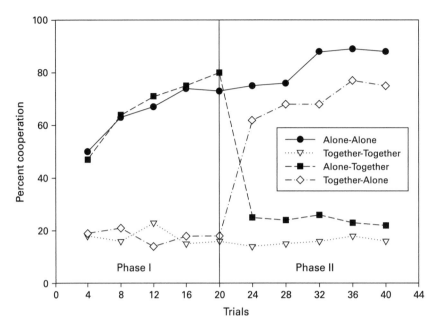

Figure 7.7
Results obtained by Brown and Rachlin (1999) with rewards of 1, 2, 5, and 6 nickels.

Dilemma situations where the players have no common interest, this probability is inherently lower.

A third experiment by Brown and Rachlin (1999) further tested the analogy between self-control and social cooperation. The crucial variable in this experiment was patterning of trials. Patterning of trials ("soft commitment") has been shown to increase self-control of pigeons and humans under conditions of ambivalence (Rachlin 1995). The effect of patterning is to broaden temporal scope—to cause decisions to be based on more abstract rather than more particular contingencies. If social cooperation is a consequence of correspondingly abstract choices, then patterning should also increase social cooperation. In this third experiment with the game board, four new groups of participants all played the game together at all times. The game board illustrated in figure 7.5 was used except, as in the experiment of figure 7.7, there were 5 and 6 nickels rather than 3 and 4 nickels in the left and right upper boxes. Instead of alone versus together, the conditions of the game were patterned versus unpatterned trials. The *unpatterned* trials condition was the same as the together condition of the experiment of figure 7.7. In the *patterned* trials condition, however, both participants playing together made four decisions at once. They indicated on a piece of paper out of the other player's view whether, on each of the next four trials, they would choose the left box or the right box. Then, the four trials were played out one by one. The player might have a red or green key on any of the four trials, but her choice on each trial was predetermined before the four-trial sequence began. The experimental design was again the standard transfer design with one group playing 40 patterned trials, one group playing 40 unpatterned trials, and the other two groups switched in the middle. The results were that patterning significantly increased cooperative behavior, just as it had increased self-control in prior experiments (Rachlin 1995).[2] This is further evidence that self-control and social cooperation are corresponding processes.

What Is Addiction?

As other chapters in this volume attest, addicts tend to have steep delay-discount functions. But what does it mean to have a steep delay-discount function? It does not mean that somewhere in the nervous system is a representation of a hyperbolic discount function and that this function is consulted whenever a choice is to be made among delayed rewards. A discount function is a form of utility function and, like utility functions, serves only as a tool for the observer (including the person himself as an observer of his own behavior) to make predictions from one situation to the next—as a means of "revealing a person's preferences" (Samuelson 1973). In economics, discount functions enter into utility functions and serve to bring rewards of various delays into the same arena. Actual choices of the behaving organism are best described, as we have found, by hyperbolic delay-discount functions. Hyperbolic discount functions are not encoded in the heads of behaving organisms any more than parabolic functions are encoded inside baseballs or elliptical functions inside the planets. If, contrary to fact, hyperbolic functions could be inside anyone's head, they would be inside the head of the theorist, not the behaving organism.[3]

For our purposes, delay-discount functions measure the degree of effective temporal integration of choices. Addicts are people whose choices can be described only in narrow temporal terms. ("*This* person chooses to have *this* cigarette at *this* time.") Such choices maximize utility over narrow time spans and, in self-control situations, fail to maximize utility over long time spans. The choices of nonaddicts, on the other hand, may be described in broader terms ("This person chooses to be a social drinker") and maximize utility over long time spans.

As we have seen in the experiments of Brown and Rachlin (1999), the degree of integration of the choices of our participants (college students) over time exceeded the degree of integration of their choices over social space. They were more cooperative with themselves at later times than they were with other Stony Brook students. (The same pattern has been found among students at the University of Rhode Island [Silverstein et al. 1998].) Assuming that the behavior of these participants is typical of that of nonaddicts we may characterize the behavior of addicts: *Addicts treat themselves at other times as nonaddicts treat other people. In other words, relative to nonaddicts, addicts defect against their own long-term interests; their future selves are strangers to them.*

This implies that, in addition to the standard behavioral treatments for addiction, addicts need to be trained in organizing their behavior into wide temporal patterns—effectively making friends with their own future selves.

Notes

1. I am grateful to Alex Kacelnik for pointing out to me the relevance of Hamilton's Rule to social discounting.

2. The single-trial participants playing together cooperated on an average of 26% of the trials across the two phases—about the same as together participants in figures 7.6 and 7.7. The patterned-trial participants playing together cooperated on an average of 38% of the trials across the two phases. The difference is statistically significant—although there is still a long way to go in engendering cooperation in this relatively simple and transparent two-player game.

3. Of course, they are not in the theorist's head either, but explicitly in her behavior—whereas, they are only implicitly in the behavior of the choosing organism.

References

Ainslie, G. (2001). *Breakdown of Will*. Cambridge: Cambridge University Press.

Brown, J., and Rachlin, H. (1999). Self-control and social cooperation. *Behavioural Processes* 47: 65–72.

Camerer, C. F. (2003). *Behavioral Game Theory: Experiments in Strategic Interaction*. Princeton, NJ: Princeton University Press.

Fehr, E., and Fischbacher, U. (2003). The nature of human altruism. *Nature* 425: 785–791.

Hamilton, W. D. (1964). The genetical evolution of social behaviour. *Journal of Theoretical Biology* 31: 295–311.

Herrnstein, R. J., and Prelec, D. (1992). A theory of addiction. In G. Loewenstein and J. Elster, eds., *Choice Over Time*. New York: Russell Sage Foundation.

Jones, B. (2007). Social discounting: Social distance and altruistic choice. Dissertation, Psychology Department, Stony Brook University.

Koffka, K. (1955). *Principles of Gestalt Psychology*. Oxford: Routledge and Kegan Paul.

Mantel, H. (2005). *Beyond Black*. New York: Picador.

Rachlin, H. (1978). A molar theory of reinforcement schedules. *Journal of the Experimental Analysis of Behavior* 30: 345–360.

Rachlin, H. (1995). The value of temporal patterns in behavior. *Current Directions* 4: 188–191.

Rachlin, H. (2000). *The Science of Self-Control*. Cambridge, MA: Harvard University Press.

Rachlin, H., and Jones, B. (2008). Social discounting and delay discounting. *Journal of Behavioral Decision Making* 21: 29–43.

Samuelson, P. A. (1973). *Economics: An Introductory Analysis*, 9th ed. New York: McGraw-Hill.

Silverstein, A., Cross, D. V., Brown, J., and Rachlin, H. (1998). Prior experience and patterning in a Prisoner's Dilemma game. *Journal of Behavioral Decision Making* 11: 123–138.

8 The Core Process in Addictions and Other Impulses: Hyperbolic Discounting versus Conditioning and Cognitive Framing

George Ainslie

It has been clear since Plato that we have a strong tendency to act against what we ourselves see as our rational interests. Rationality has been defined with increasing precision since economist Paul Samuelson's "Note on the Measurement of Utility" (1937), in what has come to be called *expected utility theory* or, more broadly, *rational choice theory* (RCT; Boudon 1996). Antirational tendencies have been cataloged in departures from the norms of RCT, many of which have been identified both in the laboratory (Herrnstein 1990) and in real-life choices (Jolls, Sunstein, and Thaler 1998). Graphically, RCT predicts that a person's valuation of a prospective event can be plotted over delay as an exponential curve, losing a constant proportion of its remaining height for every unit of delay (figure 8.1A):

$$\text{Present value} = \text{Value}_0 \times \delta^{\text{Delay}} \qquad\qquad \text{(formula 1)}$$

where Value_0 = value if immediate and $\delta = (1 - \text{discount rate})$. Any other function, if it does not generate a straight line, will generate curves from a given amount that sometimes cross the curves from some other amounts at other moments, simply because of the passage of time; that is, it will describe inconsistent preference. Inconsistent preference leaves a person susceptible to being a money pump, that is, opens her to exploitation by a competitor who repeatedly buys from her when her valuations fall below their exponentially discounted value and sells back to her when they rise (Arrow 1959; Conlisk 1996). Inconsistent preference also implies that a person can expect to make future choices that she does not currently want. Competition for survival is usually thought to have selected for people who value future events consistently, in markets and, perhaps, in the evolution of species (but see Cubitt and Sugden 2001).

This comprehensive model of choice leaves unanswered the question of why we often make choices that defeat our own plans—that is, why *impulses* or temporary preferences arise for alternatives that usually seem inferior. The diagnosis of impulse control disorder now covers a wide range of behaviors that lie at the extremes of ordinary bad habits, including pathological gambling, compulsive shopping, intermittent explosive disorder, binge eating, and "problematic Internet use" (Hollander and Stein

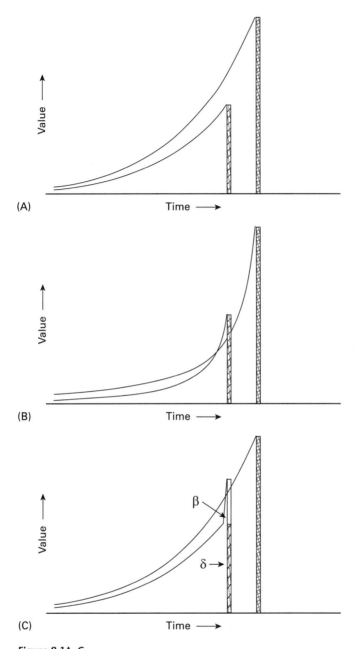

Figure 8.1A–C
(A) Exponential curves drawn according to formula 1 from two alternative expected rewards that are available at discrete moments, depicting value as a function of delay. (B) Hyperbolic curves drawn according to formula 2 from the same rewards as in 8.1A. (C) $\beta - \delta$ curves drawn according to formula 3, where $0 < \beta < 1$ if Delay $\neq 0$; $\beta = 1$ if Delay $= 0$. Immediacy raises the effective height of the SS reward.

2006), which have joined the classical substance abuse disorders in the realm of addictions. Much can be ascribed to naivete; incipient addicts often fail to anticipate the problems that will ensue. It has also been proposed that addiction, conceived broadly, does not violate RCT, but is a rational choice by people with low valuations of the future (Becker and Murphy 1988). However, both the naivete theory and the steep but consistent devaluation theory fail to account for the frequent experience of addicts themselves, who report strenuous efforts at recovery that are undermined by temporary preferences to resume their habits, often with full knowledge of the consequences. The problem confronting RCT has a tougher core: Why do experienced addicts and even highly sophisticated nonaddicts keep making choices that they know they will regret? In other words, what causes the basic tendency to form temporary preferences, in the absence of new information, for alternatives that usually seem poorer?

This question is usually answered by a resort to common experience: a temporary craving (but why temporary?), a passionate nature (but how does passion interact with other motives?), or a weak will (but why should will be required in the first place?). The commonsense approach is developed most fully in the works of Baumeister and his collaborators (1994): An impulse is defined only as "a specific motivation or desire to perform a particular action" (132) but implies a "lower process" overriding a "higher process" (8) and represents a failure of "strength" (17–20), which these authors equate with willpower. By analogy to a muscle, willpower is said to become exhausted with effort in the short run, but strengthened by repeated efforts. These are familiar experiences, but an appeal to them does not advance our understanding of impulsive choice. What directs the will, against what, and what factors make the will strong against one kind of impulse at the same time that it is weak against another? An explicit theory of impulsiveness—and control—must specify the properties of an evaluation process that enables or prevents temporary preferences in particular circumstances. To assure coherence, such a theory should make it possible to depict its predictions as a plot of the values of alternatives over time.

The temporary preference phenomenon implies an upward shift in the value of a poorer reward that makes a plot of its value over time look more bowed than an exponential curve—*hyperconcavity*. Hyperconcavity is an anomaly in any model that depicts consistent valuation of the future. Several mechanisms have been proposed for why temporary preferences occur (reviewed in Ainslie 1992, 24–55), but only three kinds have received serious discussion in the current experimental literature on impulsiveness. Under the *visceral reward hypothesis*, stimuli in your environment that you associate with a rewarding activity come to induce appetite for this activity, so that you suddenly experience an amplified desire for it when those stimuli appear. The *hyperbolic discounting hypothesis* (my proposal) holds that the basic discount curve is more deeply bowed than an exponential curve, leading smaller, sooner (SS) rewards to loom temporarily over larger, later (LL) ones, in the same way that a building can temporarily hide a taller one behind it as you approach. Under this hypothesis the value of imminent rewards is always amplified, and the flattening of curves into the exponential shape reflecting consistent choice is what needs explanation. Finally, *cognitive framing* hypotheses hold that your categorization of the available options may shift with changing distance in ways that disrupt continuous exponential discounting, inducing miscalculations that yield de facto hyperconcavity and thus cause temporary preferences for SS rewards. In this chapter I will evaluate these three kinds of theory. In particular, I will compare how the first two can be extended beyond their heretofore inadequate coverage of "conditioned appetite," and will find in this comparison an additional basis for choosing between them.

Visceral Reward and Conditioning

Visceral reward theory is recognizable as the heir to the earliest psychological theory of impulsiveness, classical conditioning. In the early days of experimental psychology classical conditioning seemed to be the obvious explanation for impulsive choices. When experimenters created animal analogues of human choice, Thorndike represented the intuitively familiar process of goal-directed learning in a theory of response selection by "satisfiers" (Thorndike 1898; see Chance 1999). Subsequently, Pavlov reported what seemed to be a different kind of response selection: When an event could "reflexively" elicit a specific response, this response came to occur after an arbitrarily selected stimulus that had been paired with the event (Pavlov 1927). However, he did not say that this was a special kind of learning; he described responses that were "conditional" on the occurrence of a stimulus, but his term was mistranslated as "conditioned" (Dinsmoor 2004). Seemingly a minor change, the implication of substituting the verb for the adjective was that a process beyond ordinary learning about the predictiveness of environmental events was taking place. Subsequent theorists took "conditioned" responses to be selected by an unmotivated response transfer process.

The relationship of Thorndike's selection by goals and the goal-independent selection imputed to Pavlov was ambiguous until Skinner (1935) proposed a methodological dichotomy): *Operant* responses were those selected by reward, and were thus goal-directed. In addition, there existed some events (*unconditioned stimuli*, UCSs) that elicited reflexive responses (*unconditioned responses*, UCRs). UCSs could select for the transfer of UCRs to arbitrarily designated stimuli (*conditioned stimuli*, CSs) that predicted their occurrence, regardless of whether the CSs predicted that the transferred responses (now called *conditioned responses*, CRs) would be rewarded. Authors soon noted that all effective UCSs had a motivational valence (Hull 1943; Miller 1969), but since this valence could be in the direction of either reward or its opposite, aversiveness, it still did not seem possible that conditioned responses were selected by the same mechanism as goal-directed ones. Unmotivated conditioning was apparently necessary to explain a subject's participation in unwanted experiences such as fear, rage, and craving for addictive substances.

Since people often say that they do not want to do the impulsive things that they are in fact doing, and since the event that selects for these impulsive behaviors usually follows the behaviors closely, many authors from Watson (1924) on have ascribed disowned behaviors to classical conditioning. However, analytic experiments on conditioning itself have found it not to be a selective mechanism for behaviors. The pairing of novel stimuli with UCSs produces only CSs, not CRs (Mackintosh 1983; Rescorla 1988). That is, only information is learned by association; the occurrence and timing of "CRs" depends on what incentives are created by this information. Thus the sight of drugs on television, for instance, could not induce an involuntary drug-taking response. Even the nature of the CR was recognized very early not to depend on what response is elicited by the UCS; only a few CRs happen to be the same, in detail or even in approximate kind, as the UCS (Upton 1929; Zener 1937). This difficulty required theorists to modify the proposal of conditioning as a mechanism for impulsive choice.

In 1947, O. H. Mowrer proposed a two-factor theory of motivation. In Mowrer's theory, an organism comes to associate a stimulus with a rewarding or punishing event through simple pairing, and thus experiences the relevant motivation whenever that stimulus appears (first factor). This motivation is then the basis for goal-directed behavior (second factor). The sight of drugs on television creates an appetite for the drug, which then motivates drug taking. However, the television show has not given the addict more information about either how available the drug is or how rewarding its consumption would be. To account for its motivational effect, conditioning theory has to postulate an extrainformational factor. This is the role of conditioned appetite or its close relative, conditioned emotion.[1] This factor is what is said to explain impulsive preference. Both emotions and appetites are clearly responses, that is, processes that are separate from the perceptions that usually give rise to them. In fact, some emotions, mainly fear, were included in the work that found conditioning to transfer only information, not responses (Estes and Skinner 1941). Furthermore, in avoidance experiments signs of emotion appear after a longer latency than the behavior that the emotion supposedly motivates (Solomon and Wynne 1954). Thus, two-factor theory has also been held to be inadequate (Mackintosh 1983, 99–170).[2]

Elicitation of strong appetites and emotions by reminders such as television shows is a familiar experience, but it is not adequately explained by the association process that has been studied in the laboratory under the name "classical conditioning." What emerges from such studies is how efficient CRs are in the laboratory. In parametric experiments CRs anticipate the occurrence of UCSs with great accuracy. If a CS occurs or begins well before a UCS is due, subjects learn to estimate the delay and emit the CR just before the UCS (Kehoe, Graham-Clark, and Schreurs 1989; Savastano et al. 1998).

With appetites specifically, cue-induced craving for cigarettes and skin conductance and salivation related to craving are strongly dependent on whether puffing is available within the next minute (Carter and Tiffany 2001; Field and Duka 2001). Thus in the laboratory involuntary responses closely track the prediction of reward. Furthermore, if the general process of learning behavioral contingencies in daily life counts as conditioning—the usual assumption—then nonanticipatory appetites are an anomalous variant here as well. Where the consumption of an addictive substance never happens in a given circumstance, humans do not crave it: Opiate addicts and alcoholics in programs that allow consumption only on certain days report absence of craving on other days (Meyer 1988), and observant orthodox Jews, who never smoke on the Sabbath, are reported not to crave cigarettes then (Dar et al. 2005; Schachter, Silverstein, and Perlick 1977). Classical conditioning, which is just associative learning, does not explain appetites that are disproportionate to the prospect of consuming and that change without changes in this prospect. It is true that some cue-induced appetites/emotions have been reported to grow without further contact with UCSs (Eysenck 1967); but these reports have not stood up under careful controls (Malloy and Levis 1990) and in any case go beyond passive association, thus requiring explanation themselves.

Cues that give new information about expectable rewards have the effects depicted in straightforward reward theory. The motivational effect of uninformative cues— mere reminders—remains to be explained. Why should a television show, or sometimes just a reverie about a drug, temporarily change someone's preference? I will argue that none of the three theories described here accounts for this phenomenon as they have so far been developed; and I will propose a rationale for the needed mechanism. This mechanism works most parsimoniously with the second basic hypothesis, which I will now summarize.

Hyperbolic Discounting

The discovery that spontaneous discount curves are hyperbolic has offered an alternative explanation for impulses, although it, too, is incomplete. Hyperbolic or other hyperconcave discounting has been proposed as the basis of a revision of RCT that might serve as the model of motivation in all the behavioral sciences (Gintis 2007). The hypothesis that humans and nonhumans alike have a basic tendency to discount delayed events in a hyperconcave curve has two roots. The economist Robert Strotz (1956) pointed out that people might recognize nonexponential discount curves in themselves and thus expect themselves to reverse their own current plans in predictable ways as time goes by; and behavioral psychologists Shin-Ho Chung and Richard Herrnstein (1967) reported that pigeons working for food on two nonexclusive, unpredictable (concurrent VI VI) schedules distributed their pecks in proportion to the inverses of the mean delays to food delivery, demonstrating that Herrnstein's matching law applies to delay. Application of the matching law to predictable rewards at specific delays (discrete trials) yields a hyperbolic function of value as a function of delay (Ainslie 1975), which was given its most-cited form by Mazur (1987):

Present value $= \text{Value}_0/[1 + (k \times \text{Delay})]$ (formula 2)

where $\text{Value}_0 =$ value if immediate and k is degree of impatience. This function predicts that for some cases where smaller rewards precede larger alternatives, individuals will prefer the larger reward when both are distant, but will change to preferring the smaller reward as time elapses, an example in very basic terms of the predictable preference reversal that Strotz discussed (figure 8.1B).

The first discrete trial experiment to look for hyperbolic discounting did not test the exact shape of the curve, only its property of predicting motivation to forestall a future choice (Ainslie 1974). Preference reversal as a function of delay was observed directly soon afterward (Ainslie and Herrnstein 1981; Green et al. 1981).[3] In the same year economist Richard Thaler (1981) reported that discount rates inferred from human subjects' self-reports declined as hypothetical delays became longer, implying hyperconcavity. The first preference-reversal experiment with human subjects offered college students temporary relief from irritating background noise (Solnick et al. 1980). The subjects preferred shorter, immediate respites to longer, delayed ones, but reversed their preference when the wait before each respite was lengthened by only 15 seconds. Soon preference reversal was found to occur even for cash prizes, both real and hypothetical (Ainslie and Haendel 1983). Precise curve-fitting came soon afterward (Mazur 1987; Rodriguez and Logue 1988) and has become increasingly fine-tuned (Grace 1996; Green, Fry, and Myerson 1994; Green and Myerson 2004; Kirby 1997; Mazur 2001).

However, scrutiny of the hyperbolic model has brought up several apparent inadequacies: With some methods hyperbolic discounting cannot be elicited (Harrison, Lau, and Rutström 2005) or is inconsistent with the observed choice pattern (Read 2001; Read and Roelofsma 2003; Rubinstein 2003). Its greatest limitation for explaining impulsive choice in humans has been that in its basic form it does not predict the sudden craving elicited by stimuli associated with reward consumption, when these stimuli do not predict increased availability or proximity of this consumption (Loewenstein 1996; Laibson 2001). In craving induced by uninformative cues, some amplifying factor beyond immediacy is clearly operating. Conditioned appetite has been the obvious alternative.

The conditioned appetite model meshes with the experience of sudden temptation that often precedes impulses. Many authors have continued to rely on conditioned appetite/emotion as an explanation for temporarily amplified valuations (Drummond et al. 1995; O'Brien 1997). Furthermore, brain correlates of rewarding events have recently become observable through functional magnetic resonance imaging (fMRI), and have been interpreted as revealing two separate motivational systems, one of which is based, in effect, on conditioned emotional reward and the other on consistent exponential discounting (McClure et al. 2004). There are also other phenomena for which differential reward alone has seemed not to be an adequate explanation: Both humans and nonhumans sometimes seek outcomes that they do not like, even for as long as the moderately short times characteristic of impulses (Berridge and Robinson 1998); that is, they seem to *want* something at the same time as they *dislike* it. Also, the attention and engagement necessary for aversive experiences such as fear and pain have never been incorporated into a motivational model without being depicted as a reflex or a conditioned reflex. Thus there have been several reasons to stick to the classical conditioning hypothesis, of which *visceral reward theory* is the latest formulation.

Does Classical Conditioning Amplify Motivation?

Although conditioning is generally a process of information transfer, a larger role in some cases has been proposed. Ordinarily, conditioning entails the straightforward prediction of events, and thus should not create motives disproportionate to this prediction. However, Loewenstein has proposed an expanded role for conditioning in the case of a special, visceral class of motives, so that it alters "the relative desirability of different goods and actions" (Loewenstein 1999, 235) beyond what the information it conveys would do. Appetite need not then be commensurate with information.

Visceral factors include drive states such as hunger, thirst, and sexual desire, moods and emotions, physical pain, and, most importantly for addiction, craving for a drug. . . . At intermediate levels, most visceral factors, including drug craving, produce similar patterns of impulsivity, remorse, and self-binding. At high levels, drug craving and other visceral factors overwhelm decision making altogether, superseding volitional control of behavior. (Ibid.)

In situations where reward is imminently available, visceral reward theory predicts a spike of the motivation to consume it just as hyperbolic discounting theory does. The difference is hypothesized to be in the specific shape of the spike as consumption becomes possible—a sudden step upward from an exponential curve of what would be the value without appetite:

$$\text{Present value} = \text{Value}_0 \times \beta \times \delta^{\text{Delay}} \qquad \text{(formula 3)}$$

where Value_0 = value if immediate and β has one of only two values, $0 < \beta < 1$ or $\beta = 1$; $\delta = 1 -$ discount rate (McClure et al. 2004; figure 8.1C). This step function contrasts with a monotonic hyperbolic curve drawn from the height of the spike (formula 2; figure 8.1B).

When the prospect of a reward is imminent, the value of visceral reward theory is mainly formal. The economist David Laibson originally adopted this theory's dual "hyperboloid" curve from an article on intergenerational transfers of wealth (Phelps and Pollack 1968) because "the discount structure [of the curve] mimics the qualitative property of the hyperbolic discount function, while maintaining most of the analytical tractability of the exponential discount function" (Laibson 1997, 450). However, as noted above, spikes of appetite for many kinds of reward occur without any cue that predicts greater availability or proximity of the reward. These seem to be visceral rewards—indeed the occurrence of these spikes has been used as a defining property of viscerality, as in the passage above. The addict suddenly gets intense cravings while watching a show about drugs. Since such sudden cravings are often implicated in relapses (Tiffany 1995), the question naturally arises of whether a sudden evocation of viscerality might have the same effect as immediacy in sending β to 1.0. This hypothesis converts Laibson's original proposal from a straightforward discounting theory to a two-factor, conditioning-and-exponential-discounting theory (figure 8.1D).

Neurophysiological Evidence

Recent neurophysiological findings have been cited as evidence for qualitatively different processing of visceral rewards. McClure et al. (2004) reported that relative activity in cortical planning areas (lateral prefrontal and lateral orbitofrontal cortex; "δ areas") and limbic craving areas (ventral striatum, medial prefrontal cortex, posterior cingulate cortex; "β areas") predicted whether student subjects would choose to wait for LL rewards. The authors suggested that these two kinds of center are the seats of (presumably conditioned) visceral reward and rational reward, the bases of the spike and the exponential curve, respectively, in the step function in figures 8.1C–E. They found activity in the limbic centers only when the subjects could get the rewards, Internet gift certificates, on the same day, and none at all for two- or four-week delays. They interpreted this finding as support for the β–δ step function of visceral reward theory—rational, exponential discounting as a function of delay interrupted by a sudden spike of appetite from activity in a time-insensitive visceral center (figure 8.1C):

Our results help to explain why many factors other than temporal proximity, such as the sight or smell or touch of a desired object, are associated with impulsive behavior. If impatient behavior is driven by limbic activation, it follows that any factor that produces such activation may have effects similar to that of immediacy. (McClure et al. 2004, 506)

In a recent review of the fMRI literature, Montague and colleagues used the McClure group's findings as a basis for rejecting hyperbolic discounting as a factor in choice:

[Hyperbolic discounting] begs several important questions. Why should not exponential discounting, as it is expressed in reinforcement-learning models, account adequately for the variety of valuation and learning behaviors [in experiments the authors had reviewed]? ... A second, more fundamental question is, How does one justify hyperbolic discounting—where it is observed—in terms of the rational agent model favored by standard economic theory? One answer to these questions is to assume that hyperbolic discounting reflects the operation of more than a single valuation mechanism. The simplest version of this view suggests that there are two canonical

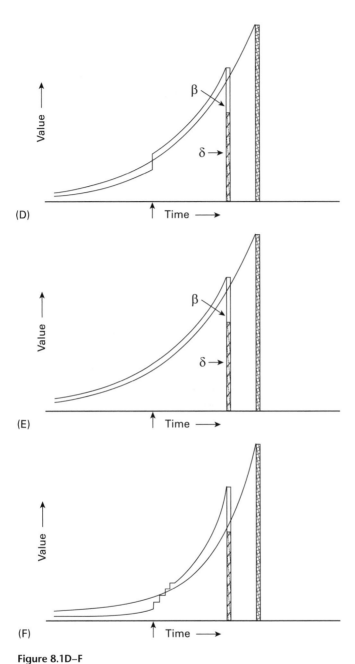

(D)

(E)

(F)

Figure 8.1D–F

(D) $\beta - \delta$ curves drawn according to formula 3, where $0 < \beta < 1$ before a CS occurs, and $\beta = 1$ afterward. The CS elicits a CR (appetite) that raises the effective height of the SS reward. (E) $\beta - \delta$ curves at equilibrium drawn according to formula 3, where $0 < \beta < 1$ before a CS occurs, and $\beta = 1$ afterwards. Repeated elicitation of appetite by a CS should make the rise in SS height expectable, leading 8.1E to converge with 8.1A. (F) Recursive evaluations of the prospect of an SS reward according to formula 2, with increasing height reflecting both change in rewardingness due to appetite and change in probability of consuming. Increasing appetite → increasing probability of consuming → increasing appetite.

mechanisms: one that has a very steep discount function (in the limit, valuing only immediate rewards), and one that treats rewards more judiciously over time with a shallower discount function. (Montague, King-Casas, and Cohen 2006, 434)

However, it is premature to say that these fMRI reports demonstrate a discontinuity between visceral-or-immediate and nonvisceral-and-delayed valuations. Gift certificates for goods that would have to be chosen after the session and then mailed to the subjects are odd examples of visceral rewards. And β centers are not unresponsive at nonzero delays. When Monterosso, Ainslie, and London (2006) studied the response of the same β centers to the prospect of puffs on cigarettes during a period of deprivation they found that these centers show activity to prospects at least a week away. Furthermore, even within β centers delay sensitivity is not uniform, but can be pinpointed in the striatum by a graded map with ventroanterior regions tracking more immediate rewards and dorsoposterior regions tracking more delayed ones (Tanaka et al. 2004).[4]

McClure et al. (2007) have recently revised their model to allow for (exponential) discounting by β centers, but at a greater rate than discounting by δ centers. Valuation by the two centers would be added together to form the individual's operative motivation:

$$\text{Present value} = \text{Value}_0 \times \{(\acute{\omega} \times \beta^{\text{Delay}}) + [(1 - \acute{\omega}) \times \delta^{\text{Delay}}]\} \qquad \text{(formula 4)}[5]$$

where $\text{Value}_0 = $ value if immediate, β and δ are one minus their respective discount rates, and $\acute{\omega}$ is a weighting factor. Graphically, this function would smooth out the abrupt step upward in figure 8.1D, more or less, depending on the β discount rate. With three parameters, formula 4 would undoubtedly improve the curve's fit with hyperconcave discounting data, but the supposedly short range of β discounting would still leave it unable to account for the hyperbolic shapes reported when the shortest delays are months (Green, Myerson, and Macaux 2005) or years (Harvey 1994). More seriously, Glimcher, Kable, and Louie (2007) have reported that, although several brain regions respond proportionately to a subject's valuation of rewards (striatum, posterior cingulate gyrus, medial prefrontal cortex), they all track declines in valuation at the same rate.

Valuation clearly takes place in a number of brain locations, which may process rewards with different zones of delay duration (Tanaka et al. 2004), degrees of predictability (Daw, Niv, and Dayan 2005), or incentive salience (Berridge 2007; see below). However, there has been no evidence against their interacting to create a single internal marketplace, with the common currency—reward—that many authors have argued to be theoretically necessary (Ainslie 1992, 28–32; Cabanac 1992; McFarland and Sibley 1975; Montague and Berns 2002; Shizgal and Conover 1996).

As for whether nonimmediate rewards are discounted hyperbolically or exponentially, no fMRI study has produced data precise enough to discriminate between these shapes, although Glimcher, Kable, and Louie (2007) found fMRI activity to be "linearly correlated" with hyperbolic discounting curves computed from subjects' choices. In addition, a study of single cells in the pigeon brain area analogous to the mammalian prefrontal cortex (Nidopallium caudolaterale) has reported activity that is better fitted by a hyperbolic temporal discount function than by an exponential one (Kalenscher et al. 2005). A neurophysiological answer that is more than suggestive will have to await better data.

For now, the evaluation of conditioned appetite as a theory of sudden craving depends on the interpretation of behavioral data, as I discussed in the previous section. Seen simply at the level of evident motivation, a basic problem for visceral reward theory appears in plots of motivation against expected delay: Visceral reward theory does not make it clear why the associative process should not lead visceral rewards that are amplified by appetite to be anticipated and discounted like any other reward, so that they become consistently preferred where the amplification is great enough—a progression from the pattern in figure 8.1D to that in figure 8.1E. After all, rewards are usually remembered as consumed in the presence of appetite; adjusting their value for satiety is a distinct process (Balleine and Dickinson 1998).

However, a straightforward application of hyperbolic discounting theory also fails to predict spikes of appetite in response to cues that do not convey new information; if a reward is no closer and no more probable, its value should not increase. And the framing effects proposed by cognitive theories have not been based on visceral or appetitive situations at all. Something more is needed.

A Solution: Recursive Self-Prediction

An extension of either conditioning or hyperbolic discounting theory can handle the occurrence of explosive appetites/emotions. I will argue that this extension works well only for the hyperbolic theory; but the hyperbolic model also requires a radical revision of our assumptions about the selection of subjectively involuntary processes. First conditioning, then.

Recursive Self-Prediction of CRs
The rewards in laboratory experiments are outside of the subject's control. Signs of appetite are studied as a function of when the experimenter signals their availability. In daily life, by contrast, goods that might be consumed impulsively are available much of the time, and their consumption is limited by a person's decisions. The information predicting reward in life situations will be very different from predictive information in the laboratory.

Modern conditioning theory no longer holds that CSs have to be concrete stimuli. They can be just temporal patterns, interpreted stochastically by the subject (Gallistel 2002), a finding that can be summarized by saying that the expectation of a UCS, in whatever form, functions as a CS. In humans, and possibly other organisms to a limited extent, expectation includes estimation of the individual's own future behavior. If a person always carried out her intentions, such estimation would serve no purpose; she could predict her behavior directly by examining these intentions. But behavior in even the near future is increasingly recognized as beyond the scope of such examination (Wegner 2002, esp. 63–144), and may depend on the dynamics of a population of competing processes (Ainslie 2001, 39–44). This means that expectation is apt to be recursive, with an expectation of a UCS, for instance taking cocaine, functioning as a CS and inducing the CR of appetite. But where the availability of cocaine is not a limiting factor, an increase in appetite will itself increase the likelihood of taking the cocaine. If this likelihood increases, the CS of expecting cocaine should increase, and in turn the CR of appetite again.

For cases where a person's consumption is limited mainly by her own choice, appetite can be a positive feedback system of the kind first described by Darwin, James, and Lange:

The free expression by outward signs of an emotion intensifies it. On the other hand, the repression, as far as this is possible, of all outward signs softens our emotions. He who gives way to violent gestures will increase his rage; he who does not control the signs of fear will experience fear in greater degree. (Darwin 1872/1979, 366)

Their proposal has sometimes been interpreted as meaning that an individual feels fear because she notices somatic signs of fear, but this interpretation has not held up to empirical scrutiny (Rolls 2005, 26–28). However, it is still possible that such a feedback process modulates a given response once the individual has focused on it. Whenever an arbitrary stimulus has been associated with consumption in the past, the appearance of that stimulus might accurately predict an increased current likelihood of consumption, and accordingly function as a conventional CS. A sudden spike of appetite could thus come from the existence of positive feedback conditions. These conditions may obtain whenever the person's consumption is determined mainly by her choice about a readily available consumption good, but are apt to have the strongest effect when there is weak-to-moderate resolve not to consume: Where a person is not trying to restrain consumption she will keep appetite relatively satisfied; where she is confident of not consuming regardless of appetite (as in cases of opiates in scheduled addicts and smoking in orthodox Jews) she will not expect appetite to lead to consumption. In both of these cases a stimulus associated with consumption should be only a trivial CS and thus not lead to an exceptional CR. In a recovering addict or restrained eater, by contrast, cues predicting that she might lapse could elicit significant CRs.

However, since conditioning is simply the acquisition of information, the power of this recursive model is limited. Even if we concede the existence of CRs in the case of appetites, they are supposed just to be UCRs that have been passively transferred to CSs because CSs predict their UCSs. If CRs are only such anticipatory responses, their amplitude should be limited to no more than that of their UCRs. If a person's expectation of consumption increases by x%, her appetite (CR) should increase by no more than x% of the UCR—at most x% of what the CR would be when certainty is 100% and delay is zero. Since we are discussing delays that are significantly greater than zero—the cases where hyperbolic curves per se do not explain the upward spiking of motivation—the increase in appetite should be markedly less than x%. Conversely, if a person's appetite increases by x%, the increase in estimated probability of consumption that this causes should also be fractional, reflecting the proportion of times when that much increase in appetite has been followed by actual consumption.

Take the case of a recovering addict who has moderate resolve not to relapse. An initial confrontation with a drug stimulus should increase her likelihood of relapsing by only a marginal amount. This increase should in turn have only a small effect on her conditioned craving (CR), which would be expected to increase her expectation of relapse by an even smaller amount again. The positive feedback effect should be damped down unless the percentage of each increase is perfectly preserved, and even in that case the CR will be capped at the level of the UCR and discounted for whatever delay she expects. The qualitative elements for explosive craving are there, but quantitatively the argument struggles uphill.

Recursive Self-Prediction of Motivated Processes

If appetites are selected not by the simple transfer of a UCS but by reward for their activity, as I have proposed elsewhere (Ainslie 2001, 48–70, 161–174), this limitation disappears. A recursive reward-seeking model predicts the same observations as a conditioning model, but without the damping effect: A stimulus associated with consumption will be a cue for generating appetite if the potential for consumption to be rewarding (nonsatiety) exists. When consumption is limited by self-control—probably the case only in humans—appetite itself has the potential to obtain fast-paying reward by motivating the abandonment of (slow-paying) self-control. The most rewarding amount of appetite, then, may be not that which optimizes the expected experience of consumption, but rather that which makes consumption most probable. The most productive timing of such appetite will take the form of concentrated attempts on discrete occasions; if appetite does not succeed in inducing consumption on a particular occasion it is unlikely to increase its chances by prolonged activity, and may indeed fatigue with repetition like many other physiological processes. Occasions for appetites could be arbitrary, especially at higher levels of deprivation, but the occasions that are the most apt to promise successful attempts must be limited in frequency—an external reminder, or a circumstance where they have succeeded in the past. In this view, the force of symbols and other reminders in relapse comes from their providing reward-based appetites with focal occasions to try to overturn self-control.

In a marketplace model reward-dependent processes compete for acceptance on the basis of the current, hyperbolically discounted value of the prospective reward for these processes. The fact that preferability among a set of processes can shift as a function of time alone puts these processes in a limited warfare relationship with each other (Ainslie 1992, 154–179; 2001, 90–100). That is, they will operate as independent agents that have some but not all interests in common, on the basis of what are common contingencies of reward but differently discounted valuations of them.[6] An appetite in this model arises when an individual perceives the opportunity for consumption that can be made either more rewarding or more likely by this appetite. Appetites still have some physical constraints such as nonsatiety, but the final selective factor for their arousal is the contingent prospect of reward.

The contingencies that determine whether appetite as a quasi-independent agent asserts itself in a given situation will be roughly the same as those determining whether a pet begs its owner for food or the chance to excrete. Begging is a low-cost behavior and is apt to occur whenever a nonsatiated pet encounters satisfaction-related cues; again, continuous begging will not be worthwhile. But if the pet is never fed or let out in a particular circumstance the begging gradually extinguishes, unless the biological need is extreme. Likewise, if gratification is so available that significant deprivation does not occur, begging adds no value.[7] By analogy, the restrained eater or recovering addict has an opportunity to experience intense reward by indulging in immediate consumption. Insofar as appetite makes consumption look even a little more likely it will pay for itself, and any signs of weakening will serve as cues that still more appetite may succeed in motivating consumption (figure 8.1F). The low cost of appetite may explain why it must go unrewarded consistently over many trials in a given circumstance to extinguish—for instance, why the orthodox Jews who do not get cravings on the Sabbath do get cravings when they know they must not smoke at work (Dar et al. 2005).

In short, appetite as a reward-seeking process can be subject to the same positive feedback mechanism as conditioned appetite. The important difference from the feedback conditioning model is that the degree of appetite will not be limited to mere anticipation, but can be whatever increases the prospect of reward. There will still be constraints—appetite depends on nonsatiety; in modalities where unsatisfied appetite brings hunger pangs or withdrawal symptoms, these will be deterrents; and appetite without occasions of limited frequency will extinguish (see Ainslie 2001, 166–171)—but the explosive appetite that so often ends people's efforts at controlled consumption can be understood as a motivated process that is rewarded in the short run when it detects these efforts.

It remains a question why a person who has generated sudden appetite in a certain circumstance does not come to anticipate the higher value of the SS reward with that appetite, and thus come to prefer it consistently, as illustrated in the case of exponential curves by the progression from figure 8.1D–E. Failure to develop consistent preference is easily accounted for by discount curves with a hyperbolic shape, as in figure 8.1B. Failure to anticipate the sudden occurrence of the responsible appetite at short delays may happen because a person avoids rehearsing the situation in advance, for fear of triggering the appetite by doing so.[8]

The model of appetite as an operant cued by recursive self-prediction appears to be the only one proposed so far that can account explicitly for explosive appetite—that is, for why a cue that is associated with consumption but does not predict increased availability of a consumption good should lead to a great increase in appetite. In this model the cue is needed only to give occasion, that is, to select one moment over another for a focused attempt at reversing the dominant preference. The model depends on the hyperconcave shape of the discount curve, since an individual with consistent preferences over time would have no short-range motive to undermine her own resolutions, or indeed any long-range motive to make resolutions in the first place. It might still work with the "hyperboloid" (β–δ) step function hypothesized by visceral reward theory; but this shape describes the explosive appetite that, according to the damping argument presented above, the theory's conditioning mechanism would be inadequate to produce. That is, the only viable mechanism for the β–δ hyperboloid discount curve is for discount curves to have an elementary hyperbolic or other hyperconcave shape to begin with.

Are Appetites Selected by Reward?

The above argument requires that an appetite respond to differential reward for that appetite, which is not a trivial change in the conventional view of appetite. But I have argued elsewhere that hyperbolic discount curves permit involuntary and even aversive processes to be incorporated into a unified motivational marketplace (Ainslie 2001, 48–70). All that is needed is to strip the selective factor, "reward," of its connotations of pleasure and reduce it to its defining function: that which selects for a process that it follows.[9] Briefly, the argument is that temporary preferences are apt to be cyclic, impulses that satiate and recover over a continuum of durations that define the periods of the cycles (figure 8.2). A binge may last for days before sickness sets in, but the urge to emit a tic lasts for only seconds until it is spent, and the urge to respond to a painful stimulus with pain emotion (Melzack and Casey 1970) lasts, hypothetically, for just a moment before its negative consequences are felt. The value of this model is that both positive and negative appetites can be seen as luring individuals into participating in them, rather than springing up automatically like reflexes, outside of the marketplace of choice. As long as it is discounted hyperbolically, reward can then be

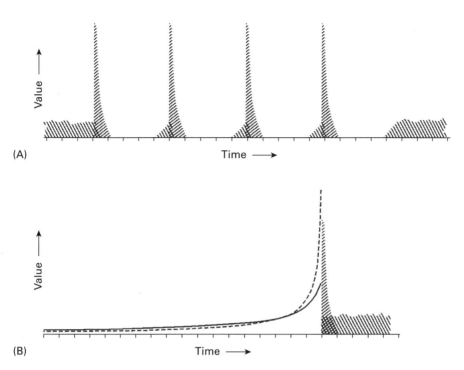

Figure 8.2A–B

(A) Aversion as a cycle of brief, intense reward (rightward hatching) that interrupts an ongoing baseline reward (leftward hatching) for a relatively longer time (from Ainslie 1992). Units of time might vary from weeks to a few milliseconds. (B) Hyperbolic discount curves drawn from a single spike in an aversion sequence such as that in 8.2A. (Each curve is the sum of the curves from each moment of reward.) The spike has less area than the baseline reward to which it is an alternative; but because it is taller it will be preferred just before it is available (from Ainslie 1992).

the selective factor not only for long-enduring pleasures, but for temporary, regretted pleasures and for urges that do not feel pleasurable at all.

This argument is bolstered by recent reports of an extensive borderline area, which can be seen as lying halfway between the phenomena of addiction and frank aversion. Berridge and his colleagues have analyzed activities that subjects have strong tendencies to repeat despite a lack of pleasure that is evident either from self-reports, or, in the case of nonhumans, facial expressions (Berridge and Robinson 1998; Berridge 2003). These authors were suspicious of supposed "pleasure centers" that induced avid self-stimulation despite reported sensations that patients said they did not enjoy and that rats would not cross their cages to initiate after periods of interruption. Using increasingly precise physiological mapping techniques they have separated brain centers that subtend pleasurable activities and centers for activities that are "wanted but not liked," which subjects perform repeatedly despite evident distaste for them (Peciña, Smith, and Berridge 2006). The authors interpret the latter findings as evidence of a dissociable component of decision making, response selection by "salience." This interpretation remains controversial (O'Doherty 2004), partly because of the difficulty of separating attention from preference (Maunsell 2004; Schultz 2006); the motivational properties of salience have been especially difficult to define. Despite the "wanting" label, the Berridge group calls this kind of selection "nonhedonic" (Berridge 2003); a wanted, disliked goal is nevertheless "a motivational magnet" (Berridge 2007) or "a false pleasure" (Peciña, Smith, and Berridge 2006). They make it clear that wanting is still motivation, and must interact with hedonic reward to determine which motor behavior a subject will perform—a conclusion that temporal difference theory, an interpretation that partially incorporates incentive salience theory, also supports (McClure, Daw, and Montague 2003).

A possible form of this interaction is intertemporal conflict. That is, wanted-but-not-liked activity may have the same motivational valence as pleasurable activity, but only temporarily. The normal course of learning is for wanted behaviors to be evaluated for liking and replaced if they fail that test (Berridge 2007), but the effect of delay per se on choice has not been studied in these experiments. There do exist ordinary human behaviors that are wanted only briefly and that interfere with other rewards, so that from a distance people try to prevent them or buy cures for them. Activities of daily life that can be described as wanted but not liked include tics, speech mannerisms, psychogenic itches, and itch-like activities such as nail biting and hair pulling. The interaction of these disliked behaviors with liked alternatives obeys the same cyclic motivational math as binges with hangovers, but it has a much shorter periodicity (figure 8.2). Both addictive and itch-like activities are avoided at a distance but sought when up close, but you have to be much closer to a disliked activity before you want it.

From the case of wanted-but-not-liked it is not a great leap to given-in-to-but-not-wanted; the same cyclic mechanism may explain seemingly unmotivated responses generally. If the "wanted" phase of an option is too short to motivate even brief approach behaviors, it might still attract attention and negative appetites/emotions. Maunsell has suggested that the reward/salience controversy has arisen from too narrow a definition of reward: "If reward is defined to include all motivating factors, then there may be no differences between attention and expectation of reward" (Maunsell 2004, 264). He thus implies that the concept should extend beyond the wanted to the attended-to. Berridge's definition of incentive salience still excludes magnets for attention per se; however, the urge to pay attention to an aversive process might be how the very truncated "wanting" for this process is experienced—not in a consciously discriminable approach phase, but merged with its alternating avoidance phase as in flicker fusion. The reward that selects for this attention thus cannot last long, but also cannot be slight if the urge is strong; hence it might be represented as the recurring tall, thin spikes of figure 8.2.

Certainly the evaluation of pain has been reported to involve the same brain centers as that of reward (ventral striatum, sublenticular extended amygdala, ventral tegmentum, and orbital gyrus [Becerra et al. 2001]), and in all but the striatum the response to pain is in the same direction as that to reward, which "suggests that they may constitute a general circuitry processing both rewarding and aversive information" (ibid., 942). Even in the striatum other authors have reported increased activity after both reward and punishment, and decreased activity after the unexpected nondelivery of either (O'Doherty 2004). The processes that have been said to be based on "salience" (e.g., Zink et al. 2003) thus include delivery of both reward and punishment but not their omission, and "unwanted" motor behaviors. As O'Doherty points out, if the striatum were merely tracking salience, its activity should increase for the unexpected omission of reward or punishment as well as their delivery. The common attribute of these processes is better characterized as brief attractiveness.

The possibility that reward and the selective principle in UCSs are identical has been proposed before (reviewed in Pear and Eldridge 1984; Donahoe, Burgos, and Palmer 1993) but has not been pursued extensively, perhaps because a separate selective principle has seemed necessary to explain why aversive experiences can compete for attention, and perhaps because no other hypotheses have hinged on this identity. But hyperbolic discounting implies that a separate selective principle is not necessary to account for attention to aversive experiences, as I have just described. Of course, it may turn out that this attention can be better explained by other hypotheses that integrate reward and nonreward in close temporal proximity, or even simultaneity, as the processes underlying motivational salience are analyzed (e.g., Berridge and Robinson 1998, 348–349). The neurophysiological dissociability of wanting from liking is certainly relevant; but so far there has been no other hypothesis at the behavioral level about how wanting—or dreading—interact with liking in the marketplace of choice. As to whether any behavioral hypotheses depend on the question of one versus two basic selective factors, the very reason for including the foregoing section in this chapter is to support the possibility that explosive appetite is based on recursive self-prediction. I have argued above that the sudden occurrence of appetite when its object is no nearer requires appetite to be reward dependent—that is, selected by the same factor as motor behavior.

Can Cognitive Framing Models Replace Hyperbolic Discounting?

In addition to the activity in conditioning research, new proposals have been made to explain preference reversal over time as a purely cognitive phenomenon, the result of how subjects frame their choices. Research since the 1960s has revealed many instances where people reason erroneously or frame choices in ways that deviate from RCT (Wason 1966; Kahneman and Tversky 1984). These deviations have often been shown to be reduced or eliminated when problems are posed to subjects in terms of familiar experience (Gigerenzer 2000), and most of them do not involve preference reversal. However, several authors have suggested that the apparently hyperbolic shape of discount curves is an artifact of cognitive framing processes.

People's Theories of Value

Human subjects' choice sometimes follows the same pattern as that of nonhuman subjects. When concrete rewards are available at short delays, these rewards seem to shape human subjects' choices in the same way that they do nonhumans' choices, for example, fruit juice (Logue et al. 1986) or escape from noxious noise (Solnick et al. 1980); and when they do, these choices imply hyperconcave curves. Surprisingly, their choices of token rewards such as money, both hypothetical and real, often follow specifically hyperbolic curves as well; these are shallower but no less hyperbolic in normal adults than in various kinds of addict (Bickel and Marsch 2001). However, humans conceive of reward in complex ways that complicate our choice process beyond what is evident in nonhumans. We often make choices not by weighing the possible experiences but by interpreting them according to what could loosely be called *theories of value*, sometimes using identifiable heuristics. The difference can be seen with a melioration procedure (Herrnstein and Prelec 1992), a series of discrete nondelayed binary choices where choice of a larger reward in one trial leads to a reduction of both options in the next, and a choice of a smaller reward leads to an increase of both options in the next. Nonhuman subjects regularly choose larger options. Humans soon learn to choose smaller options when the options are stated in amounts of money; but they continue to choose larger options when the differences are in (unstated) delays before the next trial. When the subjects go by the feel of the alternatives they choose early payoffs, but when they go by the numbers they look for maximizing solutions. In the latter case they have gone beyond their impressions and adopted a cognitive method of evaluating their payoffs, a theory of value.

People's theories of value do not replace their spontaneous motives, but rather anticipate and provide incentives to manipulate these motives, as Mischel's painstaking work with 4- to 6-year-old children showed (e.g., Mischel and Mischel 1983). It was not enough for the children to conclude that a marshmallow later was worth more than a cracker now. They had to develop commitment tactics such as distracting themselves or "thinking cool thoughts," tactics that are still discernible in the coping mechanisms of adults (Vaillant 1971). Thus it is only half true that

the connection between findings on pigeons or even monkeys and the behavior of humans seems rather tenuous. We commonly believe that an animal does not understand the choice it is facing in the same way that a human being does. (Rubinstein 2003, 1209)

Paul MacLean (1990) likened the evolutionarily older parts of our brains to a horse, which is ridden rather than supplanted by our neocortex. To study motivation in nonhuman animals is to study the horse, an endeavor that reveals as much about human decision making as study of the theory-spinning rider does. This is especially true since horse and rider must share a common hedonic outcome, of which most of the functionality seems to be located in the horse.

Theories of value do not necessarily make reward-seeking more efficient. When children begin to develop heuristics for getting rewards their performance initially falls off in comparison with younger children who are still letting their choices be shaped as nonhumans' are (Sonuga-Barke, Lea, and Webley 1989). To prevail against spontaneous preference, their theories of value often dictate the development of committing devices to restrain gut reactions; but committing devices reduce their responsiveness to ongoing experience. Even in adults, "flying on instruments" may lead to rigidity and poor ability to exploit the environment. Most schools of psychotherapy do not target our impulsiveness as much as our overgrown controls, the products of "cognitive maps" (Gestalt), "conditions of worth" (Rogerian), "musterbating" (cognitive), and of course punitive superegos (psychoanalytic; Corsini 1984).

A person's theory of value must obviously deliver the means to get actual rewards—the process that selects behavior—or she will eventually abandon it for better-paying theories. However, the separate contributions of theories of value and direct shaping are hard for an observer to measure, because imagination can reward in its own right. This capability permits theories of value to be partially self-confirming when they propose tasks that function as cognitive games. If you have a theory that money, for instance, is a good source of reward, then getting money becomes an occasion for a positive emotion like satisfaction, relief, or gloating, benefits of winning per se that are above and beyond the prospect of enjoying what you will buy (see Lea and Webley 2006). A quest for distant goals requires the establishment of milestones to mark progress; if these milestones are achieved with adequate rarity and unpredictability they can become durable occasions for emotion, with only enough constraint by their ostensible purposes to keep winning from becoming too easy. Once you "believe in" the value of finding bargains, or having acquaintances remember your name, or winning arguments, sufficiently difficult feats in these areas will occasion rewarding feelings regardless of their practical effects.

Thus when experimenters study people's evaluation of their options, we usually see an admixture of reward that does not depend on the objective outcomes. Although we may detect a quantum of prospective value that is actually constrained by the physical nature of the goal—sweetness, say, or drug effect—this is mixed with an often larger internal component determined by a subject's theories of value through both the commitments and game-like incentives that these theories set up. When we ask about preferences for money, even money that will actually be delivered as chosen, we cannot expect to sample the feel of the consumption of what the money will buy, only the conventions that the person has developed for what represents doing well in money-getting games. Fortunately, the multiplicity and interrelatedness of games that share money as a common counter have given some consistency to these conventions. Even more fortunately, subjects mostly do not subject their imagination of future money to their norm of "rational" economic behavior, so we can see their tendency to form temporary preferences even for money. Discount curves for expected money are robustly hyperbolic even though they are describing a token in a cognitive game; but their Ks (formula 2) vary among human subjects by hundredfolds, whereas Ks among nonhumans of a given species usually vary by single digits (Monterosso and Ainslie 1999). Such wide variation is unlikely to reflect differences in innate endowments, but rather reflects the differences in the cognitive games and commitments to which various subjects' theories of value have led them.[10]

Cognitive Framing Theories

Cognitively based objections to hyperbolic (or other hyperconcave) discounting as an underlying principle of motivation have been based on several kinds of finding. Most basic has been the failure to find hyperbolic discounting in amount versus delay choice experiments. More subtly, hyperconcavity has been said to be an artifact of various ways of framing choices: Human subjects have been reported to discount future payoffs more steeply when delays are broken into shorter periods, and when smaller amounts are at stake. Subjects' heuristics, such as grouping outcomes into the categories of similar versus dissimilar, or treating outcomes abstractly versus concretely, have also been identified as possible causes of inconsistent choice.

It is well known that some prospects come to be valued as occasions for anticipatory imagination beyond what they are in themselves, that is, for what they would be if they occurred immediately or otherwise without anticipation. Thus subjects say that they would defer a kiss from a movie star in order to savor it (Loewenstein 1987), or arrange sequences of experiences so that the prospect is always for improvement (Frank 1992; Read and Powell 2002). There are even cases where people arrange to savor an event to the exclusion of ever experiencing it, for instance by repeatedly deferring a dream vacation. Conversely, people often prefer to hasten the occurrence of painful events so as to avoid the development of dread (Berns et al. 2006). Such cases are seen only in humans and illustrate the human ability to use imagination to occasion reward. Nonhumans have never been observed to prefer delay of a reward, and they will choose to hasten punishment to reduce it only when this earlier punishment will still be distant (Deluty et al. 1983). Savoring and dread have been held up as counterexamples to hyperbolic discounting, but they count as such only if we disregard subjects' generation of emotional reward, as just described, using external events as occasions.

The skill of harnessing the expectation of future events to manipulate current reward depends on a person's theories of value, and the success of this skill is apt to be a major factor in selecting these theories in turn. The most systematic of these theories is the dominant principle of modern finance, RCT. The ability to make choices as if the effect of future reward decayed in a relatively shallow exponential curve is obviously adaptive in competitive markets. Commitment to evaluate prospects exponentially, at least in one's more important mental accounts (Thaler 1985), may be motivated by the prospect of greater success in one's own long-range projects, but is perhaps motivated more strongly by protection against being money-pumped by competitors (Ainslie 1991). This motivation will be insufficient if one attempts to adhere to too shallow a normative curve, and it will not be present in choices that are unimportant or unlikely to be repeated—probably including many choices made when serving as a subject in an experiment. However, to the extant that subjects regard their commitment to rational investment as applicable, they are apt not to display hyperbolic preference patterns. For instance, in an amount versus delay experiment Harrison, Lau, and Rutström (2005) reported that adults exhibited consistent exponential discount rates over delays from one to 24 months. The authors theorized that this result came from not using delays of less than one month for their SS rewards; but other experiments that used delays of a month or more for SS rewards have found preference reversals in adult subjects (Green, Myerson, and Macaux 2005; Ainslie and Haendel 1983). The consistent preferences seen in the Harrison experiment are more likely to be a result of an experimental design that encouraged prudent choice: Subjects chose between large amounts of real money ($450 to $1840, which they had a 10% chance of winning); choices were presented in ascending numeric order to avoid the "computational complexity" of the usual shuffled order; and, most important, the equivalent annual interest rate was listed next to each choice. There has never been doubt that people can often achieve the consistent financial planning displayed in this example. But according to the hyperbolic discounting model people must construct the necessary valuations strategically on the basis of an underlying hyperbolic function, a function that is discernible when conditions encourage subjects to choose according to their spontaneous impressions of value. The conditions of this experiment did not do so.

Bringing preferences under rational marketplace discipline has clearly been the most important example of how people's theories of value modify choices by framing them. However, others have become apparent in the numerous experiments conducted on human discounting during the last two decades. For example, Read (2001) and Read and Roelofsma (2003) report several experiments in which human subjects were asked their preferences between SS and LL rewards, as with Harrison et al. "in the context of investment decisions" (145), but without the prompts about interest rates. The authors computed implied discount rates from preferences between SS and LL rewards. Unlike previous researchers they compared discount rates for a particular period with the aggregate of discount rates when the period was broken into shorter, equal segments and preferences were elicited over each segment. They found neither rational choice nor hyperbolic discounting, but "*subadditive* discounting," a tendency for people to report discount rates that are higher the shorter the period they cover, regardless of whether the period will begin immediately or up to two years later. Since almost all amount versus delay experiments thus far have used lengthening periods between choices as delays get longer, these authors suggest that subadditivity might be responsible for the resulting curves' hyperbolic shape. The phenomenon stood up in the authors' own replication and may represent a significant heuristic that people use in estimating discount rates. However, these experiments do not suggest an adequate substitute for hyperbolic discounting as a basic property of response selection. Crucially, as the authors acknowledge, subadditivity does not predict temporary preference for SS over LL rewards, which is the key implication of the hyperbolic shape. Furthermore, although there has been almost no discounting research using equal delay increments, one nonhuman experiment that used them found that decreased discounting, as evidenced by preference reversals, still occurred as delays became longer, a finding predicted by hyperbolic but not subadditive discounting (Ainslie and Herrnstein 1981). Furthermore, the hyperbolic shape of curves from single, discrete choices is only one manifestation of Herrnstein's matching law, which describes the same inverse proportionality of value to delay in competing, simultaneous schedules of unpredictably timed rewards (concurrent VI-VI; Chung and Herrnstein 1967), where subadditivity would not be a factor.

Read and Roelofsma's interpretations are complicated by the fact that they did find increased rates of discounting as delays decreased—hyperconcave discounting—but in an irregular shape that deviated from hyperbolic. They attributed this finding to people's tendency to discount larger rewards less steeply than smaller ones (the *magnitude effect*). This mechanism had already been proposed by Green and Myerson (1993), who pointed out that steeper discounting might cause an exponential curve from an SS reward to start above that from an LL reward but fall below it as delay increased. However, further analysis by the same authors showed that true hyperbolic curves fit the choice data better than do exponential curves with different slopes (Green and Myerson 1996). In any case, the magnitude effect has been reported only for amounts differing by factors on the order of ten or more, not for amounts within the twofold range such as were used by Read and Roelofsma. For instance, Kirby (2006) found that the discounted value of a series of three rewards is exactly the same as the sum of the discounted values of the individual rewards. The magnitude effect is not seen at all in nonhumans or in humans when both amounts offered are large (Green and Myerson 2004), suggesting that it reflects the increasing salience of the rational choice norm as amounts go from trivial to important, rather than a basic way of evaluating future options. Subadditive discounting and the magnitude effect thus probably both arise from people's heuristics for estimating the value of reward, and can be expected to influence their choices to some extent, but not sufficiently to account for temporary preferences.

Ariel Rubinstein (2003) has pointed out that human subjects use a *similarity heuristic* in evaluating monetary choices. That is, they treat values of either amount or delay that are close to each other as equal, and decide according to any conspicuously dissimilar values involved. For instance, when amounts of reward are close enough to each other to be judged as similar, the change from "different" delays (e.g., none versus a year from now) to "similar" delays (e.g., 10 years versus 11 years—1210) could be responsible for a switch in preference between a pair of amounts offered at those delays. However, the greater perceived similarity of 10 to 11 years than of 0 to 1 years should itself be seen as a manifestation of hyperbolic discounting, or at least of the widely applicable psychophysical principle that changes in quantity are perceived in proportion to the baseline quantity. This principle, the Weber-Fechner law, is sometimes hypothesized to be the basis of hyperbolic discounting (Gibbon 1977). That is, the greater similarity of two delays that are separated by a given amount when the delays are long is based on the same principle as the lesser impact of the delay between SS and LL rewards when both are distant. Whether or not to call the corresponding hyperbolic curves measures of similarity will be a matter of taste.

Rubinstein goes beyond the similarity-with-distance effect to report three amount versus delay experiments in which the results actually contradict hyperbolic discounting. The key to those findings seems to have been that, to get the necessary rejection of the predicted offer in each of the experiments, the gain for waiting for the LL reward had to be minuscule: $467.39 versus $467.00, $1000 versus $997, and $960 versus $958, respectively; even so, no choice was endorsed by as many as 70% of the subjects. It should not be controversial that people often estimate values by rules of thumb; an astute familiarity with these rules adds to many merchants' profit margins. Operating with small relative differences that are close to indifference points may indeed let a similarity heuristic determine choice, but this shows little about the more robust motives that challenge self-control.

Another familiar experience—that one sees trees when close but forests when distant—has been proposed as a factor in temporary preference, under the name of *temporal construal* (Trope and Liberman 2000, 2003). The authors take notice of extensive overlap with hyperbolic discounting, in that the "low-level construals" with which people perceive imminent events often get their value from short-term reward or cost, whereas "high-level construals" are often designs for long-range reward. Their first two experiments (as described in both articles) do not discriminate between hyperbolic and temporal construal theories. However, experiments 3 and 4 "were designed to rule out hyperbolic discounting" (2000, 882). In experiment 3, students imagined that they would buy one of two clock radios, either a good radio with a poor clock or a poor radio with a good clock. They strongly preferred the good radio, but the strength of this preference was greater when they imagined the purchase "a year from now" than when it was to be "tomorrow" ($N = 190, p < .05$). In experiment 4, students rated how much they were interested in taking part in two prospective experiments: four sessions of an interesting task separated by boring "filler," or four sessions of a boring task separated by interesting filler. Subjects strongly preferred the interesting task, but again the strength was greater when the experiment was to be run in 4–6 weeks than when it was to be run "tomorrow" ($N = 64$, $p < .05$). The authors ascribed the results of both experiments to the higher-level construal of radio over clock and main task over filler. These experiments do seem to rule out hyperbolic discounting within their own designs, in that the alternative payoffs (and costs) were not to occur at different delays. However, they did not produce preference reversal, and they do not contradict a role for hyperbolic discounting in situations where preference reversal occurs.

There have been many failures to find hyperbolic discounting, the vast economic literature on efficient investment choices being the largest example. Disseminating the theory that exponential discounting reveals the true value of reward has been one of the great historical projects of civilization. People's limited ability to conform their choices to their belief in this tenet has been one of the great historical puzzles of civilization. In the framing experiments just described, subjects revealed additional theories of value, and these have been proposed as solutions to the puzzle; but these theories seem to have a relatively small motivational impact. The magnitude effect has been the most demonstrable, but it probably represents subjects' greater belief in exponential valuation when amounts are of investable size. Subadditive discounting, the similarity heuristic, and temporal construal have required finely tuned designs to separate them from more robust discounting patterns, and have so far not been shown to induce temporary preference.

Summary

Temporary preference for smaller, sooner (SS) over larger, later (LL) rewards is not usually the result of simply coming too close to the SS rewards. Most of us spend a great deal of time "too close" to such rewards, in the sense that unhealthy foods, tobacco, and alcohol are easily available, as is often the case as well with recreational drugs, sexual adventure, dangerous driving, unwise purchases, and certainly procrastination. Proximity does increase their attraction relative to LL rewards, but in all of these cases except for procrastination sudden craving can arise after mere reminders, or with no obvious precipitant at all. In straightforward application, none of the three kinds of explanation currently proposed in the literature accounts for sudden craving in the absence of new information about availability.

The explanation that has had the most commonsense appeal is that conditioned stimuli (CSs) that predict rewards—at least a special class of "visceral" rewards—can elicit overwhelming appetite. However, in systematic experiments CSs only convey information, and only elicit responses (CRs) insofar as they have accurately predicted the unconditioned stimuli (UCSs). CRs cannot exceed UCRs, and they are attenuated from the UCRs as expected delay increases. Mere reminders should not be able to elicit the intense conditioned appetites that are the hypothesized mechanism of preference reversal. Nor does hyperbolic discounting in itself predict preference reversal in response to mere reminders. The third class of theories, that changes in cognitive framing can overshadow the discounting factor, have been shown to predict substantial effects only in the familiar case where a norm of financial rationality modifies inconsistent choice toward exponential discounting. Framing may contribute to rationality, but not in any major way to temporary preferences for poorer rewards.

I have argued here that either conditioning or hyperbolic discounting might be adequate to account for sudden appetite if consumption is predicted recursively. That is, in cases where consumption is limited not by availability but by the person's own choice, spontaneous increases in appetite can increase the likelihood of consuming, which can induce further increases in appetite, a potentially explosive positive feedback system. However, the passive information transfer involved in conditioning should damp down any positive feedback system that depends on it. Only if appetite can be a reward-seeking process, an implication of hyperbolic discounting, can significant amplification be expected. Conversely, the need to account for this amplification joins other arguments that appetite is a reward-dependent process. The hyperbolic form of the basic discount curve is a necessary and sufficient mechanism for temporary preference phenomena in general, including sudden craving in response to uninformative stimuli.

Acknowledgments

I am grateful to Kent Berridge and John Monterosso for comments on drafts of this chapter.

Notes

1. For simplicity I am focusing on appetite, but some studies of emotion provide examples that are lacking for appetite. Emotion might be regarded as appetite without an object of consumption, and even that distinction is unclear in borderline cases such as rage and lust.

2. Nevertheless, many emotions and appetites lack external signs and are apt to be innately connected to particular kinds of expectation, making it unclear to what extent the disproof of conditioning as a mechanism of response selection applies to them. Mackintosh (1983, 65) himself hedged on this disproof: "A CS paired with a reinforcer will acquire some of the affective properties of that reinforcer"—that is, it will become an emotional CR. CRs might still exist in the form of appetites or emotions. This ambiguity has not been resolved.

3. Rachlin and Green (1972) had observed both preference reversal and behavioral commitment, but a requirement of 26 responses to make each choice prevented interpretation of these effects as functions of pure delay.

4. As for people's sometime ability to behave according to the rational agent model, this is discussed elsewhere (Ainslie 1991).

5. Modified from their formula 5 to express momentary value.

6. A limited warfare relationship implies that consistent choice has to be achieved strategically by some kind of precommitment. I have proposed recursive self-prediction, such that a person sees her current choice as a test case of whether she will choose a whole bundle of similar LL rewards in the future, as the mechanism of willpower and of related phenomena such as sudden failures of will and the experience of freedom of will (Ainslie 2001, 90–104; 2005). The recursive mechanism for sudden appetite in the absence of new information, proposed here, follows the same dynamic as sudden failure of will, and could sometimes constitute the initial phase of it.

7. In this model the pet's own appetite, as well as its begging behavior, is contingent on the prospect of gratification, but the analogy is still valid.

8. There may be no intrinsic line between evaluating a behavior and initiating it. Edward Tolman's (1939) original concept of vicarious trial and error, in which a subject estimates the reward for alternative choices by serially initiating them without committing to them, has recently been validated with single hippocampal neurons (Johnson and Redish 2007). To the extent that appetites are reward-dependent, the same process may govern them.

9. This definition modifies Rolls's behavioral definition—"A reward is anything for which [a subject] will work" (1999, 60–61)—to recognize the potentially split-second duration of some preferences, too short to motivate work. Berridge (2003) makes a similar extension of the concept with "nonhedonic" reward.

10. McClure et al. (2007) have observed a related variability in what rewards people's brains respond to as visceral. They report that a prospect of getting immediate coupons that will take days to exchange generates activity in subjects' β centers, whereas a juice reward has to be delivered within one minute to do this. But in another laboratory, a promised cigarette in a week produces β activity (Monterosso, Ainslie, and London 2006).

References

Ainslie, G. (1974). Impulse control in pigeons. *Journal of the Experimental Analysis of Behavior* 21: 485–489.

Ainslie, G. (1975). Specious reward: A behavioral theory of impulsiveness and impulse control. *Psychological Bulletin* 82: 463–496.

Ainslie, G. (1991). Derivation of "rational" economic behavior from hyperbolic discount curves. *American Economic Review* 81: 334–340.

Ainslie, G. (1992). *Picoeconomics: The Strategic Interaction of Successive Motivational States within the Person*. Cambridge: Cambridge University Press.

Ainslie, G. (2001). *Breakdown of Will*. New York: Cambridge University Press.

Ainslie, G. (2005). Précis of *Breakdown of Will. Behavioral and Brain Sciences* 28 (5): 635–673.

Ainslie, G., and Haendel, V. (1983). The motives of the will. In E. Gottheil, K. Druley, T. Skodola, and H. Waxman, eds., *Etiology Aspects of Alcohol and Drug Abuse*, 119–140. Springfield, IL: Charles C. Thomas.

Ainslie, G., and Herrnstein, R. (1981). Preference reversal and delayed reinforcement. *Animal Learning and Behavior* 9: 476–482.

Arrow, K. J. (1959). Rational choice functions and orderings. *Economica* 26: 121–127.

Balleine, B., and Dickinson, A. (1998). Goal-directed action: Contingency and incentive learning and their cortical substrates. *Neuropharmacology* 37: 407–419.

Baumeister, R. F., Heatherton, T. F., and Tice, D. M. (1994). *Losing Control: How and Why People Fail at Self-Regulation*. New York: Academic.

Becerra, L., Breiter, H. C., Wise, R., Gonzalez, R. G., and Borsook, D. (2001). Reward circuitry activation by noxious thermal stimuli. *Neuron* 32: 927–946.

Becker, G., and Murphy, K. (1988). A theory of rational addiction. *Journal of Political Economy* 96: 675–700.

Berns, G. S., Chappelow, J., Cekic, M., Zink, C. F., Pagnoni, G., and Martin-Skurski, M. E. (2006). Neurobiological substrates of dread. *Science* 312: 754–758.

Berridge, K. C. (2003). Pleasures of the brain. *Brain and Cognition* 52: 106–128.

Berridge, K. C. (2007). The debate over dopamine's role in reward: The case for incentive salience. *Psychopharmacology* 191: 391–431.

Berridge, K. C., and Robinson, T. (1998). What is the role of dopamine in reward: Hedonic impact, reward learning, or incentive salience? *Brain Research Reviews* 28: 309–369.

Bickel, W. K., and Marsch, L. A. (2001). Toward a behavioral economic understanding of drug dependence: Delay discounting processes. *Addiction* 96: 73–86.

Boudon, R. (1996). The "rational choice model": A particular case of the "cognitive model." *Rationality and Society* 8: 123–150.

Cabanac, M. (1992). Pleasure: The common currency. *Journal of Theoretical Biology* 155: 173–200.

Carter, B. L., and Tiffany, S. T. (2001). The cue-availability paradigm: The effects of cigarette availability on cue reactivity in smokers. *Experimental and Clinical Psychophamacology* 9: 183–190.

Chance, P. (1999). Thorndike's puzzle boxes and the origins of the experimental analysis of behavior. *Journal of the Experimental Analysis of Behavior* 72: 433–440.

Chung, S., and Herrnstein, R. J. (1967). Choice and delay of reinforcement. *Journal of the Experimental Analysis of Behavior* 10: 67–74.

Conlisk, J. (1996). Why bounded rationality? *Journal of Economic Literature* 34: 669–700.

Corsini, R. J. (1984). *Current Psychotherapies*, 3rd ed. Rockland, MA: Peacock.

Cubitt, R. P., and Sugden, R. (2001). On money pumps. *Games and Economic Behavior* 37: 121–160.

Dar, R., Stronguin, F., Marouani, R., Krupsky, M., and Frenk, H. (2005). Craving to smoke in orthodox Jewish smokers who abstain on the Sabbath: A comparison to a baseline and a forced abstinence workday. *Psychopharmacology* 183: 294–299.

Darwin, C. (1872/1979). *The Expressions of Emotions in Man and Animals*. London: Julan Friedman.

Daw, N. D., Niv, Y., and Dayan, P. (2005). Uncertainty-based competition between prefrontal and dorsolateral striatal systems for behavioral control. *Nature Neuroscience* 8: 1704–1711.

Deluty, M. Z., Whitehouse, W. G., Mellitz, M., and Hineline, P. N. (1983). Self-control and commitment involving aversive events. *Behavior Analysis Letters* 3: 213–219.

Dinsmoor, J. A. (2004). The etymology of basic concepts in the experimental analysis of behavior. *Journal of the Experimental Analysis of Behavior* 82: 311–316.

Donahoe, J. W., Burgos, J. E., and Palmer, D. C. (1993). A selectionist approach to reinforcement. *Journal of the Experimental Analysis of Behavior* 60: 17–40.

Drummond, D. C. , Tiffany, S. T., Glautier, S., and Remington, B. (1995). *Addictive Behavior: Cue Exposure Theory and Practice*. Chichester: Wiley.

Estes, W. K., and Skinner, B. F. (1941). Some quantitative properties of anxiety. *Journal of Experimental Psychology* 29: 390–400.

Eysenck, H. J. (1967). Single trial conditioning, neurosis and the Napalkov phenomenon. *Behavior Research and Therapy* 5: 63–65.

Field, M., and Duka, T. (2001). Smoking expectancy mediates the conditioned responses to arbitrary smoking cues. *Behavioural Pharmacology* 12: 183–194.

Frank, Robert H. (1992). Frames of reference and the intertemporal wage sequence. In G. Loewenstein and J. Elster, eds., *Choice Over Time*, 371–382. New York: Sage.

Gallistel, C. R. (2002). Frequency, contingency and the information processing theory of conditioning. In P. Sedlmeier and T. Betsch, eds., *Frequency Processing and Cognition*. Oxford: Oxford University Press.

Gibbon, J. (1977). Scalar expectancy theory and Weber's law in animal timing. *Psychological Review* 84: 279–325.

Gigerenzer, G. (2000). *Adaptive Thinking: Rationality in the Real World*. Oxford: Oxford University Press.

Gintis, H. (2007). A framework for the unification of the behavioral sciences. *Behavioral and Brain Sciences* 29: 1–61.

Glimcher, P. W., Kable, J., and Louie, K. (2007). Neuroeconomic studies of impulsivity: Now or just as soon as possible? *American Economic Review* 97: 1–6.

Grace, R. (1996). Choice between fixed and variable delays to reinforcement in the adjusting-delay procedure and concurrent chains. *Journal of Experimental Psychology: Animal Processes* 22: 362–383.

Green, L., Fisher, E. B., Jr., Perlow, S., and Sherman, L. (1981). Preference reversal and self-control: Choice as a function of reward amount and delay. *Behaviour Analysis Letters* 1: 43–51.

Green, L., Fry, A., and Myerson, J. (1994). Discounting of delayed rewards: A life-span comparison. *Psychological Science* 5: 33–36.

Green, L., and Myerson, J. (1993). Alternative frame-works for the analysis of self-control. *Behavior and Philosophy* 21: 37–47.

Green, L., and Myerson, J. (1996). Exponential versus hyperbolic discounting of delayed outcomes: Risk and waiting time. *American Zoologist* 36: 496–505.

Green, L., and Myerson, J. (2004). A discounting framework for choice with delayed and probabilistic rewards. *Psychological Bulletin* 130: 769–792.

Green, L., Myerson, J., and Macaux, E. W. (2005). Temporal discounting when the choice is between two delayed rewards. *Journal of Experimental Psychology: Learning, Memory, and Cognition* 31: 1121–1133.

Harrison, G. W., Lau, M. I., and Rutström, E. E. (2005). Dynamic consistency in Denmark: A longitudinal field experiment. Working Paper 5-02, Department of Economics, College of Business Administration, University of Central Florida, January, 2005.

Harvey, C. M. (1994). The reasonableness of non-constant discounting. *Journal of Public Economics* 53: 31–51.

Herrnstein, R. J. (1990). Rational choice theory: Necessary but not sufficient. *American Psychologist* 45: 356–367.

Herrnstein, R. J., and Prelec, D. (1992). Melioration. In G. Loewenstein and J. Elster, eds., *Choice Over Time*, 235–264. New York: Sage.

Hollander, E., and Stein, D. J. (2006). *Clinical Manual of Impulse-Control Disorders*. Washington, D.C.: American Psychiatric Publishing.

Hull, C. L. (1943). *Principles of Behavior*. New York: Appleton-Century-Crofts.

Jolls, C., Sunstein, C. R., and Thaler, R. (1998). A behavioral approach to law and economics. *Stanford Law Review* 50: 1471–1550.

Johnson, A., and Redish, A. D. (2007). Neural ensembles in CA3 transiently encode paths forward of the animal at a decision point. *Journal of Neuroscience* 12: 483–488.

Kahneman, D., and Tversky, A. (1984). Choices, values, and frames. *American Psychologist* 39: 341–350.

Kalenscher, T., Windmann, S., Diekamp, B., Rose, J., Gunturkun, O., and Colombo, M. (2005). Single units in the pigeon brain integrate reward amount and time-to-reward in an impulsive choice task. *Current Biology* 15: 594–602.

Kehoe, E. J., Graham-Clark, P., and Schreurs, B. G. (1989). Temporal patterns of the rabbit's nicti-
tating membrane response to compound and component stimuli under mixed CS-US intervals.
Behavioral Neuroscience 103: 283–295.

Kirby, K. N. (1997). Bidding on the future: Evidence against normative discounting of delayed
rewards. *Journal of Experimental Psychology: General* 126: 54–70.

Kirby, K. N. (2006). The present values of delayed rewards are approximately additive. *Behavioural
Processes* 72: 273–282.

Laibson, D. (1997). Golden eggs and hyperbolic discounting. *Quarterly Journal of Economics* 62:
443–479.

Laibson, D. (2001). A cue-theory of consumption *Quarterly Journal of Economics* 66: 81–120.

Lea, S. E. G., and Webley, P. (2006). Money as tool, money as drug: The biological psychology of a
strong incentive. *Behavioral and Brain Sciences* 29: 161–209.

Loewenstein, G. (1987). Anticipation and the valuation of delayed consumption. *Economic Journal*
97: 666–685.

Loewenstein, G. (1996). Out of control: Visceral influences on behavior. *Organizational Behavior
and Human Decision Processes* 35: 272–292.

Loewenstein, G. (1999). A visceral account of addiction. In J. Elser and O.-J. Skog, eds., *Getting
Hooked: Rationality and Addiction*. Cambridge: Cambridge University Press.

Logue, A. W., Pena-Correal, T. E., Rodriguez, M. L., and Kabela, E. (1986). Self-control in adult
humans: Variations in positive reinforcer amount and delay. *Journal of the Experimental Analysis
of Behavior* 46: 113–127.

MacKintosh, N. J. (1983). *Conditioning and Associative Learning*. New York: Clarendon.

MacLean, P. D. (1990). *The Triune Brain in Evolution: Role in Paleocerebral Functions*. New York:
Plenum.

Malloy, P. F., and Levis, D. J. (1990). A human laboratory test of Eysenck's theory of incubation: A
search for the resolution of the neurotic paradox. *Journal of Psychopathology and Behavioral Assessment* 12: 309–327.

Maunsell, J. H. R. (2004). Neuronal representations of cognitive state: Reward or attention? *Trends
in Cognitive Sciences* 8: 261–265.

Mazur, J. E. (1987). An adjusting procedure for studying delayed reinforcement. In M. L. Commons, J. E. Mazur, J. A. Nevin, and H. Rachlin, eds., *Quantitative Analyses of Behavior V: The Effect
of Delay and of Intervening Events on Reinforcement Value*. Hillsdale, NJ: Lawrence Erlbaum.

Mazur, J. E. (2001). Hyperbolic value addition and general models of animal choice. *Psychological
Review* 108: 96–112.

McClure, S. M., Daw, N. D., and Montague, P. R. (2003). A computational substrate for incentive
salience. *Trends in Neurosciences* 26: 423–428.

McClure, S. M., Laibson, D. I., Loewenstein, G., and Cohen, J. D. (2004). The grasshopper and the ant: Separate neural systems value immediate and delayed monetary rewards. *Science* 306: 503–507.

McClure, S. M., Ericson, K. M., Laibson, D. I., Loewenstein, G., and Cohen, J. D. (2007). Time discounting for primary rewards. *Journal of Neuroscience* 27: 5796–5804.

McFarland, D. J., and Sibley, R. M. (1975). The behavioural final common path. *Philosophical Transactions of the Royal Society of London B* 270: 265–293.

Melzack, R., and Casey, K. L. (1970). The affective dimension of pain. In M. B. Arnold, ed., *Feelings and Emotions*, 55–68. New York: Academic.

Meyer, R. E. (1988). Conditioning phenomena and the problem of relapse in opioid addicts and alcoholics. In B. Ray, ed., *Learning Factors in Substance Abuse*, 161–179. NIDA Research Monograph series 84. Washington, D.C.: NIDA.

Miller, N. (1969). Learning of visceral and glandular responses. *Science* 163: 434–445.

Mischel, H. N., and Mischel, W. (1983). The development of children's knowledge of self-control strategies. *Child Development* 54: 603–619.

Montague, P. R., and Berns, G. S. (2002). Neural economics and the biological substrates of valuation. *Neuron* 36: 265–284.

Montague, P. R., King-Casas, B., and Cohen, J. D. (2006). Imaging valuation models in human choice. *Annual Review of Neuroscience* 29: 417–448.

Monterosso, J., and Ainslie, G. (1999). Beyond discounting: Possible experimental models of impulse control. *Psychopharmacology* 146: 339–347.

Monterosso, J., Ainslie, G., and London, E. D. (2006). Delay discounting based on activation in the ventral striatum. Poster session presented at the 68th annual meeting of the College on Problems of Drug Dependence, Scottsdale, Arizona, June 2006.

Mowrer, O. H. (1947). On the dual nature of learning: A re-interpretation of conditioning and problem solving. *Harvard Educational Review* 17: 102–148.

O'Brien, C. (1997). A range of research-based pharmacotherapies for addiction. *Science* 278: 66–70.

O'Doherty, J. P. (2004). Reward representations and reward-related learning in the human brain: Insights from neuroimaging. *Current Opinion in Neurobiology* 14: 769–776.

Pavlov, I. P. (1927). *Conditioned Reflexes: An Investigation of the Physiological Activity of the Cerebral Cortex*. Trans. G. V. Anrep. Oxford: Oxford University Press.

Pear, J. J., and Eldridge, G. D. (1984). The operant-respondent distinction: Future directions. *Journal of the Experimental Analysis of Behavior* 42: 453–467.

Peciña, S., Smith, K. S., and Berridge, K. C. (2006). Hedonic hot spots in the brain. *Neuroscientist* 12: 500–511.

Perkins, C. C., Jr. (1968). An analysis of the concept of reinforcement. *Psychological Review* 75: 155–172.

Phelps, E. S., and Pollack, R. A. (1968). On second-best national saving and game-equilibrium growth. *Review of Economic Studies* 35: 185–199.

Rachlin, H., and Green, L. (1972). Commitment, choice, and self-control. *Journal of the Experimental Analysis of Behavior* 17: 15–22.

Read, D. (2001). Is time-discounting hyperbolic or subadditive? *Journal of Risk and Uncertainty* 23: 5–32.

Read, D., and Powell, M. (2002). Reasons for sequence preferences. *Journal of Behavioral Decision Making* 15: 433–460.

Read, D., and Roelofsma, P. H. M. P. (2003). Subadditive versus hyperbolic discounting: A comparison of choice and matching. *Organizational Behavior and Human Decision Processes* 91: 140–153.

Rescorla, R. A. (1988). Pavlovian conditioning: It's not what you think it is. *American Psychologist* 43: 151–160.

Rodriguez, M. L., and Logue, A. W. (1988). Adjusting delay to reinforcement: Comparing choice in pigeons and humans. *Journal of Experimental Psychology: Animal Behavior Processes* 14: 105–117.

Rolls, E. T. (1999). *The Brain and Emotion*. Oxford: Oxford University Press.

Rolls, E. T. (2005). *Emotion Explained*. Oxford: Oxford University Press.

Rubinstein, A. (2003). "Economics and psychology"? The case of hyperbolic discounting. *International Economic Review* 44: 1207–1216.

Samuelson, P. A. (1937). A note on measurement of utility. *Review of Economic Studies* 4: 155–161.

Savastano, H. I., Hua, U., Barnet, R. C., and Miller, R. R. (1998). Temporal coding in Pavlovian conditioning: Hall-Pearce negative transfer. *Quarterly Journal of Experimental Psychology* 51: 139–153.

Schachter, S., Silverstein, B., and Perlick, D. (1977). Psychological and pharmacological explanations of smoking under stress. *Journal of Experimental Psychology: General* 106: 31–40.

Schultz, W. (2006). Behavioral theories and the neurophysiology of reward. *Annual Review of Psychology* 57: 87–115.

Shizgal, P., and Conover, K. (1996). On the neural computation of utility. *Current Directions in Psychological Science* 5: 37–43.

Skinner, B. F. (1935). Two types of conditioned reflex and a pseudo type. *Journal of General Psychology* 12: 66–77.

Solnick, J., Kannenberg, C., Eckerman, D., and Waller, M. (1980). An experimental analysis of impulsivity and impulse control in humans. *Learning and Motivation* 2: 61–77.

Solomon, R., and Wynne, L. (1954). Traumatic avoidance learning: The principles of anxiety conservation and partial irreversibility. *Psychological Review* 61: 353–385.

Sonuga-Barke, E. J. S., Lea, S. E. G., and Webley, P. (1989). Childrens choice: Sensitivity to changes in reinforcer density. *Journal of the Experimental Analysis of Behavior* 51: 185–197.

Strotz, R. H. (1956). Myopia and inconsistency in dynamic utility maximization. *Review of Economic Studies* 23: 166–180.

Tanaka, S. C., Doya, K., Okada, G., Ueda, K., Okamoto, Y., and Yamawaki, S. (2004). Prediction of immediate and future rewards differentially recruits cortico-basal ganglia loops. *Nature Neuroscience* 7: 887–893.

Thaler, R. (1981). Some empirical evidence on dynamic inconsistency. *Economics Letters* 8: 201–207.

Thaler, R. (1985). Mental accounting and consumer choice. *Marketing Science* 4: 199–214.

Thorndike, E. L. (1898). Animal intelligence: An experimental study of the associative processes in animals. *Psychological Monographs* 2: 1–109.

Tiffany, S. T. (1995). Potential functions of classical conditioning in drug addiction. In D. C. Drummond, S. T. Tiffany, S. Glautier, and B. Remington, eds., *Addictive Behavior: Cue Exposure Theory and Practice.* Chichester: Wiley.

Tolman, E. C. (1939). Prediction of vicarious trial and error by means of the schematic sowbug. *Psychological Review* 46: 318–336.

Trope, Y., and Liberman, N. (2000). Temporal construal and time-dependent changes in preference. *Journal of Personality and Social Psychology* 79: 876–889.

Trope, Y., and Liberman, N. (2003). Temporal construal. *Psychological Review* 110: 403–421.

Upton, M. (1929). The auditory sensitivity of guinea pigs. *American Journal of Psychology* 41: 412–421.

Vaillant, G. (1971). Theoretical hierarchy of adaptive ego mechanisms. *Archives of General Psychiatry* 24: 107–118.

Wason, P. C. (1966). Reasoning. In B. M. Foss, ed., *New Horizons in Psychology*, 135–151. Hammondsworth: Penguin.

Watson, J. B. (1924). *Behaviorism.* New York: The Peoples Institute.

Wegner, D. M. (2002). *The Illusion of Conscious Will.* Cambridge, MA: MIT Press.

Zener, K. (1937). The significance of behavior accompanying conditioned salivary secretion for theories of the conditioned response. *American Journal of Psychology* 50: 384–403.

Zink, C. F., Pagnoni, G., Martin, M. E., Dhamala, M. and Berns, G. S. (2003). Human striatal response to salient nonrewarding stimuli. *Journal of Neuroscience* 23: 8092–8097.

9   Measuring Dispositions to Bundle Choices

David Spurrett and Ben Murrell

One fertile framework for thinking about addiction is Ainslie's picoeconomics (e.g., Ainslie 1992, 2001). Like other behavioral theories,[1] picoeconomics holds that hyperbolic delay discounting can help explain addictive choices. It includes distinctive and partly speculative views about the internal processes of a hyperbolically discounting chooser, as its name (indicating micro-microeconomics, or the economy within the entities typically taken to be the objects of standard microeconomics) suggests. Ainslie also makes some specific proposals regarding how some agents can resist available temptation in favor of options more in line with their long-term interests, and so behave in ways more consistent with a single set of preferences. In this chapter, some evidence regarding this bundling process is reviewed with a view to considering specific ways in which addicted subjects might turn out to differ interestingly from nonaddicted ones. A specific technical question regarding the generation of choices between single pairs of differently delayed rewards, and sets of them spread over time, is investigated in more detail.

Delay discounting is the change (usually a reduction) in the present value of a reward as a function of the delay before its receipt or consumption. That delayed rewards should generally be valued less makes sense—the passage of time before delivery sees changes including accumulation of uncertainty about the chance of successful delivery, reduced remaining lifespan of the recipient after delivery, chances to secure substitutable rewards by other means reducing the marginal value of a later reward of a given magnitude, and sometimes (in the case of monetary rewards) inflation. Delay is not the only sort of separation relative which the value of a reward might be discounted. The other main target of empirical study is discounting as a function of lower certainty of reward delivery (Rachlin, Raineri, and Cross 1991; Green and Myerson 2004). Some work with nonhuman animals has investigated discounting as a function of spatial distance (Stevens et al. 2005). Other plausible candidates for study are the effort required to obtain the reward, and the value of a reward delivered to another as a function of varying genetic relatedness. Recent work with humans has attempted to measure the change in the value of a reward for another individual as a function of the social distance of that individual from the experimental subject (Jones and Rachlin 2006; Rachlin, this volume). Despite the variety of sorts of discounting, there are good reasons for the popularity of focus on discounting for delay, and those reasons relate to the promise that work on delay specifically has for explaining temporary preferences, including those of addicted subjects who sometimes know in advance that they will regret their consumption, yet engage in it anyway.

Only exponential delay discount curves (so called because the delay term appears in them as an exponent) have the property that the ranking of all rewards irrespective of their sizes and delays remains constant over time, because the fraction of value lost for a given unit of time is constant.[2] Here is a simple example, where V is discounted value, V_0 value at no delay, D delay, and k a discount rate:

$$V = V_0(1 - k)^D \tag{1}$$

Although there are some controversies on details and some technical issues,[3] many behavioral researchers currently agree that discounting for delay in humans and a variety of animals is nonexponential and more specifically that it is approximately hyperbolic. That this should be so was suggested as an extension of the matching law (Herrnstein 1976; and other papers collected in Herrnstein 1997), previously observed in the case of frequency of reinforcement in pigeons behaving under concurrent variable-interval reinforcement schedules (Herrnstein 1961). The matching law states that allocation of behavior to mutually exclusive activities that are both available will be in proportion to the rate of reinforcement consequent on each behavior. In the case of delay this suggests allocation in inverse proportion to the magnitude of the delay.

For many purposes, Mazur's (1987) formula provides a good fit to experimentally approximated indifference points for delayed rewards. Here is the equation, with the same symbols[4] as above:

$$V = V_0(1 + kD) \tag{2}$$

Among the nonhuman animal studies in which this equation, or a similar hyperbolic function, has provided a better fit to indifference points for delayed rewards are those by Mazur (1984, 1987, 1997). Among the studies with humans that defend the same claim is that by Green and Myerson (2004). Human and nonhuman animal findings are separated here because there are grounds for holding that the significance of D in the case of human studies differs from that of work on nonhuman animals. Animal subjects in a typical procedure measuring effects of delay on reinforcer value experience the entire delay before reward is delivered, and the properties of the delay are often experimentally controlled—for example, by making it consist of exposure to a conditioned reinforcer.[5] Human subjects, on the other hand, are typically asked questions about intervals substantially longer than the experiment or task, often for hypothetical rewards, and with little control over the real or imagined content of the intervals in question, which typically include weekends, holidays, subject-specific deadlines, paydates, birthdays, and so on.[6] This isn't a purely pedantic concern—there's reason to think that the differences in procedure make a difference to what is measured. So, Reynolds, Richards, and De Wit (2006) report that administration of alcohol led to no change in k-value as measured by a standard question-based discounting task, but it did when subjects indifference points were approximated using an apparatus (the *Experiential Discounting Task*) closer to paradigm nonhuman methods, using only relatively short delays all experienced in the course of the experiment, and paying out relatively small sums, but in cash at every trial within a block.

A better fit to the data can sometimes, although this point is contested, be found with a hyperbola-like or "two parameter" formula where the denominator of the hyperbola is raised to a power (*S*).[7] Among those arguing in favor of this "hyperbola-like" curve are Myerson and Green (1995), who favor the following formula:

$$V = V_0(1 + kD)^S \tag{3}$$

If the empirically determined value of *s* is close to 1, we get a formula close to equation (2). The *k*-values using the one-parameter formula have been found to be interestingly discriminating in various empirical settings (see below), so the relative inconvenience of working with two parameters is rarely justified.[8] The additional parameter can *sometimes* be important, a point to which we return below. For the rest of this paper, when we say "hyperbolic discounting" without qualification we intend to refer indifferently to equations (2) and (3) and variants of them.

Although the empirical literature on discounting would benefit from inquiries into some of the issues we've noted,[9] for many purposes whether equation (2) or (3) or some minor variant of one of them best fits the data matters less than that any of them, or any curve approximately like them, explains at least some intertemporal inconsistency. This is because the fraction of value discounted for a given interval of time depends on total delay to delivery, and is fastest when delivery is imminent, whereas with exponential curves value decreases by the same fraction for any two time periods of the same size irrespective of absolute delay to delivery.

The thesis of hyperbolic discounting pays its way in other ways too. Among them, it makes sense of the repeatedly observed preference (e.g., Herrnstein 1964) of experimental subjects for variable schedules of reward over fixed ones when the overall rate of reinforcement for the schedules is constant. Mazur (1984) shows that a simple extension of equation (2) explains the preference for variable delays, where *P* is a measure of the probability of delivery of each reinforcer:

$$V = \sum_{i=1}^{n} P_i \left(\frac{V_0}{1 + kD_i} \right) \tag{4}$$

If this formula is correct, early reinforcers in a variable sequence will contribute disproportionately more (than later ones, compared to the case where they're exponentially
discounted) to the value of the sequence as a whole even where average total rates of
reinforcement are equal.[10] As Mazur (1997) notes, this formula permits testable (and
successful) *predictions* of the size of the preference for variability in experimental subjects for which k has been measured.

Another reason for declining to engage with detailed worry over whether equation
(2) or (3) or some variant best describes the data is that the single subject-specific "k-
value" in equation (2) has been found to discriminate addicts from controls for a range
of addictions, including heroin, cocaine, alcohol, and nicotine (for a review see Bickel
and Marsch 2001). That is, groups of addicted subjects turn out to have higher k values
than otherwise comparable nonaddicts. As noted, k values using the one-parameter
formula are enough to distinguish addicted subjects from controls, and are also predictive in other areas where degree of intertemporal inconsistency matters (e.g., academic
success, where working more and earlier rather than procrastinating directly affects
outcomes—see, e.g., Kirby, Winston, and Santiesteban 2005). This should not be surprising. Hyperbolic discounting explains temporary preferences and tells us that individuals with higher k values will be more troubled by temporary preferences. Addicts
are troubled by temporary preferences. It is an association in the *opposite* direction
that would be perplexing.

A small reward available soon (*SS*) can be temporarily preferred to a larger one available later (*LL*), given certain relative sizes and delays of the two rewards and steepness
of the discount curve. These reversals will tend to be more frequent if k is higher, for
otherwise identical subjects and environments. That is, individual differences in k
values might help explain the distribution of addictive choosing, even if we'd then
want to know what explained the individual differences. (At the conference from
which the papers in this volume are drawn, some light was shed on this by James
MacKillop, who spoke about polymorphisms in genes relating to the dopamine system
and behavioral measures of impulsivity [Einsenberg et al. 2007b], and other work relating season of birth, dopamine receptors, and later impulsivity [Einsenberg et al.
2007a].)

Given that we discount hyperbolically, the mysterious thing becomes that we resist
temptation. To draw on a distinction used by Marc Potenza at the conference, we can
ask whether people who resist temptation better have more effective "brakes," or less
effective "motors," or conversely whether the impulsive have faulty brakes or over-
active motors. (Such explanations could, of course, be complementary.) It's not so
surprising that we can make use of external opportunities to restrict our exposure to
temptations from a distance, when our longer-run preferences are in charge (e.g., the
drinker who chooses a route home that avoids going past a bar). It's more interesting

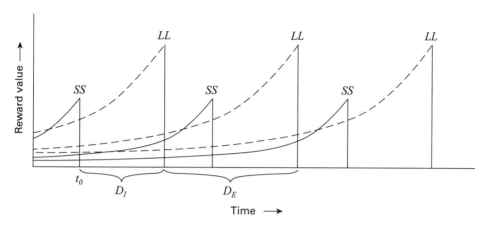

Figure 9.1
Series of hyperbolically discounted smaller, sooner (SS) and larger, later (LL) rewards. This figure represents three such choices—the discussion considers larger numbers. (Figure by Hugh Pastoll.)

that, even as hyperbolic discounters, we can turn off the TV and do some work, or be the alcoholic who turns down a drink when she's actually at a party.

One answer Ainslie proposes is that we do so by *bundling*, or choosing in accordance with *personal rules*. Bundling is something we can do with a collection of rewards, or, better, of choices between them, that are spread out over time. The first key idea is that options can be grouped together.

For simplicity[11] here we will consider (see figure 9.1) a collection of choices between mutually exclusive SS and LL rewards that are regularly spaced, and where the first choice on its own is an impulsive choice (SS is temporarily preferred) but later ones need not be, considered from the range of times at which the first choice is impulsive. We'll use D_I for the delay between SSn and LLn (the "internal" delay between options) and D_E for the delay between successive SS rewards (the "external" delay between choices).

Grouping two series of hyperbolically discounted rewards, one of SSs and one of LLs, can produce a ranking for the groups different from that of the first choice alone, if the present value of each group is the sum of the discounted values of each member of the group:

because hyperbolic curves are relatively high [compared to exponential curves] at long delays, bundling rewards together predicts an increase in the hyperbolically discounted value of the LL rewards relative to the hyperbolically discounted value of the SS rewards... even where the discounted value of the most imminent smaller reward greatly exceeds the discounted value of its LL alternative. (Ainslie 2005, 640)

How, though, might this grouping come to be *motivating*? Why, that is, should the fact that some *bundle* of choices has a certain property bear on the desirability of a current impulsive option? Ainslie reasons that if the situations and choices are viewed as relevantly similar, to the extent that current choice is the target for learning, and for the formation of expectations about what will happen in future situations of the same sort, then the currently preferred, later nonimpulsive options come to be *at stake* in the present choice, and so present impulsive choice can come to involve *losing* something (later choices for *LL*) presently valued more than the corresponding future impulsive options:

Insofar as you interpret your current choice as information predicting your own future choices between similar rewards, the incentives bearing on your current choice will... include the bundle of future rewards that this choice predicts. That is, the current choice... if perceived as a *test case*, will come to predict a whole bundle of LL rewards in the future, and thus be valued more than it would be by itself. (Ibid.)

So the bundler *wagers*, in a sense, the uncertain value of repeatedly choosing nonimpulsively (discounted for delay, and for the probability of being offered the choices and of choosing the same way again) against the value of the series of temptations, and the present choice is itself a consideration in determining the value of each option. This way of resisting temptation is unavoidably unstable—partly because there are many alternative ways of classifying rewards and so unavoidable uncertainty about the extent to which a rule fits, and about whether a situation is unusual enough for the taking of an impulsive option to be an acceptable exception or a predictor of a pattern of later impulsivity (Ainslie 2001, chapter 6).

This is an elegant and exciting set of ideas. It would be useful to have some idea of where it stood with the evidence. We do not offer a comprehensive review here, but indicate some encouraging empirical investigations and then move on to consider a specific technical question regarding generating monetary choices for the purposes of investigating bundling.

There is a wide-ranging set of arguments and evidence of various kinds, including thought experiments, and experiments in which behavior in groups of people suggests ways in which subpersonal agents may interact, in Ainslie's work (especially Ainslie 1992, 2001, this volume). An alternative approach not discussed here would be to build computational models that attempted to include as many features as Ainslie discusses as possible, with the hope of coming up with an existence proof of a system that had the right internal and external dynamics. Our focus here is on "real" experiments and empirical data that bear directly on bundling. We will look at evidence regarding the value of series of rewards, precommittment, and precedent.

Bundling is a complicated phenomenon—even if it happens exactly as Ainslie says (and not everything he says *is* very exact), it won't be possible rigorously to observe it, because it's a collection of different things happening at once, and happening in ways that are contextual (in relation to what other options are available at the time and in the future), historical (involving the subject's recollection of previous choices), and recursive (partly because the subject is involved, and in an interested way, in the classification process that determines whether rules are being followed, but lives with the effects of classification choices on credibility in future instances). There are no clean measurements of the whole phenomenon to be had.

Experimenters can, though, hope to set up situations in which one or more components of bundling are (relatively) isolated, and attempt to see whether things favor Ainslie's more detailed model or not. Some of the components that one might hope to isolate are:[12]

- Summing of multiple rewards at different delays.
- Effects of previous choices with respect to current ones.
- Effects of expectations about future choices.
- Self-prediction and choice.
- Categorical choice.
- Exceptions and lapses.

Empirical data relating to these can draw on real-world choices, choices in experiments, and additional measurements such as brain scans during experiments.

In the case of summing of multiple delayed rewards, the evidence is encouraging. This is also very important—recall that given hyperbolic discounting we should *expect* summing to make regular series the first option of which is an impulsive choice to become collectively nonimpulsive as the series gets longer. Mazur (1997) reports on a series of "adjusting-delay" procedures with nonhuman animals in which one reward is a regularly spaced series of rewards, concluding that the value of a series is the sum of the hyperbolically discounted values of the members of the series (see equation (4) above, assuming $P = 1$). Other work has found results suggesting that the required summing relationship holds in rats (Ainslie and Monterosso 2003) and human subjects (Kirby 2006). Also, students who were offered five weekly choices of an SS amount of money immediately or a delayed LL amount picked the LL amounts more frequently if they had been offered the option of all the SS rewards or all the LL rewards than if they made each choice separately. The effect was larger for pizza than money (Kirby and Guastello 2001). One complication relating typical work with nonhuman animals and procedures on humans is that the value of D in the discounting equation in laboratory work with nonhuman animals is better regarded as the duration of exposure to a conditioned reinforcer (Mazur 1997). It's not so clear *what* it represents with humans, because typically the delays are hypothetical or much longer than the experiment and include considerable variation in quality (weekends, holidays, paydays, etc.). Some light could be shed on what difference this makes with the recent (Reynolds, Richards, and De Wit 2006) *Experiential Discounting Task* where delays are more like those in nonhuman experiments. Nonetheless the evidence so far is more encouraging for the hypothesis that the present value of a series of rewards is the sum of the present hyperbolically discounted values of the individual members of the series than for any alternative hypothesis, and this itself is further evidence that discounting for delay is hyperbolic.

There's quite a lot of evidence, more than we could begin to survey here, that some of the time people (a) learn about themselves on the basis of observation of (what they take to be) their own behavior, and (b) make choices that build or maintain self-perceptions they value. The first point is illustrated by split-brain and other confabulation and self-interpretation findings (Dennett 1991; Wegner 2003; Wegner and Sparrow 2007; Dutton and Aron 1974). The second is illustrated by experiments such as that of Quattrone and Tversky (1984) who found that subjects led to believe that tolerance for pain of a hand in cold water was diagnostic of good or bad heart condition reacted by extending or shortening the period that they tolerated the pain. Though this might seem straightforwardly to confuse diagnostics with causality, it might instead be thought of as paying a cost (the disutility of discomfort) in order to have or maintain a preferred belief (preferred because of the expected utility consequent on credibly having it, which is just what the bundler supposedly gets from choosing non-impulsively now). We know of no experiments that have specifically sought to examine these phenomena in the areas of addiction or intertemporal inconsistency. It would not be surprising if the present cost a subject would bear in order to maintain a belief about a desired future state had something to do with the present delayed value of that state. But it's an open question, and an interesting one, whether (some) addicts differ over and above that—for example, in being less likely to work now for future credibility to themselves—and if so, why.

Turning to context and precedent, there's a growing body of work on the effect of locating a choice in a series of similar choices, some of it directly inspired by Ainslie. There are different ways in which choices may be related to subsequent choices, not all of them relevant to bundling, some of them dependent on reidentification of a situation type. One possibility is that whatever they think, subjects may in fact tend to choose the same way in the same cases, because they have the same dispositions. This isn't a *precedent* effect: later choices and earlier ones merely have a *common cause*. Another possibility (not fully mutually exclusive) is that earlier choices somehow (through this or that series of intermediate steps including reinforcement, planning, and memory) increase the likelihood of similar choices being made in the future.

Rachlin's view is that there may be a preference for pattern in choices, which would link earlier and later choices in an appropriate way. One example of this is reported by de la Piedad, Field, and Rachlin (2006). Pigeons were more likely to switch from pecking one key to another, even when the prospective reward from both keys was held constant, after smaller amounts of pecking had been allocated to the first. This persistence is a pigeon equivalent of committing the sunk cost fallacy. A third possibility is that subjects may view their current choice as a determinant of the likelihood of future similar choices, and this assessment may bear on the determination of the value of the current choice. This is the kind of relationship required for bundling.

Among the relevant results in this area, Read, Loewenstein, and Kalynaraman (1999) found that when subjects picked three rental movies sequentially (that is, making a single choice on each of three occasions) rather than choosing for all occasions simultaneously, they were less likely to include "high-brow" films. Simultaneous choice for each of three viewings allowed precommitment, and the proportion of "high-brow" films (typically allocated to the second and third screening sessions) increased.

Khan and Dhar (2007) found among other things that the rate of opting for "vice" (such as a chocolate chip cookie) over "virtue" (such as low-fat yoghurt) *increased* when subjects expected to have the same options later. Khan and Dhar hypothesised, partly in light of the well-documented optimism bias, that the prospect of future opportunities to be virtuous put present vice in a better overall light, providing a "guilt-reducing justification." And assuming that their vices and virtues corresponded to impulsive and restrained choices for a hyperbolic discounter, that makes provisional sense: agents only thinking of a small set of choices could conclude after a *little* contemplation that the series of choices *SS*, *LL*, *LL* is the best package. A little more contemplation or a bit of experience might be expected to see some subjects shift away from taking that proposal seriously. Some evidence for this comes from work by Kirby and Guastello (2001). They offered subjects unimodal choices between different amounts, one more delayed than the other, of money and pizza. Prior choice tasks had identified individual impulsive choices (that is, ones where a smaller reward would be temporarily preferred as long as offered relatively soon), and the subjects were then offered an impulsive choice again in one of a variety of conditions. In the case of pizza but not for money, subjects prompted to view their initial choice between an *SS* and *LL* reward as a predictor of their later choices were significantly more likely to chose nonimpulsively than subjects who were not so prompted. For both pizza and money, subjects given a forced choice between all the *SSs* and all the *LLs* were much more likely to opt for the *LLs*.

In order to conduct experiments of the general sort done by Kirby and Guastello (2001), where bundling is studied in the same way as discounting, we need to be able to generate multiple choices, between different amounts and at different delays, and we need the series to be spread out over some specific intervals. Kirby and Guastello come up with a specific procedure for the purposes of their experiment; we want here to discuss the task of generating choices more generally. If we assume that the *SS* and *LL* rewards are of the same two sizes, then here are two constraints that the choices offered in a bundling experiment should satisfy.

First is the *initial impulsive choice* condition, that SS_1 now must be preferred over LL_1 in D_I days (or whatever the unit of delay—we'll continue to say "day" here) time. Assuming Mazur's formula, and given a subject-specific value for k, the following inequality expresses the first constraint for a given subject:

$$SS_1 > \frac{LL_1}{1 + kD_I} \tag{5}$$

Unless a given SS is tempting relative to the corresponding LL, choices for LL cannot readily be regarded as informative about restraint or bundling. So it seems clear enough that the choices in *any* bundling task should satisfy this constraint.

Second is the *nonimpulsive series* condition. This requires that the summed discounted value of the series of SS rewards be less than that for the summed discounted series of LL rewards:

$$\sum_{n=0}^{i} \left(\frac{LL}{1 + k(D_I + nD_E)} \right) > \sum_{n=1}^{i} \left(\frac{SS}{1 + k(nD_E)} \right) \tag{6}$$

Unless *this* condition is met, so that a bundle of the *LLs* really is collectively worth more than a bundle of the *SSs*, then no choice for LL or a series of LLs can be safely regarded as showing anything about restraint or bundling under the conditions in question. Both of these conditions can generally be satisfied for positive reward magnitudes (where LL is greater than SS) and positive values of k, D_I, and D_E. So, for example, one can fix LL, D_I, and D_E and then ask what range of values of SS satisfies both constraints. The inequality stating the relationship is long and not very interesting to look at. Here it is for a series where the number of choices has been set to three:

$$\frac{LL}{1 + kD_I} < SS < \frac{(1 + D_E k)(1 + 2D_E k)(3 + 6(D_I + D_E)k + (3 + D_I^2 + 6D_I D_E + 2D_E^2)k^2)LL}{(1 + D_I k)(1 + D_I k + 2D_E k)(1 + (D_I + D_E)k)(3 + 2D_E k(3 + D_E k))} \tag{7}$$

Since there is some noise in experimental determinations of indifference points and hence of discount curves, it would be useful to have values of SS that are not close to the values represented by the constraints. One possible solution is to choose values of LL, D_E, D_I and the number of choices in the series such that the range of useful SSs is as large as possible, and then pick an SS in the middle of the bounding values of that range. The further the bounds of useful SSs are from the selected SS, the more a subjects discounting behavior as represented by their choices in the bundling experiment must deviate from their empirically determined k value to violate one of the two conditions. The range for a given set of values is:

$$\text{Range} = \frac{k^2 LL D_I D_E(3 + 8kD_E + 6k^2 D_E^2 + kD_I(3 + 4kD_E))}{(1 + kD_I)(4 + 9kD_E + 4k^2 D_E^2)(1 + k^2 D_I^2 + 3kD_E + 2k^2 D_E^2 + kD_I(2 + 3kD_E))} \tag{8}$$

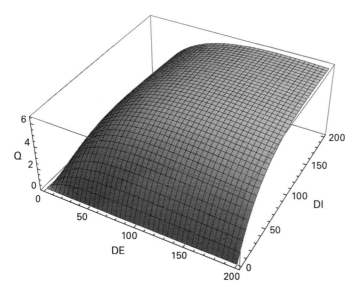

Figure 9.2
This figure shows the influence of *DE* and *DI* on range (*Q*) when *LL*, *N*, and *k* are fixed. (*LL* = 100.)

The effect of the magnitude of the two delays (D_E and D_I) in a series on the range when *LL* and *SS* are fixed for a given (arbitrary) *k* is represented in figure 9.2. As expected, the range of values of *LL* that would make bundling worthwhile is smallest at short delays, where the temptation due to hyperbolic discounting is strongest. (Although this can't be seen from figure 9.2, it is also unsurprisingly the case that the range of values of *LL* that would make bundling worthwhile rises as the number of repeated choices increases.)

It is of more interest to the student of addiction to see the effect of changes in *k* given a fixed number of choices. The two panels of figure 9.3 show the surface of ranges of *SS* satisfying the constraints for each of two different *k* values when *LL* and *N* are fixed. The range of values for temptations that a bundler could be inclined to resist in favor of a series of larger later rewards is visibly smaller for a subject with a higher *k*, and the period in which a large range of *SS* rewards could likely be resisted is concentrated in the relatively immediate future.

On the one hand, this is not surprising—in subjects with higher *k* values the decline in value as a function of delay is steeper for short delays, so of course it is more difficult to incentivize them to resist temptation with future rewards that are further delayed, even if there are multiple such delays. On the other, it is methodologically important—it is going to be tricky trying to find ways of generating experimental choices to offer subjects with varying *k* values that don't merely tell us what we already know

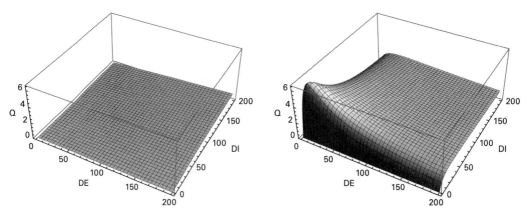

Figure 9.3
This figure shows two surfaces for range of values of *SS* satisfying the two constraints with *N* fixed. (Again, *LL* = 100.) In the left hand panel *k* is 0.007, in the right hand panel it is 0.15.

given variation in *k*, instead of telling us about more specific ways in which subjects, especially addicted ones, might differ with respect to their facility for bundling.

One way of approaching the matter is to measure something else as well, to see whether addicted subjects vary in that as well as showing less propensity to bundle. As Rachlin (this volume) suggests, partly on the basis of an experiment that related temporal discounting and discounting over social distance, nonaddicted subjects learn to cooperate with their future selves while still acting appropriately "selfishly" toward other people, whereas addicts "treat themselves at other times as nonaddicts treat other people" (Rachlin, this volume). Perhaps the nonbundling addict doesn't regard the future rewards that should be factored into appraising the bundle as *hers* as vividly as the nonaddict.

Something else that would be worth measuring is executive function, in the cognitive sense.[13] In general, cognitive psychology emphasizes the acquisition and manipulation of knowledge and the control of action in its approach to decision making, and neglects questions of desirability or hedonic value, relative to behaviorists and evolutionary thinkers. Cognitive psychologists care more than behaviorists about the architecture and representational structure of the processing systems involved in decision making. Cognitive neuroscientists agree that the frontal lobes and especially the prefrontal cortex of the brain are important for a range of abilities, including "executive" or "goal-directed" cognition. Many of the defects associated with damage to or dysfunction of parts of the frontal lobes are clearly important to bundling.

The prefrontal cortex (PFC) is an interconnected set of brain areas that together are richly connected with most sensory and motor systems in the cortex, and with a number of subcortical structures, including core parts of the midbrain reward system. PFC also has extensive back projections to the same areas, allowing the modulation of sensory processing and motor control via influence on brain processes specialized for those tasks (reviewed in Miller 2000; Fuster 2004). A growing range of types of theories is being used to interpret results regarding executive cognition, including different models of working and semantic memory (Tulving 1972), dynamic filtering (Shimamura 2000), and global workspace processing (Dehaene, Kerszberg, and Changeux 1998). Subtle experiments have demonstrated that at least some sorts of tasks show the PFC to be organized as a cascade of processes progressively recruited as the informational demands of a task increase (Koechlin, Ody, and Kouneiher 2003). Promising computer models have replicated human-like performance on some standard tests of PFC function, such as the Wisconsin Card Sorting Task (Rougier et al. 2005).

Resisting impulsive choice is the kind of task that requires integration of knowledge across multiple modalities, and evaluation of options or outcomes (such as better health or financial security in later life) about which relevant information is generally not cued by current sensory stimulation, in contrast to (for example) the current presence of a cigarettes on display in the convenience store.

Among the deficiencies noted in subjects with frontal lobe damage are "loss of ego" in the form of loss of interest in longer run projects, or in the future generally (Knight and Grabowecky 1995), and greater tendency to what are called "perseverative" errors. The Wisconsin Card Sorting Task is designed to detect the latter. Subjects sort cards according to their shape, color, or the number of symbols appearing on them. Experimenters provide feedback on whether or not the subject is sorting correctly, but without ever stating the rule that decides what counts as correct. When a subject correctly follows one rule, the experimenter switches to another without announcing that fact. PFC-damaged subjects (who also tend to score normally on IQ tests and other measures) tend to find the first rule as reliably as other subjects, but subsequently fail to abandon it when the rule changes (Milner 1963). Monkeys with PFC lesions perform badly at a task designed to be analogous to the Wisconsin task (Dias, Robbins, and Roberts 1996).

It has been found independently that subjects with frontal lesions are worse than controls at goal-oriented tasks, such as purchasing the items on a short shopping list, which require simple goals to be consistently pursued for a period of time (Shallice and Burgess 1991). The subjects with frontal lesions, who could perform individual subtasks (such as "buy a loaf of bread") effectively, tended to spend too much time on single subtasks, or otherwise got distracted entirely from pursuit of the goals. A variety of other results suggests that frontal-lobe damage impairs ability to retain a representation of a response when that representation needs to be maintained over a delay, or otherwise show greater susceptibility to distraction (Goldman-Rakic 1992; Chao and Knight 1995; McCarthy et al. 1994).

It is now clear that addicted subjects show specific performance deficits in Stroop paradigm tasks. (In the default Stroop task subjects are asked to name the color in which a word is displayed. Some trials are "incongruous," with, for example, the word "red" appearing in green letters. Subjects typically take longer to answer on incongruous trials and make more mistakes.) For example, Rugle and Melamed (1993) and Regard et al. (2003) found that non-substance-dependent pathological gamblers were impaired at a Stroop task compared to control subjects. Additional studies have found that addicts have specific reaction-time deficits when presented with cues associated with the target of their addiction, even if these cues are irrelevant to the task. (For example, the task might be to say of a word whether it is monosyllabic or polysyllabic; then a heroin addict may take longer to respond when the word is "needle.") This effect has been found with, among others, regular cannabis users (Field et al. 2006), cocaine users (Hester, Dixon, and Garavan 2006), and disordered gamblers (Boyer and Dickerson 2003). (For a recent review see Cox, Fadardi, and Pothos 2006.) This suggests that these subjects have specific difficulties with regulating their attention in general, and more specifically when cued by stimuli associated with their addiction.

All of these phenomena are related to reward bundling. To be effective a personal rule must be remembered, and the series of individually nonimpulsive choices it describes must promise more reward than the series of impulsive choices starting with the current threat to the rule. This, like executive cognition, requires reconstructing and maintaining representations of goal states including considerations that are independent from the immediate context. Failures to regulate attention could manifest in lapsing into context-cued choosing even after recalling and perhaps being temporarily motivated by a rule. Failures of memory could manifest in failure successfully to recall or reconstruct the considerations in light of which the rule promises any benefit at all. Such failures would perhaps be instances of what Marc Potenza suggested were "faulty brakes" explanations of addictive choice. We suggest that it would be very illuminating were somebody to design and perform an experiment in which the varying cognitive demands studied by, for example, Koechlin, Ody, and Kouneiher (2003) in which rules needed to be flexibly applied depending on context and other considerations, were implemented in a properly economic setting, so that the decisions made by subjects were amenable to behavioral as well as cognitive study, and furthermore included impulsive options. This could help shed light on the involvement of executive processes in resisting impulsivity, the cognitive demands of bundling-like rule-guided choice, and perhaps ways in which (some) addicted subjects differ from nonaddicts.

In conclusion, if Ainslie's proposal regarding how some of use resist temptation by bundling choices is approximately correct, it suggests various ways in which addicts may differ from nonaddicts. For reasons made clear in our discussion of generating choices for the purposes of studying bundling, it may be that variation in impulsivity captured by differing k values is sufficient to explain why the more impulsive find it more difficult to bundle—it is simply harder for equivalent future rewards to motivate them. Series of rewards need to be composed of bigger rewards, get delivered sooner, and have more members to be equivalently attractive to subjects with higher k values. Subjects might also differ in their facility at detecting appropriate groupings of choices, especially in real-world contexts where choices can be classified in a range of plausible ways. They may, independent of variations in impulsivity, be differently adept at detecting or exploiting natural or conventional chunkings of time, such as weekends, and using them to pace their consumption of relatively impulsive rewards. They may differ in their confidence in their future restraint, perhaps because of differences in their capacity to learn from their successes and failures. They might differ in their capacity to recall and represent as valuable future rewards not cued by features of the present environment. They might differ, again independent of differences in impulsivity, in the extent to which they regard the rewards available to their future selves as valuable to their present selves. All of these, and other possibilities, await further empirical investigation.

Acknowledgments

We thank the participants at the third "Mind and World" conference, and John McCoy for helpful discussion of various issues in this chapter.

Notes

1. The two main behavioral alternatives that need mentioning here, but which are not discussed further in this paper, are Loewenstein's theory of visceral cravings (Loewenstein 1999) and Rachlin's theory (e.g., Rachlin 2000) emphasizing the fact that targets of addictive consumption are close substitutes for social interaction. For Loewenstein the addict is prone to cravings cued by stimuli that have become associated with the addictive behavior, and these aversive cravings are better relieved by additional addictive behavior (such as taking the relevant drug) than alternatives, as well as being resistant to deliberate control (hence "visceral"). According to Rachlin the fact that addicts consume things that are close substitutes for social interaction makes sense partly because early consumption can increase the cost of social interaction and decrease the reward from it (for example, with disapproval, or failed interactions) and this increases the relative attractiveness of close substitutes, leading to a cycle of increased allocation culminating in addiction. See section 5 of Ross's chapter in this volume.

2. That is, as long as there is a single discount rate for all commodities or reward modalities, or if all values are represented on a single scale. This isn't generally true: food is typically discounted at higher rates than money (e.g., Kirby and Guastello 2001), and the targets of addictive consumption at higher rates than money (e.g., Madden et al. 1997). Nonetheless, questions about consistency can be posed for a single-reward modality, such as money. There too only exponential curves avoid intertemporal inconsistency.

3. Some current topics of debate in this area are discussed in Ainslie's chapter in this volume.

4. The k value here is not a discount rate in the same strict sense as in the exponential equation, because the rate of change of value for a given unit of time with a hyperbolic curve is not independent of the magnitude of the delay—the very feature that makes hyperbolic discounting a candidate explanation for intertemporal inconsistency. In this chapter we'll refer to "k values" and not "hyperbolic discount rates." Also, V_0 is often interpreted to indicate value, whereas Mazur was clear that it was *amount* of reinforcement, assumed only to be monotonically related (under experimental conditions, for example with small quantities of food and hungry animals) to physical quantity (e.g., mass of food). See Mazur and Herrnstein 1988.

5. Mazur (1997, 139–141) refers to several studies in which preferences of an experimental animal varied between cases where delay and reward were unchanged, but in some conditions the delay was spent exposed to a conditioned reinforcer.

6. Gene Heyman suggested at the conference that part of the *point* of conventional aggregations of time, including weekends, was to simplify the task of pacing different kinds of rewards. In related work, Ariely and Wertenbroch (2002) found that people who had the option of precommitting to a series of deadlines did better at a task, and met the deadlines better, than subjects who could submit at any time up to the final deadline. They were beaten in both categories by subjects who had evenly spaced deadlines imposed upon them.

7. There is some variation regarding whether the whole denominator is raised to a power (e.g., in Green, Myerson, and Ostaszewski 1999), or whether the kD term alone is (e.g., in the discussion in Mazur 1997). We'll not discuss these details further here. Mazur (1997, 134–135) describes some studies in which the hyperbolic equation with the kD term raised to a power does not fit the data as well as the simple hyperbolic equation.

8. Another approach sometimes used but not further discussed here calculates the area under the curve defined by a number of empirically determined indifference points and uses this quantity for comparing subjects (Myerson, Green, and Warusawitharana 2001). Although this sidesteps dealing with the shape of the curve in detail and gives a univariate basis for comparing individuals or groups, it leads to problems comparing data across studies (unless they use the same delays), and sometimes—including the present as we'll see below—it is exactly the shape of the curve that is of interest.

9. It is also becoming clear that the manner of determination of indifference points, for discounting procedures that depend on determining them rather than determining k values assuming the Mazur formula (e.g., as in Kirby and Marakovic 1996), is not methodologically innocuous. For example, the order of presentation of questions makes a difference to response to delay (Robles and Vargas 2007). Measured sensitivity to risk differs depending on whether the same uncertain options are presented as frequencies or percentages (Yi and Bickel 2005). Alternatively, conventional "titration" procedures that home in on indifference points through a series of questions involving large delays do not find an effect of increased impulsivity with consumption of alcohol, yet an "experiential" process that pays out for every choice and uses short delays that are experienced as part of the experiment does find such an effect (Reynolds, Richards, and De Wit 2006).

10. Contrast, following (Mazur 1997, 135–136), a reinforcement schedule where a 10-second delay is followed by food, and one where delays vary between 1 second and 19 seconds followed by the same amount of food. The average delay in both cases is 10 seconds, and the amount of food is constant. Hyperbolic discounting explains the preference, because it predicts that the average value of the reinforcers delayed at 1 and 19 seconds will be greater than for reinforcers consistently delayed at 10 seconds.

11. This is a major simplification, in the interests of experimental investigation of selected aspects of bundling. Real-world self-control choices often depend on classification of complex rewards into categories, and credible natural classifications are rare. The subject can then be involved in complicated ways in the process of determining how to classify options—deciding, yet also having multiple competing stakes in, what counts as "getting some exercise" or a "healthy" lunch, or "having two drinks" (how many drinks is one Long Island Iced Tea?). For extended discussion of some of these problems see Ainslie 2001, Part II. Redish (this volume) also discusses the importance of classifying situations for decision making.

12. This is not an exhaustive list; some of the items on it do or can overlap, and there are different ways of breaking down Ainslie's proposal.

13. This paragraph, and the following seven, retrace steps made in Ross et al. 2008, section 4.6.

References

Ainslie, G. (1992). *Picoeconomics*. Cambridge: Cambridge University Press.

Ainslie, G. (2001). *Breakdown of Will*. Cambridge: Cambridge University Press.

Ainslie, G. (2005). Précis of *Breakdown of Will*. *Behavioral and Brain Sciences* 28: 635–673.

Ainslie, G., and Monterosso, J. R. (2003). Building blocks of self-control: Increased tolerance for delay with bundled rewards. *Journal of the Experimental Analysis of Behavior* 79 (1): 37–48.

Ariely, D., and Wertenbroch, K. (2002). Procrastination, deadlines, and performance: Self-control by precommitment. *Psychological Science* 13: 219–224.

Bickel, W. K., and Marsch, L. A. (2001). Conceptualizing addiction: Toward a behavioral economic understanding of drug dependence: delay discounting processes. *Addiction* 96: 73–86.

Boyer, M., and Dickerson, M. (2003). Attentional bias and addictive behaviour: Automaticity in a gambling-specific modified Stroop task. *Addiction* 98: 61–70.

Chao, L., and Knight, R. (1995). Human prefrontal lesions increase distractibility to irrelevant sensory inputs. *Neuroreport* 6: 1605–1610.

Cox, W., Fadardi, J., and Pothos, E. (2006). The addiction–Stroop test: Theoretical considerations and procedural recommendations. *Psychological Bulletin* 132: 443–476.

Dehaene, S., Kerszberg, M., and Changeux, J.-P. (1998). A neuronal model of a global workspace in effortful cognitive tasks. *Proceedings of the National Academy of Sciences USA* 95: 14529–14534.

de la Piedad, X., Field, D., and Rachlin, H. (2006). The influence of prior choices on current choice. *Journal of the Experimental Analysis of Behavior* 85: 3–21.

Dennett, D. C. (1991). *Consciousness Explained*. New York: Little, Brown.

Dias, R., Robbins, T., and Roberts, A. (1996). Primate analogue of the Wisconsin Card Sorting Test: Effects of excitotoxic lesions of the prefrontal cortex in the marmoset. *Behavioral Neuroscience* 110: 872–886.

Dutton, D. G., and Aron, A. (1974). Some evidence for heightened sexual attraction under conditions of high anxiety. *Journal of Personality and Social Psychology* 30: 510–517.

Eisenberg, D. T. A., Campbell, B., MacKillop, J., Modi, M., Beauchemin, J., Dang, D., Lisman, S. A., Lum, J. K., and Wilson, D. S. (2007a). Season of birth and dopamine receptor associations with impulsivity, sensation seeking, and reproductive behaviors. *PLoS ONE* 7 (11): e1216.

Eisenberg, D. T. A., Campbell, B., MacKillop, J., Modi, M., Lum, J. K., and Wilson, D. S. (2007b). Polymorphisms in the dopamine D_2 and D_4 receptor genes and reproductive, sexual, and life history behaviors. *Evolutionary Psychology* 5: 696–715.

Field, M., Eastwood, B., Bradley, B., and Mogg, K. (2006). Selective processing of cannabis cues in regular cannabis users. *Drug and Alcohol Dependence* 85: 75–82.

Fuster, J. (2004). Upper processing stages of the perception–action cycle. *Trends in Cognitive Sciences* 8: 143–145.

Goldman-Rakic, P. (1992). Working memory and the mind. *Scientific American* 267: 110–117.

Green, L., and Myerson, J. (2004). A discounting framework for choice with delayed and probabilistic rewards. *Psychological Bulletin* 130 (5): 769–792.

Green, L., Myerson, J., and Ostaszewski, P. (1999). Amount of reward has opposite effects on the discounting of delayed and probabilistic outcomes. *Journal of Experimental Psychology: Learning, Memory, and Cognition* 25: 418–427.

Herrnstein, R. (1961). Relative and absolute strength of response as a function of frequency of reinforcement. *Journal of the Experimental Analysis of Behavior* 4: 267–272. (Reprinted in Hernnstein 1997.)

Herrnstein, R. (1964). Aperiodicity as a factor in choice. *Journal of the Experimental Analysis of Behavior* 45: 305–315.

Herrnstein, R. (1976). Towards a law of response strength. *Psychological Bulletin* 83 (6): 1131–1153. (Reprinted in Hernnstein 1997.)

Herrnstein, R. (1997). *The Matching Law: Papers in Psychology and Economics*. Ed. Howard Rachlin and David I. Laibson. Cambridge, MA: Harvard University Press.

Hester, R., Dixon, V., and Garavan, H. (2006). A consistent attentional bias for drug-related material in active cocaine users across word and picture versions of the emotional Stroop task. *Drug and Alcohol Dependence* 81: 251–257.

Jones, B., and Rachlin, H. (2006). Social discounting. *Psychological Science* 17: 283–286.

Khan, U., and Dhar, R. (2007). Where there is a way, is there a will? The effect of future choices on self-control. *Journal of Experimental Psychology: General* 136 (2): 277–288.

Kirby, K. (2006). The present values of delayed rewards are approximately additive. *Behavioural Processes* 72: 273–282.

Kirby, K. N., and Guastello, B. (2001). Making choices in anticipation of similar future choices can increase self-control. *Journal of Experimental Psychology: Applied* 7 (2): 154–164.

Kirby, K. N., and Marakovic, N. N. (1996). Delay-discounting probabilistic rewards: Rates decrease as amounts increase. *Psychonomic Bulletin and Review* 3: 100–104.

Kirby, K. N., Winston, G. C., and Santiesteban, M. (2005). Impatience and grades: Delay-discount rates correlate negatively with college GPA. *Learning and Individual Differences* 15: 213–222.

Knight, R., and Grabowecky, M. (1995). Escape from linear time: Prefrontal cortex and conscious experience. In M. Gazzaniga, ed., *The Cognitive Neurosciences*, 1357–1371. Cambridge, MA: MIT Press.

Koechlin, E., Ody, C., and Kouneiher, F. (2003). The architecture of cognitive control in the human prefrontal cortex. *Science* 302: 1181–1185.

Loewenstein, G. (1999). A visceral account of addiction. In J. Elster and O.-J. Skog, eds., *Getting Hooked*, 235–264. Cambridge: Cambridge University Press.

Madden, G. J., Petry, N., Badger, G., and Bickel, W. K. (1997). Impulsive and self-control choices in opioid-dependent subjects and non-drug using controls: Drug and monetary rewards. *Experimental and Clinical Psychopharmacology* 5: 256–262.

Mazur, J. E. (1984). Tests of an equivalence rule for fixed and variable reinforcer delays. *Journal of Experimental Psychology: Animal Behavior Processes* 1: 374–396.

Mazur, J. E. (1987). An adjusting procedure for studying delayed reinforcement. In M. L. Commons, J. E. Mazur, J. A. Nevin, and H. Rachlin, eds., *Quantitative Analyses of Behavior*, vol. 5: *The effect of Delay and of Intervening Events on Reinforcement Value*, 55–73. Hillsdale, NJ: Lawrence Erlbaum.

Mazur, J. E. (1997). Choice, delay, probability, and conditioned reinforcement. *Animal Learning and Behavior* 25 (2): 131–147.

Mazur, J. E., and Herrnstein, R. J. (1988). On the functions relating delay, reinforcer value, and behavior. *Behavioral and Brain Sciences* 11: 690–691.

McCarthy, G., Blamire, A., Puce, A., Nobre, A., Bloch, G., Fahmeed, H., Goldman-Rakic, P., and Shulman, R. (1994). Functional magnetic resonance imaging of human prefrontal cortex activation during a spatial working memory task. *Proceedings of the National Academy of Sciences* 91: 8690–8694.

Miller, E. (2000). The prefrontal cortex and cognitive control. *Nature Reviews Neuroscience* 1: 59–65.

Milner, B. (1963). Effects of different brain lesions on card sorting. *Archives of Neurology* 9: 90–100.

Myerson, J., and Green, L. (1995). Discounting of delayed rewards: Models of individual choice. *Journal of the Experimental Analysis of Behavior* 64: 263–276.

Myerson, J., Green, L., and Warusawitharana, M. (2001). Area under the curve as a measure of discounting. *Journal for the Experimental Analysis of Behavior* 76 (2): 235–243.

Quattrone, G., and Tversky A. (1984). Causal versus diagnostic contingencies: On self-deception and on the voter's illusion. *Journal of Personality and Social Psychology* 46: 237–248.

Rachlin, H. (2000). *The Science of Self-Control*. Cambridge, MA: Harvard University Press.

Rachlin, H., Raineri, A., and Cross, D. (1991). Subjective probability and delay. *Journal of the Experimental Analysis of Behavior* 55: 233–244.

Read, D., Loewenstein, G. F., and Kalynaraman, S. (1999). Mixing virtue and vice: The combined effects of hyperbolic discounting and diversification. *Journal of Behavioral Decision Making* 12: 257–273.

Regard, M., Knoch, D., Guetling, E., and Landis, T. (2003). Brain damage and addictive behavior: A neuropsychological and electroencephalogram investigation with pathological gamblers. *Cognitive Behavioral Neurology* 16: 47–53.

Reynolds, B., Richards, J., and De Wit, H. (2006). Acute-alcohol effects on the Experiential Discounting Task (EDT) and a question-based measure of delay discounting. *Pharmacology, Biochemistry, and Behavior* 83: 194–202.

Robles, E., and Vargas, P. A. (2007). Functional parameters of delay discounting assessment tasks: Order of presentation. *Behavioural Processes* 75 (2): 237–241.

Ross, D., Sharp, S., Vuchinich, R., and Spurrett, D. (2008). *Midbrain Mutiny: The Picoeconomics and Neuroeconomics of Disordered Gambling*. Cambridge, MA: MIT Press.

Rougier, N., Noelle, D., Braver, T., Cohen, J., and O'Reilly, R. (2005). Prefrontal cortex and flexible cognitive control: Rules without symbols. *Proceedings of the National Academy of Sciences USA* 102: 7338–7343.

Rugle, L., and Melamed, L. (1993). Neuropsychological assessment of attention problems in pathological gamblers. *Journal of Nervous and Mental Diseases* 181: 107–112.

Shallice, T., and Burgess. P. (1991). Deficits in strategy application following frontal lobe deficits in man. *Brain* 114: 727–741.

Shimamura, A. (2000). The role of the prefrontal cortex in dynamic filtering. *Psychobiology* 28: 207–218.

Stevens, J., Rosati, A., Ross, K., and Hauser, M. (2005). Will travel for food: Spatial discounting in two new world monkeys. *Current Biology* 15 (20): 1855–1860.

Tulving, E. (1972). Episodic and semantic memory. In E. Tulving and W. Donaldson, eds., *Organization of Memory*, 381–403. New York: Academic Press.

Wegner, D. M. (2003). *The Illusion of Conscious Will*. Cambridge, MA: MIT Press.

Wegner, D. M., and Sparrow, B. (2007). The puzzle of coaction. In Don Ross, David Spurrett, Harold Kincaid, and G. Lynn Stephens, eds., *Distributed Cognition and the Will*, 17–38. Cambridge, MA: MIT Press.

Yi, R., and Bickel, W. K. (2005). Representation of odds in terms of frequencies reduces probability discounting. *Psychological Record* 55: 577–593.

10 Neural Recruitment during Self-Control of Smoking: A Pilot fMRI Study

John R. Monterosso, Traci Mann, Andrew Ward, George Ainslie, Jennifer Bramen, Arthur Brody, and Edythe D. London

This chapter presents pilot data from a neuroimaging study that recorded changes in functional magnetic resonance (fMRI) signal (an indirect indication of changes in brain activity) while overnight abstinent cigarette smokers were given opportunities to smoke, but were asked to try to resist the temptation to do so. This is the first study of which we are aware that has used fMRI to identify substrates of self-control of an addictive behavior.

Inhibitory Control in Addiction Research

Until recently, neuroscience research on addiction has focused primarily on mechanisms of reinforcement. In the mid-twentieth century, *negative* reinforcement dominated the field, as relief of withdrawal (including "conditioned withdrawal") was viewed as the primary underlying basis for pathological drug use (Jelinek 1960). For reasons that included a spike in use of crack cocaine, which is associated with much less obvious withdrawal symptoms than alcohol and opioids, emphasis in the late twentieth century shifted away from negative reinforcement. Withdrawal cannot account for all pathological cocaine use, particularly since conditioned responses to cocaine-related cues generally are more drug-*like* than drug-opposite (e.g., tachycardia rather than bradycardia; Carter and Tiffany 1999). Indeed, *positive* affect is a common trigger for relapse to cocaine abuse (Shulman 1989). It became clear that positive reinforcement is central to pathological drug use. Dramatic progress was made in the neuroscience of drug reward during the late twentieth century (Koob 1996; Schultz 1997; Wise and Rompre 1989). Especially important in this regard was the recognition that midbrain dopaminergic neurons that project to the nucleus accumbens participate prominently in mediating reward from all drugs of abuse (Pontieri et al. 1996).

Still, negative and positive reinforcement alone do not fully describe the territory that the science of addiction must address. Consider the smoker who wants to quit. This person might utilize a pharmacological aid that reduces withdrawal from smoking cessation (e.g., nicotine replacement therapy) or that reduces the positive reinforcement from smoking (e.g., varenicline, a partial agonist for nicotinic receptors, that, among other effects, reduces the reward from smoking). But in addition, this person also *tries* to quit. What does it mean to try to quit drug use, that is, to try not to continue using? This aspect of addiction is, we think, central to everyday thinking about the topic. It is this aspect of the phenomenon that the eminent psychologist Frank Logan had in mind when he wrote, "Principles of animal behavior can provide a basis for a theory of human drug use and abuse, but voluntary control of addictive behavior requires uniquely human cognitive processes" (Logan 1993, 291).

In the last decade, addiction researchers have paid more attention to understanding the basis of "voluntary control of addictive behaviors" and its failing (Goldstein and Volkow 2002; Jentsch and Taylor 1999; London et al. 2000). Grant (2004) described this as the beginning of a third and as yet unproven wave of addiction research (negative and positive reinforcement being the first two). The research on voluntary control has proceeded in parallel along several lines, variously labeled as investigations of *inhibitory control, executive function, impulse control, cognitive control, self-control, self-regulation,* and *willpower.* This chapter uses Logan's descriptive phrase "voluntary control of addictive behaviors" throughout, and does not attempt to interrelate the various processes or subcategories of the constructs named above. We will, however, describe three approaches to the area of research in order to provide the context for the study presented here. We say from the outset that we do not think it inevitable, or even likely, that all cognitive processes that underlie voluntary control of addictive behaviors will be able to be mapped onto identifiable neurobiology (see Ross 2005). However, even in the absence of complete reductionism, there may well be an opportunity to illuminate neural substrates relevant to the voluntary control of addictive behaviors.

Good Decision Making and the Voluntary Control of Addictive Behavior

Abstinence from drugs of abuse is a *rational* (i.e., utility-maximizing) choice given anticipated negative consequences of continued drug taking. Individual differences in the capacity for rational decision making may therefore constitute a substantial determinant of problem drug use. Laboratory tasks have been constructed to isolate aspects of decision making that are thought to be relevant to drug use (Bechara and Damasio 2002; Bechara, Dolan, and Hindes, 2002; Kirby, Petry, and Bickel 1999; Rogers et al. 1999). Typically, these tasks require individuals to select repeatedly from sets of alternatives designed to isolate one or more factors, such as *risk, uncertainty,* or *delay.* The most common approach has been to compare the performance of drug abusing and nonabusing participants on such tasks, and in some cases, to pair the tasks with neuroimaging. This research asks, "What decision-making factors differ between drug abusers and comparison subjects who do not abuse drugs?" and, in some cases, "How do drug abusers and comparison subjects differ in neural activity associated with decision making?"

Although generalizing is complicated by the myriad factors that differ from one study to another, including the history and severity of drug dependence, the duration of abstinence prior to assessment, and specifics of the methodology employed, drug-abusing and non-drug-abusing populations appear to differ with respect to decision making. In particular, drug-abusing subjects appear to be less risk averse (Fishbein et al. 2005; Rogers and Robbins 2001), less sensitive to unpredictable penalties (Bartzokis et al. 2000; Bechara 2001; Fishbein 2000; Grant, Contoreggi, and London 2000; Mazas, Finn, and Steinmetz 2000), more driven by reinforcement history in the most immediate past (Paulus et al. 2002, 2003), more prone to behave in accordance with local versus global reinforcement rates (Heyman and Dunn 2002), and more willing to trade reward value for reward immediacy (Bickel, Odum, and Madden 1999; Cairns and van der Pol 2000; Coffey et al. 2003; Fuchs 1982; Kirby and Petry 2004; Kirby, Petry, and Bickel 1999; Mitchell 1999; Moeller and Dougherty 2002; Petry 2003; Reynolds et al. 2004; Vuchinich and Simpson 1998).

Studies comparing neural activation (inferred through neuroimaging) during performance of decision-making tasks have revealed significant anomalies among drug abusers. Although there is some inconsistency, most studies have reported hypofrontality among drug abusers during decision making, especially within the dorsolateral prefrontal cortex (DLPFC) (Bolla et al. 2003, 2005; Ersche et al. 2005; Paulus et al. 2002, 2003). Of course, cohort studies that compare drug abusers and nonabusers suffer shortcomings including indeterminacy regarding whether group differences predated substance abuse. In an important extension of cohort comparison findings, low recruitment during a two–choice guessing task within a network of regions involved in decision making (including the right middle frontal gyrus, middle temporal gyrus, and posterior cingulate) was associated with subsequent relapse among abstinent methamphetamine abusers (Paulus, Tapert, and Schuckit 2005).

Although repeated reports of decision-making anomalies among drug abusers suggests the importance of decision making to the behavior, decision-making tasks may not capture processes engaged during the struggle between a strong desire to use drugs and conflicting goals such as commitments made to abstain from drug use. Indeed, while small amounts of money have been put at stake in some decision-making tasks, the majority of the research in this area has used hypothetical choices (Madden et al. 1997; Monterosso et al. 2001) or decision-making games where "points" provide the only task incentive (Bechara and Damasio 2002; Rogers et al. 1999). Although a steeper discounting of reward as a function of delay has, for example, been repeatedly shown in drug abusers (Bickel, Odum, and Madden 1999; Cairns and van der Pol 2000; Coffey et al. 2003; Fuchs 1982; Kirby and Petry 2004; Kirby, Petry, and Bickel 1999; Mitchell

1999; Moeller and Dougherty 2002; Petry 2003; Reynolds et al. 2004; Vuchinich and Simpson 1998), the difference appears as a *preference*. An individual who says that she would, hypothetically, choose $10 today over $20 in a week may be making a bad decision, possibly even reflecting a tendency that puts her at risk for substance abuse. But (to our knowledge) there is no evidence that the decision entails the type of ambivalence or motivational struggle that is associated with voluntary control of an addicted behavior.

Behavioral Inhibition and the Voluntary Control of Addictive Behavior

An alternative approach to studying the voluntary control of addictive behavior looks at capacity for *behavioral inhibition*. According to this idea, behavioral inhibition, which can be loosely defined as the *intentional suppression of prepotent responses that are goal-inappropriate*, is critical to recovery from addiction, because recovery requires the suppression of rapid, conditioned responses so that slower mechanisms can guide behavior (Fillmore 2003; Jentsch and Taylor 1999). If this conjecture is correct, deficiency in behavioral inhibition could serve as a behavioral phenotype for substance-abuse disorders, facilitating the search for genetic linkages and physiological markers. Established paradigms that tax behavioral inhibition are easily paired with imaging methodologies. Below we consider first the construct of behavioral inhibition, and then the limits of evidence linking it to addiction.

Several behavioral inhibition subtypes have been proposed, with perhaps the most agreed-upon subclassifications being "response inhibition" versus "interference control" (Barkley 1997). *Response inhibition* is the intentional cancellation of a behavior already underway, as when a baseball batter attempts to stop ("check") his swing at a pitch outside the strike zone, or as when a speaker attempts to cut off an utterance she realizes is inappropriate. *Interference control* refers to protecting ongoing processes from interference so that they *can* be completed, as when a speaker tries to avoid distraction by a neighboring conversation. Although both functions are generally included under the heading of inhibitory control, performance on response inhibition tasks such as the Stop Signal (SST) and go/no-go tasks is not strongly correlated with performance on interference control tasks such as the Color-Word Stroop Task and the Flanker Task (in Friedman and Miyake 2004, $r = .15$; in Avila et al. 2004, $r = -.11$).

The clinical literature has strongly implicated the frontal lobes in both types of behavioral inhibition. Frontal lobe lesions cause dramatic impairment on both response inhibition and interference control tasks (Aron et al. 2003; Perret 1974). There has been a recent spate of studies that have paired behavioral inhibition tasks (especially the Stroop, go/no-go, and SST) with neuroimaging methodologies (Bush et al. 1999; Garavan et al. 2002; Hester and Garavan 2004; Kaufman et al. 2003; Peterson et al. 1999; Rubia et al. 2005). In general, these studies corroborate findings from the clinical literature, demonstrating an association between performance on inhibitory tasks and activation of the frontal lobes (we will defer discussion of more specific localization for the time being).

Several studies have reported an association between deficits in behavioral inhibition and substance-abusing populations (Fillmore and Rush 2002; Monterosso et al. 2005; Salo et al. 2005). In addition, two studies pairing versions of the go/no-go task with fMRI found less recruitment in the frontal cortex and in the anterior cingulate cortex and presupplementary motor area among cocaine abusers than in control subjects (Hester and Garavan 2004; Kaufman et al. 2003). As with cohort comparisons of decision-making anomalies, it is not possible to determine whether impairment in response inhibition follows drug use (as a consequence) or precedes (perhaps predisposes to) drug abuse.

Although it has been argued that the ability to resist temptation relies on the capacity for behavioral inhibition (Mahone et al. 2002), it is unclear how much behavioral inhibition, as measured by speeded cognitive tasks, captures functioning that is important for maintaining abstinence. Errors on behavioral inhibition tasks result from prepotent responses that are only transiently dominant, and such errors depend on the speeded nature of the tasks. Typically a respondent is aware of committing an error even while completing the response, and would correct it promptly if given the chance. By contrast, even when drugs are readily available, using them requires the execution of an action plan that remains dominant for seconds; and although the user may experience ambivalence, self-correction does not reliably occur at all, let alone within a few hundred milliseconds. In short, although behavioral inhibition *may* be integral to self-control of drug taking, dissimilarities between the phenomena warrant skepticism regarding whether speeded inhibition tasks really correspond to resisting everyday temptation.

The "Self-Control Challenge"

There is emerging interest in studying the voluntary control of addictive behavior with laboratory tasks that more directly model the real-world phenomenon. For example, Childress and colleagues conducted an imaging protocol in which they assessed what circuitry was recruited when individuals actively attempted to suppress craving for cocaine (Childress et al. 2003, 2004). Following the most well-established technique for eliciting craving in drug abusers during brain image acquisition (Childress et al. 1999; Grant et al. 1996), Childress and colleagues presented video cues depicting drug use to a group of cocaine abusers. Participants were instructed to allow themselves to crave in one condition, and to attempt to stop their craving in another condition. Preliminary reports of that work indicated that relative to the condition in which craving was not suppressed, attempts to inhibit craving recruited robust activation in inferior frontal

gyri (Childress et al. 2003, 2004). A similar design was recently used in a study of cigarette smokers; attempt to suppress the urge to smoke resulted in activation of the dorsal anterior cingulate cortex (dACC) and posterior cingulate cortex (Brody et al. 2007).

Although the suppression of craving may constitute a more direct model of the voluntary control of an addictive behavior than a speeded cognitive task like the Stroop, it
is also problematic. Since the relationship between craving and drug abuse is itself not
straightforward (Tiffany 1999; Tiffany et al. 1993), it is unclear how much the explicit
target of inhibitory control (craving) is relevant in achieving abstinence. For example,
empirical evidence suggests that at least in early recovery, the difference between more
and less effective treatment is not reflected in the amount of craving reported, but
rather in the frequency of drug use given the presence of high craving (Weiss et al.
2003). The recent development of methodologies for delivering primary rewards during fMRI (e.g., (McClure, Berns, and Montague 2003) allows for more direct analysis
of this phenomenon.

Pilot Study of Smoking Self-Control

We used a specialized MRI-compatible device for delivering cigarette smoke to allow us
to study the brain activity associated with the voluntary control of smoking behavior
in regular cigarette smokers. The goals were (1) to establish the viability of the method
for use in larger studies, and (2) to collect preliminary evidence regarding the brain
regions that are active when abstinent cigarette smokers voluntarily abstain from an
opportunity to smoke.

Method

Ten smokers, who were not seeking treatment, were recruited from a list of previous
research participants who gave permission for further contact. All had been previously
screened for the presence of Axis I disorders. At a baseline screening session, participants were given a full explanation of the procedures and provided informed consent
in accordance with the University of California Institutional Review Board. They completed a magnetic resonance imaging safety screening form, and were in good general
health, right handed, and 18–50 years of age. They reported smoking 10 or more cigarettes per day, and had $\geq$ 18 ppm CO in their expired breath in the screening session.
Potential participants were excluded if they reported a history of neurological disease
(e.g., stroke) or of head trauma, reported claustrophobia (which would preclude fMRI),
or were pregnant.

During the baseline test session, the participants were trained to smoke through the
''MRI-Hookah,'' a specialized smoking device that is compatible with the MR environment. To approximate the scanning environment, participants were positioned supine
on a cot, and fit with their own Silastic mask. After smoking through the apparatus,

participants were asked to rate the experience of smoking through the hookah on a scale between -10 and $+10$ with the following anchors provided: $-10 =$ "very unpleasant," $-5 =$ "moderately unpleasant," $0 =$ "neither pleasant or unpleasant," $+5 =$ "moderately pleasant," and $+10 =$ "very pleasant—equal to normal smoking." Participants in the baseline session were invited to participate in fMRI testing only if they reported (1) smoking > 10 cigarettes per day, had CO scores > 18 ppm, and rated smoking through the MRI-Hookah as at least a "$+5$" (moderately pleasant). Participants included in the study were predominantly female (6 of 10) and Caucasian (8 of 10). The mean age of participants was 30.3 ± 4.5 and the mean number of cigarettes smoked per day (according to self-report) was 16.3 ± 3.2.

Subjects were instructed to abstain from smoking for 12 hours before their scheduled participation in the Smoking Self-Control Challenge. CO was assessed at the beginning of the test session to verify abstinence (≤ 8 ppm was required). After completing the Smoking Self-Control Challenge (described below) subjects were again assessed for CO in expired breath. Participants were then asked to indicate how difficult they found it to refrain from smoking on "self-control" test blocks. To increase the desire to smoke during the task, participants were informed that an additional 1.5 h of monitored abstinence would be required after they completed the task.

Self-Control Challenge Task Design

Prior to the Smoking Self-Control Challenge, participants were read task instructions and given a practice of several trials (outside the scanner). Most important, the instructions informed participants that there would be times during the task in which they would have access to cigarette smoke, but during which they should try to refrain; "We'd really like it if you could try not to smoke on as many of these rounds as you can manage.... We realize that it may be difficult to resist smoking, but try your best." Our goal in choosing this particular wording was both to encourage self-control efforts, but at the same time, to convey that failure was not tantamount to breaking the rules of the experiment. Figure 10.1 provides a schematic of a single trial of the Smoking Self-Control Challenge. Each trial began with a 12–second video clip of smoking cues (e.g., a cigarette being lit). After the clip, subjects were asked to indicated whether or not they wished to smoke (see below). If they responded in the affirmative, depending on the particular trial, subjects were either informed by the computer (1) "Smoke available— but try not to," or (2) "Valve closed, smoke unavailable"). An experimenter outside the scanner room signaled to an assistant inside the scanner room which type of trial was about to begin, and the assistant positioned the valve accordingly. During self-control trials, the assistant inside the scanner room watched the cigarette that was held in tubing within the MRI-Hookah (see figure 10.2). Inhalation on the part of the participant was readily detected as a brightening of the ambers at the end of the cigarette. The

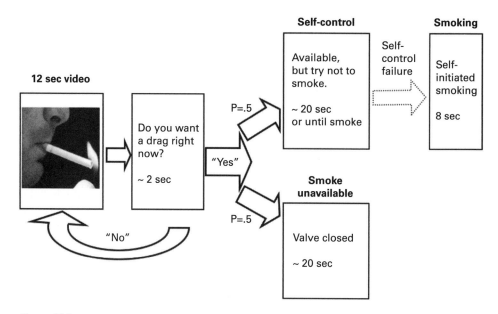

Figure 10.1
Schematic of one trial of the Self-Control Challenge. Each of two task runs consisted of twelve trials.

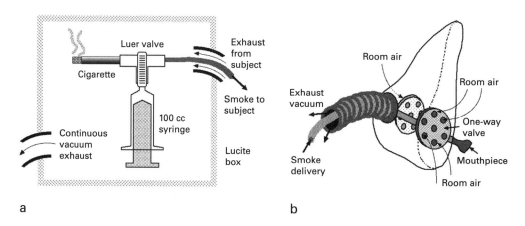

Figures 10.2
MRI-Hookah. A. Schematic representation of the fully enclosed continuously vented smoking apparatus. B. Facemask used by the subject to inhale smoke. The smoke is delivered through the center cannula of a concentric dual hose apparatus. The expired smoke is exhausted through the outer tube.

occurrence of inhalation was signaled to the experimenter, who recorded the event through a button press on the computer that ran the experimental task. During these trials, if subjects smoked, the computer presented the word "Smoking" to the participant for 5 sec. On "Smoke Unavailable" trials, the aforementioned "Valve closed, smoke unavailable" message appeared on the screen for the trial duration. Each task run was conducted until 6 Smoke-Unavailable and 6 Self-Control trials were completed (regardless of how many times the participant abstained on those trials). Each participant completed two task runs lasting approximately 8 minutes, separated by a short break. After completing each imaging session, participants were asked to rate how difficult they found it to *not smoke* on self-control trials.

The MRI-Hookah

The MRI-Hookah was developed to allow cigarette-smoke inhalation simultaneous to image acquisition (*R21 DA13627–02; Enabling Technologies in fMRI and Cigarette Smoking*, PI Cohen). The device introduces no MRI artifacts, allows the subject to inhale and exhale both smoke and room air through nose or mouth, and quickly removes smoke and excess odors so that these secondary reinforcers may be kept under experimental control. It delivers smoke to the subject through a close-fitting Silastic mask, which includes a mouthpiece that the subject places comfortably in his or her teeth (figure 10.2a and 10.2b).

Use of a standard surgical oxygen mask ensured that the subjects are able to breathe through both the nose and mouth. Air was expired through a low-velocity vacuum system, which draws air continuously through a large-bore tube, fitted concentrically around the smoke delivery tube. When cigarette smoke was made available, a gated valve within the MRI-Hookah was opened, allowing smoke to be drawn through the mouthpiece. When the subject was not inhaling cigarette smoke, one-way valve ports on the side of the mask passed room air freely. In this way the smoke odor, which might act as a secondary reinforcer and therefore a contaminant in experiments, was removed from the environment as quickly as possible.

MRI Data Acquisition

Imaging parameters We used a 3-Tesla Siemens Allegra system for all acquisitions (see note for details[1]). Stimuli were displayed on magnet-compatible video goggles (Resonance Technology, Northridge, CA). This display presents VGA screen resolution (800 × 600 pixels with 24-bit color depth) with a nominal visual angle of about 30° horizontally and 20° vertically. Correction for individual myopia or hyperopia was accomplished by the insertion of lenses. During the scans, subjects responded to the "yes/no" question regarding whether they wanted to smoke by pressing a two-button magnet-compatible keypad. The touch pad was placed under the fingers of the subject's dominant hand (right only, per inclusion criteria).

Image Analysis

Functional image processing and analysis   Preprocessing procedures are described in the note below.[2] Subsequent to preprocessing, both task runs for each subject were analyzed individually in the first level of analysis. For each participant, a second-level analysis combined the Z-statistical maps from the task runs (except for one participant, for whom one run was discarded due to excessive head motion). The resulting statistical maps from these second-level analyses (also Z-statistic maps) served as inputs for group analyses ("third level"). Activation maps for main effect consist of voxels with $Z > 2.3$, with cluster-level significance (correcting for whole brain search) of $p < .05$.

Results of Smoking Self-Control Challenge Pilot Study

Subjects voluntarily abstained on 56.2% of Self-Control trials. No subject smoked on all Self-Control trials, and only one subject abstained on all Self-Control trials. Subsequent to the experiment, the participants reported a mean rating of difficulty in maintaining self-control of 6.9 ± 2.1 (of a possible 10). For the primary contrast, we assessed the difference between fMRI signal during Self-Control trials in which the participant succeeded (Voluntary Abstinence) and Smoke-Unavailable trials. Self-Control trials in which the participant smoked were excluded from this contrast, in part because of artifacts related to smoking.

The primary imaging results are presented in figure 10.3 (*in radiological space*). Three clusters were identified in which the fMRI signal was greater during Voluntary Abstinence trials, relative to Smoke Unavailable trials. The largest cluster (1,769 voxels; fig. 10.3, top right and bottom right) included portions of the dorsal anterior cingulate cortex (dACC, BA32) and supplementary motor area (SMA BA8 and BA6). A second cluster of significant extent (654 voxels; fig. 10.3, bottom left) was observed in the right superior and middle frontal gyri (SFG, MFG, BA9; encompassing more medial aspects of the DLPFC). A third cluster of significant extent (577 voxels; fig. 10.3, top left, top right, and bottom left) was centered in the right inferior frontal gyrus and encompassed part of the insula as well (IFG, BA 47, extending to BA 45).

Deactivations in the primary contrast (i.e., clusters in which BOLD signal was greater during Smoke-Unavailable than Voluntary Abstinence trials) were also identified (though are not presented visually). The largest cluster of deactivation (1,532 voxels) was observed in the posterior cingulate cortex (PCC) and extended dorsally into the precuneus (BA 30 and 31). The next largest cluster (895 voxels) was observed in the ventral portion of the medial frontal gyrus and in the orbital gyrus (BA 11). The third cluster of deactivation (711 voxels in extent) was observed in the dorsomedial frontal gyrus and paracentral lobule (BA 6 and 5). The smallest cluster of deactivation (605 voxels in extent) was centered on the border between the angular gyrus and postcen-

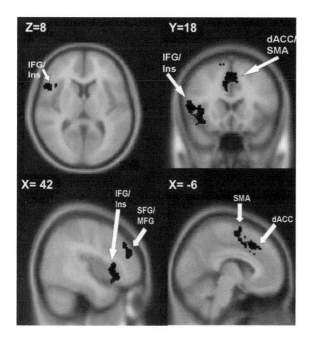

Figure 10.3
Results from whole brain results in radiologic space for Voluntary Abstinence—Smoke Unavailable with significant activations in black (voxel $z > 2.3$, maximum $z = 3.7$, cluster level corrected significance of $p < .05$). Increases in BOLD signal during Voluntary Abstinence were observed in a large cluster encompassing portions of the dACC and SMA, and smaller clusters in the right DLPFC (SFG/MFG) and the right VLPFC (IFG), which encompassed part of the insula as well.

tral gyrus, encompassing portions of each within the right hemisphere (BA 2, 3, and 40).

Discussion

Our primarily goal was to develop a methodology for examining the neural activity during voluntary control of smoking behavior. In order to accomplish this, we developed a method for making cigarette smoke available in the scanner (*R21 DA13627–02; Enabling Technologies in fMRI and Cigarette Smoking*, PI Cohen). Smokers were then faced with a situation in which the opportunity to smoke was available, though discouraged, on some trials, whereas it was unavailable on other trials. It was necessary that the procedure be sufficiently comfortable for participants that the relevant opportunity to smoke remained attractive. The fact that participants' self-reports indicated that they found it difficult to not smoke on the trials in which smoke was available (6.9 on a 10-point scale) indicates that this objective was met.

Although both sides of the contrast included no physical behavior, relative to trials in which smoke was not available, voluntary abstinence recruited activity in a network of regions predominantly within the prefrontal cortex. In characterizing their influential integrative theory of prefrontal cortical functioning, Miller and Cohen (2001, 171) write: "We assume that the PFC serves a specific function in cognitive control: the active maintenance of patterns of activity that represent goals and the means to achieve them. They provide bias signals throughout much of the rest of the brain, affecting not only visual processes but also other sensory modalities, as well as systems responsible for response execution, memory retrieval, emotional evaluation, etc." At a very general level, the activation of lateral portions of the prefrontal cortex may have served the top-down biasing of the action plan to *not smoke*. The network of regions "deactivated" (i.e., those regions that showed relatively diminished activity during the Voluntary Abstinence trials) in the primary contrast (including the ventromedial prefrontal cortex and posterior cingulated cortex) are consistent with the "resting network"/"default network" identified during fMRI (i.e., the set of brain regions observed to consistently deactivate during active task states; Buckner and Vincent 2007). This provides further indication that not smoking when smoke was available was associated with more cognitive processing than was not smoking when cigarette smoke was not available.

Although current knowledge of the functional specificity of the aforementioned brain regions is insufficient to permit conclusive "reverse inferences" from region to underlying function, we can offer some further speculation. The observed network is consistent with the functional characterization of voluntary abstinence as including top-down maintenance of task goals in working memory (prominently linked to the dorsolateral prefrontal cortex; Levy and Goldman-Rakic 2000), monitoring of conflict or errors with respect to behavior and task goals (the anterior cingulate cortex; van Veen et al. 2001), and the cancellation of initiated prepotent behaviors (the right ventrolateral prefrontal cortex; (Aron, Robbins, and Poldrack 2004). Robust recruitment in supplementary motor areas is also intriguing, particularly in light of the fact that the contrast included only those trials in which the participant did not smoke. It is possible that recruitment in these areas reflects motor ideation (behavior that was planned but not executed). The high similarity between the identified network of regions and activation reported during inhibitory control tasks like the Stroop (e.g., Bush et al. 1999) provides some support for the suggestion that inhibitory control tasks tap functions that are relevant to voluntary control of drug taking.

Differential Craving as a Potential Confound

There is an experimental confound related to craving in the present study that warrants discussion. The primary contrast subtracted fMRI signal while smoke was not available from those blocks in which participants voluntarily abstained from smoking. Our goal was to isolate activity recruited by self-control efforts of the participant. However, the two above conditions may have included different levels of craving. If, for example, most self-control trials during which there was strong craving were dropped from this contrast because the participants smoked, then, *all else being equal*, the average craving during Voluntary Abstinence trials would have been lower than that of Smoke Unavailable trials. Alternatively, the availability of cigarette smoke on Self-Control trials may have led to stronger craving on Voluntary Abstinence trials relative to Smoke Unavailable trials; it has, for example, been repeatedly observed that the expectation of imminent smoking increases craving (Carter and Tiffany 2001; Dols et al. 2000, 2002; Juliano and Brandon 1998). If craving differed across conditions, then significant differences in neural recruitment may have reflected differences in craving rather than self-control efforts. We have taken steps to disambiguate these factors in an ongoing larger study using a similar methodology.

Taking Stock: What Needs to Be Done

In our view, the present study demonstrated the feasibility of measuring brain function during a "self-control challenge" in cigarette smokers. However, we did not demonstrate that the brain activity we observed was associated with success in the challenge, much less that it was *causally relevant* to success. There is nothing in the data that were collected that, for example, indicates that higher activation within the prefrontal cortex during Smoke Available trials was associated with a lower rate of smoking. Ongoing research is directed at this question. Assuming such an association is present, of course, still does not establish that observed brain activity is a relevant determinant of the behavior. In order to establish causal influence, it will be necessary to show that the behavior is disrupted by alteration of function in the candidate brain regions. One exciting possibility along these lines is to use repetitive transcranial magnetic stimulation (rTMS) to temporarily "knock out" a targeted brain region. This is feasible for regions on or very near the surface of the cortex. With respect to the brain regions identified in our analysis, certainly the dorsolateral prefrontal region would be a reasonable target for rTMS. It would be interesting to see if voluntary abstinence was reduced when activity in this region was temporarily disrupted.

Even if the above steps were successfully taken, it is important to note that we would not have established that the experimental paradigm described captures the sort of functioning most relevant to actual success in overcoming an addiction. Indeed, we have argued elsewhere (Ainslie 1975, 1992, 2001; Monterosso and Ainslie 2007) that the most critical factor in gaining control over an addiction is the conceived connection between individual temptation and expectation regarding future behavior (e.g., the idea that *this one* tempting cigarette is not really *just this one*, because there is something more significant in the balance; see chapters 5, 8, and 9 in this volume). The experimental situation that participants were placed in was not likely to engender the cycles of resolution and regret that characterize the real-world struggle of addiction. By instructing participants in such a way as to suggest that it was expected that they would smoke some of the time, participants were likely always in a psychological state that is incompatible with sustained cessation of addiction. For participants in the study, *not smoking* did not take on the status of a personal rule that needed to be followed without fail. That is to say, smoking was maintained as an option throughout. Successfully sustained cessation of an addiction may require that the behavior be seen as off-limits at least most of the time.

The robust prefrontal activity observed during voluntary relative to involuntary abstinence may well reflect the effortful control of attention away from smoking ideation (the imagery of the act that, left unchecked, leads smoothly to its initiation). It has been argued that the essence of willpower involves the skillful direction of attention. Philosopher Michael Bratman (1999) considers the mechanism of willpower to be an avoidance of reconsidering one's resolutions, and this idea dates back to at least William James: "The effort by which [a drunkard] succeeds in keeping the right name unwaveringly present to his mind proves to be his saving moral act" (James 1890, 565). But as we have recently argued elsewhere (Monterosso and Ainslie in press) the control of attention is not itself the essence of willpower, and it probably cannot provide a basis for sustained cessation of drug use because it is not sufficiently reliable over long time periods. Nevertheless, such control may well play a supporting role, increasing the chances of successfully resisting specific challenging temptations when, for whatever reason, resolve is vulnerable. We believe that the reported study represents an initial step toward understanding the dynamics of this control, and that future research efforts in this area can profit from looking at the relationship between brain function and actual behavior during attempts at smoking cessation.

Acknowledgments

This research was supported by the National Institute on Drug Abuse (J.M. [R01 DA021754]). The authors thank Xochitl Cordova for technical support in conducting this research.

Notes

1. First, we performed a rapid localization study in the sagittal plane using gradient echo methods (TR/TE 68/7.5 ms, matrix 256×128, flip angle $30°$, FOV 26 cm, 5-mm thickness and gap, scan time 35.6 s) (Frahm, Merboldt, and Hanicke 1993). Based on this localizer, we then used an EPI-based shimming procedure (Reese, Davis, and Weisskoff 1995) to establish a typical r.m.s. field uniformity of <15 Hz (<0.12 ppm) over the entire head. Next, two functional runs of the Self-

Control Challenge were acquired using standard gradient-echo EPI scanning (TR = 2000 ms, TE = 45 ms). Data were acquired with 3.125 mm² pixels within plane, and with slice thickness of 4 mm with 1 mm skip, acquiring 26 slices. After completion of the test runs, we collected a scan series of high-resolution EPI images (Cohen and Weisskoff 1991) in the same planes (TR 6s, TE 54 ms, 128 × 128 matrix, 20-cm FOV, 4 NEX, scan time 24 s). These T2-weighted images have the same bandwidth and, therefore, the same shape distortions (Cohen and Weisskoff 1991) as the functional data and as such are valuable in providing accurate image registration and localization.

2. Each BOLD time series was motion-corrected using MCFLIRT, part of FSL (FMRIB Software Library) (Smith et al. 2004). The data sets were smoothed with a nonlinear algorithm designed to preserve image structure by only smoothing over voxels classified as the same tissue type (5-mm kernel) (Smith and Brady 1997). Each data set was subjected to a multiple-regression analysis, using a prewhitening technique (Woolrich et al. 2001) to account for the intrinsic temporal autocorrelation of BOLD imaging (Zarahn, Aguirre, and D'Esposito 1997). Z scores and parameter estimates were computed for the comparison of the time course of each intracranial voxel to the HRF-smoothed stimulus waveform using FEAT, part of FSL. Functional data from each run were normalized first to the matched bandwidth high-resolution T2 scan, and then to an FSL standard space template in MNI space.

References

Ainslie, G. (1975). Specious reward: A behavioral theory of impulsiveness and impulse control. *Psychological Bulletin* 82: 463–496.

Ainslie, G. (1992). *Picoeconomics: The Strategic Interaction of Successive Motivational States within the Person.* New York: Cambridge University Press.

Ainslie, G. (2001). *Breakdown of Will.* Cambridge: Cambridge University Press.

Aron, A. R., Fletcher, P. C., Bullmore, E. T., Sahakian, B. J., and Robbins, T. W. (2003). Stop-signal inhibition disrupted by damage to the right inferior frontal gyrus in humans. *Nature Neuroscience* 6: 115–116.

Aron, A. R., Robbins, T. W., and Poldrack, R. A. (2004). Inhibition and the right inferior frontal cortex. *Trends in Cognitive Science* 8 (4): 170–177.

Avila, C., Cuenca, I., Felix, V., Parcet, M. A., and Miranda, A. (2004). Measuring impulsivity in school-aged boys and examining its relationship with ADHD and ODD ratings. *Journal of Abnormal Child Psychology* 32 (3): 295–304.

Barkley, R. A. (1997). *ADHD and the Nature of Self-Control.* London: Guilford Press.

Bartzokis, G., Lu, P. H., Beckson, M., Rapoport, R., Grant, S., Wiseman, E. J., et al. (2000). Abstinence from cocaine reduces high-risk responses on a gambling task [letter]. *Neuropsychopharmacology* 22 (1): 102–103.

Bechara, A. (2001). Neurobiology of decision-making: risk and reward. *Seminars in Clinical Neuropsychiatry* 6 (3): 205–216.

Bechara, A., and Damasio, H. (2002). Decision-making and addiction (part I): Impaired activation of somatic states in substance dependent individuals when pondering decisions with negative future consequences. *Neuropsychologia* 40 (10): 1675–1689.

Bechara, A., Dolan, S., and Hindes, A. (2002). Decision-making and addiction (part II): Myopia for the future or hypersensitivity to reward? *Neuropsychologia* 40 (10): 1690–1705.

Bickel, W. K., Odum, A. L., and Madden, G. J. (1999). Impulsivity and cigarette smoking: Delay discounting in current, never, and ex-smokers. *Psychopharmacology* 146 (4): 447–454.

Bolla, K. I., Eldreth, D. A., London, E. D., Kiehl, K. A., Mouratidis, M., Contoreggi, C., et al. (2003). Orbitofrontal cortex dysfunction in abstinent cocaine abusers performing a decision-making task. *Neuroimage* 19 (3): 1085–1094.

Bolla, K. I., Eldreth, D. A., Matochik, J. A., and Cadet, J. L. (2005). Neural substrates of faulty decision-making in abstinent marijuana users. *Neuroimage* 26 (2): 480–492.

Bratman, M. E. (1999). *Faces of Intention: Selected Essays on Intention and Agency.* Cambridge: Cambridge University Press.

Brody, A. L., Mandelkern, M. A., Olmstead, R. E., Jou, J., Tiongson, E., Allen, V., Scheibal, D., London, E. D., Monterosso, J. R., Tiffany, S. T., Korb, A., Gan, J. J., Cohen, M. S. (2007). Neural substrates of resisting craving during cigarette cue exposure. *Biological Psychiatry* 62: 642–651.

Buckner, R., and Vincent, J. (2007). Unrest at rest: The importance of default activity and spontaneous network correlations. *Neuroimage* 37: 1091–1096.

Bush, G., Frazier, J. A., Rauch, S. L., Seidman, L. J., Whalen, P. J., Jenike, M. A., et al. (1999). Anterior cingulate cortex dysfunction in attention-deficit/hyperactivity disorder revealed by fMRI and the Counting Stroop. *Biological Psychiatry* 45 (12): 1542–1552.

Cairns, J., and van der Pol, M. (2000). Valuing future private and social benefits: The discounted utility model versus hyperbolic discounting models. *Journal of Economic Psychology* 21 (2): 191–205.

Carter, B. L., and Tiffany, S. T. (1999). Meta-analysis of cue-reactivity in addiction research. *Addiction* 94 (3): 327–340.

Carter, B. L., and Tiffany, S. T. (2001). The cue-availability paradigm: The effects of cigarette availability on cue reactivity in smokers. *Experimental and Clinical Psychopharmacology* 9 (2): 183–190.

Childress, A., Wang, J., Listerud , J., Sciortino, N., Derenick, D., Fornash, A., et al. (2003). Which brain regions are activated when cocaine patients are activated when cocaine patients attempt to inhibit ("STOP!") cue-induced craving? Paper presented at the Society of Neuroscience, Washington, D.C.

Childress, A., Wang, Z., Wang, J., Listerud, J., Sciortino, N., Detre, J., et al. (2004). Do the brain substrates differ for "attempted" vs. "successful" inhibition of cue-induced craving? Paper presented at the College on Problems of Drug Dependence, San Juan.

Childress, A. R., Mozley, P. D., McElgin, W., Fitzgerald, J., Reivich, M., and O'Brien, C. P. (1999). Limbic activation during cue-induced cocaine craving. *American Journal of Psychiatry* 156 (1): 11–18.

Coffey, S. F., Gudleski, G. D., Saladin, M. E., and Brady, K. T. (2003). Impulsivity and rapid discounting of delayed hypothetical rewards in cocaine-dependent individuals. *Experimental and Clinical Psychopharmacology* 11 (1): 18–25.

Cohen, M. S., and Weisskoff, R. M. (1991). Ultra-fast imaging. *Magnetic Resonance Imaging* 9 (1): 1–37.

Dols, M., van den Hout, M., Kindt, M., and Willems, B. (2002). The urge to smoke depends on the expectation of smoking. *Addiction* 97 (1): 87–93.

Dols, M., Willems, B., van den Hout, M., and Bittoun, R. (2000). Smokers can learn to influence their urge to smoke. *Addictive Behavior* 25 (1): 103–108.

Ersche, K. D., Fletcher, P. C., Lewis, S. J., Clark, L., Stocks-Gee, G., London, M., et al. (2005). Abnormal frontal activations related to decision making in current and former amphetamine- and opiate-dependent individuals. *Psychopharmacology (Berlin)* 188 (3): 364–373.

Fillmore, M. T. (2003). Drug abuse as a problem of impaired control: Current approaches and findings. *Behavioral and Cognitive Neuroscience Review* 2: 179–197.

Fillmore, M. T., and Rush, C. R. (2002). Impaired inhibitory control of behavior in chronic cocaine users. *Drug and Alcohol Dependence* 66 (3): 265–273.

Fishbein, D. (2000). Neuropsychological function, drug abuse, and violence: A conceptual framework. *Criminal Justice and Behavior* 27 (2): 139–159.

Fishbein, D., Eldreth, D., Hyde, C., Matochik, J., London, E. D., Contoreggi, C., et al. (2005). Risky decision making and the anterior cingulate cortex in abstinent drug abusers and nonusers. *Cognitive Brain Research* 23: 119–136.

Frahm, J., Merboldt, K.-D., and Hanicke, W. (1993). Functional MRI of human brain activation at high spatial resolution. *Magnetic Resonance in Medicine* 29 (1): 139–144.

Friedman, N. P., and Miyake, A. (2004). The relations among inhibition and interference control functions: a latent-variable analysis. *Journal of Experimental Psychology: General* 133 (1): 101–135.

Fuchs, V. R. (1982). Time preference and health: An exploratory study. In V. R. Fuchs, ed., *Economic Aspects of Health*, 93–120. Chicago: University of Chicago Press.

Garavan, H., Ross, T. J., Murphy, K., Roche, R. A., and Stein, E. A. (2002). Dissociable executive functions in the dynamic control of behavior: inhibition, error detection, and correction. *Neuroimage* 17 (4): 1820–1829.

Goldstein, R. Z., and Volkow, N. D. (2002). Drug addiction and its underlying neurobiological basis: Neuroimaging evidence for the involvement of the frontal cortex. *American Journal of Psychiatry* 159 (10): 1642–1652.

Grant, S. (2004). Let's not be impulsive: Comments on Lubman et al. (2004). *Addiction* 99 (12): 1504–1505; discussion 1506–1507.

Grant, S., Contoreggi, C., and London, E. D. (2000). Drug abusers show impaired performance in a laboratory test of decision making. *Neuropsychologia* 38 (8): 1180–1187.

Grant, S., London, E. D., Newlin, D. B., Villemagne, V. L., Liu, X., Contoreggi, C., et al. (1996). Activation of memory circuits during cue-elicited cocaine craving. *Proceedings of the National Academy of Sciences of the USA* 93 (21): 12040–12045.

Hester, R., and Garavan, H. (2004). Executive dysfunction in cocaine addiction: Evidence for discordant frontal, cingulate, and cerebellar activity. *Journal of Neuroscience* 24 (49): 11017–11022.

Heyman, G. M., and Dunn, B. (2002). Decision biases and persistent illicit drug use: An experimental study of distributed choice and addiction. *Drug and Alcohol Dependence* 67 (2): 193–203.

James, W. (1890). *The Principles of Psychology* (vol. 2). New York: Henry Holt.

Jelinek, E. M. (1960). *The Disease Concept of Alcoholism.* New Haven: Hill House Press.

Jentsch, J. D., and Taylor, J. R. (1999). Impulsivity resulting from frontostriatal dysfunction in drug abuse: Implications for the control of behavior by reward-related stimuli. *Psychopharmacology (Berlin)* 146 (4): 373–390.

Juliano, L. M., and Brandon, T. H. (1998). Reactivity to instructed smoking availability and environmental cues: Evidence with urge and reaction time. *Experimental and Clinical Psychopharmacology* 6 (1): 45–53.

Kaufman, J. N., Ross, T. J., Stein, E. A., and Garavan, H. (2003). Cingulate hypoactivity in cocaine users during a GO-NOGO task as revealed by event-related functional magnetic resonance imaging. *Journal of Neuroscience* 23 (21): 7839–7843.

Kirby, K. N., and Petry, N. M. (2004). Heroin and cocaine abusers have higher discount rates for delayed rewards than alcoholics or non-drug-using controls. *Addiction* 99 (4): 461–471.

Kirby, K. N., Petry, N. M., and Bickel, W. K. (1999). Heroin addicts have higher discount rates for delayed rewards than non-drug-using controls. *Journal of Experimental Psychology: General* 128 (1): 78–87.

Koob, G. F. (1996). Hedonic valence, dopamine, and motivation. *Molecular Psychiatry* 1 (3): 186–189.

Levy, R., and Goldman-Rakic, P. S. (2000). Segregation of working memory functions within the dorsolateral prefrontal cortex. *Experimental Brain Research* 133 (1): 23–32.

Logan, F. A. (1993). Animal learning and motivation and addictive drugs. *Psychological Reports* 73 (1): 291–306.

London, E. D., Ernst, M., Grant, S., Bonson, K., and Weinstein, A. (2000). Orbitofrontal cortex and human drug abuse: Functional imaging. *Cerebral Cortex* 10 (3): 334–342.

Madden, G. J., Petry, N. M., Badger, G. J., and Bickel, W. K. (1997). Impulsive and self-control choices in opioid-dependent patients and non-drug-using control participants: Drug and monetary rewards. *Experimental and Clinical Psychopharmacology* 5 (3): 256–262.

Mahone, E. M., Cirino, P. T., Cutting, L. E., Cerrone, P. M., Hagelthorn, K. M., Hiemenz, J. R., et al. (2002). Validity of the behavior rating inventory of executive function in children with ADHD and/or Tourette syndrome. *Archives of Clinical Neuropsychology* 7 (7): 643–662.

Mazas, C. A., Finn, P. R., and Steinmetz, J. E. (2000). Decision-making biases, antisocial personality, and early-onset alcoholism. *Alcoholism: Clinical and Experimental Research* 24 (7): 1036–1040.

McClure, S. M., Berns, G. S., and Montague, P. R. (2003). Temporal prediction errors in a passive learning task activate human striatum. *Neuron* 38 (2): 339–346.

Miller, E., and Cohen, J. (2001). An integrative theory of prefrontal cortex function. *Annual Review of Neuroscience* 24: 167–202.

Mitchell, S. (1999). Measures of impulsivity in cigarette smokers and non-smokers. *Psychopharmacology* 146: 455–464.

Moeller, F. G., and Dougherty, D. M. (2002). Impulsivity and substance abuse: What is the connection? *Addictive Disorders and Their Treatment* 1: 3–10.

Monterosso, J., and Ainslie, G. (2007). The behavioral economics of will in recovery from addiction. *Drug and Alcohol Dependence* 90 (Suppl. 1): S100–111.

Monterosso, J., and Ainslie, G. (in press). The picoeconomic approach to addictions: Analyzing the conflict of successive motivational states. *Addiction Research and Theory*.

Monterosso, J., Aron, A. R., Cordova, X., Xu, J., and London, E. D. (2005). Deficits in response inhibition associated with chronic methamphetamine abuse. *Drug and Alcohol Dependence* 79 (2): 273–277.

Monterosso, J., Ehrman, R., Napier, K. L., O'Brien, C. P., and Childress, A. R. (2001). Three decision-making tasks in cocaine-dependent patients: Do they measure the same construct? *Addiction* 96 (12): 1825–1837.

Paulus, M. P., Hozack, N., Frank, L., Brown, G. G., and Schuckit, M. A. (2003). Decision making by methamphetamine-dependent subjects is associated with error-rate-independent decrease in prefrontal and parietal activation. *Biological Psychiatry* 53 (1): 65–74.

Paulus, M. P., Hozack, N. E., Zauscher, B. E., Frank, L., Brown, G. G., Braff, D. L., et al. (2002). Behavioral and functional neuroimaging evidence for prefrontal dysfunction in methamphetamine-dependent subjects. *Neuropsychopharmacology* 26 (1): 53–63.

Paulus, M. P., Tapert, S. F., and Schuckit, M. A. (2005). Neural activation patterns of methamphetamine-dependent subjects during decision making predict relapse. *Archives of General Psychiatry* 62 (7): 761–768.

Perret, E. (1974). The left frontal lobe of man and the suppression of habitual responses in verbal categorical behavior. *Neuropsychologia* 12: 323–330.

Peterson, B. S., Skudlarski, P., Gatenby, J. C., Zhang, H., Anderson, A. W., and Gore, J. C. (1999). An fMRI study of Stroop word-color interference: Evidence for cingulate subregions subserving multiple distributed attentional systems. *Biological Psychiatry* 45 (10): 1237–1258.

Petry, N. M. (2003). Discounting of money, health, and freedom in substance abusers and controls. *Drug and Alcohol Dependence* 71 (2): 133–141.

Pontieri, F. E., Tanda, G., Orzi, F., and Di Chiara, G. (1996). Effects of nicotine on the nucleus accumbens and similarity to those of addictive drugs. *Nature* 382 (6588): 255–257.

Reese, T., Davis, T., and Weisskoff, R. (1995). Automated shimming at 1.5 T using echo-planar image frequency maps. *Journal of Magnetic Resonance Imaging* 5: 739–745.

Reynolds, B., Richards, J. B., Horn, K., and Karraker, K. (2004). Delay discounting and probability discounting as related to cigarette smoking status in adults. *Behavioral Processes* 65 (1): 35–42.

Rogers, R. D., Everitt, B. J., Baldacchino, A., Blackshaw, A. J., Swainson, R., Wynne, K., et al. (1999). Dissociable deficits in the decision-making cognition of chronic amphetamine abusers, opiate abusers, patients with focal damage to prefrontal cortex, and tryptophan-depleted normal volunteers: Evidence for monoaminergic mechanisms. *Neuropsychopharmacology* 20 (4): 322–339.

Rogers, R. D., and Robbins, T. W. (2001). Investigating the neurocognitive deficits associated with chronic drug misuse. *Current Opinion in Neurobiology* 11 (2): 250–257.

Ross, D. (2005). *Economic Theory and Cognitive Science*, vol. 1: *Microexplanation*. Cambridge, MA: MIT Press.

Rubia, K., Lee, F., Cleare, A. J., Tunstall, N., Fu, C. H., Brammer, M., et al. (2005). Tryptophan depletion reduces right inferior prefrontal activation during response inhibition in fast, event-related fMRI. *Psychopharmacology (Berlin)* 179 (4): 791–803.

Salo, R., Nordahl, T. E., Moore, C., Waters, C., Natsuaki, Y., Galloway, G. P., et al. (2005). A dissociation in attentional control: Evidence from methamphetamine dependence. *Biological Psychiatry* 57 (3): 310–313.

Schultz, W. (1997). Dopamine neurons and their role in reward mechanisms. *Current Opinions in Neurobiology* 7 (2): 191–197.

Shulman, G. (1989). Experience with the cocaine trigger inventory. *Advances in Alcohol and Substance Abuse* 8 (2): 71–85.

Smith, S., and Brady, J. (1997). SUSAN—a new approach to low level image processing. *International Journal of Computer Vision* 23: 45–78.

Smith, S. M., Jenkinson, M., Woolrich, M. W., Beckmann, C. F., Behrens, T. E. J., Johansen-Berg, H., Bannister, P. R., De Luca, M., Drobnjak, I., Flitney, D. E., et al. (2004). Advances in functional and structural MR image analysis and implementation as FSL. *Neuroimage* 23: 208–219.

Tiffany, S. T. (1999). Cognitive concepts of craving. *Alcohol Research and Health* 23 (3): 215–224.

Tiffany, S. T., Singleton, E., Haertzen, C. A., and Henningfield, J. E. (1993). The development of a cocaine craving questionnaire. *Drug and Alcohol Dependence* 34 (1): 19–28.

van Veen, V., Cohen, J. D., Botvinick, M. M., Stenger, V. A., and Carter, C. S. (2001). Anterior cingulate cortex, conflict monitoring, and levels of processing. *Neuroimage* 14 (6): 1302–1308.

Vuchinich, R. E., and Simpson, C. A. (1998). Hyperbolic temporal discounting in social drinkers and problem drinkers. *Experimental and Clinical Psychopharmacology* 6 (3): 292–305.

Weiss, R., Griffin, M., Mazurick, C., Berkman, B., Gastfriend, D., Frank, A., et al. (2003). The relationship between cocaine craving, psychosocial treatment, and subsequent cocaine use. *American Journal of Psychiatry* 160 (7): 1320–1325.

Wise, R. A., and Rompre, P. P. (1989). Brain dopamine and reward. *Annual Review of Psychology* 40: 191–225.

Woolrich, M., Ripley, B., Brady, M., and Smith, S. (2001). Temporal autocorrelation in univariate linear modeling of FMRI data. *Neuroimage* 14: 1370–1386.

Zarahn, E., Aguirre, G., and D'Esposito, M. (1997). Empirical analyses of BOLD fMRI statistics. I. Spatially unsmoothed data collected under null-hypothesis conditions. *Neuroimage* 5: 179–197.

11 Anticipatory Processing as a Transdisciplinary Bridge in Addiction

Mark S. Goldman, Jack Darkes, Richard R. Reich, and Karen O. Brandon

When stripped of characteristics that cannot be seen but instead must be inferred (e.g., "compulsivity," "psychological dependence"), addiction comes down to the repetition of a behavior accompanied by a desire to refrain from that behavior, an apparent lack of control over the behavior, and expressions by the behaving party of "feeling bad" (dysphoric) when they cannot engage in the behavior (see, e.g., Koob and Le Moal 2008). Instead of reacting skeptically, we often judge such accounts credible because the observed behavior seems both excessive (to us) and to result in serious adverse consequences—consequences that (seemingly) no one would choose to endure if he or she could manifest control. In the classic diagnostic scheme (e.g., DSM IV) these characteristics (loss of control, continued use despite adverse consequences, reports of dysphoria upon cessation) are then used to infer a category; one is either addicted or not addicted (although more or less severe addiction is often discussed). Leaving aside the many discussions regarding the role of discrete assignment and dimensional criteria in diagnosis (see Helzer, van den Brink, and Guth 2006; Muthen 2006), a predominance of evidence from a range of domains related to the etiology of "addiction" suggests a more continuous reality, which encompasses a wide range of normal processes that together can produce "abnormal" behavior; individuals vary across multiple dimensions (endophenotypes, intermediate phenotypes, environmental contexts) that ultimately can result in wide variations in the course and severity of involvement with the behavior in question. Among these dimensions are: genetically based individual differences in sensitivity, reactivity, and metabolism (when substances are involved) (for review, see MacKillop, McGeary, and Ray this volume); individual differences in neurobiologically based learning and motivational pathways; individualized neuropsychological processes of self-regulation; varying family/social/peer influences; varying experiences and environmental exposures; and varying cultural norms. These dimensions are of course not independent; each may interact with the others, or even reflect the same overall processes addressed at different levels of explanation.

Few, if any, scientists can acquire deep expertise in, and remain abreast of, developments across all these dimensions. Instead, researchers tend to focus on components that have been parsed horizontally into separate disciplines or vertically into different levels of explanation. This compartmentalized conceptual structure has in recent years facilitated impressive scientific advances in genetics, neuroscience, cognitive science, and affective/motivational science that can be applied to the understanding of "addiction," as well as related problematic behaviors that fall short of full addiction.

Compartmentalization also may impede progress, however. It can isolate researchers and promote competition for primacy of explanation (and often funding and journal space). Contrary to the cliché, nature has no such joints; advances in any area must ultimately be integrated into and evaluated in light of the whole; full understanding cannot be achieved in the absence of a transdisciplinary approach aimed at identifying common processes and properties. A truly transdisciplinary approach (as opposed to just applying approaches and findings from different domains in a kind of "parallel play") calls for a conceptual framework that can meld findings across disciplines and levels of explanation.

Expectancy as Fundamental Process of Adaptation

This chapter describes and updates such a framework for integrating disparate domains while maintaining respect for local explanations. It is not our intent to diminish domain-specific theory and research, but to offer a synthetic framework in the hope of facilitating crosstalk and encouraging interweaving of emerging findings. The synthesis offered is based on the concept of expectancy, which was applied originally to general learning theory by Tolman (1932). More recently, this concept was applied in the alcohol field to explain alcohol placebo effects (manifestation of alcohol effects in the absence of consumption; e.g., Marlatt, Demming, and Reid 1973), and to predict consumption (patterns and levels of use based on anticipated outcomes of consumption; e.g., Brown, Goldman, and Inn 1980).

Recent research suggests, however, that the expectancy concept, which emphasizes the role of anticipation, is more fundamental to behavior than these specific applications to substance use might indicate; it may represent a fundamental adaptive quality involved in behavior across several domains and at several levels of explanation. Our intent, then, is to review findings regarding the basic nature of anticipatory systems, and then to integrate those notions into our understanding of addiction.

The concept of anticipatory processing has emerged as an explanatory factor independently in increasingly diverse scientific venues, including basic behavioral processes such as operant (Dragoi and Staddon 1999) and classical conditioning (Kirsch et al. 2004; Van Hamme and Wasserman 1994), comparative judgment (Heekeren et al. 2004; Ritov 2000), models of memory (Bower 2000), the neurobiology of animal and human reward and reinforcement (Breiter et al. 2001; Kupfermann, Kandel, and Iversen 2000; McClure, Laibson, and Loewenstein 2004; Schultz 2004; Schultz, Dayan, and Montague 1997), perception of motion (Kerzel 2005), development of language (Colunga and Smith 2005), time perception (Correa, Lupiáñez, and Tudela 2005), brain electrophysiology (ERP; Donchin and Coles 1988), visual orienting behavior in early infancy (Haith, Hazan, and Goodman 1988), and the learning of complex motor skills (e.g., Wulf and Prinz 2001), among others. Expectancy has also been related to more complex processes such as expert sport performance (e.g., Gray, Beilock, and Carr 2007) and social functioning, including the neurobiology of interpersonal trust (King-Casas, Tomlin, and Anen 2005); Gray, Beilock and Carr (2007, 669) note that "the governing nodes of motor control hierarchies are the intended environmental changes that actions should create," suggesting that a focus on expected outcomes facilitates athletic expertise, and Kilner et al. (2004, 1299) conclude that "mere knowledge of an upcoming movement [in another person] is sufficient to excite one's own motor system, enabling people to anticipate, rather than react to, other's actions." Social functioning involves, of course, more than just the anticipation of movements; for instance, Baron-Cohen, Knickmeyer, and Belmonte (2005, 819) describe empathy as "the capacity to predict and to respond to the behavior of agents (usually people) by inferring their mental states and responding to these with an appropriate emotion." Even the psychological appreciation of music has been explained via expectation (Huron 2006).

Expectancy also appears to function at even more basic levels; for instance, "Homeostatic regulation is often anticipatory" (Kupfermann, Kandel, and Iversen 2000, 1007). This anticipation of biological demands need not elicit only acute adjustments, but may foreshadow longer-term adaptation as well. Adjustment of the homeostatic set point to anticipate repeated stressors (i.e., allostasis) has been implicated in alcohol and drug addiction (Koob and Le Moal 2008) and may be considered a fundamental version of expectancy.

Expectancy theory also has informed the clinical domain (see Kirsch 1999). In that area, it has been related to mood dysfunction, fear, pain reduction, sexual dysfunction, asthma, drug abuse, alcohol abuse and alcoholism, smoking, placebo (Price, Finniss, and Benedetti 2008; Wager 2005; Wager, Rilling, and Smith 2004; Petrovic et al. 2005) and nocebo effects (psychologically induced illness or even death), psychotherapy, hypnosis, and therapeutic effects of psychotropic (Kirsch and Scoboria 2001), and analgesic medications (Waber et al. 2008). Placebo effects (the experience of anticipated relief) may even contribute significantly to what are purportedly well-established drug effects; in a meta-analysis of drug trial data, Kirsch et al. (2008) found that drug versus placebo differences only emerged at the most severe levels of depression and even then drug superiority to placebo was relatively small. In addition, experienced placebo analgesia has been observed to increase as a function of the expected value of the placebo treatment; those informed that a treatment under investigation would be more expensive reported less pain (Waber et al. 2008). Conditioned (placebo) analgesia as a function of pretreatment with morphine has also been demonstrated; training doses of morphine lead to reduced pain in the presence of training cues during competition (Benedetti, Pollo, and Colloca 2007).

Given this widespread application of expectancy, it should be clear that the concept we describe here is attached neither to a single domain of science nor any specific theorist. In fact, naming the concept itself *expectancy* is not critical, nor are any particularized theoretical approaches to expectancy that have been developed in the specialized fields in which it has been used. We have adopted the word "expectancy" because of its common use within our domain of research and because we wish to relate this domain (centered on overt human cognitive/behavioral output) to the larger research enterprise that addresses the same anticipatory processes. Referring to the processes we describe, some investigators have used the word "anticipation," others "prediction," and still others "preparation." For example, consider Calvin and Bickerton (2000, 58): "you won't go far wrong if you think of your brain as always preparing for action, trying to guess what happens next, and gathering sensory information in aid of tentative plans for action."

In its most expansive sense, expectancy may even be regarded as the functional outcome of epigenesis, an increasingly popular and ever-evolving term in this age of genomics. As described by Gottesman and Hanson (2005) the concept originated in embryology in reference to the emergence of complex organisms from undifferentiated cells, but has come to be understood by molecular biologists as encompassing the mechanisms by which gene expression is influenced to alter cell structure and function and then transferred to future cells in that cell line (Jablonka and Lamb 2002). Even broader definitions refer to gene expression profiles that include behavioral outcomes (Gottesman, Shields, and Hanson 1982). Although it is not our purpose to review the term in these pages, Gottesman and Hanson (2005, 267) relate epigenetics to "the complexities of how multiple genetic factors and multiple environmental factors become integrated over time through dynamic, often nonlinear, sometimes nonreversible, processes to produce behaviorally relevant endophenotypes and phenotypes."

To link this notion with expectancy requires only noting that such behavioral relevance rests on the integration of genetic and environmental factors in order to facilitate anticipation of upcoming circumstances. Put another way, this process may be construed as the transfer, via multilevel biological processes, of experience with external circumstances into biological tissue (and neurophysiological processes sustained by this tissue) that represents those experiences, so as to prepare the organism for future encounters with similar circumstances. In the current context, such processes can easily be construed as the substrate for "decision making" in a broad sense; such a decision-making perspective should not be considered in conflict with the arguments made in this chapter. The multilevel biological processes of interest range from those occurring within the nuclei of cells, to those that occur within single cells, to those complex processes that regulate the function of proximal groups of cells, and ultimately to distributed cell groupings that constitute brain "systems" (Breiter and Gasic 2004). Some of these processes are discussed later.

It is our belief that expectancy/anticipatory processes can serve as a means of creating a transdisciplinary framework because of their consistency with epistemological concepts that have emerged as conceptual bridges across scientific domains (see Goldman 2002). The first of these concepts is consilience; E. O. Wilson (1998, 8), quoting Whewell (1840/1967), explained that consilience "takes place when an Induction, obtained from one class of facts, coincides with an Induction, obtained from a different class." Wilson's argument that consilient concepts are fundamentally advantaged in the search for scientific explanation stems from his belief in the underlying unity of knowledge. The spontaneous emergence of expectancy (anticipatory processes) across so many domains exemplifies the prototype of a consilient concept with a natural capacity to amalgamate disparate findings. The expectancy concept is also consistent with three other cross-cutting concepts in biological science: conservation (the repeated observation of similar function and structure), contingency (describing both the responses of biological elements [e.g., individual cells] and intact organisms to varying external conditions), and emergence (phenomena that arise from complex combinations and interactions [e.g., of genes and neurons]). Expectancy may be seen as a function that is conserved across domains and levels of explanation, underpins contingent responding, and explains the emergence of complex behavior from the operation of simpler processes.

The essence of the expectancy concept is captured by reference to six interconnected and defining aspects: (a) anticipation/prediction, (b) comparison of stored information patterns with incoming stimulus arrays to influence outputs, (c) constrained perception of incoming stimuli by stored information patterns; (d) representation of anticipatory templates via changes in the physical neural substrate, (e) the equivalence of expectancy/anticipation and "memory," and (f) inseparability of memory, cognition, and affect/emotion. In earlier papers (Goldman 1999, 2002; Goldman, Reich, and Darkes 2006), we reviewed literature that supported these aspects of expectancy function. The present chapter will selectively update this material. It does not attempt to be comprehensive; the vastness of this literature has now grown well beyond the scope of any single paper. As has been noted previously, although we will refer to the notion of expectancy, in some instances, the research that underpins these ideas uses the term "expectancy"; in other cases, it may highlight only one or more of the above aspects, or use terms such as "anticipation," "prediction," or "preparation." What is key, however, is that whenever scientists find a mechanism for *reacting* to a circumstance or event, they must further look for mechanisms that *anticipate* the circumstance or event; complex functioning is built upon these anticipatory processes.

Aspects of Expectancy Operation

Anticipation/Prediction

Even theoretical physicists are struck by the fact that the "arrow of time" is unidirectional; it always moves forward. In this incessant march forward, no environment is static. Each is momentary, instantly changing into the next context, and that context into the subsequent one. Changes may not be uniform or universal; some elements may change as others do not, some may change at different rates, and some changes may be quite noticeable and others barely perceptible. Nonetheless, context shifts from moment to moment; ultimate survival (success) relies on organismic adjustments that move the organism in the proper direction, that proactively anticipate and prepare for the next shift, both biologically and behaviorally (domains that are, of course, not truly separable). This ubiquitous but often overlooked characteristic of nature has placed evolutionary pressure on organisms to anticipate (predict) and subsequently negotiate future circumstances, and nervous systems have evolved in response to that pressure. "Anticipating the future has a decided evolutionary advantage, and researchers have found many evolutionarily conserved mechanisms by which humans and animals learn to predict future events" (Brembs 2003, 218). In fact, brains themselves are best thought of, according to Dennett (1991, 177), as "in essence, just anticipatory machines."

Calvin and Bickerton (2000, 34) also point out the adaptive efficiency of basing future actions on past experience: "We, like most other creatures, are built to make generalizations on inadequate evidence at very short notice, because that works better, in terms of evolutionary fitness, than making 100% correct generalization after a long period of cogitation." The "common coding" (i.e., shared storage) of anticipated outcomes of actions with the motor programs that produce those actions (and outcomes) confers a distinct advantage (Wulf and Prinz 2001). Our perception of the moment and the experience of common visual illusions may even be a function of such anticipatory processes; Changizi et al. (2008, 495) suggested that "the visual system possesses mechanisms that attempt to compensate for neural delays while in ecologically typical forward motion" such that "it is reasonable to expect that the visual system will have been selected to have compensation mechanisms by which it is able to, via using the stimulus occurring at time t, generate a perception at time $t + 100$ msec that is probably representative of the scene as it is at time $t + 100$ msec. In short, we should expect visual systems have been selected to 'perceive the present,' rather than to perceive the recent past" (ibid., 460). In essence, to stay ahead of its own processing requirements and perceive the world in "real time," the system must predict the future. Fortunately, most missteps, such as visual illusions, due to this prediction or rapid approximation fall within tolerance limits for survival; lethal mistakes apparently remain below a critical threshold (from the perspective of species survival), or natural selection would favor a different working arrangement.

Anticipation, of course, is not unitary; a course cannot be determined and irrevocably set. As the next moment arrives, will the organism be best served by maintaining an ongoing behavioral sequence, or by changing behavioral output to accommodate altered contextual conditions? Beyond the next moment, to what time span should behavioral output be accommodated? Is responding keyed to anticipation of relatively immediate payoffs, or to longer-term but potentially higher-value rewards? Could a distortion in the neural systems that "make" these decisions, which balance anticipated probability, latency, and value of reinforcement, lie at the heart of risk for addiction?

As research addresses these questions, it becomes clearer that there are many anticipatory mechanisms, each operating on different time scales and with different functions (see the Brembs quote above). For example, while discounting functions address reward delay that might occur over a considerable time frame, components of brain event-related potentials (ERPs) reflect the adjustment of attention within a few hundred milliseconds to note change and accommodate unexpected events or shifts in context (Donchin and Coles 1988). And context and reward availability are not the only bases upon which anticipatory decisions are made; space and time can themselves serve as anticipatory cues. Targets appearing at unexpected locations elicit faster and/or more accurate responses and amplification of visual evoked potentials (Posner, Snyder, and Davidson 1980), and response times are shorter when the temporal expectancy for a target and the time interval that *actually* precedes its presentation coincide (Nobre 2001). Cuing also need not be explicit; expectancies can be based on information of which the observer is unaware. Attention may be allocated as a function of implicit knowledge of the context in which a stimulus appears (Johnson et al. 2007).

Recent research has revealed brain circuitry that is differentially responsive in anticipation of the smaller of two rewards (as opposed to simply responding to reward magnitude; Glimcher and Lau 2005; Minamimoto, Hori, and Kimura 2005), of shorter- and longer-term payoffs (McClure, Laibson, and Loewenstein 2004), and of discrepant probability of rewards (Tobler, Fiorillo, and Schultz 2005). Recasting the common understanding of dopaminergic pathways as the substrate for reward itself, Montague and Berns (2002) described this system's function as reward prediction, contending specifically that the level of dopamine pathway activity signals, in advance of consummatory behaviors, that rewards available in a particular context differ from rewards anticipated. Such a mechanism obviously would serve to adjust ongoing behavior toward the most beneficial expected outcomes. Such a model of dopamine activity links the literature on classical conditioning with the computational literature on machine learning (Cohen and Blum 2002).

Research with monkeys has shown that orbitofrontal neurons activate differentially in anticipation of the different phases of the reward sequence (Schultz et al. 2000). Three distinctive types and stages of activity were found: responses to reward-predicting instructions, activation in the period immediately preceding reward, and responses following reward. Schultz, Tremblay, and Hollerman (2000, 272) concluded that "The processing of reward expectations suggests an access to central representa-tions of rewards which may be used for the neuronal control of goal-directed behav-ior," in essence suggesting a mechanism for the role of common coding of outcome expectancy and motor programs facilitating those desired outcomes (Wulf and Prinz 2001).

The developing discipline of neuroeconomics (see Lee 2005; Lowenstein, Rick, and Cohen 2008), closely connected to the models described in other chapters in this book, has applied economic theories of utility and games to the operation of neurons, and has found that the output of neuronal circuits often corresponds to mathematical models of decision making and outcome prediction (Breiter et al. 2001; Cohen and Ranganath 2005; Glimcher and Rustichini 2004; Schultz 2004). That is, the neural machinery that computes discounting functions may be understood as the basis for generation of anticipatory behavior in circumstances that signal the applicability of the computation. Even interpersonal trust, a quintessential aspect of human social be-havior, is fundamentally anticipatory in nature, and can be modeled using economic exchange theory (King-Casas, Tomlin, and Anen 2005). Miller (2005, 36) notes that King-Casas et al.'s "results also suggest that trust isn't purely noble—it may stem from a cold calculation of expected rewards."

Comparison of Stored Information Patterns with Incoming Stimulus Arrays to Influence Outputs

The second key aspect of expectancy relates to its mode of operation. Grossberg (1995, 1) underscores this mode of operation and that it is built upon the nexus between be-havior and biology, noting that "Neural networks that match sensory input with learned expectations help explain how humans see, hear, learn and recognize informa-tion." However, all these operations cannot be supported by a single mechanism (Brembs 2003). Hence, expectancy is best understood as an emergent principle; that is, it is not a distinct function of a single system, but a functional approach to adapta-tion and survival that has emerged and been manifested over evolutionary time in multiple biological systems using different structures and processes. This principle, however, is not just an abstraction. We also may theorize a common functional sub-strate, sometimes using common underpinnings in the nervous system and sometimes with distinctive underpinnings that accomplish the same function.

Regardless of the specific mechanism in question, the common function seems based on the storage of information about previous circumstances, followed by comparison of the newly encountered circumstances with this stored information. Given sufficient overlap, behaviors are performed that were effective in these circumstances (in the orig-inal encounter, behavioral options may have developed through trial and error or algo-rithmic computation, i.e., deliberative thought). The stored information is not simply a static "photograph"; it incorporates the temporal course of the original circumstance, as well as a wide variety of other characteristics specific to that encounter (Leutgeb et al. 2005). It also generalizes by incorporating elements that vary from the original but fall within tolerance within newly encountered circumstances. When reactivated, it can unfold over time to represent the temporal parameter of the original experience. Of course, the more experiences one has with a particular circumstance, the more indelible this record might be (Martin and Gotts 2005) and the more likelihood that common coding of context, action, and outcome will result (Wulf and Prinz 2001). Such a process is demonstrated when the performance of experts is facilitated by a focus on outcomes rather than execution (Gray, Beilock, and Carr 2007).

Consider the experience of driving home from work over a very familiar route; we often arrive home with little recollection of the drive. The "map" that directed our movements unfolded automatically, even though we might not have registered (looked at) exactly the same external cues as in preceding trips. And the "map" would not just include the space external to the automobile's windshield. It might include information on the size and shape of the car's interior, and even the type of transmission in the automobile one was driving (e.g., how one would shift gears; Leutgeb et al. 2005), as well as a representation of the ultimate expected outcome of the drive that would also activate the motor actions that would have previously lead to that outcome. Indeed, as we leave work we visualize the anticipated outcome (arriving home), and without intervention, the actions attendant to that outcome unfold.

Nor must a precise match occur for the production of linked behavior. The new stimulus configuration need only be within a given confidence interval of the stored template; a decision must often be made based on partial information using "fuzzy" logic (i.e., decisions built on stochastic processes). Furthermore, recent research suggests that the most simple (i.e., first-order) version of pattern matching (i.e., straightforward comparison of one "picture" to another) cannot fully account for the manner in which previously recorded experience is generalized to every new, and somewhat different, situation (Poggio and Bizzi 2004). Although the Poggio and Bizzi (2004) model for matching in the visual system is quite complex, for the present purposes it is sufficient to note that it posits multidimensional "tuning" of a linear combination of hierarchically arranged neurons to an optimal stimulus. In fact, the tuning of inferotemporal cortex cells is accomplished using a hierarchical set of cortical stages that successively agglomerate responses from neurons tuned to simpler features; patterns among simple features detected at the lowest stage are recognized at the next stage up in the processing hierarchy. Such patterns at each level are in turn recognized as even higher-order patterns or combinations at a further step up in processing. Feedback loops in this hierarchical system increase the power of these detection devices considerably over simple first-order pattern detectors (Poggio and Bizzi 2004). We have described a simplified version of such a system in an earlier paper (see Goldman 2002, 740).

Because the emission of contextually appropriate behaviors is the essential adaptive function of these anticipatory mechanisms, representations of broad motor patterns, the beginnings of motor activity appropriate to the recognized stimulus inputs, must be completely integrated. These motor patterns are arranged in a manner that is essentially the inverse of sensory recognition patterns (Saper, Iversen, and Frackowiak 2000). At the highest level, stored information constitutes an abstract action pattern laid out over a temporal dimension. A useful way of conceptualizing this type of expectancy is as a script, a dynamic blueprint for an action sequence that is activated by the encoded anticipated outcome of those actions. As activation proceeds down the movement hierarchy, scripts are translated into more specific sequences of planned muscle activity that in turn control actual movements. The common experience that such motor programs run most efficiently when allowed to run automatically is borne out by research showing that attention to their execution causes a decrement in performance, whereas attention to the expected outcomes is related to increased performance (Gray, Beilock, and Carr 2007).

Constrained Perception of Incoming Stimuli by Stored Information Patterns

The human sensory system is constantly bombarded by a vast array and amount of sensory stimulation. Not only is detailed information received by all the senses in parallel, but, as noted above, incoming information is changing from moment to moment. It has been estimated that potentially billions of bits of information impinge on the human senses every second, whereas studies have shown that, after processing, no more than 50 bits of information per second are available to consciousness (Norretranders 1991). Even allowing for substantial additional capacity to process some information outside of consciousness, organisms must dramatically reduce the degrees of freedom in information during processing, while simultaneously remaining responsive to the information that matters most for survival and adaptation.

The anticipatory systems described above reduce incoming information to a manageable level; that is, they control and constrain active search for and processing of expected inputs. This may, in fact, be one central purpose for a memory system; to provide a director, a filter for such incoming stimuli. The information to which the organism is biased (selectively responsive) is governed by the nature of our sensory systems that has been honed over evolutionary time, and by our encoding of past sensory–perceptual configurations collected throughout our experience. As one example, the visual system has receptive elements configured to be sensitive to particular stimulus arrays (e.g., lines in various orientations, patterns, movement; Maunsell 1995). But much of that selectivity is based on past experience; complex adaptations require plasticity. Many receptive elements can be altered by experience (Grossberg 1995). Even basic elements of the visual system, once thought to be hardwired, have been found to be adaptable (plastic; Singer 1995; Tsodyks and Gilbert 2004). In addition, these filtering mechanisms do not operate passively; they actively identify, process, and compare information to create whole perceptions from available information. Grossberg (1995, 439; credited to Richard Warren) offered an interesting example:

Suppose you hear a noise followed immediately by the words "eel is on the...." If that string of words is followed by the word "orange," you hear "peel is on the orange." If the word "wagon" completes the sentence, you hear "wheel is on the wagon." If the final word is "shoe," you hear "heel is on the shoe."

In this example, Grossberg suggests that expectations activated by the final word in the sequence provide a means to fill in incomplete data and influence perception of the first word. One substrate for this type of active process that completes a pattern in the absence of full and precise information (but not necessarily in this specific verbal example) has been shown to be an area of the hippocampus containing massively interconnected pyramidal cells (CA3; Nakazawa, Quirk, and Chitwood 2002). It has been suggested (Miyashita 2004, 436) that because "the configuration of environmental stimuli and their behavioral context in daily life are unique and rarely repeated exactly," the brain must be able to recover a complete memory from stimulus conditions that supply only partial cues.

Similarly, nonhuman primates categorize stimuli based on important features rather than all available visible information (Hampson et al. 2004). Because only a small number of particular hippocampal neurons were found to fire in relation to the categorization task, the researchers concluded that it was the *pattern* of activating neurons that conveyed the information. Most interestingly, the importance of specific features differed by individual monkey, leaving Hampson et al. (2004, 3189; emphasis added) to conclude that "firing of category neurons in hippocampus may herald the presence of items that are similar to past events and therefore *through prior experience*, have a high probability of being significant to the individual... the presence of such neurons may be critical for the ability to detect and/or encode critical features present in ambiguous stimuli."

The tendency to use limited cues to create a percept that anticipates future events extends beyond completion of spatial or auditory patterns; primates have been shown to anticipate multiple action sequences based on slight changes in the context of an initial action (Fogassi, Ferrari, and Gesierich 2005). Monkeys predicted the outcome of movement sequences when the object involved and the initial movements were identical and only the ultimate repository of the object differed. Recent work on "mirror neurons" underscores that human and primate brains are wired to anticipate intentions and behavioral patterns of other living actors in their environments (Iacoboni et al. 2005) and that these "mirror" representations are modifiable by experience (Catmur, Walsh, and Heyes 2007). In related work, rodents were trained to distinguish circles and squares, and the corresponding neuronal activation patterns were mapped (Wills, Lever, and Cacucci 2005). When ambiguous blends of these stimuli were presented along a continuum, the firing patterns corresponded to either the circle or square, with abrupt shifts in firing occurring at about the midpoint of the transformation. The human phenomenon of "false memory" (in which "remembered" stimuli were never actually experienced) is analogous to these animal paradigms in which novel stimuli evoke responses similar to those observed to familiar stimuli. Such false memory errors have been referred to as "intelligent" (Roediger and McDermott 2000) in that they expose the operation of processes that are critical for adaptive cognition. The paradigm used to demonstrate such errors will be covered in more detail later.

Representation of Anticipatory Templates via Changes in the Physical/Neural Substrate
How are information patterns that anticipate upcoming circumstances and constrain perception stored? The complete answer to this question would encompass an extensive array of neurophysiological mechanisms. For present purposes, however, a limited point suffices: Our senses register information in a manner that mirrors the actual physical input created by external stimulation. The visual system registers patterns of light using sensors that are sensitive to these patterns (Frishman 2001), the auditory system registers where on a vibrating membrane sound waves produce the most displacement (Moore 2001), and so on. Consequently, the virtual storage of input patterns may involve actual physical enhancement of the pathways that move sensory input through the nervous system (Chklovskii, Mel, and Svoboda 2004; Fitzpatrick 2005; Winocur, Moscovitch, and Fogel 2005). This point was underscored when Tarr (2005) suggested that, in the human visual system, object recognition depends on our astonishing memory capabilities, which facilitate the encoding of much of what we see as originally experienced. Buzsaki (2005, 568) further noted that "ensembles of hippocampal 'place cells' form a map-like representation of the environment." Such representations, then, can serve as templates that constrain perception and anticipatory impending events.

   Such flexibility sounds simple, but it is extremely profound; experience modifies our ability to perceive and process future sensations. For instance, Kandel and Squire (2000, 1119) further point out that cerebral "cortices can be reshaped by experience. In one experiment, monkeys learned to discriminate between two vibrating stimuli applied to one finger. After several thousand trials, the cortical representation of the trained finger became more than twice as large as the corresponding areas of the other fingers." More recently, evidence has emerged that regionally specific reshaping of the cortex based on increased myelination occurs in children who began piano lessons relatively early in life (before age 11), as compared with children who began later (Bengtsson et al. 2005), suggesting a means whereby experience might be translated into enhanced neural processing (and also suggesting that such flexibility may, in some cases, be time limited). Evidence also suggests that receptive fields of (visual) cortical cells are routinely remapped so that more processing resources (cells) are devoted to behaviorally important objects than to those less important (Bundesen, Habekost, and Kyllingsbaek 2005). Both Kandel and Squire (2000) and Miyashita (2004) refer to altered gene expression, increased protein synthesis, growth of new synaptic connections, and reorganization of neural circuits as the mechanism that underlies such physical changes. Hence, core cellular mechanisms are mustered in the nervous system for the building and organizing of neural tissue that stores information. Once again, this is not storage for storage's sake; the storage of such information serves an adaptive function, facilitating processing of similar information in the future. Such patterns of adaptation may be conceived of as expectancy templates.

Recent study of somatosensory receptive fields in rodents has considerably advanced understanding of the mechanisms of cortical plasticity (Feldman and Brecht 2005). Each rodent whisker has a columnar receptive field for which it is the primary source of input and these radial columns are arranged into a "barrel map." The functional arrangement of these maps is, however, quite plastic; they continually restructure in response to sensory input. Such investigations of the processes of plasticity make it apparent that simple Hebbian principles (i.e., simple enhancement of the most frequently activated pathways) will not suffice to explain the full range of changes. Instead, it appears that there is interplay between the intrinsic organization of neural tissue and sensory experience that stimulates modification of this tissue. Among the many plastic changes observed: different cortical layers respond differently, unused tissue may recede in addition to utilized tissue elaborating, and different layers may be differentially responsive to changes at different points in development. The fundamental point remains that neural tissue is constructed and modified to reflect experience in a manner that is in some way (perhaps loosely) isomorphic to the input it receives. And, as noted below, experience is preserved not as a record of the past, but rather as a map that shows the way to the future.

Equivalence of Expectancy/Anticipation and "Memory"

Because anticipatory adjustments can only be based on information obtained in similar past circumstances (either long–term or immediate past), we conventionally refer to this stored information as memory. The word memory, and the concept that commonly underlies it, likely evolved to capture the subjective experience of searching within ourselves to recall information and ability to report that "I remember." The notion of recall, by its very nature, implies looking "backward" in time to locate and bring forward information. But memory operation is most often inferred from alterations in current or future behavior based on what the organism has encountered in the past. Hence, while the mystique of memory is in reminiscence, the function of memory seems to be to anticipate upcoming circumstances, and to make adjustments accordingly. To serve this anticipatory function, multiple memory storage mechanisms exist, and exhibit reciprocal influence, in an intact organism (Miyashita 2004). "Memory" systems are ubiquitous in higher organisms; even the immune system is often considered to be a memory system, wherein templates are stored to guide later responses (e.g., Lanzavecchia and Sallusto 2002). Despite humans' subjective sense of memory as a device for looking backward, memory perhaps is better understood as a means of looking forward (Goldman 2002). The capacity of human memory to produce conscious recollection may be simply a serendipitous consequence of advanced cortical development; as Holland and Gallagher (2004, 148) note, "The utility of learning and memory lies not in reminiscence about the past, but in allowing us to act in anticipation of future events."

It is beyond scope of this chapter to thoroughly review the functional distinctions between "types" of memory and the structures that support memory. For a review of one memory taxonomy, please consult Miyashita (2004). A few points should be made in this context, however. First, common taxonomies of memory distinguish between long- and short-term stores. All long-term memory can be viewed as implementing the anticipatory function; that is, stored information that allows comparison of a current context with previous exposures to similar or related contexts. But even short-term (working) memory can be posited as serving, in part, this function: Because multiple mechanisms may operate in tandem to anticipate behavioral adaptations, and these mechanisms may compete (i.e., lead to different behavioral outputs), working memory (as an element of what is often called "executive functioning") may enter into adjudication between potential outputs. Recent research has indicated that prefrontal neurons accomplish just this memory-comparison process (Latham and Dayan 2005; Machens, Romo, and Brody 2005). Once again, though, the function of this decision making is to optimize behavioral outputs for achieving payoffs in upcoming circumstances, a function that is of great importance to the process of addiction given that most payoffs themselves are at least partially a function of prior experience. (Optimization is not always achieved; see the next section for a discussion of these payoffs.)

Second, although distinctions have been made between explicit (declarative) and implicit (nondeclarative) memory, it is important to recognize that a number of discriminable memory processes can be subsumed under these umbrellas (see Miyashita 2004)—processes that do not necessarily handle the same information, and do not, therefore, represent a single repository of either explicit or implicit information. Tasks designed to access such information cannot be assumed to be interchangeable. At the same time, however, research in cognitive psychology has suggested that many of these processes and subprocesses interrelate on a continuing basis, and may not be measurable at the behavioral level as truly distinct (Roediger, Buckner, and McDermott 1999). As we shall show later, anticipatory processes (in the extended sense we are describing) are not confined to either explicit or implicit domains, or to any of their subprocesses. In fact, early in this chapter, we noted that some of the subprocesses within the implicit domain as described by Miyashita (2004; e.g., simple conditioning) have been explained using the expectancy concept.

Third, information used as reference points (expectancy templates) in anticipatory processing need not be restricted to specific memory pathways; such information might be assembled from brainwide networks in deliberate response to top-down signals from the frontal cortex (active retrieval), or automatically, using a retrieval signal from the temporal cortex. To some as yet unknown extent, such assemblies integrate information that resides in the memory pathways described above. These integrations of information seem to arise automatically in particular contexts based on the principles of associationism (see Miyashita 2004), and can also be understood as supporting the anticipatory function described above. Associational relationships represent the "glue" that binds together otherwise disparate objects or events and renders them useful for anticipating upcoming circumstances.

Inseparability of Memory, Cognition, and Affect/Emotion—Logic of the Linkage

Associationist principles (e.g., Nelson, McEvoy, and Pointer 2003) provide an effective starting point for understanding how initially disconnected information may be "bonded" into a larger whole in the appropriate context. Such bonding assures that relevant information can be reassembled efficiently and effectively repeatedly as needed. Quickly and effectively searching the information in the brain, and assembling such information into coherent and situationally appropriate wholes, is a formidable task. In some circumstances faced by modern humans (e.g., many modern information service jobs, academic testing, completing many laboratory-based cognitive tasks), searches that assemble purely abstract information may even be sufficient to produce adequate behavioral output.

A full explanation of the control of behavior in the real world requires, however, additional theoretical elements that encourage the translation of pure information into overt behavior. After all, human memory systems evolved before the existence of many of the abstract tasks modern humans encounter. It must be the case, therefore, that evolutionary (selection) pressures (e.g., adaptation, survival) influenced the development of these memory systems. We can identify mechanisms built into the biological fabric of each individual that serve as proxies for monitoring evolutionary success. These mechanisms are what we typically mean when we refer to the constructs motivation, reward, incentive, reinforcement (positive and negative), and punishment. Hence, to govern real-world behavior, information that is accessed by associational search at some point must be associated with information about reward and punishment (Schultz 2004). It is this final, critical information that specifies what searches will be undertaken and what behaviors will be carried out to consummate reward via approach or avoidance.

In higher organisms, at least two kinds of motivational pathways may be distinguished. In the first, basic needs are regulated by physiological signals that indicate that the internal system has moved, or will soon move, outside an acceptable biological range (e.g., hunger, thirst, etc.). Such signals activate an associational search for behavioral programs that will bring the system back into balance (some adjustments do not require overt behavioral outputs and occur purely at the physiological level; e.g., homeostasis).

The second kind of pathway accommodates rewards that go beyond the adjustment of basic biological parameters. In this pathway, contextual stimuli are compared with existing representations to signal (via a number of neural pathways) that a rewarding condition may be achieved. Information that in some fashion represents the behavioral steps that may be anticipated to achieve reward is then accessed via an associational pathway. Because many rewarding circumstances are not of the variety that would call for activation of the first kind of pathway (they signal an enhancement of status rather than a biological necessity for return to equilibrium), organisms have neural systems that appear designed to signal the availability of reward; that is, systems that use contextual signals to anticipate that reward is imminent (Berridge and Robinson 1998). In humans, rewards even may be anticipated into the distant future; such long-term rewards are most often called goals (Bargh et al. 2001) that are served by the attainment of immediate or interim reward. It must also be noted that these pathways are not independent; the second system may signal payoffs for behaving in a manner that anticipates (and wards off) strong activation of the first pathway. Although a thorough examination of motivational systems is beyond the scope of this chapter, central to this process is the fact that motivation must be linked to cognition in the control of behavior; as noted by Holland and Gallagher (2004, 148), "Recently, conventional associative learning paradigms have been adapted to allow systematic study of expectancy and action in a range of species, including humans.... 'expectancy' refers to the associative activation of such reinforcer representations by the events that predict them, before the delivery of the reinforcer itself."

Reinforcing circumstances go far beyond the traditional basic biological needs. It is becoming clearer that our nervous systems are set up to register (and anticipate) consequences that are related to evolutionary "fit" (Glimcher 2002). For example, successful jockeying for status in the social hierarchy may be noted by motivational systems because such status makes reproductive success more likely. Glimcher refers to genetic survival as the ultimate cause of behavior and notes the correspondence between work on this notion and formal economic theory. He also notes, however, that behavior of individuals often fails to optimize long-term (evolutionary fit) or sometimes even short-term outcomes, perhaps because people are "tuned" to inaccurately evaluate longer-term payoffs, or because emotion overrides logical thinking. As he suggests, individual decision making may be stochastic; but, when outcomes of these stochastic processes are distributed across many individuals, they may result in collective outcomes that optimize survival (passing on of genes) at the population level.

In sum, to produce behavior, associational pathways at some point must result in anticipation or prediction of payoffs, be they mitigation of basic needs or related to evolutionary fit. Contextual signals of the availability of payoffs are made salient within the total pattern of neural activation by brain mechanisms that highlight the presence of those signals (see below). Complex associational pathways then link the highlighted activation patterns to the internal representations of behaviors (i.e., scripts, templates) that have some probability of achieving available outcomes. The essence of the expectancy model is that context engenders both *anticipation/prediction* of payoffs and the emission of reward-achieving behaviors. In this way, expectancy serves as the theoretical amalgam of cognition (association) and motivation/emotion.

Selection of Biologically Meaningful Inputs

Even if one accepts that cognition and emotion must be linked, the question remains of how biologically meaningful inputs are culled from the vast array of stimuli impinging on the organism. Neuroscientists currently identify a number of brain pathways for registering biological significance. As an example of that process, it has been noted that one of these pathways, dopaminergic neurons running from the striatum to the nucleus accumbens and on to the frontal lobes, is thought to convert "an event or stimulus from a neutral 'cold' representation (mere information) into an attractive and 'wanted' incentive that can 'grab' attention" (i.e., incentive salience; Berridge and Robinson 1998, 313). Further, Kupfermann, Kandel, and Iversen (2000, 1010; emphasis added) note that "dopaminergic neurons encode *expectations* about external rewards." More recent work by Matsumoto and Tanaka (2004, 178) indicates that the prefrontal cortex (anterior cingulate cortex) links these signals of biologically important inputs with actions "based on goal expectation and memory of action–outcome contingency." Given the conceptualization presented in these pages, memory of action–outcome contingency would be, of course, the essence of the expectancy. It is this "memory" that is reenacted in anticipation that the action will again lead to reward.

A second means of indexing biological significance centers on the amygdaloid complex, an important area in the expression of emotion (Holland and Gallagher 2004; Iversen, Kupfermann, and Kandel 2000). Obviously, a neural system supporting the experience of pleasure and aversion would be instrumental in encouraging certain behaviors and discouraging others. Once again, however, the close linkage between this source of emotional expression and systems that undergird information processing makes certain sensed patterns of information more salient, and therefore more likely to be attended to, stored, and acted on (Holland and Gallagher 2004; Phelps 2004; Schultz 2004). This link is suggested by connections observed between motivational areas such as the nucleus accumbens and amygdala, and information-processing areas such as the hippocampus and frontal cortex (Cardinal and Everitt 2004; Phelps 2004). Corticosteroids released by the hypothalamic-pituitary-adrenal (HPA) axis in response to threatening circumstances also influence hippocampal memory storage (Heinrichs and Koob 2004). This linkage between neural processing of information and motivation/emotion is well captured by the expectancy concept, and researchers in this domain routinely apply expectancy in describing its function (Holland and Gallagher 2004; Phelps 2004).

The "somatic marker hypothesis" by Bechara, Damasio, and Damasio (2000) widens the spectrum of signals that may arise from bioregulatory processes to influence decision making. They aver that final oversight of decisions (resolution of the competition between anticipatory pathways) is not just a function of the orbitofrontal ("executive") cortex, but arises from large-scale systems that subsume both cortical and subcortical structures. Among these structures are the amygdala, the somatosensory/insular cortices, and the peripheral nervous system. In fact, it has been noted that one function of the amygdala is to register unexpected or ambiguous inputs; the sort of inputs that might interrupt ongoing processing and suggest that a more automatic pathway between input and output might not be appropriate to the current context (Kagan 2007).

Complex Behavior as Anticipatory

Because the anticipatory mechanisms discussed in this chapter can be used to conceptually integrate biobehavioral functioning vertically (across levels of explanation) as well as horizontally, it follows that overarching and consistent human behavioral patterns (e.g., personality) also can be understood by viewing functional outputs through this same lens. Infants clearly have identifiable behavioral propensities (temperament), even at birth (perhaps even in utero; e.g., DiPietro et al. 1996). As newborns react to environmental contexts in accord with their propensities (e.g., approach, avoidance), they accrue experience with payoffs and failures as a function of their behavioral outputs in these contexts. The creation of anticipatory patterns results. Over time, successive experiences (representing the interplay between innate behavioral propensities and ensuing exposures to the specific environments they select/encounter) will result in apparently consistent behavioral patterns, or what we term personality. (However, to the extent that contexts are never identical, the performance of these patterns also will be variable and probabilistic.) Given that accrual of experience is crucial to the establishment of these patterns, it seems no happenstance that the term "personality" has not typically been applied in relation to the behavioral consistencies of children (see Caspi, Roberts, and Shiner 2005). Although temperament may reflect general tendencies to respond to simulation, discrete anticipatory patterns may more slowly regularize into what is commonly meant by personality.

Because complex behavioral patterns always reflect interweaving of tonic propensities (e.g., temperaments, affective tone), more phasic affective reactions to triggering stimuli (e.g., approach or avoidance), and previously learned behavioral templates, the neurophysiology of these tonic propensities and phasic affective reactions may influence behavioral outputs. The most elemental source of these propensities is, of course, gene expression and the activation of consequent neurophysiological processes. Research on the genetics of these processes has accelerated in recent years, and it is much better understood how the genetics of neurophysiological pathways for reward, behavioral control, and stress response interact with environments to produce the anticipatory patterns of behavior that underlie addiction (see Goldman, Oroszi, and Ducci 2005).

For more extensive discussion of the overlap between expectancy and personality, please consult Goldman 1999. Recently, however, Smith and Anderson (2001) have shown that even after years of accrual of these reciprocal events humans continue to acquire new expectancies as a function of preexisting personality patterns. Anderson, Schweinsburg, and Paulus (2005) have linked these "personality" processes to brain functioning; greater inhibitory reactivity (an indicator of trait-like inhibition) on functional magnetic resonance imaging (fMRI) predicted fewer expectancies of cognitive and motor improvement from alcohol use, but more expectancies of cognitive and motor impairment. This process, which emphasizes the role of preexisting tendencies in the formation of anticipatory patterns, has been referred to as acquired preparedness (Smith and Anderson 2001).

Application to Substance Use, Abuse, and Dependence

We have been emphasizing how anticipatory function can serve as a conceptual bridge between cognitive/information-processing systems and emotional/motivational influences. Because recent research has shown that substance use can be characterized as arising from the integrated operation of these influences, the concept of anticipatory processing, including the distinguishing aspects explored above, is very clearly applicable to substance use, abuse, and dependence. In relation to substance use, the anticipatory processes described earlier place everyday stimuli that co-occur with the availability of substances into memory as information templates. In addition, substances prone to abuse themselves impact the system for tagging stimuli as biologically significant (via direct effects on the dopamine system; i.e., "incentive salience"), and on emotional/motivational systems, to make use-related memories more indelible and salient and thereby more influential within the overall decision-making process that leads to (or eludes) use.

That the physical neural substrate reacts in anticipation of events related to alcohol and substance use has been shown by using neuroimaging techniques. Sell et al. (2000, 208), noted that "PET scanning...noted activation in midbrain structures by both heroin and heroin-related cues," further summarizing that "the target regions of the mesolimbic dopamine system are implicated in the expression of an urge to use heroin in response to heroin-related cues and in the effects of the drug itself in human heroin addicts" (ibid., 213). Although this anticipatory reaction might be viewed as an example of a classically conditioned response, recall that some major theories of classical conditioning are expectancy-based. Even more important, however, is the fact that the brain regions activated in response to drug-related cues are the very areas that have been suggested to be implicated in the learning and storage of expectancy (memory) templates that guide future behaviors. By using fMRI to directly address the brain region and neurotransmitter system noted by Kupfermann, Kandel, and Iversen (2000) to encode expectancies, Robinson and Berridge (2000, S100; citing work by Breiter et al. [1997]) note, "One region to show bilateral activation during a saline retest was the nucleus accumbens, which the authors speculate could be related to expectancy for cocaine."

Given that the substrate for storing memories to anticipate and prepare for future events exists in all of us, are we all then at risk for excessive substance use? This review of the processes involved suggests that, in the right circumstances, we all do share some level of risk; environments can either encourage or discourage particular levels and patterns of use. At the population level, after all, the most important predictor of substance use and substance-related problems is availability (e.g., Gruenewald, Millar, and Treno 1993). In addition, drinking across the academic year among first-year college students varies over time with holiday periods that increase the availability of time for alcohol use (Del Boca et al. 2004).

After holding availability constant, however, differential risk largely reflects individual differences. The individual difference characteristics routinely invoked, such as emotional reactivity, personality, and sensitivity to alcohol (see MacKillop, McGeary, and Ray, this volume), are the very mechanisms highlighted above as making memories more or less salient in anticipatory processing. For example, Katner, Kerr, and Weiss (1996, 669) compared genetically bred alcohol-preferring (P) rats with Wistar rats, concluding that "the mere expectation of ethanol availability enhances the efflux of DA (dopamine) in the Nac (nucleus accumbens) of the P, but not the Wistar rat, which may play a role in the initiation or maintenance of ethanol seeking behavior in the P line."

To examine similar processes in humans, McCarthy et al. (2000) assessed self-reported alcohol expectancies in individuals who differed genetically in the alcohol dehydrogenase allele (ALDH2; those with this allele metabolize alcohol less effectively and may find use more aversive). They reported that one mechanism by which the allelic variation may influence use is by lowering positive expectancies and reducing the expectancy–drinking relationship. A follow-up study (McCarthy et al. 2001) provided preliminary evidence that it is indeed the level of response to alcohol that mediates the relationship between ALDH2 status and expectancies. Among men, those with the ALDH2 allele had more adverse reaction to alcohol and increased expectancies for cognitive impairment. Statistical modeling showed that the ALDH2-expectancy relationship was fully explained (mediated) by the level of response to alcohol. In females, having the ALDH2 allele decreased the likelihood that women would view alcohol as tension-reducing, but a mediational relationship was not found.

Underscoring the conclusion that positive expectancies partially mediate the relationship between level of response to alcohol and alcohol use is work by Schuckit et al. (2005, 181–182) showing that "the level of response to alcohol, . . . [a] well established . . . genetically influenced phenotype related to alcoholism risk," operated "both directly and through alcohol expectancies" in the prediction of alcohol-related outcomes. Not only does level of response to alcohol influence the nature of expectancies held and decisions to drink by an individual, but self-reported anticipated effects of alcohol influence actual response to alcohol once drinking begins (Park and Grant 2005). Indeed, Park and Grant concluded that positive expectancies override the negative outcomes that occur when actual drinking takes place.

Furthermore, it is well established that differences in temperament and/or personality and psychopathology place people at differential risk for problematic use (e.g., Sher, Grekin, and Williams 2005), and that these differences may influence drinking through the operation of expectancies (Darkes, Greenbaum, and Goldman 2004; Finn et al. 2005; Ham et al. 2005). Because it is also well established that such individual differences may have heritable components, it would not be surprising to find that some piece of the complex expectancy process might also be heritable. A small body of studies using genetically informative designs suggests that genetic differences contribute a small, but significant, amount of variance in explaining differences in expectancies in individuals who drink regularly (Merrill et al. 1999; Vernon et al. 1996). Apparently in contrast, Slutske, Heath, and Madden (2002) found that shared experiences, rather than genetic variation, explained most of the variation in positive alcohol expectancies in a large twin sample of young women. However, when only twin pairs in which both members drank were included in the analyses, a significant genetic effect was found for performance enhancement expectancies. Consistent with the idea that expectancies reflect the impact of experience on genetically influenced mechanisms for selecting and retaining information, all genetically informative studies found that nonshared environmental influences predominated in determining expectancy variation. In sum, it is the interplay between basic mechanisms of incentive salience, emotional reactivity, and alcohol reactivity, some aspects of which may be inherited, and contextual influences from the environment, that sculpts expectancies and, at least in part, determines subsequent usage patterns.

Language-based Access to Expectancies

Explicit "Questionnaire" Approaches

Since 1989, more than 15,000 studies have investigated expectancy/anticipatory processes as they relate to human alcohol use (based on a Google Scholar search using "alcohol" and "expectancies" as key words). The vast majority of these studies has related responses from children, adolescents, and adults to verbal items about anticipated outcomes from drinking to patterns of alcohol use (also self-reported via questionnaire). The relationship between expectancies and alcohol use measured by questionnaires has proven robust: Measured expectancies are correlated with drinking in all groups, accounting for up to 50% of the variance in drinking outcomes when analyzed with statistical methods that attenuate error (e.g., Darkes, Greenbaum, and Goldman 2004; Leigh and Stacy 1993); measured well before drinking began, expectancies predicted drinking as children matured into adolescence (Christiansen et al. 1989) and even many years later, into adulthood (Stacy, Newcomb, and Bentler 1991); as drinking increased, so did expectancies (Smith et al. 1995); as drinking showed its typical decrease in young adulthood, so did expectancies (Sher et al. 1996). The relationship between psychometrically measured expectancies and drinking was also found in longitudinal designs to be reciprocal: Higher expectancies led to higher drinking, which, in turn, led to higher expectancies (Smith et al. 1995). Expectancies, as measured by questionnaires, could also be inferred to exert causal influence: In the context of appropriate designs (Baron and Kenny 1986), expectancies were shown to mediate up to 50% of the variance of other known antecedents of consumption levels (e.g., Darkes, Greenbaum, and Goldman 2004; Finn et al. 2000; Henderson et al. 1994; Scheier and Botvin 1997).

Recent Implicit Approaches

These conclusions using questionnaire-based measures of alcohol expectancies, which are considered explicit in nature (i.e., require conscious deliberation by respondents), have been recently supplemented using "implicit/indirect" cognitive measures for accessing stored anticipatory information. Implicit approaches may be of great importance; given that much of the decision process that leads to alcohol use is theorized to take place outside of awareness, indirect assessments may more closely mirror the natural process of access and activation of anticipatory templates. To what extent probing implicit (or, indeed, explicit) language-based processes might reveal the output of neurally based decisional activity described earlier remains an open question, of course, one we shall revisit later.

One of the critical questions regarding distinctions between explicit and implicit language-based measures (not to mention distinctions among these measures and neurophysiological measures of anticipation) arises from an in-depth consideration of the processes by which individuals might select responses to such measures. Expectancy questionnaires are typically considered explicit in nature, meaning that responses are thought to be largely influenced by conscious retrieval and decision making. However, although agree/disagree or Likert-type response formats *may* be completed via conscious deliberation, it is not possible to say with complete certainty what processes might underlie such responses. For example, simply changing questionnaire item order can affect observed factor structure, suggesting an implicit priming effect of items that appear earlier (Weinberger et al. 2006). To respond to expectancy instruments, respondents *may* deliberately recollect specific experiences from "autobiographical memory," or simply "go with" their subjective feeling or impression. The latter strategy is somewhat difficult to distinguish from implicit processing, and experts in this area have noted inherent difficulty in parsing one type of processing from the other, regardless of the techniques used (see Roediger 2003).

While our discussion of implicit assessment of expectancies emphasizes our own work, we acknowledge substantial work by others in connection with implicit memory processes and alcohol use (e.g., Houben and Wiers 2006; Palfai and Wood 2001; Stacy 1997; Wall et al. 2001; Wiers et al. 2002). Each of these studies has demonstrated that the association between expected effects of alcohol and alcohol use can be measured implicitly, specifically showing that, when primed with alcohol cues, heavy drinkers have strong associations for positive and/or arousing effects of alcohol.

Our own investigations of memory processes in alcohol expectancy operation (and concomitantly, implicit anticipatory processes) began with mapping expectancy associational space in accord with Estes's (1991, 12) observation that memory "traces can be viewed as vectors or lists, as nodes in a network, or as points in multidimensional space." Our mapping began with the collection of individual associations to the prompt, "Alcohol makes one...," subsequently placing scaled responses to this prompt into a hypothetical memory network using multidimensional scaling (MDS). In adults (Rather and Goldman 1994; Rather et al. 1992) and children (both prior to, and subsequent to drinking experience; Dunn and Goldman 1996, 1998), the resulting network was well described using two orthogonal dimensions, valence (positive–negative) and arousal (sedation–excitation). Each associate could be located in space by its coordinates on these two dimensions. Although responding to the cue required attention and deliberation, participants did not explicitly compare pairs of items and did not directly create networks generated based on the relationships among all expectancy items; the derived structure could be inferred to reflect a network of implicit relationships between anticipated effects of alcohol and served as models of implicit memory storage that could later be tested empirically in experimental studies. (An instrument based on conversion of this MDS solution into confirmatory factor structure for use in prediction equations was recently derived as well; Goldman and Darkes 2004.)

Proximal words in these networks were viewed as more likely to co-activate than words more distant. Ancillary analyses showed that heavier drinkers were more likely to associate positive and arousing outcomes with drinking and to have "tighter" relationships (closer associations in "space") among anticipated outcomes than did lighter drinkers. If viewed as causal models of drinking, the increased likelihood of co-activation of positive and arousing outcomes would increase heavier drinkers' likelihood of drinking. Interestingly, preadolescent children's maps suggested that they were more likely to activate negative expectancies but, as age increased into adolescence (these were cross-sectional studies), gradual shifts toward an increased likelihood of activating positive/arousing expectancies, whether drinking had been initiated or not, occurred. That is, changes in the expectancy network anticipated later drinking, moving toward patterns seen in drinkers.

These maps of the expectancy association network were recently confirmed using free association (Nelson, McEvoy, and Dennis 2000) to directly quantify the strength of association between memory concepts as the probability that given one word or concept (e.g., *salt*) another will be produced (e.g., *pepper*). These probabilities can be used to derive process models of memory operation (e.g., Nelson, McEvoy, and Pointer 2003). Free associations were first obtained from 1,465 children in the 2nd to 12th grades, and then from 4,585 college students. Children's free associations essentially replicated the previous work using the MDS approach, validating the earlier MDS maps (Dunn and Goldman 2000). Obtaining free associates from a large number of students allowed us to accomplish a task that not only clarified the incentive matrix for drinking, but also was informative for future research in general cognitive psychology, which generally has not emphasized individual differences in memory processes. Previous free association research (Nelson, McEvoy, and Dennis 2000) had established general population norms for common words by obtaining first associates to a limited list of prompts from groups of 100 to 200 participants. By iterating this procedure many times to many prompts, norms were derived that would characterize the average response for all English-language speakers (Nelson, McEvoy, and Schreiber 1998). In contrast, our sizeable sample of responses to a single prompt was used to establish norms for subgroups of drinkers (i.e., individual differences in alcohol cognitions; Reich and Goldman 2005). As drinker level increased, free associate norms showed a steady shift from negative and sedating expectancies toward arousing and positive expectancies, providing direct confirmation that lighter and heavier drinkers activated different concepts in response to an alcohol prompt, and showing that humans differ in their associational network as a function of individual differences.

These models of alcohol expectancy network structure provided the initial framework for investigating the multistep process noted earlier: that context activates anticipatory cognitions/affects that, in turn, influence behavioral output. Next, we tested whether the activation process suggested by these memory network models could be demonstrated via the experimental manipulation of alcohol cues. A series of studies were conducted using tasks developed by cognitive psychologists to test memory activation following implicit primes. The first of these studies used the Stroop technique (Kramer and Goldman 2003); following an alcohol (e.g., *vodka*) or alcohol-neutral (e.g., *milk*) prime, expectancy target words were ink-(color) named and expectancy acti-vation was indexed as the relative difference in latency to ink-name alcohol and neu-tral primed trials (interference; the greater the activation, the slower the ink-naming). Expectancy activation differed as a function of prime (alcohol/neutral), level of cus-tomary consumption, and location of the expectancies in a network defined by the valence/arousal dimensions. Following an alcohol cue, the heaviest drinkers had slower latencies (greater activation) to ink-name arousing expectancy words compared to other target words, whereas lighter drinkers had greater activation (interference) to sedating expectancy words; context differentially activated particular expectancies as a function of individuals' experience with alcohol. Reich, Noll, and Goldman (2005) then demonstrated expectancy activation consistent with the network models via pri-ming in a word-list memory study in which the experimental manipulation was simply a change in the first word on the study list. The study list was made up of alcohol ex-pectancy words from the list of free associates noted earlier and grocery words (50% each). The first word on the list studied was either "MILK" or "BEER." Although either word can be considered a grocery word, participants presented with BEER as the first word recalled more alcohol expectancy words than those who saw MILK. Further, this effect resulted from an interaction between drinker type and type of expectancy word recalled. Heavy drinkers tended to remember proportionately more alcohol expectancy words, predominantly reflecting positive expectancies, than lighter or nondrinkers. In other words, a slight change in the initial study stimuli seemingly activated different memory patterns, and these patterns reflected differences that would be expected by different drinker types.

Another study (Reich, Goldman, and Noll 2004) used the false memory paradigm (Deese 1959; Roediger and McDermott 1995) to test the structure of the modeled net-works. In this paradigm, several 12-word lists (e.g., *hot, chilly, frigid, wet*) that are each associated to one nonstudied word (e.g., *cold*) are studied. In previous studies, about 80% of participants remembered studying the nonpresented word (associate). This par-adigm was extended to expectancies by developing a study list of alcohol expectancy words and excluding three high-frequency positive and arousing expectancy words that, according to our network maps, should have been part of that list. Participants studied this list in either a simulated bar or an alcohol-neutral room, to allow for the evaluation of the role of context in activating the alcohol expectancy elements that in-tentionally were not presented. Participants were also split into heavier, lighter, and nondrinkers, to explore how context affected individuals with different patterns of consumption. After controlling for the tendency to falsely remember any type of word, heavier drinkers' false recognition for the three nonpresented positive/arousing words was significantly higher in the bar context than in the neutral room, whereas false memory rates were similar across context for the other drinker groups. In other words, the alcohol context created sufficiently strong memory activation in heavier drinkers so that they "remembered" positive and arousing expectancies that were never presented.

Because many alcohol expectancy studies invoking implicit techniques, in our lab and others, have used widely different implicit tasks (e.g., reaction time, recall, free associates), Reich, Below, and Goldman (in press) conducted a meta-analysis of studies including both an implicit and an explicit measure of alcohol expectancies. The purpose was twofold: (1) to review and summarize the results from this range of studies available, and (2) to compare implicit methods with the more traditional explicit methods, which, as indicated earlier, have accounted for up to 50% of the variance in drinking in error-attenuated models (Goldman, Darkes, and Del Boca 1999).

In 10 out of the 15 studies reviewed, implicit and explicit measures were significantly correlated with one another, albeit with relatively small effect sizes (mean $r = .25$). Hence, a small degree of measurement overlap exists between the two methods. Perhaps more interesting, in 12 of the 15 studies, explicit measures accounted for more drinking variance than implicit measures (in 12 out of 13 studies accounting for unique variance). This qualitative impression of a difference was supported by the significant difference observed in the statistical comparison of mean correlation values. Comparisons of unique variance explained did not reach statistical significance, but were in the same direction as the correlations. It is noteworthy that even though explicit measures explained a relatively large amount of variance in drinking, implicit measures accounted for significant incremental drinking variance. This pattern of results supports the use both explicit and implicit measures of alcohol expectancy and similar associative processes to predict drinking.

One advantage of using implicit measures of alcohol expectancy is their sensitivity to very subtle contextual shifts. For example, priming effects vastly differ with only slight changes in stimuli; Reich, Noll, and Goldman (2005) demonstrated this sensitivity to slight modifications in alcohol expectancy task stimuli by simply varying the first word of a list to be later recalled (beer versus milk). Recently, Reich, Kwiatkowski, et al. (2008) tested whether alcohol-expectancy memory associations changed as a function of the assessment context. Undergraduate drinkers provided up to five responses to the free associate (FA) cue "Alcohol makes me _____" in either an alcohol-neutral room or a simulated bar. Participants then rated each associate on valence and arousal. Results revealed both a qualitative and quantitative difference in the associates given; more positive associations (e.g., *happy*) were given in the alcohol context, an effect confirmed by a significant effect in the valence ratings of the first FA given. Interestingly, in the alcohol context, although valence and arousal ratings of the first FA were not significantly related to typical drinking quantity, the ratings for FA 2 through 5 *were* associated with quantity. This pattern of results suggests that ongoing, trait-like, alcohol-expectancy memory associations measured in an alcohol-neutral context are good predictors of *typical* drinking, but in a drinking context, positive associations become more salient for *all drinkers,* and are therefore less related to typical drinking. It may be, however, that these context-dependent associates reflect state-like memory network activation that predicts immediate drinking. Future studies should test this possibility.

This response sensitivity to very subtle contextual differences may provide insight into the function of implicit cognitive processes (see Gawronski, LeBel, and Peters 2007). Perhaps truly implicit processes are "meant" to be sensitive to short- or medium-term fluctuations in context. Cognitive scientists have acknowledged that this might be the case. For example, Nelson, McEvoy, and Pointer (2003) applied a model originally used in quantum physics, in which associative patterns exist in a state of "superposition" (undifferentiation), and are only "collapsed" into their functional state upon exposure to a particular context. Widdows (2004) also applied quantum theory to describe the operation of semantic associates. He used the ambiguous word "bass" as an example. When not in a "bass" context, memory associations to "bass" can be many words simultaneously, including words that are nearly orthogonal like "fisherman" and "guitar." In other words, in a neutral context each of these associates is equally likely to be given on a free associate task. But given a context, such as music, the associations take one form, that of the word "guitar" and the like. These conceptual applications underscore the role of context and environmental stimuli in determining what memory associations are activated. Our next line of studies illustrates the importance of understanding this memory activation process.

Having shown that elements within the network models could be activated as predicted by the associational structure, it is important to note whether cognitions activated by alcohol cues translate into actual drinking. Priming techniques and a disguised beer "taste test" were used in two studies to demonstrate increased alcohol consumption as a function of the presentation of alcohol-consistent cues. Roehrich and Goldman (1995) placed participants in a "memory" study where they were primed with either alcohol expectancy words or alcohol-neutral words and viewed one of two video clips from network television comedies. The clips were similar in content, while differing centrally in the contextual location of the show: One show took place in a bar (*Cheers*; alcohol prime), the other in an inn at a breakfast table (*Newhart*; alcohol-neutral prime). Following the manipulation, participants exposed to alcohol primes consumed more alcohol during what they believed was an entirely separate "taste test" study; increased alcohol priming led to more alcohol consumption. Those exposed to both alcohol-consistent primes drank most, the group that had both alcohol-neutral primes drank least, and the other two groups with discrepant primes fell in between. These results supported the inference of a causal relationship between expectancy activation and alcohol consumption.

Because the above study did not directly assess activation of the memory networks flowing priming, a further study (Stein, Goldman, and Del Boca 2000) used a similar design, but included a recognition task to determine whether priming had activated alcohol expectancies. Again, the level of consumption increased as the level of alcohol cues presented increased, and greater priming (activation) effects occurred for heavier drinkers. Other similar studies also have shown increases in consumption following exposure to alcohol expectancy–like cues (Carter et al. 1998; Palfai, Monti, and Ostafin 2000).

In sum, this line of research, from both our own and other laboratories, supports the validity of language-based memory models of alcohol expectancies, shows that these hypothesized networks can be activated implicitly, and shows that, as theorized, these models accurately reflect individual differences in previous drinking and that both alcohol contexts and these individual differences influence actual drinking prospectively.

Moving toward Non-Language-Based Measures

Environmental cues (primes) used to activate alcohol-expectancy memory networks clearly do not depend on language to influence cognition or behavior. Simulated bars, pictures, or even television programs have been used successfully. The question arises, however, whether responses (outcomes) can be measured without using language-based approaches. This question has partially been answered by the demonstration of consumption differences following non-word cues (e.g., Roehrich and Goldman 1995; Stein, Goldman, and Del Boca 2000). It remains to be determined whether cognition can be measured using non-language-based approaches. To this end, we have begun by relating language-based expectancy measures to brain activation that precedes verbal output. Fishman, Goldman, and Donchin (2008) measured the P300 component of the event-related potentials (ERPs) to detect violations of individually held alcohol expectancies. This study showed (1) that word-based violations of alcohol expectancy can be measured electrophysiologically, and (2) that expectancy effects occur within a few hundred milliseconds of stimulus presentation—faster than conscious decision making. These results demonstrated concordance between language-based measures of alcohol expectancies and activation in the brain. Additionally, Drobes, Carter, and Goldman (2009) used the startle eye-blink reflex as a measure of appetitive or aversive response to visually presented alcohol cues. Drinkers showed weaker startle (greater appetitive response) to alcohol cues than to neutral cues. The degree to which these responses are related to alcohol expectancies using verbal approaches has yet to be elucidated, but work continues in this vein.

A Fundamental Question Raised by Expectancy Challenge Findings

How do language-based measures of expectancies correspond to the anticipatory processes discussed earlier in this chapter? To begin this discussion, we will briefly divert into what has become an increasingly controversial area of expectancy research, expectancy challenge. The expectancy challenge originally was designed to experimentally test alcohol expectancies' causal role in drinking; although the plethora of findings from correlational designs suggested a robust relationship, the assertion of causality required the use of an experimental design, a protocol created to manipulate expectancies, and the subsequent examination of resultant changes in drinking. In the two original studies conducted in our laboratory (Darkes and Goldman 1993, 1998), groups of 10–15 moderate to heavy drinking males consumed, during interaction in a bar environment, beverages that they were told might or might not contain alcohol (i.e., alcohol or placebo beverages designed to mimic alcoholic beverages, randomly distributed). They then were asked to identify which of their peers had consumed actual alcohol and were unable to do so at better than chance levels. It appeared that the experience of being unable to reliably identify drinkers based on observed behaviors, which challenged their existing associations between drinking and its outcomes, coupled with information about alcohol expectancies, resulted in both expectancy and drinking decreases as much as six weeks following the procedure.

These initial studies stimulated a number of follow-ups that tested challenge protocols modified from the original procedure in various ways. Exclusively female groups have been used (Dunn, Lau, and Cruz 2000); mixed gender, rather than same-sex, groups have been used (e.g., Wiers et al. 2005); nonexperiential challenges that do not administer alcohol-containing beverages have been used (Corbin, McNair, and Carter 2001); the number of sessions (e.g., Corbin, McNair, and Carter 2001; Lau-Barraco and Dunn 2008; Wiers et al. 2005) and nature of the protocol (Wood et al. 2007) have been modified; and video-taped (Keillor, Perkins, and Horan 1999) and computer-based challenges have been conducted (Hunt, Darkes, and Goldman 2005). Given the wide variability in procedures, the varying degree to which challenge studies have replicated the original results is not surprising; in some cases, certain findings have not replicated the original research, although most studies have also not replicated what have been proposed as central elements (Darkes et al. 2003) of the protocol and design. These elements and the variability in sample, procedure, and protocol are often not taken into account in reviews of the challenge literature; yet some reviewers (e.g., Jones, Corbin, and Fromme 2001a,b) have suggested that these latter incomplete replications raise questions about the value or applicability of expectancy as an explanatory process.

Given the extensive body of research we have reviewed here from widely divergent fields of study that have converged on some version of an expectancy (anticipation, prediction, preparedness) process as an explanatory device, inconsistent findings in a single expectancy-based paradigm do not seem to pose serious questions about the concept of anticipatory function (Del Boca and Darkes 2001). Even within the alcohol field, the range of studies using research designs from surveys to true experiments that have shown expectancies to predict drinking and to mediate the influence of other variables on drinking should support continuing research in this vein. If discussion is restricted to variations on the expectancy challenge itself, it may of course eventually be concluded that this particular approach to disrupting anticipatory pathways, although effective at changing expectancies, has a less reliable or durable influence on drinking. Many other factors that have been reviewed here, such as context, personality, and individual differences (e.g., gender), also strongly influence drinking and may interact with the expectancy challenge to influence outcomes. Hence, it remains possible that continued investigation of variables related to this paradigm, including treatment dose and duration, the need for a true drinking experience, the role of other individual difference characteristics, the need for expectancy specificity in challenge protocols, and the temporal relationship between explicitly or implicitly measured expectancy changes and drinking changes, will lead to a more reliable procedure. Full tests of these parameters of the challenge remain to be fully evaluated.

These considerations do lead, however, to a more fundamental question related to the multidimensional and multilevel characterization of anticipatory processes. If, as asserted herein, the expectancy principle is manifested via a number of different mechanisms that may, or may not, process similar information, to what extent are these anticipatory pathways consistent in their outputs? A related question is to what extent can assessment of higher-order (i.e., language-based) pathways inform about more basic neurophysiological pathways, or even about each other (i.e., explicit to implicit, or vice versa)? Given the range of stimulus inputs handled by these kinds of systems, there is no reason that they should be entirely redundant and consistent in the outputs at which they might arrive. In fact, distinct evolutionary advantage might accrue from the generation of somewhat divergent outputs, because variations in "recommendations" for final outputs would offer more flexibility and adaptability than a unitary system that always offered the same choice. (As noted by Glimcher [2002], some degree of randomness might also be advantageous.) Of course, some means of adjudicating among varied output recommendations would have to be available. As noted earlier, this seems to be the function of specific nuclei in the prefrontal cortex (Latham and Dayan 2005; Machens, Romo, and Brody 2005). As a consequence of the multiple pathways for this kind of decision making, there is no reason to believe that assessing one will automatically provide information about what is going on in another.

Within the explicit domain alone, expectancy instruments have been found to show overlap (Darkes, Greenbaum, Goldman 1996). And, as noted earlier, a recent meta-analysis shows small but reliable overlap between explicit and implicit measures (Reich, Below, and Goldman in press). Within the implicit domain alone, the question of overlap (i.e., a common underlying construct) arises also. We do not yet know the extent to which implicit measures overlap. For a variety of methodological reasons (e.g., measures priming later measures), studies of possible overlap within the implicit domain are difficult to carry out. In addition, although implicit processes need not be verbal in nature, as we have noted, much of the research in this domain uses language-based stimuli. Therefore, some empirical findings may not reflect the implicit–explicit distinction per se, but instead reflect the nature and function of the human language system. And even within the human language system, the general cognitive literature indicates the activity of at least two types of implicit processes; Blaxton (1989) has shown both perceptually based and conceptually based implicit processing for text read from a page or computer screen.

Given these unknowns about the overlap in anticipatory processes, there is no reason to assume that specific interventions designed to affect nonspecific expectancy pathways will necessarily impact all of the pathways involved in influencing particular decisions (assuming, of course, that they effectively influence *any* decisional pathway), any more than we might assume that any single measure of such processes taps *all* relevant information. For example, should a verbal intervention inexorably influence a classically conditioned response, even if both were construed as based on anticipatory processes? It is possible, therefore, that a particular pathway could be influenced without (fully) influencing the decisional end point. If expectancy challenge procedures turn out to be erratic in their influence, this could be one reason why.

Conclusion

We offer this transdisciplinary synthesis in the spirit suggested by Reber's (1997, 52) cautionary admonition: "Psychologists just can't seem to resist dichotomies.... We like to be able to decide that one theory is right and the other wrong.... We seem ineluctably drawn to setting up poles rather than recognizing continua. Alas, this tendency often functions as a hindrance to doing good science." It is this often all-too-reflexive parsing that we have sought to address. Even if the expectancy concept ultimately turns out not to be the optimal integrating device, the diverse literature presented in these pages begs us to decipher common themes that should be capitalized upon to advance the understanding of human decision making in general, and decision making related to alcohol use, abuse, and dependence, in particular.

References

Anderson, K., Schweinsburg, A., and Paulus, M. (2005). Examining personality and alcohol expectancies using functional magnetic resonance imaging (fMRI) with adolescents. *Journal of Studies on Alcohol* 66 (3): 323–331.

Bargh, J. A., Gollwitzer, P. M., Lee-Chai, A., Barndollar, K., and Trotschel, R. (2001). The automated will: Nonconscious activation and pursuit of behavioral goals. *Journal of Personality and Social Psychology* 81: 1014–1027.

Baron, R. M., and Kenny, D. A. (1986). The moderator-mediator variable distinction in social psychological research: conceptual, strategic, and statistical considerations. *Journal of Personality and Social Psychology* 51: 1173–1182.

Baron-Cohen, S., Knickmeyer, R. C., and Belmonte, M. K. (2005). Sex differences in the brain: Implications for explaining autism. *Science* 4: 819–823.

Bechara, A., Damasio, H., and Damasio, A. (2000). Emotion, decision making and the orbitofrontal cortex. *Cerebral Cortex* 10: 295–307.

Bengtsson, S. L., Nagy, Z., Skare, S., Forsman, L., Forssberg, H., and Ullén, F. (2005). Extensive piano practicing has regionally specific effects on white matter development. *Nature Neuroscience* 8: 1148–1150.

Benedetti, F., Pollo, A., and Colloca, L. (2007). Opioid-mediated placebo responses boost pain endurance and physical performance: Is it doping in sport competitions? *Journal of Neuroscience* 27: 11934–11939.

Berridge, K. C., and Robinson, T. E. (1998). What is the role of dopamine in reward: Hedonic impact, reward learning, or incentive salience? *Brain Research and Brain Research Reviews* 28: 309–369.

Blaxton, T. A. (1989). Investigating dissociations among memory measures: Support for a transfer appropriate processing framework. *Journal of Experimental Psychology: Learning, Memory, and Cognition* 15: 657–668.

Bower, G. (2000). A brief history of memory research. In E. Tulving and F. I. M. Craik, eds., *The Oxford Handbook of Memory*. New York: Oxford University Press.

Breiter, H. C., Aharon, I., Kahneman, D., Dale, A., and Shizgal, P. (2001). Functional imaging of neural responses to expectancy and experience of monetary gains and losses. *Neuron* 30 (2): 619–639.

Breiter, H., and Gasic, G. P. (2004). A general circuitry processing reward/aversion information and its implications for neuropsychiatric illness. In M. Gazzaniga, ed., *The Cognitive Neurosciences*, 3rd ed. Cambridge, MA: MIT Press.

Breiter, H. C., Gollub, R. L., Weisskoff, R. M., Kennedy, D. N., Makris, N., Berke, J. D., Goodman, J. M., Kantor, H. L., Gastfriend, D. R., Riorden, J. P., Mathew, R. T., Rosen, B. R., and Hyman, S. E. (1997). Acute effects of cocaine on human brain activity and emotion. *Neuron* 19: 591–611.

Brembs, B. (2003). Operant reward learning in aplysia. *Current Directions in Psychological Science* 12 (6): 218–221.

Brown, S. A., Goldman, M. S., and Inn, A. (1980). Expectations of reinforcement from alcohol: Their domain and relation to drinking patterns. *Journal of Consulting and Clinical Psychology* 48 (4): 419–426.

Bundesen, C., Habekost, T., and Kyllingsbaek, S. (2005). A neural theory of visual attention: Bridging cognition and neurophysiology. *Psychological Review* 112 (2): 291–328.

Buszaki, G. (2005). Similar is different in hippocamal networks. *Science* 309: 568–569.

Calvin, W. H., and Bickerton, D. (2000). *Lingua ex Machina: Reconciling Darwin and Chomsky with the Human Brain.* Cambridge, MA: MIT Press.

Cardinal, R. N., and Everitt, B. J. (2004). Neural and psychological mechanisms underlying appetitive learning: Links to drug addiction. *Current Opinion in Neurobiology* 14: 156–162.

Carter, J. A., McNair, L. D., Corbin, W. R., and Black, D. H. (1998). Effects of priming positive and negative outcomes on drinking responses. *Experimental and Clinical Psychopharmacology* 6: 399–405.

Caspi, A., Roberts, B. W., and Shiner, R. L. (2005). Personality development: Stability and change. *Annual Review of Psychology* 56: 453–484.

Catmur, C., Walsh, B., and Heyes, C. (2007). Sensorimotor learning configures the human mirror system. *Current Biology* 17: 1527–1531.

Changizi, M. A., Hsich, A., Nijhawan, R., Kanai, R., and Shimojo, S. (2008). Perceiving the present and systematization of illusions. *Cognitive Science* 32: 459–503.

Chklovskii, D. B., Mel, B. W., and Svoboda, K. (2004). Cortical rewiring and information storage. *Nature* 431: 782–788.

Christiansen, B. A., Smith, G. T., Roehling, P. V., and Goldman, M. S. (1989). Using alcohol expectancies to predict adolescent drinking behavior at one year. *Journal of Consulting and Clinical Psychology* 57: 93–99.

Cohen, J., and Blum, K. (2002). Reward and decision. *Neuron* 36: 193–198.

Cohen, M. X., and Ranganath, C. (2005). Behavioral and neural predictors of upcoming decisions. *Cognitive, Affective, and Behavioral Neuroscience* 5 (2): 117–126.

Colunga, E., and Smith, L. B. (2005). From the lexicon to expectations about kinds: A role for associative learning. *Psychological Review* 112 (2): 347–382.

Corbin, W. R., McNair, L. D., and Carter, J. A. (2001). Evaluation of a treatment-appropriate cognitive intervention for challenging alcohol outcome expectancies. *Addictive Behaviors* 26: 475–488.

Correa, A., Lupiáñez, J., and Tudela, P. (2005). Attentional preparation based on temporal expectancy modulates processing at the perceptual level. *Psychonomic Bulletin and Review* 12 (2): 328–334.

Darkes, J., Del Boca, F. K., Goldman, M. S., and Brandon, K. O. (2003). The expectancy challenge: What are the essential elements? Paper presented at the 2003 Annual Scientific Meeting of the Research Society on Alcoholism, Ft. Lauderdale, FL.

Darkes, J., and Goldman, M. S. (1993). Expectancy challenge and drinking reduction: Experimental evidence for a mediational process. *Journal of Consulting and Clinical Psychology* 61 (2): 344–353.

Darkes, J., and Goldman, M. S. (1998). Expectancy challenge and drinking reduction: Process and structure in the alcohol expectancy network. *Experimental and Clinical Psychopharmacology* 6: 1–13.

Darkes, J., Greenbaum, P. E., Goldman, M. S. (1996). Positive/arousal and social facilitation alcohol expectancies and concurrent alcohol use. Paper presented at the 1996 Annual Scientific Meeting of the Research Society on Alcoholism, Washington, D.C.

Darkes, J., Greenbaum, P. E., and Goldman, M. S. (2004). Alcohol expectancy mediation of biopsychosocial risk: Complex patterns of mediation. *Experimental and Clinical Psychopharmacology* 12 (1): 27–38.

Deese, J. (1959). On the prediction of occurrence of particular verbal intrusions in immediate recall. *Journal of Experimental Psychology* 58: 17–22.

Del Boca, F. K., and Darkes, J. (2001). Is the glass half full or half empty? An evaluation of the status of expectancies as causal agents. *Addiction* 96 (11): 1670–1672.

Del Boca, F. K., Darkes, J. Greenbaum, P. E., and Goldman, M. S. (2004). Up close and personal: Temporal variability in the drinking of individual college students during their first year. *Journal of Consulting and Clinical Psychology* 72 (2): 155–164.

Dennett, D. C. (1991). *Consciousness Explained.* New York: Little, Brown.

DiPietro, J. A., Hodgson, D. M., Costigan, K. A., and Johnson, T. R. B. (1996). Fetal antecedents of infant temperament. *Child Development* 67: 2568–2583.

Donchin, E., and Coles, M. G. (1988). Is the P300 component a manifestation of context updating? *Behavioral and Brain Sciences* 11 (3): 357–427.

Dragoi, V., and Staddon, J. E. R. (1999). The dynamics of operant conditioning. *Psychological Review* 106 (1): 20–61.

Drobes, D. J., Carter, A. C., and Goldman, M. S. (2009). Alcohol expectancies and reactivity to alcohol-related and affective cues. *Experimental and Clinical Psychopharmacology* 17 (1): 1–9.

Dunn, M. E., and Goldman, M. S. (1996). Empirical modeling of an alcohol expectancy network in elementary school children as a function of grade. *Experimental and Clinical Psychopharmacology* 4 (2): 209–217.

Dunn, M. E., and Goldman, M. S. (1998). Age and drinking-related differences in the memory organization of alcohol expectancies in 3rd-, 6th-, 9th-, and 12th-grade children. *Journal of Consulting and Clinical Psychology* 66 (3): 579–585.

Dunn, M. E., and Goldman, M. S. (2000). Validation of multidimensional scaling-based modeling of alcohol expectancies in memory: Age and drinking-related differences in expectancies of children assessed as first associates. *Alcoholism: Clinical and Experimental Research* 24 (11): 1639–1646.

Dunn, M. E., Lau, H. C., and Cruz, I. Y. (2000). Changes in activation of alcohol expectancies in memory in relation to changes in alcohol use after participation in an expectancy challenge program. *Experimental and Clinical Psychopharmacology* 8: 566–575.

Estes, W. K. (1991). Cognitive architectures from the standpoint of an experimental psychologist. *Annual Review of Psychology: Neuropsychology* 8: 464–475.

Feldman, D. E., and Brecht, M. (2005). Map plasticity in somatosensory cortex. *Science* 310: 810–815.

Finn, P. R., Bobova, L., Wehner, E., Fargo, S., and Rickert, M. E. (2005). Alcohol expectancies, conduct disorder and early-onset alcoholism: Negative alcohol expectancies are associated with less drinking in non-impulsive versus impulsive subjects. *Addiction* 100 (7): 953–962.

Finn, P. R., Sharkansky, E. J., Brandt, K. M., and Turcotte, N. (2000). The effects of familial risk, personality, and expectancies on alcohol use and abuse. *Journal of Abnormal Psychology* 109: 122–133.

Fishman, I., Goldman, M. S., and Donchin, E. (2008). The P300 as an electrophysiological probe of alcohol expectancy. *Experimental and Clinical Psychopharmacology* 16: 341–356.

Fitzpatrick, D. (2005). Zooming in on cortical maps. *Nature Neuroscience* 8: 264.

Fogassi, L., Ferrari, P. F., and Gesierich, B. (2005). Parietal lobe: From action organization to intention understanding. *Science* 308 (5722): 662–667.

Frishman, L. J. (2001). Basic visual processes. In E. B. Goldstein, ed., *Blackwell Handbook of Perception*. Malden, MA: Blackwell.

Gawronski, B., LeBel, E. P., and Peters, K. R. (2007). What do implicit measures tell us? Scrutinizing the validity of three common assumptions. *Perspectives on Psychological Science* 2: 181–193.

Glimcher, P. W. (2002). Decisions, decisions, decisions: Choosing a biological science of choice. *Neuron* 36 (2): 323–332.

Glimcher, P. W. (2005). Indeterminacy in brain and behavior. *Annual Review of Psychology* 56: 25–56.

Glimcher, P. W., and Lau, B. (2005). Rethinking the thalamus. *Nature Neuroscience* 8: 983–984.

Glimcher, P. W., and Rustichini, A. (2004). Neuroeconomics: The consilience of brain and decision. *Science* 306 (5695): 447–452.

Goldman, D., Oroszi, G., and Ducci, F. (2005). The genetics of addictions: Uncovering the genes. *Nature Reviews: Genetics* 6: 521–532.

Goldman, M. S. (1999). Expectancy operation: Cognitive and neural models and architectures. In I. Kirsch, ed., *How Expectancies Shape Experience*. Washington, D.C.: American Psychological Association.

Goldman, M. S. (2002). Expectancy and risk for alcoholism: The unfortunate exploitation of a fundamental characteristic of neurobehavioral adaptation. *Alcoholism: Clinical and Experimental Research* 26 (5): 737–746.

Goldman, M. S., and Darkes, J. (2004). Alcohol expectancy multi-axial assessment (A.E.Max): A memory network-based approach. *Psychological Assessment* 16: 4–15.

Goldman, M. S., Darkes, J., and Del Boca, F. K. (1999). Expectancy mediation of biopsychosocial risk for alcohol use and alcoholism. In I. Kirsch, ed., *How Expectancies Shape Experience*. Washington, D.C.: American Psychological Association.

Goldman, M. S., Reich, R. R., and Darkes, J. (2006). Expectancy as a unifying construct in alcohol-related cognition. In R. W. Wiers and A. W. Stacy, eds., *Handbook of Implicit Cognition and Addiction*, 105–121. Thousand Oaks, CA: Sage Publications.

Gottesman, I. I., and Hanson, D. R. (2005). Human development: Biological and genetic processes. *Annual Review of Psychology* 56: 263–286.

Gottesman, I. I., Shields, J., and Hanson, D. R. (1982). *Schizophrenia: The Epigenetic Puzzle*. London: Cambridge University Press.

Gray, R., Beilock, S. L., and Carr, T. H. (2007). "As soon as the bat met the ball, I knew it was gone": Outcome prediction, hindsight bias, and the representation and control of action in expert and novice baseball players. *Psychonomic Bulletin and Review* 14: 669–675.

Grossberg, S. (1995). The attentive brain. *American Scientist* 83: 438–449.

Gruenewald, P., Millar, A., and Treno, A. (1993). Alcohol availability and the ecology of drinking behavior. *Alcohol Health and Research World* 17 (1): 39–45.

Haith, M. M., Hazan, C., and Goodman, G. S. (1988). Expectation and anticipation of dynamic visual events by 3.5-month-old babies. *Childhood Development* 59: 467–479.

Ham, L. S., Carrigan, M. H., Moak, D. H., and Randle, C. L. (2005). Social anxiety and specificity of positive alcohol expectancies: Preliminary findings. *Journal of Psychopathology and Behavioral Assessment* 27 (2): 115–121.

Hampson, R. E., Pons, T. P., Stanford, T. R., and Deadwyler, S. A. (2004). Categorization in the monkey hippocampus: A possible mechanism for encoding information into memory. *Proceedings of the National Academy of Sciences* 101: 3184–3189.

Heekeren, H. R., Marrett, S., Bandettini, P. A., and Ungerleider, L. G. (2004). A general mechanism for perceptual decision-making in the human brain. *Nature* 431 (7010): 859–861.

Heinrichs, S. C., and Koob, G. F. (2004). Corticotropin-releasing factor in brain: A role of activation, arousal and affect regulation. *Journal of Pharmacology and Experimental Therapeutics* 311 (2): 427–440.

Helzer, J. E., van den Brink, W., and Guth, S. E. (2006). Should there be both categorical and dimensional criteria for substance use disorders in DSM V? *Addiction* 101 (suppl. 1): 17–22.

Henderson, M. J., Goldman, M. S., Coovert, M. D., and Carnevalla, N. (1994). Covariance structure models of expectancy. *Journal of Studies on Alcohol* 55: 315–326.

Holland, P. C., and Gallagher, M. (2004). Amygdala-frontal interactions and reward expectancy. *Current Opinion in Neurobiology* 14: 148–155.

Houben, K., and Wiers, R. W. (2006). Assessing implicit alcohol associations with the Implicit Association Test: Fact or fiction? *Addictive Behaviors* 31: 1346–1362.

Hunt, W. M., Darkes, J., and Goldman, M. S. (2005). Effects of participant engagement on alcohol expectancies and drinking outcomes for a computerized expectancy challenge intervention with college student drinkers. *Alcoholism: Clinical and Experimental Research* 29: 73A.

Huron, D. (2006). *Sweet Anticipation: Music and the Psychology of Expectation*. Cambridge, MA: MIT Press.

Iacoboni, M., Molnar-Szakacs, I., Gallese, V., Buccino, G., Mazziotta, J. C., and Rizzolatti, G. (2005). Grasping the intentions of others with one's own mirror neuron system. *Public Library of Science Biology* 3 (3): 529–535.

Iversen, S., Kupfermann, I., and Kandel, E. R. (2000). Emotional states and feelings. In E. R. Kandel, J. H. Schwartz, and T. M. Jessell, eds., *Principles of Neural Science*, 4th ed. New York: McGraw-Hill.

Jablonka, E., and Lamb, M. J. (2002). The changing concept of epigenetics. *Annual Proceedings of the New York Academy of Sciences* 981: 82.

Johnson, J. S., Woodman, G. F., Braun, E., and Luck, S. J. (2007). Implicit memory influences the allocation of attention in visual cortex *Psychonomic Bulletin and Review* 14: 834–839.

Jones, B. T., Corbin, W., and Fromme, K. (2001a). A review of expectancy theory and alcohol consumption *Addiction* 91: 57–72.

Jones, B. T., Corbin, W., and Fromme, K. (2001b). Half full or half empty, the glass still does not satisfactorily quench the thirst for knowledge on alcohol expectancies as a mechanism of change. *Addiction* 96 (11): 1672–1674.

Kagan, J. (2007). A trio of concerns. *Perspectives on Psychological Science* 2: 361–376.

Kandel, E. R., and Squire, L. R. (2000). Neuroscience: breaking down scientific barriers to the study of brain and mind. *Science* 290: 1113–1120.

Katner, S. N., Kerr, T. M., and Weiss, F. (1996). Ethanol anticipation enhances dopamine efflux in the nucleus accumbens of alcohol-preferring (P) but not Wistar rats. *Behavioral Pharmacology* 8: 669–674.

Keillor, R. M., Perkins, W. B., and Horan, J. J. (1999). Effects of videotaped expectancy challenges on alcohol consumption of adjudicated students. *Journal of Cognitive Psychotherapy: An International Quarterly* 13 (3): 179–187.

Kerzel, D. (2005). Representational momentum beyond internalized physics. Embodied mechanisms of anticipation cause errors in visual short-term memory. *Current Directions in Psychological Science* 14 (4): 180–184.

Kilner, J. M., Vargas, C., Duval, S., Blakemore, S.-J., and Sirigu, A. (2004). Motor activation prior to observation of a predicted movement. *Nature Neuroscience* 7: 1299–1301.

King-Casas, B., Tomlin, D., and Anen, C. (2005). Getting to know you: Reputation and trust in a two-person economic exchange. *Science* 308 (5718): 78–83.

Kirsch, I., ed. (1999). *How Expectancies Shape Experience*. Washington, D.C.: American Psychological Association.

Kirsch, I., Deacon, B. J., Huedo-Medina, T. B., Scoboria, A., Moore, T. J., and Johnson, B. T. (2008). Initial severity and antidepressant effects: A meta-analysis of data submitted to the Food and Drug Administration. *PLoS Medicine* 5: 260–268.

Kirsch, I., Lynn, S. J., Vigorito, M., and Miller, R. M. (2004). The role of cognition in classical and operant conditioning. *Journal of Clinical Psychology* 60 (4): 369–392.

Kirsch, I., and Scoboria, A. (2001). Apples, oranges, and placeboes: Heterogeneity in a meta-analysis of placebo effects. *Advances in Mind-Body Medicine* 17: 307–309.

Koob, G. F., and Le Moal, M. (2008). Addiction and the brain antireward system. In S. T. Fiske, D. L. Schacter, and R. Sternberg, eds., *Annual Review of Psychology*. Palo Alto: Annual Reviews.

Kramer, D. A., and Goldman, M. S. (2003). Using a modified Stroop task to implicitly discern the cognitive organization of alcohol expectancies. *Journal of Abnormal Psychology* 112 (1): 171–175.

Kupfermann, I., Kandel, E. R., and Iversen, S. (2000). Motivational and addictive states. In E. R. Kandel, J. H. Schwartz, and T. M. Jessell, eds., *Principles of Neural Science*. New York: McGraw-Hill.

Lanzavecchia, A., and Sallusto, F. (2002). Progressive differentiation and selection of the fittest in the immune response. *Nature Reviews: Immunology* 2: 982–987.

Latham, P. E., and Dayan, P. (2005). Touché: The feeling of choice. *Nature Neuroscience* 8 (4): 408–409.

Lau-Barraco, C., and Dunn, M. E. (2008). Evaluation of a single-session expectancy challenge intervention to reduce alcohol use among college students. *Psychology of Addictive Behaviors* 22: 168–175.

Lee, D. (2005). Neuroeconomics: Making risky choices in the brain. *Nature Neuroscience* 8: 1129–1130.

Leigh, B. C., and Stacy, A. W. (1993). Alcohol outcome expectancies: Scale construction and predictive utility in higher order confirmatory models. *Psychological Assessment* 5: 216–229.

Leutgeb, S., Leutgeb, J. K., Barnes, C. A., Moser, E. I., McNaughton, B. L., and Moser, M.-B. (2005). Independent codes for spatial and episodic memory in hippocampal neuronal ensembles. *Science* 22 (309): 619–623.

Lowenstein, G., Rick, S., and Cohen, J. D. (2008). Neuroeconomics. In S. T. Fiske, D. L. Schacter, and R. Sternberg, eds., *Annual Review of Psychology*. Palo Alto: Annual Reviews.

Machens, C. K., Romo, R., and Brody, C. D. (2005). Flexible control of mutual inhibition: A neural model of two-interval discrimination. *Science* 307: 1121–1124.

Marlatt, G. A., Demming, B., and Reid, J. B. (1973). Loss of control drinking in alcoholics: An experimental analogue. *Journal of Abnormal Psychology* 81 (3): 233–241.

Martin, A., and Gotts, S. J. (2005). Making the causal link: Frontal cortex activity and repetition priming. *Nature Neuroscience* 8: 1134–1135.

Matsumoto, K., and Tanaka, K. (2004). The role of the medial prefrontal cortex in achieving goals. *Current Opinion in Neurobiology* 14: 178–185.

Maunsell, J. H. R. (1995). The brain's visual world: Representation of visual targets in cerebral cortex. *Science* 270 (5237): 764–768.

McCarthy, D. M., Brown, S. A., Carr, L. G., and Wall, T. L. (2001). ALDH2 status, alcohol expectancies, and alcohol response: Preliminary evidence for a mediation model. *Alcoholism: Clinical and Experimental Research* 25 (11): 1558–1563.

McCarthy, D. M., Wall, T. L., Brown, S. A., and Carr, L. G. (2000). Integrating biological and behavioral factors in alcohol use risk: The role of ALDH2 status and alcohol expectancies in a sample of Asian Americans. *Experimental and Clinical Psychopharmacology* 8: 168–175.

McClure, S. M., Laibson, D. I., and Loewenstein, G. (2004). Separate neural systems value immediate and delayed monetary rewards. *Science* 306 (5695): 503–507.

Merrill, K., Steinmetz, J. E., Viken, R. J., and Rose, R. J. (1999). Genetic influences on human conditionability: A twin study of the conditioned eyeblink response. *Behavior Genetics* 29 (2): 95–102.

Miller, G. (2005). Economic game shows how the brain builds trust. *Science* 308: 36.

Minamimoto, T., Hori, Y., and Kimura, M. (2005). Complementary process to response bias in the centromedian nucleus of the thalamus. *Science* 308 (5729): 1798–1801.

Miyashita, Y. (2004). Cognitive memory: cellular and network machineries and their top-down control. *Science* 306 (5695): 435–440.

Montague, P. R., and Berns, G. S. (2002). Neural economics and the biological substrates of valuation. *Neuron* 36 (2): 265–284.

Moore, B. C. J. (2001). Basic auditory processes. In E. B. Goldstein, ed., *Blackwell Handbook of Perception*. Malden, MA: Blackwell.

Muthen, B. (2006). Should substance use disorders be considered as categorical or dimensional? *Addiction* 101 (suppl. 1): 6–16.

Nakazawa, K., Quirk, M. C., and Chitwood, R. (2002). A requirement for hippocampal CA3 NMDA receptors in associative memory recall. *Science* 297 (5579): 211–218.

Nelson, D. L., McEvoy, C. L., and Dennis, S. (2000). What is free association and what does it measure? *Memory and Cognition* 28 (6): 887–899.

Nelson, D. L., McEvoy, C. L., and Pointer, L. (2003). Spreading activation or spooky action at a distance. *Journal of Experimental Psychology: Learning, Memory, and Cognition* 29 (1): 42–51.

Nelson, D. L., McEvoy, C. L., and Schreiber, T. A. (1998). The University of South Florida word assocaiation, rhyme, and word fragment norms. Retrieved November 21, 2000, from http:// w3.usf.edu/~fan/.

Nobre, A. C. (2001). Orienting attention to instants in time. *Neuropsychologia* 39 (12): 1317–1328.

Norretranders, T. (1991). *The User Illusion: Cutting Consciousness Down to Size*. New York: Penguin.

Palfai, T. P., Monti, P. M., and Ostafin, B. (2000). Effects of nicotine deprivation on alcohol-related information processing and drinking behavior. *Journal of Abnormal Psychology* 109 (1): 96–105.

Palfai, T., and Wood, M. D. (2001). Positive alcohol expectancies and drinking behavior: The influence of expectancy strength and memory accessibility. *Psychology of Addictive Behaviors* 15 (1): 60–67.

Park, C. L., and Grant, C. (2005). Determinants of positive and negative consequences of alcohol consumption in college students: Alcohol use, gender, and psychological characteristics. *Addictive Behaviors* 30 (4): 755–765.

Petrovic, P., Dietrich, T., Fransson, P., Andersson, J., Carlsson, K., and Ingvar, M. (2005). Placebo in emotional processing—induced expectations of anxiety relief activate a generalized modulatory network. *Neuron* 46: 957–969.

Phelps, E. A. (2004). Human emotion and memory: Interactions of the amygdala and hippocampal complex. *Current Opinion in Neurobiology* 14: 198–202.

Poggio, T., and Bizzi, E. (2004). Generalization in vision and motor control. *Nature* 431 (7010): 768–774.

Posner, M. I., Snyder, C. R. R., and Davidson, B. J. (1980). Attention and the detection of signals. *Journal of Experimental Psychology* 109: 160–174.

Price, D. D., Finniss, D. G., and Benedetti, F. (2008). A comprehensive review of the placebo effect: Recent advances and current thought. In S. T. Fiske, D. L. Schacter, and R. Sternberg, eds., *Annual Review of Psychology*. Palo Alto: Annual Reviews.

Rather, B. C., and Goldman, M. S. (1994). Drinking-related differences in the memory organization of alcohol expectancies. *Experimental and Clinical Psychopharmacology* 2 (2): 167–183.

Rather, B. C., Goldman, M. S., Roehrich, L., and Brannick, M. (1992). Empirical modeling of an alcohol expectancy memory network using multidimensional scaling. *Journal of Abnormal Psychology* 101 (1): 174–183.

Reber, A. S. (1997). How to differentiate implicit and explicit modes of acquisition. In J. D. Cohen and J. W. Schooler, eds., *Scientific Approaches to Consciousness*. Hillsdale, NJ: Lawrence Erlbaum.

Reich, R. R., Below, M. C., and Goldman, M. S. (in press). Explicit and implicit measures of expectancy and related alcohol cognitions: A meta-analytic investigation. *Psychology of Addictive Behaviors*.

Reich, R. R., and Goldman, M. S. (2005). Exploring the alcohol expectancy memory network: The utility of free associates. *Psychology of Addictive Behaviors* 19: 317–325.

Reich, R. R., Goldman, M. S., and Noll, J. A. (2004). Using the false memory paradigm to test two key elements of alcohol expectancy theory. *Experimental and Clinical Psychopharmacology* 12 (2): 102–110.

Reich, R. R., Kwiatkowski, J. L. V., Lombardi, S. E., Nicklaus, H. M., Wooten, C. L., Below, M. C., and Goldman, M. S. (2008). Context and alcohol expectancies: How location changes free associates. Paper submitted for presentation to the Annual Scientific Meeting of the Research Society on Alcoholism, June 2008, Washington, D.C.

Reich, R. R., Noll, J. A., and Goldman, M. S. (2005). Cue patterns and alcohol expectancies: How slight differences in stimuli can measurably change cognition. *Experimental and Clinical Psychopharmacology* 13: 65–71.

Ritov, I. (2000). The role of expectations in comparisons. *Psychological Review* 107: 345–357.

Robinson, T. E., and Berridge, K. C. (2000). The psychology and neurobiology of addiction: An incentive-salience view. *Addiction* 95 (suppl. 2): S91–S117.

Roediger, H. L. (2003). Reconsidering implicit memory. In J. S. Bowers and C. J. Marsolek, eds., *Rethinking Implicit Memory*, 3–18. New York: Oxford University Press.

Roediger, H. L., Buckner, R. L., and McDermott, K. B. (1999). Components of processing. In J. K. Foster and M. Jelicic, eds., *Memory: Systems, Process, or Function*. New York: Oxford Univeristy Press.

Roediger, H. L., and McDermott, K. B. (1995). Creating false memories—remembering words not presented in lists. *Journal of Experimental Psychology: Learning, Memory, and Cognition* 21 (4): 803–814.

Roediger, H. L., and McDermott, K. B. (2000). Tricks of memory. *Current Directions in Psychological Science* 9: 123–127.

Roehrich, L., and Goldman, M. S. (1995). Implicit priming of alcohol expectancy memory processes and subsequent drinking behavior. *Experimental and Clinical Psychopharmacology* 3 (4): 402–410.

Saper, C. B., Iversen, S., and Frackowiak, R. (2000). Integration of sensory and motor function: The association areas of the cerebral cortex and the cognitive capabilties of the brain. In E. R. Kandel, J. H. Schwartz, and T. M. Jessell, eds., *Principles of Neural Science*, 4th edition. New York: McGraw-Hill.

Scheier, L. M., and Botvin, G. J. (1997). Expectancies as mediators of the effects of social influences and alcohol knowledge on adolescent alcohol use: A prospective analysis. *Psychology of Addictive Behaviors* 11: 48–64.

Schuckit, M. A., Smith, T. L., Danko, G. P., Anderson, K. G., Brown, S. A., Kuperman, S., Kramer, J., Hesselbrock, V., and Bucholz, K. (2005). Evaluation of a level of response to alcohol-based structural equation model in adolescents. *Journal of Studies on Alcohol* 66: 174–184.

Schultz, W. (2004). Neural coding of basic reward terms of animal learning theory, game theory, microeconomics, and behavioural ecology. *Current Opinion in Neurobiology* 14: 139–147.

Schultz, W., Dayan, P., and Montague, P. R. (1997). A neural substrate of prediction and reward. *Science* 275: 1593–1599.

Schultz, W., Tremblay, L., and Hollerman, J. R. (2000). Reward processing in primate orbitofrontal cortex and basal ganglia. *Cerebral Cortex* 10 (3): 272–283.

Sell, L. A., Morris, J., Bearn, J., Frackowiak, R. S., Friston, K. J., and Dolan, R. J. (2000). Neural responses associated with cue evoked emotional states and heroin in opiate addicts. *Drug and Alcohol Dependence* 60: 207–216.

Sher, K. J., Grekin, E. R., and Williams, N. A. (2005). The development of alcohol use disorders. *Annual Review of Clinical Psychology* 1 (1): 493–523.

Sher, K. J., Wood, M. D., Wood, P. K., and Raskin, G. (1996). Alcohol outcome expectancies and alcohol use: A latent variable cross-lagged panel study. *Journal of Abnormal Psychology* 103: 561–574.

Singer, W. (1995). Development and plasticity of cortical processing architectures. *Science* 270: 785–764.

Slutske, W. S., Heath, A. C., and Madden, P. (2002). Personality and the genetic risk for alcohol dependence. *Journal of Abnormal Psychology* 111 (1): 124–133.

Smith, G. T., and Anderson, K. G. (2001). Personality and learning factors combine to create risk for adolescent problem drinking: A model and suggestions for intervention. In P. M. Monti, S. M. Colby, and T. A. O'Leary, eds., *Adolescents, Alcohol, and Substance Abuse: Reaching Teens through Brief Interventions*. New York: Guilford Publications.

Smith, G. T., Goldman, M. S., Greenbaum, P. E., and Christiansen, B. A. (1995). Expectancy for social facilitation from drinking: The divergent paths of high-expectancy and low-expectancy adolescents. *Journal of Abnormal Psychology* 104: 32–40.

Stacy, A. W. (1995). Memory association and ambiguous cues in models of alcohol and marijuana use. *Experimental and Clinical Psychopharmacology* 3 (2): 183–194.

Stacy, A. W. (1997). Memory activation and expectancy as prospective predictors of alcohol and marijuana use. *Journal of Abnormal Psychology* 106 (1): 61–73.

Stacy, A. W., and Leigh, B. C. (1993). Memory accessibility and association of alcohol use and its positive outcomes. *Experimental and Clinical Psychopharmacology* 2 (3): 269–282.

Stacy, A. W., Newcomb, M. D., and Bentler, P. M. (1991). Cognitive motivation and problem drug use: A 9-year longitudinal study. *Journal of Abnormal Psychology* 100: 502–515.

Stein, K. D., Goldman, M. S., and Del Boca, F. K. (2000). The influence of alcohol expectancy priming and mood manipulation on subsequent alcohol consumption. *Journal of Abnormal Psychology* 109 (1): 106–115.

Tarr, M. (2005). How experience shapes vision. Psychological Science Agenda Website. Available at http://www.apa.org/science/psa/july05.pdf.

Tobler, P. N., Fiorillo, C. D., and Schultz, W. (2005). Adaptive coding of reward value by dopamine neurons. *Science* 307 (5715): 1642–1645.

Tolman, E. C. (1932). *Purposive Behavior in Animals and Man.* New York: Appleton-Century-Crofts.

Tsodyks, M., and Gilbert, C. (2004). Neural networks and perceptual learning. *Nature* 431 (7010): 775–781.

Tulving, E. (1999). Study of memory: Processes and systems. In J. K. Foster and M. Jelicic, eds., *Memory: Systems, Process, or Function*, 11–30. New York: Oxford University Press.

Van Hamme, L. J., and Wasserman, E. A. (1994). Cue competition in causality judgments: The role of nonpresentation of compound stimulus elements. *Learning Motivation* 25: 127–151.

Vernon, P. A., Lee, D., Harris, J. A., and Jang, K. L. (1996). Genetic and environmental contributions to individual differences in alcohol expectancies. *Personality and Individual Differences* 21 (2): 183–187.

Waber, R. L., Shiv, B., Carmon, Z., and Ariely, D. (2008). Commercial features of placebo and therapeutic efficacy. *Journal of the American Medical Association* 299: 1016–1017.

Wager, T. D. (2005). The neural bases of placebo effects in anticipation and pain. *Seminars in Pain Medicine* 3: 22–30.

Wager, T. D., Rilling, J. K., and Smith, E. E. (2004). Placebo-induced changes in fMRI in the anticipation and experience of pain. *Science* 303 (5661): 1162–1167.

Wall, A. M., Hinson, R. E., McKee, S. A., and Goldstein, A. (2001). Examining alcohol outcome expectancies in laboratory and naturalistic bar settings: A within-subject experimental analysis. *Psychology of Addictive Behaviors* 15 (3): 219–226.

Weinberger, A. H., Darkes, J., Del Boca, F. K., Greenbaum, P. E., and Goldman, M. S. (2006). Items as context: The effect of item order on factor structure and predictive validity. *Basic and Applied Social Psychology* 28: 17–26.

Whewell, W. (1840, 1967). *The Philosophy of the Inductive Sciences.* London: Cass Publishing.

Widdows, D. (2004). *Geometry and Meaning.* Stanford, CA: CSLI Publications.

Wiers, R. W., Van de Luitgaarden, J., Van den Wildenberg, E., and Smulders, F. T. Y. (2005). Challenging implicit and explicit alcohol-related cognitions in young heavy drinkers. *Addiction* 100: 806–819.

Wiers, R. W., van Woerden, N., Smulders, F. T. Y., and de Jong, P. J. (2002). Implicit and explicit alcohol-related cognitions in heavy and light drinkers. *Journal of Abnormal Psychology* 111 (4): 648–658.

Wills, T. J., Lever, C., and Cacucci, F. (2005). Attractor dynamics in the hippocampal representation of the local environment. *Science* 308 (5723): 873–876.

Wilson, E. O. (1998). *Consilience: The Unity of Knowledge.* New York: Knopf.

Winocur, G., Moscovitch, M., and Fogel, S. (2005). Preserved spatial memory after hippocampal lesions: Effects of extensive experience in a complex environment. *Nature Neuroscience* 8 (3): 273–275.

Wood, M. D., Capone, C., Laforge, R., Erickson, D. J., and Brand, N. H. (2007). Brief motivational intervention and alcohol expectancy challenge with heavy drinking college students: A randomized factorial study. *Addictive Behaviors* 32: 2509–2528.

Wulf, G., and Prinz, W. (2001). Directing attention to movement effects enhances learning: A review. *Psychonomic Bulletin and Review* 8: 648–660.

12   Impulsivity and Its Association with Treatment Development for Pathological Gambling and Substance Use Disorders

Nancy M. Petry

Pathological gambling is a disorder of impulse control that often occurs in conjunction with substance use disorders. Research is beginning to examine the association between these disorders, especially with regard to impulsivity and discounting and how these constructs may inform treatment development. This chapter initially outlines the diagnosis and prevalence rates of pathological gambling, including its association with substance use disorders. It then describes studies assessing constructs of impulsivity in pathological gamblers and substance abusers. Finally, a treatment strategy for substance use disorders, known as contingency management, is detailed. Adaptations of this intervention for use with pathological gamblers are suggested.

Pathological Gambling: Prevalence Rates and Comorbidities

The *Diagnostic and Statistical Manual of Mental Disorders*, fourth edition (DSM-IV), defines pathological gambling as persistent and recurrent gambling that is disruptive to one's personal life, family, or vocation (American Psychiatric Association 1994). For a diagnosis, one must meet at least five out of ten criteria: (1) preoccupation with gambling; (2) need to gamble with increasing amounts of money; (3) repeated unsuccessful attempts to stop or reduce gambling; (4) restlessness and/or irritability when trying to reduce or stop gambling; (5) gambling in order to escape unpleasant emotions; (6) chasing losses; (7) lying to others to hide the extent of gambling; (8) committing illegal acts to finance gambling; (9) placing a relationship, job, or educational opportunity at risk by gambling; and (10) seeking assistance from others to relieve desperate financial situations caused by gambling.

Although not considered a diagnosis according to the DSM-IV, *problem gambling* is a term commonly used for individuals who meet some of these diagnostic criteria but not the five necessary for a diagnosis (Petry 2005). The term *disordered gambling* will be used throughout this chapter to refer to the combined group of both problem and pathological gamblers.

Three nationally representative surveys have been conducted examining the prevalence rates of disordered gambling in the United States. Gerstein et al. (1999) surveyed

2,417 randomly selected residents by phone in the National Gambling Impact Study. They reported a 0.8% prevalence rate of pathological gambling and a 1.3% rate of problem gambling. Welte et al. (2001) found lifetime prevalence rates of pathological and problem gambling of 2.0% and 2.8%, respectively, in a phone survey of 2,638 adults from across the country. From the National Epidemiology Survey of Alcohol and Related Disorders (NESARC), which involved an in-person survey of over 43,000 randomly selected adults throughout the United States, Petry, Stinson, and Grant (2005a) found that lifetime prevalence rates of pathological gambling were 0.4%.

These three national surveys also examined the relationships between pathological gambling and substance use disorders, and all reported positive associations. For example, Gerstein et al. (1999) found that 9.9% pathological gamblers also had alcohol dependence, compared with 1.1% of nongamblers. Welte et al. (2001), similarly, noted that pathological gamblers had much higher rates of alcohol dependence (25%) than nongamblers (1.4%). In the NESARC study, Petry, Stinson, and Grant (2005) reported alcohol dependence was five times higher in pathological gamblers than nonpathological gamblers. Petry, Stinson, and Grant (2005) also found that pathological gambling increased the odds of an illicit drug use disorder 4.4–fold, with 38.1% of lifetime pathological gamblers having one or more illicit substance use disorder versus 8.8% of nonpathological gamblers.

Treatment samples also show high rates of comorbidity between gambling and substance use disorders. Shaffer, Hall, and Vander Bilt (1999) estimate rates of pathological gambling among substance abusers to be 14% across 18 surveys of adults in treatment for substance use disorders; this rate is significantly higher than the 0.4–2.0% rate of lifetime pathological gambling in general population surveys (Gerstein et al. 1999; Petry, Stinson, and Grant 2005; Welte et al. 2001). Large studies of treatment-seeking substance abusers also show that 10–13% of substance-dependent individuals meet criteria for pathological gambling (e.g., Cunningham-Williams et al. 2000; Langenbucher et al. 2001; Toneatto and Brennan 2002). Conversely, persons seeking treatment for pathological gambling either through Gamblers Anonymous (GA) or professional treatment programs are more likely to meet the diagnostic criteria for a substance use disorder than the general population (Ibanez et al. 2001; Ladd and Petry 2003; Maccallum and Blaszczynski 2002; Specker et al. 1996). Thus, all the available epidemiological data indicate that substance use and gambling disorders have high rates of comorbidity, and some data suggest these relationships stem from a common underlying trait of impulsivity as described below.

Impulsivity in Disordered Gamblers and Substance Abusers

Personality Indexes

Cross-sectional studies show that levels of impulsiveness as assessed by standardized personality questionnaires are associated with substance use and abuse, as well as gambling, in general populations of college students (e.g., Jaffe and Archer 1987). Numerous studies likewise demonstrate that substance-dependent individuals score higher than controls on personality inventories of impulsivity (Allen et al. 1998; Chalmers, Olenick, and Stein 1993; Cookson 1994; Eisen et al. 1992; McCormick et al. 1987; Patton, Stanford, and Barratt 1995; Rosenthal et al. 1990; Sher and Trull 1994). In addition, longitudinal research finds that impulsivity assessed in childhood appears to be a marker for later development of substance abuse and gambling problems (Dawes, Tarter, and Kirisci 1997; Vitaro, Arsenault, and Tremblay 1997, 1999; White et al. 1994).

Although the DSM-IV classifies pathological gambling as a disorder of impulse control, the relation between impulsivity and this disorder is ambiguous. Some studies find high levels of impulsivity on standardized personality measures in pathological gamblers (Blaszczynski, Steel, and McConaghy 1997; Carlton and Manowitz 1994; Castellani, Wootton, and Rugle 1996; McCormick et al. 1987; Steel and Blaszczynski 1998), whereas others report no difference, and in some cases even lower scores, on personality scales assessing impulsivity and related traits (Allcock and Grace 1988; Blaszczynski, Wilson, and McConaghy 1986; Blaszczynski, McConaghy, and Frankova 1990; Dickerson, Hinchy, and Fabre 1987). These discrepancies might be explained partially by the comorbidities of gambling and substance use disorders. As noted earlier, up to 50% of pathological gamblers have a history of drug or alcohol use disorders (Ibanez et al. 2001; Ladd and Petry 2003; Maccallum and Blaszczynski 2002; Petry, Stinson, and Grant 2005; Specker et al. 1996), and studies reporting a relation between impulsivity and pathological gambling may simply have drawn a larger sample of substance-dependent gamblers than other studies that failed to find this association. Failure to report drug use histories in many of the early studies of impulsivity in pathological gamblers makes it difficult to assess this hypothesis with existing data.

Another potential explanation for the differences in findings across studies is that impulsiveness is a multidimensional construct (Gerbing, Ahadi, and Patton 1987) and includes orientation toward the present, diminished ability to delay gratification, behavioral disinhibition, risk taking, sensation seeking, proneness to boredom, sensitivity to probabilistic events, hedonism, and poor planning. Some types of impulsiveness characterize substance use disorders, such as sensation seeking, while other aspects may be more closely related to pathological gambling, such as sensitivity to probabilistic rewards. Other facets of impulsivity may be reflective of both disorders, such as present orientation, disinhibition, and poor planning (Vitaro, Arseneault, and Tremblay 1999). To date, not much data are available examining these multiple aspects of impulsivity in pathological gamblers.

Using behavioral tasks to measure aspects of impulsivity may have some benefits over personality inventories for uncovering the nature of impulsivity and its relationship to these disorders. Compared to personality questionnaires, behavioral tasks may represent more construct-relevant indicators of impulsivity. Below, some behavioral measures of impulsivity are described, along with findings in pathological gamblers with and without substance use disorders.

Behavioral Measures

Iowa Gambling Task   The inability to tolerate long delays to reinforcer presentation, or preference for smaller, more immediate rewards over larger, more delayed rewards, is one type of impulsivity that can be assessed behaviorally (Rachlin and Green 1972). Ainslie (1975) extended this definition of impulsivity to include choices for a small, short-term gain at the expense of a larger, long-term loss. This definition seems representative of both pathological gambling and substance use disorders. The choice to gamble or use drugs may produce immediate pleasurable sensations or excitement, but these effects can come at the expense of legal, financial, and social problems.

Bechara et al. (1994, 1997) developed the Iowa Gambling Task (IGT), which captures Ainslie's (1975) definition and has surface similarities to the long-term losses associated with heavy substance use and gambling. Subjects select cards from four decks that vary in probability and magnitude of gains and losses. Two decks yield a large gain (e.g., $100) with each draw, but continuing to draw from these decks results in a long-term net loss because of occasional substantial losses (e.g., $150–$1250). Selecting from these decks may reflect hypersensitivity to large gains and/or insensitivity to large losses, characteristics of addictive disorders. Drawing cards from the other two decks provides smaller wins (e.g., $50) but results in a long-term net gain because the occasional losses are relatively modest (e.g., $25–$250). Substance abusers make more impulsive choices than controls on this task (Dom et al. 2006; Petry, Bickel, and Arnett 1998; Verdejo-Garcia, Perales, and Perez-Garcia 2007).

Several groups of investigators have examined disordered gamblers' performance on the IGT. Petry (2001c) evaluated performance of disordered gambling substance abusers, nondisordered gambling substance abusers, and controls. Subjects also completed several personality inventories of impulsivity. Principal components analyses revealed that the personality inventories measured three distinct aspects of impulsiveness: impulse control, novelty seeking, and time orientation, while choices on the IGT loaded on a unique factor and tapped a different dimension of impulsivity. Disordered gambling substance abusers selected cards from the disadvantageous decks significantly more often than their nondisordered gambling counterparts, and the presence of disordered gambling and substance abuse had an additive effect. Although pathological gamblers without drug use disorders were not included in the above study, Goudriaan et al. (2006) reported that pathological gamblers with no history of drug or alcohol dependence also chose from disadvantageous decks significantly more often than nondisordered gambling controls.

Delay discounting Another aspect of impulsivity that can be measured behaviorally is the choice of a smaller, sooner reward over a larger, delayed reward, often referred to as *delay discounting*. In these studies, subjects selected between a larger-later reward and an immediate reward, the magnitude of which is adjusted until the subject is indifferent between the two. At the indifference point, the magnitude of the immediate reward provides the subjective value of the larger-later reward. When indifference points are determined across a range of delay intervals, a curve can be plotted that describes the rate at which the value of a reward decreases with increasing delays to its receipt. Mazur (1987) proposed a hyperbolic function that fits these data:

$$V_d = A/(1 + kd) \tag{1}$$

In this equation, V_d is the present value of the delayed reward (indifference point), A is the amount of the delayed reward, d is the delay duration, and k is an empirically derived constant proportional to the degree of delay discounting.

Substance abusers' discounting rates have been extensively studied, and virtually all studies find increased discounting in drug-abusing populations compared to controls. Bickel, Odum, and Madden (1999), Vuchinich and Simpson (1998), and Madden et al. (1997), for example, each found that cigarette smokers, heavy drinkers, and heroin-dependent patients, respectively, discounted hypothetical amounts of money more rapidly than controls. Effects are similar if the reward is hypothetical or real (e.g., Kirby, Petry, and Bickel 1999).

A few studies have examined delay discounting in pathological gambling. Petry and Casarella (1999) investigated delay discounting of hypothetical monetary rewards among disordered gambling substance abusers, substance abusers with no history of gambling problems, and controls. Groups with either or both addictive disorders discounted delayed rewards significantly more than controls. Further, substance abusers with gambling problems discounted delayed rewards at about three times the rates of substance abusers without gambling problems, and at nearly ten times the rate of controls. Others have replicated these findings, with both Dixon, Marley, and Jacobs (2003) and MacKillop et al. (2006) finding higher discounting rates in disordered gamblers than controls. However, Holt, Green, and Myerson (2003) reported no difference in discounting rates between disordered gamblers and controls. The reasons behind these discrepant findings are unclear. Dixon, Marley, and Jacobs (2003) asked their gamblers to delay discount in an offtrack betting parlor, and their subsequent research (Dixon, Jacobs, and Sanders 2006) suggests that this setting may increase rates of delay discounting when compared with the nongambling settings in which control data were collected in their earlier study. A shortcoming of some of these studies is failure to report prevalence of substance use disorders in the samples. These comorbidities, as outlined earlier, could influence delay discounting, as substance use itself is associated with rapid discounting.

Other studies have examined delay discounting in pathological gamblers while controlling for substance use status. Petry (2001b) examined discounting in individuals with a primary diagnosis of *pathological gambling* separated into groups with and without substance use problems. Pathological gamblers with and without a history of substance use disorders had higher delay discounting rates than controls, and gamblers with substance use disorders had the highest discounting rates. Strikingly, the two studies (Petry 2001b; Petry and Casarella 1999), which comprised entirely different patient populations, had nearly identical discounting rates for individuals with dual addictive disorders (gambling and substance abuse), regardless of which was their primary problem. Likewise, discounting rates were nearly identical for subjects with one disorder (either pathological gambling or substance use). Together, these data suggest that gambling and substance use disorders lie along a continuum with respect to delay discounting. Moderately high rates of discounting may be a risk factor for developing a problem with either drugs or gambling, while higher rates of discounting may put an individual at risk of developing multiple impulse-control problems such as pathological gambling and substance abuse. Longitudinal research will be necessary to confirm or refute this hypothesis.

Contingency Management Treatments for Substance Use Disorders

Gambling, similarly to substance use, can be considered an operant behavior, guided by its consequences. Choices to use substances or to gamble are considered along with their converse decisions, which do not involve using or wagering. If the delayed effects of using or gambling are substantially discounted, then their negative values may fail to compete with the benefits of using or gambling, leading to an addictive or excessive behavior pattern. On the other hand, if the positive effects of not using or not gambling are made more salient and are immediately and positively reinforced, gamblers and substance abusers may cease the harmful behavior and engage in behaviors in concert with recovery.

Contingency management (CM) is such a form of behavioral therapy that has been widely applied to substance abusers. CM treatments are derived from basic behavioral principles that any behavior that is reinforced will increase in frequency. In these interventions, clinicians typically provide a tangible reinforcer, such as a voucher exchangeable for retail goods and services, every time patients provide objective verification of drug abstinence. CM is generally not provided as the sole treatment. Rather, it is usually added to another form of therapy (supportive, behavioral, and/or pharmacological) to improve outcomes. Growing evidence suggests that CM therapies can be expanded to behaviors beyond abstinence and to a variety of patient populations.

Early research on CM studied its efficacy in reducing use of various drugs among patients receiving methadone maintenance treatment for opioid dependence. These studies demonstrated that providing supplemental methadone doses or take-home methadone dosing contingent upon abstinence (submission of drug-negative urine toxicology screens) could effectively reduce illegal drug use in methadone patients (Stitzer et al. 1986; Stitzer, Iguchi, and Felch 1992). However, these reinforcers were only applicable to patients receiving an agonist medication therapy.

Higgins and colleagues utilized another form of reinforcement—vouchers—for treating patients with a primary cocaine use disorder (Higgins et al. 1994; Higgins, Wong, et al. 2000). These CM interventions provide points worth a specific amount of money whenever a patient submits a urine sample negative for cocaine. The points are recorded on vouchers that can be exchanged for products of monetary value, such as restaurant gift certificates, clothing, or electronics. An important component of a voucher program is that the value of vouchers earned increases with each consecutive instance of the desired behavior, and voucher values reset to an initially low value when a target behavior is not demonstrated, thus providing a powerful incentive to sustain abstinence over time (Roll and Higgins 2000; Roll, Higgins, and Badger 1996).

An early study of voucher-based CM compared an intensive individual therapy alone to that same therapy provided in conjunction with voucher CM (Higgins et al. 1994). There was a significant difference between groups in the proportion of patients who remained in treatment for 24 weeks, with 75% in the CM group and 40% of patients who did not receive vouchers completing treatment. Longest duration of continuous cocaine abstinence differed between groups as well. Patients in the voucher group achieved an average of 11.7 ± 2.0 weeks of continuous abstinence from cocaine, whereas patients in the no voucher group achieved an average of 6.0 ± 1.0 weeks of continuous abstinence. Durations of abstinence achieved during treatment are highly predictive of long-term abstinence outcomes (Higgins, Badger, and Budney 2000; Petry, Martin, and Simcic 2005).

Other research on CM suggests that the magnitude of reinforcement and timing of voucher delivery can affect treatment outcomes (Kirby et al. 1998). Specifically, better outcomes are observed when the initial value of vouchers is high and they are provided immediately after a negative urine specimen, suggesting that immediate reinforcement and high magnitude incentives may be particularly important. Lower voucher amounts reduce efficacy (Stitzer and Bigelow 1984), but a variant on the voucher-based CM approach provides for immediate chances to win prizes of different magnitudes (Petry et al. 2000, 2004; Petry, Peirce, et al. 2005; Petry, Martin, and Simcic 2005; Petry, Alessi, et al. 2005). In this system, large ($100) prizes can be awarded even in early stages of treatment, and the variable ratio schedule of reinforcement allows for an overall reduction in costs, without comprising efficacy. This prize-based CM approach has similar efficacy of voucher CM, even when the arranged magnitude of reinforcers is lower (Petry et al. 2007).

Two independent meta-analyses find CM treatments to be superior to control treatments in facilitating abstinence (Lussier et al. 2006; Prendergast et al. 2006). These meta-analyses also demonstrate that CM procedures are efficacious across a range of patient populations, including cocaine-, opioid-, marijuana-, alcohol-, and nicotine-dependent samples. Hence, the techniques are highly generalizable.

While most CM studies target abstinence for reinforcement, other behaviors can also be reinforced using voucher- or prize-based techniques. Several studies reinforced compliance with goal-related activities that relate to improvement of education, employment, legal, family, or social/recreational or medical/psychiatric status (e.g., Petry et al. 2000; Petry et al. 2004; Petry, Alessi, et al. 2005). A full description of the process and methods of verification for reinforcing goal-related activities is provided in Petry, Tedford, and Martin (2001). Briefly, activities that are often reinforced include such things as attending Alcoholics Anonymous (AA) or Narcotics Anonymous meetings, going to doctor's appointments, keeping daily track of medication consumption, completing housing application forms, signing up for and exercising at gyms, writing letters to non-drug-using relatives, and so on.

Reinforcing social network development using such techniques was a focus in a study of alcohol-dependent patients. This study was designed to determine if a socially focused treatment can change social networks from one that reinforces drinking to one that reinforces sobriety. Litt et al. (2007) randomly assigned 210 alcohol-dependent patients to one of three conditions: Network Support (NS), NS+CM, or Case Management (CaseM, a control condition). Analysis of drinking 15 months posttreatment indicated a significant treatment by time interaction effect, with both NS conditions yielding better outcomes than CaseM. Analyses of social network variables posttreatment indicated that NS conditions did not reduce social support for drinking, but did increase social support for abstinence as well as AA involvement, which itself is based on CM principles in that each day of abstinence is reinforced socially with increased reinforcement (e.g., special celebrations, sponsor status) for sustained abstinence. Both network support and AA involvement variables were significantly correlated with drinking outcomes. These findings indicate that drinkers' social networks can be changed by a treatment that is specifically designed to do so, and that these changes contribute to improved drinking outcomes.

Similar approaches may be warranted when adapting CM for treatment of pathological gamblers. Because no objective indicator of gambling abstinence exists, CM treatments have instead focused on increasing behaviors incompatible with gambling, such as attending Gamblers Anonymous (GA) meetings, or becoming involved with non-gambling social networks. We are currently conducting a trail in which 210 pathological gamblers are being randomly assigned to psychoeducational sessions (a control condition), cognitive-behavioral therapy (CBT) for pathological gambling as described in Petry et al. (2006) and Petry (2005), or CBT+CM, in which patients earn escalating amounts of vouchers for completing homework assignments and engaging in non-gambling-related social activities (attending Gamblers Anonymous meetings, joining a book club, volunteering at their child's school, etc.). Initial data suggest that CM is efficacious in increasing number of GA meetings attended and homework assignments completed. CM may facilitate the development of coping skills for handling high-risk situations for gambling such that temporal horizons can be extended so that the long-term negative consequences of gambling are considered during the decision-making process of whether or not to gamble. Ultimately, we will ascertain whether CM's effects are associated with overall improvements in long-term gambling outcomes and if reductions in gambling are mediated by changes in coping skills and discounting rates.

Summary

Studies reviewed in this chapter suggest that if the delayed aversive outcomes associated with substance use disorders and pathological gambling (e.g., loss of income, deterioration of social relations, and legal difficulties) are substantially discounted, then their diminished negative value may fail to deter gambling in much the same way that the long-term consequences of cigarette smoking or drug use fail to deter these behaviors in drug-dependent individuals (Odum et al. 2000; Odum, Madden, and Bickel 2002; Petry 2003). The hyperbolic shape of the delay-discounting function as shown in equation 1 predicts preference reversals between self-control and impulsive choices. For example, tendencies toward self-control (e.g., going home after work to save money to pay the rent instead of heading to the casino) give way to impulsive choices as the benefits of these choices become more immediately available (e.g., while driving past the casino on the way home). With the thrills of gambling imminent, their value far outweighs the discounted value of avoiding an eviction notice at the end of the month. As higher rates of discounting increase the probability of preference reversals, pathological gamblers' delay intolerance may make their road to recovery a difficult journey filled with relapses, despite good intentions.

A related account of the importance of delay discounting is Rachlin's (2000) *string theory*. According to this theory, gamblers take account of their wins and losses after experiencing wins. Some wins occur after the first bet, and because they are immediate, they retain their full reward value. Other wins follow a string of losses, such that the net effect at the end of the string is a negative value. If these negative value events were only modestly discounted, they would guard against gambling. However, high discounting rates characteristic of pathological gamblers render the delayed net loss greatly devalued. In other words, when gamblers take a mental accounting of the sums of immediate undiscounted gains and delayed (and discounted) losses, the net value of gambling is positive. Individuals who discount delayed rewards at a lower rate are more likely to be affected by the net loss of funds following the long strings of losses leading up to a win. Their mental accounting may be closer to the reality that gambling is a net losing activity, hence reducing their gambling substantially, if not completely.

These accounts of discounting appear useful in designing treatments for pathological gambling. To date, the study of the relation between discounting and addictive behaviors has primarily assumed a trait approach (i.e., documenting the correlation between discounting and the variety of addictive disorders), but there is also evidence that experiential variables can affect discounting rates. For example, Williams and Dayan (2005) speculated that high rates of delay discounting may be adaptive in environments in which delayed rewards are unlikely to be available after the delay. A lifetime of learning not to trust others to deliver what they promise in the future may play a role in delay discounting rates (Takahashi, Ikeda, and Hasegawa 2007), and the tendency to take whatever is immediately available may be important in the decision to gamble or use drugs (Reynolds, Patak, and Shroff 2007). These theories may explain at least in part the extraordinarily high rates of pathological gambling found in Southeast Asian refugees in the United States (Petry et al. 2003).

Consistent with a role of learning in discounting, cognitive strategies can help children better tolerate delays to a larger reward (Mischel, Shoda, and Rodriguez 1989). Research conducted with animals also suggests that long-lasting patterns of delay tolerance can be taught even without mediating verbal strategies (Mazur and Logue 1978). That substance users might acquire self-control skills leading up to a successful quit attempt is supported to some degree by data showing that abstinent cigarette smokers, intravenous drug users, and alcoholics have lower delay discounting rates compared to active users (Bickel, Odum, and Madden 1999; Bretteville-Jensen 1999; Petry 2001a). Further evidence for this hypothesis comes from two studies demonstrating that pre-quit delay discounting rates are predictive of success in interventions designed to promote cigarette abstinence (Dallery and Raiff 2007; Yoon et al. 2007). Of course, an equally viable trait-based interpretation of these findings is that some individuals with lower discounting rates will, for unrelated reasons, develop a substance use or gambling disorder and their lower rate of discounting enhances their chances of a successful quit attempt. Whether lower delay discounting rates can be systematically taught, and the effects of this learning on clinical outcomes, is an important topic for future research. For example, AA and other 12-step interventions emphasize making decisions based on "one day at a time," or even "one hour at a time." The clinical significance of these approaches has yet to be systematically studied.

CM interventions, similarly to 12-step interventions, take into account the truncated time horizons of substance abusers and pathological gamblers and provide relatively immediate and tangible reinforcers for abstinence or development of behaviors incompatible with substance use and gambling. These interventions have demonstrated efficacy in treating a variety of substance abusing populations and are beginning to be applied to gamblers as well. Future research should examine how discounting rates may change in response to these interventions and if extensions of one's time horizon can mediate reductions in addictive behaviors.

Acknowledgments

This chapter was supported in part by NIH grants R01-MH60417, R01-MH60417-Supp, R01-DA021567, R01-DA13444, R01-DA14618, R01-DA018883, R01-DA016855, P50-AA03510, P50-DA09241, and M01RR006192. Amy Novotny is thanked for assistance with manuscript preparation.

References

Ainslie, G. (1975). Specious reward: A behavioral theory of impulsiveness and impulse control. *Psychological Bulletin* 82: 463–496.

Allcock, C. C., and Grace, D. M. (1988). Pathological gamblers are neither impulsive nor sensation-seekers. *Australian and New Zealand Journal of Psychiatry* 22: 307–311.

Allen, T. J., Moeller, F. G., Rhoades, H. M., and Cherek, D. R. (1998). Impulsivity and history of drug dependence. *Drug and Alcohol Dependence* 50: 137–145.

American Psychiatric Association (1994). *Diagnostic and Statistical Manual of Mental Disorders*, 4th ed. Washington, D.C.: American Psychiatric Association.

Bechara, A., Damasio, A. R., Damasio, H., and Anderson, S. W. (1994). Insensitivity to future consequences following damage to human prefrontal cortex. *Cognition* 50: 7–15.

Bechara, A., Damasio, H., Tranel, D., and Damasio, A. R. (1997). Deciding advantageously before knowing the advantageous strategy. *Science* 275: 1293–1295.

Bickel, W. K., Odum, A. L., and Madden, G. J. (1999). Impulsivity and cigarette smoking: delay discounting in current, never, and ex-smokers. *Psychopharmacology* 146: 447–454.

Blaszczynski, A., McConaghy, N., and Frankova, A. (1990). Boredom proneness in pathological gambling. *Psychological Reports* 67: 35–42.

Blaszczynski, A., Steel, Z., and McConaghy, N. (1997). Impulsivity in pathological gambling: The antisocial impulsivist. *Addiction* 92: 75–87.

Blaszczynski, A. P., Wilson, A. C., and McConaghy, N. (1986). Sensation seeking and pathological gambling. *British Journal of Addiction* 81: 113–117.

Bretteville-Jensen, A. L. (1999). Addiction and discounting. *Journal of Health Economics* 18: 393–407.

Carlton, P. L., and Manowitz, P. (1994). Factors determining the severity of pathological gambling in males. *Journal of Gambling Studies* 10: 147–157.

Castellani, B., Wootton, E., and Rugle, L. (1996). Homelessness, negative affect and coping among Veterans with gambling problems who misused substances. *Psychiatric Services* 47 (3): 298–299.

Chalmers, D., Olenick, N. L., and Stein, W. (1993). Dispositional traits as risk in problem drinking. *Journal of Substance Abuse* 5: 401–410.

Cookson, H. (1994). Personality variables associated with alcohol use in young offenders. *Personality and Individual Differences* 16: 179–182.

Cunningham-Williams, R. M., Cottler, L. B., Compton, W. M., Spitznagel, E. L., and Ben-Abdallah, A. (2000). Problem gambling and comorbid psychiatric and substance use disorders among drug users recruited from drug treatment and community settings. *Journal of Gambling Studies* 16: 347–376.

Dallery, J., and Raiff, B. R. (2007). Delay discounting predicts cigarette smoking in a laboratory model of abstinence reinforcement. *Psychopharmacology* 190: 485–496.

Dawes, M. A., Tarter, R. E., and Kirisci, L. (1997). Behavioral self-regulation: Correlates and 2 year follow-ups for boys at risk for substance abuse. *Drug and Alcohol Dependence* 45: 165–176.

Dickerson, M., Hinchy, J., and Fabre, J. (1987). Chasing, arousal and sensation seeking in off-course gamblers. *British Journal of Addiction* 82: 673–680.

Dixon, M. R., Jacobs, E. A., and Sanders, S. (2006). Contextual control of delay discounting by pathological gamblers. *Journal of Applied Behavior Analysis* 39: 413–422.

Dixon, M. R., Marley, J., and Jacobs, E. A. (2003). Delay discounting by pathological gamblers. *Journal of Applied Behavior Analysis* 36: 449–458.

Dom, G., De Wilde, B., Hulstijn, W., van den Brink, W., and Sabbe, B. (2006). Behavioural aspects of impulsivity in alcoholics with and without a cluster-B personality disorder. *Alcohol and Alcoholism* 41: 412–420.

Eisen, S. V., Youngman, D. J., Grob, M. C., and Dill, D. L. (1992). Alcohol, drugs, and psychiatric disorders: A current view of hospitalized adolescents. *Journal of Adolescent Research* 7: 250–265.

Gerbing, D. W., Ahadi, S. A., and Patton, J. H. (1987). Toward a conceptualization of impulsivity: Components across the behavioral and self-report domains. *Multivariate Behavioral Research* 22: 357–379.

Gerstein, D. R., Volberg, R. A., Toce, M. T., Harwood, H., Johnson, R. A., Buie, T., et al. (1999). *Gambling Impact and Behavior Study: Report to the National Gambling Impact Study Commission*. Chicago: National Opinion Research Center, University of Chicago.

Goudriaan, A. E., Oosterlaan, J., de Beurs, E., and van den Brink, W. (2006). Psychophysiological determinants and concomitants of deficient decision making in pathological gamblers. *Drug and Alcohol Dependence* 84: 231–239.

Higgins, S. T., Badger, G. J., and Budney, A. J. (2000). Initial abstinence and success in achieving longer term cocaine abstinence. *Experimental and Clinical Psychopharmacology* 8: 377–386.

Higgins, S. T., Budney, A. J., Bickel, W. K., Foerg, F. E., Donham, R., and Badger, G. J. (1994). Incentives improve outcome in outpatient behavioral treatment of cocaine dependence. *Archives of General Psychiatry* 51: 568–576.

Higgins, S. T., Wong, C., Badger G., Ogden, D. E., and Dantona, R. L. (2000). Contingent reinforcement increases cocaine abstinence during outpatient treatment and 1 year follow-up. *Journal of Consulting and Clinical Psychology* 68: 64–72.

Holt, D. D., Green, L., and Myerson, J. (2003). Is discounting impulsive? Evidence from temporal and probability discounting in gambling and non-gambling college students. *Behavioural Processes* 64: 355–367.

Ibanez, A., Blanco, C., Donahue, E., Lesieur, H. R., Perez de Castro, I., Fernandez-Piqueras, J., and Sáiz-Ruiz, J. (2001). Psychiatric comorbidity in pathological gamblers seeking treatment. *American Journal of Psychiatry* 158: 1733–1735.

Jaffe, L. T., and Archer, R. P. (1987). The prediction of drug use among college students from MMPI, MCMI, and sensation seeking scales. *Journal of Personality Assessment* 51: 243–253.

Kirby, K., Marlowe, D. B., Festinger, D. S., Lamb, R. J., and Platt, J. J. (1998). Schedule of voucher delivery influences initiation of cocaine abstinence. *Journal of Consulting and Clinical Psychology* 66 (5): 761–767.

Kirby, K. N., Petry, N. M., and Bickel, W. K. (1999). Heroin addicts have higher discount rates for delayed rewards than non-drug-using controls. *Journal of Experimental Psychology: General* 128: 78–87.

Ladd, G. T., and Petry, N. M. (2003). A comparison of pathological gamblers with and without substance abuse treatment histories. *Experimental and Clinical Psychopharmacology* 11: 202–209.

Langenbucher, J., Bavly, L., Labouvie, E., Sanjuan, P. M., and Martin, C. S. (2001). Clinical features of pathological gambling in an addictions treatment cohort. *Psychology of Addictive Behaviors* 15: 77–79.

Litt, M. D., Kadden, R. M., Kabela-Cormier, E., and Petry, N. (2007). Changing network support for drinking: Initial findings from the network support project. *Journal of Consulting and Clinical Psychology* 75: 542–555.

Lussier, J. P., Heil, S. H., Mongeon, J. A., Badger, G. J., and Higgins, S. T. (2006). A meta-analysis of voucher-based reinforcement therapy for substance use disorders. *Addiction* 101: 192–203.

Maccallum, F., and Blaszczynski, A. (2002). Pathological gambling and comorbid substance use. *Australian and New Zealand Journal of Psychiatry* 36: 411–415.

MacKillop, J., Anderson, E. J., Castelda, B. A., Mattson, R. E., and Donovick, P. J. (2006). Divergent validity of measures of cognitive distortions, impulsivity, and time perspective in pathological gambling. *Journal of Gambling Studies* 22: 339–354.

Madden, G. J., Petry, N. M., Badger, G. J., and Bickel, W. K. (1997). Impulsive and self-control choices in opioid-dependent patients and non-drug-using control participants: Drug and monetary rewards. *Experimental and Clinical Psychopharmacology* 5: 256–262.

Mazur, J. E. (1987). An adjusting procedure for studying delayed reinforcement. In M. L. Commons, J. E. Mazur, J. A. Nevin, and H. Rachlin, eds., *Quantitative Analysis of Behavior*, vol. 5: *The Effect of Delay and of Intervening Events of Reinforcement Value*, 55–73. Hillsdale, N.J.: Erlbaum.

Mazur, J. E., and Logue, A. W. (1978). Choice in a "self-control" paradigm: Effects of a fading procedure. *Journal of the Experimental Analysis of Behavior* 30: 11–17.

McCormick, R. A., Taber, J., Kruedelbach, N., and Russo, A. (1987). Personality profiles of hospitalized pathological gamblers: The California Personality Inventory. *Journal of Clinical Psychology* 43: 521–527.

Mischel, W., Shoda, Y., and Rodriguez, M. I. (1989). Delay of gratification in children. *Science* 244: 933–938.

Odum, A. L., Madden, G. J., Badger, G. J., and Bickel, W. K. (2000). Needle sharing in opioid-dependent outpatients: Psychological processes underlying risk. *Drug and Alcohol Dependence* 60: 259–266.

Odum, A. L., Madden, G. J., and Bickel, W. K. (2002). Discounting of delayed health gains and losses by current, never- and ex-smokers of cigarettes. *Nicotine and Tobacco Research* 4: 295–303.

Patton, J. H., Stanford, M. S., and Barratt, E. S. (1995). Factor structure of the Barratt impulsiveness scale. *Journal of Clinical Psychology* 51: 768–774.

Petry, N. M. (2001a). Delay discounting of money and alcohol in actively using alcoholics, currently abstinent alcoholics, and controls. *Psychopharmacology* 154: 243–250.

Petry, N. M. (2001b). Pathological gamblers, with and without substance use disorders, discount delayed rewards at high rates. *Journal of Abnormal Psychology* 110: 482–487.

Petry, N. M. (2001c). Substance abuse, pathological gambling, and impulsiveness. *Drug and Alcohol Dependence* 63: 29–38.

Petry, N. M. (2003). Discounting of money, health, and freedom in substance abusers and controls. *Drug and Alcohol Dependence* 71: 133–141.

Petry, N. M. (2005). *Pathological Gambling: Etiology, Comorbidity, and Treatment*. Washington, D.C.: American Psychological Association.

Petry, N. M., Alessi, S. M., Hanson, T., and Sierra, S. (2007). Randomized trial of contingent prizes versus vouchers in cocaine-using methadone patients. *Journal of Consulting and Clinical Psychology* 75 (6): 983–991.

Petry, N. M., Alessi, S. M., Marx, J., Austin, M., and Tardif, M. (2005). Vouchers versus prizes: Contingency management for treatment of substance abusers in community settings. *Journal of Consulting and Clinical Psychology* 73: 1005–1014.

Petry, N. M., Ammerman, Y., Bohl, J., et al. (2006). Cognitive-behavioral therapy for pathological gamblers. *Journal of Consulting and Clinical Psychology* 74: 555–567.

Petry, N. M., Armentano, C., Kuoch, T., Thonguanh, N., and Lien, S. (2003). Gambling participation and problems among South East Asian refugees to the United States. *Psychiatric Services* 54 (8): 1142–1148.

Petry, N. M., Bickel, W. K., and Arnett, M. (1998). Shortened time horizons and insensitivity to future consequences in heroin addicts. *Addiction* 93: 729–738.

Petry, N. M., and Casarella, T. (1999). Excessive discounting of delayed rewards in substance abusers with gambling problems. *Drug and Alcohol Dependence* 56: 25–32.

Petry, N. M., Martin, B., Cooney, J., and Kranzler, H. R. (2000). Give them prizes and they will come: Contingency management for the treatment of alcohol dependence. *Journal of Consulting and Clinical Psychology* 68: 250–257.

Petry, N. M., Martin, B., and Simcic, F. (2005). Prize contingency management for cocaine dependence: Integration with group therapy in a methadone clinic. *Journal of Consulting and Clinical of Psychology* 73: 354–359.

Petry, N. M., Peirce, J. M., Stitzer, M. L., et al. (2005). Effect of prize-based incentives on outcomes in stimulant abusers in outpatient psychosocial treatment programs: A national drug abuse treatment clinical trials network study. *Archives of General Psychiatry* 62: 1148–1156.

Petry, N. M., Stinson, F. S., and Grant, B. F. (2005). Comorbidity of DSM-IV pathological gambling and other psychiatric disorders: Results from the National Epidemiologic Survey on Alcohol and Related Conditions. *Journal of Clinical Psychiatry* 66: 564–574.

Petry, N. M., Tedford, J., Austin, M., et al. (2004). Prize reinforcement contingency management for cocaine abusers: How low can we go and with whom? *Addiction* 99: 349–360.

Petry, N. M., Tedford, J., and Martin, B. (2001). Reinforcing compliance with non-drug related activities. *Journal of Substance Abuse Treatment* 20: 33–44.

Prendergast, M., Podus, D., Finney, J., Greenwell, L., and Roll, J. (2006). Contingency management for treatment of substance use disorders: a meta-analysis. *Addiction* 101: 1546–1560.

Rachlin, H. (2000). *The Science of Self-Control*. Cambridge, MA: Harvard University Press.

Rachlin, H., and Green, L. (1972). Commitment, choice and self-control. *Journal of the Experimental Analysis of Behavior* 17: 15–22.

Reynolds, B., Patak, M., and Shroff, P. (2007). Adolescent smokers rate delayed rewards as less certain than adolescent nonsmokers. *Drug and Alcohol Dependence* 90: 301–303.

Roll, J., and Higgins, S. T. (2000). A within-subject comparison of three different schedules of reinforcement of drug abstinence using cigarette smoking as an exemplar. *Drug and Alcohol Dependence* 58 (1–2): 103–109.

Roll, J., Higgins, S. T., and Badger, G. J. (1996). An experimental comparison of the three different schedules of reinforcement of drug abstinence using cigarette smoking as an exemplar. *Journal of Applied Behavior Analysis* 29 (4): 495–505.

Rosenthal, T. L., Edwards, N. B., Ackerman, B. J., Knott, D. H., and Rosenthal, R. H. (1990). Substance abuse patterns reveal contrasting personal traits. *Journal of Substance Abuse* 2: 255–263.

Shaffer, H. J., Hall, M. N., and Vander Bilt, J. (1999). Estimating the prevalence of disordered gambling behavior in the United States and Canada: A research synthesis. *American Journal of Public Health* 89: 1369–1376.

Sher, K. J., and Trull, T. J. (1994). Personality and disinhibitory psychopathology: Alcoholism and antisocial personality disorder. *Journal of Abnormal Psychology* 103: 92–102.

Specker, S. M., Carlson, G. A., Edmonson, K. M., and Johnson, P. E. (1996). Psychopathology in pathological gamblers seeking treatment. *Journal of Gambling Studies* 12: 67.

Steel, Z., and Blaszczynski, A. (1998). Impulsivity, personality disorders and pathological gambling severity. *Addiction* 93: 895–905.

Stitzer, M. L., and Bigelow, G. E. (1984). Contingent reinforcement for carbon monoxide reduction: Within-subjects effects of pay amounts. *Journal of Applied Behavior Analysis* 17: 477–483.

Stitzer, M., Bickel, W. K., Bigelow, G., and Liebson, I. (1986). Effect of methadone dose contingencies on urinalysis test results of polydrug-abusing methadone-maintenance patients. *Drug Alcohol Dependence* 18: 341–348.

Stitzer, M. L., Iguchi, M. Y., and Felch, L. J. (1992). Contingent take-home incentive: Effects on drug use of methadone maintenance patients. *Journal of Consulting and Clinical Psychology* 60: 927–934.

Takahashi, T., Ikeda, K., and Hasegawa, T. (2007). A hyperbolic decay of subjective probability of obtaining delayed rewards. *Behavioral Brain Functioning* 3: 52.

Toneatto, T., and Brennan, J. (2002). Pathological gambling in treatment-seeking substance abusers. *Addictive Behaviors* 27: 465–469.

Verdejo-Garcia, A. J., Perales, J. C., and Perez-Garcia, M. (2007). Cognitive impulsivity in cocaine and heroin polysubstance abusers. *Addictive Behaviors* 32: 950–966.

Vitaro, F., Arseneault, L., and Tremblay, R. E. (1997). Dispositional predictors of problem gambling in male adolescents. *American Journal of Psychiatry* 154: 1769–1770.

Vitaro, F., Arseneault, L., and Tremblay, R. E. (1999). Impulsivity predicts problem gambling in low SES adolescent males. *Addiction* 94: 565–575.

Vuchinich, R. E., and Simpson, C. A. (1998). Hyperbolic temporal discounting in social drinkers and problem drinkers. *Experimental and Clinical Psychopharmacology* 6: 292–305.

Welte, J., Barnes, G., Wieczorek, W., Tidwell, M. C., and Parker, J. (2001). Alcohol and gambling pathology among U.S. adults: Prevalence, demographic patterns and comorbidity. *Journal of Studies on Alcohol* 62: 706–712.

White, J. L., Moffitt, T. E., Caspi, A., Bartusch, D. J., Needles, D. J., and Stouthamer-Loeber, M. (1994). Measuring impulsivity and examining its relationship to delinquency. *Journal of Abnormal Psychology* 103: 192–205.

Williams, J., and Dayan, P. (2005). Dopamine, learning, and impulsivity: A biological account of attention-deficit/hyperactivity disorder. *Journal of Child and Adolescent Psychopharmacology* 15: 160–179.

Yoon, J. H., Higgins, S. T., Heil, S. H., Sugarbaker, R. J., Thomas, C. S., and Badger, G. J. (2007). Delay discounting predicts postpartum relapse to cigarette smoking among pregnant women. *Experimental and Clinical Psychopharmacology* 15: 176–186.

13 Medical Models of Addiction

Harold Kincaid and Jacqueline A. Sullivan[1]

Biomedical science has been remarkably successful in explaining illness by categorizing diseases and then identifying localizable lesions such as a virus and neoplasm in the body that cause those diseases. Not surprisingly, researchers have aspired to apply this powerful paradigm to addiction. So, for example, in a review of the neuroscience of addiction literature, Hyman and Malenka (2001, 695) acknowledge a general consensus among addiction researchers that "addiction can appropriately be considered as a chronic medical illness," or as Koob and Le Moal (2006, 1) put it, addiction "is a chronically relapsing disorder." Working from this perspective, researchers have put much effort into characterizing the symptomology of addiction and the brain changes that underlie them. Evidence for involvement of dopamine transmission changes in the ventral tegmental area (VTA) and nucleus accumbens (NAc) have received the greatest attention. Kauer and Malenka (2007, 844) put it well: "drugs of abuse can co-opt synaptic plasticity mechanisms in brain circuits involved in reinforcement and reward processing."

Our goal in this chapter to provide an explicit description of the assumptions of medical models, the different forms they may take, and the challenges they face in providing explanations with solid evidence of addiction.

What Does a Medical Model Entail?

In its purest or simplest form, a medical model of disease asserts that:

1. there is characteristic set of objectively observable symptoms manifested both synchronically and diachronically;
2. those symptoms are caused by a physical condition that represents a deviation from normal functioning;
3. that deviation can in principle be localized somewhere in the body; and
4. the physical condition is necessary and sufficient to have the disease.

Objectively observable symptoms are those that are not in the eye of the beholder. They do not depend on social conventions. They are measurable by reliable and valid methods in the technical sense that different observers get the same results and measurements correspond to real phenomena. A medical model also says that there is sufficient understanding of normal biological function and biological systems to identify deviations from normality that cause the disease. The deviation is a state of the physical body that can be localized, is present in all cases of the disease, and when present makes the disease inevitable.

Of course, less simple models may be called for. The localization may not be as simple as a tumor at a specific site; the lesion may only make it probable that the disease will occur; and different lesions in different individuals may produce the same disease (though this latter situation usually calls for finer subdivisions in disease categories).

Note two important implications of medical models for the study of addiction. First, either one has the disease or one does not. Addiction is a categorical, not a dimensional variable: there is a point at which addiction "takes hold." Nosology begins by identifying characteristic symptoms. However, in the end, the key element is a specifiable lesion or malfunction—the etiology of the disease that divides the phenomena into kinds. For addiction, the hope is that changes like those found in the reward system mentioned above will be the "molecular switch" (Adinoff 2004) that does so.

Additionally, if we stick strictly to the medical model, we are committed to localizing the causes of the disease—in this case, addiction—inside the person. This is what Koob and Le Moal (2006, 8) mean when they say addiction is a biological phenomena, not a social one. Of course everybody agrees that addiction results from a complex interplay between genetics, neurobiology, and the environment. Obviously, access to drugs or the relevant activity is presupposed. Social and environmental factors may be involved in acquiring the relevant lesion. Maybe even environmental stimuli may trigger the behavior associated with the disease that is a preexisting state of the body. However, the larger the role of these environmental factors and the more they involve complex social relationships rather than simple external stimuli, the more the spirit of the medical model is being violated. If the factors involved in the transitions from limited use, addiction, remission, and relapse depend significantly on social factors, then we do not have a medical model.

As we noted, researchers often explicitly treat addiction as a disease in the full medical sense. However, at the same time they can be considerably more ambiguous when spelling out details. The language used will be familiar. It will be said that the biological fact is "involved in," "associated with," or "implicated in" the addiction. The part of the brain will be described as a "locus for" or "the substrate for" addiction. The addiction "results from" the biological process identified.

These descriptions are ambiguous when it comes to deciding if the process is necessary and sufficient, and it is quite common never to get a precise statement about what is being claimed. Claims about loci and substrates seem to be more clearly about something being required or necessary for addiction. Claims about being associated with or implicated in addiction may not be asserting that all cases of addiction include the identified area. Identifying the substrate or locus for addiction may entail that, given normal background conditions, the area in question is sufficient for addiction—that addiction is always present when the process in question is operative.

The pure medical model for addiction described above can be weakened in various ways by relaxing the assumptions we have noted. There might be different neurobiological changes in different addictions or a change common to all that is combined with other type-specific differences.

We think the eventual goal for addiction research should be to formulate clear causal claims about the role of specific neurobiological changes in addiction. Clarity requires stating exactly which of the various different possible claims described above is at stake.

Despite the ambiguous formulations, the medical model is an ideal that is strived for by addiction researchers. It can shape research by providing the background assumptions that are inevitably needed in providing evidence and explanation. Medical models can set the range of hypotheses that are considered plausible possible competitors. They can determine the kinds of causes taken to be important and how they should be described as well as what causes can be ignored. We will detail some of these influences below.

What Would a Medical Model Explain?

Addiction is a complex phenomenon with multiple aspects. If a medical model is an ideal to shoot for, we need to be clear what we want the model to explain. We believe that greater precision on these issues can help avoid unnecessary confusion and help show where progress toward a medical style explanation of addiction is most likely and where it is most likely to run into problems. We focus on two issues: the extent to which the commonsense notion of addiction groups together similar phenomena suitable to the same scientific, medical type explanation; and the aspects of the dynamics of addiction that the medical model is supposed to explain.

Medical models of addiction entail that there are in principle clear criteria for the differential diagnosis of addiction. However, types specified in the *Diagnostic and Statistical Manual of Mental Disorders* (DSM) may not pick out homogeneous phenomena, as Ross et al. (2008) note for addiction, and as Horwitz (2003) notes in general for DSM. The DSM provides a set of criteria. To have the DSM disorder is to have a specified number of those criteria. The criteria are not weighted. The end result is that individuals with different characteristics can get the same diagnosis.

Furthermore, the screens that are used to operationalize the DSM work in the same way. Take, for example, diagnosis of substance disorder using the common World

Health Organization (WHO) substance-dependency screen. The questions in the screen are:

How often have you had a strong desire or urge to use?
How often has your use led to health, social, financial, or legal problems?
How often have you failed to do what was normally expected of you because of your use?
Has a friend or a relative ever expressed concern about your use?
Have you ever tried and failed to control, cut down, or stop using?

These questions are given either a 5- or 3-element Likert scale for severity and scored. The scores are based on a straight linear combination of the question scores with a cut-off point determining who has a severe problem and who does not. Individuals who have made no attempt to stop but have families and friends who disapprove of all drug use, controlled or not, can be grouped with individuals who make repeated efforts to stop using but who have friends that express little concern over drug use because they are also serious users. The other items can be similarly traded off.

A further complication is that the criteria or questions themselves sometimes are not so clearly objectively observable. The problem comes from the standard inclusion of harmful consequences as a criterion for addiction. Physical harm may be fairly non-controversial. But there many people who act compulsively and make repeated attempts to stop who have not yet done serious physical harm to themselves. Thus the harm in question is almost always defined more broadly as involving harm to relationships and work. This broader conception of harm leaves plenty of room for social conventions and norms as well as other factors such as income to be essential aspects determining what causes harm. A wealthy individual whose drug use is financially inconsequential and whose family and friends do not disapprove may exhibit the same behaviors that in a different individual and social context might indeed cause harm in a sense broader than physical harm. This variability is an obstacle to successful medical models of addiction.[2]

There are at least two worries here: what individuals themselves experience as harm will vary with social context and what practitioners count as social harm will vary from individual to individual and from practitioner to practitioner. We are uncertain how serious these problems are, but believe they are worth keeping in mind. Research in clinical populations in treatment may present fewer problems in practice—particularly for the most severe frequent relapse cases (see below) where the harm is blatantly obvious. For epidemiological research, which is essential for understanding the full range of addiction phenomena such as spontaneous remission in the general population, the problem may be serious. This argues for the importance of longitudinal studies.

We know that many concepts in science are not easily defined in terms of straightforward traditional necessary and sufficient conditions and that nevertheless such concepts do not prevent scientific progress. Yet it is undeniable that clear definitions allowing for clear operationalizations are something to be valued. We think that the problems with DSM-style categorizations of addiction as well as with their specific instantiations are an obstacle to progress in addiction research. That obstacle should be recognized and routes around it pursued.

We would suggest two possible, related paths are worth pursuing in trying to find more scientifically palatable categorizations of addiction. There is nothing to prevent researchers from going beyond the "any five of the following ten criteria" method of categorizing addicts. It is possible to weight components and to determine statistically which components are doing the most work in the classification processes. Researchers have begun to take such steps in the pathological gambling literature. Even when research samples are based on the DSM criteria, it is possible to report on differences in results by differences in which subcriteria are met.

The loose nature of the DSM categorization might also be dealt with by investigating the possibility that the commonsense notion of addiction that underlies the DSM-based categorization covers heterogeneous phenomena that are best separated (Ross et al. 2008). Those who get labeled addicts may fall into two distinct groups: the severe, biochemically challenged individuals, perhaps best picked out by serious (resource-using) repeated failed attempts to quit, and another set of individuals who exhibit a range of behaviors such as episodic use, movement between binge and controlled use, and so on. The individual who uses alcohol daily in a controlled way a large part of the time perhaps should not be classified with the individual who has been in detox repeatedly and who returns to binge drinking each time.

If we are serious about a medical model for addiction, then separating the severe addicts from the others may be essential. Science often takes commonsense notions and then fragments them into components, finding some amenable to some kinds of explanation and not others. Medical models that give relatively minimal place to social and environmental factors in explaining addiction are likely to be more plausible for the severe addicts described above than for the full plethora of behaviors that get labeled as addiction. Pursuing a strong medical model for all behaviors that get labeled as addiction may be letting the medical model dictate hypotheses and possible causes where it should not be doing so.

We have been discussing the extent to which the commonsense notion of addiction groups together similar phenomena suitable to the same scientific, medical type explanation. We also need to look at the aspects of the dynamics of addiction that the medical model is supposed to explain. This is an important complication and one that is probably under-discussed in the research literature where the medical model predominates. The problem is there is not one thing—"addiction"—to explain. This is not the problem raised above by diverse behaviors associated with the commonsense notion of addiction. Rather, this is a problem that would surface even if we had quite clear necessary and sufficient conditions for being addicted. The problem is that we do not want to explain just the state of being addicted. It would be nice to have an explanation for much more. We want to know what explains onset—what explains the transition of nonproblem user to addict? We also want to explain the course of addiction, in particular the high spontaneous remission rate (though it is unclear if there is evidence about remission among the severe cases—assuming that it is not definitionally impossible on the grounds that if you go into remission you were not a severe addict in the first place).[3]

It should be obvious that what explains one of the various aspects of addiction need not logically explain the other aspects. Indeed, some theories of a current state of addiction are logically incompatible with explaining other aspects. If current-state addiction is explained by a medical model describing a biological transformation in the brain, that very same change cannot explain spontaneous remission. The dearth of discussion of spontaneous remission in medical-model-inspired addiction research is thus not so surprising; it is perhaps another place where strong medical models may be skewing what is investigated in potentially unhelpful ways. *Note that in general a medical model might be a good explanation for one stage of addiction but not another.*

To What Extent Have We Gotten a Neurobiological Model?

Up to this point we have been talking about medical models of addiction in the abstract. Addiction, it is said, is a disease of the brain. In this section we ask in what sense addiction has been located as a disease of the brain. Contemporary addiction researchers cling to the hope that all addictions (whether natural, e.g., sex; substance, e.g., cocaine, alcohol; or behavioral, e.g., gambling) may prove to be successfully treated by some *common* therapeutic intervention. So, the predominant goal is to provide what might best be termed a "common pathway account" of the causes of addiction. However, in the literature we encounter multiple idealized common pathway models of addiction pitched at varying levels of analysis. The interesting question, then, is how such models can be fit together into a unified causal account that locates addiction as a disease in the brain. It is the strides that have been made toward such a unified account of the mechanisms of addiction and the challenges that still remain with which we concern ourselves in this section.

The best-articulated systems-level model of addiction consists in the hypothesis that addicts have a dysfunction in "the mesocorticolimbic dopaminergic and glutaminergic pathways" (Adinoff 2004). As Nestler (2005, 1445) claims:

There is now considerable evidence, from animal models and more recently from humans, that all drugs of abuse converge on a common circuitry in the brain's limbic system. Most attention has been given to the mesolimbic dopamine pathway, which includes dopaminergic neurons in the ventral tegmental area of the midbrain and their targets in the limbic forebrain, especially the nucleus accumbens (NAc).

Details of this hypothesis differ across individual advocates, but there are enough common elements to define a common approach and research program. At the systems level, changes in the function of brain systems are appealed to in order to explain at least some of the behavioral phenomena of addiction (e.g., loss of control, relapse). The most prevalent and widely accepted systems-level explanation is in terms of two competing systems. According to Bickel and Yi (this volume), "choices of addicts result from two separate competing processes—one that is hyperactive and one that is hypoactive." The hypoactive system is executive functioning, which is subserved by the prefrontal cortex. It is claimed that addicts "exhibit a variety of deficits in what is often called executive function." The hyperactive process is "the impulsive system" or "the reward system." This system, at this level of analysis, is taken to comprise two pathways: the mesocortical and mesolimbic pathways (described below). Addiction occurs when "the impulsive system overwhelms the executive system"—"if signals triggered by the impulsive system were relatively strong, they would have the capacity to hijack the top-down goal-driven cognitive resources needed for normal operation and exercising the willpower to resist drugs" (Bickel and Yi, this volume).[4] Goldstein and Volkow (2002, 164) put the claim another way: "top-down processes are reduced, releasing behaviors that are normally kept under close monitoring."

This general picture is multilevel, as it includes reference to brain systems and neuronal networks. But it is pitched at a relatively abstract level. Below we will look at a complementary account that ties addiction more closely to details at the synaptic, cellular, and molecular levels. We believe that such details are important because medical models at the systems level do not by themselves get us very far with respect to identifying the causes of addiction. We worry that the causal stories they provide are dictated too much by what fMRI can measure. It seems to us that the use of the fMRI naturally encourages oversimplification in explanations, as experimental tools are prone to do. What can be measured is treated as an isolable cause despite background knowledge that suggests that the system in question is much more complex. To see this in practice in the addiction literature, look at the reasoning in these two quotations:

"Neuroimaging studies generally observe decreased activity among addicts relative to controls in those regions that compose the prefrontal cortex (PFC), which is an evolutionarily younger brain region found in humans and higher mammals. For example, studies have demonstrated decreased activity or volumetric reduction of the PFC" (Bickel and Yi, this volume).

"The frontal cortex is a brain region that supports logical thinking, goal setting, planning and self control. Numerous MRI studies have documented that addictive drugs cause volume and tissue composition changes in this region. . . . Several structural MRI studies have shown enlargement of the brain's basal ganglia in addicts compared to controls. . . . In one study, methamphetamine dependence and poor decision making correlated with reduced activation of the PFC" (Fowler et al. 2007, 6).

Here the experimental tool, after much data analysis, produces a result—a small probability of seeing a small decrease or increase in blood-oxygen-level-dependent (BOLD) signal by chance in some region of the brain.[5] That is then taken to show that the region in question is "less active." From "less active" comes the move to the conclusion that the region is dysfunctional, and it is so because, being less active, it is less able to control other brain regions. These hydraulic explanations come from taking what the experiment is able to isolate as an isolable cause. But from a molecular or synaptic perspective, we are not sure that the idea that different parts of the brain are more or less *causally* forceful has a clear sense—there is burst firing, phasic firing, and many other biochemical processes all going on at any one time throughout the brain. The "resting" brain—one that is not engaged in a task or receiving an experimental stimuli—is quite "active" as measured by fMRI (Sonuga-Barke and Castellanos 2007).

There are further issues to worry about with respect to explanations at this level insofar as they are supported by fMRI. First, an important problem calling for further investigation concerns the extent to which brain differences in addicts is the result of addiction or the cause of addiction (or some combination of both). Ideally, we would like to see prospective, longitudinal studies using fMRI to help sort this out. Such studies would be valuable.

We also know that there is high comorbidity in addiction, particularly in the severe cases, with disorders such as depression, and we know that depression is also associated with lower PFC volume and signal. Having been addicted could be a common cause of lower signal in both cases, but the signal could also be the result of prior differences. Moreover, depression is not the only such confounder. The lower PFC and higher striatum activation pattern also show up in antisocial personality disorder, for example (Silbersweig et al. 2007). These are issues that still need to be sorted out if the system-level medical model of addiction is to make progress.

Finally, we note that the fMRI evidence points to a more complicated medical model at the systems level, though these complications are sometimes not fully acknowledged. fMRI results in addicts show that in addition to differences in the orbitofrontal cortex (OFC), VTA, anterior cingulate cortex (ACC), and NAc there are differences between addicts (active and abstinent) and controls in activation in:

Right posterior cingulate, an area that may be "involved in" risky decision making. Parietal cortex, which is involved in attentional, inhibitory, imagery, episodic memory retrieval, and consciousness of self. PET studies have found similar activity differences in these areas.

Occipital-temporal regions, particular the superior temporal gyrus, which is involved in action planning and identifying salient events, among other things. These regions show greater activation in addicts compared to controls.

Thus there is some evidence that the causes of addiction are more widely distributed in the brain than the systems-level executive versus reward systems story allows.

Better medical models at this level will need to take such causal complexity into consideration.

Researchers working in the neurobiology of addiction accept the basic story behind the executive versus reward systems-level model of addiction (e.g., Hyman and Malenka 2001; Kalivas and Volkow 2005; Kauer and Malenka 2007; Nestler 2005). Their task has been predominantly to identify the synaptic, cellular, and molecular mechanisms that play a permissive role in the reward system coming to dominate over executive function in addiction. Or, at least, they are interested in explaining the phenomena they take to be common across addictions including binging, withdrawal, recovery, relapse, and the *persistence* that defines addiction. A handful of basic experimental strategies have been employed for this purpose, including behavioral experiments in which organisms are trained in addiction paradigms and the effects of drugs of abuse on behavior, synaptic physiology, and/or molecular activity are investigated. In other experiments, animals are injected with the drug of interest (e.g., cocaine) either one time or repeatedly; their brains are later removed (e.g., 24h following injection) to produce midbrain slices that are used to investigate, *in vitro*, potential physiological and morphological changes at synapses of interest (e.g., VTA-NAc synapse) that occur *in vivo* in response to drugs of abuse (see, e.g., Hyman and Malenka 2001; Kauer and Malenka 2007; Ungless et al. 2001).

The general consensus among neurobiologists is that research efforts ought to be directed at identifying the cellular and molecular mechanisms involved in persistent activity-dependent changes in synaptic strength in those synapses that are assumed to be "hijacked" in addiction, so that treatment strategies may be aimed directly at preventing or reversing such changes (e.g., Kauer and Malenka 2007). Yet, how far has such research gotten us toward a neurobiological medical model of addiction of the kind investigators want?

To date, neurobiological research on the whole has yielded evidence that has been used to substantiate several different neurobiological models of addiction. The common denominator across all models is the important role ascribed to the *mesolimbic dopamine pathway*. This pathway consists of dopamine neurons that originate in the VTA of the midbrain and terminate on medium spiny neurons in the NAc. We want to consider this basic model to determine how good the evidence for it is and to see how far it takes us in explaining addiction. Other, more elaborate models have been introduced to overcome this model's shortcomings, and we will consider the merits of these models with respect to achieving this goal later in this section.

Explanations of addiction that appeal to this synapse span multiple levels of organization (e.g., cells, synapses, and molecules). First, VTA dopamine neurons in this pathway are ascribed several different functional roles under "normal" or "natural" conditions. For example, they burst fire (i.e., release a number of action potentials within a very short temporal window, and consequently release a significant amount of dopamine into the synaptic cleft, which remains there for a prolonged period of time, given the time it takes for the reuptake of such a large amount of dopamine) in response to stimuli considered to be naturally rewarding for an organism, such as food and sex. Second, they burst fire in response to stimuli that predict the occurrence of such rewarding stimuli, or in response to stimuli that have come to be associated with such stimuli (e.g., via classical conditioning) (see, e.g., Schultz 2000). Third, their firing pattern reflects when an expected reward differs from the actual reward received (see, e.g., Schultz 2002). A fourth function is also ascribed to dopamine neurons and the dopamine signal. In reinforcement learning paradigms, increased release of dopamine into the synaptic cleft is hypothesized to act as a primary reinforcer, making it more likely that those behaviors that preceded its release into the synaptic cleft will be repeated (see, e.g., Hyman and Malenka 2001). It is also supposed that medium spiny neurons in the NAc "[are] involved in responding to the motivational significance of stimuli" whereas "the dorsal striatum is involved in the learning and execution of behavioral sequences that permit an efficient response to those cues" (Hyman and Malenka 2001, 697).[6]

One basic explanation for addiction offered on this neurobiological model is as follows. Drugs of abuse and certain kinds of behaviors cause VTA dopamine neurons to burst fire and release a significant amount of dopamine for a sustained period of time into the synaptic cleft. Repetitive drug use causes the repetitive significant and prolonged release of dopamine into the synaptic cleft, which repeatedly activates NAc neurons. Such repetition is accompanied by a *strengthening* of this synapse, because VTA dopamine neurons repeatedly cause NAc neurons to fire, and according to the Hebbian rule, "cells that fire together wire together." The organism exposed to the drug is motivated to take it again, given the reinforcing properties of dopamine. In turn, plastic changes downstream of the VTA-NAc synapse are also hypothesized to occur in order to explain the changes in behavior that accompany addiction. Such changes are used to explain repetitive drug use and the phenomenon of binging. Furthermore, following repeated drug use, natural rewards (e.g., food, sex) no longer elicit the same kind of dopamine release of which they were previously capable (i.e., they become *less* rewarding). This contributes to the organism subsequently engaging in drug-seeking behaviors. Overall basal levels of dopamine or tonic release of dopamine in the synaptic cleft between the VTA and NAc (i.e., release that occurs in the absence of rewarding stimuli) are decreased, yet, stimuli that are associated with the drug of abuse or behavior and the use of the drug or engagement in the behavior itself both continue to result in a significant release of dopamine into the synaptic cleft. On Robinson and Berridge's (1993, 2001, 2003) model, the synapse becomes "hypersensitized" to the drug. Such hypersensitivity is also appealed to in order to explain drug-seeking behavior and relapse. Furthermore, stimuli that often co-occurred with drug-taking and subsequent dopamine release come to be associated with the drug experience or its effects; this is taken to occur via the co-release of (1) glutamate from pyramidal cells that synapse onto medium spiny neurons in the NAc from limbic structures traditionally involved in associative learning (e.g., hippocampus, bed nucleus of the stria terminalis [BNST] and the amygdala) and (2) dopamine (i.e., the "reward" signal) from VTA dopamine neurons. Subsequent exposure to such stimuli may then come to trigger dopamine release in the absence of the drug or, during periods of withdrawal and even recovery, trigger relapse and repeated drug use. All of these causal factors are taken to contribute to addictions being so difficult to treat and beat.

Yet neurobiological explanations for addiction do not stop at the synaptic level. For such synaptic level changes are thought to require changes in cells and molecules. Neurobiologists, accepting the aforementioned synaptic model of addiction, have recently been concerned with investigating the cellular and molecular mechanisms that result in hypersensitization or strengthening of the VTA-NAc dopamine synapse. Long-term potentiation (LTP), an activity-dependent *increase* in synaptic strength, and long-term depression (LTD), an activity-dependent *decrease* in synaptic strength, are the two candidate mechanisms that have been identified as causally responsible for such drug-induced changes at this synapse. It is supposed that drugs of abuse, in part because they lead to persistent changes in behavior, co-opt the synaptic, cellular, and molecular machinery traditionally involved in learning and synaptic plasticity and that, in fact, "addiction represents a pathological, yet powerful form of learning and memory" (Kauer and Malenka 2007, 844).

Activity-dependent changes in synaptic strength occurring under "natural" learning conditions have been predominantly studied in glutamatergic synapses in brain structures such as the hippocampus and amygdala. LTP and LTD are produced by artificial stimulation, but cellular and molecular research on these two forms of synaptic plasticity has been used to shed light on how those plastic changes that are thought to underlie learning are achieved in the brain. In one form of LTP, NMDA-receptor-dependent LTP, (NMDA-LTP), activation of NMDA receptors following artificial stimulation results in Ca^{2+} influx into postsynaptic neurons. This is thought to trigger the activation of second-messenger signaling cascades (e.g., extracellular signal-regulated kinase [ERK]), which are poised to send signals from the synapse to the nucleus and ultimately result in downstream physical changes at the synapse (e.g., new spine growth, AMPA and NMDA receptor trafficking) that mediate changes in synaptic strength. So, addiction research at the molecular level has been primarily directed at identifying the kinds of extracellular and intracellular changes in molecular activity that occur in VTA neurons in response to drugs of abuse (see Thomas, Kalivas, and Shaham 2008). More recent work has sought to move beyond the VTA to study changes in synaptic strength at the VTA-accumbens synapse, as well as in projections from the amygdala to the accumbens.

So, at the molecular level the hypothesis is that the same molecular mechanisms that are operative in traditional forms of LTP and LTD are recruited in response to drugs of abuse, and ultimately result in persistent changes at the VTA-NAc synapse that underlie systems-level accounts of addiction and the behavioral phenomena of addiction (see, e.g., Hyman, Malenka, and Nestler 2006; Hyman 2005). The consensus is that interventions exclusively at the molecular level may prevent those changes in synaptic plasticity at the VTA-NAc synapse that accompany addiction. It should also be noted, however, that this traditional causal story is typically supplemented by noting that individuals who become addicts have certain "early" molecular vulnerabilities to addiction, such as low availability of D2 or D3 dopamine receptors in the ventral striatum (see, e.g., Everitt et al. 2008 [review]; Dalley et al. 2007).[7]

To summarize, the predominant working medical model of addiction based on the mesolimbic dopamine system spans multiple levels from molecules to behavior. It attributes primary roles in the etiology of addiction to the VTA-NAc synapse, dopamine neurons in the VTA and medium spiny neurons in the NAc, dopamine molecules/release, and cellular and molecular machinery implicated in synaptic plasticity at the VTA-NAc synapse. It hypothesizes a role for glutamatergic inputs from limbic association areas to medium spiny neurons in the NAc in both addiction and relapse, and it acknowledges that there must be consequences downstream of this synapse that result in changes in behavior. It is, in itself, a bold, interesting, and parsimonious hypothesis that is the result of an integration of research findings and methodologies across multiple levels of analysis. It, in some form or other, currently plays a crucial role in all medical models of addiction and drives neurobiological research on addiction. But how far does it actually take us toward a robust medical model that localizes addiction in the brain? How good is the evidential support for this model, and what types of phenomena is it actually able to explain?

Remember that a medical model of a disease ideally requires that the disease in question be identified by a set of objectively verifiable symptoms. It must be the result of a physical condition that represents a deviation from normal functioning. This condition must be in principle localizable somewhere in the body and it must be both necessary and sufficient to have the disease. We have suggested that two problems may arise with respect to providing a traditional medical model of addiction. First, the model may fail to be exhaustive with respect to identifying the phenomena of addiction. It may identify some phenomena, while remaining silent about or placing less weight on others. Second, descriptions of the causes of addiction phenomena may suffer from ambiguity or vagueness.

Since the explanation of addiction that is offered on this model makes reference to at least some of the stages of addiction observed at the level of the behaving organism, it seems worthwhile to approach our analysis of this model with respect to these stages and with respect to the type of evidential support offered for each stage.

First, an obvious prerequisite for becoming an addict is exposure to a drug of abuse. The best evidence to suggest that drugs of abuse elicit persistent changes at the VTA-

NAc synapse in response to a one-time exposure to a drug of abuse is data obtained from *in vitro* midbrain slices prepared from the brains of mice 24h after administration (via injection) of cocaine or saline (control) (Ungless et al. 2001). The type of plastic change observed in such cases was a change in excitatory postsynaptic currents in VTA dopamine neurons. This was shown to be mediated in part by increased expression of AMPA receptors at the cell surface in these neurons. There are several things worthy of note about such data. First, as Kauer and Malenka (2007) point out, these studies only investigated changes in VTA dopamine neurons and were not concerned with investigating whether other types of plastic changes had taken place in the brains of these mice as a result of the cocaine injection. So, these data do not rule out the possibility that the onset of addiction involves more brain areas than just the VTA-NAc synapse. What is required to validate this explanation of the onset of addiction on the VTA-NAc model would be data that demonstrated that these plastic changes in response to drugs of abuse were unique to the VTA, and this would have to be shown for each and every drug of abuse, not just cocaine.[8] So, one suggestion, which is aligned with Kauer and Malenka's admission of the limitations of this study, would be to investigate whether plastic changes are observed in brain structures upstream and downstream of the VTA following acute exposure to each drug of abuse.

Of course, few investigators are committed to the idea that an individual becomes an addict after a one-time exposure to a drug of abuse. It is thought to take *multiple* trials. In fact, the predominant method employed to study addiction in rodent and primate models is the self-stimulation paradigm, in which rat or monkey subjects come to develop what is identified as an addiction only over *repeated* self-controlled exposure to a drug. But, if repetition is necessary for addiction (at least in some if not all cases), what is the threshold? How many times is enough for the requisite plastic changes to take place to make an individual an addict? Or how much of the drug is enough? This is not so odd a question, given that activity-induced synaptic plasticity in other brain structures, such as the hippocampus, is thought to require stimuli of a particular frequency, intensity, and duration. A further question we may ask is whether the thresholds for the induction, expression, and maintenance of plasticity vary or are consistent across different drugs of abuse and different people. For example, might there be synaptic, cellular, or molecular changes that can be appealed to in order to explain why some individuals never develop an addiction even after repeated exposure to a drug, whereas other individuals do? Do thresholds for addiction vary across individuals? These are merely some of the questions that may be raised with respect to onset. And investigators have sought to provide answers to such questions, but this does not mean that they have considered all of the potential causes that may contribute to variability in the onset and expression of addiction across individuals.

There is an additional issue relative to the specific methodology of studying drug-induced plasticity one set of synapses at a time. We may anticipate that the kinds of plastic changes observed when an animal is administered a drug via injection will differ from those plastic changes observed in the brain of an animal that has been trained in a self-stimulation paradigm, in which it learns to lever-press to receive a drug stimulus. In the latter case, other brain areas besides the VTA are likely to be involved in the process of the animal becoming an addict, given that it is in an operant learning situation. The activation of other brain areas that send neuronal projections to the VTA and NAc will most likely have an impact on the kind of plastic changes that are observed at the VTA-NAc synapse. This is an obvious and worthwhile avenue for exploration, namely, to tease apart plastic changes caused by the drug alone versus plastic changes that may occur in addition to such changes as a result of the learning. In any case, experimentalists will face obvious challenges in trying to link data obtained from these two methodologies up into a neat causal story of addiction that validates the current working medical model.[9]

Another issue with respect to the onset of addiction relative to this model presents itself. As Kauer and Malenka (2007) acknowledge, recent neurobiological research has been directed at understanding plastic changes that occur at the VTA-NAc synapse— that is, to understand postsynaptic changes in NAc medium spiny neurons in response to drugs of abuse. Little to date is known about plastic changes in these neurons and the story will presumably be complex for several reasons. First, these neurons have multiple dendritic spines, which each receive inputs from multiple different neuronal types originating in multiple different brain systems (e.g., hippocampus, amygdala, VTA, prefrontal cortex [PFC]). NAc medium spiny neurons are integrators of information coming from each of these different regions. Types of information include (1) the reward or any number of other signals from dopamine neurons in the VTA, (2) spatial and temporal information from pyramidal cells (GLU) originating in the hippocampus, and (3) emotional information from pyramidal cells (GLU) originating in the amygdala. Now, the VTA-NAc model makes it seem as if at the time that an individual is presented with or takes a drug of abuse for the first time, that is, prior to the onset of addiction, there is nothing going on in his or her brain apart from the reward signal from dopamine neurons—and that the only time that these other brain areas exert their influence in addiction is at the stages of drug-seeking and withdrawal, resulting in relapse. But there are several interesting questions we may raise for this model: First, how is it that the dopamine signal comes to be rewarding if these other brain structures and neurotransmitter systems are not operative prior to onset? Isn't "reward" dimensional—having emotional, temporal, and even spatial dimensions? Some investigators have suggested so (e.g., Berridge and Robinson 2003). And aren't organisms learning all the time? But if these other brain areas are operative from the get-go, then isn't it possible that important changes in synaptic plasticity are happening in these regions as early as the first exposure to a drug of abuse? And if so, then, what role do they play? Sometimes, when addiction is explained in light of the working model, the role of these other systems tends to be overlooked. Yet it is not obvious that the key to solving addiction isn't in these other brain areas as well as in the reward system—or that maybe the area currently designated as the reward system should be more broadly circumscribed.

Another important point is that when an individual crosses the threshold from non-addict to addict, there is an obvious behavioral signature: the individual engages in drug-seeking behaviors even when doing so is to his or her own or others' detriment. In order to establish that such changes in behavior are the result of plastic changes in brain synapses, neurobiological investigators have intimated that it would be helpful to understand how changes at the VTA-NAc synapse actually lead to these downstream behavioral consequences. Whereas the hypothesis at the systems-level is that there is an inhibition of executive function that explains this apparent loss of control, and that this is mediated in part by changes in synaptic plasticity in dopaminergic projections from the VTA to the PFC, plastic changes occurring at the VTA-PFC synapse have yet to undergo investigation; merely establishing that VTA cells exhibit some plastic changes in response to drugs of abuse does not provide insight into the downstream consequences of such plastic changes. Furthermore, neurobiological investigators seem more interested in understanding the synaptic events occurring directly downstream of the NAc. For example, evidence to date suggests that the excitability of NAc neurons is depressed in response to chronic drug exposure, yet the downstream behavioral consequences of such depression are not well known. It is supposed that such changes occur rapidly in response to repeated drug exposure and are crucial for the persistence of addiction. But although the pathways via how such changes may occur have been identified, the mechanisms are not yet known.

We take it that it is in response to considerations like these that other circuit models of addiction have begun to proliferate in the neurobiology of addiction literature. Although some of the components of these models are not appealed to in order to explain the early stages of addiction, researchers have at least agreed that more complex models[10] necessarily have to be posited in order to explain the later stages of addiction, which include the phenomena of withdrawal and relapse. Withdrawal is said to be accompanied by responses typically classified as "emotional." Relapse may be the result of stress, or the result of encountering contextual stimuli that have become previously associated with the drug during use.

What these more complex models really suggest, however, is that the causes of addiction could potentially be distributed throughout the whole brain. And this casts doubt on the feasibility of a strict localization of the causes of addiction across all types of addictions and across all persons who are addicts, as is required by a strict understanding of the medical model in combination with the goals of contemporary addiction research. Furthermore, these newer models, insofar as they suggest a diffuse interaction among different brain systems, cell types, and neurotransmitter systems, make the prospect of a very localized therapeutic intervention in addiction unlikely. This does not mean that the project of finding one is doomed from the start, but rather that investigators must continue to be more inclusive in their search for a cure. And this may mean, as we claim in the next section, considering causal factors outside of the brain.

We want to draw the reader's attention to a final issue that we mentioned in the previous section. The rates of spontaneous remission among diagnosed addicts are actually quite high. Although neurobiological models identify potential causes involved in becoming addicted, being addicted, and staying addicted, these models are silent with respect to these phenomena. And, there is no obvious mechanism in the context of such models to which we might appeal to explain them. If such remission is the result of plastic changes somewhere in the brain, where are such plastic changes taking place and what is the impetus for them? Even if we claim that there is still an underlying addiction, there must be something that we can point to in order to accommodate the lack of expression of addiction in the individual's behavior. We think it is worthwhile to raise such questions, given that understanding why some addicts go into spontaneous remission—that is, understanding what the mechanisms are—may shed light on novel avenues to pursue in the search for effective treatments for addiction.

How Far Can a Medical Model Get Us without Bringing in the Social?

A final challenge for medical models of addiction is to incorporate a richer picture of the social environment when that is needed. Whether it is needed is, of course, an open question. There is little direct discussion in the papers in this volume of social factors in addiction, whereas there is much attention to the kind of neurobiological detail of medical models we have sketched above. However, that does not preclude us from asking if and how we would add social elements to our explanations of addiction if those factors do indeed play a causal role.

We should remember that this question must be refined along two dimensions: according to the various aspects or stages in the course of addiction and perhaps according to whether we are focusing on addiction in its broad sense or only the most severe addicts. That social factors determine accessibility of addictive drugs is uncontroversial. What role they play in ongoing addiction, spontaneous remission, relapse, and treatment is more controversial. We saw Koob and Le Moal (2006) expressing the hardest line, namely, that after onset, the explanation is biological, not social. In this final section we sketch reasons for thinking things are not this simple and identify some open issues about social influences that we think might usefully be pursued.

There are some general considerations that make it likely that social and cultural factors have to be an important part of the story. As MacKillop, McGeary, and Ray (this volume) point out for alcoholism, genetic findings about addiction always point to gene–environment interactions, and social and cultural factors are likely to be part of that environment. We also know from neurobiology that the amygdala is strongly involved in addiction and that the amygdala plays a central role in the emotions. Emotions, however, are often shaped and elicited by social relations.

Aside from such general considerations, there is significant research on the importance of specific social factors:

1. Both smoking and heroin use can be learned substance use (use that takes effort prior to addiction) in that both can be initially very unpleasant and individuals have to make repeated efforts before they find anything pleasurable about the activity. The learning is usually done with the help, support, and peer pressure of friends and family. Social factors in this case are importantly involved in the transition from use to addiction.

2. Stress is a major contributor to relapse (Sinha 2007). Stress is very much social in nature. It works through family, peer group, and work relationships. Life events such as the loss of a job or the breakup of a relationship are prime ways to undergo stress.

3. Access to resources is a key factor in determining whether a regular or past user experiences major problems of the sort that are used to define addiction—individuals with extensive financial support can sometimes lead fairly normal lives without the disruption of social roles.

4. Heavy heroin users in Vietnam mostly transitioned to abstinence or controlled use on their return from the war. Change in the social environment—family and work responsibilities, for example—was probably part of the explanation.

5. Hajema and Knibbe (1998) found that drinking in a Dutch sample declined significantly after marriage and employment.

6. Frankenstein, Hay, and Nathan (1985) found that alcoholics in marital therapy spoke more often to each and more positively after consuming alcohol. Apparently alcohol use can sometimes have positive social functions.

7. Steady but nonbinging drinkers tend to live in families with positive family environments (Dunn et al. 1987).

8. Substance abusers score lower on relationship functioning than controls (Wright and Wright 1990).

9. Deliberate and planned family rituals—regular meals, holiday celebrations together—among married individuals whose parents were alcoholics and who themselves drank show less alcoholism among their offspring (Bennett and Wolin 1990).

10. Spouse coping skills predict transition to problem drinking (Hurcom, Copello, and Orford 2000).

11. Bandura's social learning theory based on individual "modeling" behavior of others led to research supporting the finding that such learning occurs in drug use onset (Rotgers, Morgenstern, and Walters 2006).

12. Sobell et al. (1993) found that spousal support was an important factor in spontaneous remission among problem drinkers.

13. Several clinical trials have shown that voucher programs providing rewards for being drug free are effective (Budney et al. 2000).

14. The price of valued, nondrinking rewards influence relapse (Vuchinich and Tucker 1996), with social interaction being a substitute commodity (Rachlin 1997). Addicts are price sensitive. Smokers, for example, are quite price sensitive, showing elasticities of .8.

We have some specific causal claims here with some supporting evidence about the role of social factors in onset, current addiction, remission, and relapse. These are piecemeal causal claims. There is a more systematic story about social interaction in addiction that would nicely incorporate these claims. The story falls into the domain of suggestive but imprecise social science, but it is worth keeping in mind as we think about the social side of addiction.

The more systematic account comes primarily from the social interactionist literature in sociology as well as the behavioral learning tradition in psychology and behavioral economics. On this picture, individuals come to their self-identity in interaction with and negotiation with others who do the same. They have roles that are identified by the expectations of others, and they have different levels of commitment to their roles. Roles may expand in that a subject may identify it with in a wide range of circumstances. Reference groups are those who expectations define the role. Roles can conflict. Roles require expenditures of effort, and individuals can have difficulty in achieving them. Some roles are more similar than others, and the more similar the role, the easier it is to adopt it. Adopting roles involves learning of various kinds. Classical conditioning, operant learning, Bandura's modeling processes, and higher-order cognitive decision making can all be involved.

From this perspective, being an addict is a role. Individuals assume the addict role in part to the extent that families and friends label them as such—the labeling process is part of the learning process. Moreover, it is not just the drug experience that is rewarding. The role itself can be rewarding—although addicts may forgo certain kinds of social interaction and that is a cost, there are nonetheless various social interactions built into being addict that can themselves be rewarding. Spontaneous remission can result from what social scientists call role strain—the costs of being an addict—and from the extent to which the addict can commit to new and past nonaddict identities. One way this can happen is through 12 step programs. Addiction in disadvantaged individuals occurs in part because of the restricted number of roles there are for them to occupy.

This picture is suggestive but sketchy. Nonetheless, it seems clear that social processes of some sort are importantly involved in addiction. How are medical models to incorporate them? The pure medical models, which explain only via localizable internal dysfunctions, will not do the job. However, we take it that the social processes we describe can be complements to the kind of neurobiological details that medical models emphasize. The effect on the dopamine system helps explain why the addict role can be rewarding and how individuals learn to adopt that role, and thus why the role may be hard to abandon. The success of voucher programs suggests that rewards differ in their ability to compete with drugs, and this fact ought to have a neurobiological substrate if not a complete explanation. Such explanations could also help flesh out how family relations make a difference to various aspects of addiction. There is no reason that the biological and the social have to be competing as Koob and Le Moal claim—unless one persists in requiring a full–on, pure medical model.

It is also important to remember our distinction between the broad common sense–based varieties of addictive behavior and that of the most severe addicts who make serious repeated attempts to quit and fail. It is possible that for the latter the medical model is closer to the truth and that social factors are much more important for the less severe addictive phenomena. If no contingencies in the environment short of incarceration will deter the addictive behavior, then the environment drops out for these individuals after the onset of addiction. At that point it would not be the case that the kinds of factors that influence human behavior in general explain ongoing addiction as Heyman (this volume) asserts they can.

Ross et al. (2008) provide some evidence for thinking that there are such severely addicted individuals for whom the medical model is appropriate. We think there are some further interesting empirical issues about this hypothesis that could be fruitfully pursued. We would like to know if people fall on a continuum of failed times attempting to quit or if there is sharp cutoff—a sharp peak in the frequency histogram pointing to a distinct group. Do we see successes at stopping after X number of tries but never at some larger X? That would give us further evidence that the severe addicts are a distinct group and represent a homogeneous phenomenon. A related empirical question is whether the social factors that seem to influence remission and relapse such as social support, for example, are irrelevant for these individuals—do they show repeated failed attempts to quit despite high social support or other social factors that might explain remission and relapse in the less severe addicts, picked out by the broad sense of addiction? These questions call for going beyond the DSM-based screens and regressions based on them, for they are not set up to find such differences even if they exist.

Finally, if there is a distinct group of severe addicts where the medical model is plausible, they will probably be individuals with other axis I comorbidities such as depression. What is the causal relation between the two? How are the neurobiological causes of the two related? Of course, these are big questions, but the ideal medical model that we might aspire to would provide us with their answers.

Conclusion

Medical models of addiction as exemplified by the dysfunctional dopamine reward system hypothesis are bold, interesting, and parsimonious accounts. They have served to direct a research program that has produced many important results. However, we think that progress requires, first, being clearer on what exactly they claim and to what extent they actually are medical models, and second, trying to incorporate the more complex causal nexus that is involved in addiction running from the neurobiological to the social. We hope to have contributed in a small way to that enterprise.

Notes

1. The listing of authors is alphabetical.

2. See Manson, this volume, for a discussion of related problems applied specifically to problem gambling.

3. Orthogonal to these dimensions, if we think there is a genetic component to addiction—and the evidence for this is strong, if not perhaps for the large effects claimed—it will surely be an effect that consists in a vulnerability. If you live in an alcohol-free environment, your alcoholism gene is not going to make martinis for you at happy hour. So we may explain the vulnerability for each of the above aspects of addiction cited above. On our view, explaining behavioral tendencies more generic and fundamental than addiction may be a better target for medical models. See MacKillop, MacKillop, McGeary, and Ray, this volume.

4. For example, "compulsive cocaine use has been hypothesized to result from a failure in top-down executive control over maladaptive habit learning," which is hypothesized to "reflect the diminishing influence of prefrontal cortical function, as behavioral control devolves from the ventral to dorsal striatum" (Belin et al. 2008, 1352).

5. Sometimes it is claimed that the activation is "significant." This is the elementary fallacy of confusing statistical significance with clinical causal significance.

6. It should be noted that the functions that we are itemizing for dopamine neurons here are only a small sample of the many functions that have been attributed to dopamine in the literature. Wolfram Schultz (2007, 277) puts it best in claiming: "Scholars have numerous and mutually exclusive views on dopamine function based on the fallacy that there should be only one major role for every brain system. Results from individual experiments using different methods suggest a role in movement, reward, punishment, salience, learning, cognition, and many other processes." He adds that dopamine may serve all these diverse functions in light of the different time courses at which dopamine neurons can operate.

7. One possible explanation as to why persons with low D2/D3 receptors are more vulnerable to becoming addicts is that following acute exposure to a drug of abuse, the reuptake of dopamine in the ventral striatum is slow due to the low number of reuptake receptors. In turn, the dopamine

remains in the synaptic cleft for a longer duration of time, causing the repeated firing of accumbens neurons after a one-trial exposure. This will make such individuals more likely to become drug abusers. Yet, after chronic exposure to a drug of abuse (e.g., shown for cocaine), low D2 and/or D3 dopamine receptor availability has been observed in dorsal striatum.

8. Of course, this is true only if the assumption is made that drugs of abuse share common cellular and molecular pathways. It is, however, possible that different drugs of abuse will set different kinds of synaptic changes in motion—that is, even if the functional consequences (i.e., addiction and the behaviors associated with it) of such changes are ultimately identical across different drugs of abuse or even types of addiction. Nestler (2005) points to the possibility of there being a common molecular pathway for addiction.

9. Note that a common way to infer a causal relationship between a drug-of-abuse-induced form of synaptic plasticity and a change in behavior at the level of an organism is to reverse, via pharmacological interventions, the drug-induced synaptic plasticity and then subsequently observe a corresponding change in the behavior. As Thomas, Kalivas, and Shaham (2008, 328) claim in reference to experiments using cocaine, "a stringent criterion to infer causality between a specific physiological process that underwent cocaine-induced neuroplasticity and a specific behavioural effect of cocaine is that reversal of cocaine-induced neuroplasticity of the physiological process to a drug-naïve state leads to decreases in the behavioral effect of cocaine." Of course, though we may accept this criterion for establishing causality, in all of the cases cited by Thomas et al. (2008), plastic changes at the synapse (e.g., increases in AMPA receptor surface expression) are assumed to be blocked because the activity of certain molecules that are upstream of such plastic changes at the synapse (e.g., ERK), when blocked, is accompanied by a cessation of a drug-related behavior (e.g., drug-seeking). However, such data are only correlational—although suggestive, they are insufficient to establish that changes in synaptic plasticity actually *cause* the changes at the level of behavior.

10. For example, Goldstein and Volkow (2002, 1642) posit what they refer to as "an integrative model of drug addiction that encompasses intoxication, bingeing, withdrawal, and craving," which includes the mesocortical (VTA-PFC) as well as the mesolimbic dopamine system (VTA-NAc) and takes into account the possible pathways via which these two systems may interact. For example, dopamine projections from the VTA are sent directly to the NAc, the medial dorsal thalamus (via the ventral pallidum), and the medial prefrontal cortex (mPFC or anterior cingulate). The model takes into account the fact that both the PFC and the NAc receive glutamatergic inputs from the amygdala and hippocampus. It also acknowledges reciprocal projections from the PFC to the VTA (glutamatergic), the PFC to the NAc (glutamatergic), and the NAc to the VTA (GABAergic). This model suggests that the neurons contained in the different brain areas identified may interact in complex ways, which might make it difficult to understand which neurotransmitter systems and physiological signals are implicated in the purported plastic changes that underlie addiction. Yet even this model is an idealized model that abstracts away from the actual connectivity of these different systems and neuron types.

Kalivas and Volkow (2005) have put forward another model, namely, the extended amygdala model, that takes into account GABAergic/neuropeptide projections from the extended amygdala (including the central nucleus of the amygdala [CeA], stria terminalis, and shell of the NAc), which can serve to regulate the activity of dopamine neurons. It also acknowledges an important role for the ventral pallidum, a structure intermediary between the NAc, VTA, and medial dorsal thalamus. This structure sends GABA projections to the VTA and NAc and also receives a GABAergic projection from the NAc. This suggests that there are various points of control in the network, and understanding the plasticity of one may necessarily involve understanding the plasticity of the others. On this model, "plasticity in [those] neural systems converging on the nucleus accumbens and dorsal striatum" are "usurped by chronic drug self-administration" (Everitt and Wolf 2002, 3312). Yet even this model, though more complex than the interactive and mesolimbic models, remains an idealization compared to the actual neural circuitry that is likely to become activated or play a role in addiction. Furthermore, within these systems-level models are distinct neurotransmitter and neuromodulator systems that have become targets of neurobiological investigations. For example, some investigators (e.g., Koob 2008; Koob and Le Moal 2008) aim to understand the role of molecular pathways involved in stress (e.g., corticotrophin-releasing factor [CRF] within the extended amygdala) that contribute to addiction.

References

Adinoff, B. (2004). Neurobiological processes in drug reward and addiction. *Harvard Review of Psychiatry* 12 (6): 305–320.

Belin, D., Mar, A., Dalley, J., Robbins, T., and Everitt, B. (2008). High impulsivity predicts the switch to compulsive cocaine-taking. *Science* 320: 1352–1355.

Bennett, L. A., and Wolin, S. J. (1990). In R. L. Collins, K. E. Leonard, and J. S. Searles, eds., *Family Culture and Alcoholism Transmission*, 194–219. New York: Guilford Press.

Berridge, K., and Robinson, T. (2003). Parsing reward. *Trends in Neuroscience* 26 (9): 507–13.

Budney, A. J., Higgins, S. T., Radonovich, K. J., and Novy, P. L. (2000). Adding voucher-based incentives to coping-skills and motivational enhancement improves outcomes during treatment for marijuana dependence. *Journal of Consulting and Clinical Psychology* 68: 1051–1061.

Dalley, J., Fryer, T., Brichard, L., Robinson, E., Theobald, D., Lääne, K., Peþa, Y., Murphy, E., Shah, Y., Probst, K., Abakumova, I., Aigbirhio, F., Richares, H., Hong, Y., Baron, J., Everitt, B., and Robbins, T. (2007). Nucleus accumbens D2/3 receptors predict trait impulsivity and cocaine reinforcement. *Science* 315 (5816): 1267–1270.

Dunn, N. J., Jacob, T., Hummon, N., and Seilhamer, R. A. (1987). Marital stability in alcoholic-spouse relationships as a function of a drinking pattern and location. *Journal of Abnormal Psychology* 96: 99–107.

Everitt, B., Belin, D., Economidou, D., Pelloux, Y., Dalley, J., and Robbins, T. (2008). Neural mechanisms underlying the vulnerability to develop compulsive drug-seeking habits and addiction. *Philosophical Transactions of the Royal Society of London, Series B, Biological Sciences* 363: 3125–3135.

Everitt, B., and Wolf, M. (2002). Psychomotor stimulant addiction: A neural systems perspective. *Journal of Neuroscience* 22 (9): 3312–3320.

Fowler, J., Volkow, N., Kassed, C., and Chang, L. (2007). Imaging the addicted human brain. *Science and Practice Perspectives*: 4–16.

Frankenstein, W., Hay, W. M., and Nathan, P. E. (1985). Effects of intoxication on alcoholics' marital communication and problem solving. *Journal of Studies on Alcohol* 46: 1–6.

Goldstein, R., Alia-Klein, N., Tomasi, D., Zhang, L., Cottone, L., Maloney, T., Telang, F., Caparelli, E., Chang, L., Ernst, T., Smaras, D., Squires, N., and Volkow, N. (2007). Is decreased prefrontal cortical sensitivity to monetary reward associated with impaired motivation and self-control in cocaine addiction? *American Journal of Psychiatry* 164 (1): 43–51.

Goldstein, R., and Volkow, M. (2002). Drug addiction and its underlying neurobiological basis: Neuroimaging evidence for the involvement of the frontal cortex. *American Journal of Psychiatry* 159: 1642–1652.

Hajema, K.-J., and Knibbe, R. A. (1998). Research report: Changes in social roles as predictors of changes in drinking. *Addiction* 93: 1717–1727.

Horwitz, A. (2003). *Creating Mental Illness*. Chicago: University of Chicago Press.

Hurcom, C., Copello, A., and Orford, J. (2000). The family and alcohol: Effects of excessive drinking and conceptualizations of spouses over recent decades. *Substance Use and Misuse* 35 (4): 473–502.

Hyman, S. (2005). Addiction: A disease of learning and memory. *American Journal of Psychiatry* 162 (8): 1414–1422.

Hyman, S., and Malenka, R. (2001). Addiction and the brain: The neurobiology of compulsion and its persistence. *Nature Reviews* 2: 695–703.

Hyman, S., Malenka, R., and Nestler, E. (2006). Neural mechanisms of addiction: The role of reward-related learning and memory. *Annual Review of Neuroscience* 29: 565–598.

Kalivas, P., and Volkow, N. (2005). The neural basis of addiction: A pathology of motivation and choice. *American Journal of Psychiatry* 162: 1403–1413.

Kauer, J., and Malenka, R. (2007). Synaptic plasticity and addiction. *Nature Reviews Neuroscience* 8 (11): 844–858.

Koob, G. (2008). A role for brain stress systems in addiction. *Neuron* 59 (1): 11–34.

Koob, G., and Le Moal, M. (2006). *Neurobiology of Addiction*. London: Elsevier.

Koob, G., and Le Moal, M. (2008). Neurobiological mechanisms for opponent motivational processes in addiction. *Philosophical Transactions of the Royal Society of London, Series B. Biological Sciences* 363 (1507): 3113–3123.

Nestler, E. (2005). Is there a common molecular pathway for addiction? *Nature Neuroscience* 8 (11): 1445–1449.

Rachlin, H. (1997). Four teleological theories of addiction. *Psychonomic Bulletin and Review* 4: 462–473.

Robinson, T., and Berridge, K. (1993). The neural basis of drug craving: An incentive sensitization theory of addiction. *Brain Research, Brain Research Reviews* 18 (3): 247–292.

Robinson, T., and Berridge, K. (2001). Incentive-sensitization and addiction. *Addiction* 96 (1): 103–114.

Robinson, T., and Berridge, K. (2003). Addiction. *Annual Review of Psychology* 54: 25–53.

Ross, D., Sharp, C., Vuchinich, R., and Spurrett, D. (2008). *Midbrain Mutiny: The Picoeconomics and Neuroeconomics of Disordered Gambling: Economic Theory and Cognitive Science.* Cambridge, MA: MIT Press.

Rotgers, F., Morgenstern, J., and Walters, S. (2006). *Treating Substance Abuse.* New York: Guildford Press.

Schultz, W. (2000). Multiple reward signals in the brain. *Nature Reviews Neuroscience* 1 (3): 199–207.

Schultz, W. (2002). Getting formal with dopamine and reward. *Neuron* 36 (2): 241–263.

Schultz, W. (2007). Multiple dopamine functions at different time courses. *Annual Review of Neuroscience* 30: 259–288.

Silbersweig, D., Clarkin, J., Goldstein, M., and Kernberg, O. (2007). Failure of frontolimbic inhibitory function in the context of negative emotion in borderline personality disorder. *American Journal of Psychiatry* 164 (12): 1832–1842.

Sinha, R. (2007). The role of stress in addiction relapse. *Current Psychiatry Reports* 9 (5): 388–395.

Sobell, L. C., Sobell, M. B., Toneatto, T., and Leo, G. I. (1993). What triggers the resolution of alcohol problems without treatment? *Alcoholism: Clinical and Experimental Research* 17: 217–224.

Sonuga-Barke, E., and Castellanos, F. (2007). Spontaneous attentional fluctuations in impaired states and pathological conditions: A neurobiological hypothesis. *Neuroscience and Biobehavioral Reviews* 31 (7): 977–986.

Thomas, M., Kalivas, P., and Shaham, Y. (2008). Neuroplasticity in the mesolimbic dopamine system and cocaine addiction. *British Journal of Pharmacology* 154 (2): 327–342.

Ungless, M., Whistler, J., Malenka, R., and Bonci, A. (2001). Single cocaine exposure in vivo induces long term potentiation in dopamine neurons. *Nature* 411 (6837): 583–587.

Volkow, N. (2004). Imaging the addicted brain: from molecules to behavior. *Journal of Nuclear Medicine* 45 (11): 13N-24N.

Volkow, N., Fowler, J., and Wang, G. (2004). The addicted human brain viewed in the light of imaging studies: Brain circuits and treatment strategies. *Neuropharmacology* 47 (1): 3–13.

Vuchinich, R. E., and Tucker, J. A. (1996). Alcoholic relapse, life events, and behavioral theories of choice: A prospective analysis. *Experimental and Clinical Psychopharmacology* 4: 19–28.

Wright, P. H., and Wright, K. D. (1990). Measuring codependents' close relationships: A preliminary study. *Journal of Substance Abuse* 2: 335–344.

14 Addiction and the Diagnostic Criteria for Pathological Gambling

Neil Manson

Introduction

A philosophical question divides the field of addiction research. Can a psychological disorder count as an addiction absent a common underlying physical basis (neurological or genetic) for every case of the disorder in the category? Or is it appropriate to categorize a disorder as an addiction if the symptoms of and diagnostic criteria for it are sufficiently similar to those of other disorders also classified as addictions—regardless of whether there is some underlying physical basis common to each case of the disorder? The question concerns the scope and validity of the scientific concept of addiction and, more broadly, what is required for a psychological concept to count as scientific.

The case of pathological gambling (PG) raises this question nicely. "Should pathological gambling be considered an addiction?" asks Howard Shaffer (2003, 176). He specifies the question further (2003, 177–178): "When clinicians and scientists identify a behavior pattern as an addiction, even if they can identify it reliably according to DSM criteria, how do they know that it is indeed an addiction?" He warns that, as it stands, "the concept of addiction represents a troublesome tautology" (2003, 178): a subject S is addicted if and only if S engages in repetitive behavior with negative consequences against S's better judgment. The problem with this concept is that it provides no way to distinguish behavior that cannot be controlled from behavior that is merely in fact not controlled. This "lay" concept is of little scientific value, Shaffer (2003, 179) argues, saying that "for addiction to emerge as a viable scientific construct …investigators need to establish a 'gold standard' against which the presence or absence of the disorder can be judged." PG has no such gold standard, says Shaffer. What would such a gold standard be? Shaffer suggests "neurogenetic or biobehavioral attributes" (ibid.). Such attributes will have to be identified because "if pathological gambling represents a primary disorder orthogonal both to its consequences and the laws of probability, then clinicians and scientists should be able to identify the disorder without knowing the winning or losing status of the gambler" (ibid.).

Stanton Peele (2003, 210) denies that there must be such a gold standard, claiming that researchers like Shaffer "fall prey to the reductionist fallacy" of thinking that pathological gambling must be fitted to "the disease model" if it is to count as an addiction.

This logic is exactly backwards—with drugs and with gambling. If a model does not begin to explain the behavior in question, then any number of associations with biological mechanisms and measurements will fail to provide an explanation (and, by extension, a solution) for the problem. Science is the creation of accurate and predictive models, not an exercise in laboratory virtuosity to show, for example, how drugs impact neurochemical systems. No work of this kind will ever explain the most basic elements of addiction, including that many people show the ability to be addicted to an array of dissimilar substances and activities, that different people react differently to the same addictive activities and substances even though the same neurological systems are implicated for all of these individuals, and—most patently—that people addicted to an involvement at one time and place cease to be addicted at a different time and place. (Ibid.)

In response to perceived encroachments from neurochemical reductionists, Peele (2003, 212) defends the autonomy of phenomenological psychology, claiming that "addiction is best understood from an experiential and behavioral perspective."

Shaffer (2003, 179) is right when he says clinicians should be able to identify PG "without knowing the winning or losing status of the gambler." However, as they currently stand, the accepted diagnostic criteria for PG fail to provide the desired ability. They rely on tacitly considering the fact that the gambling subject has actually suffered significant monetary losses. Because the obtaining of this fact is partially extrinsic to the subject (since gambling outcomes are partially a matter of chance), meeting the current diagnostic criteria for PG is neither necessary nor sufficient for being a pathological gambler. The criteria allow gambling outcomes to be determinative of PG when it should be the decisions gamblers make that play this role. The solution to this problem is to revise the screening instruments for PG so that they do not rely on knowledge of gambling outcomes. Clinicians need new diagnostic tools that are much more discriminating regarding the gambles being taken by the subjects they diagnose. Some new metrics for gambling quality are proposed, including metrics with a normative element.

Problems with the DSM-IV Criteria for PG

The American Psychiatric Association's *Diagnostic and Statistical Manual of Mental Disorders* proposes that meeting five or more of the following diagnostic criteria is sufficient for classifying someone as a pathological gambler (assuming that "the gambling behavior is not better accounted for by a manic episode.")

(1) Preoccupation Subject is preoccupied with gambling (e.g., preoccupied with reliving past gambling experiences, handicapping or planning the next venture, or thinking of ways to get money with which to gamble)

(2) Tolerance   Subject needs to gamble with increasing amounts of money in order to achieve the desired excitement

(3) Withdrawal   Subject is restless or irritable when attempting to cut down or stop gambling

(4) Escape   Subject gambles as a way of escaping from problems or relieving dysphoric mood (e.g., feelings of helplessness, guilt, anxiety, depression)

(5) Chasing   After losing money gambling, subject often returns another day to get even ("chasing" one's losses)

(6) Lying   Subject lies to family members, therapist, or others to conceal the extent of involvement with gambling

(7) Loss of Control   Subject has repeated unsuccessful efforts to control, cut back, or stop gambling

(8) Illegal Acts   Subject has committed illegal acts such as forgery, fraud, theft, or embezzlement to finance gambling

(9) Risking Significant Relationships   Subject has jeopardized or lost a significant relationship, job, or educational or career opportunity because of gambling

(10) Bailout   Subject relies on others to provide money to relieve a desperate financial situation caused by gambling

(American Psychiatric Association 1994, 615)

Intuitively, meeting five or more of the preceding descriptions is an indication that a subject has a gambling problem. A closer look, however, reveals that at least one of the criteria—(9), "Risking Significant Relationships"—is dubious insofar as it depends on factors partially extrinsic to the subject. If it really is a valid criterion, then a community, or even just a single person, could make a pathological gambler out of a subject meeting four of the above criteria just by breaking off relationships with that subject. Whether or not someone is a pathological gambler could depend, say, on whether he or she lives in a conservative community that shuns gambling on religious grounds. This criticism has been made by Wakefield (1997), who notes that criterion (9) is "inconsistent with DSM IV's own definitions of mental disorder which assert that symptoms must not be due to conflict with society." It is hard to see how there could be a Shafferian physical "gold standard" connecting PG with addiction if PG itself cannot be diagnosed without reference to the subject's community.

These reflections on the problem with criterion (9) suggest that if we seek a Shafferian "gold standard" for addiction, then a general restriction must be enforced on diagnostic criteria for any proposed addictive behavior: the criteria must not make reference to factors extrinsic to the subject. What is it for a factor to be "extrinsic to the subject"? The general answer to this question is far from clear, yet that does not mean there are no particular factors we can declare extrinsic. It is an open question whether a subject's being accepted or rejected by her community reflects the state of the subject more than the state of the community. Clearly, however, whether three cherries do or do not come up on a slot machine has nothing to do with the subject, and the idea that a subject's having a psychological disorder might depend on whether three cherries come up is simply bizarre.

The outcomes of the events wagered on by a gambler are at least partially outside of the gambler's control. Yet most of the DSM-IV criteria tacitly assume that the subject does, in fact, lose money on his or her gambles. That the DSM-IV criteria rely on this extrinsic consideration generates some glaring counterexamples to the claim that those criteria are adequate. Consider the following two cases.

(A) Mr. Lucky: The subject wins millions of dollars at a slot machine on his first visit to a casino. The subject subsequently becomes a frequent casino patron, playing slot machines exclusively and for long sessions. Due to the limits on the size of the wagers accepted by the slot machines, the subject is never in a position to risk a significant reduction is his overall slot machine winnings. After two years of frequent, intensive slot-machine play during which the subject suffers no significant monetary losses from his gambling, by chance he participates in a clinical study of gambling behavior and finds himself the subject of diagnosis.

(B) Mr. Unlucky: The subject is a brilliant young student of mathematics and psychology. After inheriting a significant amount of money, he decides to embark on a career as a professional poker player. He reads and fully grasps the best books on poker strategy, practices by playing low-stakes games online (with great success), receives tips and training from other professionals regarding how to read other players, learns to calculate the odds for all relevant poker situations in his head, and masters the art of keeping his "poker face." In short, he demonstrates all the requisite skills to be one of the world's best poker players. Finally, he moves to Las Vegas and begins playing poker for high stakes. Although he plays in a way that the other professionals regard as brilliant, he suffers an extremely long string of bad cards and "bad beats." After two years, all of his inheritance has been lost at the poker tables. He goes back to his parents, penniless and in need of their financial support. While home, the subject by chance participates in a clinical study of gambling behavior and finds himself the subject of diagnosis.

How would clinical psychiatrists, armed with the DSM-IV criteria for PG, diagnose our two hypothetical subjects?

Mr. Lucky almost certainly would not regard himself as a pathological gambler, and would not have sought treatment if he had not by chance participated in a clinical study of gambling behavior. But if he somehow found himself under the clinician's scrutiny, he would not be classified as a pathological gambler if that clinician relied solely on the DSM-IV criteria for PG. He does not exhibit withdrawal (3) because he never attempts to cut down or stop his gambling. It is not true that he gambles to escape his problems (4), seeing as his millions of dollars have alleviated whatever problems bothered him. He does not chase (5) insofar as there are no overall losses for him to chase; he is ahead millions of dollars. Rather than lying (6), the subject makes his gambling public; indeed, he brags about it as a way of attracting admirers and hangers-on. He never exhibits loss of control (7) because he has never had any reason to cut back or stop his gambling; after all, gambling made him a millionaire. He has never committed illegal acts (8) or requested bailout (10) because he has never needed to do so.

Despite all of this, intuitively Mr. Lucky has a serious gambling problem. Intuitively, no psychologically healthy person, when gifted with a prize of millions of dollars, would use it to spend his waking life playing slot machines—even if doing so never risked a significant loss of his money. Intuitively, there is something wrong with playing slot machines all day, even if doing so happens not to cause any financial hardship for the slot machine player. Mr. Lucky, it seems, is a pathological gambler if ever there was one—yet he would not be classified as such according to the DSM-IV criteria for PG. Thus meeting the DSM-IV criteria for PG is not required for someone to be a pathological gambler.

Meeting the DSM-IV criteria for PG is also not enough for someone to be a pathological gambler, as the case of Mr. Unlucky shows. If, as we have supposed, Mr. Unlucky is a brilliant poker player, then he is rightly preoccupied (1) with playing poker. Assuming that he gets a normal distribution of cards in his playing career, he rationally expects to make a significant amount of money in the long run by playing poker. In connection with this, he exhibits restlessness or irritability (3) if he is prevented from playing poker; after all, the less often he plays, the less money he can expect to make. Playing poker is his job, so not being able to do his job makes him restless and irritable. Whenever he loses, he comes back to play again (5). Given that he is a brilliant poker player, playing as much poker as he can is the smart thing for him to do, whether he has won or lost the day before. Because he seems to be cursed with ill luck, his friends abandon him (9), even though it is arguably irrational on the part of his friends to do so. (Can a subject be made a pathological gambler just by being abandoned by his friends—friends who believe in jinxes and curses?) Lastly, the subject is reduced to begging his parents for money (10).

Despite all of this, intuitively Mr. Unlucky is not a pathological gambler—or, if he is, then by parity of reasoning, there should also exist the categories "pathological investing," "pathological entrepreneurship," and so on. Yet clearly these fictional pathologies are bogus, unless we decide that the mere act of engaging in activities having high financial risks is pathological. Incidentally, the truncated life story of Mr. Unlucky, though fictional, mirrors that of known poker professionals, some of whom testify that early in their careers they started out with runs of extremely bad luck. These professionals testify that, though plagued by doubt, they continued to believe in themselves, and eventually their fortunes turned. We can say of these professionals that they did the right thing in continuing to play despite their losses. This is because skill at poker is an objective property of a person—at least, just as much an objective property as skill at investing, skill at starting up a business, and so on. The skilled business owner whose first enterprise fails through misfortune clearly does the right thing by trying to start up another business. Indeed, a skilled business owner does the right thing in trying to start up another business no matter how many prior businesses have failed.

Of course, the failure of many business ventures is good evidence that the business owner is not, in fact, skilled, but rather is inept. But this epistemic point is irrelevant here. Supposing that the business owner *really is* skilled, bad luck with past business ventures is no reason to abandon future ventures (and if the APA cared to identify a new disorder, "pathological entrepreneurship," they would have to find a way of identifying it that did not depend on knowing whether a subject's businesses succeeded or failed). Likewise, supposing Mr. Unlucky *really does* have all of the skills necessary to be one of the world's greatest poker players, initial bad luck is no reason for him to stop playing poker. *A fortiori* it is no reason to classify him as a pathological gambler.

Note that a person need not know or be confident that he possesses an ability to possess that ability. Some teachers are familiar with the phenomenon of students insisting they just do not understand certain material, even though all objective tests show that the students have mastered that material.[1] Suppose Mr. Unlucky is likewise plagued with doubt about his skill. He might mistakenly attempt to cut down on his poker playing, yet fail to do so, thus exhibiting loss of control (7). He might also wrongly feel ashamed of his losses, attributing them to lack of skill rather than bad luck, and thus might lie about his gambling (8). In this case, Mr. Unlucky would meet seven out of the ten criteria for PG. Nonetheless, intuitively Mr. Unlucky is not a pathological gambler. He has simply (i) started off with an exceptionally bad run of luck, and (ii) mistakenly attributed his losses to himself rather than to the bad run of luck.

The case of Mr. Unlucky shows that meeting the DSM-IV criteria for PG is not sufficient for someone to be a pathological gambler; that is, it does not guarantee that someone is a pathological gambler. The case of Mr. Lucky shows that meeting those criteria is not necessary for someone to be a pathological gambler. Thus meeting the DSM-IV criteria for PG is neither necessary nor sufficient for being a pathological gambler. Meeting the criteria does not entail that the subject is a pathological gambler, and not meeting the criteria does not entail that the subject is not a pathological gambler. The source of the problem is that the APA has tacitly made the status "having lost significant money"—a status partially extrinsic to the gambler—be criterial of PG.

What is the practical import of this problem with the DSM-IV criteria for PG? As Stinchfield, Govoni, and Frisch (2007, 205) note, the DSM-IV criteria are the standard criteria in PG research:

In response to the need for instruments to detect and measure problem gambling, a number of instruments have been developed. The SOGS is the most commonly used assessment instrument and has accumulated the largest volume of psychometric research to date, but new DSM-based instruments are generating a good deal of research momentum. DSM-IV diagnostic criteria have been paraphrased into questions that are used to diagnose clients in gambling treatment programs (e.g., DIGS), measure prevalence rates of PG in epidemiological surveys (e.g., DSM-IV-MR, NODS, and GAM), and measure gambling treatment outcomes (e.g. GAMTOMS).

Petry's (2005, 35–54) survey of PG screening instruments comports with that of Stinchfield, Govoni, and Frisch. Except for SOGS—the South Oaks Gambling Screen (Lesieur and Blume 1987), which was informed by DSM III—every screening instrument mentioned by Petry was either modified or developed directly in light of the DSM-IV criteria for PG. If the DSM-IV criteria for PG are fundamentally inadequate (as argued above), then any search for a gold standard for PG based on those criteria is bound to fail. The question that arises is how the DSM-IV criteria might be amended or supplemented to put the classification on a more solid footing.

Developing a Metric of Gambling Quality

The problem with the DSM-IV criteria seems to have arisen due to ignorance on the part of the psychiatric and psychological communities regarding some relevant specifics of gambling. They have treated gambling as a blob. They have used the term "gambling" as a mass noun and seen all forms of it as essentially alike. The following characterization of gambling is typical:

It is well accepted that statistical principles of probability applied to gambling indicate that payout rates and overall advantage always favor the house. The cost of each gamble is a combination of the proportion of each bet retained for taxes and the "house edge," with the remainder allocated to a prize pool for distribution amongst winners. This means that the longer one gambles, the greater the likelihood of losing. Under these conditions, an economically prudent person would minimize risk by limiting exposure to gambling. (Blaszczynski and Nower 2007, 323–324)

Yet gambling is not a blob; there is a tremendous variety of events on which a person may stake a wager. The events wagered on and the kinds of wagers made defy reduction to the sorts of easy generalizations made above. First, not all gambling involves competition against "the house," as suggested by the above quotation. For example, poker is played against other players, with the house charging a fee, either in the form of taking a percentage of each pot or in the form of an explicit entry fee for poker tournaments. Second, it is not true that "all gambling outcomes are determined by chance," if this is taken as meaning skill has no role in gambling; again, the case of poker illustrates this. The false generalization that gambling is "all a matter of chance" helps explain the befuddlement of some researchers at the fact that "gamblers rated their peers who won as more competent than those who lost" (Blaszczynski and Nower 2007, 330). Although it is true for many forms of gambling that there is no such thing as skill with respect to them, some games do involve some level of skill. Depending on the type of game, winning might indeed be a sign of competence. Finally, although it is true that "payout rates and overall advantage always favor the house," games differ tremendously in their payout rates and the overall advantage they provide to the house (the "house edge"). Some games have a fast rate of play and the house edge on each wager is high; others have a slow rate of play and the house edge on each wager is relatively low. The concern shown by casinos for marketing specific games, and for placing specific games in specific areas of the casino, attests to these facts. The differences in rate of play and house edge are crucial in evaluating the gambling engaged in by the subjects in PG studies. Yes, most gamblers wager against the house, make wagers for which the house has a considerable edge, and exercise little or no skill when they gamble; but not all do. The DSM-IV criteria for PG are blind to this fact.

Instead of diagnostic criteria that tacitly refer to the losing status of the gambler, PG research needs criteria that incorporate a refined, multidimensional metric of the games being played—a metric that ties in directly to the comparative quality of the decisions made by the gambler. Some researchers have made efforts to develop general metrics of gambling behavior and gambling decisions, but these metrics neglect the nuts and bolts of the specific games on offer, both in casinos and elsewhere. For example, in "Quantification and Dimensionalization of Gambling Behavior," Currie and Casey (1997, 163) identify the dimensions of gambling activity as "participation status, frequency, expenditure, duration, and type of game played." Yet their account of the dimension "type of game played" (ibid., 168) is thin: "There are literally hundreds of different gambling activities, each with its own set of rules, odds of winning, and payout schedule," they note. "Gambling types can be categorized across several dimensions: single-player (e.g., blackjack) versus multiplayer (e.g., bingo); passive (e.g., sports betting) versus active (e.g., poker); continuous (e.g., slot machines) versus non-continuous (e.g., lottery)." This list of distinctions provides a helpful start, but much more detail is needed.

A more refined metric should include at least the following dimensions: (a) the *expected value* of the wager in question; (b) the *rate of play* at which the wager in question is being made; (c) the degree to which the making of the wager and the observation of the outcome require *social interaction*; (d) the degree to which *strategic thinking* is required for the placement of the wager; and (e) the degree to which the wager involves *competition* against other agents. This list of dimensions is not put forth as exhaustive. Perhaps others need to be considered. But the ones offered here have two advantages. First, unlike the binary dimensions offered by Currie and Casey, each of these dimensions is scalar, so a metric based on them allows for more refined classifications than does that of Currie and Casey. Second, collectively they incorporate and supplant those suggested by Currie and Casey. "Rate of play" supplants "continuous versus non-continuous." "Social setting" supplants "single player versus multiplayer." "Strategic thinking" and "competition" supplant "passive versus active." Below I give more detailed descriptions of each of these proposed dimensions.

(a) Expected value   The concept of expected value is explained in connection with casino games by Manson (2003). We can simply note here that attached to each wager is a number representing the percentage of the dollar amount wagered that the gambler can expect to get in return "in the long run"—that is, the average return on each specific wager if that specific wager were to be made over and over again. This number is also sometimes represented as the "house edge," which is simply 100% minus the expected value. Thus for roulette (with two zeros), every wager (but one) has an expected value of 94.7% and thus a house edge of 5.3%. The "pass line" bet in craps has an expected value of 98.6%; furthermore, making it entitles the bettor to place a true "odds" bet (a bet with an expected value of 100%) of much greater value than the pass line bet. Thus the overall expected value of a pass line plus odds bet can get extremely close to 100% (if the bettor stakes a lot of money). Depending on one's strategy and on the rules of the house for it, the expected value for a hand of blackjack can approach 99%. At the opposite extreme, in most state-run lotteries the expected value of a $1 ticket is at or below 50¢.

(b) Rate of play   The rate of play refers to the rapidity with which the gambler makes each individual wager (say, one hand of blackjack per minute). Slot machines typically have the highest rate of play; gamblers can wager perhaps ten times in a minute on certain machines. For craps, the time between each roll of the dice can range anywhere from fifteen seconds (if the table consists of only a single player making a single bet) to several minutes (if the table is full and players are making a variety of bets). Likewise, the speed at which hands of blackjack are dealt or spins of the roulette wheel are made depends on the number of players at the table and the size and variety of their bets. Poker hands vary depending on these factors plus the time it takes players to make decisions. For lotteries and sports wagers, on the other hand, there is a significant gap in time—sometimes several days—between the placing of the wager and the occurrence of the event wagered on.

Several points need making here. First, typically the expected value and rate of play bear an inverse relationship to one another. The lower the house edge is, the more rapidly the game is played; the slower the game, the bigger the house edge. The dynamic is just like that in retail sales. Some businesses sell items at low marginal profit but make up for it with a high sales volume, whereas purveyors of luxury items sell their wares at large markups because luxury items are rarely bought.

Second, seemingly small differences in the expected values of two bets can lead to a very large difference in the overall expected returns of series of those bets. In craps, the expected value of a "proposition bet" on the number 12 is 86.1%, whereas the expected value of a pass line bet is 98.6%, as is the expected value of a "come" bet. Suppose two players go to a craps table, each with $1,000. On every roll of the dice the one makes a $10 proposition bet on 12, while the other makes either a $10 pass line bet or a $10 "come" bet. Each plays craps for five straight hours. If the dice were tossed at a rate of once per minute, each player has placed $3,000 in wagers. This is possible because it is not necessary to have $3,000 to make $3,000 worth of bets over the course of five hours—unless one loses every single bet, which is extremely unlikely. Mathematically, the first player would be expected to lose $425, the second only $45. The first player is expected to lose about $85 per hour, the second about $8 an hour. Arguably, the second player might count as the "economically prudent person" mentioned by Blaszczynski and Nower once the various perquisites of casino gambling (free drinks, entertainment, and so on) are considered. At the very least, the second player is engaged in a leisure activity with a per-hour cost comparable to those of other leisure activities (bowling, golf), with one exception: the per-hour cost of gambling is variable, whereas the per-hour cost of other leisure activities is fixed. Unlike other leisure activities, gambling involves risk with respect to cost.

Third, just as having a negative expected value does not necessarily make it irrational (not "economically prudent") to engage in a form of gambling, having a positive expected value does not necessarily make it rational to engage in a form of gambling. Consider a hypothetical game in which a slow-churning, robotically controlled machine mixes 4,999 red balls in an urn along with 5,001 white balls. Every ten minutes, a ball is drawn, its color is noted, and then it is placed back in the urn. The casino offers to pay even money to bettors who correctly predict the color of the ball drawn; the maximum bet is $10. Given these rules, the player playing this game nonstop can be expected to make $10 every seven days. The game involves no strategy and no competition (two dimensions of gambling to be discussed shortly), and it is intensely monotonous. Intuitively, anyone who did play this game repeatedly would be irrational, even though the gambler would be expected to make money playing it. This suggests that judging a form of gambling to be rationally engaged in or not involves a much more complex judgment than just that the form of gambling has a negative expected value. Additional dimensions besides expected value and rate of play must have some role. I suggest three such additional dimensions below.

(c) Social interaction Intuitively, any metric of gambling behavior that wants to detect PG should capture whether the subject's behavior involves significant social interaction. The dimension "single player versus multiplayer" of Currie and Casey indirectly gets at the relevant question: is the gambler engaged in his or her activity alone, or in the company of others? To divide the question more precisely, is the wager placed alone, and is the outcome observed alone? For some gambles (e.g., slot machines and lotteries), both the placement of the wager and the observation of the outcome typically occur alone. For others (e.g., sports bets), the wager is typically placed alone but the outcome is typically observed communally. For some games (e.g., roulette, craps, and blackjack), the placement of the wager and the observation of the outcome typically both occur in a crowd (though it is possible to find just a single player at a roulette, craps, or blackjack table). Other games (e.g., poker) necessarily involve the joint effort of gamblers. And for almost all of these games, the degree to which other people are involved varies. For example, one can play blackjack alone if one finds a table with no other players. Note that the degree of social interaction is typically related to the rate of play; the more people that are involved in a game, the longer it takes for the result of each particular wager to be determined.

(d) Need for strategy For some games, the decisions made by the gambler affect the expected value of the wager made. This is obviously the case in games such as poker, which involve such decisions at every stage. Bets on roulette wheels, on the other hand, involve no strategic decision making. But many games involve strategy to some degree. Blackjack is an obvious example; whether to "stay" or take a "hit" affects the probability that the player will win his or her wager. Knowing when to stay and when not to involves some knowledge; that is why there are various strategy "systems" for blackjack, spelled out clearly in pricey books and pamphlets. Even craps involves decisions regarding which bets to make, with the bets varying with respect to their expected values; to that extent, craps involves strategy, even if the outcomes of the dice rolls themselves are completely beyond human control.

Such decisions engage the intellect. Insofar as it is intrinsically better for an activity to engage the intellect than not, games that require such decisions are, other things being equal, better than games that do not. Strategic games reflect better on those who engage in them than do nonstrategic games. Other things being equal, it is better to play chess than tic-tac-toe. Likewise, other things being equal, it is better to play poker than slot machines. This value difference can be captured if we measure games along dimension (d).

(e) Degree of competition Some games involve outthinking and outplaying another agent, or at least an artificial agent. Chess requires paying attention to one's opponent, figuring out her patterns, anticipating her next move, and so on. Chess thus engages the intellect in a way that few other games do, though the kinds of thinking involved with competing against another agent are distinct from those mentioned in the "strategy" dimension discussed above. Thus there is an element to playing chess against an opponent (real or virtual) that is missing from, say, roulette. Insofar as it is intrinsically better for an activity to engage the intellect than not, games that feature competition are, other things being equal, better than games that do not. Competitive games reflect better on those who engage in them than do noncompetitive games. The value difference between competitive and noncompetitive forms of gambling should be accounted for in any metric for game quality. This value difference can be captured if we measure games along dimension (e).

Intuitively, poker, which involves direct competition against other gamblers, is a form of gambling that speaks better of those engaging in it than slot machines. Aside from the varieties of poker, no other casino games involve competition. This assumes we do not view the casino itself as an agent, but rather as an automaton; this assumption is justified, because, unlike even a computerized opponent in chess, the house always follows a predesignated and preannounced strategy. However, some forms of noncasino gambling (e.g., sports wagering) do involve some degree of competition. The important point for researchers and clinicians is that the degree of competition a game features is relevant in assessing the person making the decision to play that game. That a form of gambling taps into human competitive instincts is surely just as much a factor in its attractiveness as the fact that it offers those playing it a chance to make money.

Indeed, the desire to compete is plausibly regarded as virtuous. In *The Politics* Aristotle proposed that a good political structure would discourage conflict but encourage competition (Skultety 2009). Aristotle held that competition is intrinsically good because it promotes excellence, and that it is derivatively good because it develops virtues such as courage. Plausibly, the development of courage requires the suppression of risk-aversion instincts. Although some forms of gambling (e.g., slot machines) may desensitize gamblers to risk in the wrong way (by encouraging impulsive action), others (e.g., poker) may do so in the right way (by encouraging strategic thinking and deliberation). Undoubtedly, few of the gambling activities people engage in actually do develop virtues such as bravery or judgment, and the absence of those virtuous traits from most forms of gambling is doubtless part of what makes subjects who routinely engage in those forms of gambling disordered. To repeat, the important point for researchers is that what might contribute to making a form of gambling bad is that it involves no competition, or that it involves a degenerate form of competition—not just that those engaging in it can be expected to lose money.

Conclusion

The import of the preceding discussion should be clear. There is a strong cognitive component to gambling behavior. It is the cognitive features of gambling decisions that PG researchers need to measure, not the outcomes of those decisions, if we ever hope to find a gold standard for PG. Yes, significant gambling losses correlate strongly with a subject's being a bad decision maker with respect to gambling, but that is no excuse for making gambling losses criterial of PG. Doing so makes factors extrinsic to the subject be determinative of PG. This would rule out the possibility of a gold standard for PG and cast grave doubt on whether PG could properly be considered an addiction.

Note

1. As a long-time logic teacher, I have known students who insisted they did not know how to complete proofs in symbolic logic—yet they successfully completed all of their assigned proofs.

Their success was a mystery to them. One student occupied my office hours trying to get me to explain where he was going wrong in his proofs. When I told him his proofs were flawless (just as all his prior work had been), he was incredulous.

References

American Psychiatric Association (1994). *Diagnostic and Statistical Manual of Mental Disorders*, 4th edition. Washington, D.C.: American Psychiatric Association.

Blaszczynski, A., and Nower, L. (2007). Research and measurement issues in gambling studies: Etiological models. In Garry Smith, David C. Hodgins, and Robert J. Williams, eds., *Research and Measurement Issues in Gambling Studies*, 323–344. New York: Elsevier.

Currie, S. P.. and Casey, D. M. (1997). Quantification and dimensionalization of gambling behavior. In Garry Smith, David C. Hodgins, and Robert J. Williams, eds., *Research and Measurement Issues in Gambling Studies*, 155–177. New York: Elsevier.

Lesieur, H. R., and Blume, S. B. (1987). The South Oaks Gambling Screen (SOGS): A new instrument for the identification of pathological gamblers. *American Journal of Psychiatry* 144 (9): 1184–1188.

Manson, N. A. (2003). Probability on the casino floor. In Gerda Reith, ed., *For Fun or Profit? The Controversies of the Expansion of Gambling*, 293–307. Amherst, N.Y.: Prometheus Books.

Peele, S. (2003). Is gambling an addiction like drug and alcohol addiction? Developing realistic and useful conceptions of compulsive gambling. In Gerda Reith, ed., *For Fun or Profit? The Controversies of the Expansion of Gambling*, 208–218. Amherst, N.Y.: Prometheus Books.

Petry, N. M. (2005). *Pathological Gambling: Etiology, Comorbidity, and Treatment*. Washington, D.C.: American Psychological Association.

Shaffer, H. J. (2003). A critical view of pathological gambling and addiction: Comorbidity makes for syndromes and other strange bedfellows. In Gerda Reith, ed., *For Fun or Profit? The Controversies of the Expansion of Gambling*, 175–190. Amherst, N.Y.: Prometheus Books.

Skultety, S. (2009). Competition in the best of cities: Agonism and Aristotle's politics. *Political Theory* 37: 44–68.

Stinchfield, R., Govani, R., and Frisch, G. R. (2007). A review of screening and assessment instruments for problem and pathological gambling. In Garry Smith, David C. Hodgins, and Robert J. Williams, eds., *Research and Measurement Issues in Gambling Studies*, 179–213. New York: Elsevier.

Wakefield, J. S. (1997). Diagnosing DSM-IV, part 1: DSM-IV and the concept of disorder. *Behavior Research and Therapy* 36: 633–649.

15   Irrational Action and Addiction

Timothy Schroeder

Conventional wisdom has it that rational actions are the ones that maximize expected desire satisfaction. Addiction poses a challenge to this view. Addicts seem to want their addictive goods very, very much. Following the conventional wisdom, then, it would seem that addicts are often rational in choosing to use their addictive goods. And yet, using these goods often seems irrational.

It is common in philosophical circles to cite these facts as a reason to reject the conventional wisdom about rational action. But in this chapter, I defend the conventional wisdom by arguing for a surprising claim. Although addicts are often highly motivated to choose their addictive goods, and although they often feel strongly about obtaining their addictive goods, they nonetheless do not desire these goods with a proportionate intensity. In addiction, what a person feels and what a person is moved to do come apart from what a person actually wants. Of course, addicts do desire their addictive goods. But they do not desire them as much as they seem to. This is why they often act irrationally in choosing to use. So, at least, I will argue.

This chapter will combine ideas from neuroscience and the philosophy of mind. Neuroscience can tell us an enormous amount about what is going on in the brains of addicts. Applying philosophical work on the mind can allow this neuroscientific information to be interpreted in terms of desires. And doing so reveals a gap between what addicts desire and how they are moved to feel or act.

I begin, though, with a more careful statement of the problem.

1   The Puzzle

To make things concrete, think for a moment about nicotine addiction. There are many factors that influence nicotine use by nicotine addicts. Nicotine use increases alertness, affords and maintains social bonds with other users, contributes to one's social cachet, relieves withdrawal symptoms, gives structure to moments in one's life, passes the time, and so on. For nicotine users, these can all be good reasons to continue using. For some users, they are such good reasons that they make using rational. But rationality (according to conventional wisdom) is a matter of trading expected costs against expected benefits, and of course nicotine use has its costs as well as its benefits. Most of its benefits are associated with ingesting it by smoking tobacco, but smoking tobacco also harms one's health and (increasingly) acts as a social barrier as much as a social lubricant. It is also expensive relative to the means of many users.

These costs and benefits trade off differently for different people, depending on their desires and their expectations. The person who knows she has a family history of lung cancer has stronger reasons not to smoke than the person who knows that her family history shows a marked resistance to that disease, assuming they have the same desires for health. And the person who very much desires to be seen as cool has a stronger reason to smoke than the person who is not much concerned with how she is perceived. So I make no universal claims.

Nonetheless, it seems to me that most of the people I know who smoke do so irrationally. Most of the people I know who smoke gain few benefits from it and very much want the health and financial benefits of not smoking. Furthermore, most of them have tried to quit smoking—evidence that they themselves consider their smoking to be irrational. So it seems that many of these people smoke irrationally.

Still, there remains a pull toward the opposite conclusion. If rationality really is doing what one expects will maximize desire satisfaction, then it is hard to see how quitting can be rational until the day one finally quits—because, up until that day, it seems that one still *wants* to smoke, and wants to smoke more than one wants to quit.

There are some—economists, mostly—who think that addicts by and large are doing what is rational in using their addictive goods (e.g., Becker and Murphy 1988). I do not intend to directly address these sorts of arguments, but I want to acknowledge their force.[1] These sorts of arguments gain their plausibility from two assumptions, both very plausible themselves. The first is that the conventional wisdom is right about rational action. And the second is that people reveal what they want most in their choices, or their feelings, or both. In this chapter, I show that this second assumption is in fact mistaken, and show that its being mistaken is the beginning of an explanation of how it is that addicts often act irrationally.

2 The Neuroscience of Reward

To understand how addicts could count as irrational even according to the most conventional understanding of rational action, it will help to begin with the neuroscience of reward, because addictive drugs have their most distinctive effects through action on the brain's reward system.[2]

The output structures of the brain's reward system are very small and located deep in the brain, but they reach out to almost all of the brain, and are split into two subdivisions. The substantia nigra, pars compacta (SNpc) reaches out specifically to the motor striatum, a structure important in action production. The ventral tegmental area (VTA) reaches out to almost every other part of the brain. When active, the SNpc and VTA release dopamine.

The reward system has a certain baseline level of activity. Momentary deviations from this baseline are caused when organisms represent that the world contains more rewards than expected or fewer, so that the moment-to-moment changes in dopamine release take the value of x in the calculation $x =$ (actual reward) − (expected reward). An organism representing that the world contains more rewards than expected will have a momentary increase in dopamine release, whereas an organism representing fewer will have a momentary decrease.[3]

The point of this pattern is to implement reward-based learning.[4] In reward-based learning, an organism has an idea of how full of rewards the world is, an idea that it is constantly updating. Updates that say the world has more rewards than expected result in positive learning: whatever was just done will be more likely to be repeated in the future. Updates that say the world has fewer rewards than expected result in negative learning: whatever was just done should probably not be repeated. Reward-based learning is suited to produce operant conditioning of behavior, but in theory it should also be able to influence patterns of thought, perceptual sensitivities, and more. And in fact, there is good reason to believe that the brain's reward system has all of these effects.[5]

(It is important to note here, if only in passing, that the sort of learning caused by the reward system is unconscious: this sort of learning causes changes in the disposition of one perception or thought to lead to another, or of a perception or thought to lead to an action. It is not the sort of learning that causes later conscious recollection of an event and its conscious factoring into decision making.[6])

In addition to having an effect on learning, fluctuations in the reward signal also affect immediate motivation and feelings. Fluctuations in the reward signal from the SNpc into the motor striatum are directly influential on action production, so much so that a complete absence of such input results in paralysis (this is the limit case of Parkinson's disease; Mink 1996). And fluctuations in the reward signal from the VTA into the nucleus accumbens and perhaps the ventral pallidum would appear to be directly influential on feelings, such that increases in reward signal cause feelings from positive mood through to euphoria (Berridge 2003).

Part of the point of the last few paragraphs might be missed if it is not emphasized. The reward system is not defined by its effects on behavior, nor is it defined by how its activity makes one feel. These are both *downstream effects* that are *caused* by the reward system. In and of itself, the reward system is a *learning* system: a mechanism by which the brain can change itself in response to good and bad events in the world.[7]

In human beings and other animals like us, various thoughts and perceptions can activate the reward system. When we are hungry, the arrival of food triggers the reward system. When playing a game that requires cooperation, being cooperated with triggers the reward system. That is, a whole range of stimuli, both perceptually available and cognitively grasped, simple and complex, are capable of triggering the reward system. When it is triggered, the reward system directly causes unconscious learning and indirectly causes motivational effects and positive feelings. This, in a nutshell, is how the reward system works in ourselves and in animals like us.

3   Interpreting the Reward System

Elsewhere, I have argued at length that the best way to understand the reward system is that it realizes desires (Schroeder 2004). In this section, I summarize the main lines of evidence for this idea.

Desires are the causes of the effects we associate with them. So what are these effects? Consider a range of desires: a desire to eat, a desire to see a particular abstract painting, a desire that someone cooperate with you, and a desire for world peace. These desires are all, obviously, quite different. And yet they all share certain effects in common. Most saliently, desires bring about action and cause strong feelings. The person who has a desire to eat is a person who will tend to eat, and who will tend to feel good if he gets to eat, or bad if he does not. The person who desires to see a particular abstract painting is a person who will tend to gaze on the painting, and who will tend to feel good at doing so, or bad if denied the chance to see the painting. Likewise for the person who desires cooperation. Even the person who desires world peace will be more inclined to take certain actions that might contribute to world peace than will the person who does not desire peace: the person who desires world peace is more likely to make a donation to a UN charity, for instance. And certainly such a person would feel good if world peace were achieved, and will sometimes feel bad that world peace remains so far off.

Back in section 2, I claimed that the reward system plays these two roles, among others. The reward system makes a prominent causal contribution to action, and it makes a prominent causal contribution to pleasure and displeasure. So if desires also play these two roles, this is a reason to think that desires and the reward system are the same thing known under two different labels.

Now consider another line of evidence: the relation of desires to rewards. What sorts of things would count as rewards for me? A raise in pay would be a reward for my hard work, and a kiss would be a reward for being a sweet boyfriend. Sustained applause is a reward for giving a good talk—and perfunctory applause is a punishment for giving a bad one. How are these rewards related to my desires? It seems clear that, for each thing that would be a reward for me, it is also something I desire. I desire a raise in pay, I desire a kiss from my girlfriend, I desire sustained applause after talks—and dread brief applause.[8] What is desired is the same as what is rewarding, it seems. There are certain exceptions to this: although I want the universe to be closed rather than open, no one can reward me for anything I do by making the universe be closed, for example. But by and large, what is a reward is the same as what is desired. This is a reason to think that the system that *makes* things rewards—the reward system—makes the same things *desired*. And this is another reason to think that desires are made out of the reward system.

For these sorts of reasons, it is reasonable to develop a theory of desire in terms of reward. Here is such a theory, which can be called the *reward theory of desire*: to desire something is for one's reward system to treat it as a reward. And for one's reward system to treat something as a reward is for the reward system to take representations of that thing as positive inputs into a calculation of how many rewards the world contains versus how many it was expected to contain. Thus, to desire food is for one's reward system to treat food as a reward. And for one's reward system to treat food as a reward is for the reward system to take representations of eating food (from the senses, or the hypothalamus, perhaps) as positive inputs to a calculation of how rewarding the world is versus how rewarding it was expected to be.

What are desires like, if such a theory is correct? The first thing to note is that, if the theory is correct, then what desires *are* is different from the best-known things that desires *do*. The reward system is a learning system that contributes its output to action and emotion systems as well. If the reward theory of desire is correct, then this is true of desires too. Desires *are* drivers of operant conditioning and related learning. But what desires are best known for are some of their *effects*: on actions and emotions. This is crucial to the present discussion. If the reward theory of desire is correct, then it is possible in principle for people to have strong motivations without having strong desires, or to have strong feelings without having strong desires. There are other theories of desires on which one or both of these results would be impossible—theories on which desiring is nothing more than being motivated, or having some suitable feeling, for example.[9]

The second thing to note is that, if the reward theory of desire is correct, then most desires are stable, enduring features of our psychologies. For it is generally a stable, enduring fact about one's psychology that a representation of a certain state of affairs serves as a positive input into the calculation of how rewarding the world is. Of course, often this input results in no special output: representing that my father is healthy today does not produce an increase in dopamine release in me. But that is simply because the positive contribution made by representing my father as healthy was already expected: I expected him to be healthy, and he was, so the world was no more rewarding than expected, and so dopamine release did not change. But even so, it is a stable fact about me that representations of my father being healthy factor positively into such calculations, even when the net result of the calculation is zero. Hence, on the reward theory of desire, it turns out that my desire that my father be healthy is a stable, enduring fact about my psychology. I always want my father to be healthy, even when

I am busy thinking about a philosophical problem and I am not attending to the question of his health.

Although desires are stable, according to the reward theory of desire, their effects are not. The effects of having a desire are variable, depending on a host of other factors. So if I want my father to be healthy, then representations of him being healthy stably factor into a calculation of how rewarding the world is. If things are just as I expect them to be, then this desire will contribute nothing to changing my reward signal, and so contribute nothing to my current motivations or feelings. But if I believe my father to be unwell with arthritis, and then learn that, if only he would start a new treatment, he would be much healthier, then that will produce an increase in dopamine signaling: I will get excited at the thought of my father being healthier, and I will become motivated to try to get him on the new treatment. These effects—the excitement and the motivation—are not constant, but are caused by the new information I have received.

Some might interpret these effects as the onset of a new desire. Before, I did not want my father on the new treatment; now I do. But according to the reward theory of desire, this is not the clearest way to see the situation. According to the reward theory, my ultimate desires have not changed at all, but I have new information about how to achieve them, and that new information is causing me to be motivated to do new things, and to feel excited in response to new thoughts. The significance of all this will become clearer as the argument of this chapter is developed.

4 Addiction and the Reward System

Return now to the topic of addiction. Using the goods to which people naturally become addicted triggers responses in the reward system. Nicotine, cocaine, alcohol, and the like all cause the reward system to release dopamine at levels above baseline. They do so via a variety of mechanisms, with different intensities, timecourses, and the like. But a common feature to them all is that they cause this response.

Another common feature of addictive goods is that the way in which they trigger the reward system is deviant. They do not rely on the normal mechanism of calculating how rewarding the world looks and how rewarding it is expected to be. Instead, addictive goods have the power to trigger the release of dopamine by the reward system independently of how reward-laden the world is represented to be. Jon Elster has characterized this as a "hijacking" of the reward system (Elster 1999), and the term is apt. Nicotine, cocaine, alcohol, and the like all cause the reward system to release dopamine by getting into the brain and directly stimulating the reward system. This makes them very different from ordinary triggers of the reward system—food, cooperation, or whatnot—which only trigger the reward system through their representation in a calculation of changes in how rewarding the world looks to be.

In the short term, the immediate effects of the increased reward signal caused by addictive goods are seen most clearly on motivation and feelings. People using a good that causes a sharp, transient increase in reward signaling are generally motivated to continue using, and generally have elevated mood. Using a good that causes a sharp prolonged increase in reward signaling generally gives less reason to continue using immediately, but it also generally provides longer-lasting pleasure.

In the long term, the lasting effects of an increased reward signal are seen most clearly in tolerance and dependency effects. But as is widely known, tolerance and dependency effects are far from the most important long-term effects of using addictive goods. As Hyman (2005, 1414) writes, if tolerance and dependency were the main factor in addiction, "treatment could simply consist of locking addicted people away in a protective environment until withdrawal symptoms were comfortably behind them, issuing a stern warning about future behavior, and having done with it." But things are not so simple. People who become addicts, then cease using, are perfectly capable of ending their dependencies and losing their tolerances, while still being particularly vulnerable to returning to using.

We can call such people *abstinent addicts*. Abstinent addiction is what makes it so hard to stop smoking tobacco or crack, or to stop using any other addictive good. Even when one has passed through whatever withdrawal there might be, and even after one has lost whatever tolerance one once possessed, one is likely to be subject to periodic attacks of craving, in which one feels very strongly the absence of one's former addictive good, and in which one is highly motivated to obtain one's former addictive good (see, e.g., Gjelsvik 1999 for discussion).

It has been claimed that these attacks of craving are what constitute addiction (Lowenstein 1999), and the claim has considerable merit. To my mind, the powerful pull to return to use even after one has stopped using, beaten withdrawal, and lost tolerance is the essence of what it is to be an addict. Addiction, after all, is what actively using and abstinent addicts have in common, and this common feature is not a pattern of use, a fear of withdrawal, or a degree of tolerance. It is simply being subject to powerful attacks of craving, and sudden, habitual impulses to use.

The long-term effects of the reward system offer a good explanation of abstinent addiction, for they explain both felt cravings and impulses to use.

First, consider the way in which abstinent addicts are subject to very strong feelings. Once withdrawal is over, abstinent addicts are not subject to constant anguish at the lack of their addictive goods, nor to constant hope for their return. Their feelings about their addictive goods are, often, strong in a way familiar from other sorts of ordinary strong desires. Sometimes, however, abstinent addicts are subject to extremely powerful feelings of craving, longing, excitement, deprival pain, and the like. These feelings are out of proportion with the feelings they have at other times, and in the grip of these feelings non-use is particularly difficult. These feelings are correlated with the experiencing of familiar places and things associated with use of the addictive good.[10] Thus, a former smoker can miss smoking, be nostalgic for the ease with which he could be instantly accepted into a group of fellow smokers, and so on, without these feelings being particularly powerful or moving. And then, that same former smoker can one day walk into the bar where he did much of his smoking and be assailed by a feeling of craving to smoke far out of proportion with any experienced for years.

This feeling seems tied to activity in the reward system and appears to be a product of past unconscious learning. In the past, this particular environment was associated with nicotine ingestion. What does that mean? It means that in the past, representation of the bar occurred just before the release of a powerful reward signal, directly stimulated by the ingestion of nicotine. This powerful reward signal caused a number of learning effects, including an effect on the brain's system for representing expected rewards. The result was that the brain came to expect a powerful reward signal to follow the perception of the bar environment again in the future, an expectation that would be factored into future calculations of actual minus expected reward. As a result of all this, years later when the bar is experienced again, the brain encodes an expectation of large reward, an expectation learned through past association of the bar with a powerful reward signal. Since actual reward remains constant (the former smoker does not actually smoke), the calculation of actual minus expected reward generates a negative result, and this causes a negative emotional state, one worsened if the former smoker continues to think about smoking. A miserable craving for a cigarette is the result.

Second, consider the inclination to return to use found in abstinent addicts. Some of these behavioral inclinations follow felt cravings, but far from all. Sometimes an abstinent addict will find himself acting "on autopilot," as it were, accepting a drink after years of sobriety without even thinking about it, or asking a smoker for a cigarette without even feeling any particular craving. Nicotine addicts have also reported to me their motivation to smoke cigarettes in excess of their need for nicotine. Doing so is often unpleasantly nauseating, but knowledge of this does not prevent them from sometimes smoking excess cigarettes. This suggests that there are craving-independent motivations in actively using addicts as well.

These are actions that appear to be taken out of habits, habits formed while using the addictive good. And the long-term effects of the reward system appear to explain them just as much as they explain felt cravings. Evidence strongly suggests that connections in the motor striatum realize habits, and these habits are shaped by input from the reward system through familiar operant conditioning effects (see, e.g., White 1996, 1997; Knowlton, Mangles, and Squire 1996). Hence the reward signals that come from asking for, and receiving, a cigarette (for example) can leave traces in habitual patterns of action, patterns that are later activated even after long abstinence.

5   Reward System Realizations of Desires and Addiction

Are the desires identified by the reward theory of desire responsible for addiction? No. For the desires identified by the reward theory are not responsible for the powerful feelings of craving to which addicts are subject, nor are they responsible for the powerful tendencies to act out of habit to which addicts are subject. And these feelings of craving and habitual actions are what make up addiction.

To begin, consider feelings of craving. Certainly, desires as identified by the reward theory can give rise to feelings of craving. I desire the experience of eating fine French chocolate, and sometimes I feel strong cravings for French chocolate as a result. So it would be a mistake to hold that an addict cannot crave an addictive good as a result of desiring to consume that good. But the question is not whether some of the feelings of craving had by addicts are the products of their desires to use. The question is whether the feelings of craving that are *especially distinctive of addiction* are the products of their desires to use. These are the feelings of craving that strike abstinent addicts occasionally, when they are presented with "triggers"—with things they strongly associate with past use—as described in the last section. No doubt they also frequently strike actively using addicts as well, though it is more difficult to separate them out from other things when an addict is engaged in ongoing use.

Consider, then, how the reward system generates strong feelings in the case of abstinent addicts exposed to triggers of craving. As the previous section held, it seems that these feelings stem entirely from the addicts' reward systems representing a coming large reward, as a result of detecting something (a familiar bar, a needle, a crack pipe . . .) strongly associated with past large reward signals. So a representation of coming large reward is the cause of the strong feeling. If the reward theory of desire is correct, this is a representation that a strong desire needs to be satisfied, for rewards are just desired things, according to the theory.

But notice that the representation need not be correct. Every representation is capable of misrepresentation, at least in principle. A representation of movement can be a misrepresentation if one is exposed to an optical illusion, for instance, and a representation of honesty can be a misrepresentation if one is exposed to a talented liar. Likewise, a representation that a powerful desire needs to be satisfied can also be a misrepresentation.

Even if it is possible in principle that the reward system's representation could be a misrepresentation, why think that it is? (Why, in particular, think that the misrepresentation would be a misrepresentation of the strength of the desire that looks to be satisfied?) To see why, consider again the reward theory of desire. According to the reward theory, for something to be a reward is for it to be treated as a reward by the reward system. For a thing to be treated as a reward by the reward system is for a representation of the thing to positively contribute to the calculation of actual reward in the production of a reward signal. So for an addict's reward system to treat using an addictive good as a strong reward is for a representation of using the addictive good to positively contribute to the calculation of actual reward in the production of a strong reward signal.

This is where a gap appears. The strength of the reward signal that would be produced by a representation of using an addictive good will tend to be less than the reward system expects. This is because using has always caused a *stronger* reward signal than would be generated by a representation of using alone, and predicted reward is based on what reward signals have actually been generated in the past. Use of addictive goods causes abnormally strong reward signals because what is distinctive of addictive goods is that, in addition to whatever reward signal they generate through representation of their use, they also generate a reward signal directly, by direct action on the brain, as described in section 4. Thus it turns out that the predicted reward coming from using an addictive good will tend to be greater than the reward signal that would be generated merely from a representation of the consumption of that good. And this effect should be particularly strong when the prediction of reward is being generated by stimuli that have the strongest past association with the powerful reward signals generated by use: with "triggers," in other words.

In terms of desire, this means that the predicted desire satisfaction from using an addictive good will tend to be greater than the actual strength of the desire, and so "trigger" stimuli especially will tend to make a person have stronger feelings than would ordinarily be produced by a desire of the same strength for a nonaddictive good.

None of this is meant to imply that addicts do not actually desire their addictive goods. Although some addicts do not really seem to desire their addictive goods in and of themselves, others do seem to do so. But even among addicts who desire their addictive goods, and who would miss them as abstinent addicts, the very powerful cravings to which they are subject do not reflect the true strength of their desires.

In some addicts, what is ultimately wanted is relief from feelings of self-loathing (this seems to have motivated many of the alcoholics who have written memoirs about their experiences). In these individuals, there seems to be little or no desire to use the addictive good as such. In his memoir *Dry*, for example, Augusten Burroughs relates that his body tolerates alcohol so poorly that he has always needed to consume antihistamines when drinking. For him, it seems, drinking has little value in itself. It is the ability of alcohol to block out certain thoughts that gives it its value. For Burroughs, perhaps, a powerful craving to drink would be almost entirely a product of misrepresented coming desire satisfaction, induced by the perception of some trigger.

In other individuals, what is ultimately wanted might well come to include the addictive good itself. In her memoir *How to Stop Time*, Ann Marlowe relates how her heroin addiction was driven in part by her fascination with the criminal and the forbidden: with what is outside "straight" society. The reader gets the impression that this less instrumental relationship to heroin led Marlowe to want to use heroin as an end in itself. Marlowe seems to have related to heroin a little like the way she might have related to a pair of sunglasses: as something at first to be worn (consumed) for its chic, but then over time something that one comes to like wearing (consuming) just because one has grown fond of it. For Marlowe, perhaps, a powerful craving to use heroin would be a combined product of a genuine desire producing a modest feeling of craving, plus an extra element of felt craving produced by misrepresentation.

Turn now to acting out of habit. Cravings and habits together make up addiction, and showing that desires as identified by the reward theory are not responsible for cravings does not show that such desires are not responsible for habitual behavior.

As it happens, however, it is relatively easy to show that habits are impulses to behavior that are independent of desires as identified by the reward theory. To see this, it is only necessary to compare how the reward system directly contributes to action with how habits directly contribute to action. The reward system directly contributes to action by acting as input to the motor striatum, changing its current activity, as section 2 described. But habits are realized in the internal connections between structures in the motor striatum, rather than in its current activity, as described in section 4. So impulses to action that come from habit are not impulses to action that come from what the reward theory identifies as desires.

As a result, the desires realized by the reward system cannot explain what addicts do. And if they cannot explain what addicts do, then these desires cannot be what makes addicts rational in using their addictive goods. If anything makes addicts rational in using their addictive goods, it must be desires realized in some other way. But where else could these desires be hiding? They must be hiding in the cravings themselves, or in the habits themselves—or both—if there are to be desires that explain addiction. The next two sections will consider these possibilities in turn.

6 Interpreting Cravings

Suppose felt cravings for addictive goods were themselves desires for these goods. Then it would turn out that there are strong desires for these goods after all, even if they are desires not derived from the reward system. These desires would be short lived—as short as the felt craving itself—and so quite unlike desires derived from the reward system. But they might simply be a different form of desire.

The view that addictions are constituted by powerful but suddenly appearing, short-lived desires appears in work by Jay Wallace (1999) and George Lowenstein (1999). Wallace does not attempt to explain why it is that addicts, but not casual users, are particularly prone to these strong desires. In fact, because Wallace sees his explanation of addicts' behavior as assimilating such behavior to the behavior of ordinary people subjected to strong temptations (Wallace 1999, 648), Wallace is not really in a position to explain why it is that addicts are special in this way. Certainly, someone who has used cocaine in the past and enjoyed it, and who has an opportunity to use again, will often be struck by a pang of longing for the euphoric rush of the high and be tempted to use again even if it seems like a bad idea overall. But a casual user faced with these thoughts is not in the same vulnerable position as the abstinent addict, and explaining why this is so is important. So I take it that Wallace's position is problematic from the outset.

Lowenstein's account of addictive behavior is better positioned to explain abstinent addiction and relapse than Wallace's. Lowenstein explains that the strong desires he has in mind are responses to "cue conditioned cravings" (Lowenstein 1999, 244). The onset of cravings, that is, powerful short-lived desires, in response to familiar cues associated with use of one's addictive good, is what defines addiction, in Lowenstein's view, and a good is addictive insofar as repeated exposure to it tends to produce cue-conditioned cravings for it. Cravings are strong unpleasant feelings, and they provoke a strong desire to use in order to escape them (Lowenstein 1999, 243). Thus, repeated use of an addictive good gives one a tendency to crave it when one sees the friend with whom one normally uses, or the good itself, or the kind of setting where one normally uses. These tendencies persist even if one becomes an abstinent addict; thus the abstinent addict is occasionally assailed by strong desires to use, desires that come about when the abstinent addict is reminded of the days when she or he used, and when cravings then ensue.

There are several problems for Lowenstein's approach, however. These problems stem from the options available for linking these supposed desires to predictions of coming reward.

One could hypothesize that these craving-desires are identical to the brain's expectations of coming reward. This hypothesis is problematic, though. Expectations of coming reward are beliefs, or belief-like cognitive states, and desires are not beliefs. An expectation that a reward is coming is a belief that a reward is coming, which is true if a reward is coming and false if it is not. But a desire for an addictive good is not true if a reward comes, or false if it does not—desires cannot be true or false.[11]

One could also hypothesize that these craving-desires are caused by the brain's expectations of coming reward, though they are distinct from them. But where are they? Somewhere, presumably, that realizes a state of consciousness, for cravings are feelings. That means that craving-desires would not be realized in the reward system or the motor striatum, for these are deep-brain structures, buried far below the neocortical systems that appear to realize feelings. Suppose, then, that the cravings are realized in some emotional or perceptual system. They can then be expected to have an impact on our behavior just like the impact of other feelings. But as Lowenstein (1999, 243) notes, "even mild craving seems to have a profound effect on behavior, an effect equivalent to that exerted by other visceral factors only at extreme levels of intensity." This suggests that, although addicts might be moved to use the addictive goods they crave in order to relieve unpleasant feelings of craving, this is not the explanation of the *differential* effect of addiction on using addictive goods. What lies outside of consciousness—the action of the reward system—seems much more important in explaining this differential than what lies in consciousness.

As these options seem exhaustive, I conclude that felt cravings do not realize or generate desires that might make using addictive goods more rational for addicts than for nonaddicts.

7 Interpreting Habits

Consider a familiar sort of habit: Heidi drives northward to work along a certain route every day, and comes to be in the habit of making certain turns. In particular, she comes to be in the habit of making a right turn off of a thoroughfare in order to enter the university. Having this habit makes Heidi distinctively vulnerable to certain sorts of errors. If one day she is driving northward toward a destination on a route that takes her past the university, and if she is not paying attention to what she is doing, she is likely to make the habitual turn and end up at the university instead of her intended destination.

Ending up at the university would *seem* to be an error. But it need not be. If acting out of habit is acting out of a desire, then perhaps Heidi really does do what she wants most to do, and so does not take any irrational action (though she might make an intellectual error about where she is going). This possibility is one that must be taken seriously if one is to hold—contrary to my thesis—that the habits that move addicts to pursue their addictive goods realize desires for these goods.

So perhaps Heidi's habit of turning right at the university when approaching it by car from the south is the result of Heidi's tendency to have a strong desire to turn right whenever she approaches the university by car from the south. That is, the context creates a strong desire in her, and Heidi has a tendency to give in to this desire by turning to the right.

There are two difficulties for this view. First, Heidi's conscious practical reasoning does not respond to her habit as though it were responding to a new and particularly strong desire. While driving and finding herself inclined to turn right, she never begins to consider the relative merits of changing her plans and going to the university rather than continuing on with her plans and going to, say, the dance club. If she had a sudden impulse instead to go home and curl up with *The Divine Comedy* she would be likely to weigh it, think of the ramifications of each decision, and so on. But if she is like most people, she treats her habit as if it were a strong gust of wind, blowing her car toward a right turn. To claim that a habit realizes a desire commits one to more than just plunking the label "desire" on the habit: it commits one to the claim that habits realize a mental state that is quite recognizable as a desire. But this just seems false.

Second, Heidi's emotional responses are not those she would have if she had a particularly strong desire to go to the university. When one has a particularly strong desire, it normally is pleasant to satisfy it, and unpleasant to leave it frustrated. But this is not how it feels to Heidi when she is moved by habit, nor is it how it feels to most of us. Turning to the university is not pleasant, nor is overriding the habit unpleasant. In fact, it is frustrating to act purely out of habit: as soon as Heidi realizes that she has taken a wrong turn, she will be annoyed. These facts suggest that, if Heidi has any desire at all to turn right, it is much weaker than her desire to go to the dance club, to see her friends, and so on. But, if the desire is much weaker, then how is it capable of overriding her other desires? This cannot be explained in rationalizing terms. Some nondesire factor must be at work. And this is just what I am arguing is the central feature of habits.

8 Conclusion

Addictions are the forces that drive actively using and abstinent addicts toward the use of their addictive goods: felt cravings and habits of use. If felt cravings or habits of use are realized by desires, then when addicts use because of their addictions, they are doing what they most want to do. And if this is true, then it would seem that addicts are acting rationally—which is implausible. To show that addicts are not doing what they most want to do, it is necessary to show that nothing known to be a desire should be thought of as a felt craving or a habit, and to show that nothing known to be a felt craving or habit should be thought of as a desire. Insofar as this chapter has been successful, it has done just that. Though addicts are powerfully moved by their addictions on various occasions, these are not occasions on which they are equally powerfully moved by their desires. Their desires no doubt play *some* role in what they do. But insofar as addicts are moved by their addictions, they are moved by forces other than desires. And so they are moved irrationally.

Acknowledgments

Thanks to the philosophy departments at CalTech and University of California, Riverside; to members of Gary Watson's research group on addiction; and to the students in my seminar on addiction in the fall quarter of 2006 for opportunities to present much earlier versions of this work. Thanks also to Nomy Arpaly, Ben Caplan, and Giddeon Yaffe for helpful discussions.

Notes

1. For a direct response, see, e.g., Skog 1999.

2. Similar summaries can be found in Gardner and David 1999, Hyman 2005, and Robinson and Berridge 2000.

3. See, e.g., Schultz and Romo 1990, Romo and Schultz 1990.

4. See, e.g., Montague, Dayan, and Sejnowski 1996.

5. See the results cited in Schroeder 2004, chapter 2.

6. See, e.g., Packard and Teather 1997.

7. This is not an uncontested claim. Compare, e.g., Berridge and Robinson 1998.

8. This is as good a point as any to bring up punishment. There is both theoretical and empirical reason to think that the brain must produce a punishment signal that is the counterpart of the brain's reward signal. But unfortunately, no experiment has conclusively identified a punishment signal or its effects, and so it is not possible to write about punishment with the same level of detail as one can write about reward.

9. Smith (1987) offers a clear statement of the view that desiring is nothing other than being disposed to be motivated. Strawson (1994, 2010) offers a similarly clear version of the view that desiring is nothing other than being disposed to have certain feelings.

10. A fact particularly emphasized by George Lowenstein. I will return to Lowenstein's work below.

11. I also suspect that predictions of coming reward are realized in the nucleus accumbens, a deep brain structure so unlike those neocortical structures normally thought to realize consciousness (in vision, audition, etc.) that there are further reasons to doubt it could realize *feelings* of craving. But the localization of these predictions is disputed, and I will place no particular weight on my suspicions here.

References

Becker, G., and Murphy, K. (1988). A theory of rational addiction. *Journal of Political Economy* 96: 675–700.

Berridge, K. (2003). Pleasures of the brain. *Brain and Cognition* 52: 106–128.

Berridge, K., and Robinson, T. (1998). What is the role of dopamine in reward: Hedonic impact, reward learning, or incentive salience? *Brain Research Reviews* 28: 309–369.

Burroughs, A. (2003). *Dry: A Memoir.* St. Martin's Press.

Elster, J. (1999). *Strong Feelings: Emotion, Addiction, and Human Behavior.* Cambridge, MA: MIT Press.

Gardner, E., and David, J. (1999). The neurobiology of chemical addiction. In J. Elster and O. Skog, eds., *Getting Hooked: Rationality and Addiction*, 93–136. Cambridge: Cambridge University Press.

Gjelsvik, O. (1999). Addiction, weakness of the will, and relapse. In J. Elster and O. Skog. eds., *Getting Hooked: Rationality and Addiction*, 47–64. Cambridge: Cambridge University Press.

Hyman, S. (2005). Addiction: A disease of learning and memory. *American Journal of Psychiatry* 162: 1414–1422.

Knowlton, B., Mangles, J., and Squire, L. (1996). A neostriatal habit learning system in humans. *Science* 273: 1399–1402.

Lowenstein, G. (1999). A visceral account of addiction. In J. Elster and O. Skog, eds., *Getting Hooked: Rationality and Addiction*, 235–264. Cambridge: Cambridge University Press.

Marlowe, A. (1999). *How to Stop Time: Heroin from A to Z*. New York: Basic Books.

Mink, J. (1996). The basal ganglia: Focused selection and inhibition of competing motor programs. *Progress in Neurobiology* 50: 381–425.

Montague, P., Dayan, P., and Sejnowski, T. (1996). A framework for mesencephalic dopamine systems based on predictive Hebbian learning. *Journal of Neuroscience* 16: 1936–1947.

Packard, M., and Teather, L. (1997). Double dissociation of hippocampal and doral-striatal memory systems by posttraining intracerebral injections of 2-amino-5-phosophopentanoic acid. *Behavioral Neuroscience* 111: 543–551.

Read, D., and Roelofsma, P. (1999). Hard choices and weak wills: The theory of intrapersonal dilemmas. *Philosophical Psychology* 12: 341–356.

Robinson, T., and Berridge, K. (2000). The psychology and neurobiology of addiction: An incentive-sensitization view. *Addiction* 95 (suppl. 2): S91–117.

Romo, R., and Schultz, W. (1990). Dopamine neurons of the monkey midbrain: Contingencies of response to active touch during self-initiated arm movements. *Journal of Neurophysiology* 63: 592–606.

Schroeder, T. (2004). *Three Faces of Desire*. New York: Oxford University Press.

Schultz, W., and Romo, R. (1990). Dopamine neurons of the monkey midbrain: Contingencies of response to stimuli eliciting immediate behavioral reactions. *Journal of Neurophysiology* 63: 607–624.

Skog, O. (1999). Rationality, irrationality, and addiction—Notes on Becker's and Murphy's theory of addiction. In J. Elster and O. Skog, eds., *Getting Hooked: Rationality and Addiction*, 173–207. Cambridge: Cambridge University Press.

Smith, M. (1987). The Humean theory of motivation. *Mind* 96: 36–61.

Strawson, G. (1994). *Mental Reality*. Cambridge, MA: MIT Press.

Strawson, G. (2010). *Mental Reality*, second edition. Cambridge, MA: MIT Press.

Wallace, R. J. (1999). Addiction as defect of the will: Some philosophical reflections. *Law and Philosophy* 18: 621–654.

White, N. (1996). Addictive drugs as reinforcers: Multiple partial action on memory systems. *Addiction* 91: 921–949.

White, N. (1997). Mnemonic functions of the basal ganglia. *Current Opinion in Neurobiology* 7: 164–169.

16 Defining Addiction and Identifying the Public Interest in Liberal Democracies

Peter Collins

Introduction

The perspective of this chapter is significantly different from that of previous chapters. Previous chapters have been mainly concerned with debates about how best to understand addiction for the purpose of studying it scientifically. This chapter focuses on issues relating to the definition of addiction as they arise in political debates about what public policy should be in relation to addiction.

I do not, of course, wish to suggest that these perspectives and purposes are incompatible with or necessarily hostile to one another. On the contrary, as almost all concerned—elected officials, civil servants, relevant professional practitioners, as well as scientists—acknowledge, it is desirable that in the area of addiction, as in all others, public policy should be "evidence based." And indeed the purpose of this chapter is precisely to prepare the ground—space constraints prevent me from planting it more productively—for exploring what ought to be the implications of the best scientific investigations of addiction, as described in the rest of this book, for the formulation of the best possible public policy toward the phenomenon of addiction. This, incidentally, intimates formulations of what should be the best research strategy for the future and who should fund that research and why.

There are, however, two crucial and related differences between the concerns of the scientist and the concerns of the policymaker in relation to addiction—as to many other issues.

The first difference flows from the fact that scientific knowledge about addiction—as about much else—is incomplete (there is much we don't yet know) and contested (there is much we still disagree about). In the face of scientific ignorance, the efforts of scientists are properly directed toward trying to reduce this ignorance by carrying out more and better scientific investigations. Public officials, by contrast, are typically faced with a different question when compelled to acknowledge deficiencies and limitations in the state of current scientific knowledge. The question they confront is: "which, of the available policy choices open to us *now*, should we adopt given the current inconclusiveness of scientific evidence?" Or more generally: "How should we navigate faced with an uncertain future?"

One reason that governments have to make decisions before the scientific evidence becomes more or less conclusive is that they have to allocate scarce resources now —including resources to fund research, prevention, and treatment in the area of addiction—in circumstances where there are many other claims on the public purse generally and for spending on particular items of scientific research and on health care, in particular.

Another reason why the determination of public policy has for the present to precede the resolution of scientific debates is that the public often thinks—rightly, I believe, in the case of addiction—that we simply can't wait for the scientific community to reach consensus: we need, for the purposes of alleviating suffering or promoting welfare, to be doing things *now*. This typically means reaching conclusions about policy on the basis of exercising *judgment* about what the evidence concerning any public policy issue seems to suggest so far, in relation to the probable consequences of different policies on the problem in question, their likely impact on other policies, and their comparative costs and benefits in the greater scheme of government spending. In all this we can produce reasons for thinking that we will do more good than harm although we can't be sure.

The second basic difference between the concerns of scientists and policymakers (at least in democracies) in relation to defining addictions relates to value judgments. Scientists *qua* scientists ought not to be concerned about whether the world as they find it is as they would wish it to be—nor should anyone else whose concern is with truth. However, moral agents, individually and collectively (and, of course, scientists are moral agents too), are necessarily concerned with how they think the world ought to be and how they can conduct themselves so as to make the world conform more closely to their notion of what is desirable. This means that not only every voter has to be concerned with value judgments but also that policymakers need to be equally attentive to the values of all these voters. No doubt, they should pay special attention to the factual claims made by scientists, but there is no reason to think that the moral values of scientists are more deserving of respect than anyone else's.

Notoriously, in the case of addiction, different stakeholders, including different scientists, have conflicting values, and even when values are broadly agreed on among scientists (and others) there is often sharp disagreement about how to implement them.

It is, of course, also true that policymakers in practice have to try to accommodate not only competing values but also competing interests. Indeed, on some accounts of politics, that is all they can and should try to do. But the fact is that in addressing competing interests, one of the things governments have to decide is which are legitimate and which are illegitimate interests—and that is, of course, itself a value question, and, moreover, one that is particularly acute when legislating about alleged vices.

Abuse of the Concept of Addiction in Public Policy Debates

My central contention in this chapter is that the way addiction and cognate terms are used in public policy debates is profoundly corrupted by covert ideological agendas based on puritanical ethics and even more covert and illegitimate interests based on commercial protectionism. This, in turn, leads to a lot of dishonest or simply incompetent (and usually bought) "scientific" research that appears to support prohibitionist or restrictionist public policy, and which those who have ideological or commercial interests in such policies ensure is widely disseminated to a credulous public. That at present bad research is adduced mainly in support of restrictionist political agendas with respect to the supply of gambling is, of course, a merely sociological accident. Bad research has also commonly been harnessed to political advocacy of more liberal policies toward gambling, particularly in relation to the economic benefits that are alleged to flow from permitting increasing the availability of gambling machines.

In democracies, so I shall argue, all bad research has particularly grave consequences, because democracy essentially means government by public opinion. Consequently, in the case of addictions, the dishonest but effective propaganda disseminated nowadays mainly by puritans and protectionists makes a rational and humane consensus about addiction policy unachievable. I shall illustrate this thesis mainly with reference to gambling addiction because that is the area I know best and because that is also perhaps the area where the corruption of public policy debate is most clearly identifiable. It may well be, however, that the issue of bad addiction policy based on bad science and moral prejudice is more serious and causes more unnecessary human suffering in relation to drugs policy.

I shall also focus on the problem of formulating good public policy about addiction in liberal democracies rather than in autocracies because, for reasons that will become clear, the problem takes a unique and uniquely difficult form in societies committed *both* to the protection and promotion of liberal political principles and to a democratic form of government.

However, although I am critical on moral grounds of both puritanism and protectionism, my purpose is ultimately not to mount a critical argument against these moral or political positions. It is rather to try to develop a constructive position that does justice to the complexity of the value issues involved and, in particular, to the views of partisans of competing values so that something like a rational and broadly acceptable consensus about what is truly in the public interest can be reached—at least about gambling policy, and perhaps about policy relating to other addictions as well.

Common Sense, Science, Sound Policy, and the Definition of Addiction

To make plain that the concept of "addiction" is widely abused, it is helpful to see how much both policymakers and scientists, as well as the general public, would agree on if they were only concerned with morally neutral, practical, working definitions.

If that were their concern it seems to me fairly uncontroversial to identify the main criteria for addiction of the sort that governments should "do something about" and that scientists could usefully investigate. At least, these criteria are uncontroversial in the scientific literature I have read as well as in the role they play in honest discussions between individuals concerned, as citizens, with improving public policy. There are four in particular:

- All potential addictions involve people engaging, at least initially, in an activity mainly because it affords them *pleasure*.
- They also all involve doing something to *excess*. But we can speak quite reasonably but usually metaphorically of "mild addictions," of "harmless addictions," of "being addicted to golf, newspapers," and so on.
- However, we get interested politically and demand government action only when addictions refer to excessive behaviors that cause substantial *harm*, primarily to the addict but also often to others.
- We also get interested politically only when the addict seems *powerless* to refrain from engaging in the damaging behavior or start engaging in it harmlessly.

Other signs of severe addictions identified by addicts themselves and often noted by family members as well as by clinicians include:

- Thinking *obsessively* about the activity; that is, thinking about past and future engagements in it for much of the time when not actually indulging.
- Using the activity as a means of *escaping* the pain of existence instead of enhancing its pleasures.
- Being—again, at least initially—*incapable of feeling good or at ease* except when under the influence or at least assured of the next fix.
- Really believing *fantasies* about being attractive, powerful, peculiarly skillful or lucky, or even of possessing an identity at all only when indulging in the addictive behavior of choice.

Utility and Liberalism

If these criteria were agreed to be adequate for the purpose of discriminating between addiction and mere recreational indulgence, public policy could comparatively easily be derived from classic utilitarian principles of happiness maximization—or, indeed, from more modern economic principles of preference satisfaction.

First, since *ex hypothesi* potentially addictive activities afford considerable pleasure to at least many of those who indulge in them, our basic position would be that those who enjoy them harmlessly should not be prevented by governments from doing so. Indeed, we would only be interested in addictions to the extent that they had the potential to do *severe* harm to individual indulgers or to others. We would not typically be interested in "addictions" or mere excessive indulgence in playing games (like Sudoku or gin rummy), but we might be worried about children playing violent computer games to excess.

Second, we would want to ensure that potentially dangerous pleasures were not available to those who were highly likely to become addicted to them. This might include all children. If it also constituted a very large percentage of potential adult indulgers—as with cigarettes, absinthe, or crack cocaine—we might well support prohibition, but we would not do this in the case of drinking generally, most gambling, and at least some drug use, where the vast majority of those who indulge do so without causing any significant harm either to themselves or others. We would also not do it without recognizing that all prohibition has a moral cost in terms of respect for the freedom of individuals to live their lives as seems best to them even if this means that they make choices that they subsequently regret.

Third, depending on how widespread and harmful the addictive behavior was in relation to other health and social problems, we would invest resources in trying to ascertain the causes of addiction and the best ways of preventing it or curing it. Some of this might not involve much more than ordinary consumer education.

No doubt there are other consumer-protection policy measures we would adopt as well, but, in general, our utilitarian policy would be to do nothing to interfere with the enjoyment of those who indulge harmlessly in the activity concerned, while ensuring the minimization of the suffering of those for whom the temptation to engage in the activity would otherwise be well-nigh irresistible and for whom the consequences of succumbing to temptation would be to render their lives and those of others seriously miserable.

Moreover, it would be perfectly possible to justify such a policy on liberal grounds. J. S. Mill agonized somewhat about what could legitimately be done in a free society about someone who chose to spend all day poisoning himself with drink in the privacy of his own home. Mill concluded that one could attempt persuasion and prevent negligence and other harms, but one certainly could not legitimately invoke the coercive power of the law to impose prohibition (Mill 1859/1974, 167; see also chap. 4 and elsewhere in chap. 5). However, if the addict really isn't capable of choice—if, as seems likely, there is a neurological deficiency that makes self-control impossible—then by preventing addicts from indulging, or compelling them to undergo treatment, we are not interfering with their freedom of choice since they don't have any in respect of their addiction.

Indeed, arguably we are enlarging their freedom of choice to the extent that we are able to release them from the tyranny of their compulsions.

In the case of nonaddicts, however, Mill—who incidentally makes no use of the concept of addiction, deeming what we now classify as addictions to be character flaws—is quite clear that the best way of maximizing the greatest happiness of the greatest number of people is to allow individuals to decide for themselves how they will live their own lives provided only that they do not wrongfully harm others. This is because the individual "is the person most interested in his own well-being. . . . With respect to his own feelings and circumstances the most ordinary man or woman has means of knowledge immeasurably surpassing those that can be possessed by anyone else" (1859/1974, 142–143.)

If all this is so, the question arises: Why does policy relating to allegedly addictive activities remain so frequently and deeply illiberal and anti-utilitarian in societies broadly committed to liberal and/or utilitarian politics? The answer clearly relates to the role played, albeit usually in disguise, by the concept of *vice*.

Vice

The essence of a vice is that it is an activity that is deemed to be wicked even though engaging in it does not apparently do harm to innocent third parties. On a broad conception of vice—one influenced by Greek ethics—vices are dispositions to behave in ways that are ultimately damaging to the real and long-term interests of the agent. Thus extravagance and cowardice are vices as well as imprudence and intemperance. The commoner conception of vice in cultures influenced by established religions is that it involves *pleasures* that are deemed to be intrinsically wicked. Indulging in them is contrary to the will of God and is incompatible with the living of a truly godly life. Vices are thus a species of sin and are therefore certain to lead to all the terrible consequences to which sin (unabsolved and unatoned for) inevitably leads, if not in this world, then in the next.

What counts as a vice even within the doctrines of established religions varies over time. It used to be the case that visiting the theater was thought of as being not much better than visiting a brothel, and actors were thought of as not much better than prostitutes (and could not, therefore, be buried in hallowed ground). Still earlier, reading was regarded by the Church as a dangerous vice that might imperil the safety of one's immortal soul. On the other hand, a religious context is not necessary for the widespread moral disapproval of particular pleasures. Not only do atheistical ideologies such as Marxism and some forms of nationalism have strong puritanical tendencies toward condemning the vices identified by traditional religions; it is also the case that in contemporary secular societies activities like smoking or eating fast foods, which were until recently, for the most part, morally uncontroversial, now seem to be viewed by many as not merely foolish or dangerous but also as evidence of moral delinquency. (Conversely, few pulpits, including, most remarkably, Roman Catholic ones, seem not to condemn sex before marriage with anything like their official anti-gay, anti-divorce, or anti-contraceptive passions. They are also silent on the heavy petting and oral sex that young people intelligently engage in as a safe-sex measure that doesn't also require extreme frustration.)

The existence of vices, understood as pleasures that are disapproved of by some people on moral grounds, presents a major problem for modern liberal democracies. In liberal theory, there can be no case for prohibiting or restricting the supply of drugs (including alcohol and probably heroin) or of gambling or sexual services, which most people will enjoy harmlessly, provided of course that they are properly alerted to the risks. Nor, at least if consumer surplus clearly outweighs all other costs, can a utilitarian case be made for prohibition or severe restriction. And yet, our policies in liberal democracies with respect to the addictive substances and activities once deemed to be vices seem to violate natural understandings of what a liberal utilitarianism such as Mill's requires.

Nor, of course, are our policies consistent in this area. Thus we prohibit drugs, which are widely used recreationally, but permit alcohol and fail to prohibit smoking. We restrict the supply of gambling, regulate it and tax it extensively, for the most part in a manner that is both discriminatory and regressive. We are also highly ambivalent about pornography and prostitution.

It is not my purpose here to discuss the merits of particular policies regarding the regulation by governments of pleasures that many people enjoy and many others regard as immoral. It is rather, first, to show how this general issue has come to make it exceptionally difficult for governments in liberal democracies to formulate and implement rational policies about addiction. Second, I hope to show both that and how these difficulties are exacerbated by abuse of the concept of addiction by interested parties. Such parties, as I have indicated, seek to camouflage what are really moral or commercially self-interested objections to liberal policies about allegedly dangerous pleasures by dressing them up as objections based on the desire to minimize harm. The harm is supposedly caused by the addiction to which the activities in question lead. For the individual addict the harm consists in paralysis of the will. For third parties, including families and taxpayers, addiction allegedly imposes great psychological and financial costs. It is these arguments that effectively ensure that it is still possible in liberal societies to make vice a crime, contrary to the fundamental principles of Millian (and indeed all other coherent versions of) liberalism.

In this context two fallacies about addiction (and vice) are particularly pernicious and pervasive. The first is that because indulging in pleasures addictively is bad, indulging in them at all is bad. The second is that all pleasures that are morally reprehensible are addictive. The first fallacy yields the position that there is no such thing as, for example, harmless or recreational gambling or drinking because at the very least one is putting oneself at risk of becoming an addict—which might in theory be true but seems not to be (Ross et al. 2008).

The second fallacy yields the view that those who, for example, like having a lot of promiscuous sex are "sex addicts." Again, this view seems to be not warranted by the scientific evidence (Ross, this volume). More generally, it leads to a failure to discriminate, even sometimes among scientists, between enthusiastic indulgers—those who drink a lot or gamble a lot because they really enjoy it—and those who do themselves serious and involuntary harm because they are addicted.

Totalitarian Aristocracies

The reason the regulation of alleged vices poses a particular problem for liberal democracies is that until quite recently governments have been neither liberal nor democratic, and, moreover, most people were convinced that it would be disastrous for the well-being of the public if they were either. Throughout most of history, and in much of the world still, it has been and is taken for granted in both political theory and political practice that government should be neither liberal nor democratic. Instead it should be totalitarian in the strict sense of being concerned with all aspects of the well-being of its subjects. It should also be aristocratic (or meritocratic) in the literal sense of ensuring that political power resides exclusively in the hands of those who are best fitted to exercise it. The most comprehensive and persuasive case for totalitarian and meritocratic government remains that to be found in Plato's *Republic* where he argues that all aspects of people's lives should be regulated by moral experts ("philosopher rulers") who possess both the necessary wisdom to know where other people's true interests lie and the necessary virtue that will ensure that they place the interests of others before their own.

Since Plato, in respect of rejecting liberalism, it has seemed in the past to almost everyone—and still seems to some—self-evident that the purpose of government is to ensure that, in all areas of their lives, individual subjects live the best possible lives of which they are capable. This means that governments should legislate for all aspects of human conduct including family relations and private pleasures; that is, governments should be totalitarian and legislate for the totality of human conduct. This is the opposite of the liberal view that individual subjects should be as free as possible to decide for themselves how they will live their own lives consistent with (a) everyone else enjoying the same degree of freedom and (b) no one exercising his or her freedom so as to harm others wrongfully. Consequently, according to liberalism, the purpose of government is restricted to preventing individuals from wrongfully harming one another and (what seems to me to amount to the same thing) protecting their legitimate rights. Instead of being totalitarian, the legal restrictions on engagement in self-chosen activities should be kept to a minimum, because the less issues of conduct are decided by governments the more they will be decided by individuals. And, of course, there are whole areas of human conduct, including the domain of "private" pleasures, which ought to be immune from government interference. The key passage in Mill's *On Liberty* that summarizes this position is the following:

The sole end for which mankind are warranted, individually or collectively, in interfering with liberty of action of any of their members is self-protection.... The only purpose for which power can rightfully be exercised over any member of a community, against his will, is to prevent harm to others. His own good, either physical or moral, is not a sufficient warrant. He cannot be rightfully compelled to do or forbear because it will be better for him to do so, because it will make him happier, because, in the opinions of others, to do so would even be wise or even right.... The only part of conduct of anyone for which he is amenable to society is that which concerns others. In the part which merely concerns himself, his independence is, of right, absolute. Over himself, over his own mind and body the individual is sovereign. (1859/1974, 68)

It has also seemed in the past to almost everyone—and still seems so to many—that societies ought not to be governed democratically. Democracy means that the ultimate power to decide how coercion by the state shall be used and shall be contained rests with all citizens equally. Thus, those who govern are compelled to conform at least most of their conduct to the wishes of at least the majority of those whom they govern. They are compelled to do so through the mechanism of free, fair, and frequent elections, which ensures that they are constantly concerned to make themselves popular enough with their electorates to guarantee that they retain office rather than forfeiting it to an opposition who promises to govern more in accordance with what most people want.

It is not difficult to see why almost everyone who has reflected on forms of government from Plato until comparatively recently has thought that democracy was obviously an undesirable form of government. Its central defect lies in the fact that democracy means government in accordance with public opinion instead of government in accordance with expert opinion. But, so it is alleged by Plato and others, the government of communities is an area that self-evidently requires a high degree of expertise for at least three reasons.

First, most people (the majority who exercise ultimate political power in democracies) simply cannot be expected to know which of a range of possible policies will in fact lead to the optimal promotion of the public interest. It requires expertise in many different areas to formulate the best possible policies for preventing civil disorder; for avoiding or prosecuting wars; for regulating trade, sexual relations, child-rearing, and religious observance; for fostering the arts and sciences; for commissioning public works; for promoting public health; and generally for ensuring the stability and effectiveness of government itself. In other words, good government requires that decisions be taken by the people best versed in a variety of empirical sciences so that they can predict accurately what, in fact, will be the consequences of pursuing one policy rather than another.

Second, and perhaps more important, those who govern—those who make and enforce laws binding on all members of the community—must not only be scientific experts: they must be moral experts too. This means that they must know where the true public interest lies, what the moral ideals ought to be which set the goals of political activity in a community, and what is really the best—most satisfying, most fulfilling, most admirable—kind of life that human beings are capable of living. This, after all, is the kind of life that governments must ensure that as many of its citizens as possible actually do live. Unfortunately, most people simply lack the moral understanding to see where their own true interests lie, and consequently they are blind to what would be best for their communities as a whole. Most people will simply want to maximize personal pleasure and possessions and will, since in a democracy they are able to do so, compel their rulers to govern so as to maximize short-term satisfactions and minimize short-term privations even though such policies will lead to much greater misery for all in the longer term.

Finally, and most seriously of all, in a democracy those who rule—even if they understand the real public interest and understand the objectively best ways of securing it—will not, in fact, prefer the public interest to their own private interests. Typically they will follow Machiavelli's advice and make themselves as popular as possible with the masses while protesting (hypocritically) their selfless devotion to the public interest. They will, therefore, secretly do everything they can to get and retain power (and its accoutrements) by ruthlessly ignoring all conventional moral principles that require consideration of the interests of others. The main talent they will need is a talent for demagoguery—which deliberately makes the worse cause appear the better—and falsely convinces voters that they will provide them with instant gratification and simultaneously pander to their basest predilections and prejudices.

In other words, democracy—according to its critics—guarantees that we are governed by hypocritical scoundrels who exploit public office to promote their private interests. Instead, we need to ensure that government is conducted by a moral, as well as an intellectual, elite who really are committed to placing the public interest above their personal and private interests. In short, for good government, we need political power to reside exclusively with those who combine knowledge with virtue—with those who are not only polymathic scientists but also saints. Democracy ensures that we get the antithesis of this and is therefore a deplorable form of government.

Vice in Totalitarian Aristocracies

Moreover, it is easy to see why the regulation of vices, that is, of pleasures widely enjoyed but also widely thought to be immoral, presents no problem for societies based on the political theory of totalitarian aristocracy or meritocracy. Such societies include, of course, not only Plato's ideal state but the actual forms of government that prevailed in the great religious empires of Christianity and Islam; in the governance of "more primitive" peoples by "civilized ones" under European imperialism; in the theory and practice of communism in much of the twentieth century, and in much of today's world; in monarchical (or dictatorial) societies, past and present, where an elite ruler appeals to the values—religious or otherwise—of an alleged national culture.

In such societies, it is the business of government to work for what the Book of Common Prayer (1662) identifies as something we should pray that our rulers may deliver to us: "the removal of wickedness and vice." Vices are immoral—regardless of what account is given of what makes them immoral—and it is the business of government to stamp out immorality. Therefore, government should enforce prohibition of whatever activities it deems—in its elite moral wisdom—to constitute vices. End of story.

There may be practical difficulties about, say, enforcing monogamy, and a good deal of hypocrisy may need to be tolerated, but, in principle, if it is decreed (and usually broadly agreed as well) that sexual relations are only permitted to members of opposite sexes who are married to one another and everything else is vicious and immoral, then everything else ought to be criminal as well. The same logic applies to drinking alcohol and taking other psychotropic drugs and to gambling.

Notoriously, also, governments may want to cause their subjects to believe that certain activities are morally deplorable for reasons that are (usually economically) self-interested. Thus, in England in the past, governments have banned gambling because they wanted their young men to practice archery on Sundays instead of gambling, or because they were worried about landed estates passing from the aristocracy to the bourgeoisie, or because they disapproved of the working classes choosing their own forms of fun.

But the general point remains: if an activity comes to be widely deemed immoral then the government can and should use the full force of the law to stop people engaging in it.

The two principles of totalitarian autocracy in respect of legislating for vice are consequently (from Platonism, through theocracy to Marxism and nationalism) clear:

- The government knows best how people ought to behave in all aspects of their lives.
- The government has a duty to use the law to ensure that people behave as they ought to.

Liberal Principles and the Regulation of Vice

These propositions are anathema to the prevailing ideology of liberalism, which began life as a an intellectually and politically radical movement in England in the seventeenth century, which was exported to France and the United States with great revolutionary success in the eighteenth century, was virulently criticized but also significantly assimilated by Marx and his communist collaborators in the nineteenth century and thereafter, and which now provides the official ideological rhetoric of most of the world.

The fundamental difference between liberalism and authoritarianism in its many previous guises is the view that the business of government is not to make people good but to enable then to be free. In particular, liberals think—for many different reasons—that individuals should, as far as possible, be able to choose for themselves how to live their own lives, regardless of whether others think their choices foolish, wicked, dangerous, or contrary to the will of God (or their rulers, or their psychiatrists, or the interpreters of the inexorabilities of history).

This means that the business of government is not to promote virtue, to eliminate vice, to build utopia, to secure maximum happiness and minimum distress for as many people as possible, or generally to protect people from the consequences of their own choices, however foolish these may be. The business of government—indeed the sole business of government—on a liberal view is to protect the right of individuals to live their lives as seems best to them, provided only that they do not illegitimately harm others. The consequence is that citizens, in a liberal society, have, in matters where others are either unaffected or consenting, an inalienable right to behave badly—to make foolish, dangerous, self-destructive, immoral choices that are likely to damage their real long-term self-interest—for example, by marrying unsuitable partners or pursuing careers at which they are well-nigh certain to fail.

This is not an anarchic doctrine that holds that the government has no role whatsoever. The business of government is to ensure maximum equal liberty by enabling as well as allowing everyone to live their lives as far as possible in accordance with their own preferences.

The particular consequence of this is that the onus of justification for proposals to prevent others from enjoying themselves is always on those who wish to do the preventing. Thus governments (and others) must demonstrate that some particular pleasurable activity unwarrantably restricts the freedom of others or otherwise wrongfully harms them. And, of course, in the case of most addictions this is extraordinarily difficult to demonstrate honestly and objectively, except in the case of the few substances that are almost universally seriously harmful to their consumers or have a clear and widespread propensity to do nontrivial harm to others.

Perhaps of all the vices, gambling provides the greatest challenge to prohibitionists who operate in a liberal society and who therefore wish (and electorally need) to show that prohibiting gambling does not violate the central principle of liberalism. After all, most gamblers do not spend much more than they can afford gambling any more than they do on shopping. And although it is certainly regrettable that the families of gambling addicts suffer from some avoidable poverty, this is too rare a social evil to warrant universal prohibition and one that can, in any case, be more effectively mitigated by less drastic means.

On liberal principles, there is no doubt that the government should not try to stop people from gambling, if that's something they enjoy. Nor should the government prevent people from charging customers for providing that particular form of enjoyment—other than by preventing force and fraud, ensuring real consumer choice, charging equitable taxes, and imposing sensible health and safety regulations, as they would for any other commercial activity. In a society founded on liberal principles, in other words, trade should be as free in respect to commercial gambling as it is with respect to anything else.

On this view, individuals have the right to indulge in, even devote their lives to whatever vices they choose—since indulgence in vices by definition doesn't wrongfully harm others.

Notoriously, however, indulgence in vices such as gambling, and other morally disapproved-of activities, is not left to the free choice of the individual.

Democracy and the Regulation of Vice

The reason why, in ostensibly liberal societies, there is no free indulgence, let alone free trade, in gambling and other pleasures deemed by some to be immoral is that these societies are not unwavering in their commitment to liberal values. They are also typically committed to democracy, which often yields very different policy conclusions, especially in respect to pleasures that arouse strong and hostile passions.

Thus democracy requires that government conform its activities to what most people want, and if most people want hard drugs or prostitution banned then in principle the government should ban them. Conversely, of course, if most people want people to be able to trade freely in narcotics or sexual services, the government should not use the law to prevent them from doing so.

For most of the time, we don't notice this potential conflict between our commitments to liberal politics and our commitments to democratic politics. There is, after all, a democratic consensus that people should be free to decide for themselves what to believe and how to behave in matters of religion. A large majority of us also think that people should be allowed to express their own political preferences and convictions, to try to persuade others to share them, and to engage in voting and related activities to ensure that legislators will be as committed to the same broad policies as they are themselves.

In other areas, it is not always so easy to know whether to trust to liberalism: are there really no limits to what consenting adults can portray on camera for commercial gain or what drugs may be bought and sold, or should we go along in these matters with what overwhelming public opinion endorses? On the other hand, it is sometimes very difficult both in practice and in principle to subscribe to pure demo-cratism. Clearly government cannot rightfully permit, let alone engage in, the per-secution of minorities even if an overwhelming majority of electors would apparently like them to. And to what extent is it right to decide the issue of capital punishment democratically?

My contention with respect to the regulation of vice is that—regardless of what the scientific evidence shows—we are in fact locked into a fundamental conflict between our commitment to liberalism and our commitment to democracy.

The fact is that a smallish but active minority in most societies, otherwise committed to liberal values, believes that certain residual types of pleasure-seeking are immoral, namely, traditional vices, and that government should ensure that the less vice there is in society the better. They may—typically do—believe this on traditional religious grounds, which not only distinguish authoritatively what is vicious pleasure-seeking from what is not but also accept without question that it is the business of government to stamp out immoral pleasure-seeking.

A more numerous and therefore democratically more crucial group, however, is also likely to feel uneasy about vices like pornography and gambling, in a way that they do not about eating candy or riding roller coasters. They would prefer not to have too much vice around, especially in the particular communities where they and their chil-dren live. On the other hand, they are also uneasy about government interference with private pleasures generally. They don't want gambling or pornography banned, but they don't want too much of it; and they think it is sufficiently different from other pleasures to warrant especially tight government regulation. They are thus ambivalent about prohibitionist policies relating to traditional vices.

What all this means is that with respect to many (but not all) traditional vices, the democratic majority is undecided in relation to the regulation of vices.

Political Consequences

The political consequences of this ambivalence in liberal democracies are, of course, profound because electorates can be swayed either way. Nor is it just the permissivists and the puritans who are competing for the people's vote.

The most vigorous and expensive lobbying of elected officials and campaigning for democratic votes is likely to be undertaken by those who have a commercial, vested in-terest, either as potential new entrants into an existing gambling (or other) market or as existing suppliers of gambling and other services who want the law to protect them from new and unwelcome competition.

In addition, because sensational antivice stories sell better than stories to the effect that, for example, problem gambling is a small and shrinking problem, the media will be more interested in prohibitionist than in permissivist stories—unless they can be suborned.

It should also be frankly acknowledged that most of us have gut feelings about vices that have been inculcated into us from an early age, and which most of us have seen no more reason to change than our gut feelings about cabbage or bacon.

When these moral or quasi-moral issues are combined with powerful economic interests for which governments are responsible and have a clear interest—notably by raising taxes that are relatively unresented and generating investment in job-creating projects—the question of what good government requires in relation to an issue like gambling becomes extremely complex, even intractable.

"Addiction" in Democratic Debate about Gambling and Other Addictions

At all events, the complexity of the real democratic debate and the ferocious competition to secure the support of the genuinely ambivalent middle ground among electors has a clear consequence for the terms in which public debate is conducted. This consequence is that democratic debate is conducted (mostly dishonestly and ignorantly) around the issue of gambling addiction—what it is, how widespread it is and will become if the law is changed, and what are its costs and consequences for non-problem-gamblers and for nongamblers (all of whom are also taxpayers).

As we have already noticed, J. S. Mill does not use the term "addiction." He is as convinced as any Victorian that drunkenness, drug-taking, promiscuity, and gambling are vices. Where he heroically differs from many of his contemporaries is in thinking that vices shouldn't be treated as crimes. Today, in liberal democracies, that argument has been largely won, and won spectacularly, in many other areas not addressed by Mill—such as the treatment of homosexuals.

This victory, however, has had awkward political consequences for those who still think that many vices should be outlawed. It is now much harder—and in some cases impossible—to get a prohibitionist agenda accepted by electorates if you rely solely on the claim that the wickedness of the activity is self-evident and therefore ought to be banned. First you face the difficulty that most voters may not agree with you about the obvious wickedness of the activity concerned, and second—and more politically disastrous—they are likely to believe that even wicked activities that don't harm others should not be legislated against.

In this situation, the prohibitionist must play the liberal-democratic game.

They must claim that the prohibition of the activity in question, say, gambling, is fully compatible with liberal and democratic principles. And the only way they can do this is by claiming that all or almost all indulgence in morally disapproved-of pleasures is, in fact, severely addictive.

Prohibitionists need to persuade electorates of three mutually reinforcing propositions if they are to make a successful cumulative case that even in liberal and democratic societies people should be prevented by the law from pursuing whatever pleasures they like provided only that they don't harm others in the process.

First they must argue that enthusiastic indulgence, in gambling or drink or food or sex or whatever, is really a case of being driven by morbid compulsions. As such, indulgence in these activities is not really a free choice and therefore escapes the liberal requirement that people should be free to choose for themselves how to live their own lives.

Second, prohibitionists must argue that it is an illusion that "self-indulgence" in vices does not really and seriously impact on the lives of others. Addicts are typically said to ruin the lives of lovers, children, and others close to them. This certainly happens sometimes and is extremely distressing for the addicts themselves and those who love them. To deny the intense misery sometimes caused by addiction to many different people is both ignorant and callous. What is not clear is whether a policy of prohibition (or restriction) would most effectively alleviate that suffering. Does not prohibition merely drive addicts underground and so exacerbate their wretchedness (as allegedly does the criminalization of prostitution)? Is it really plausible to say that an increase in availability automatically causes increases in addiction? (The evidence suggests not.[1]) After all, may not individuals who get themselves and their families into trouble by gambling too much be just as or even more likely to create comparable havoc as a consequence of other comorbid behavioral and psychological deficiencies from which they suffer, for example, being unable to control their temper or being likely to drink too much? (The evidence suggests that this is at least worth looking at.) Finally, on the issue of harm to others, addicts are also said to generate huge costs for society in terms of treatment programs, welfare payments, and so on. The literature on this is carefully and comprehensively reviewed in Walker 2007. But it is not necessary to get into scholarly economic debate to realize that the revenues generated by what have come to be categorized by the technical term "gambling privilege taxes" (in whatever form they take) far exceed any possible costs to the public purse in health and welfare payments. Moreover, if the consumer surplus enjoyed by non-problem-gamblers is taken into account then the economic benefits clearly outweigh the costs.

Third and lastly, prohibitionists who want to make their case in a liberal democracy need to persuade the electorate that the government has a duty to protect people from harming themselves. In the case of addiction, this means persuading governments that restricting and rigorously regulating (if not actually prohibiting) the supply of allegedly addictive substances and activities is no more illiberal than making people obey speed limits or wear seat belts, or stopping them from committing suicide.

The difficulty for prohibitionists here is not that sometimes governments should indeed (or at least arguably) protect their citizens from the damage they would otherwise be likely to do themselves and their families—as in the seat-belt case—with all the real and substantial public health and other costs that might otherwise be incurred. The difficulty is that with many potentially addictive activities, including undoubtedly drinking alcohol and gambling, the vast majority of those who enjoy these activities never become addicted or otherwise disposed to do themselves significant harm.

To deal with this problem prohibitionists have to talk falsely as if all gamblers were somehow problem gamblers and as if everyone who indulges in any potentially addictive activity is thereby irrevocably embarked on the slippery slope that leads to full-blown addiction (and the road to fatal perdition that runs beside it).

Unfortunately, one of the more regrettable consequences, from a scientific point of view, is that the definition of "addiction" gets altered in the scientific literature. In particular, the cutoff point in the various screens that identify problem gamblers according to how many out of a set of questions they answer affirmatively may be raised to show that there are fewer gambling addicts than previously supposed. Other people (including myself and some recovering problem gamblers surveyed in Collins and Barr 2001) tend to make claims to the effect that (for example) real gambling addicts score at least 14 on the Gamblers Anonymous 20 questions.[2] Alternatively, it may get reduced to show that anyone who scores even one affirmative on any test is "at risk" and therefore on the above-mentioned slippery slope. What this shows is the inherent ambiguity in the notion of addiction and, perhaps also, that scientists themselves have pro- and antigambling biases.

Values and Addiction

Even when used by scientists, it is beyond doubt that "addiction" is sometimes employed as a value-laden term. Everyone may claim that addiction is simply a disease, but that is not how it's treated.

We really don't want our children to be addicts, and not just because it's a dangerous illness like diabetes. Addiction, also, attracts shame where other illnesses mostly attract pity. Moreover, there are few straightforwardly clinical illnesses for which one of the best treatments is sitting around with other addicts sharing "experience, strength, and hope."

In short, addiction arouses psychological fascination and moral horror, and that is why we don't treat it as simply an illness—which may indeed be a comparatively unimportant and tractable one by comparison with many others.

The reason for this brings together themes that have been running through other discussions in this chapter. We don't treat addicts as we treat, say, diabetics, because large numbers of those who can vote and run for elective office disapprove of addictive behaviors on moral grounds—whether sincerely, rationally, or simply opportunistically. This compels legislators—and students of public policy—to ask difficult questions about not only intrinsic values but also about competing values.

It is, of course, (comparatively) easy to decide whether, say, smoking or gambling is something that one thinks that oneself, one's children, and/or others ought not to do. It is considerably more difficult to decide whether adults should be forbidden from doing these things by law, and much more difficult to decide where and how the line should be drawn between what the law ought to permit and what it should ban. This difficulty is exacerbated if there are some things the law currently permits—say, children's violent video games—which perhaps it ought to ban, and some things the law currently bans which perhaps it ought to permit—say, consuming cannabis in licensed cafés as in Holland. The reason for the increasing levels of difficulty is that as the questions grow more complex, so the number of moral principles that need to be taken into account grows and the competition between them becomes more difficult to disentangle.

Thus, it is fairly uncontroversial that we should not, on the whole, encourage our children to engage in activities that may harm them in various ways. But surely we should also not expect the law to prevent them from taking risks of any kind. Still less with adults should the law forbid them from engaging in activities—ranging from driving a motorbike to hang-gliding—if they know the risks and accept them. Nor indeed should the law put out of business those who have earned a legitimate livelihood selling hamburgers because some people are now prone to eat nothing else and others think this activity is, in every sense, unedifying.

Yet a part of us, at least, feels tempted to do all these things in the name of protecting people from themselves—which is only another way of prohibiting them from engaging in vice. By and large a part of a large number of us still wants the law to remove wickedness and vice, and this means we democratically demand illiberal laws. But of course we can't put it like that: our liberal commitments are too strong and we know that declaring our paternalism would lose us votes.

As we have seen, it is not only the puritan but also the democrat in all of us who is tempted to exaggerate greatly the extent to which vices undermine *liberal* ideals of free choice. Thus, we are disposed to believe that *all* drug use leads to addiction and *no* drug users are exercising free choice. Moreover, all soft drug use leads to hard drug use, and almost all hard drug use leads to horrible death by overdose.

Exactly the same happens with gambling. Those who want gambling banned or severely restricted start by arguing that they wouldn't want heir children to grow up to spend most of their time gambling (and losing). They then go on to say that buying a lottery ticket is the start of the slippery slope that will lead to harder forms of gambling. These harder forms will (almost) inevitably lead to addiction, which will in turn lead to the ruination of their own lives and those of their families as well as incurring huge costs for taxpayers.

In short, the prohibitionist case relies on a putative set of claims about the nature, causes, and progress of addictive diseases for which we lack adequate scientific warrant, and which seem, on the evidence that we do have, to be in many cases false. Nevertheless our atavistic nervousness, which in many cases serves us well in making practical judgments where there are no unequivocal scientific answers, inclines us to caution. Do we really want slot machines wherever there might be a market for them, including hospital waiting rooms, supermarket checkouts, bus and rail stations, senior citizens' frail-care centers, and Junior Common rooms? Maybe. Maybe not.

Unfortunately, we cannot expect the press and politicians to be really interested in good—subtle, complex, highly qualified, and cautious—science; they are interested in plausible scientific sound bites that advance their own political agenda.

The result is that whether one is talking about internet gambling policy in the United States, VLTs in Canada, Pokies in Australia, casinos in the U.K., or lotteries in Europe, policy is almost wholly uninformed by the best science and conspicuously fails to deliver the laudable and sensible public interest goals that it ostensibly sets out to deliver. And the reason is not that we have incompetent scientists or wicked politicians. The reason is that we are not full-fledged liberals in our attitude to other people's pleasure. We remain partially democrats who think that if enough of us share the same moral views about how others should and should not be able to enjoy themselves harmlessly, these views should be enshrined in law and those who have different ideas about enjoying themselves should be punished. And this widespread and partial illiberalism can be easily amplified and given spurious scientific support by those who will benefit from protection from commercial competition and will consequently be willing to pay for the necessary advocacy research and public relations work.

In this way the tendency emerges in public debate to define anyone who overindulges in particular pleasures that I disapprove of as an addict and anyone who enjoys what I don't disapprove of as exercising freedom of choice. In short, we are ambivalent between our commitment to democracy and our commitment to freedom.

Conflicting Values

Conflicts between values in politics and in private life are not to be resolved by choosing sides—by declaring one conflicting value supreme over another. They are to be resolved by doing justice to the best that can be said against all sides of the argument and trying to reach an accommodation that is widely persuasive—at least to those more interested in reason and evidence than in passion and prejudice.

I shall try here to set out the principal value judgments that all—including the most dispassionate scientists—have to think about if they are to form conclusions about how policymakers should address the phenomenon of addiction and how scientists can help them to do it.

1. The pure politics of autocratic totalitarianism ("benevolent despotism" if the term is preferred) are not acceptable in liberal democracies and certainly not likely to be acceptable with respect to the private enjoyment of harmless pleasures. But particular items of totalitarian policy may be retained because disapproval of them enjoys the support of the democratic majority.

2. Pure liberalism will conflict with the principle of pure democracy (majority rule) in many areas, including the regulation of allegedly addictive pleasures deemed by some citizens to be immoral.

3. The consequences of different policies in relation to allegedly addictive pleasures are uncertain: prohibition may not lead to a reduction in addiction and may have substantial incidental costs relating to the activities of organized crime. Permitting a free market in allegedly addictive substances and activities may or may not lead to a reduction or increase in addiction: its incidental consequences are also unknown. The same arguments apply to regulated supply depending on whether the regulation is principally prohibitive or permissive.

4. Other things being equal, existing vested interests should not be disturbed without a clear basis in public welfare being demonstrated (though protectionism is not a legitimate interest).

5. Illegitimate (criminal) interests should be frustrated both by making illegal trade more difficult and by avoiding the creation of further opportunities for illegal trade.

6. No laws should be passed that, because they are difficult to enforce, bring the law generally into disrepute.

Consequences for Addiction Policy in the West

The history of the "war on addiction" in the West has not been a happy one. I don't know, nor can I see any easy way of finding out, the extent to which the abuse of the concept of addiction has been causally implicated in the stupendous failure of Western governments to reduce the suffering caused by excessive indulgence in potentially addictive activities, most notably drugs. I believe that some of this failure has been in the past due to unclear and inaccurate thinking among both scientists and policymakers about addiction. But many of the original fallacies that the original antidrugs campaigns emphasized seem to have been dropped in light of better science and its influence on policymakers.

Thus not all soft drug-taking is now said to lead to hard drug-taking. Many addicts recover spontaneously. Most addicts do not, in fact, die horrible deaths. I also suspect that we have learned a lot about how to teach the young sensibly rather than censoriously about addiction.

The Past

Defining excessive and self-destructive indulgence in potentially dangerous pleasures as "addiction" was originally deemed to be a progressive step, because by categorizing such behavior as diseased and in need of therapy we removed it from the realm of activities that should be accounted wicked and therefore as suitable cases for punishment. The danger, now, may be the opposite one that we are using the notion of "addiction" as a way of selling under false pretenses prohibition, restriction, or excessive regulation and taxation of activities (morally disapproved of by a minority) to majorities of democratic voters who maybe enjoy the activity in question, but don't really understand or have strong feelings about the policy issues involved.

In one sense disease models of addiction—and the public health models that typically accompany them—may well be benign. They are, however, also likely to be expensive simply because every addict becomes a suitable case for treatment at the expense of the public purse. This economic fact is likely to grow in importance as demands on health budgets grow generally. (Who is really going to spend thousands of dollars supposedly curing someone who can't stop betting too much at the racetrack?)

On the other hand, whatever else may be said about addicts, they don't choose to ruin their lives, and if they could reasonably easily cure their addictions they would. A humane society will surely go on offering them sympathetic and skilled therapy of whatever kind and in whatever affordable doses they can rather than leave them to rot. Similarly, a humane society will also do what it can to prevent people from getting into trouble in the first place. This is roughly how addiction is treated around the more affluent world. But the results are not yet impressive.

What Is to Be Done by Scientists?

Certainly, our present programs are not enough. Too many people become addicts. Too few know of the existence of treatment. Of those who do know of its existence, too few seek treatment. Of those who seek treatment, too few stay the course. Of those who stay the course, too many relapse.

This brings us back to the divergent perspectives of scientists and policymakers and the need to bring them closer together.

Clearly we need, first and foremost, better science, which means better-funded science. There is huge hope for progress from, on the one hand, brain research, and, on the other, from studies like the American National Comorbidity Study. I am also confident that we will make important progress in South Africa in understanding the particularities of these issues in the environment of developing countries.

In respect of neuroscience, we obviously need to know much more about the brains both of problem gamblers and also of enthusiastic and regular gamblers who don't experience problems. Much pioneering work has already been done in these areas. (See, in particular, Ross et al. 2008 with its extensive references to others who have worked productively in this field.)

We already know that some pathological gambling—at least—is a potentially treatable neurophysiological disorder. We also know that some forms of disordered gambling respond well to relatively short treatments. On the other hand, there is much that we simply don't know—for example, whether mechanically interrupting the enjoyment of non-problem-gamblers really helps problem gamblers.

All these issues need to be explored further by unbiased scientists who are best equipped, morally as well as materially, to engage in the disinterested pursuit of truth. The money to pay for this should be fairly easily forthcoming because both governments and the industry have a formidable financial interest in knowing the answers to these questions.

The Future: What Is to Be Done by Policymakers?

But, however good the science, there is for at least quite some time going to remain my original question: What do we do now in the absence of comprehensive and uncontested scientific knowledge? Part of the answer, of course, is that scientists and policymakers must each try to better understand the preoccupations of the other. Both, in their way, are fundamentally interested in truth, but scientists are also interested in the esteem of fellow scientists and policymakers are interested in the acclaim that accompanies making the world a (slightly) better place. This requires science that is better explained in terms that legislators, businesspeople, journalists, and the general public can understand. It also requires a more serious and honest (as opposed to a merely public-relations) approach to science by those involved in the world of practical affairs.

To some extent we also clearly have no alternative in the absence of more conclusive science than to adopt a scattershot approach to the treatment and preventative measures that we have some reason to think may work in a not insignificant number of cases. We may, however, achieve nothing. We are unlikely to make matters worse. Probably we shall do a bit of good, though not so much as we could and would if we had better science.

But in making an appeal for better science, I have a broader notion of what constitutes better knowledge of the kind we are seeking than that which is dominant in scientific psychology.

Psychological knowledge of the sort that current science provides involves (roughly) carefully and imaginatively constructed experiments, properly interpreted and well-designed accumulations of data from case histories and surveys whose results are subjected to appropriate statistical techniques. There is, however, another kind of psychological knowledge that forms part of what philosophers typically categorize as "practical" rather than "theoretical" knowledge.

This kind of practical knowledge is indispensable for the determination and implementation of public policy. In briefly describing it I build on the account of intelligent political activity elaborated most eloquently by Michael Oakeshott, especially in his inaugural lecture at the London School of Economics in 1952, later reprinted as "Political Education" in *Rationalism in Politics* (Oakeshott 1956). I also rely on the account of how the politics of a "decent" society in which values often conflict will be informed by historical knowledge to be found throughout the writings of Isaiah Berlin, especially in his essay "The Pursuit of the Ideal" (Berlin 1990).

Oakeshott argues for a way of understanding and engaging in politics in particular, and practical activity in general, that consists neither in identifying general principles and values and then working out their implications and applications in particular cases nor in relying for understanding and guidance merely on irrational intuitions and impulses. This way of understanding is what Oakeshott famously calls "the pursuit of intimations," and he sees it as a *via media* between these two clearly mistaken extremes. To explain what people engaged in successful practical activity are doing, we need to see them as choosing creatively among a range of possibilities the course of action that seems to them the most appropriate way of proceeding within a traditional manner of behaving in a particular set of current circumstances. His own favorite examples are cooking and clothes design, where success can clearly neither be reduced to the application of formulas but nor is it simply a matter of ineradicably subjective taste. Rather it is a matter of educated and experienced judgment.

To illustrate what is meant here for the notion of psychological understanding as it applies to gambling, consider playing poker. A poker player must reach a conclusion about a matter of psychological fact concerning what an opponent is trying to signal by raising the ante in a game of poker. Two bodies of scientific knowledge, the psychology of decision under risk and uncertainty, and the game-theoretic account of strategic dominance in zero-sum games, are *potentially* relevant here, and would be used by a scientist studying the situation. However, the poker player in real time lacks access to the evidence she'd need to infer the other's intention from generalizations of cognitive science, and she has no program at hand telling her what constitutes implementation of dominant play on the hand in question.[3] Despite the unhelpfulness of science in such situations, some poker players will be more consistently right in judging the significance of their opponent's behavior. The good poker player will exercise intelligent and informed judgment, and the better poker player will exercise better judgment. Looking at the results is how one verifies claims about who is the better player.

This is a simple version of the much more complex situation in which businesspeople and politicians find themselves all the time. Sure, they should study odds. Sure, they should study the scientific laws of psychology—and of much else. They may also benefit from the specific study of decision making in various contexts. But in the end, poker players, businesspeople, and politicians will exercise judgment. The quality of their judgment will be based mainly on daily experience of human relations and human transactions, both individual and collective. Their judgment is also likely to be enhanced by knowledge of human actions and interactions in both factual history and in stories.

These considerations suggest the conclusion that to understand addiction and to formulate good policy and good practice for dealing with it, we indeed need to know as much as we can about what the relevant science can currently tell us, but we also need to understand how addiction and its treatment fit into the web of values that constitutes our cultural life and what the resources of our political traditions, for better or worse, make both possible and impossible.

More generally, as Berlin puts it:

The best that can be done, as a general rule, is to maintain a precarious equilibrium that will prevent the occurrence of desperate situations, of intolerable choices—that is the first requirement for a decent society; one that we can always strive for, in the light of the limited range of our knowledge, and even of our imperfect understanding of individuals and society. A certain humility in these matters is very necessary. (Berlin 1990, 17–18)

Politicians should take note of this in pursuing their own engagements, and scientists and other citizens need to do so in order to understand the constraints within which their political leaders navigate.

Acknowledgments

I am very grateful to Harold Kincaid who read the first version of this chapter and made a number of proposals for corrections and improvements, which I have been happy to incorporate. I am also especially grateful to Don Ross for alerting me to the material about the relationship between science and poker and for proposing amendments to my original text that eliminated error and facilitated clarity in my discussion of the role of judgment in practical affairs.

Notes

1. Some of this evidence is summarized in the introduction to Collins and Barr 2006.

2. See especially section A: "Theoretical Considerations" in Collins and Barr 2001.

3. The world's leading professional money winner at poker, Chris "Jesus" Ferguson, uses game theory to select dominant strategies (Harford 2008, chapter 2). This may eventually become common as more people gain easy access to ever more powerful and convenient computers, which threatens the long-run sustainability of poker. However, the situation I describe is that of nearly all current poker players.

References

Berlin, I. (1990). The pursuit of the ideal. In Henry Hardy, ed., *The Crooked Timber of Humanity*. London: John Murray.

Collins, P., and Barr, G. (2001). *Gambling and Problem Gambling in South Africa*. South African National Responsible Gambling Trust. www.responsiblegambling.co.za.

Collins, P. and Barr, G. (2006). *Gambling and Problem Gambling in South Africa.* (Third study in series.) South African National Responsible Gambling Trust. www.responsiblegambling.co.za.

Harford, T. (2008). *The Logic of Life.* New York: Random House.

Mill, J. S. (1859/1974). *On Liberty.* Edited and with an introduction by Gertrude Himmelfarb. London: Penguin Books.

Oakeshott, M. (1956). *Rationalism and Politics.* London: Methuen.

Ross, D., Sharp, C., Vuchinich, R., and Spurrett, D. (2008). *Midbrain Mutiny: The Picoeconomics and Neuroeconomics of Disordered Gambling.* Cambridge, MA: MIT Press.

Walker, Douglas M. (2007). *The Economics of Casino Gambling.* Berlin: Springer.

Contributors

George Ainslie   Veterans' Affairs Medical Center, Coatesville, Pennsylvania

Jennifer D. Bellegarde   Yale University

Warren K. Bickel   University of Arkansas for Medical Sciences

Jennifer Bramen   University of California at Los Angeles

Karen O. Brandon   University of South Florida

Arthur Brody   University of California at Los Angeles

Peter Collins   Salford University, UK

Jack Darkes   University of South Florida

Mark S. Goldman   University of South Florida

Gene M. Heyman   McLean Hospital and Harvard Medical School

Harold Kincaid   University of Alabama at Birmingham

Edythe D. London   University of California at Los Angeles

James MacKillop   University of Georgia

Traci Mann   University of Minnesota

Neil Manson   University of Mississippi

John E. McGeary   Providence Veteran's Administration Medical Center

John R. Monterosso   University of Southern California

Ben Murrell   University of KwaZulu-Natal

Nancy M. Petry   University of Connecticut

Marc N. Potenza   Yale University

Howard Rachlin   State University of New York, Stony Brook

Lara A. Ray   University of California at Los Angeles

A. David Redish   University of Minnesota

Richard R. Reich   University of South Florida

Don Ross   University of Cape Town, University of Alabama at Birmingham

Timothy Schroeder   Ohio State University

David Spurrett   University of KwaZulu-Natal

Jacqueline A. Sullivan   University of Alabama at Birmingham

Andrew Ward   Swarthmore College

Richard Yi   University of Arkansas for Medical Sciences

Index

DATE DUE